Law and Public Administration in Ireland

Law and Public Administration in Ireland

By
Dr Fiona Donson
LLB, LLM, PhD

Dr Darren O'Donovan
BCL, PhD

Published by
Clarus Press Ltd,
Griffith Campus,
South Circular Road,
Dublin 8.

Typeset by
Deanta Global Publishing Services

Printed by
Clondalkin Print Group,
Dublin

ISBN
978-1-905536-70-2

Disclaimer
Whilst every effort has been made to ensure that the contents of this book are accurate, neither the publisher, nor authors can accept responsibility for any errors or omissions or loss occasioned to any person acting or refraining from acting as result of any material in this publication.

Fiona would like to dedicate this book to Aoife and Oisín
Darren would like to dedicate this book to Aoibheann

PREFACE

It is often said that administrative law is notoriously difficult to study and to teach because its doctrines are abstract and nuanced, moving across a wide array of statutes and aspects of legal practice. This book is an attempt to defend administrative law as an exciting and dynamic subject which is central to meeting the future challenges facing Irish public governance.

Law and Public Administration in Ireland inevitably focuses heavily upon judicial review, as the central aspect of the legal regulation of governance, providing a firm backstop against government abuse of power. In our account of the grounds of judicial review, we have sought to track the movement within the case-law, rather than simply overview existing precedents. Administrative law is a deeply contextual subject, one in which formal doctrinal language obscures the competing principles of public policy and the role played by the complicated fact patterns of cases. This underlying connection with purpose and pragmatic sensitivity to context are essential for any student, practitioner or decision-maker dealing with judicial review cases, and we have sought to anchor our text in this emphasis.

Alongside this formal legal analysis, this book also seeks to engage with broader issues concerning the reform of Irish public administration and the availability of non-judicial forms of review. A distinct focus is upon the crucial role of Parliament in administrative law. It will be obvious to the reader that administrative law has direct implications for citizens, the executive and the courts, with each usually constituting the applicant, the respondent and the adjudicator respectively. Yet, outside the narrow confines of individual cases, it is the Oireachtas which is the primary actor in our administrative justice system. This book stresses the fact that in discharging its legislative mandate, the Oireachtas must create consistent frameworks for resolving disputes between citizen and government. In our discussion of the Office of the Ombudsman, public inquiries in Ireland and parliamentary review generally, we argue that a greater commitment to improving the machinery of administrative justice is key to disentangling the Oireachtas from executive dominance, and ensuring that the executive is answerable to the public. Thus, *Law and Public Administration in Ireland* looks to connect judicial and non-judicial mechanisms to the broader goal of accountability.

Ultimately, the core question which this book poses is, simply put, what do we want from administrative law? This, to us, is the fundamental question of the subject. Rather than a focus upon inherited principles, it is important to locate the ongoing value judgments shaping judicial decisions and the design of our institutions. For the courts and practicing lawyers, we would submit that this question was central to recent refinements to judicial review principles such as occurred in *Meadows v Minister for Justice*. Such cases, and broader debates regarding the reform of the Irish administrative state, reflect the fact that Irish legal scholarship continues to question which administrative structures and approaches best reflect, and practically secure, the values of Bunreacht na hÈireann. We hope that this book contributes to this vital conversation.

Fiona Donson and Darren O'Donovan,
23rd February 2015

ACKNOWLEDGEMENTS

We are very proud of this book as combining both traditional and newer themes in administrative law scholarship. This book was a truly collective endeavor, in which we attempted to draw out our best strengths, in both substance and process. Thanks must go to David McCartney at Clarus Press, who has proved remarkably patient with the book, willing us freedom to pursue a work with the broadest coverage. We would also like to thank Danielle Fleming and Samantha Williams for their research assistance during the initial stages of the book.

Darren would like to thank all the staff at Bond University. While acknowledgements cannot be exhaustive, in particular, I would like to thank Professor Gerard Carney, for having provided me with my first start in Australia. I am also grateful to Professor Patrick Keyzer for his continuing support and for having helped my integration in the Australian legal context. This book strongly benefitted from discussions with my fellow teacher of administrative law, Narelle Bedford, whose knowledge and affection for the subject has been a wonderful resource. Thanks to Linsday Stevenson Graf for providing me with a forum, in her clinical legal placement subject, for the discussion of access to justice themes. Thanks Professor Laurence Boulle, Professor John Farrar and other members of our faculty book club, for our discussions on Lord Bingham's *The Rule of Law*. I am grateful also to the editors and members of the Human Rights in Ireland website for providing a testing ground for critical themes on the Irish administrative state, and for their patience with my infrequent blogging over the course of writing this book. I would also like to pay tribute to the staff of the law faculty, University College Cork. It is impossible to single out each individual, as every member of staff seems to have provided me with support or inspiration over my four years on staff there and beyond. Thanks as always, to Professor Siobhan Mullally, who, as my PhD supervisor, laid the foundations of my academic career. Thanks also to all my fellow graduates of the PhD programme at UCC, which has produced so many new scholars over the past decade. To my parents, Alfred and Nuala, and my siblings Adrian, Ronan and Eimear. To Iresha, thank you for your love and patience throughout this process. And finally, to my new daughter Aoibheann, in the hope you will grow up with a passion for improving Irish society.

Fiona would like to thank her colleagues at University College Cork. Specific mention should go to Professor Maeve McDonagh for generously sharing her thoughts on Freedom of Information, particularly the 2014 Act and Dr Maria Cahill for invaluable discussions around Parliamentary oversight under the Irish Constitution. Thanks should also be extended to those who tutored Administrative Law in UCC over the past years and shared discussions around both administrative law concepts and the challenges of teaching the subject. Generally I would like to express my appreciation for friends and family for all their support and encouragement. Particular thanks are extended to my parents, Ted and Cathy, who have always encouraged my intellectual and personal efforts, no matter what direction they have taken; and my sister Mary for her ever present voice of reason and support. Finally, and most significantly, I would like to thank Niall, Aoife and Oisín for sharing your home life with this book — your patience, energy and love has supported me through this project.

CONTENTS

TABLE OF CASES

TABLE OF LEGISLATION

Secondary Legislation

Rules of Court

International Conventions

Other Jurisdictions

CHAPTER ONE

ADMINISTRATIVE LAW: VALUES AND TENSIONS

Introduction

The failure of public administration and political oversight that underwrote [1–01] the collapse of the Irish economy in 2008 has provoked widespread reflection upon the need for public law reform. While much of the popular imagination has fixated upon the process of constitutional reform initiated by the Constitutional Convention, there is also a need to ensure Ireland's administrative state is restructured to ensure more effective governance, accountability and oversight. The authors initially considered calling this book *Administrative Justice in Ireland*, which was intended as a deliberate, though small, provocation. The idea of administrative justice has never been settled, as Ombudsmen, lawyers, political scientists and governments have clashed over what it should include and who should be responsible for its delivery. Yet, in the Ireland of today, it is clear that traditional structures, cultures and approaches have failed. Many of the chapters in this book testify to the shortcomings of parliamentary culture, the failures of regulatory bodies and the need for more accessible and effective remedies for individuals who are the victims of maladministration. While flaws are easy to point out, the cures are more difficult, and even if we could settle on a definition, how significant a role can and should *legal* institutions play in cultivating administrative justice? There is no doubting the centrality of judicial review to the practice of administrative law, but we must not forget, in the words of Harlow and Rawlings that "behind every theory of administrative law there lies a theory of the state".[1] At a time of much contestation regarding the structure and operation of the Irish State therefore, practitioners, students and administrators must survey the emerging institutional and regulatory landscape alongside traditional doctrinal principles.

Administrative Law as a Branch of Law

The Subject of Administrative Law

In introducing the subject, we must first acknowledge that, unlike other [1–02] law subjects such as contract or constitutional law, its scope may not be easily and immediately identified. This book reflects the wide definition of

---

[1] C Harlow and R Rawlings, *Law and Administration* (3rd ed) (Cambridge University Press, Cambridge, 2009) at p 1, hereinafter "Harlow and Rawlings (2009)".

administrative law forwarded by de Smith and Brazier, who described it as the law, which:

> "...relates to the organization, composition, functions and procedures of public authorities and special statutory tribunals, their impact on the citizen and the legal restraints and liabilities to which they are subject."[2]

As we will see over the course of this chapter however, beyond this conventional definition, agreement often fractures. Indeed the authors of a leading Australian administrative law book have commented that the subject's definition is "a topic on which few commentators can reach agreement, because it ultimately depends on what they want out of administrative law".[3]

[1–03] Another remarkable feature of administrative law is that its existence is, to an extent, a recent phenomenon, tied to the expansion of the modern State's activities.[4] Administrative law consists of the general principles which apply to the exercise of public power across a variety of contexts, from refugee law, housing law, planning and development to the operation of regulatory agencies. Thus, at times, it seems that most of the material could be relocated somewhere else on a standard curriculum. Yet, equally, subjects such as taxation law can be viewed as specialized branches of administrative law. The key point is that whereas some law subjects can be more easily isolated from others, administrative law elements attach to virtually all areas of practice. In this sense the subject lays down a fundamental legal grammar which can apply across a wide variety of contexts. This is particularly important in the current era of legislative hyperactivity, where more and more fields of life are regulated; a trend that will continue apace as more statutes carry within them regulatory structures and enforcement frameworks.

What is the "Administrative" in Administrative Law?

[1–04] Apart from defining the subject, there are also difficulties in defining the key term: administrative. What precisely does the term "administrative" cover? The origins of the word lie in the 18 century, coined from the Latin verb

---

[2] S de Smith and R Brazier, *Constitutional and Administrative Law* (7th ed) (Penguin Books, London, 1994) at p 577.

[3] M Aronson, B Dyer and M Groves, *Judicial Review of Administrative Action* (3rd ed) (Law Book Company, Sydney, 2004) at p 1.

[4] See the famous comment of Lord Reid in *Ridge v Baldwin* [1964] AC 40, at 72 that "we do not have a developed system of administrative law – perhaps because fairly recently, we did not need it".

administrare, meaning to manage. The popular present day understanding would be that an administrator has the task of taking government policy and implementing them at ground level. In this way an administrator can be understood to manage the operation of government. In getting behind the *legal* connotations of the term "administrative", this "implementation" element is often more prominent than the "management" element. For the lawyer, an "administrative matter" is often one which lies at the other end of a spectrum from a "policy matter". Policy decisions are of general application usually involving an abstract choice between broad principles e.g. a vote on approving the regional planning strategy. An administrative decision, on the other hand, is often an act affecting a specific individual, where an administrator has established the facts and circumstances and applied the relevant policy e.g. a specific planning permission. Of course, between these two artificially defined ends of the continuum, there are a range of combinations, and indeed, administration may involve the balancing of policy factors.

Further insight into the defining elements of "administrative" action may   **[1–05]**
be gained from Australian jurisprudence, as the key statute entitling individuals to judicial review of administrative acts in that jurisdiction is limited to decisions which possess "an administrative character".[5] The courts have avoided any precise definition of the term but have supplied some general indicators:

> "Administrative carries with it the notion of 'managing', 'executing' or 'carrying into effect...laws".[6]

> "Administration includes the application of a general policy or rule to particular cases; the making of individual decisions".[7]

Beyond these more general indicators, a further consideration will often be the nature of the institution under the spotlight. In practice, administrative law is often most focused upon executive acts rather than legislative ones.

The Primary Actors of Administrative Law

Who are the primary *actors* of administrative law? Throughout this book   **[1–06]**
we focus upon two main groupings: firstly, *the instruments of government*,

---

[5] Administrative Decisions (Judicial Review) Act (Cth), s 3(1).
[6] *Burns v Australian National University* (1982) 40 ALR 707 at 713.
[7] *Hamblin v Duffy (No 1)* (1981) 34 ALR 333 at 339.

a category embracing the government (cabinet), government departments and agencies, public bodies and local authorities; and secondly, *the instruments of accountability*, a category embracing oversight or integrity agencies such as ombudsmen, tribunals, parliament and the courts. In relation to the latter category we must stress the importance of recognizing the diverse mechanisms of securing accountability, and how these have significantly expanded the scope of administrative law. Law is just one form of regulation, and increasingly, the traditional principles of judicial review now sit alongside other forms of oversight, as Professor Margaret Allars notes:

> "The power to review administrative decisions has been distributed amongst a variety of institutions and access to the relief available from such institutions made available to a broad range of individuals. Although general legal principles can still be discerned, their content has become uncertain as courts and tribunals struggle to fashion responses to the challenge of the expansion and complexity of the executive branch of government…On account of this blurring of the boundaries between principles whose sources are clearly legal and those which are regarded as sourced in other disciplines, the scope of administrative law defies neat definition."[8]

[1–07]   In relation to the *instruments of government*, the category clearly contains a number of obvious organisations such as central government, public bodies and local government (which we cover directly). This category does, however, extend beyond this core to include a far wider variety of organisation operating under the wider heading of government and beyond. The changing nature of government has posed conceptual challenges for this group of bodies. For instance, one of the more confusing terminological debates we must note is that relating to whether an entity is a State body or a semi-State body. A definition of some of the distinctive features of a core State body can be generated from reading the judgment of McMenamin J in *Health Service Executive v Commissioner of Valuation*.[9] This case arose when the respondent body sought payment of rates from the HSE in relation to an office block. A decision that the building was rateable was made despite the existence of Valuation Act 2001, s 15 which exempted all buildings occupied by "the State including…any Department or Office of the State". In ruling that the HSE was an exempted public body

---

[8] M Allars, *Introduction to Australian Administrative Law* (Butterworths, Sydney, 1990) at p 1.
[9] [2010] 4 IR 23.

under the legislation, McMenamin J focused upon four key elements: the HSEs statutory function, the manner in which the Minister could influence through policy formulation and Ministerial direction the actions of the HSE, that its funding was provided through the Appropriation Act and that its staff were recruited in according the Public Service Management (Recruitments and Appointments Act) 2004. In short, McMenamin J ruled that the HSE was a State body as it was "closely integrated into the process of government".[10] This decision provides an interesting reflection on how public bodies can be considered part of central government or alternatively can be more peripheral, State-sponsored semi-State entities. That question ultimately turns on "the degree of integration of such authorities to the core functions of government".[11] However, it is important to emphasise at this stage that the question of what is a State body is separate from whether a decision taken by an entity is reviewable as a public law matter, which is a question of law we deal with later in this book.[12]

The Interface Between Administration and Policy

In understanding the everyday realities of central government administration, it is perhaps important to note the exact division of labour and interaction between policy and administrative roles. A fundamental principle in the administrative-policy interface is that of individual ministerial responsibility. This traditional, under-enforced constitutional convention holds that a Minister is responsible to the Dáil for most actions which occur in his or her department. This doctrine is discussed in more detail in chapter 2 where the reader will find an analysis of why the traditional approach is an ineffective accountability mechanism which has triggered few resignations in modern Ireland. A more consolidated, legal map of the actual relationship between the Minister and his or her department is laid down in the Public Service Management Act 1997. Section 4(1) bestows "the authority, responsibility and accountability" over administrative tasks[13] upon the principal civil servant in the department,

[1–08]

---

[10] *ibid* at para 60.

[11] *ibid*.

[12] The public/private divide is discussed in the context of the ambit of procedural fairness, see chapter 10, paras [10.10]–[10.17].

[13] These are defined by s 4 to include:
- Managing the Department, implementing government policies and delivering outputs;
- Preparing and submitting to the Minister a Strategy Statement with a three year horizon;
- Providing advice to the Minister in relation to Departmental expenditure;

the Secretary General. Despite this recognition, his or her authority is not free-standing, as under s 6 the Secretary General is made accountable to the Minister even for actions covered by s 4(1). The Act also affirms the principle of ministerial responsibility[14] and the sole right of the Minister "to determine matters of policy".[15] In doing so, it allows Government or the responsible Minister to give directions in relation to any of the Secretary General's obligations (apart from human resources and staff allocation).[16] No clear picture emerges from this weak accountability framework; the basic terms "policy" and "administration" are not defined, and their interactions are not clearly mapped. It is therefore of little surprise that following the crash of the Irish economy in 2008, Minister Pat Rabbitte TD committed to developing a legislative definition of this critical political/administrative interface, in order to foster clearer lines of accountability[17]:

> "As a minister, I value the relationship between the civil service and the minister. This key relationship is built largely on trust but it is also by its nature ambiguous and lacking in clarity as to the specific roles of the players. Ambiguity is defended on the basis that it supports a flexible and collaborative public service, where the elasticity of individual roles allows for a quick response to changing demands. But ambiguity also allows for vagueness as to who is responsible for what and to whom are they accountable."[18]

The current Programme for Government, under a heading of Empowering the Civil Service, includes a commitment to

---

- Ensuring arrangements are in place to facilitate an effective response to cross cutting matters;
- Ensuring resources are used appropriately;
- Examining and developing means to improve cost effective public services; and
- Managing all matters related to the appointment, performance, discipline and dismissal of staff below the Principal Officer grade.

[14] s 3, Public Service Management Act 1997.

[15] s 4(1), *ibid*.

[16] s 4(1), s 6 and s 7, *ibid*.

[17] See generally the work of the Independent Panel on Strengthening Civil Service Accountability and Performance, *Report of the Independent Panel on Strengthening Civil Service Accountability and Performance*, 30 May 2014 http://www.per.gov.ie/civil-service-accountability-consultation-process/ (date accessed 31 July 2014).

[18] P Rabbitte, *Reform agenda not a knee-jerk response to political corruption*, speech presented at McGill Summer School, 26 July 2012, available at http://www.labour.ie/press/listing/134333961410222143.html (date accessed 31 July 2014). For further discussion see B Connaughton, "Ministers and their Departments: Inside the 'Black Box' of the Public Policy Process" in E O'Malley and M MacCarthaigh, *Governing Ireland*, (Institute of Public Administration, Dublin, 2011) at pp 61-88.

"Legislate for a reformulated code of laws ... which will spell out the legal relationship between Ministers and their civil servants and their legal accountability for decisions and for management of Departments."[19]

The proposals are then fleshed out in the Government's Consultation Paper on the Civil Service where the distinction is drawn between Ministers' responsibilities for "strategic direction, setting policy priorities and the outcomes achieved" and civil servants' responsibilities for "implementation".[20] However, even here the blurred nature of these two areas is apparent:

"It is clear, however, that it is not possible to draw a line through the policy process after which no more ministerial involvement is required. The process of implementing a particular scheme can raise policy issues that will often require a minister to make further political judgments. When policy has been set it does not mean a minister will have no further involvement; the implementation of policies can be as politically sensitive as the policy decision itself and may require direct ministerial involvement at different times to ensure successful implementation."[21]

These two contributions from Minister Pat Rabbitte TD and the Government **[1–09]** consultation paper return us to the idea of a policy-administration spectrum rather than a sharp division between the two activities. It also opens up space for a final introductory question which we often ask our students: do you think administrators possess a lot of power? And what gives them their power? The most strident academic answer to this question was perhaps supplied by Max Weber, the German sociologist, who firmly believed that a defining quality of modern governance would be the delegation of significant power by legislators to administrative agencies.[22] In effect, Weber predicted that bureaucrats would play an enormously significant part in who effectively "governs" democratic societies. Clearly a wide range of perspectives exist on the nature and legitimacy of administrative power, some of which will be analysed as we move through this chapter.

---

[19] Programme for Government 2011-2016, available at http://www.taoiseach.gov.ie/eng/Work_Of_The_Department/Programme_for_Government/Programme_for_Government_2011-2016.pdf (date accessed 10 October 2014) at p 29.

[20] Government Reform Unit, *Strengthening Civil Service Accountability and Performance: Consultation Paper on Programme for Government Commitments*, 9 January 2014 at p 23.

[21] *ibid.*

[22] See generally, M Weber, *The Theory of Social and Economic Organization*, Translated by AM Henderson and Talcott Parsons (Collier Macmillan Publishers, London, 1947).

[1–10]   For the moment, however, we would merely stress one key aspect which often emerges in legally focussed classrooms: the existence of discretion. If administrative power is the power to execute or apply the laws to individual, then a key part to determining its scope lies in the relationship between *rules* and *discretion*. The latter concept is perhaps best defined by the Canadian Supreme Court, in *Baker v Canada*:

> "The concept of discretion refers to decisions where the law does not dictate a specific outcome, or where the decision-maker is given a choice of options within a statutorily imposed set of boundaries."[23]

Clearly, when we ask students to reflect upon the amount of power belonging to administrators, we tend to get in response anecdotal stories of injustice. This in turn brings us to the idea that the subject of administrative law is ultimately about locating the actions of administrators against the backdrop requirement of the rule of law. How deeply does the law structure and confine an administrators' discretion? What impact do differing types of rules have on the flexibility available to administrators? These are the core questions in understanding how the law interacts with the everyday task of administrative decision-making.

[1–11]   Having provided this basic, descriptive orientation into the processes and actors which are examined in this book, we must now proceed to reflect upon the founding normative principles of the subject. This in turn will help the reader develop a deeper understanding of the functions and underlying values of this branch of law.

Traditional or Red Light Values

The Rule of Law and the *Ultra Vires* Principle

[1–12]   Ireland's colonial heritage has meant that the shape of its administrative state has been powerfully influenced by the system of law of England and Wales. The dominant shaping force upon traditional accounts of law and government in this context was AV Dicey, whose theory installed the principle that law should function as a brake on state action. This red light understanding of administrative law has as its central project the control of government power, required as it is to protect individual liberty and the rule of law. This latter, deeply rooted, yet highly controversial, principle of

---

[23] *Baker v Canada (Minister of Citizenship & Immigration)*, [1999] 2 SCR 817 at para 52.

Western legal thinking refers to the binding of government itself to the law. For Dicey the rule of law consisted, *inter alia*, of the following key principles:

1. That law should be supreme over arbitrary power: "no man is punishable...except for a distinct breach of the law established in the ordinary legal manner before the ordinary courts of the land"[24];
2. Legal Equality: that all classes should be equally subject to the ordinary law as administered by the ordinary courts;
3. The rule of law was to be protected by ensuring that individual public servants are responsible to the ordinary courts of the land for their use of statutory powers.[25]

These basic pre-requisites generate the *ultra vires* principle, a foundational   **[1–13]** tenet of administrative law, which essentially holds that, in the words of Lord Bingham:

> "Ministers and public officers at all levels must exercise the powers conferred on them reasonably, in good faith, for the purpose for which the powers were conferred and without exceeding the limits of such powers".[26]

Thus, while public representatives have been delegated by citizens to create laws and the government and its administrators are authorised to carry these into effect, the executive cannot act otherwise than in strict accordance with the laws laid down by parliament. Under this model, the judiciary, through judicial review, "are auditors of legality",[27] tasked with ensuring the lawfulness of administrative action.[28] The "courts and public authorities are ultimately regarded as combatants",[29] with the courts representing the bulwark to ensure that power is not abused. The principle

---

[24] A V Dicey, *Introduction to the Study of the Law of the Constitution* (10th ed) (Macmillan, London, 1959) at p 188, hereinafter "Dicey".

[25] The account of these three elements is featured in Dicey at pp 188-196.

[26] T Bingham, *The Rule of Law* (Allen Lane, London, 2010) at pp 37 and 60, hereinafter "Bingham".

[27] *ibid* at p 61.

[28] These traditional accounts of Administrative law often boast extremely legalistic definitions of accountability, see for instance, the statement of Justice Gaudron of the Australian High Court:
> "Accountability can be taken to refer to the need for the executive government and administrative bodies to comply with the law, and in particular, to observe relevant limitations on the exercise of their powers"
Corporation of the City of Enfield v Development Assessment Commission (2000) 199 CLR 135.

[29] M Elliott, J Beatson and M Matthews, *Beatson, Matthews and Elliott's Administrative Law Text and Materials*, (4th ed) (Oxford University Press, Oxford, 2011) at p 3.

of legality's most basic and fundamental consequence is to introduce the distinction between an appeal and review. Judges are tasked with undertaking the latter process, which is concerned not with the merits of the decision or substituting a new result, but centres upon the validity of the decision and whether it lies within the scope of the agency's power. In keeping administrators within the bounds of their power, the courts are ensuring that the will of the legislature is carried out. It is important to note that in identifying the will of the parliament, legislation will of course be read according to the presumption of constitutionality.

[1–14] In traditional red light understandings, administrative law serves a "thin" conception of the rule of law, aimed at overseeing a broader *culture of authority* which is anchored in:

> "...a political division of labor: the existence of distinct institutions for distinct spheres of public life, each best equipped to act in its sphere, and accountable for its actions within that sphere. As far as judicial review is concerned, this means that the main task of judicial review is policing the borders of this division of labor, and making sure that each institution is operating within its sphere and bounds of authority. Within these bounds an institution is not regularly required to justify its actions, but merely to identify the legal source of its authority to act."[30]

The concept of the rule of law represents "the driving force behind — and the normative basis of — modern administrative law"[31] and the different approaches to it will be discussed throughout the chapter.

[1–15] Alongside the rule of law, it is clear that the separation of powers also has a powerful effect upon administrative law doctrine. As can be seen from the above quote, a Diceyan conception of administrative law reflects a particular conception of the separation of powers.[32] This is of a unitary democracy founded on the sovereignty of parliament, a body which possesses a legislative monopoly. In Ireland, the primacy of the Oireachtas as law

---

[30] M Eliya-Cohen and I Porat, "Proportionality and the Culture of Justification", 59 *Am J Comp L* 463 (2011) at p 476.

[31] M Elliott, *The Constitutional Foundations of Judicial Review*, (Hart Publishing, Oxford, 2001) at p 104.

[32] There should be no doubting the substantial differences which exist between a state operating under a written constitution, and one where the limits of the authority of the different branches of government rest upon historical accommodations and political and legal theories.

maker is secured through Article 15.2.1°.[33] While clearly initially intended as a muscular affirmation of the new Irish Parliament's absolute status and to expunge any past relationship with the Westminster Parliament [34] the article has in modern times functioned as an injunction against judicial activism in the protection of rights.

Parliamentary sovereignty carries within it a vision of accountability of the administrative state. Fundamental to this, is the ideal that parliament controlled the executive, and is then itself controlled by the people. A faithful fulfilment of the *ultra vires* principle thus requires the legitimation of law through effective parliamentary scrutiny. An Irish reader at this point will likely be concerned about questions regarding the functional realism, as distinct from the normative idealism, of the theory. As we outline throughout this book, Ireland's parliamentary culture is at a low ebb. In our analysis of the Office of the Ombudsman in chapter 4 we address the allegation that prior to the crash, parliamentary oversight of the executive was in danger of becoming something of a "charade".[35] Such criticism has continued into the post-crash era, as exemplified by the lack of faith in parliamentary representatives to hold the banking inquiry, and the defeat of the Oireachtas inquiries referendum. In the context of judicial review, we also see tensions around the extensive use of delegated legislation and a lack of oversight of the transposition of European Union norms into Irish law. [1–16]

Discretion and the Rule of Law

A further element which has often accompanied red light accounts is a scepticism of administrative discretion. For early writers, the "uncertain and crooked cord of discretion" was insufficiently protective of liberty, and stood in stark contrast to the "golden and straight metwand of the law".[36] Dicey reflected this preference even as he espoused the ultra vires principle: [1–17]

---

[33] This sub-article provides that "The sole and exclusive power of making laws for the State is hereby vested in the Oireachtas: no other legislative authority has power to make laws for the State." Bunreacht na hÉireann, Art 15.2.1°.

[34] See D Morgan, *The Separation of Powers in the Irish Constitution* (Round Hall Sweet & Maxwell, Dublin, 1997) at pp 261-263.

[35] E O'Reilly, *Executive Accountability and Parliamentary Democracy,* speech given at "Executive Accountability and Parliamentary Responsibility", NUIG, 26 March 2011. Available at: http://www.ombudsman.gov.ie/en/News/Speeches-Articles/2011/Executive-Accountability-and-Parliamentary-Democracy.html (date accessed 31 July 2014).

[36] Sir Edward Coke, *Institutes of the Lawes of England (Volume 4)*, (William S Hein Co., Buffalo, NY, 1986), at p 41.

> "[The rule of law] means, in the first place, the absolute supremacy or predominance of regular law as opposed to the influence of arbitrary power, and excludes the existence of arbitrariness, of prerogative, or even of wide discretionary authority on the part of the government. Englishmen are ruled by law, and by law alone...."[37]

The association of discretion with arbitrariness, and the preference for the ex-ante rule which sets clear expectations and boundaries is somewhat evident even in Lord Bingham's modern, and more expansive, account of the rule of law. One chapter of his landmark book, *The Rule of Law*, even bears the strident title "Law not discretion".[38] This is moderated by his statement of principle that follows however, which provides that:

> "Questions of legal right and liability should ordinarily be resolved by application of the law and not the exercise of discretion."[39]

[1–18] Nevertheless, there is no doubt that this is more than a little puzzling to regulatory scholars,[40] who view law as just one tool of the broader process of regulation. From their perspective, the rule of law's goal of consistency and certainty is merely one aspect of a regulator's task, and to pursue it as an absolute value is not realistic. In some senses, discretion will always accompany rules, with it being inevitable that judgments will have to be made in applying legal standards to factual situations. The open-textured quality of language means that, for Professor Julia Black, a foremost regulatory theorist:

> "...[claims that] discretion can be 'managed' both to confine its exercise to certain actors and to limit the way that those actors use the discretion given, is thus ambitious, if not misguided."[41]

[1–19] Yet despite the seemingly conflicting nature of the starting points adopted by lawyers and regulatory scholars, it is important to note that the debate is not one of polar opposites but rather of subtle continuums. Both sides signal an initial, emotive mistrust of discretion or legal control, but then proceed to cede a role for both. Even by the end of his chapter, Lord

---

[37] Dicey, above n 24 at pp 202-3.

[38] Bingham above n 26, chapter 4.

[39] *ibid* at p 48.

[40] The authors apologise for treating such a diverse group holistically, but it is a necessary evil for the purposes of an introductory account.

[41] J Black "Managing Discretion", Australia Law Reform Commission Conference Papers – *Penalties: Policy, Principles and Practise in Government Regulation*, June 2001 at p 2, hereinafter "Black".

Bingham appears to have moved further down the road of recognizing the inevitability of discretion, stating that:

> "... the rule of law does not require that official or judicial decision-makers should be deprived of all discretion, but it does require that no discretion should be unconstrained so as to be potentially arbitrary."[42]

Somewhat ironically by adopting this ending point, Lord Bingham appears to have passed Professor Black, who is travelling in the opposite direction. Black seems to envisage a much more subtle role for the law than merely ruling out arbitrariness. Ultimately, for her, legal regulation can influence decision-makers to:

> "...act within the law, and in accordance with principles of rationality, proportionality, consistency, non-discrimination, transparency and due process."[43]

[1–20]

Ultimately, it appears that the deep distrust of many classical red light accounts of administrative discretion can be rendered less strident. However, it does remain a point of emphasis.

Imbalances and Tensions in the Red Light Understanding of Administrative Law

Diceyan Legacies and the Evolution of the State

There is no doubt that Diceyan understandings of administrative law often reflect a distrust of the administrative state and an emphasis upon avoiding mistakes. As we will discuss in the context of the tribunals and of parliamentary inquiries, it is possible to argue that Irish administrative law has had a tendency to mistrust justice when it is not dispensed via court procedures, with tribunals often viewed as "unsatisfactory and injurious to the freedom of the citizen and to the welfare of society".[44] It is important to note that in writing his initial works Dicey was reacting to what he

[1–21]

---

[42] Bingham above n 26 at p 54.

[43] Black above n 41 at p 12. For a more extensive discussion of the contrasting views of discretion see D Kalderimis, C Nixon and T Smith, "Certainty and Discretion in New Zealand Regulation", published online as part of Victorian University of Wellington/Law Foundation of New Zealand's Regulatory Toolkit project: http://www.regulatorytoolkit.ac.nz/resources/papers/book-3/chapter-4-certainty-and-discretion-in-new-zealand-regulation (date accessed 10 October 2014).

[44] This viewpoint was described (and condemned) by W Robson, *Justice and Administrative Law, A Study of the British Constitution*, (Stevens, London, 1951) at p xiii.

perceived as the woeful operation of the French *droit administratif*, a system of specialised administrative courts. Dicey preferred to avoid such an approach, and argued that the "ordinary" courts should handle cases, as in most respects the "relationships of citizens with public officials are not — and should not be radically different from relations between citizens and public bodies".[45] At the end of his long career, however, Dicey had moved to a position whereby he acknowledged that the French system appeared effective in controlling abuse of power and that some elements of it were influencing British governance structures.[46] Yet fundamentally, Dicey's vision of the constitutional State was one which protected the fundamental rights of the citizen, but was not involved in collectivist projects such as the provision of services for the benefit of its citizens. The rise of the welfare and regulatory State, with the concomitant growth in discretionary power were unforeseen developments postdating his theory.

The Ambiguity of the *Ultra Vires* Principle

[1–22] Secondly, the *ultra vires* principle, in its focus upon legal authority, relies on concepts which are at best increasingly muddy and at worst perhaps entirely indeterminate. As will be seen throughout the judicial review section of this book, the distinction between the "law" (which the judiciary are to declare) and the "merits" (the preferable result in a particular administrative matter) has been fundamental to the understanding of the role of the courts under the principle of legality. Yet, concepts such as reasonableness and proportionality which are now at the core of modern administrative law seem transgressive to this borderline. Thus as we see in our discussion of errors of law and errors of fact and law in chapter 7, the distinction between "law" and "merits" is increasingly a marker of an anxiety for the courts rather than a determinative bright line. This reflects the fact that the exercise of statutory power will often be dependent upon the existence of factual conditions defined by the law e.g. the ability to grant a social welfare payment to a person "injured" in the "course of their employment". To allow the decision-making agency a completely free hand in construing such conditions could result in the expansion of their power beyond that contemplated by legislators, but too interventionist an approach could lead to judicial control. While we are at this stage merely

---

[45] Harlow and Rawlings (2009), above n 1 at p 9.

[46] A V Dicey "The Development of Administrative Law in England", (1915) 31 LQR 148, a fuller discussion of this is available in Harlow and Rawlings (2009), above n 1 at pp 8-9.

linking to more extensive discussions later in this book, it is useful to set out the provocative perspective of Sir John Laws, who concluded that:

> "[the *ultra vires* principle has] nothing to say as to what a court will *count* as a want of power in the deciding body; and so of itself illuminates nothing. It amounts to no more than a tautology, *viz*, the court will strike down what it chooses to strike down".[47]

While this reflects a British viewpoint, it is fair to say that some of the volatility around the meaning of reasonableness and of jurisdictional error, indicates that the demands and contours of the *ultra vires* principle are not inevitable.

The Centrality of Parliament

One of the strongest benefits to commend the red light account of administrative law is its emphasis upon *input legitimacy*, i.e. the concept that administrative agencies and bureaucrats gain their power solely from the democratic process and through direct legal authorisation. This means that administrative actions, no matter how laudable or far sighted, cannot be legitimate if they have not been authorised through the democratic process. This contrasts with those accounts which argue for a mix of input and *output legitimacy*[48]: whereby the agency is legitimated by the outcomes it secures through using its discretion, as well as by the direct mandate given to it by the democratically elected parliament. In an era of growing regulatory complexity and transnational structures, output legitimacy is increasingly being relied upon, particularly in the economic fields.[49] Red light understandings stress the importance of tying the power of administrators to a grant of power by parliament: thereby promoting input

[1–23]

---

[47] Sir John Laws, "Illegality: The Problem of Jurisdiction" in M Supperstone and J Goudie (eds), *Judicial Review* (2nd ed) (Butterworths, London, 1997) at p 52.

[48] These terms were first coined by Fritz Sharpf in 1970, who divided democratic legitimacy into *output*, assessed in terms of effectiveness of outcomes for people, and *input* judged in terms of responsiveness to the citizen's concerns as a result of participation by the people. For lawyers specifically, output legitimacy refers to the degree to which laws solve the relevant problems they seek to address, whereas input legitimacy in such circumstances would refer to the quality of the public debate and the extent of participation of citizens in the creation of the law. For further discussion see V A Schmidt, "Democracy and Legitimacy in the European Union Revisited: Input, Output and 'Throughput'" (2013) *Political Studies* Vol 61, at p 2.

[49] The overreliance of the European Union upon output legitimacy has been criticized by Scharpf, see F W Scharpf *Governing in Europe*, (Oxford University Press, Oxford, 1999) and F W Scharpf, "The Asymmetry of European Integration, or Why the EU Cannot be a Social Market Economy" 2010 8(2) *Socio-Economic Review* 211-50.

legitimacy through the public debate and scrutiny of proposed legislation. Such an emphasis clearly corresponds with Ireland's republican character, which, at the level of theory, would seem to make most executive actions contingent upon legislative authorisation.

Yet we should also consider whether there are certain fields or circumstances where the executive does have the ability to pursue its own policies without such authorisation. While this was a bigger issue for the UK with its constitutional monarchy, we have seen traces of Irish judicial affinity with notions of free-standing executive authority. In chapter 7 examining narrow *ultra vires*, we discuss the recent High Court case of *Prendergast v Higher Education Authority*,[50] which in our view underlined the unclear footing of executive power in Ireland. A further threat to the red light school's goals can be seen in the growth of delegated legislation, with regulations and orders issued by departments now far more expansive and technical than could have been foreseen.

The Rule of Law: Narrow and Broad Understandings

[1–24] A clear tension within the traditional Diceyan account is its reliance on a particular conception of the rule of law. The rule of law is at once the foundation stone of administrative law as a subject, but also the wellspring of contestation as various legal theorists argue that traditional *ultra vires* principles are an insufficient definition of the concept. Red light theories have thus often been accused of relying upon unduly "thin" or "transmission" versions of the rule of law. Such "thin" understandings merely require that law possess some formal properties, beyond which the actual law which Parliament passes may have any content. Some critics therefore argue that Dicey's understanding of the rule of law is so minimal that it in fact constitutes rule *by law* rather than the rule of law.[51] The allegation that "thin", Diceyan understandings of the rule of law are insufficiently protective of the rights of individuals was most evident in debates regarding another "thin" account, that of Lon Fuller. Fuller

---

[50] *Prendergast v Higher Education Authority & Ors* [2009] 1 ILRM 47.

[51] See for example R Stein, "Rule of Law: What Does it Mean", (2009) *18 Minn J. Int'l. L.* 293 at p 299. It is important to note that even Dicey's account does contain certain substantive values, with judicial independence for example, implicit in the theory. For further general discussion on the debate between formalist and substantive understandings of the rule of law see: P Craig "The Formal and Substantive Conceptions of the Rule of Law: An Analytical Framework" (1997) *Public Law* 467.

proposed an updated version of the rule of law,[52] made up of eight virtues which a law must possess in order to be valid:

- Laws should be general and contain rules prohibiting or permitting behaviour;
- Laws must be widely promulgated, i.e. advertised and accessible to the public;
- Laws should not be retrospective;
- Laws must be clear, with citizens able to adapt their conduct to ensure compliance;
- Laws should be non-contradictory;
- Laws should not ask the impossible;
- Laws should not change frequently or be so volatile as to make it difficult of citizens to adapt their behaviour;
- Finally there should be congruence between what written statutes declare and how officials enforce those statutes.

Clearly a number of these principles are particularly significant for administrative law, and can be enforced through the classic *ultra vires* principles and doctrines such as legitimate expectation and natural justice. Fuller claimed that these eight principles represented an internal morality for the legal system. This claim was strongly disputed by HLA Hart, who argued that even undemocratic, despotic regimes could satisfy Fuller's criteria.[53] Thus Fuller, and other thin accounts of the rule of law, can be criticised for failing to address fundamental values such as human rights and democracy and how these shape and legitimate the legal system.   **[1–25]**

The Hart-Fuller exchange is representative of the debate regarding whether thin definitions of the rule of law should seek to move towards more substantive or thicker ideals, which can be developed through the inclusion of fundamental rights, democracy or the requirements of justice. It has historically been quite tempting for the judiciary to settle for the common baseline offered by the minimum requirements of formal, red light commentators rather than engage in a wide ranging, contentious jurisprudential inquiry. Yet, as we shall see later in this chapter, the increasing   **[1–26]**

---

[52] L Fuller, *Morality of Law*, rev. ed. (Yale University Press, New Haven, 1969), at p 39. Fuller discusses each criterion in depth at pp 46–90.
[53] HLA Hart, "Positivism and the Separation of Law and Morals", (1958) 71 *Harv L Rev* 593, 595–96.

role of human rights law in public administration disturbs some of those traditional baselines. Perhaps the most prominent effort to defend a thicker conception of the rule of law was undertaken by Lord Bingham, writing after his retirement from the House of Lords. He proposed that the rule of law should be taken as being made up of the following reservoir of principles:

1. The law must be accessible and so far as possible intelligible;
2. Questions of legal right and liability should ordinarily be resolved by application of the law and not the exercise of discretion;
3. The laws of the land should apply equally to all, save to the extent that objective differences justify differentiation;
4. The law must afford adequate protection of human rights;
5. Means must be provided for resolving disputes, without prohibitive cost or inordinate delay;
6. Ministers and public officers at all levels must exercise the powers, conferred on them reasonably, in good faith, for the purposes for which the powers were conferred and without exceeding the limits of such powers;
7. Adjudicative procedures provided by the state should be fair;
8. The state must comply with its obligations under international law.[54]

[1–27] Lord Bingham's account of the rule of law is significant, not merely for its alternative (more expansive) content, but also for the manner in which it was constructed.[55] Rather than representing a philosophically framed, universally valid definition of the rule of law, his work is rather an attempt

---

[54] Bingham, above n 26. These principles are elaborated in chapters 3-10.

[55] While we focus upon Lord Bingham's account here, it is important to note that judges from other countries have also considered the rule of law implicit in their constitutional frameworks. Particularly noteworthy in this regard is the contribution of Justice Anthony M Kennedy of the US Supreme Court, who formulated the following substantive conception of the rule of law:

"1. The law is superior to, and thus binds, the government and its officials.
2. The Law must respect and preserve the dignity, equality and human rights of all persons. To these ends the Law must establish and safeguard constitutional structures necessary to build a free society in which all citizens have a meaningful voice in shaping and enacting the rules that govern them,
3. The Law must devise and matinain systems to advise all persons of their rights, and it must empower them to fulfill just expectations and seek redress of grievances without fear of penalty or retalisation"

See A M Kennedy, "The Rule of Law, Written Constitutions and the Common Law Tradition", Speech at the American Bar Association Annual Meeting, 5 August 2006, Honolulu, Hawaii. This conception is extensively discussed by Stein, above n 51, at pp 299-300.

to locate the rule of law as it stood at the time of writing in England and Wales. Thus in understanding the roots of Irish administrative law, it is necessary for lawyers and commentators to locate an *Irish* conception of the rule of law. This would not be dependent upon academic debate regarding the merits of particular theoretical approaches, but rather upon construing key constitutional provisions and philosophies. The Irish Constitution remains a primary resource for locating an Irish rule of law, whether it be of a "thin" or "thick" conception. Thus, while it may be said that Irish administrative law has Diceyan tendencies, the justification for this would likely lie in existing approaches to Article 15.2.1° of our Constitution. Further, to the extent that Ireland's rule of law may reach beyond the *ultra vires* principle towards more expansive ideals, this would be rooted in the fact that our constitution requires that the State defend and vindicate the fundamental rights of the citizen. As we will see later in chapter 10 in our discussion of the cases of *Dellway Investments Ltd v National Asset Management Agency*[56] and *Mallak v Minister for Justice*,[57] the right of a citizen to procedural fairness has deep foundations within our constitutional framework. It is very important, therefore, to acknowledge the powerful gravitational pull that constitutional law debates regarding the proper role and competences of judges and the separation of powers has upon administrative law as a subject. Such forces were evident in the Supreme Court's discussion of proportionality analysis in the case of *Meadows v Minister of Justice*,[58] which we discuss in chapter 9. If, in the words of Criddle, "administrative law serves as the rule of law's handmaid",[59] we encourage students and practitioners to see the value of reflecting upon which of the competing conceptions the subject's doctrines are serving.

Administrative Law Viewed From Below: Green Light Values

The Importance of Facilitating and Encouraging Government Action

We have already seen that Diceyan approaches were rooted in a conservative viewpoint of the State, being grounded in the need to defend

[1–28]

---

[56] [2011] 4 IR 1.
[57] [2012] 3 IR 297.
[58] [2010] 2 IR 701.
[59] E Criddle, "Mending Holes in the Rule of (Administrative) Law", 104 *Nw. U. L. Rev. Colloquy* (2010) 309, at p 1271. Available at http://www.law.northwestern.edu/lawreview/colloquy/2010/8/LRColl2010n8Criddle.pdf (date accessed 10 October 2014).

liberty against encroachment. With the rise of the welfare State, and the expansion of modern governance and regulation, voices emerged which called for less scepticism of government's role and expressed a desire for administrative law to be more facilitative of government action. Harlow and Rawlings dubbed such approaches green light theories, a description which was not to be understood as a wholly permissive or "hands off" approach. Instead these theorists acknowledged the public interest benefits of government action and therefore saw administrative law as being more facilitative than preventive. In addition green light theorists were less concerned with court based controls and more interested in political and administrative forms of accountability:

> "Because they look in at administration from outside, lawyers traditionally emphasise external control through adjudication. To the lawyer, law is the policeman; it operates as an external control, often retrospectively. But a main concern of many green light writers was ... to *minimise* the influence of courts: courts, with their legalistic values, were seen as obstacles to progress, and the control that they exercise as unrepresentative and undemocratic. 'The lawyers', said Robson, 'still regard themselves as champions of the popular cause; but there can be little doubt that the great departments of state ... are not only essential to the well-being of the great mass of the people, but also the most significant expressions of democracy in our time'".[60]

[1–29]   The reader will see that portions of this book, in their emphasis upon non-judicial forms of review, reflect such outlooks. Our desire to locate administrative law within a broader conversation regarding effective regulation and public participation is a marker of green light influences. The green light approach is particularly important to Ireland due to the court-centrism which has often marred discussion of administrative law in our law schools and professions. It also allows us as lawyers to initiate conversations regarding the perception and use of law within government departments and amongst those working within other disciplines such as politics and government. There is no doubt that such encounters can, however, lead to conflict. In one instance, Professor John Willis criticised the legalistic approach of Ontario's Inquiry into Civil Rights' in the 1968, which focussed almost entirely upon the provision of judicial review

---

[60] Harlow and Rawlings (2009), above n 1 at p 37 quoting W Robson, *Justice and Administrative Law* (3rd ed) (Stevens, London, 1951) at p 421.

remedies. Enraged by the narrow formalism of the approach, Willis wrote his law journal riposte, he admitted, "in a mood of irritated dissent":

"...[C]onsider what these terms of reference assume. It is the government — and not the predatory real-estate developers, suppliers of goods and services, salesmen of mining shares etc. who the government, by its action, tries to control — that is suspected of encroaching on 'the freedom of the individual.' It is the powers conferred on paper by the statutes and regulations, and not what the civil servants actually do under them, that are to be examined. It is the statutory powers of civil servants, and not some attitudes of some civil servants to the citizen — still less the attitude of the citizen himself to 'authority' or to what his 'fundamental freedoms' are - that may need changing...[Willis noted the entire Commission team consisted of lawyers]... And consider the normal lawyer's biases. Because he acts for individuals he necessarily empathizes with the individual. Because he is steeped in the common law he views with alarm any departures from the eighteenth century Constitution which he finds in the law reports. Because he lacks experience in the facts of governmental life he has little interest in what actually happens there. Because he is familiar with law as a shield to be used in the defence of his clients he overestimates the importance of legal safeguards and underestimates the importance of the, to him, less familiar but more efficacious ones of fair-minded civil servants, a vigilant press, and a 'watch that government' atmosphere in the general public".[61]

This represents a call for an integrated, socio-legal understanding of administrative law as a subject.[62] Though, perhaps contra Willis' optimism above, the reader may notice that we are a great deal more jaundiced regarding the current state of our political oversight and the responsiveness of government at this juncture in Irish history.[63]

Critiquing Legal Formalism

So what would an administrative law facilitative of government action [1–30] look like? Firstly, it would attempt to moderate, if not wholly eschew, formalism. Harlow and Rawlings argue that law often obstructs effective

---

[61] J Willis, "The McRuer Report: Lawyer's Values and Civil Servant's Values" (1968) 17 UTLJ 351 at p 353.

[62] Willis himself referred to his desire to "talk administrative law with a civil servant and political science accent", to be both "a government man" and a "what actually happens man". *ibid*.

[63] One vote being the central mechanism to condemn so many individual failures, the electoral system provides only a diffuse form of accountability, and must be supplemented by other participative mechanisms to make government more responsive.

governance with excessive formalism — what they describe as "hair-splitting distinctions and terminological contortions".[64] Clearly, not all legal reasoning suffers from such technicality, but the red light school can be seen to view the law as a matter for judicial cultivation and declaration; a sealed off regime of internal logic belonging to the judiciary For green light commentators, judicial review needs to be viewed as a form of *communicative legality*, with the standards and principles identified by the courts eventually migrating to the administrative context, where they can be integrated proactively into everyday functioning and decision-making. Harlow and Rawlings note the fundamentally different approach of administrators and lawyers to "the law":

> "Judicial review of administrative action is primarily retrospective, although it can possess a prospective element if the administration accepts that judicial precedent establishes the limits of its future conduct. Legislation is primarily prospective. Like the banks of the river, legislation controls administrative activity by prescribing its limits. When an administrator asks, 'May I do X?', the lawyer replies 'if the law permits'. He knows where to find the law: statutes, regulations, precedent etc., and he knows how to rank it when it has been found. Lawyers like to assume that administrators approach the law in the same way...Generally speaking, [however,] neither administrators nor politicians seek their mandate in law but in policy; they are, in other words, policy-oriented. Administrators see law positively as a set of pegs on which to hang policies; viewed negatively, the law may be series of hurdles to be jumped before policy can be implemented...".[65]

---

[64] C Harlow and R Rawlings, *Law and Administration* (2nd ed) (Cambridge University Press, Cambridge, 2006) at p 31. Though a better and more extensive definition supplied by Michael Taggart: including "a highly technical approach to problems; the employment of formal, conceptual and logical analysis, often related to literalism and sometimes originalism; a belief that law is an inductive science of principles drawn from the cases, rather than the application of broad, overarching principles to particular disputes; ... a downplaying of the role of principle, policy, values and justice in adjudication; and in extreme forms a denial of judicial law-making".
M Taggart, "Australian exceptionalism in judicial review", (2008) 36 *Federal Law Review* 1 at p 7.

[65] *ibid* at p 77. While this quote best serves our current purposes, it is worth noting that the position was somewhat revised by Harlow and Rawlings in the third edition of their book in 2009, perhaps to reflect the greater visibility of judicial review:
"Legislation is prospective in that it controls administrative activity by prescribing its bounds. Judicial review of administrative action is primarily retrospective, although it alos possesses a prospective dimension. Lawyers assume and administration tacitly accepts that judicial rulings set boundaries for future conduct".
Harlow and Rawlings (2009), above n 1 at p 40.

It is a matter of great concern, therefore, that there are a number of judicial   [1–31]
review grounds that are currently encrusted with technicality and
uncertainty.[66] In particular, in our discussion of reasonableness in chapter 9,
we will see that judges have adopted a powerfully "contextual" approach to
review, whereby general principles are avoided in preference to fact specific
judgment. We argue very strongly for greater clarity following the landmark
Meadows judgment, based on the concern that our law is now overly
impressionistic. Apart from the difficulties in fixing core doctrines, we would
also note a failure to empirically study how government departments react to
significant judicial review cases. Unlike other jurisdictions, there has been
little research carried out of the on the ground, systemic impact of judicial
rulings on Irish administrators — we are left to question the means and extent
by which legal norms and rulings migrate into bureaucratic contexts.

Law and Regulation

Green light scholars also underline that the positive *exercise* of public   [1–32]
power, not merely the procedural conditioning of its exercise, lies at the
heart of the subject. This reflects the view that the courts are not the primary
actors of administrative law, but rather that administrative justice "is today
the work of many hands".[67] Even de Smith, in his pioneering text, famously
said of judicial review that it was "inevitably sporadic and peripheral" to
the daily realities of administrators.[68] The green light theory is useful
because it avoids excessive legalism in the pursuit of good administration.

---

[66] In terms of the accessibility of our law, it bears remarking that we are not helped by the fact
we are a small country. The resulting lower volume of cases raises the stakes at play when
a particular issue comes to a head, and makes the possibility of correction or adaptation
slower than in larger jurisdictions. An interesting acknowledgement of this was made in
the New Zealand context *in Lab Tests Auckland Ltd v Auckland District Health Board* [2009]
1 NZLR 776 (CA (NZ)). There Hammond J noted that in such contexts there is often "an
intermittent and somewhat mad-headed chase after the 'latest case' on the part of the bar
and commentators, and seminars sprout up as if there has been a seismic shift when one case
is decided". Ironically therefore, Irish administrative law may feature rapid accelerations
and longer periods of stagnation, which can irritate the natural judicial tendency towards
incrementalism and refinement.

[67] The Rt Hon Dame Sian Elias, GNZM, Chief Justice of New Zealand, *National Lecture on
Administrative Law*, Australian Institute of Administrative Law Conference, 2013, at p 7.

[68] S A de Smith, *Judicial review of Administrative Action* (1st ed) (Stevens, London, 1959), at p 1.
Though the 1995 edition of his masterwork was to reverse course, reflecting the opening up
of previous mindsets by acknowledging that "the effect of judicial review on the practical
exercise of power has [...] become constant and central." S A de Smith, H Woolf and J A
Jowell, *Judicial Review of Administrative Action*, (5th ed) (Sweet & Maxwell, London, 1995)
at p vii.

A legalistic definition of administrative justice would equate compliance with the grounds for judicial review, with a "good" decision. Certainly reading some books in the area, one gets the impression that a good decision is said to be one that is reasoned, is based on relevant and not irrelevant material, is procedurally fair, adheres to the legislative standards and involves a genuine exercised of discretion. In short compliant with judicial review principles.[69] For many, however, the modern project of administrative law should seek a broader frame: searching out interdisciplinary insights into what might be best practice approaches to decision-making and accountability. Adopting this approach with its resultant deeper definition, we may return to judicial review and reflect on how it can support the promotion of good administration. It is possible, for instance, that the recent strengthening of legitimate expectation and proportionality can promote an increased visibility of administrative reasoning and consistency.

[1–33] One of the most significant recent commentators reflecting upon this legal/regulatory interface has Professor Cass Sunstein, whose book (co-authored with Richard Thaler) *Nudge*, sought to persuade lawyers to moderate their oppositional tendencies towards discretion and administrative judgment, to use law to structure and influence individual or corporations' choices rather than as a series of rigid commands.[70] One of the underlying principles of this approach has been Sunstein's longstanding desire to shift administrative law from a subject addressing merely "procedural rules to discipline the exercise of power by bureaucrats" to one which addresses what he terms "administrative substance": namely what works and does not work in regulating the conduct of administrators.[71] Sunstein is, therefore, one of a line of commentators who have criticised what Dean Edward Rubin has bracingly dubbed the "prehistoric" fear of administrative discretion, and who have sought to foster a more complex narrative about

---

[69] For a discussion of this theme see J McMillan, *Can Administrative Law Foster Good Administration*, the Whitmore Lecture 2009, Council of Australian Tribunals, New South Wales Chapter, Sydney, September 16 2009. Available at: http://www.ombudsman.gov.au/files/16_September_2009_Can_administrative_law_foster_good_administration.pdf (date accessed 31 July 2014).

[70] C Sunstein and R Thaler, *Nudge: Improving Decisions about Health, Wealth and Happiness*, (Penguin Books, New York, 2009).

[71] C R Sunstein, "Administrative Substance" (1991) Vol 40(3) *Duke Law Journal* 607 at pp 608-9.

how law can structure and guide administrators to reason through the choices in front of them.[72]

Non Judicial Forms of Review

Another way in which the standard Irish administrative law doctrines are being exposed to green light philosophies is through the growing role and influence of European institutions in our legal and regulatory systems. The values of the common law constructed administrative law have often been framed in opposition to continental Europe's versions — with Dicey himself directly criticising France's *droit administratif* while defending his differing understanding of government-citizen relations. Yet, as the process of European integration continues, it is important to acknowledge the differing legal and administrative infrastructure which Union members possess, and how these may be reflected in the Union's legal instruments and judicial philosophies. For non-common law countries, the relationship between the citizen and the executive branch is often regulated by an entirely separate regime of norms and precedent, administered by specialist tribunals rather than by the general courts. Readers may, for instance, be familiar with the Counseil d'Etat, which is the peak body for an entire system of administrative tribunals in France. As we discuss throughout this book, Ireland's system of first instance tribunals is scattershot and certainly not systematised. Core areas in environmental law are largely reliant upon judicial review rather than an Environmental Appeals Tribunal, for instance. The development of tribunals in Ireland has often been reactively tied to the perceived needs of particular areas rather than the product of a clear vision of the benefits of merits based review.[73] The under-development of such bodies has access to justice implications, but also means that a best practice standard of merits review is often limited, or simply unavailable. This regularly lies at the core of cases taken against Ireland internationally, as we see in chapter 14 on European Union and chapter 15 on the European Convention on Human Rights. These chapters highlight that the indirect pressure on our courts to offer more supple versions of judicial review to meet the expectations of European actors may, in part, be traced to our failure to diversify our review and appeal systems.

[1–34]

---

[72] E Rubin, *Beyond Camelot* (Princeton University Press, Princeton, New Jersey, 2005) at p 84.

[73] See our discussion of the Refugee Appeals Tribunal in chapter 11 and our treatment of the independence of the Social Welfare Appeals Tribunal in chapter 15.

[1–35]   That an amalgam of common law and continental administrative law is possible can be seen, oddly enough, from Australia, where for the past thirty years, the Australian Administrative Appeals Tribunal has functioned.[74] The AAT attempts to provide systematised appeal for over four hundred individual statutes, and is superior to existing Irish decision-making structures due to the following features:

- There is greater security of tenure for tribunal members, as well as statutorily mandated independence;
- The AAT has available to it on the merits decisions drafted by leading experts (while always presided over by a judge of high standing, the AAT is made up experts from a wide range of cognate areas including medical and financial experts);
- The tribunal stands in "the shoes of original decision-maker", tasked with finding "the correct and preferable decision". This is an antidote to the restricted frame of analysis and remedies available through judicial review.
- While Ministerial policy is applied by the AAT (as it would be by the original decision-maker), this would at least bring administrative decision-making out into the open, and model proper conduct for ground level decision makers. Tribunal decisions embody for instance the obligation to find individualised justice even in the face of ministerial policy and reflect upon how the two should interact.
- There is an emphasis on self-represented litigants, alternative dispute resolution mechanisms such as neutral case evaluation, case appraisal and mediation. The timelines and procedures of the AAT regularly outstrip any best practice Irish examples.[75]

[1–36]   Green light accounts thus adopt a systematic and collectivist perspective. This is evident even in their view of accountability which champions the need to supplement the private individual's right to natural justice with broader rights available to the public as a whole, such as rights to access under freedom of information laws. The Irish administrative State has historically lacked such an overarching "design" perspective in areas of enforcement and regulation. This flaw has also been contributed to by the

---

[74] Established by the Administrative Appeals Tribunal Act 1975 (Cth).

[75] For an overview of the operation of the Australian Administrative Appeals Tribunal, as well as tribunals in the UK and the US, see P Cane, *Administrative Tribunals and Adjudication*, (Hart Publishing, Oxford, 2009).

legal community, with Irish administrative law's traditional emphasis upon judicial review having resulted in the subject's diversity and wider systemic importance being underappreciated

Imbalances and Tensions in the Green Light Understanding

The Integrity Branch of Government

While we have so far painted green light accounts as eager to promote the effective use of Government power, this should not be taken as implying that such scholarship is not critical of maladministration. Rather, it emphasises the need to proactively *design* frameworks to avoid such negative practices rather than centre the subject upon the reactive, individualistic remedy of judicial review. Thus we see a call for a renewed emphasis upon more diverse schemes of accountability and regulation, upon "administrative substance" as Sunstein describes it.[76] In chapters such as that on the Office of the Ombudsman, we note the rise of an "integrity branch" of government, embracing a range of institutions which are increasingly regarded as an essential supplement to the classical branches of judiciary, legislature and executive. This additional "integrity branch", first championed by Professor Bruce Ackerman, seeks to combat the gaps and inertia produced by traditional judiciary-executive-legislature divisions.[77] For Buck, Kirkham and Thompson, the existence of institutions such as the Ombudsman:

[1–37]

> "provides strong evidence that in the modern administrative state the institutions of the tripartite model by themselves are incapable of upholding the full range of values that underpin the constitution".[78]

In examining parliamentary inquiries, Commissions of Inquiry and the Office of the Ombudsman, we underline that Irish experiences and reforms endorse these outlooks, and that integrity institutions will be core to future efforts to diversify and re-centre traditional Irish administrative philosophies.

---

[76] Above n 71.

[77] See B Ackerman, "The New Separation of Powers" (2000) 113(3) *Harvard Law Review* 633 at pp 694-696.

[78] T Buck, R Kirkham and B Thompson, *The Ombudsman Enterprise and Administrative Justice*, (Ashgate, Farnham, 2010), at p 18.

The Need for a Supportive Political Culture

[1–38] It is, however, very important to note judicial oversight's unique and abiding importance to the fight for quality in government decision-making. For administrators, the possibility of the judge looking over their shoulders, potentially intervening to ensure legality, rationality and procedural fairness represented the first iteration of administrative justice. It also represents the fundamental and most secure backstop against the abuse of government power, being constitutionally grounded with significant protection of their independence. While the notion of the "integrity branch" represents an alluring label to attach to so much vital work done by many diverse institutions in public life, there is an inherent brittleness to bodies which require legislative foundations, whose independence is conditioned by resource constraints provided by the State and the need to maintain constructive relationships with government departments. As we illustrate in the Ombudsman chapter in particular, notions of an integrity branch often end up cast adrift upon the fickle tides of our underlying political culture. The current very low level of public opinion regarding both Parliament and independent regulatory agencies leads inescapably to a conclusion that there is a need for a fundamental normative and institutional redesign in order to restore a diverse, green light vision of accountability in the Irish State.

[1–39] Ultimately, green light accounts should not pursue an oppositional relationship with the courts or lawyers generally, but rather administrators, regulators and lawyers should work synergistically. The authors' experiences of teaching a topic such as the Ombudsman to law students in Ireland and Australia is revealing of this relationship. We have noted a form of identity politics in the classroom, where legally minded students recoil from the sheer "softness" of much of the Ombudsman's work — and regard it as a deeply compromised, negotiational body. We hope that some parts of our book will play a small part in alleviating any rigid belief that judicially enforced legal commands are the sole reliable fount of administrative justice. As Abraham Maslow warned, "I suppose it is tempting, if the only tool you have is a hammer, to treat everything as if it were a nail".[79] Equally, the authors' encounters with non-lawyers often reveal a mindset that regards judicial review as disconnected from the

---

[79] A Maslow, *The Psychology of Science: A Reconnaissance* (Gateway, Chicago, 1966), at p 15.

central policy issues, islanded within its own technical language.[80] We would suggest that this approach fails to appreciate, the powerful systematic effects which judicial review has. Even beyond its specific outcome, the public platform which it gives applicants has led to it making a powerful discursive contribution to broader political debates and policy issues. However, there are moments in this book where the reader will identify our underlying doubt that a *system* of administrative justice exists in Ireland. This is perhaps most evident in our discussions of the Ombudsman, the parliament and the planning system. The proactive reform necessary to deliver upon green light accounts is contingent upon an alignment of public support and political interests which has not regularly presented itself during the history of the State. Irish governance has, on the whole, been reactive and fragmented in terms of regulatory design — as seen by the profusion of semi-State bodies (Irish solutions for Irish problems?), and by the lack of any consolidated vision of merits appeals. We would encourage the reader to reflect upon the development of legislation in core governmental areas and to ask the question to what extent are substantive obligations underpinned by a sustained vision for administrative implementation and oversight?

The Era of Rights: Building a Culture of Justification

As mentioned earlier in our discussion of the *ultra vires* principle, the [1–40] increasing prominence of human rights law is often viewed as having powerful effects upon public law generally. The impact which human rights norms have had upon the standard doctrines of administrative law is quite controversial, with some arguing that human rights law stands apart as a specialised field of statute or constitutional law and does not fundamentally affect the overall grammar of how courts oversee

---

[80] Harlow and Rawlings (2009), above n 1, at pp 37-8, quote extensively the views of Hutchinson, who delivers a stinging rebuke of what he sees as the core failings of judicial review:

"Courts ... take an overly historical approach to deciding disputes; they rely on an adversarial process; they limit the amount of relevant information on which decisions can be made; they are ignorant of bureaucratic concerns and workings; they allow access to only a limited number of individuals; they fail to monitor the impact of their own decisions; they ignore the claims of the collective interests; they adopt a negative cast of mind; and they are imbued with an individualistic philosophy. In short, the work of the courts is qualitatively incoherent and quantitatively ineffective."

A Hutchinson, "Mice under a chair: Democracy, courts and the administrative state" (1990) 40 UTLJ 374, at p 375.

administrators.[81] Yet there is no doubt, as members of the Supreme Court acknowledged in *Meadows* that rights discourse is now near ubiquitous in Irish public law matters, with nearly every matter capable of being framed in terms of individual rights.[82] While a healthy dose of scepticism regarding "new eras" is always called for, there is no doubt that rights discourse shines a renewed light on the uneven remainders and conceptual looseness of many traditional doctrines.

[1–41]   While the Irish Constitution remains the primary (long established) source of human rights within our jurisdiction, the main challenges to traditional understandings have come from the growing influence of the Charter of Fundamental Rights of the European Union and the European Convention on Human Rights. As we discuss extensively throughout this book, these instruments appear to require judges to supervise more closely the actions of administrators where individual rights are adversely affected. This is primarily achieved through requiring that decisions be proportionate, a standard which seems to be more invasive and merits based than the traditional *Wednesbury* reasonableness requirement. Those who focus upon the role of human rights in this area, argue that many human rights norms carry within them an implicit vision of a more interventionist administrative law — one which would expand the role of judicial review.[83] According to this understanding, human rights law is not merely made up of discrete obligations which must be complied with or enforced, but rather a process of *rights reasoning* which structures administrators' discretion.

[1–42]   It is also clear, however, that agreeing the extent and nature of "rights reasoning" in government decision-making is extremely divisive, even amongst its supporters. As we see in our chapter on reasonableness and proportionality, the Supreme Court in *Meadows* struggled to articulate how the fact that a matter involves interfering with fundamental rights might change the courts' approach to reviewing it. Is the traditional requirement of reasonableness enough? Or is a renewed test of proportionality required? Does Irish judicial review measure up to the standards expected under

---

[81] For an evaluation of such arguments see JNE Varuhas, The Reformation of English Administrative Law? Rights, Rhetoric and Reality', [2013] CLJ 369-413.

[82] *Meadows,* above n 58, judgment of Hardiman J at 782-3.

[83] The leading advocates of this position in an international context include Thomas Poole, 'The Reformation of English Administrative Law'', (2009) 68 CLJ 142 and Michael Taggart, "Reinventing Administrative Law", in N Bamfroth and P Leyland, *Public Law in a Multi-Layered Constitution*, (Hart Publishing, Oxford, 2003), at pp 331-340.

European Union law and the European Convention on Human Rights? While these questions are often portrayed as being caused by international legal trends, their prominence can also attributable to the silences and gaps in existing Irish jurisprudence. Irish public law features extensive judicial and academic analyses of the scope and method of reviewing the constitutionality of *legislation*,[84] but there has been nowhere near the same level of reflection regarding how to review *administrative decisions* affecting fundamental rights.

The Culture of Justification and Rights Reasoning

Let us return for now to the vision of administrative law that may underlie human rights norms. We might start by asking why rights discourse is so confronting for red light and green light advocates? This is largely due to human rights law apparent insensitivity to administrative law's traditional values. Firstly, rights norms often appear to require greater judicial intervention than under the red light school's "culture of authority". Rather than merely asking whether the decision is authorised by statute, the judge is often tasked with assessing the relative proportionality of the benefits of a decision to the adverse effects on the individual's rights. For the green light school, human rights offer another avenue for the over-judicialisation of administrative discretion: at worst resulting in the colonisation of expert decision-making with legal norms and requirements. In addition, rights norms are focused upon ends, i.e. asking whether a decision is sufficiently protective of rights, rather than the procedural or functional allocation-focused approaches of the red and green light schools.

[1–43]

Ultimately we argue that human rights norms are able to supplement the values of both the red and green light schools, specifically by requiring a culture of justification in government decision-making. In this approach, even after authority has been assigned, the authorised body needs to provide a justification for its decisions. This idea of a "culture of justification" was first forwarded by the South African academic, Etienne Maureinik, who argued for the following obligations:

[1–44]

---

[84] This is further discussed by H Biehler, "Curial Deference in the Context of Judicial Review of Administrative Action Post Meadows" [2013] 48(1) *Irish Jurist* 28 at pp 44-45.

1. Prior to the making of decisions, the individual should enjoy an extensive right to procedural fairness, including the right to partici- pate in the decision-making process;
2. Upon the making of the decision, the reasons for it should be given;
3. Judicial review should embrace a wider ground of reasonableness, which in Mureinik's should require that:
   (a) The decision-maker has considered all the serious objections to the decision taken, and has answers that plausibly meet them;
   (b) The decision-maker has considered all the serious alternatives to the decision taken, and has discarded them for plausible reasons; and
   (c) There is a rational connection between the premises and conclusion: between the information (evidence and argument) before the decision-maker and the decision that it reached.[85]

The culture of justification is, however, not merely an academic theory. Indeed, we would argue that increasingly, practice in comparator jurisdictions such as Canada and England and Wales reflect the approach set out by Mureinik. Even within our own jurisdiction it is clear that administrative law has recently undergone some significant modifications which are indicative of Mureinik's typology — with enhanced protection now recognised for the right to reasons and procedural fairness, together with some limited movement towards proportionality analysis.

Proportionality Analysis

[1–45] The rise of a deeper notion of a culture of justification is most visible in two key fault-lines in administrative law reasoning. The first, as we have already indicated, is proportionality analysis. Proportionality offers a structure to identify where there is a conflict between interests or rights and how these interests or rights may be rationally harmonised. It consists of four stages:

---

[85] This summary of core principles is drawn from E Mureinik, "A Bridge to Where? Introducing the Interim Bill of Rights", (1994) 10 *South African Journal on Human Rights* 31 at p 31 and E Mureinik, 'Reconsidering Review: Participation and Accountability', [1993] Acta Juridica 35. On Mureinik's work generally, see D Dyzenhaus, "Law as Justification: Etienne Mureinik's Conception of Legal Culture", (1998) 14 *South African Journal on Human Rights* 11 at p 11. See also Elias, above n 67 at pp 62-66.

- An examination of whether there is a legitimate aim being pursued by the action proposed (*legitimate aim requirement*);
- A consideration of whether the measure proposed is rationally connected to the legitimate aim (*rational connection of means to aims requirement*);
- A requirement that the action should not impair the rights adversely affected more than is necessary to achieve the legitimate aim (*minimal impairment requirement*);
- A requirement that there be an overall proportionality between what is achieved by the measure and the overall impact on the rights adversely affected (*fair balance requirement*).

The difference between such a stepped approach and the traditional framing of the reasonableness question which asks "was the decision so extreme in its defiance of logic or accepted moral standards…?" seems striking.[86] Under the proportionality approach decisions which affect rights have to be shown to, on the balance of probability, pursue a legitimate aim, be means-end rational, represent the least restrictive means and be balanced overall. As Thomas Poole has noted, this seems to have the immediate effect of "prioritising and protecting rights":

[1–46]

> "This aspect of the proportionality principle has led some commentators to talk about the creation of a "culture of justification" surrounding new, rights-based judicial review. But this cannot be quite right – what else was "traditional" review but a mechanism for demanding from government (certain kinds of) of justification for (certain kinds of) impugned decisions? Better to say that proportionality review offers the possibility of a different — and potentially deeper — inquiry into the reasons offered by government for its interference with rights and similar interests".[87]

---

[86] This approach is to be found in the traditional reasonableness test as set out in *The State (Keegan) v Stardust Compensation Tribunal* [1986] IR 642, at 658 and *O'Keeffe v An Bord Pleanála* [1993] 1 IR 39.

[87] T Poole, "The reformation of English administrative law", (2009) 68(1) *Cambridge Law Journal* 142 at p 147. Despite Poole's point, we are exercising academic's discretion to provoke by using the culture of justification heading for this section. This reflects Mureinik's own work, whereby he felt that justification should be *substantive* and that mere formalist reliance upon legal authority was insufficient to earn the moniker "justification". Further discussion of whether justification should be viewed as an aim of the *ultra vires* principle is seen in D Dyzenhaus, M Hunt and M Taggart, "The Principle of Legality in Administrative Law: Internationalisation and Constitutionalisation" (2001) 1 *Oxford University Commonwealth Law Journal* 5 at p 29.

[1–47]   The second key fault-line which features in many debates regarding an expanded culture of justification, is the idea of deference. This has become prominent because of a fundamental question which proportionality leaves unaddressed: the institutional question of how the court and the administrator are to co-operate in running a proportionality analysis. As Rivers notes:

> "In itself, [proportionality] is merely the structure of rational decision-taking, neutral on the question of who should take the decision. In order to function as a legal doctrine of constitutional or administrative review, it has to be combined with a theory of institutional competence and responsibility."[88]

Indeed it is this key floating variable to proportionality analysis which led Poole to remark that "proportionality is plastic" and "can in principle be applied almost infinitely forcefully or infinitely cautiously".[89]

Doctrine of Deference

[1–48]   Deference may be defined as requiring courts to give weight to the conclusions of an administrative decision-maker in its reasoning, with the possible result that the court will elect not to substitute its own perspective on the issues before it. Both red and green light accounts support notions of deference by judges towards administrators' decisions. Red light approaches stress the division between law and non-law, requiring judges to defer on any matters related to the merits, while green light approaches at times stress the need to defer to the needs of efficiency and not to colonise complex decisions with legal principles. The culture of justification school views deference as a concept which interacts with proportionality, but one that needs to be spelt out more clearly, and its use more closely justified. Rather than merely relying on the fact that a decision is carried out by a particular institution, a judge should look closely at why that institution's decision is worthy of respect. Merris Amos has argued that the amount of deference accorded to a decision-makers actions should be determined by three factors; how well democratic mechanisms are working in addressing the underlying issues, whether the decision-maker has conducted a thoroughly reasoned inquiry and the seriousness of their engagement with

---

[88] J Rivers, "The Presumption of Proportionality", (2014) 77 *Modern Law Review* 409 at p 413.
[89] Above n 87 at p 147.

the proportionality question.[90] In effect, what we see is that judicial constraint based on institutional concerns is being made subject to a process of justification, rather than being declared based on abstract separation of powers concerns or due to the mere identity of the body.

The role which deference can play is best explained through three judgments delivered by the House of Lords: *Begum*,[91] *Huang*[92] and *Miss Behavin' Ltd*.[93] The latter case concerned a decision made by Belfast City Council as to whether the buying of pornographic literature in a retail property should be permitted. It did so without any detailed consideration, explicit or implicit, of the proportionality of its interference with the applicant's rights under the European Convention on Human Rights. The House of Lords stressed that:

          "...the views of the local authority are bound to carry less weight where
          the local authority has made no attempt to address that question."[94]

Consequently, the Court regarded itself as being in a position to balance the relevant interests. In doing so however, the Court stressed, that local government bodies or parliament may possess obvious advantages in measuring the impact of a particular decision upon those who may be indirectly affected, and in obtaining information and consultations. In order for its judgment to be accorded the fullest extent of deference, however, it should bring such advantages to bear upon the matter in front of it. In short, the institutional advantages of the decision-maker are not merely assumed by the court, but there must be evidence in the decision-making process that the relevant advantages have been employed.

In *Begum*, a case which concerned a decision to ban the jilbab (a form of Islamic dress) at a secondary school in England, the Court stressed the importance of consultation in the decision-making process. The carrying out of a consultation process in such a context could function as evidence

[1–49]

[1–50]

---

[90] M Amos, "Separating human rights adjudication from judicial review - Huang v Secretary of State for the Home Department and Kashmiri v Secretary of State for the Home Department" (2007) *European Human Rights Law Review* 679.

[91] *R (Begum) v Head Teacher and Governors of Denbigh High School* [2007] 1 AC 100.

[92] *R (Huang) v Secretary of State for the Home Department* [2011] EWHC 2069 (Admin), [2011] All ER (D) 87.

[93] *Miss Behavin' Ltd v Belfast City Council* [2007] UKHL 19; [2007] 1 WLR 1420.

[94] *ibid* at para 37.

of expertise given that efforts had been made to gather all relevant evidence, and in effect trigger a "earned deference" to be recognised by the court. In the case at hand, the school had:

> "...taken immense pains to devise a uniform policy which respected Muslim beliefs but did so in an inclusive, unthreatening and uncompetitive way. The rules laid down were as far from mindless as uniform rules could ever be".[95]

[1–51] In *Huang*, the Court debated a number of possible ways to describe the contours of judicial deference, but displayed a preference for a pragmatic approach rejecting unnecessarily complex attempts to define, what it viewed ultimately as:

> "...the ordinary judicial task of weighing up competing considerations on each side and according appropriate weight to the judgment of a person with responsibility for a given subject matter and access to special sources of knowledge and advice."[96]

What emerges therefore is a debate which looks to avoid notions of "spatial" deference, whereby the decision-maker is insulated from review or their perspective is given particular weight due to their *identity* as a particular body. Instead the approach requires a consideration of whether an expert judgment is manifest in the reasons supplied and in the overall conduct of the decision-maker in the matter before it. This form of "earned" deference is intriguing, as it offers courts an opportunity to incentivise and affirm systemic efforts such as consultation with the public, organisational expertise and internal debate while reviewing a particular matter. This has been criticised, as will be seen below, as involving judicial review in process chasing or moving its concern outside of the result or content of the decision. Regardless, it at least foregrounds the question of how best to divide labour between the courts and administrative bodies in seeking to ensure that rights reasoning is diffused in across government.

[1–52] As we see later in this book, Ireland's current positioning in relation to these two conceptual fault-lines is somewhat controversial. While Ireland has, through the judgment in *Meadows*, recognised a form of proportionality, it is far from clear whether this is the structured conception outlined above. Rather, it often appears that Irish judges undertake an impressionistic

---

[95] Above n 91 at para 34.
[96] Above n 92 at para 16.

approach, merging the stages into a general question of fair balance. This reflects the fact that the Supreme Court in *Meadows*, indicated that the times when a decision will be held to be disproportionate will be rare.

In terms of the concept of deference, while it appears to exist in Irish law, **[1–53]** it has not been structured or conceptually mapped. It is clear that *contextual* factors are absolutely vital in Irish judicial review for reasonableness/proportionality, but there is, as yet no overarching theory or consolidated theory of when deference will be accorded, and what its impact should be upon the court. Having said that, it is evident that the courts will defer to the expertise of An Bord Pleanála for example, though this body has itself been at the centre of recent controversy. Following the recent case of *Kelly v An Bord Pleanála*,[97] the Government announced that it will be reviewed, with the expectation that it will be made "more accountable in justifying decisions to objectors and also reporting to Oireachtas committees on its activities". [98] Alongside such specific instances of deference being accorded, the courts have also stressed their role in vindicating the rights of the individual, and the accompanying impact on the initial decision-maker:

> "It is natural…for any decision maker to be the more hesitant, the more deliberate, the more cautious as the decision he or she is considering will the more gravely trench on the rights or interests of those likely to be affected".[99]

The Irish courts' approach therefore largely eschews general principle, for a contextual approach, which may fragment into a "wilderness of single instances"[100] rather than a consolidated structure. By not tending sufficiently to concept, there is a danger that underlying values may not be debated openly. In this jurisdiction, we thus see confusion surrounding two concepts central to the production of a "culture of justification", and a

---

[97] [2014] IEHC 400.

[98] F Sheahan, "Planning Body for Review in Wake of Court Overturning Decision", 6 October 2014, *Irish Independent*, Available at: http://www.independent.ie/irish-news/politics/planning-body-for-review-in-wake-of-court-overturning-decision-30640745.html (date accessed, 13 October 2014).

[99] *Meadows* above n 58 at p 824 (per Fennelly J).

[100] "Mastering the lawless science of our law, that codeless myriad of precedent, that wilderness of single instances, through which a few, by wit or fortune led, may beat a pathway out to wealth and fame." Alfred, Lord Tennyson, *Aylmer's Field* (1793).

trend towards a contextual focus, which prefers the practical resolution of individual cases to abstract reflection on foundational principles.

Criticisms of the Culture of Justification

An Undesirable Shift from Traditional Approaches?

[1–54]   In considering criticisms in this approach we must at the outset note that even the label "culture of justification" provokes dislike on the part of those who advocate red light understandings. Such voices would argue that their account also aims for justification — by requiring legal authority for the decision through a process of political justification in parliament. In addition, they would argue that in supervising the justification, and at times overturning some decisions as substantively disproportionate, the courts are engaging in a task for which they are unsuited: an impermissible straying out of the realm of legality into the merits of the matter. The bracing dissent of Hardiman J in *Meadows*, which should be required reading for students, provided eloquent testimony for traditional red light understandings of judicial review and opposed the shift to a proportionality analysis:

> "...I am also concerned that the process of requiring "justification" of the impugned decision will in practice cast an onus on to the decision maker, here the first respondent, to justify his decision to the courts... The fact that the law puts a particular decision into the hands of a member of one of the constitutionally established organs of government, the executive, does not in my view disentitle the decision to respect and to deference as that word is used in a judicial review context. On the contrary, I believe that the democratic nature of the State and the constitutional position of the decision maker, affirmatively entitles the decision in this case to deference in that technical sense...I am forced to the view that the test now proposed to be applied has quite the contrary effect; it looks for explanation and justification from the decision maker which I believe to be inconsistent with the proper principles of judicial review, and with the view that the onus of proof remains on the applicant. This, in my view, is a revolution in the law of judicial review, differing only semantically from that which has occurred in Britain."[101]

[1–55]   A culture of justification is also criticised for process chasing. At times the focus upon getting decision-makers to reason through legal rights, by

---

[101] Above n 58 at p 793.

expressly using the four step proportionality process can seem to encrust the decision-making process with unnecessary rigidity. Furthermore, too much of an emphasis on allocating deference can actually cause judges to prioritise surrounding actions, such as whether the decision-maker used key terms such as "proportionate", rather than reviewing the actual substance of the decision. Such an emphasis was memorably derided by Lord Hoffman, who stressed in *Begum* that school teachers "cannot be expected to make such decisions with human rights law textbooks at their elbows".[102] This plea to focus upon substance is constructive in that it reflects a fear that rights could become mere markers to tick off, rather than protections to affirm in decision-making. Thus we find Dame Elias of the New Zealand Supreme Court, recalling Lord Sedley's fear that:

> "human rights may take on the "throw-away status" of Wednesbury reasonableness...if the emphasis upon "rationality in decision-making leads to a "tick the box" scrutiny of process, if rights are "balanced" to blandness, if justifications for incursions on rights are used to manage them down, then there will be set backs for human rights."[103]

Criticism of the Primacy Given to Deference

The culture of justification thesis is also heavily criticised by *rights* advocates who prefer an alternative conception of rights which understands them as being legal obligations which are to be declared and enforced by the judicial branch. The use of a doctrine of deference is particularly criticised in this regard, with the eminent UK scholar TRS Allan, a particularly strong opponent. He argues that a focus upon an abstract idea of deference can lead to an abdication of judicial responsibility, and calls upon culture of justification advocates to limit its role in their accounts of judicial review. A general doctrine of deference, he argues, invites the decision-maker to point to expertise or good procedures in primary decision-making and use this as a way of avoiding determining whether the right was violated.[104] For Allan, the answer should be found by reference to the terms of the particular finding in the particular case. Thus, as Brady notes, for Allan "due deference is a double counting mechanism" which allows the

[1–56]

---

[102] Above n 91 at para 68.

[103] Above, n 67 at p 60-61, discussing S Sedley, *Freedom, Law and Justice* (Sweet & Maxwell, London, 1999) at p 21.

[104] TRS Allan, "Human Rights and Judicial Review: a Critique of 'Due Deference'" (2006) 65 CLJ 671, at p 673.

decision-maker to advance additional external factors rather than rely on the content of the decision made.[105]

[1–57] Allan decries attempts to define general factors which might make a judge defer to an administrator's judgment, such as was attempted by Laws LJ's (dissenting) judgment in *International Transport Roth GmbH*. There Laws LJ proposed four principles which might increase the amount of deference to the decision:

- The courts should be more deferential to an Act of Parliament than to a subordinate measure or executive decision;
- Where the matter requires the balancing of interests with fundamental rights as distinct from where the relevant [convention] right was unqualified;
- Where the subject matter is within the constitutional responsibility of the decision-maker (e.g. defence or foreign affairs), more deference should be applied;
- The degree of deference should also depend on whether the subject matter lies within the expertise of the decision-maker or the court.[106]

Allan criticises this approach because it "purports to implement a separation of powers between the courts and other branches of government", whereas, for him the separation of powers instead requires "the proper application of legal principles defining the scope of individual rights".[107] As such, deference, when elevated to a free-standing concept, can result in an imbalanced impression of the proper role of the court crowding out rights protection with institutional restraint. For him, the misguidedness of the approach can be seen by the fact that it permits reliance upon expertise even where the particular decision made might be *wrong*.

[1–58] Rather than looking at the surrounding institutional context as Laws LJ proposed, Allan argues that "the court must be persuaded by the reasons… rather than impressed by expertise or procedural competence".[108] His approach is marked by a great confidence in the certainty of legal reasoning,

---

[105] A Brady, *Proportionality and Deference under the UK Human Rights Act: An Institutionally Sensitive Approach* (Cambridge University Press, Cambridge, 2012) at p 27.
[106] *International Transport Roth v Secretary of State for the Home Department* [2002] EWCA Civ 158; [2003] QB 728 at 765-767.
[107] Above n 104 at pp 675-676.
[108] *ibid* at p 672.

and the ability to identify a correct *legal* answer. The role of the courts is to define human rights and to correct decisions of public authorities that fail to comply with the courts' requirements. Yet, it can be argued that much of rights reasoning is contextual and requires a balancing of competing institutional perspectives and interests. While the statement "the role of the courts is to define rights" seems alluring, the reality is more complex, as Young suggests. She argues that, courts are ultimately a secondary decision-maker:

> "the job of the court is not to define human rights. Rather, it is to set the boundaries of lawful restrictions that can be placed by public authorities on human rights. When ascertaining these boundaries, the courts first define rights broadly, using proportionality and deference to determine the range of lawful decisions that can be taken by public authorities."[109]

Rights reasoning seems to require a willingness to recognise competing inter-institutional perspectives on their scope, and for inter-institutional dialogue regarding their protection or possible limitation. It may be, as Raine argues, that "there are no correct answers, only those that are more justifiable than others".[110] In this respect, the culture of justification is rooted in a theory of deliberative democracy, whereby rather than morally rooted, judge-led definition of rights, democracy and rights are co-original and co-dependent, with the key being to protect rights while fostering dialogue between institutions and the public. Concepts such as proportionality and deference allow the courts to pursue this dialogue, while also defending fundamental rights, where necessary. Ultimately, a lot of the criticism is rooted in the tendency of some accounts to give deference undue prominence; indeed Poole has referred to an "academic craze" for the concept.[111] Despite all the debate, the concept merely attempts to install the basic principle that judges attribute weight to the primary decision where it is justifiable to do so.   [1–59]

Conflicting Understandings of Proportionality

As can be seen from the foregoing debates around deference, advocates of a culture of justification can be accused of a form of academic   [1–60]

---

[109] A L Young, "Human Rights Adjudication and the Human Rights Act 1998" in N Bamford and P Leyland (eds), *Accountability in the Contemporary Constitution* (Oxford University Press, Oxford, 2013) at p 177.

[110] T Raine, "Judicial Review under the Human Rights Act: A Culture of Justification", (2013) *North East Law Review*, Vol 1 81 at p 108.

[111] Above n 87 at p 146.

entrepreneurship, whereby their core concepts represent little more than a mere rebranding of older ideas such as reasonableness. The criticism advanced is that the core idea — proportionality — while seeming to offer space for the closer examination of the challenged decision, in fact may end up being little more than a check upon the process of the decision rather than upon its underlying fairness. If readers look back at the four step definition of proportionality given above, they will see that the last question — the notion of "fair balance" — is quite vague in its scope. Indeed, a debate has emerged over what the extent of its role should be — with some preferring a cautious approach[112] and others supporting a more expansive understanding.[113] The former approach tends to view fair balance as a check to ensure that the benefits of the decision are not wholly disproportionate to the adverse effects upon the individual. As indicated by the use of the word "wholly", this approach tends to be somewhat cautious in finding substantive disproportion, recognising the possibility of legitimate disagreement but still defending rights in cases of serious intrusion. Under such a "state-limiting" conception of proportionality,[114] the weight of analysis should fall upon the first three steps, with the last step only occurring on rare occasions. Where it is invoked, the use of the fourth step is largely linked to traditional, if controversial, legal concepts such as vulnerability, dignity and equality.[115] Thus, proportionality is seen as flexible and contextual, particularly when combined with deference and the need to consider the fundamental nature of the statute and the rights provision before the court.

[1–61]   Such a pragmatic approach to the fourth question is not adopted by those who prefer a more expansive conception of the principle of proportionality — what may be termed the "optimising school". Such commentators,

---

[112] This generally takes the form of urging the cautious use of proportionality balancing, by stressing the need to rely on fair balance where the decision is clearly disproportionate. As we discuss in chapter 14, the proportionality principle has varied in intensity, with actual balancing contemplated by theorists such as Alexy not occurring extensively. For an excellent discussion of the dueling conceptions, see A L Young, "Proportionality is dead: long live proportionality" in G Huscroft, B Miller and G Webber, *Proportionality and the Rule of Law*, (Cambridge University Press, Cambridge, 2014).

[113] J Rivers, "Proportionality and Variable Intensity Review", (2006) 65(1) *Cambridge Law Journal*, 65 at p 180.

[114] This label was coined by Rivers to describe approaches which do not fully value the role of fair balance plays in ensuring the protection of rights is optimized.

[115] On the use of dignity in balancing, see M Kumm and D Walen, "Human Dignity and Proportionality: deontic pluralism in balancing" in G Huscroft, B Miller and G Webber, *Proportionality and the Rule of Law*, (Cambridge University Press, Cambridge, 2014).

foremost amongst them Julian Rivers, point to the continental European roots of the concept. For Rivers, it is vital for common law judges to reflect upon the fundamental differences between a common law understanding of proportionality and that which prevails in the rest of Europe. The centrality of proportionality to European Union law and to the European Convention on Human Rights makes this particularly important for the Irish legal system. The traditional common law understanding of proportionality views it as an:

> "...efficiency-based oversight to ensure that there are no unnecessary costs to rights, that sledgehammers are not used to crack nuts, or rather, that sledgehammers are only used when nutcrackers prove impotent."[116]

Rivers argues however, that a continental decision-maker, when considering whether a decision is proportionate frames things differently, namely by asking: **[1–62]**

> "...does the act realise the public interest to such an extent that, all things considered, the gain to the public interest at least balances out the cost to the right?"[117]

Such an optimizing perspective often reflects the work of German theorist Robert Alexy, who argues that rights are principles which can be given weight, and then be balanced against other principles such as the common good or the public interest.[118] This approach clearly displays enormous confidence in the idea of "balancing" the right versus the common good. Alexy has, however, been criticized by Tsakyrakis for saying "nothing about how various interests are to be weighted, and this silence tends to conceal the impossibility of measuring incommensurable values" by holding out the idea of a common system of weighting which produces a

---

[116] Above n 113, at p 180.

[117] *ibid* at p 181.

[118] R Alexy, "The Construction of Constitutional Rights", (2010) 4(1) *Law & Ethics of Human Rights*, 51 at p 21:
"Principles are norms that require something be realised to the greatest extent possible, given the factual and legal possibilities at hand." Thus principles are optimization requirements. As such, they are characterised by the fact that they can be satisfied to varying degrees, and that the appropriate degree of satisfaction that depends not only on what is legally possible. Rules aside, the legal possibilities are determined essentially by opposing principles. For this reason, principles, each taken alone, always comprise a merely *prima facie* requirement"

"correct" answer.[119] This form of proportionality appears radically transgressive to red light understandings of judicial review, seeming to promise judicial intervention on broadly substantive grounds, though it is important to stress that Alexy himself does team it with a doctrine of deference, which operates to restrain the role given to judges.[120]

[1–63] Despite arguments that such a perspective has or will be adopted by Irish judges, we believe that the currently prevailing approach to proportionality within this jurisdiction is an intuitive common law understanding, which selectively uses the "fair balance" requirement in "sledgehammer" cases of severe intrusions on rights.[121] Irish judges have clearly signaled that substantive disproportion will generally be found in rare instances, and have not, in our view, displayed the type of confidence in the balancing process that shapes the accounts of Rivers or Alexy. It is interesting to reflect that many regard the "optimizing" approach as key to compliance with the understandings of proportionality in European Union law and European Convention on Human Rights — a question we return to later in this book. Even without this international perspective, however, Ireland's scheme of constitutional rights is, in the context of the judicial review of administrative action, currently refracted through a culture of authority, central to the red light theory, rather than of justification. We encourage the reader to reflect upon the appropriateness of this, particularly when we encounter the *Meadows* case later in this book.

---

[119] S Tsakyrakis, "Proportionality: an assault on human rights?", (2009) 7(3) *International Journal of Constitutional Law* 468 at p 471.

[120] One of the reasons this is not prominent in the literature on Alexy is that he employs the term discretion instead of deference. The use of this terminology is particularly unhelpful in an administrative law context. The leading discussion of Alexy's ideas on deference is given by Brady, above n 105, at pp 62-75, which provides an in-depth breakdown of the relevant passages in R Alexy, *A Theory of Constitutional Rights*, (Oxford University Press, Oxford, 2002) at pp 403-415.

[121] We argue later in this book, in chapter 9, that greater focus should be placed upon the first three steps, evaluating whether the means are adapted to achieve the ends and whether alternatives exist. Due to the complicated and fragmented judgments in the *Meadows* case, it can be argued that these first three questions have not been recognised as required by the courts, and that proportionality in Ireland is an impressionistic, seldom used indicator of unreasonableness. In that case, the "fair balance" step is all that exists, and it is failed only where a decision is manifestly disproportionate. This reveals Ireland as somewhat unusual in relation to international debates on the nature of proportionality, at least in relation to review of administrative decisions. The Heaney proportionality test (*Heaney v Ireland* [1994] 3 IR 593) is often applied when assessing the constitutionality of *legislation*. This is far more extensive and structured.

Conclusion

As is perhaps evident by our later analysis of the reasonableness ground in   **[1–64]**
Irish law, we do not believe that judicial review of administrative decisions
will undergo a vast normative revolution in the coming years. It may,
however, be increasingly shaped by a war of position between the three
schools we have identified in this chapter. One certainty is that the subject
will not, and cannot, be shaped by inertia but by a fruitful contestation of
legitimate perspectives. We believe that the culture of justification which
lies latent within many of Ireland's human rights obligations (and, in our
view, its own constitutional framework), will continue to press the edges of
the legal authority versus legal justification distinction, it will query the
values underlying the grant of discretion to administrators and, in some
cases, it may lead to judicial intervention through the application of
proportionality analysis.

This chapter was written to provide the reader with a reservoir of values to   **[1–65]**
draw upon as we move through an analysis of doctrinal divisions and
technical details. Many accounts of administrative law, in their introductory
chapters, merely produce a set of benignly abstract general values such as
openness, fairness, participation, impartiality, accountability, honesty and
rationality. Rather than producing a talismanic laundry list of abstract
ideas which are never harmonised or reasoned off against each other, we
have sought to highlight the core approaches and political theories which
might be used to fix the content of those labels. As teachers of this subject,
we are often disappointed to see it dismissed as aridly technical,[122] entirely

---

[122] This perception is one which the teacher must fight, yet such a feeling can also be the
starting point for an awareness of how the world works. In defending administrative law's
importance, Mark Fenster has stressed its ability:
   "...to get students to see the boring and to understand why it exists. To become an
   effective government lawyer or administrative law attorney requires one to recognize
   the importance of bureaucracy, as well as the necessity of channeling it within legal
   bounds. That's essential and can be exciting; it can also quite frequently be really boring."
M Fenster, *Boring*, Available at: http://prawfsblawg.blogs.com/prawfsblawg/2012/02/
boring.html (date accessed 31 January 2014).
Perhaps the comments of David Foster Wallace in his novel, *the Pale King* should also
provoke reflection upon the real mechanics of social change:
   "Gentlemen' here is a truth: Enduring tedium over real time in a confined space is what
   real courage is. Such endurance is, as it happens, the distillate of what is, today, in
   this world neither I nor you have made, heroism. The truth is that the heroism of your
   childhood entertainments was not true valor. It was theater. [...] actual heroism receives
   no ovation, entertains no one. No one queues up to see it. No one is interested."
D F Wallace, *The Pale King*, (Little, Brown & Co., Boston, 2011) at p 231.

dwarfed in student affection by the broad, abstract conflicts of principle contained in constitutional law. This is particularly so, in Ireland, where in the authors view there is a tendency to over-constitutionalise our problems. In many respects, as is perhaps evident in our discussion of the integrity branch and proportionality analysis, there is a greater need to "administrationalise" our constitution to ensure rights are weighted and vindicated in administrative decision-making, and that our political and legal institutions cultivate the ethos of contestation and justification that is the mark of an effective system of checks and balances.

[1–66] Thus we encourage the reader to see the broader project at play behind the technicalities of the subject, and the need to marry core values and sensitivity to context. We share the views of United States Justice Felix Frankfurter, who stated that administrative law was a dynamic legal subject, one not shaped by the "mechanical application of fixed rules", but one which required sensitivity to circumstance. It should not be viewed as a subject of bright lines and hard edges, of abstractions or "universal moulds", but of practical judgment, contextual understanding and balancing. For as Frankfurter wrote:

> "In administrative law we are dealing pre-eminently with law in the making; with fluid tendencies and tentative traditions. Here we must be especially wary against the danger of premature synthesis, of sterile generalisation unnourished by the realities of law in action".[123]

---

[123] F Frankfurter, "The Task of Administrative Law" (1926) 75 *University of Pennsylvania Law Review* 614, at p 619.

CHAPTER TWO

PARLIAMENTARY OVERSIGHT OF PUBLIC ADMINISTRATION

Introduction

In considering how administrative decision making is held accountable in [2–01]
a democratic system a central mechanism should be that of parliamentary
oversight. John Stuart Mill observed that the:

> "… the proper office of a representative assembly is to watch and
> control the government; to throw the light of publicity on its acts; to
> compel a full exposition and justification of all of them which any one
> considers questionable; to censure them if found condemnable, and,
> if the men who compose the government abuse their trust, or fulfil it
> in a manner which conflicts with the deliberate sense of the nation,
> to expel them from office, either expressly or virtually appoint their
> successors."[1]

The Irish Constitution, as a matter of principle, appears to reflect this view,
by stating, in Article 28.4.1°, that "The Government shall be responsible to
Dáil Éireann".[2] There is no doubt, however, that this is an undesirably
laconic statement of constitutional principle,[3] and is not accompanied by
provisions laying down the machinery to translate principle into practice.[4]
As we shall discuss in this chapter, the recent proposed constitutional
amendments on parliamentary inquiries and the abolition of the Seanad, to
a limited extent, addressed the question of supervisory mechanisms – but
these were defeated. Unfortunately, therefore, Article 28.4.1° represents

---

[1] JS Mill, *Considerations on Representative Government*, (Arc Manor LLC, Maryland, 2008) originally published 1848 at p 69.

[2] It is important to note that this obligation refers to the Dail not to the Seanad – implying the latter body is to be more focussed upon legislative matters.

[3] Though one would comment that as a result of judicial interpretation, the similarly abstract Art 6 was viewed as mandating the holding of referenda for the approval of international agreements which involved the transfer of constitutional sovereignty. Art 6 states that "All powers of Government, legislative, executive and judicial, derive, under God, from the people, whose right it is to designate the rulers of the State and, in final appeal, to decide all questions of national policy, according to the requirements of the common good" As we shall see in our discussion of cases such as the Abbeylara ruling, judicial rulings have not resulted in constitutionally mandated powers being given to the Oireachtas in order to ensure Art 28.4.1° is complied with.

[4] It may nevertheless be inferred from other constitutional provisions that the drafters were concerned about the possibility that a strong parliament would affect the primacy of the Office of An Taoiseach. Efforts were therefore made to ensure that the Head of Government was not reliant on Parliament in certain key decisions. Art 28.9.4° allows the Taoiseach to demand the resignation of any Minister as he or she wishes. The Taoiseach can also resign and request that the President dissolve Dáil Éireann without obligation to seek approval for this from other members of the Government. Such rebalancing measures seem to carry within them an implication that subjecting such actions to parliamentary approval could have frustrated the designs of the Taoiseach.

something of a floating, unclaimed principle, currently undercut by prevailing political dynamics. Such strong statements critiquing the ability of the Oireachtas to provide a functioning oversight mechanism are likely nothing new to the reader. It has been regularly stated by politicians, academics and commentators alike that Ireland's economic crisis was in very large part caused by fundamental flaws in the oversight and accountability systems of the State, including the Oireachtas.[5]

[2–02] Unquestionably, the activities and institutional architecture of the Irish State have increased significantly in range and complexity, with this expansion raising questions regarding the efficacy or practicability of parliamentary oversight. In response other mechanisms have taken on an increased significance, and these alternatives are discussed elsewhere in this book, for example chapters 3 and 4. The growth of the integrity branch of Government, through the creation of institutions such as the Ombudsman, the Information Commissioner and the Irish Human Rights Commission, emphasises the need for accountability to operate through an enhanced system of parallel checks and balances. A conclusion that these bodies can be understood as growing out of the fundamental failures of Parliament to hold the executive to account is extremely appealing.[6] However, that does not absolve the Oireachtas of its responsibilities; rather these parallel systems require robust Parliamentary accountability to heighten public awareness of their everyday scrutiny of Government action. In chapters 3 and 4 we expand somewhat on this alternative idea of an *integrity branch* of Government established to combat the gaps and inertia produced by

---

[5] See for example, B Hayes TD "The Financial Crisis Five Years On: A Critical Reflection", Speech by Minister of State at the Department of Finance, 18 October 2013 — "The banking collapse and the national economic crisis which followed exposed major weaknesses and failures in politics, public administration and regulation. It became obvious that many of our institutions and practices were not fit for purpose. Confidence in the basic capacity of the State was undermined." Available at http://www.finance.gov.ie/news-centre/ speeches/current-minister/speech-brian-hayes-td-minister-state-dept-finance-financial (date accessed 10 July 2014) and R Boyle and M MacCarthaigh, *Fit for Purpose? Challenges for Irish Public Administration and Priorities for Public Service Reform*, (2011) Institute of Public Administration Research Paper 4. Available at http://www.ipa.ie/pdf/Fit_For_Purpose_ New_Report.pdf (date accessed 10 July 2014).

[6] For a discussion of this in the Australian context see D Solomon, "The integrity branch – parliament's failure or opportunity?", paper presented at the Australasian Study of Parliament Group Annual Conference, Perth 2 – 4 October 2013. Available at http:// www.integrity.qld.gov.au/library/document/catalogue/speeches-articles/paper_perth_ integrity_breach.pdf (date accessed 12 June 2014).

traditional judiciary-executive-legislature divisions.[7] In this chapter, however, we will directly consider those gaps as they arise particularly in the executive-legislative context.

Mapping Parliamentary Oversight in Ireland

The flaws in our Parliamentary oversight system are widely acknowledged—and were placed on the political agenda by the 2011 Programme for Government: [2–03]

> "We believe that in recent years an over-powerful executive has turned the Dáil into an observer of the political process rather than a central player and that this must be changed."[8]

Reforms were therefore promised, including an overhaul of the Oireachtas committee structures, renewed powers to carry out inquiries and improvements in the procedures for asking questions.[9] We will examine these core Parliamentary mechanisms for oversight in more detail in this chapter. However, structural changes are only one part of the solution to revitalising the accountability role of the Oireachtas.

Accountability of the executive to the people is an essential feature of democratic systems. A representative democracy clearly involves the core political accountability mechanism operating during elections — the decision to select representatives who will take part in the governing process. The role of citizens in removing or endorsing Government is therefore critical to our democratic system and in trying to ensure that Government is held to account. In practice, such discipline and punishment can be limited — elections take place often long after errors take place or are exposed, and voters can have limited choice at the ballot box. Voting is often regarded by the electorate as an unsatisfactorily diffuse form of accountability.[10]   [2–04]

---

[7] The term "integrity branch" was first used by Professor Bruce Ackerman in the context of the US Constitution. See B Ackerman, "The New Separation of Powers" (2000) 113(3) *Harvard Law Review* 633 at pp 694-696.

[8] Programme for Government 2011, p 18. Available at http://www.merrionstreet.ie/wp-content/uploads/2010/05/Programme_for_Government_2011.pdf (date accessed 16 June 2014).

[9] *ibid.*

[10] K Strøm, "Delegation and Accountability in Parliamentary Democracies", (2000) 37(3) *European Journal of Political Research* 274.

[2–05]   Although the Oireachtas is not a replica of the Westminster parliamentary model which originated in the late 1800s, it does adopt many of the characteristics. Thus the model sees Parliament as being representative of the people who elect their representatives, in the Irish system under a Proportional Representation Single Transferable Vote system to the Dáil. These elected representatives are required to hold the Government to account under Article 28 of the Constitution. To this end, under our model of democracy, Government accountability is, in theory, a core parliamentary task. Parliamentary oversight has a number of key elements by which it can make Government accountable. These include:

- Scrutiny of the finances of the State;
- Scrutiny of Government policy;
- Evaluation of the Executive's implementation of those policies;
- The protection of the rights of citizens — inherent in this is the prevention or exposure of executive action that is unconstitutional, illegal or arbitrary;
- Ensuring overall transparency and accountability of the Executive ultimately to the public.[11]

Methods designed to achieve this type of oversight are varied, and are largely developed through internal Parliamentary practice embodied in the working rules of the Oireachtas rather than in the Constitution.[12]

[2–06]   However, despite the Oireachtas' establishment as a classical oversight forum it has also been exposed as being deeply flawed. Constitutional law reminds us that in practice the separation of the executive and the legislature in Ireland is incomplete. The political fusing of the legislature and the executive has meant that the executive can exercise significant levels of control over the legislature. The increase in the power of political parties and the associated systems of control they have imposed on the institution,

---

[11] H Yamamoto, *Tools for Parliamentary Oversight: A Comparative Study of 88 Parliaments* (Inter-Parliamentary Union, Geneva, 2007).

[12] Those rules are found in the Standing Orders of the Dáil, available: http://www.oireachtas. ie/documents/proceduraldocuments/Standorders2011_revised.pdf (date accessed 10 July 2014) and the Standing Orders of the Seanad, available: http://www.oireachtas.ie/ documents/proceduraldocuments/SeanadStandingOrders2011.pdf (date accessed 10 July 2014). The primary constitutional arrangements for scrutiny are via Collective Ministerial Responsibility and Individual Ministerial Responsibility, discussed below at paras [2-15] – [2-18] and [2-19] – [2-61].

such as the whip system,[13] has effectively neutered much of the traditional accountability mechanisms. The result has been a rise in the bear pit approach to politics, with opponents seeking to effectively maul each other rather than find information and provide oversight.

The Oireachtas therefore often finds it difficult to effectively perform its core oversight responsibilities, particularly under the classical framework of Ministerial (both collective and individual) responsibility. The result is that additional methods have been identified and developed to supplement the more traditional oversight mechanisms, including a strengthened committee structure.[14]   [2–07]

Party Political Loyalty and Parliamentary Oversight

The weaknesses in the traditional mechanisms arise in large part because of the fact their origins predate the development of political parties. Gallagher notes that party loyalty is not peculiar to Ireland, but is a significant aspect of how our Parliament works: [2–08]

> "[w]hen Dáil deputies vote on issues, they do so, in most cases, as members of a party.... All across Europe, deputies follow the party line in votes in parliament and, if anything, parliamentary party cohesion is even higher in Ireland than the European average."[15]

TDs in particular are highly likely to follow the party line for fear of expulsion from their party and the belief that this is ultimately fatal to their chances of future re-election. Research undertaken by Farrell et al found only 54 examples of TDs having lost the whip after rebelling against their party in a thirty year period — 3.3% of TDs over that period.[16] The study also found

---

[13] The whip system is the primary method by which the Government and the Dáil "negotiate" the business of the Oireachtas. As MacCarthaigh describes it the office of the chief whip is "the institution that exists at the interface of the Dáil and Government". See M MacCarthaigh, *Accountability in Irish Parliamentary Politics* (Institute of Public Administration, Dublin, 2005) at p 147.

[14] See discussion below at para [2-68] onwards.

[15] M Gallagher, "The Oireachtas: President and parliament", in J Coakley and M Gallagher, *Politics in the Republic of Ireland*, (5th ed) (Routledge, Abingdon, 2010) at p 202, hereinafter Gallagher.

[16] D Farrell, P Mair, S Ó Muineacháin and M Wall, "Courting, but not always serving: Perverted Burkeanism and the puzzle of Irish Parliamentary Cohesion", (2012) Paper presented at a conference in UBC, Vancouver to mark Ken Carty's retirement. Available at http://researchrepository.ucd.ie/bitstream/handle/10197/4329/Carty_chapter_final. pdf?sequence=1 (date accessed 16 June 2014). This data predates the voting regarding the

that "[s]lightly more than half of [the] rebels, 54%, were not readmitted to their original party".[17] However, the consequences for re-election were not so severe — "[t]he results suggest that whip loss is not generally related to *any* discernible change in overall electoral performance"[18] although it did have a negative impact on career progression.[19]

[2–09]   As a result of party discipline Government TDs will naturally seek to support their Government while opposition TDs will generally seek to score political points against the Government. In this environment, scrutiny of the Government and its work becomes a more marginalised task prioritised when it coincides with these other strategic interests, particularly the opportunity to undermine an opposition party. The challenge from the party structure also extends further into opportunities for reform of accountability structures. A political party's main aim is ultimately to become Government: it is therefore unsurprising that accountability and oversight is prioritised in opposition, but underplayed when in Government.

Clientelism and Parliamentary Oversight

[2–10]   This control by political parties in the parliamentary process is reinforced in Ireland by the ongoing clientelism that distorts the process further and minimises TDs interest in accountability. The role played by parliamentarians as constituency representatives has been a predominant part of Irish politics. Komito stressed the prevalence of clientelism in 1984, finding that:

> "[t]he political broker who intervenes on behalf of constituents to help them obtain government benefits and the client who rewards the politician with his vote has become an acceptable, and even fashionable, model of Irish political life."[20]

[2–11]   It should, of course, be remembered that representation of constituency interests and clientism are not peculiar to the Irish context[21] there is also a

---

Protection of Life During Pregnancy Act 2013 which saw five Fine Gael TDs vote against their Party position. Hereinafter "Farrell".

[17] *ibid* at p 6.

[18] *ibid* at p 7.

[19] *ibid* at p 8. See J McEnroe "Party chiefs 'threaten' FG rebels over bill", 8 July 2013, http://www.irishexaminer.com/ireland/party-chiefs-threaten-fg-rebels-over-bill-236225.html (date accessed 17 November 2014).

[20] L Komito, "Irish Clientism: A Reappraisal" (1984) 15(3) *The Economic and Social Review* 173 at p 173.

[21] See M Gallagher and L Komito, "The constituency role of Dáil deputies" in J Coakley and M Gallagher *Politics in the Republic of Ireland* 5th ed, (Routledge, Abingdon, 2010) at pp 244-6.

legitimate tension to be dealt with here. TDs are constituency representatives and it is appropriate that they represent their interests in the Parliamentary process. However, there is a danger that that representation can, and has, morphed into clientelism in the Irish context. What is meant by this is that politicians are driven to focus upon individual, local casework rather than tackle structural or national problems. While portraying the TD as a "welfare officer" — intervening to help individuals access services is a little reductive, it does highlight the emphasis upon local constituency work.[22] This historical emphasis is a powerful variable in electoral campaigning. There is some evidence that TDs place an emphasis on the local over the national. Combining this with a system of strong party loyalty Farrell *et al*, we would argue correctly, conclude that

> "by encouraging the Irish TD to focus on representation at the local level while remaining deferential to the leadership in the Dáil, the electoral system has helped to undermine any real sense of parliamentary accountability, and has thereby enable the government to have a freer hand than was or is desirable. As the present economic crisis takes its toll, it might be argued that effective local representation has come with a heavy national cost."[23]

The Constitutional Ideal of Dáil Éireann as an Accountability Mechanism

The Oireachtas has generally been criticised for being a weak parliamentary structure in terms of its ability to hold Government to account. As Gallagher notes it has variously been described as "supine", "woefully inadequate" and "puny".[24] It is perhaps therefore not surprising that when the Fine Gael/Labour Government attempted to abolish the Seanad in the 32nd amendment referendum on 5 October 2013 the debate was successfully redirected by opponents from abolition into one of reform.[25]

[2–12]

The background to public cynicism about the Oireachtas, combined with recognition of a need for reform, has developed alongside revelations of

[2–13]

---

[22] *ibid.*

[23] Farrell, *supra* n 16 at pp 14-15.

[24] Gallagher, *supra* n 15 at p 201.

[25] See G Murphy, "Saving Seanad in referendum is real voice for change", *Irish Examiner*, 27 May 2013, available at http://www.irishexaminer.com/sport/columnists/tony-leen/saving-seanad-in-referendum-is-real-voice-for-change-232420.html (date accessed 10 July 2014).

corruption and incompetence since the early 1990s. Scandals over matters such as tax evasion, political collusion with the beef industry and corruption in the planning system illustrate the fact that the Oireachtas has few effective institutional safeguards embedded within its system that work to prevent the abuse of public office.[26]

[2–14] As previously noted , the constitutional framework by which the Oireachtas holds the Executive accountable is rooted in Article 28. The same article also outlines executive power, requiring that:

1. The Government shall consist of not less than seven and not more than 15 members who shall be appointed by the President in accordance with the provisions of this Constitution.
2. The executive power of the State shall, subject to the provisions of this Constitution, be exercised by or on the authority of the Government.

Thus, the Constitution regulates the size and composition of Government but it tells us little nothing about what the powers and functions of Government actually are. While one could thus describe executive power as residual to the express legislative and judicial powers, in reality the lack of definition may underline that construing the boundaries of the power is centred on political undertows than principled definitions. Government is made of up a maximum of fifteen members, including the Taoiseach who is head of the Government and elected by Dáil and formally appointed by President. The Taoiseach nominates other cabinet members, including one member to be the Tanaiste.[27] All members of the Government must be members of the Oireachtas, a maximum of two can be from the Seanad, although in practice this is rare. The Constitution sets no limit as to the number of departments; if there are more than 15 then Ministers double up and have responsibility for more than one.

---

[26] These were catalogued in a series of Tribunals of Inquiry including the Beef Tribunal 1991-1994 (to inquire into malpractice in the Irish beef processing industry), Mahon Tribunal 1997-2012 (to inquire into planning matters) http://www.planningtribunal.ie/asp/index. asp?ObjectID=310&Mode=0&RecordID=480 (date accessed 10 July 2014), and Moriarty Tribunal 1997-2011 (to inquire into payments to politicians) http://www.moriarty-tribunal. ie/asp/index.asp?ObjectID=636&Mode=0&RecordID=399 (date accessed 10 July 2014). For an examination of the operation of Tribunals of Inquiry and their role as an accountability mechanism see chapter 5.

[27] The Tanaiste primarily acts in place of Taoiseach in case of absence, illness or death.

Collective Ministerial Responsibility

In terms of how Government is to be held responsible, the Constitution provides some guidance, but not a complete account. Article 28.4 states that: **[2–15]**

> "1   The Government shall be responsible to Dáil Éireann.
>
> 2   The Government shall meet and act as a collective authority, and shall be collectively responsible for the Departments of State administered by the members of the Government."

Article 28.4.1° says nothing about the role of the Seanad, and so the flow of responsibility bypasses the upper chamber and is formally, and largely in practice, concentrated in the Dáil. Following a general election the Dáil elects a new Government and, in certain defined circumstances, has the power to remove the Government. Thus Article 28.10 states that the Taoiseach "shall resign from office upon his ceasing to retain the support of a majority in Dáil Éireann" and Article 28.11.1° provides that if the Taoiseach resigns "the other members of the Government shall be deemed also to have resigned from office". Article 13.1 also states that the Dáil nominates the Taoiseach and is responsible for approving the Government: the President is responsible for the final appointment.[28] Removal of the Government can come as a result of a vote of no confidence in the Dáil.

Despite this constitutional framework, the Dáil plays little practical role in the appointment of the Government. The nomination of the Taoiseach and approval of the Government are merely rubber stamping processes of decisions taken outside the Dáil. This is typical in a Westminster style Parliament.[29]   **[2–16]**

If the Dáil plays little role in appointment, their ability to remove a Government is equally limited in practice, not least because it is usual for a   **[2–17]**

---

[28] Article 13.1 states:
> "1   The President shall, on the nomination of Dáil Éireann, appoint the Taoiseach, that is, the head of the Government or Prime Minister.
>
> 2   The President shall, on the nomination of the Taoiseach with the previous approval of Dáil Éireann, appoint the other members of the Government.
>
> 3   The President shall, on the advice of the Taoiseach, accept the resignation or terminate the appointment of any member of the Government."

[29] For more detailed discussion of the formation of Government see Gallagher, *supra* n 15 at p 208.

Government to have a majority which protects them from attack.[30] Accordingly it has only dismissed a Government twice, first in 1982[31] and later in 1992.[32] However, it is more likely that a Government in danger of losing a vote of no confidence will choose to resign before being defeated. This has happened on eight separate occasions.[33]

[2–18] As we noted above, Article 28.4.2° states that the Government will be "collectively responsible" to the Dáil. This goes beyond appointment and removal and accounts for the fact that the Government operates as a united entity. As a matter of constitutional probity, there is to be no outward dissent from the stated Government position by Ministers. If a Minister does disagree with the Government view she should resign thus making herself able to speak freely. In addition, the Government will stand together, if the Taoiseach resigns or is removed the rest of the Government must also leave office.

Individual Ministerial Responsibility

[2–19] The other, and in practice more significant, traditional accountability mechanism is individual ministerial responsibility. Historically, the primary mechanism for holding Government to account in the Westminster model has been through the doctrine of ministerial responsibility. Government power is largely held by Ministers, appointed from the pool of TDs from the Government party or parties.[34] Ministers are the *political* heads of Government departments established under the Constitution: the departments are in turn staffed, and in practice, run by civil servants.[35]

---

[30] Although that majority is more often than not based on a coalition between two or more parties. Therefore the majority is reliant upon that remaining stable.

[31] The minority Fianna Fáil Government was defeated in a vote of no confidence by 82 to 80 votes; the Government resigned and called a general election. Although as Gallagher notes this vote has to be understood in its context — a Fianna Fáil TD had died and another was ill and unable to attend the vote, *supra* n 15 at p 206.

[32] Following a decision by the Progressive Democrats (PDs) to leave a coalition Government with Fianna Fáil they joined the opposition and a vote of no confidence followed which was carried by 88 votes to 77. *ibid.*

[33] *ibid* at pp 216-7.

[34] As already noted, Senators may serve as Ministers.

[35] The Government consists of a minimum of seven and a maximum of 15 members. The Taoiseach, the Tánaiste and the Minister of Finance must be members of Dáil Éireann. All other Ministers tend also be TDs although the Constitution does allow for two Ministers to be appointed from the Seanad. Constitution, Art 28.7.2°.

The Minister is understood to be a critical link between the machinery of Government and Parliament and in turn, the voter. Thus, under the doctrine of ministerial responsibility, ministers are *responsible* to Parliament. Traditionally the method of calling ministers to account is through parliamentary questions and debates. However, as we have already highlighted,[36] control of Parliament by the Government parties or party means that all of these methods are ultimately limited.[37]

[2–20]

Within the Irish constitutional structure, ministerial responsibility is a convention, as unlike collective ministerial responsibility it is not mentioned directly within the Constitution. It does, however, have legislative underpinning through the Ministers and Secretaries Act 1924 and Public Service Management Act 1997.[38] We find further embodiment of the doctrine in the civil service guidelines which state that

[2–21]

> "a civil servant who appears before, or provides information to, an Oireachtas Committee does so on behalf of his Minister who ... is legally responsible for the official acts of his civil servants ...".[39]

The Guidelines go on to state that:

> "The formulation of policy is the responsibility of Government. It is, accordingly, for the responsible Minister to decide how much information a committee should be given on policy matters. In general, civil servants can factually explain existing policies as outlined by Ministers/Government. However, they should not discuss the merits of particular policies or policy alternatives (including their administrative and financial feasibility) or allow themselves to be drawn into debating the merits of particular policy decisions, including expenditure decisions. If criticism is levelled at witnesses by members of committees in regard to policy decisions or related aspects which reflect on the competence, judgment or good name of the witness or other persons, the witness may point out that:
>
> - he is precluded from disclosing policy advice given to a Minister;
> - criticisms of policy decisions are appropriate to Ministers who are answerable to the Oireachtas."[40]

---

[36] See discussion above at paras [2-08] – [2-09].

[37] Parliamentary questions will be discussed in detail below at paras [2-28] – [2-29].

[38] See discussion below at paras [2-46] – [2-49].

[39] Circular 1/1984 *Guidelines for civil servants appearing before or providing information to Oireachtas Committees*, 24 February 1984. Available at http://circulars.gov.ie/pdf/circular/finance/1984/01.pdf (date accessed 10 July 2014).

[40] *ibid.*

[2–22] The roots of the doctrine itself date back further than the development of the political party system. It emerged in the Westminster system during the nineteenth century at a time when Government was small and thus had limited powers:

> "Over the course of the 19th and early 20th century the government became organised in individual departments, headed by a secretary of state. This replaced earlier models of semi independent boards, such as Local Government Board, Education Board etc.... it was practically convenient for responsibility and control to pass to individual ministers, who could be fully answerable to parliament."[41]

As a result, an accountability approach that assumed the Minister of each Department of Government was in personal control of all that went on within it made sense within the structures of the time.

[2–23] At its most basic level, the idea of ministerial responsibility is that the Minister must take both the credit and the blame for all that happens within his Department. This of course fits with the principle that civil servants remain faceless providers of information or advice and are the delegated decision makers for the Minister.[42] In practice, the concept, is much criticised as being at best ill-equipped to deal with modern Government/Parliamentary relations and at worst as providing merely an illusion of responsibility that prevents accountability operating effectively.

[2–24] The Doctrine requires that the Minister will be both answerable and accountable to Parliament, with the TDs and Senators undertaking that accountability process. However, this idea has a number of parts to it, as the UK Defence Select Committee noted in the Westland Affair, it requires that:

> "[a] Minister does not discharge his accountability to Parliament merely by acknowledging a general responsibility and, if the circumstances warrant it, by resigning. Accountability involves *accounting* in detail for actions as a Minister."[43]

---

[41] O Gay, *Individual Ministerial Responsibility,* House of Commons Library Research Paper 04/31 8 November 2012. Available online at www.parliament.uk/briefing-papers/SN06467.pdf (date accessed 16 June 2014) at p 3.

[42] The *Carltona* principle supports this. See discussion below at paras [2-37] – [2-38].

[43] Fourth report of the Defence Committee, *Westland plc: the Government's decision-making,* HC 519, 1985-86 para 235.

Thus in order to work effectively, the concept is understood to have a number of components: (a) a requirement that the minister accounts for her actions; (b) that the Minister apologises where necessary; (c) that the Minister and/or her Department acts to correct and/or prevent the problem; and (d) in some cases the Minister may have to resign.

a)   The Minister Informs and Explains to Parliament

Accountability requires as a first component, the provision of information. **[2–25]** Thus the Minister must give information to the Dáil/Seanad. This component should be a straightforward process; however, although questions might be asked to elicit information from Ministers, they can also be used to pursue other agendas such as raising the profile of an issue (whether national or local) or assisting Ministers by focusing on good news stories.[44]

This basic requirement of accountability therefore requires ministers to **[2–26]** explain their actions and policies to Parliament and inform Parliament of events or developments within their sphere of responsibility. Thus, Ministers make statements (on their own initiative, through urgent questions, or through written ministerial statements for example) on all sorts of issues from transport accidents to proposed new policy initiatives and make available detailed explanations through Parliamentary answers, consultation papers or white and green papers.

How far this information provision fully engages accountability is of **[2–27]** course reliant upon the candour of ministers. In the UK context where there is a duty under the Ministerial Code[45] not to "knowingly" mislead Parliament, Feldman states that

> "some senior civil servants and many ministers consider that it is permissible to withhold some information from Parliament without telling Parliament that it is being withheld, arguing that half the story can be true and not misleading even if it gives a different impression from the whole story."[46]

---

[44] S Martin, "Monitoring Irish Government", in E O'Malley and M MacCarthaigh (ed.) *Governing Ireland* (Institute of Public Administration, Dublin, 2010) at p 162.

[45] Ministerial Code, Cabinet Office, 2010. Available at https://www.gov.uk/government/uploads/system/uploads/attachment_data/file/61402/ministerial-code-may-2010.pdf (date accessed 4 October 2013).

[46] D Feldman, "Constitutional Conventions" in M Qvortrup, (ed.) *The British Constitution: Continuity and Change* (Hart Publishing, Oxford, 2013) at p 110.

Thus, he notes the example of Sir Robin Butler, former Cabinet Secretary, who argued that in some situations the harm caused by lying to Parliament had to be "balanced against the harm that would result from telling the truth".[47] Such a position cannot be maintained however, as it undermines the very basis of accountability within the Westminster model. However others have warned that

> "[t]he secrecy culture of Whitehall is essentially a product of British parliamentary democracy; economy with the truth is the essence of a professional reply to a parliamentary question".[48]

[2–28] In the Irish context, it is clear that Ministers do not regard themselves as having to inform the Dáil of all the relevant information. Gallagher states that the "etiquette of parliamentary questions requires not that answers be helpful or informative but only that they not be untruthful".[49] It is possible to find examples of a less than truthful and open approach to questions; the best known is possibly the circumstances surrounding the Beef Tribunal and attempts prior to that body being established by the Oireachtas to examine the details regarding the relationship between Ministers and the industry. The Chair of the Beef Tribunal later stated:

> "I think that if the questions that were asked in the Dáil were answered in the way they are answered here, there would be no necessity for this inquiry and an awful lot of money and time would have been saved."[50]

[2–29] The provision of information in this context is not always of the highest quality and it has long been recognised that there is an art to writing ministerial answers. Parliamentary question times are generally regarded as being a political point scoring opportunity for both sides. Rules nevertheless operate within the Oireachtas as to how parliamentary questions should be answered and TDs can complain to the Ceann Comhairle with the Dáil standing orders if they believe that a Minister has failed to answer a question. Standing Order 40A requires that a Minister "address each and every request for information" contained within a

---

[47] *ibid* at p 111.

[48] Sir Patrick Nairne, former permanent secretary speaking in 1987, quoted in R Norton-Taylor, *Truth is a Difficulty Concept: Inside the Scott Inquiry* (Guardian Books, London, 1995) at p 97.

[49] Gallagher, *supra* n 15 at p 217.

[50] Cited in F O'Toole, Meanwhile, *Back at the Ranch* (Vintage, London, 1995) at p 241.

question. A complaint must be made within two days and if the Ceann Comhairle upholds the complaint the Minister should then

> "furnish to the Ceann Comhairle a response in writing to each of the requests for information in relation to which there has been, in the opinion of the Ceann Comhairle, a failure to comply".[51]

For example, in October 2012 the Ceann Comhairle upheld two separate complaints against the Minister for Health James Reilly for a failure to answer parliamentary questions put to him in relation to primary care centres. [52]

In addition, question planting and the stage managing of question times [2–30] can also undermine the operation and integrity of this process. Recent evidence from the UK has highlighted the extent of this practice in Westminster; Fogg writing in *The Guardian* newspaper provided a damning critique of Prime Minister's Questions:

> "On the spectrum of stage-managed spectacles, one is tempted to place PMQs somewhere between a Punch and Judy show, a pantomime and a farce. This would be a great injustice. Those noble theatrical traditions have brought joy, laughter and colour into our lives for centuries; PMQs has brought nothing but shame and disgrace. The weekly performance is an embarrassment, the nadir of our anachronistic, elitist, dysfunctional parliamentary system."[53]

The handling of questions in the Oireachtas has not suffered as badly as in [2–31] Westminster but concerns are still raised about the practice. Thus, in early 2013 the now former Minister for Health James Reilly TD was accused by Fianna Fáil of organising Government backbenchers to ask friendly

---

[51] Standing Order 40A(4), available at http://www.oireachtas.ie/documents/ proceduraldocuments/mod20130504.pdf (date accessed 27 September 2013).

[52] N Hunter, "Reilly's Dail replies raise new issues", Irishhealth.com, 31 January 2013, available at http://www.irishhealth.com/article.html?id=21635 (date accessed 10 July 2014).

[53] A Fogg, "Stage-managed PMQs? The problems go deeper than that", *The Guardian*, 5 February 2014 available online at http://www.theguardian.com/commentisfree/2014/ feb/05/stage-managed-pmqs-problems-deeper-david-cameron (date accessed 16 June 2014). The issue gained renewed coverage in the UK after memos were revealed highlighting the efforts made by the Prime Minister's aides to control Prime Minister's Questions. E Malnick, "David Cameron's attempts to 'stage manage' Prime Minister's Questions", *The Telegraph* , 5 February 2014, available at http://www.telegraph.co.uk/ news/politics/10617436/David-Camerons-attempts-to-stage-manage-Prime-Ministers- Questions.html (date accessed 16 June 2014).

questions regarding positive developments in health service provision.[54] Allegations were made by Sinn Fein that "83 [questions were] definitely manufactured by a single hand, each of them seeking information on measures that have been taken"[55] and that the long list prevented opposition spokespersons the opportunity to speak. Undoubtedly, all TDs have the right to ask questions, and positive stories are important within the Parliamentary process, but any planting of questions would represent an inappropriate use of a key Dáil accountability opportunity.

[2–32]   The legislature therefore has opportunities to hold Ministers to account through requesting and receiving information, albeit that these opportunities are at times flawed and/or abused. However, provision of information is ultimately insufficient to meet the requirements of full and effective accountability. To regard it as the main component would be to reduce the Minister to a mere conduit for the flow of information.

b)   The Minister Apologises to Parliament

[2–33]   Part of the process of providing information to Parliament may include, in appropriate circumstances, an apology. This involves the Minister admitting an error has been made, whether personally or officials. An apology is a very public acceptance of responsibility; it also suggests some form of contrition. However, an apology with no sanction[56] or reform may ultimately be regarded as limited, and perhaps even insincere.

c)   The Minister and Their Department Acts in Response

[2–34]   A minister who is responsible for an unsatisfactory state of affairs will be expected to take appropriate remedial steps to correct it and to ensure that it should not happen again. This applies whether or not any resignations or dismissals are involved, although in some cases the remedial action may be promised and carried out by a successor in cases where the responsible minister has left office. The extent of any remedial

---

[54] See for example http://www.fiannafail.ie/news/entry/9658/ (date accessed 16 June 2014).

[55] Deputy Caoimhghín Ó Caoláin quoted in D Gantly, "A Dickensian Tale of two Houses", *Irish Medical Times*, 29 March 2013. Available at http://www.imt.ie/opinion/2013/03/a-dickensian-tale-of-two-houses.html (date accessed 16 June 2014).

[56] This may involve the resignation or dismissal of the Minister or relevant civil servant. However as we will see this does not necessarily happen. See discussion below at paras [2-33] – [2-35].

response may be difficult to see, and may well take place long after the error took place.

d) The Minister May have to Resign

Resignation, or removal from office, is the ultimate accountability sanction. It is also the most difficult to categorise and explain in terms to rules and procedures because in reality there are neither. The process is elusive and subject to the vagaries of politics, the media and public opinion. Indeed, while the other elements of individual ministerial responsibility noted above are essentially executive actions, resignation cases can develop into political, often partisan, battles. In practice, resignation can become a distraction and can undermine the effectiveness of responsibility. Nor should resignation be understood as necessarily the only sanction, though commentators often behave as if it is. Ministers might be reshuffled or demoted; a serious incident might prevent further career advancement. However, these are less visible to the public and generally are not directly linked back to any particular Ministerial or departmental failing. [2–35]

As we have already stated, there are no rules setting out when a Minister should resign. However, there is some conventional expectation that if the fault is bad enough then the Minister should go. In such a situation, then the Minister refuses to resign the Taoiseach is under a duty to dismiss them. If neither happens then resignation should follow a vote of no confidence passed by the Dáil. In reality, the party political system results in Government deputies normally providing support for the erring minister. As we will see a central flaw in the doctrine is the lack of an impartial agency to adjudicate on and enforce this doctrine. [2–36]

Resignation is ultimately a rather blunt tool of discipline and in its operation we see many of the disadvantages and limitations of the doctrine as an effective accountability mechanism. Nevertheless, it does need to be understood as a form of disciple, however weak. As Finer highlights, the doctrine's sanction changed over the years from impeachment under the old system to loss of office.[57] While resignation [2–37]

---

[57] SE Finer, "The Individual Responsibly of Ministers" (1956) 34 *Public Administration* 377 at p 393.

appears to be a voluntary action, the "choice" made by the Minister is highly dependent on external factors as Finer sets out:

> "whether a Minister resigns depends on three factors, on himself, his Prime Minister and his party... For a resignation to occur all three factors have to be just so; the Minister compliant, the Prime Minister firm, the party clamorous. This conjuncture is rare, and is in fact fortuitous. Above all, it is indiscriminate – which Ministers escape and which do not is decided neither by the circumstance of the offence not its gravity."[58]

In addition, Finer notes the unsteady nature of the process — "A remedy ought to be certain. A punishment, to be deterrent, ought to be certain".[59] The operation of Ministerial responsibility is, as the reader will see, is volatile.

Individual Responsibility in Operation

[2–38]   Examining individual responsibility in practice quickly reveals its weakness as a fully functioning accountability mechanism meeting the realities of today's State apparatus. Government has become far too complex for responsibility to be channelled through one individual standing at the head of a department. Nor can a Minister realistically take all decisions themselves: the delegation of power has therefore become essential in modern Government. We need to be careful about the term delegation here, however: under the *Carltona principle*[60] the civil servant acting under delegation *is* acting as the Minister but in practice Ministers have less oversight than ever before.

The Carltona Principle

[2–39]   Briefly, the *Carltona principle* operates to the effect that the duties and powers vested in a Minister may be performed or exercised by officials of her Department.

> "Constitutionally, the decision of such an official is, of course, the decision of the minister. The minister is responsible. It is he who must answer before Parliament for anything that his officials have done under his authority, and, if for an important matter he selected

---

[58] *ibid.*

[59] *ibid.*

[60] *Carltona Ltd v Commissioner of Works* [1943] 2 All ER 560.

an official of such junior standing that he could not be expected competently to perform the work, the minister would have to answer for that in Parliament. The whole system of departmental organisation and administration is based on the view that ministers, being responsible to Parliament, will see that important duties are committed to experienced officials. If they do not do that, Parliament is the place where complaint must be made against them."[61]

The effect of this is, as Wade points out, that:

"[s]trictly speaking, there is not even delegation in these cases. Delegation requires a distinct act conferred upon some person not previously competent to exercise it. But the authority of officials to act in their ministers' names derives from a general rule of law and not from any particular act of delegation. Legally and constitutionally speaking the act of the official is the act of the minister, without any need for specific authorisation in advance or ratification afterwards."[62]

As we analyse more fully in chapter 7, this approach has also been adopted in our jurisdiction by the Supreme Court in *Tang v Minister for Justice*[63] and *Devanney v District Judge Shields*.[64] It also has statutory support through the operation of individual ministerial responsibility.[65]

In terms of exceptions to the *Carltona doctrine*, the judiciary have preserved a possible right of intervention, where, as Denham J expressed it *Devanney v District Judge Shields*[66] the issue concerns "matters of significant importance where the Minister is expected to make the decision personally".[67] Ultimately it is clear that the *Carltona principle* and its general operation across Government departments is essential to the effective workings of   **[2–40]**

---

61 Per Lord Greene MR, in *Carltona, ibid* at 563.

62 HWR Wade and C Forsyth, *Administrative Law* (10th ed) (Oxford University Press, Oxford, 2009) at p 267.

63 [1996] 2 ILRM 46.

64 [1998] 1 ILRM 81 hereinafter *"Devanney"*.

65 Hogan and Morgan note that this is in turn supported by the Ministers and Secretaries Act 1924 which makes the minister responsible to the Dáil. G Hogan and DG Morgan, *Administrative Law in Ireland*, (4th ed) (Round Hall, Dublin, 2010) at para 3-08. Hereinafter "Hogan and Morgan".

66 *Devanney* above n 64.

67 *ibid* at 108. In this case the decision concerned the appointment of a District Court Clerk, which was legislatively vested in the Minister for Justice. The Court nevertheless found that the role of the Minister was a solely formal one, to give effect to a recommendation by officials. A similar position was taken in *Tang v Minister for Justice* [1996] 2 ILRM 46 in which a civil servant refused an application for permission to reside without consulting the Minister. Similarly the Supreme Court found the *Carltona* principle applied in the case.

individual ministerial responsibility. Any limitations there might be, as Hogan and Morgan note, most likely operate because of statutory interpretation.[68]

[2–41]   In addition to the growth in the complexity and size of Government, the doctrine also fails to deal with the growth in semi-State bodies and its inability to provide accountability outside the immediate circle of Government. The growth of such bodies has created tensions within the traditional accountability framework not least in terms of understanding the relationship between semi-state bodies and their "parent" Departments. This was noted in the OECD Public Management Review in 2008 which recommended that the role of departments and agencies be "clarified" and "clearer lines of accountability" developed.[69]

The Critchel Down Affair

[2–42]   The classic example of a Minister taking full responsibility for a failure within his Department is found in the Critchel Down affair from 1954. In that case the Minister for Agriculture, Thomas Dugdale, resigned from office when his civil servants were exposed as having misled members of the public over the re-sale of compulsorily purchased farm land. A public inquiry into events was critical of individual officials and the civil service, although the Minister had no personal knowledge or involvement in the events. During the subsequent parliamentary debate Dugdale resigned, accepting responsibility. However, no civil servant was ever disciplined.[70] This then is held up as the example of an approach where "the minister is responsible for every stamp which is stuck on in his department".[71] This example is regarded as upholding the line of responsibility between the civil service and Parliament:

---

[68] Hogan and Morgan above n 65 at para 11-155. Noting the case of *Tang v Minister for Justice* [1996] 2 ILRM 46 they note that the case provides that "the minister could not be expected to decide every immigration case personally, but there could well be certain exceptional types of cases where the stator context is such that it was clear that the Oireachtas must have intended that the decision would be personal to the minister."

[69] OECD, *Public Management Reviews: Ireland Towards an Integrated Public Service*, (OECD Publishing, Paris, 2008) at p 268. Available at https://bvc.cgu.gov.br/bitstream/123456789/3593/1/strengthening_governance.pdf (date accessed 16 June 2014) hereinafter OECD.

[70] The report was published some ten years after the original errors occurred and many of the senior officials and the Minister at the time had retired.

[71] Herbert Morrison, quoted in G Marshell (ed.) Ministeral Responsibility (Oxford University Press, Oxford, 1989) at p 7.

"The Minister is not bound to defend action of which he did not know, or of which he disapproves. But... he remains constitutionally responsible to Parliament for the fact that something has gone wrong, and he alone can tell Parliament what has occurred and render an account of his stewardship."[72]

The dynamics of briefing the Minister on all serious matters relating to their Department arose most prominently in Ireland in the events surrounding the Travers Report 2005. This concerned the illegal charging of patients in nursing homes, and the failure of the Department of Health, including successive Ministers, to recognise the existence of serious questions regarding the scheme since 1976. While we will discuss the general findings of the report later in this chapter, one specific issue which arose was whether the then Minister for Health, Micheál Martin, had received a briefing on the issues involved in a file created in 2004, which contained a draft letter to the Attorney General seeking advice on the legality of the charges and setting out the Department's position on the issue. The Secretary General at the time stated that while he did not recall giving the file to the Minister, he believed that he would have. The report concluded that Minister Martin was not fully briefed on the issue and that nothing of substance was said to him.

[2–43]

It strongly condemned the failure of civil servants to adequately inform the Minister of the serious nature of the issues and the "significant legal, financial and political consequences".[73] Such briefings where they occur were to be comprehensive, fully inclusive of all relevant facts and adequately recorded. The circulation of information within the Department was also found to be complicated by the presence of several ministerial advisers, who were not members of the civil service. These advisors had been present at one particular meeting on the need to secure legal advice, but the report stressed that special advisers were not part of the line management system and briefings to them by civil servants should not be considered as an alternative to direct briefing of the Minister.[74] The ambiguities of the Travers report underlined the

[2–44]

---

[72] Sir David Maxwell-Fyfe, HC Deb 20 July 1954 vol 530, cc 1286-7.

[73] The cost of the Estimated at two billion euros.

[74] This related to a key December 2003 meeting at a Dublin hotel where the issue of legality was discussed by ministerial advisers, CEOs of then health boards and departmental officials. Minister Martin was late to this meeting.

everyday dynamics relating to the circulation of information in Government departments must be dealt with systematically.

Distinguishing Policy from Administration: The Special Criminal Court Delisting Case

[2–45] An important distinction has also been developed by the politicians to minimise the operation of responsibility, at least for administrative matters. This can be seen in the example of the Special Criminal Court delisting case.[75] In 1996 Judge Dominic Lynch had requested permission to step down as a judge. This was granted but the decision was not communicated to the judge who continued to sit on the Special Criminal Court for a further three months. During this time he continued to exercise his judicial functions in the Court including decisions regarding bail refusals.[76]

[2–46] When the error emerged and the issue was debated in the Dáil, the Justice Minister at the time, Nora Owen, was unable to inform TDs who was responsible for the error but promised a "full, speedy and impartial inquiry" by outside officials. She however denied it was a resignation matter. The inquiry was carried out in just over a week and the report failed to identify officials in the Department of Justice responsible for the error.[77]

[2–47] The approach to Ministerial responsibility adopted by the Government of the day was that Ministers took responsibility for personal errors.[78] Minister Owen stated that she was "accountable to the Dáil" in the limited sense that she had to give information to it for administrative errors which took place in her Department. This was distinct from culpability which would require the Minister to resign.[79] The opposition argued, unsuccessfully, that she was responsible, despite it being an administrative failing, because she had failed to establish an effective system of correspondence within the Department. Although previously

---

[75] E Feldman, "Accountability: A Case Study", (1999) vol 88 no 350 *Studies: An Irish Quarterly Review* 140.
[76] Some 15 people were released because of being illegally detained as a result of this affair. They were all subsequently rearrested and recharged - *Hegarty v Governor of Limerick Prison* [1998] 1 IR 412, *Quinlivan v Governor of Portlaoise Prison* [1998] 1 IR 456.
[77] *ibid* at 142-3.
[78] 471 *Dáil Debates* Col 651, 12 November 1996.
[79] 471 *Dáil Debates* Col. 669 12 November 1996.

the Minister would have been regarded as responsible for the effective running of their Department, in practice this position is no longer sustained. The result is that the Minister is no longer responsible for every stamp and letter. This in large part reflects the reality of the operation of large Government Departments, with responsibility for administrative errors now being regarded as lying with the civil servant.

The Public Service Management Act 1997 and Ministerial Responsibility

The changed relationship between the Minister as head of the Department and the civil servants who staff the Department has been recognised in the Public Service Management Act 1997. The legislation retains the foundation of individual ministerial responsibility first established in the Ministers and Secretaries Act 1924, but it allows for transfer of responsibility, where appropriate, downwards in the civil service hierarchy. The legislation outlines the respective responsibilities and accountability functions of the Minister and the Departmental Secretary General, and in turn down through the hierarchy of the Department. Section 4 therefore states that the Secretary General has "authority, responsibility and accountability" in respect of large parts of departmental administration. This attempts to reflects the reality of the system of central Government and impose responsibility to match that.[80] Thus managerial responsibility for the Department is given to the Secretary General while the Minister retains overall responsibility for the performance of the functions of the Department and policy. The idea has been to update the concept of responsibility in order to encourage and reinforce modern managerial thinking.

[2–48]

Imposing responsibility and accountability on civil servants directly through this legislation in turn requires there to be a system of holding them to account in a way that is external to the internal civil service disciplinary system. One method of doing this has been through questioning before Oireachtas Committees.[81] The *Committees of the Houses of the*

[2–49]

---

[80] For a fuller discussion of the operation of the legislation see Hogan and Morgan above n 65 at paras 3-09-3.48.
[81] The operation of Oireachtas Committees as accountability mechanisms are discussed in more detail below at paras [2-68] onwards.

Oireachtas (Compellability, Privileges and Immunities of Witnesses) Act 1997[82] provided for *any person,* including civil servants,[83] to be directed to appear before a committee to answer questions. In practice[84] civil servants regularly appear voluntarily before committees. However, one significant limitation operates in relation to this. Section 93(1)(b) of the *Houses of the Oireachtas (Inquiries, Privileges and Procedures) Act 2013* prevents a civil servant being asked to express an opinion on the merits of Government or Ministerial policy.[85] This provision is a slightly amended version of s 15(1) of the Committees of the Houses of the Oireachtas (Compellability, Privileges and Immunities of Witnesses) Act 1997 which had raised disquiet about a restriction on speech in the committees.[86] More significantly, the limitation highlights the impossibility of disentangling policy and administration in the answer of questions. In practice, most administrative failings are attributable to poor policy choice. The prohibition on commenting on policy ultimately has a chilling effect on debating its interrelationship with administration, and damages the ability of committees to understand how the two interact in Government departments.

[2–50]   The result is that while the scope of evidence that civil servants may give to Oireachtas Committees has been extended, particularly as we will see below to new committee inquiries, limitations remain:

---

[82] Now replaced by the *Houses of the Oireachtas (Inquiries, Privileges and Procedures) Act 2013* which maintains the same compellability powers, and extends them to include inquiries. See discussion below at paras [2-93] – [2-120].

[83] Subject to certain exceptions such as the President, AG and DPP, s 10.

[84] Particularly following the decision of the Supreme Court in *Ardagh v McGuire* [2002] IR 385. See discussion below at paras [2-85] – [2-90].

[85] s 93(1)(b)

  (i)   the committee may not ask a civil servant, member of the Permanent Defence Force or the Garda Síochána, or relevant person, to express an opinion on the merits of a policy of the Government or of a Minister of the Government or the merits of the objectives of such a policy, and

  (ii) a civil servant, member of the Permanent Defence Force or the Garda Síochána, or a relevant person, may not express such an opinion.

[86] The Labour Party had previously called the impact of this provision into question and had committed itself to abolish it in its policy document "New Government, Better Government: changing a broken system", published January 2011, available online at http://www.labour.ie/download/pdf/newgovernmentbettergovernmen.pdf (date accessed 14 October 2013). At para 37 it stated that it would "introduce legislation to *repeal the "gag" clause that applies to the officers of public bodies,* preventing them from expressing an opinion on the merits of Government policy. The business of public administration can only gain from a more open system which will allow officials to express their views more freely before a Dáil committee." (emphasis in original).

[the] current prohibition on an Oireachtas Committee from asking a public servant to otherwise express an opinion on the merits of policy will be maintained. It is not expected, that disclosing specific policy advice should occur other than in exceptional circumstances where it is central to terms of reference of an inquiry. This will be set out in revised guidance for to civil servants once the legislation comes into force.[87]

In justifying the position Brendan Howlin TD stated that:

Civil servants are not accountable for policy. If one is sitting with a group of civil servants one might get a variety of contradictory or countervailing views. Bluntly, and with all due respect to senior civil servants, their policy views do not matter because they are not elected. The only person whose policy view matters is the relevant Minister whose policy can be implemented and who is accountable to the House for this policy position.... What is important is that they are required and enabled to give a factual account of matters and give evidence on how policy was formulated, but not give their view on policy.[88]

In reality, this is somewhat incomplete picture of Government policy development. While the final say on policy does lie with the Minister and the wider Government, it would be inexact to suggest that senior civil servants have no role to play in formulating that policy. Nor is it completely convincing to suggest that a bright line can be drawn between policy and administration.

The functioning of the system of responsibility following the 1997 Act **[2–51]** continues to be limited in practice as can be revealed by two significant examples of central Government maladministration. The first arises in the context of the DIRT inquiry which will be discussed further in relation to the operation of Oireachtas Committees and the Comptroller and Auditor General (CAG).[89]

---

[87] Second Stage Debate, Speech by Minister for Public Expenditure and Reform Brendan Howlin TD, 22 May 2013 available at http://oireachtasdebates.oireachtas.ie/debates%20 authoring/debateswebpack.nsf/takes/dail2013052200035?opendocument#HH00800 (date accessed 10 July 2014).

[88] Brendan Howlin TD, Select Sub-Committee on Public Expenditure and Reform, Houses of the Oireachtas (Inquiries, Privileges and Procedures) Bill 2013: Committee Stage, 5 June 2013, available at http://oireachtasdebates.oireachtas.ie/Debates%20Authoring/ DebatesWebPack.nsf/committeetakes/FI22013060500021 (date accessed 14 October 2013).

[89] See discussion below at para [2-66].

The DIRT Inquiry and Ministerial Responsibility

[2–52] Briefly, in 1999 the Dáil Public Accounts Committee (PAC) carried out what was to become known as the DIRT inquiry into bogus non-residential bank accounts established in the 1980s/90s to avoid payment of the Deposit Interest Retention Tax (DIRT). In most cases false names and British or USA addresses were supplied by customers whose true names and addresses were known to the banks. The Revenue Commissioners also knew of the practice.

[2–53] Although much of the inquiry, and the CAG report upon which it was based, was concerned with the wrongdoings of the banks, at issue was also the question of the responsibility and accountability of the Department of Finance for the fact that the Revenue Commissioners knew what was happening and had failed to fully enforce the relevant law. Evidence before the PAC indicated that civil servants were concerned about the impact of a rigorous enforcement of the law on investors— it might have resulted in money leaving the country. It was said that they "sensed" their (successive) Ministers would not have wished this. However, there was no evidence put before the committee of Ministers being formally told of these decisions, although there was evidence that they were aware of large-scale tax evasion.[90]

[2–54] The DIRT inquiry did not make findings as to whether Ministers had knowledge or were responsible. Hogan and Morgan do note, however, that they

> "seem to have accepted the implication that an unlawful failure to collect tax, on such a massive scale, was a matter of policy and, in consequence, the responsibility of the Minister for Finance".[91]

Although the DIRT inquiry is held up as a model of how committee inquiries can effectively function as accountability mechanisms, the report failed to censure or sanction any civil servant or minister for their actions in relation to the events. Condemnation was reserved for the financial institutions.

---

[90] Hogan and Morgan above n 65 at para 3-22.
[91] *ibid.*

In principle however, under the 1997 Act responsibility falls within the   [2–55]
remit of the Secretary General of the Department of Finance given that s/
he has "authority, responsibility and accountability" in respect of
departmental administration — that would include the requirement that
administration of departmental activities is carried out *according to law*.
However, it may also be the case that the decision not to enforce the law
fell within the category of a policy; a failure to take action can be a policy
as much as a decision to take action. In which case the Minister would
also be responsible for the errors.

Illegal Nursing Home Charges

A similar conclusion arises in relation to the case of illegal charging of   [2–56]
nursing home residents which took place between the 1970s and 2004. For
28 years charges were imposed on residents in long stay public institutions
without any legal basis.[92] The problem arose because under statute[93]
patients with medical cards were entitled to free in-patient services but
Health Boards were deducting money from their welfare benefits to pay for
their treatment under regulations.[94]

As far back as 1978 the Eastern Health Board had received a legal   [2–57]
opinion establishing that primary legislation could not be changed by
means of regulation and that the Oireachtas had failed to introduce
legislation to provide for the charges being made. Officials contacted
the Department of Health advising to the effect that without legislation
the charges could be challenged.[95] In addition, an Ombudsman Report
in 2001 on a related issue of patients in private nursing homes also drew
attention to the issue of legality.[96] However, the Department of Health,
under successive Ministers, appear to have ignored the *ultra vires*
levying of charges in this area.[97]

---

[92] For more detail see B Connaughton, "Reform of Politico-administrative Relations in the
Irish System: Clarifying or Complicating the Doctrine of Ministerial Responsibility", (2006)
21 (3) *Irish Political Studies* 257. Hereinafter "Connaughton".

[93] Health Act 1970, s 53.

[94] Health (Charges for In-Patient Services) Regulations 1976.

[95] Connaughton above n 92 at p 265.

[96] Office of the Ombudsman, *An Investigation by the Ombudsman of Complaints Regarding
Payment of Nursing Home Subventions By Health Boards,* (Ombudsman, Dublin, 2001).

[97] Hogan and Morgan, note that sixteen Ministers held office during the period of the unlawful
charging, only Mary Harney took action, above n 65 at para 3-23.

[2–58] An inquiry into the events was carried out by the Joint Oireachtas Committee on Health and Children which published the *Travers Report*[98] in 2005. In debating this report, the committee ultimately operated along party political lines, despite the important accountability role they were undertaking.[99] As a result the Government majority was able to focus its findings on the administrative failures of the civil service rather than any policy failures. The report itself found that there was a longstanding political failure to probe the detail of events and ask focused questions of civil servants. Despite underlining this silence, however, it went on to conclude that the primary responsibility for the failures fell within the administrative sphere. It concluded that successive civil servants had wanted to protect their Ministers and had failed to appreciate, the risk associated with continuing to allow illegal charging to continue.[100] The responsibilities were also broken down in line with administration and policy:

> "there was an overall corporate failure in the Department to deal adequately with the matter.... the failure was greater on the part of the administrators than it was on the part of the politicians. I did not exclude the politicians from responsibility for these matters, I said that the politicians should have probed more deeply over the years... this probing was not done."[101]

[2–59] These conclusions become problematic if we accept, as some of the evidence indicates, that it was well known within the Department of Health that the charges were being levied unlawfully and that a blind eye was then turned. Briefings were either not provided to Ministers or if they were, the information was not fully grasped and/or acted upon.[102] Furthermore the failure to gain knowledge when it should have been

---

[98] Joint Committee on Health and Children, Report on the Report on Certain Issues of Management and Administration in the Department of Health and Children associated with the Practice of Charges for Persons in Long-Stay Care in Health Board Institutions and Related Matters (Stationery Office, Dublin, 2005). Hereinafter "Travers report".

[99] Hogan and Morgan above n 65.

[100] Connaughton above n 92 at pp 267-8.

[101] Travers report above n 98 at p 14.

[102] For example, whether Micheál Martin TD, former Minister for Health, was briefed became a major point of disagreement between himself and a senior civil servant — F Sheahan, "The civil servant, the missing file, Micheál Martin and the €2bn bill" *Irish Examiner*, 10 March 2005. Available at http://www.irishexaminer.com/archives/2005/0310/ireland/the-civil-servant-the-missing-file-micheal-martin-and-the-2bn-bill-501903904.html (date accessed 10 July 2005).

gathered, suggests responsibility at the Ministerial level as well as the Secretary General level. We agree with Connaughton's conclusion that:

"The case illustrates that reform has not adequately clarified the responsibilities of ministers and the extent to which they can be reasonably held accountable and responsible for the actions of their departments. It may be implied that in Ireland resignation from office is seen as an admission of personal guilt on the minister's part for whatever wrong-doing or mistakes were made. Hence, the more diluted concept of 'answerability' is more prevalent."[103]

Flaws in the System

These cases studies illustrate the practical problems of the current operation of ministerial responsibility within Ireland. Despite the passing of the 1997 Act there continues to be a lack of clarity as to who bears responsibility for maladministration within central Government Departments. This is exacerbated by the apparent ability of Ministers to avoid responsibility where they had no knowledge. This in turn can produce a situation where Ministers limit their engagement with problematic issues and civil servants limit their briefings of Ministers.[104] However, we do not know how far Ministers engage with their briefings and civil servant advice because the standard practice is that such briefings are not recorded.[105] This is poor practice at central Government level and continues despite recommendations from the Travers Report in 2005 that Ministers:

[2–60]

"should insist on full and periodic briefings on key issues of policy and operational performance. This is basic sense in any system of government whereby ministers are entitled to be warned of 'skeletons in the cupboard' as was the issue in this instance given the time span

---

[103] Connaughton above n 92 at p 268.

[104] In the recent controversy around the recording and retention of telephone conversations in Garda stations the then Minister for Justice Alan Shatter was briefed by Department of Justice Officials on information provided by Garda Commissioner Martin Callinan after a two week delay. "Department of Justice releases Martin Callinan's letter" RTE News, 2 April 2014 available at http://www.rte.ie/news/2014/0401/605859-garda-recordings/ (date accessed 10 July 2014).

[105] P Rabbitte, "Public Service Reform must not let Ministers off hook", Speech at the *"Power – Its Uses and Abuses"* forum at the Burren Law School, Ballyvaughan, Co. Clare, 2 May 2010. Available at http://www.burrenlawschool.org/archive/BLS_2010_PatRabbitte.pdf (date accessed 10 July 2014).

of the case. Likewise, the civil servants should ensure that all such briefings are adequately documented."[106]

[2–61]   The traditional concept of individual ministerial responsibility therefore no longer connects with the structure of Government and civil service today. Even with the reforms of the Public Service Management Act 1997 the system tries to cling onto Ministerial responsibility while recognizing that civil servants are no longer faceless, have far more complex responsibilities and that Government cannot operate on the basis that the Minister knows or is in control of all:

> "In practice ... ministerial responsibility does not oblige ministers to resign for matters where they are not personally at fault. In such cases, they are merely required to undertake appropriate remedial actions, including the identification of those personally responsible, in other words to exercise the accountability obligations of their leadership role."[107]

[2–62]   The doctrine in fact reinforces party political dimensions to the Ministers role, overtaking the internal accountability role of the Oireachtas. Calls for Ministerial resignations now take the form of a staged engagement between Government and opposition with the need for achieving accountability outcomes lost in the posturing.

[2–63]   In addition, it provides for no subtlety in relation to sanctions whether in relation to the Minister or civil servants. It remains the case that little information is provided as to internal disciplinary processes where a civil servant is responsible for maladministration. Where a Minister (or Ministers) is at fault, the only sanction is a loss of post. This provides no gradation to reflect relative gravity of an error, nor can it provide an effective sanction where either a Minister is no longer in post or, as in the case of the nursing home affair, where multiple Ministers presided over maladministration.

---

[106] Connaughton above n 92 at p 273.

[107] R Mulgan, *Holding Power to Account: Accountability in Modern Democracies* (Macmillan, London, 2003) at p 206.

The Comptroller and Auditor General and the Public Accounts Committee

In addition to the doctrine of ministerial responsibility, the Oireachtas has also developed a range of structures and bodies designed to improve oversight. For the most part these allow for improved information gathering and investigation of the activities of Government departments, civil servants and ministers. However, the growth of semi-State bodies and the use of voluntary sector organisations to provide public services mean that oversight has also been pushed out from the central public sphere to the border between the public and private. This unsurprisingly has caused some tensions in the operation of Oireachtas accountability systems.
    [2–64]

The Comptroller and Auditor General (CAG) is tasked with the job of overseeing the use of public money by the State. As a result the office audits and reports on the accounts of public bodies, monitor the use of monies, including issues of efficiency and legality, and generally contributes to the development of accountability in relation to the public sector.
    [2–65]

The office is established under Article 33 of the Constitution and came into existence in 1926. However, for many years it was largely underfunded and ignored by the Oireachtas. In addition, the powers of the office derived principally from the Exchequer and Audit Departments Act 1866 which was outdated and unable to provide effective powers to ensure oversight in relation to modern Government.[108] This was rectified in 1993 when the Comptroller and Auditor General Act was passed; most significantly the office was given the power to carry out Value for Money audits and its remit was extended to include all non-commercial State bodies such as the HSE.[109]
    [2–66]

The CAG works in cooperation with the Public Accounts Committee (PAC) which is made up of thirteen members: six Government backbenchers, six opposition backbenchers and a chair who is by convention a leading
    [2–67]

---

[108] E Connolly, "The Government and the governmental system", in J Coakley and M Gallagher, *Politics in the Republic of Ireland*, (4th ed) (Routledge, Abingdon, 2005) at p 346.

[109] Commercial State bodies were not brought into the office's remit because they were already within the jurisdiction of the Oireachtas by way of the Joint Oireachtas Committee on State-sponsored Bodies. This committee was disbanded in 1997 and the jurisdiction is now divided up between the relevant committee for each sector.

member of the opposition. It is unusual in its operation because it is normally not subject to party politics, in part because the committee's existence dates back before party control was dominant.[110]

[2–68] The Committee is tasked with the job of examining the accounts of Government departments, a job it does through the CAGs audit reports. As part of this process civil servants are called before the Committee to answer questions and report changes and actions within departments as a result of audits. The most high profile example of the operation of the PAC was the DIRT inquiry.[111] That inquiry was facilitated by the passing of the Comptroller and Auditor General and Committees of the Houses of the Oireachtas (Special Provisions) Act 1998 which gave the PAC powers to compel people to give evidence for the purpose of the investigation. In addition, it gave the CAG the power to appoint an auditor to examine the accounts of bank customers. Generally regarded as an accountability success story, the investigation by the CAG was ultimately an information gathering exercise. As a result the report of the CAG did not make any conclusions on the events surrounding the failure to pay tax. Once the CAG had finalised its report, the PAC then carried out oral hearings based on its findings. The success of the resulting PAC investigation was in large part because the CAG report provided a sound base for those hearings.

[2–69] A key element of the work of the CAG is that it does not seek to impose or allocate blame for failings when they are found. Rather it focuses on trying to "establish whether institutional machinery has failed to work satisfactorily".[112]

Oireachtas Committees

[2–70] An effective committee system is beneficial to the role Parliaments play in effectively holding Government and Departments to account. Committees are a familiar mechanism in Parliamentary systems with some democratic systems, such as the USA placing heavily reliance upon committees because of the limited role the Parliamentary process

---

[110] DG Morgan, "Enforcing Public Accountability: A Tour D'Horizon" (2009) 27 ILT 71 at p 76. Hereinafter "Morgan (2009)".

[111] Discussed above in relation to Ministerial Responsibility – see paras [2-56] - [2-59].

[112] Law Reform Commission, Consultation Paper on Tribunals of Inquiries (LRC CP 22-2003) (LRC, Dublin, 2003) at para 4.19.

plays in their accountability processes.[113] However, in the Westminster model committees have been a relatively recent addition to the parliamentary furniture. However, they are not considered to be of central importance. Thus Strøm observes that committees are "among the most significant internal organisational features of modern Parliaments" and a basic requirement if Parliaments are to have influence over the executive.[114] Indeed, for some the committee system provides the legislature its best oversight opportunity.[115]

Parliamentary committees are made up of backbench members of Parliament who are tasked with examining issues, legislation, or finances in a manner that allows for a much higher degree of scrutiny than can ever systematically be achieved in the full chamber. In order for committees ultimately to be successful it is necessary for them to operate in some measure beyond traditional party political ties. Committee members therefore need to be committed to the purpose of their committee and to engaging in the scrutiny of Government. If members are unable to leave the political point scoring at the door then the committee will simply be a smaller version of the Parliamentary chamber and suffer from the same limitations. [2–71]

Advantages of the Committee System[116]

There are some clear benefits of Parliamentary Committees. Firstly they allow the legislature to increase its work rate by delegating the business of Parliament to smaller groups. This allows for a diversity of work to take place at the same time and improves efficiency. [2–72]

In addition, committees assist in the specialisation of the Oireachtas allowing individual politicians to either make use of pre-existing specialised knowledge or develop an area of interest. In principle therefore committees should not reward loyalty to party and allow appointments as political patronage but instead reward skills and expertise. In turn, the skills of the [2–73]

---

[113] B Schwartz, *American Constitutional Law,* (CUP, Cambridge, 2013) at p 66.

[114] K Strøm, "Parliamentary committees in European democracies", (1998) *The Journal of Legislative Studies,* 4: 1, 21 at p 55.

[115] J Lees and M Shaw (eds) *Committees in Legislatures: A Comparative Analysis* (Duke University Press, Durham, North Carolina, 1979).

[116] For a more detailed discussion of the Oireachtas Committee system see S Martin, "The Committee System" in M MacCarthaigh and M Manning (eds) *The Houses of the Oireachtas* (IPA, Dublin, 2010), hereinafter "Martin" (2010).

committee are fed back into the Parliamentary process as reports and discussions relay between committees and the full Parliamentary chambers.

[2–74] Committees facilitate easier access to the Oireachtas by civil society groups who can make direct representations to committees. This allows representatives to hear expert views in a way that previously could only really be done through the role of a parliamentarian acting in a constituency representation capacity.

[2–75] Finally, and most significantly for our purposes, committees are well positioned to gather information on the workings of Government and in turn improve the operation of departments through public scrutiny. In particular, the value of committees is the ability to directly question civil servants, in many cases the key persons making decisions. The resulting increased scrutiny of Government is an essential product of a strong committee system as the OECD noted in 2008:

> "The use of the Joint and Select Committee system by the Oireachtas allows government and public officials to be accountable to the wider electorate. It is also a valuable way of examining key policy initiatives and regulatory developments, particularly the impacts that policy developments originating from the EU will have on Ireland."[117]

However, if committees are regarded as a central component of accountability, then a consistent culture of compliance must build up, as yet the OECD report stressed that the practice and impact of committees was highly variable.[118]

Challenges to the Effectiveness of Oireachtas Committees

[2–76] In order for Committees to be effective they must have the power to oversee key areas and the capacity to carry out their oversight role effectively. However, it appears that in practice many committees struggle with this. The Economist Intelligence Unit, reporting in 2009, stated that

> "the ability of Oireachtas committees effectively to hold regulators to account [appeared] to be limited because they lack the specialist knowledge to do so".[119]

---

[117] OECD above n 69 at p 260.
[118] *ibid.*
[119] Economist Intelligence Unit *Review of the Regulatory Environment in Ireland* (Department of the Taoiseach, Dublin, 2009) at p 54. Hereinafter "Economist Intelligence Unit (2009)".

This perhaps reflects the reality that committee structures are reliant upon their members with specialised knowledge either coming from members' pre-existing backgrounds or longer term accumulation as a result of the work within committees. The Oireachtas committees system is thus still developing and not yet functioning as well as might be hoped. Committee work needs to be incentivised and committees effectively resourced.

However, Martin notes that the operation of Oireachtas Committees must be understood in the context of a Parliamentary system where the legislature is dominated by the executive. Thus, in relation to the operation of major inquiries such as the nursing home or DIRT inquiries the terms of reference largely focused on activities that were somewhat removed from Ministerial control. [120] This point is important; Committees need a non-partisan framework within which to operate. This includes the need to minimise the politicisation of the drafting of terms of reference of inquiries, their capacity to compel witnesses, as well as the internal operation and behaviour of members. The establishment of the Committee of Inquiry into the Banking Crisis[121] in May 2014 clearly illustrates the dangers of undermining the credibility of the work of committees before they even start work. The very formation of the Banking Inquiry Committee was beset with controversy when the Government added two of its senators to the Committee in order to ensure it had a majority.[122]

It is hardly surprising that party politics can have a negative impact if [2–77] committees are allowed to simply replicate the politics of the Dáil. The development of cross party cooperation is recognised ultimately as being necessary if a committee is to ever achieve anything substantial. Although it is not the case that all committees adopt this approach it is clear that it can develop for a number of reasons. Firstly, because of the lack of public/media interest in committee work there is little need or opportunity for politicians to grandstand for the headlines. Secondly,

---

[120] Martin (2010) above n 116 at p 298.

[121] For more detail of the Joint Committee see http://www.oireachtas.ie/parliament/oireachtasbusiness/committees_list/committeeofinquiryintothebankingcrisis/ (date accessed 26 August 2014).

[122] The Government's expected majority on the committee was initially lost when members of the Seanad's Committee of Selection voted for opposition senators in the absence of Government members. The Government therefore extended the membership of the inquiry committee thus restoring its majority. See M Minihan and M O'Halloran, "Government accused of 'skulduggery' over banking committee", *The Irish Times*, June 12 2014. Hereinafter "Minihan and O'Halloran".

good relationships can be nurtured through the committee structure regardless of the politics. Thirdly, many politicians are enthusiastic about the opportunity to influence policy. A committee may be the only real way in which they can do this. For many independent politicians it provides the main opportunity to access the policy and legislative process.

[2–78]   A developed Committee structure is a relatively new component of the Oireachtas. Martin notes that in their original form they were regarded as "weak" and "ineffective"[123] although there have in recent times been some significant improvements. There are a number of different types of committees:

a)   *Select committees* — whose members come from one house only. The committees are set up at discretion of the house and normally do one of two things — they either investigate or consider legislation referred to them;

b)   *Joint committees* — membership comes from both houses sitting and voting together under common orders of reference;

c)   *Standing committee* — these committees are formed automatically at the start of a new Dáil and are the most visible committees outside of the Oireachtas. The best known example is the Committee of Public Accounts (PAC);

d)   *House-keeping committees* — these are the committees dealing with the operation of internal parliamentary administration. They have no policy role but are designed to monitor and control the internal workings of the Oireachtas.

[2–79]   As currently constituted the committee structure of the Oireachtas matches well with the departmental structure of Government. At the time of going to press there are 21 committees, and 22 sub-committees, monitoring the work of Government.[124] However, in practice the committees of the Oireachtas have suffered from the typical weaknesses of many committee systems. Although parliamentarians can express a preference for particular committees, the ultimate membership of all

---

[123] *ibid* at p 285.
[124] For detailed information on Oireachtas Committees see http://www.oireachtas.ie/ parliament/oireachtasbusiness/www.oireachtas/committees/ (date accessed 26 August 2014).

committees is controlled by the party whips. Although there is only a small panel of backbenchers to choose from to populate committees, allegations of patronage remain.[125] This claim has particularly focused on the fact that certain committee positions have attracted payments.[126] The existence of paid positions, and the use of whips in small committees is odd and undermines their operation.

Although some backbenchers are enthusiastic about committee work, there remains difficulties in encouraging membership. Preference for constituency work given its significance in achieving re-election is reinforced by the perceived weakness of committees. The result is that the performance of committees varies significantly, the OECD thus noted that there was variation not only in the quality of work, but also how often committees actually met.[127]   **[2–80]**

As was noted earlier, effective committees require sufficient resources. Here too, the Irish system has suffered. Surveying its operation in 2009 the Economist Intelligence Unit found that the lack of resources and expertise meant that Oireachtas committees were in reality not well placed to engage in effective oversight of Government:[128] the Minister for Finance controls the financial purse strings of committees. However, over the past years efforts have been made to support committees including secretarial support and Parliamentary assistants provided to members and the development of a central research facility.[129]   **[2–81]**

The ability of committees to contribute to improved scrutiny of Government requires that they have the power to gather evidence in the form of documents and oral hearings that are more than merely a shadow of the political fighting of the main chamber. It is therefore worrying that Martin highlights that practice has in many committees gone no further than political grandstanding: **[2–82]**

> "[a]lthough difficult to quantify, there appears to be a problem in Oireachtas committees with some committee members not being

---

[125] Martin (2010) above n 116 at p 301.

[126] s 4 of the Oireachtas (Allowances To Members) and Ministerial, Parliamentary, Judicial and Court Offices (Amendment) Act 1998 allows for this. However, since 2009 only the Committee chairs are paid an allowance.

[127] OECD above n 69.

[128] Economist Intelligence Unit (2009) above n 119 at pp 53-4.

[129] Martin (2010) above n 116 at p 298.

particularly interested either in the questions they are asking or the answers that are being given. In some instances, a member might even pose a question and then leave before or as the answer is being given by the witness. Others have reported that committee members are sometimes more keen to ask questions than to hear answers and thus monopolise the available time. Indeed, it would seem that in many instances, appearing before an Oireachtas committee can be a wholly unfulfilling experience, ultimately because of the disinterest of committee members towards their role as policy makers and scrutinisers of government bodies and agencies."[130]

[2–83]   In theory, committees should provide an opportunity to directly question both Ministers and civil servant, as well as other relevant actors. These powers were initially provided to Oireachtas Committees by the Committees of the Houses of the Oireachtas (Compellability, Privileges and Immunities of Witnesses) Act 1997 which was passed as part of the package of reforms of the public sector.[131] The legislation empowered Committees to send for papers, people or records, including civil servants.[132] Compellability was not automatic, with the power being authorised by the sub-committee of the Committee on Procedure and Privileges (otherwise known as the compellability committee), chaired by the Government Chief Whip. This structure is important as it provides that the Government maintains control over the operation of this important power. Compellability was backed up by s 3(7) of the 1997 Act which provided for the High Court to make an order to compel attendance by a person whom a Committee had ordered to appear before it. Failure to comply with that order, without just cause or excuse, was an offence under s 3(8).

[2–84]   The 1997 Act provided important new powers to committees and the DIRT inquiry became the first instance of their exercise. It is also the main example of their effective use to date.[133] In that case the PAC established a sub-committee in 1999 which held hearings over 26 days. Proceedings were televised and the media provided widespread news coverage as the

---

[130] *ibid* at p 300.

[131] As we will discuss below at paras [2-93] - [2-120] this legislation has now been replaced by the Houses of the Oireachtas (Inquiries, Privileges and Procedures) Act 2013.

[132] s 3 of the 1997 Act, now replaced by s 67 2013 Act. s 10 of the 1997 Act allowed for any person to "whom responsibility for the performance of functions has been assigned" to appear before an Oireachtas Committee and to answer its questions.

[133] Martin (2010) above n 116 at p 295. See discussion above regarding the DIRT inquiry at paras [2-50] – [2-53].

committee examined a range of witnesses regarding 300,000 false off-shore accounts.

Impediments to the Conducting of Oireachtas Inquiries: From Abbeylara to the Proposed 30th Constitutional Amendment

The DIRT inquiry was regarded as a significant success and was quickly **[2–85]** followed by the establishment of two further inquiries. Firstly, the Joint Committee on Justice, Equality, Defence and Women's Rights established a sub-committee to examine the report of the Garda Commissioner into the fatal shooting in Abbeylara by the Gardaí.[134] Secondly, the Joint Committee on Public Enterprise and Transport established a sub-committee to examine the awarding of a contract by CIE which was budgeted to cost around €16 million but in fact cost approximately €50 million.[135] Neither investigation should have been particularly problematic but both were brought to a swift end when union representatives challenged the operation of Abbeylara committee, particularly its ability to compel witnesses and to reach findingss of fact.

The decision of the High Court and the Supreme Court in *Ardagh v* **[2–86]** *Maguire*[136] reinforced the power of the Oireachtas to operate committees but then effectively displaced their ability to compel witnesses and make findings of fact beyond a very narrow remit:

> "It is of course agreed that elected representatives should take every opportunity to inform and advise themselves on all matters relevant to their wide-ranging duties as law makers .... The information required by TDs will range from the international, technical and detailed to the parochial, popular (or unpopular) and general. The great Library of Congress in Washington is a monument to the information required by diligent legislators. Thus the right of members of the Oireachtas, whether individually or collectively, to obtain information is implicit in the Constitution and the right, in certain circumstances, to compel members of the public to provide such information under oath is expressly conferred by statute. The

---

[134] The establishment of a sub-committee on the Abbeylara shooting was made on 18 April 2001, see press release http://www.oireachtas.ie/viewdoc.asp?fn=/documents/press/180401.htm (date accessed 10 July 2014).

[135] The sub-committee on Mini CTC Signalling Project was established on 16 November 2000, http://debates.oireachtas.ie/seanad/2001/04/04/00005.asp#N2 (date accessed 10 July 2014).

[136] [2002] 1 IR 447 Supreme Court.

real concern, as I see it, relate to the power or duty of a subcommittee of the Oireachtas 'to make a finding of fact.'"[137]

[2–87]   The Court concluded that the powers of the Oireachtas to engage in inquiries were limited to the activities of Government departments. Article 28.4 of the Constitution makes Government accountable to the Dáil as we have already seen, and so a committee should operate within that remit. The terms of the Constitution were thus construed as limiting the extent to which committees can range beyond the natural territory of legislation, policy and Government administration. In addition, the Court found that the terms of reference of the Abbeylara sub-committee brought the committee into the realm of considering whether members of the Gardaí had carried out an unjustifiable killing: the consequences of such a finding would have a significant impact on the reputations of individual Garda which engaged constitutional justice. The outcome for the Abbeylara investigation was that it was transferred from the Oireachtas sub-committee to a Tribunal of Inquiry.[138]

[2–88]   The impact of this decision on the operation of committees within the Oireachtas has been profound. Following the *Ardagh* judgment, all witnesses attending before committees under the 1997 Act have appeared voluntarily thus making the compellability mechanism in that legislation meaningless in practice. By appearing voluntarily, witnesses are regarded to have given up the rights to constitutional justice which would have applied without such consent.[139]

[2–89]   Attempts to force attendance by reluctant bankers highlighted the emasculation of the committees. In 2009 Seán Fitzpatrick, former head of Anglo Irish Bank, refused to attend PAC hearings: the committee considered forcing attendance but quickly backed down. As Morgan notes, the committee was faced with significant problems as regards the *Ardagh* decision. Anglo Irish was a private bank and therefore detached from Government activity and control; furthermore the questioning of

---

[137] *ibid* per Murphy J at 575.

[138] Tribunal of Inquiry into the facts and circumstances surrounding the fatal shooting of John Carty at Abbeylara, Co. Longford, on 20 April 2000. The Tribunal was chaired by Mr Justice Barr. Tribunals of Inquiry are discussed in more detail in chapter 5.

[139] Morgan (2009) above n 110.

Fitzpatrick could easily have moved into the realm of criminal activity[140] which would have seriously hampered the process. Ultimately, the committee would have had to award their witness full constitutional justice rights.

The fear of overstepping the *Abbeylara* decision continues to haunt committees, even following the enactment of the 2013 Act, discussed below at paras [2-94] – [2-121]. In April 2014, former senior executives of Voluntary Organisation the Rehab Group refused to appear before a PAC hearing to answer questions about their pay structure and the use of public funds. The reasons given by former executives of that organisation for refusing to attend were that they were "ordinary citizens" and that PAC was going beyond its remit and ignoring constitutional justice.[141] PAC has since sought authorisation from the Committee on Procedure and Privilege to compel the attendance of Frank Flannery and Angela Kerins, however, this has been refused on the basis that questioning Flannery and Kerins would be "outside the remit" of the PAC and that "a mis-step will cost the taxpayer".[142]

[2–90]

It therefore appears that the Supreme Court decision in the *Abbeylara* case significantly hamstrung the powers of Oireachtas committees. They do not have the power to make findings of fact which could potentially damage the good name of persons who were not members of the Oireachtas. Whilst the Committees have no power of penalty over someone in relation to wrong doing, clearly if a finding is made of negligence or a failure of duty, for example, that could cause reputational damage. It is significant that both Kerins and Flannery have accused PAC members of "'a gross abuse'

[2–91]

---

[140] Seán Fitzpatrick was sent for trial on twelve charges relating to financial irregularities at Anglo Irish Bank on 1 March 2013. The Charges were brought under the Companies Act 1990, s 197, the allegations being that he knowingly or recklessly failed to disclose the true value of loans held by him and people connected to him, to the bank's auditors, http://www.independent.ie/irish-news/courts/sean-fitzpatrick-sent-for-trial-accused-of-concealing-139m-worth-of-loans-29103258.html (date accessed 9 October 2013). He was found not guilty on all counts on 16 April 2014.

[141] http://www.thejournal.ie/angela-kerins-frank-flannery-rehab-pac-1407090-Apr2014/.

[142] See RTE News, "Committee seeks more information from PAC on Rehab", 11 June 2014, http://www.rte.ie/news/2014/0611/623199-rehab/ The committee requested further information as to why PAC wants the power. S. Phelan, "PAC members claim it is being nobbled in its attempts to investigate rehab" *Irish Independent*, 12 June 2014, http://www.independent.ie/irish-news/politics/pac-members-claims-it-is-being-nobbled-in-its-attempts-to-investigate-rehab-30349258.html (date accessed 10 July 2014) and finally N. O'Connor, "Taxpayer at risk of legal costs in Dáil Rehab Probe" *Herald.ie*, 10 July 2014, http://www.herald.ie/news/taxpayer-at-risk-of-legal-costs-in-dail-rehab-probe-30420291.html (date accessed 10 July 2014).

of their position and of knowingly acting outside the law — warning there would be 'grave consequences' if the inquiry continues".[143] David Morgan noted in a paper on the Abbeylara decision that:

> "[i]n a way, the most surprising aspect of *Abbeylara* was the statement in many of the majority judgments that the Oireachtas lacked the authority to hold an inquiry, at any rate of the *Abbeylara* type.... Many commentators consider that the reasoning of the majority judges was unconvincing and that the Court majority was really influenced by the subject matter of the inquiry. This could be put right by spelling it out clearly, by way of constitutional amendment that there is a power to mount an investigation."[144]

[2–92] In 2011, the Government attempted to do this by putting to the people a proposed thirtieth amendment to the Constitution which would have effectively broadened the inquiry powers of Oireachtas Committees. In support of the change the Fine Gael/Labour coalition argued that it was necessary to improve overall accountability in public life.[145] This is supported in large part by Professor Morgan's point that

> "[i]t is surely reasonable that the Oireachtas, like the democratic powers of almost all other constitutional democracies, should have a wide power to hold inquiries".[146]

[2–93] However, what should have been a relatively straightforward change to strengthen Parliamentary oversight was rapidly destabilised because of the wording in the proposed Article 15.10.4°:

> "It shall be for the House or Houses concerned to determine, with due regard to the principles of fair procedures, the appropriate balance between the rights of persons and the public interest for the purposes of ensuring an effective inquiry....".

---

[143] J McEnroe, "PAC's bid to compel ex-Rehab chiefs looks set to fail", *Irish Examiner*, 9 June 2014, http://www.irishexaminer.com/ireland/pacrsquos-bid-to-compel-ex-rehab-chiefs-looks-set-to-fail-271422.html (date accessed 10 July 2014).

[144] DG Morgan, *Oireachtas Power of Inquiry*, Paper for Joint Committee on the Constitution, (Parliamentary Number A11/0140, 2011). Available at http://www.oireachtas.ie/viewdoc.asp?fn=/documents/Committees30thDail/J-Constitution/Submissions/Electoral_System/sub_20110128.3.doc (date accessed 10 July 2014). Hereinafter Morgan (2011).

[145] See for example, statement by Brendan Hayes TD, 20 October 2011, http://www.merrionstreet.ie/index.php/2011/10/minister-brian-hayes-on-oireachtas-inquiries-referendum/ date accessed 10 July 2014.

[146] Morgan (2011) above n 144.

This triggered a significant NO campaign involving lawyers, NGOs and academics who regarded it as a limit to judicial supervision of such inquiries, particularly on the basis of constitutional justice and the right to reputation. The debate quickly demonstrated the level of public distrust of the Oireachtas to responsibly carry out these inquiries. The amendment was therefore rejected in October 2011 not because of a lack of public desire for effective political reform, but rather a lack of trust in politicians and the Oireachtas apparatus to effectively implement reforms particularly those that appear to give extensive power to politicians.

Re-empowering Oireachtas Committees – Houses of the Oireachtas (Inquiries, Privileges and Procedures) Act 2013[147]

Having lost the referendum, the Government has now passed the Houses of the Oireachtas (Inquiries, Privileges and Procedures) Act 2013.[148] The stimulus for this legislation was the desire on the part of the Government to run a banking inquiry through an Oireachtas Committee rather than through a tribunal of inquiry mechanism.[149]   [2–94]

The legislation was passed in order to better facilitate committee inquiries within the legal context set out by the Supreme Court in the *Abbeylara* case. It is therefore a clarification of the powers of such committees in light of the view that inquiries are possible so long as they do not seek to ascribe personal responsibility to individuals outside the remit of the Oireachtas. Thus, it provides a legislative basis for five types of inquiry under a general heading of *Part 2 inquiries*.   [2–95]

1. An Inquire, Record and Report Inquiry (IRR) — Section 7

This type of inquiry operates in relation to a specific issue and can make findings of fact, so long as they are uncontested. In addition it can draw attention to any matters that are subject to dispute.[150]   [2–96]

---

[147] The 2013 Act supersedes and updates the 1997 legislation as regards compellability, privilege and immunity of witnesses in parts 6, 7 and 8.

[148] The legislation came into force in September 2013.

[149] S Connelly, "Full Tribunal would be too long and expensive, says Kenny", *Irish Examiner*, 26 June 2013, http://www.irishexaminer.com/archives/2013/0626/world/full-tribunal-would-be-too-long-and-expensive-says-kenny-235128.html date accessed 10 July 2014.

[150] s 7.

[2–97]   Such an inquiry is designed to gather and record evidence for the purpose of having it published as a public record of events. The only finding of fact that can be made relates to uncontested evidence. The forthcoming banking inquiry falls into this category, not least because given the need to respect constitutional justice in light of the *Abbeylara* decision, an inquiry that simply records evidence is less likely to engage with guilt, good reputation and justice — "by its very nature, no implications for the reputations of persons could arise."[151]

2.   A Legislative Inquiry — Regarding any Matter that the Oireachtas has or might Legislate on — Section 8

[2–98]   This second type of inquiry has been called the "looking forward inquiry" and operates to allow a committee to carry out an inquiry that will inform itself, and the Oireachtas, of matters relevant to the recognised functions of parliament. This requirement relates to the jurisdictional point decided in the *Abbeylara* case and in effect means that committees can examine any legislative measures that could be needed. As the name suggests, the inquiry does not review past events but considers possible future action with a view to making recommendations and findings within the terms of reference of the committee. In this type of inquiry, findings of fact can be made, and under s 8(2)(c) those findings can relate to misbehaviour. As we will discuss below at paragraph [2- 113] such findings can only be made in relation to those within the jurisdiction of the Oireachtas.

3.   Removal of an Officeholder Inquiry — Section 9

[2–99]   An inquiry under s 9 allows a committee to examine the removal of certain key office holders, including the power to record and report evidence, make findings of fact including ones impugning the good name of the officeholder and make recommendations. Relevant officer holders include the President under Article 12.10, the Comptroller and Auditor general under Article 33.5 and Supreme Court and High Court Judges under Article 35 of the constitution.[152]

---

[151] Brendan Howlin TD, Minister for Public Expenditure and Reform, writing in correspondence to John McGuinness TD, Chair of the Public Accounts Committee, 12 June 2012 available at http://www.oireachtas.ie/parliament/media/committees/pac/correspondence/2012-meeting490507/[PAC-R-574]-Correspondence-3C.5.pdf (date accessed 14 October 2013).
[152] s 9.

4. Conduct of a Member of the House Inquiry — Section 10

Section 10 provides for an inquiry into the conduct of a member of the   **[2–100]**
Oireachtas in relation to his or her *capacity* as a member. Findings of fact can
be made including, under s 10(2)(c) findings that "directly impugn the
good name of the member". However, a s 10 inquiry cannot take place if
the behaviour is already the subject of a complaint under s 8 of the Ethics in
Public Office Act 1995.

Outside of s 10 the Oireachtas already has a system for investigating the   **[2–101]**
behaviour of its members through the Committee on Members Interests
(of both the Dáil and Seanad). However, as the Ivor Callely Inquiry
illustrates, compliance with constitutional justice can be as much of a
challenge when a member is being investigated as it is with members of
the public. In that case, the former Fianna Fáil senator was disciplined by
the Oireachtas Select Committee on Members' Interests following a
finding that he had breached s 4 of the Standards in Public Office Act 2001
"by misrepresenting his normal place of residence for the purpose of
claiming allowances".[153] A High Court ruling that there was a breach of
fair procedure was overturned by a 4-3 majority of the Supreme Court.[154]
For our purposes it is important to note that the court found that Article
15.10 of the Constitution[155] meant that decisions made by the Oireachtas
in relation to members of the Oireachtas would not normally be justiciable.
However, as Fennelly J noted, this does not mean:

> "that a member of a House of the Oireachtas, faced with a disciplinary
> proceeding to be conducted by his or her peers, enjoys no constitutional
> protection. Every organ of the State is obliged to respect the
> constitutional rights of individuals who may be affected by its actions.
> Most relevantly to disciplinary proceedings, every organ of state, such

---

[153] "Findings and Determinations of Report of the Results of an Investigation in the Complaints
concerning Senator Ivor Callely", quoted in O'Donnell and Clarke JJ judgment [2014] IESC
26 at para 26.
[154] [2014] IESC 26. The High Court had found that the Committee had failed to uphold
constitutional justice in its procedures. *Callely v Moylan & Ors* [2011] IEHC 2.
[155] Art 15.10 states:
    Each House shall make its own rules and standing orders, with power to attach penalties
for their infringement, and shall have power to ensure freedom of debate, to protects its
official documents and the private papers of its members, and to protect itself and its
members against any person or persons interfering with, molesting or attempting to
corrupt its members in the exercise of their duties.

as, in the case, the Seanad, through one of its committees, is bound to observe the principles of natural and constitutional justice."[156]

The question as to the boundaries of the power and justifiability in such a case was a matter for the courts. On the facts of Callely's case, the majority concluded that he had benefited from fair procedures.

[2–102]   Dissenting, Hardiman J was troubled by "the contention that the jurisdiction of the High Court at the suit of a person who is a member of Seanad Eireann is *ousted or excluded* by virtue of the provisions of 15.10"[157] and that

> "the Constitution would be subverted if the legislators could, by conferring a particular function on an Oireachtas Committee, create total immunity in the discharge of an adjudicative function."[158]

[2–103]   There is somewhat of a distinction here then between the role of Oireachtas Committees in relation to members of the public and in relation to members of the Oireachtas. Although all people examined by Oireachtas Committees will have to be provided with fair procedures where their constitutional right to reputation is at stake, there is a more limited space for judicial review in the latter context.

5.   Inquiry to Hold the Government to Account — Section 11

[2–104]   This final type of inquiry allows a committee to examine the work of the Government and any person who is liable to the scrutiny of the Dáil because of their contract or statutory appointment. It is important to note here that it is the Houses of the Oireachtas and their committees who initiate an inquiry under this system. This is an important difference from the operation of Commissions of Investigation which require a decision to be made by the Government, or specific Minister, that an inquiry is needed.[159]

[2–105]   These five types of inquiry have been designed to fit with the *Abbeylara* judgment in that they limit the scope of inquiry and the possibility of contested findings of fact beyond the constitutional competence of the

---

[156] Fennelly judgment, *ibid* at para 5.

[157] Hardiman judgment, *ibid*. Emphasis in original.

[158] *ibid*.

[159] See discussion in chapter 5 and the Tribunals of Inquiry Act 1921.

Oireachtas. Only time and operation of the legislation will tell how effectively this has been done. In addition, it will be up to the committees of the Oireachtas to shake off their self-imposed timidity that has been so evident in the post-*Abbeylara* years.

Procedure

Section 12 states that a committee proposing to conduct a Part 2 inquiry shall, in accordance with the rules and standing orders made by the House, give a notice in writing of the proposal for the inquiry to any individual or committees designated by the House to receive such notice.. Standing Order 103B(1) states that the Committee on Procedure and Privileges is the "designated" committee and it will examine any proposal for an inquiry under the 2013 Act and prepare a report making recommendations for the House.[160] That report will include whether the inquiry should be held and, if so, by which committee and in what manner. The House will then pass a resolution to establish an inquiry and confirm its terms of reference.

[2–106]

Section 13 requires that the committee establish clear terms of reference before an inquiry can be conducted. Those should indicate what type of inquiry is being carried out under the Act, and whether the committee has the power to call for evidence. For inquiries to operate effectively it is in practice essential that the terms of reference be narrow and specific enough to be workable in developing a focused inquiry within a clear timeframe. The banking inquiry will be a first example of this and it illustrates already the importance of adequate terms of reference. These can have significant impacts on the scope, and ultimately the effectiveness, of an inquiry. A decision to exclude or include certain things and time periods can radically alter the findings. It appeared for some time that the inquiry may be limited to the 2008 decision to bail out the banks. Such an approach however, would have lain open to the clear criticism that in order to effectively understand how those decisions were made, a longer term review should have been undertaken. At time of going to press, the inquiry will examine the period from 1992 to 2013, broken into four modules: context, banking systems and practices; regulatory and supervisory systems and practices and crisis management and policy responses. The final module will examine the bank guarantee, the creation

[2–107]

---

[160] There is a Committee on Procedure and Privileges for both the Dáil and Seanad. Should a proposal be made by a joint committee it will be considered by both committees.

of the National Asset Management Agency, bank nationalisation and recapitalisation, the bailout programme and the question of promissory notes. Clearly, the longer the period you include the more complex the inquiry can become, [161] particularly given the multiple domestic and international actors involved. This is a difficulty for all types of inquiries — is your priority to provide the widest possible public record (leading often to long and complex inquiries) or is it to provide a manageable and affordable/efficient record of key events?

Compellability under the 2013 Act

[2–108]   The reader should already be familiar with the operation of compellability having been briefly introduced to the framework under the 1997 Act.[162] Part 6 of the 2013 Act gives committees the power to compel attendance for Part 2 inquiries. Section 67(1) provides that a committee may, *inter alia*, direct in writing any person

> "to attend before the committee on a date and at a time and place specified in the direction and there to give evidence and any document in his or her possession or control specified in the direction"

and

> "direct in writing any person to give the committee any document in his or her possession...".[163]

The President, senior judges, the Attorney General and the Director of Public Prosecutions are all excluded from this provision.[164]

[2–109]   Under s 30, there is also an obligation to preserve material in their possession or control. This includes documents and other information which relates to matters within the terms of reference of an inquiry. The obligation applies to material held by a person after the establishment of an inquiry or before an inquiry is established where it can be reasonably inferred in the circumstances that such an inquiry is likely. Where someone knowingly or is reckless as to giving misleading evidence, or

---

[161] This can be seen from the large scale tribunals of inquiry considered in chapter 5.
[162] See discussion above at paras [2-82].
[163] Similar powers are found under s 83 in relation to "other committee business and related matters".
[164] s 67(6) & (7).

fails to preserve material,[165] they are liable to be found guilty of an offence under s 32. [166]

Compellability is not, of course, unlimited. Section 77(3) ensures that a committee cannot proceed to compel a person or document without authorisation from Committee on Procedure and Privileges.[167] In addition, s 71 exempts certain evidence; this includes *inter alia*, under s 71(1)(a) discussions of Government meetings including committees appointed by Government, and under s 71(1)(c) evidence that could "reasonably be expected to prejudice any criminal proceedings".[168] The first category may cause difficulties for the forthcoming banking inquiry given that cabinet discussions will only be accessible on a voluntary basis as it is statutorily excluded from compellability powers. This exemption falls within, although in fact goes further than, the constitutional protection provided to cabinet discussions under Article 28.4.3°.[169] That provision does allow for exceptions to the rule but only in relation to court or tribunal of inquiry proceedings; the banking inquiry clearly does not fall into either. As O'Mahony has noted this restriction may not in itself be particularly harmful to the operation of the committees work as the discussions in cabinet which approved the bank bailout are covered by collective responsibility.[170] It is reported, however, that surrounding documentation prepared for the Government of the day will be accessible.[171]

[2–110]

---

[165] Under s 30.

[166] A conviction for a summary offence carries a class A fine and/or imprisonment of not more than six months (s 32(3)(a)). A conviction on indictment carries a fine of not more than €500,000 and/or imprisonment not exceeding five years (s 32(3)(b)).

[167] The definition of "appropriate committee" as the Committee on Procedure and Privileges in found in s 76.

[168] In relation to powers under s 83 noted above at n 177 similar exemptions are found in s 86.

[169] "The confidentiality of discussions at meetings of the Government shall be respected in all circumstances save only where the High Court determines that disclosure should be made in respect of a particular matter –
  i in the interests of the administration of justice by a Court, or
  ii by virtue of an overriding public interest, pursuant to an application in that behalf by a tribunal appointed by the Government or a Minister of the Government on the authority of the Houses of the Oireachtas to inquire into a matter stated by them to be of public importance."

[170] C O'Mahony, "Cabinet Confidentiality and the Banking Inquiry", Constitution Project @ UCC, July 2 2014. Available online at http://constitutionproject.ie/?p=342 (date accessed 26 August 2014).

[171] F Kelly, "Cabinet talks on bank guarantee 'off limits' to inquiry" *The Irish Times*, 26 June 2014.

[2–111]   The power of compellability is backed up with a sanction for non-cooperation; thus s 14 allows a committee to make a finding of "failed to fully co-operate". This includes failure to attend, refusing the answer, failure to provide documents, destroying evidence, interfering with witnesses and generally obstructing the inquiry. A finding under this section can lead to an additional inquiry taking place, or to the imposition of disciplinary proceedings in another forum and/or the committee making recommendations in its final report. These findings may naturally have resulting bad publicity and therefore impact on the witness's good name.

[2–112]   Section 99 provides for a procedure whereby, when a person refuses to comply with a s 67 direction, an application can be made to the High Court for an order that the person so observe that direction. The legislation also makes it an offence for someone to fail to cooperate with a s 67 direction. Section 75(1) includes failure to comply with a direction, refusal to take the oath, or acting in a manner which would amount to contempt of court.[172] In addition, where someone is found by a court to have failed to cooperate or obstructed an inquiry they may be found liable for committing one of a number of offences under s 32.

Fair Procedure

[2–113]   Part three of the Act sets out measures designed to meet the protections mandated by the Supreme Court judgment in the *Abbeylara* case. In particular the legislation establishes under s 17 that findings of fact that directly impugn the good name of people can only be made in relation to members of Houses or an office-holder or other person accountable to the Oireachtas. Nor can a committee make findings of civil or criminal liability.[173] The section goes on to state that a committee may make findings that "systems, practice, procedures or policy or arrangements for the implementation of policy" should have been carried out differently[174] and related recommendations[175] or findings of relevant

---

[172] s 75(3) states that a person found guilty of an offence under s 75 is liable

　　"(a) on summary conviction, to a class A fine or imprisonment for a term not exceeding 6 months, or both, or

　　(b) on conviction on indictment, to a fine not exceeding €500,000 or imprisonment for a term not exceeding 5 years, or both."

[173] s 17(2)(b).
[174] s 17(3)(a).
[175] s 17(3)(b).

misbehaviour.[176] However, any finding of misbehaviour must, under subsection 4, be supported by particulars relating to the finding of fact and an assessment of any prejudice cause to the inquiry.

The legislation naturally provides privileges and immunities for witnesses. In particular, a witness, whether attending voluntarily or under a direction, has equivalent court protections.[177] This is necessary where someone is being asked questions that might incriminate themselves or others. Despite this, the protections do not allow a person to refuse to answer incriminating questions or provide relevant documents. However, under s 22 a witness has a right to have their legal representative present. **[2–114]**

In an attempt to develop a framework for operating inquiries in line with constitutional justice requirement, the Committee on Procedure and Privileges has developed guidelines setting out the appropriate procedures to be followed.[178] To date these have not been published but they are already informing the development of the Banking Inquiry terms of reference. In addition, a committee chairman will be entitled to make directions under s 20 to "avoid contravention" of the legislation including directing a cessation of the giving of evidence or a particular line of questioning. **[2–115]**

A further attempt to reinforce wider concerns of fairness include a prohibition on members of a House sitting where a perception of bias might arise in a reasonable person if the committee member has been involved in an inquiry as a result of a connection, comments or other circumstances.[179] **[2–116]**

Good Name

Where a committee seeks to make an adverse finding of fact against a person within their jurisdiction, it is required that that person has full *Re Haughey* rights[180] under s 24: **[2–117]**

---

[176] s 17(3)(c).

[177] s 18.

[178] s 19.

[179] s 21.

[180] [1971] IR 217 requiring legal representations, a right to know the allegations, a right to cross examination and a right to call one's own evidence.

i)   advance notice in writing of the evidence proposed to be given against him or her;

ii)   right to cross-examine witnesses;

iii) right to give evidence to answer the allegation;

iv)   call witnesses to answer the allegation;

v)   make a submission at the close of evidence;

vi)   request the committee to call or direct specified persons to attend to give evidence or procure by direction production of specified documents.

In support of these protections a person may access the High Court to make a claim that his or her constitutional rights are not being vindicated by the inquiry.[181] Similarly, the Committee may also make a referral to the court where it is of the opinion that a report could prejudice criminal proceedings.[182]

[2–118]   Although there is a presumption that hearings will be held in public, s 31 does allow for private sessions where the committee is satisfied "it is desirable for the purposes of the inquiry or fair procedures" to have some hearings in private.[183] Evidence given at a hearing will not be admissible in any other proceedings (including disciplinary proceedings) except in relation to prosecution of offences under the Act or the offence of perjury under s 29.

Costs

[2–119]   Under s 22 witnesses are entitled to have legal representation at an inquiry. However, the costs of such legal representation are considered to be the expense of the witness and not the inquiry. The Act does, however, provide for the payment of legal costs in limited circumstances where the good name of a witness is at issue under s 47. In such circumstances, a witness must apply to the Oireachtas Commission for an order to recover those expenses. The Commission will, under s 46, prepare guidelines that will indicate whether such individuals are entitled to such costs.[184] The guidelines can include provisions for the

---

[181] s 94, Part 9 of the legislation. See discussion below.

[182] s 95.

[183] s 31(1)(a).

[184] s 46(1). At the time of writing guidelines on costs had not been published.

development of general principles in this regard, restrictions on the types of services costs will be paid for and maximum amounts. Similarly, under s 53, guidelines can be developed regarding inquiry costs. It would be hoped that the overall cost of such inquiries will not be allowed to spiral out of control. One of the major criticisms of the operation of the Tribunals of Inquiries over the past few years has been the excessive costs incurred by the state for inquiries that have seemingly resulted in little practical change.[185] It is perhaps as part of this that s 43 requires that a committee must prepare a report setting out an estimate of the costs and expenses following a decision to run an inquiry has been made under s 13.

At its conclusion, the committee shall, under s 95, resolve to publish the final report as soon as possible after the inquiry has finished. In addition it may choose to publish an interim report if it considers that the full report would have a negative impact on another inquiry. Also, if the committee thinks that a report would prejudice pending or in progress criminal proceedings it may, under s 95 apply to the High Court for directions concerning publication. This is important, as the Minister Howlin has noted "the criminal process is a separate and distinct accounting process which must follow its course without interference".[186] **[2–120]**

The operation of this legislation is already coming into sharp focus through the establishment of the banking inquiry. It is the stated intention of the Government that it will be completed before the end of the current Oireachtas, that will be at the latest 2016. Given both the size and controversial nature of the banking inquiry remit it is likely to be a challenging test. The preliminary stages of selecting members to the committee have already been fraught with political infighting. The Government's decision to impose extra members on the committee in order to ensure a Government majority has led, unsurprisingly to allegations of "gerrymandering" from opposition parties,[187] and the resignation of a key independent TD, Stephen Donnelly, because of concerns about the credibility of the inquiry: **[2–121]**

---

[185] See chapter 5: Public Inquiries and Administrative Justice.
[186] Houses of the Oireachtas (Inquiries, Privileges and Procedures) Act (Commencement) Order 2013: Statements, 24 September 2013.
[187] Minihan and O'Halloran above n 122.

"when the Taoiseach overrides the will of the Oireachtas and subverts the democratic process, and then explicitly states he is doing so in order to control the banking inquiry, my decision taken last Friday was to say 'no, I cannot be a part of this. I'm going to stand up and say I'm sorry, I don't believe this is how politics should be done.'"[188]

Conclusion

[2–122] This chapter has offered an overview of key Parliamentary systems of oversight. Although there are a variety of mechanisms, they are ultimately limited both in terms of the operational effectiveness and their impact on both central Government and the wider public administration.

[2–123] It is important to recall that the Oireachtas has the tools available to it to engage in oversight of central Government, particularly through the strengthened committee structures and newly developed inquiry system. Indeed, parliamentary questions and overall debate should also play a role in information gathering and strong debate and oversight. The operation of these mechanisms nevertheless regularly falls far short of what is needed: reinforcing fundamental distrust amongst the public in their politician's abilities to fairly and effectively operate as an accountability mechanism. Since the early 1990s there have been a series of revelations regarding political and administrative corruption and/or incompetency. However, as the Oireachtas struggles to meet these accountability needs we remain in a situation where there are few *effective* institutional safeguards against the misuse of public office at the Parliamentary level.

[2–124] A key impact of this has been a resultant loss of trust amongst the population in both Parliament and government.[189] The starkest example of which was the dramatic fall in confidence in 2010 following the bank bail out where trust in government fell to ten percent and trust in

---

[188] C D'Arcy, "Donnelly's decision to quit banking inquiry criticised" *Irish Times*, June 15 2014. Available online at http://www.irishtimes.com/news/politics/donnelly-s-decision-to-quit-banking-inquiry-criticised-1.1833092 (date accessed 26 August 2014).

[189] Although note that there are a variety of factors that contribute to this lack of trust. See for example, E O'Malley, I McMenamin, K Rafter, R Flynn, "Why are national parliaments so unpopular? Journalism, Information and Sentiment", Working Paper, (2014) available on *Social Science Research Network* http://papers.ssrn.com/sol3/papers.cfm?abstract_id=2437971 (date accessed 10 July 2014) who consider the role of critical media coverage.

Parliament was only marginally better at twelve percent.[190] While this chapter began by claiming that one of the few universally held truisms regarding the economic crash was the need to strengthen parliament, such reform has proved difficult to deliver. While the forthcoming banking inquiry will be an opportunity for the Oireachtas to start to rebuild its reputation, it may also be crowded out by party politics. A failure to discharge its constitutional mandate will also be viewed by the public as retrospectively justifying the decision to vote down the inquiries referendum in 2011. Historical experience underlines that while many governments feature the rhetoric of administrative justice reform, all have remained to content to maintain a weak legislature.

---

[190] R Boyle, *Public Sector Trends*, (2011) Institute of Public Administration Research Paper 6, p 47, available online at http://www.ipa.ie/pdf/Public_Sector_Trends_2011.pdf (date accessed 10 July 2014).

CHAPTER THREE

FREEDOM OF INFORMATION AND ITS ROLE AS AN ACCOUNTABILITY MECHANISM

Introduction

The issue of Freedom of Information ("FOI") is often overlooked in administrative law texts, being regarded as a specialised area inhabited by FOI experts. However, as we will show in this chapter, its position in administrative law, and in relation to a wider understanding of public administration, is critical. Historically Governments have not been forthcoming with information to the public, and secrecy has been the default setting regarding the States operations and decision-making. This default position has been replaced more recently with transparency being formulated as a key indicator of a healthy Government. However, in reality the extent of the impact of freedom of information on accountability is contested and in many States, including Ireland, its operation is often limited. [3–01]

Nonetheless, the development of an effective FOI system is generally regarded as being a critical component of the ability of citizens, the media and opposition parties, to hold Government to account: [3–02]

> "Freedom of information is the single thing that does the most to ensure governments are working efficiently for the majority of the people and not a privileged few. It is the friend of those politicians who work diligently for their constituents and with an eye for value for money, and the enemy of those who go into politics to accrue their own power, privilege and wealth."[1]

As we discuss more extensively in chapter 10 of this book, a failure to provide information about decisions and rules can result in people groping in the dark, unable to respond effectively to the decisions that affect their lives.[2] This "information inefficiency", whereby the citizen does not have all the information associated with their situation, effectively prevents them making good decisions in relation to their individual circumstances. [3–03]

In this chapter we will set out the key elements of FOI which complement the pursuit of judicial and non-judicial review and effectively promote [3–04]

---

[1] H Pidd, "Tony Blair memoirs: A journey sparks anger at 'self pity and mockery'", *The Guardian*, 1 September 2010, quoting Heather Brook, FOI Campaigner: available at http://www.guardian.co.uk/politics/2010/sep/01/tony-blair-memoirs-anger-unions (date accessed 12 June 2013).

[2] See discussion in chapter 10 of the right to reasons in Irish law, paras 10.27-10.49.

broader administrative justice. In particular we will focus on the role FOI can play in improving democracy and governance, strengthening public decision-making and instilling in the populace confidence and engagement in Government. In this context freedom of information can be regarded as having a central part in a democracy:

> "It is perhaps as an underpinning of democracy that freedom of information is most important. Information held by public authorities is not acquired for the benefit of officials or politicians but for the public as a whole. Unless there are good reasons for withholding such information, everyone should be able to access it. More importantly, freedom of information is a key component of transparent and accountable government. It plays a key role in enabling citizens to see what is going on within government, and in exposing corruption and mismanagement. Open government is also essential if voters are to be able to assess the performance of elected officials and if individuals are to exercise their democratic rights effectively, for example through timely protests against new policies."[3]

[3–05] These are not minor claims, and in reality FOI has been largely undervalued by both Government and the public in many jurisdictions, including Ireland. The exposure of political scandals can for a short while focus public attention on the fundamental need for transparency in public life. However, juxtaposed against this can be strong, if specious, counterarguments such as the costs and bureaucratic challenges created by FOI systems.

[3–06] As we will establish, freedom of information does make a difference in achieving effective accountability of Government, as part of wider integrity mechanisms. In addition, it also has a potential transformative effect on the culture of the public service and can ultimately be seen as a step along a road to a system of *open Government*. Although Ireland has been rather slow to move down this road, it is clear that citizens have significantly better access to information about themselves, excepting specific limitations on access such as security. In addition, general access to information has dramatically improved in recent years with a resulting change in attitudes towards the internal workings of the public sector.

---

[3] T Mendel, "Freedom of Information as an Internationally Protected Human Right" (2003) 1 *Comparative Media Law Journal* 1 at 1. Available at http://www.juridicas.unam.mx/publica/rev/comlawj/cont/1/cts/cts3.htm (date accessed 26 May 2014).

However, although FOI has become a widely accepted system both in [3–07] Ireland and globally, challenges remain to the extent of the claim to transparency and openness and its status as a putative right. In addition, there is little doubt that there remains a deeply rooted culture in many parts of Government and the public sector that access the information should be limited and at best FOI is tolerated rather than embraced.

Finally, a note of warning regarding terminology — freedom of information [3–08] is one part of a wider idea of transparency and/or openness, both of which are different:

> "Transparency ... is used primarily for the purposes of accountability whereas the purpose of openness is more than this. It is intended to provide the opportunity for individuals to participate in the policy process and to utilize information for that purpose."[4]

So the concept of open Government can include ideas of consultation but is often Government initiated and can therefore involve the publication and dissemination of information the public sector wishes to share with its citizens. The potential shortcoming of a Government driven concept of openness can be that it may be limited to information the State wishes to share because it thinks the public should know about or engage with it. This can of course be different from the information a citizen seeks through the FOI system. This is attributable to the fact open Government tends to focus on the public interest whereas FOI often involves the more private interests of the citizen. However, this should not detract from the capacity for open Government initiatives to have a significant effect on Government transparency, something which is currently gaining momentum at both local and international level.[5]

---

4 M Hunt & R Chapman, "Open Government and Freedom of Information", in M Hunt and R Chapman (eds.) *Open Government in a theoretical and practical context* (Ashgate Publishing, Aldershot, 2006), p 3.
5 R Hazell, "Commentary on Draft Freedom of Information Bill" (London, Constitution Unit, July 1999) at p 8 available at http://wwws-uat.ucl.ac.uk/spp/publications/unit-publications/48.pdf (date accessed 26 May 2014). At the international level the United Nations Public Administration Programme has developed Guidelines on Open Government Data for Citizen Engagement see http://www.unpan.org/DPADM/Themes/OpenGovernmentDataandServices/tabid/1536/language/en-US/Default.aspx (date accessed 13 October 2014). Also see the Open Government Partnership, an international organisation founded to promote transparency and openness in Government through multi-party cooperation, Ireland became a full member in 2014 – http://www.opengovpartnership.org/ (date accessed 13 October 2014).

Governance Justifications for FOI

[3–09] A primary foundation for freedom of information lies in the principle of good governance:

> "Transparency of public authorities is a key feature of good governance and an indicator of whether or not a society is genuinely democratic and pluralist, opposed to all forms of corruption, capable of criticising those who govern it, and open to enlightened participation of citizens in matters of public interest. The right of access to official documents is also essential to the self-development of people and to the exercise of fundamental human rights. It also strengthens public authorities' legitimacy in the eyes of the public, and its confidence in them."[6]

[3–10] There are, therefore, a number of distinct governance advantages to FOI. The openness that can follow allows for the exposure of corruption, mismanagement and the capture of Government by vested interests. In economic terms, it should assist in the early detection of inefficiency and corrupt practices leading in turn to a reduction in overspending and administrative waste. For example, FOI was central to the exposure of the FÁS expenses scandal by the *Sunday Independent*.[7] In turn, a more transparent system of Government, established as a result of a well-functioning FOI scheme, should reduce the need for more costly accountability mechanisms such as public inquiries and judicial review applications. As O'Connor notes:

> "The evidence ... suggests that the overall administrative costs of operating Ireland's FOI regime (estimated at c.€6.9 million in 2009) are far outweighed by the material benefits in terms of money saved.

---

[6] Council of Europe Convention on Access to Documents 2009 (Explanatory Report, II.1) available online at http://conventions.coe.int/Treaty/en/Treaties/Html/205.htm (date accessed 27 November 2013).

[7] The scandal, exposed in 2008, involved the misappropriation of funds by FÁS (Foras Áiseanna Saothair) Executives. Note that FÁS initially tried to charge €1200 for search and retrieval fees, though this was reduced to €400, see S Phelan, "Opinion: Cynical Move will only make scandals harder to uncover", *Irish Independent*, 13 November 2013. Available online at http://www.independent.ie/opinion/analysis/shane-phelan-cynical-move-will-only-make-scandals-harder-to-uncover-29749618.html (date accessed 26 November 2013). See "How freedom of information has become a farce" for original story in 2008 http://www.independent.ie/opinion/analysis/how-freedom-of-information-has-become-a-farce-26495878.html (date accessed 26 November 2013).

Preventing the need for a single tribunal of inquiry would save tens of millions of euro...."[8]

This is a particularly important point in austerity Ireland when the current financial difficulties faced by the public sector have produced the predictable claim that FOI is expensive. This is characterised in the public debate by the row over fees[9] but goes beyond that to the failure to support staff in FOI bodies in relation to their statutory duties under the legislation in our jurisdiction. However, any simplistic claims regarding costs are difficult to sustain — FOI is not a luxury, but rather an essential component of accountability systems in the modern administrative state. This extends to the positive cost benefits that FOI can produce but which are often not directly quantified by the State. However, in our own jurisdiction work carried out by journalist Ken Foxe has found evidence of a number of key savings which were brought about by FOI requests by the media.[10] These include a saving of €1.2 million per year following the closure of the FÁS science challenge programme[11] and the development of a new expenses system in the Oireachtas following the resignation of Ceann Comhairle John O'Donoghue TD.[12] As Séamus Dooley of the National Union of Journalists commented in relation to these findings:

[3–11]

"[a]ctual savings produced by the media industry through Freedom of Information are frequent but difficult to quantify. In most instances the

---

[8] N O'Connor, "An Economic Argument for Stronger Freedom of Information Laws in Ireland" (2012) TASC discussion paper at p 14, hereinafter O'Connor. Available at http://issuu.com/ tascpublications/docs/an_economic_argument (date accessed 2 July 2014).

[9] Discussed below at paras 3.108-3.115.

[10] National Union of Journalists, "Calls to block amendments as research highlights benefits of FOI in Ireland", 12 November 2013, http://www.nuj.org.uk/news/calls-to-block- amendments-foi-ireland/ (date accessed 16 December 2013), hereinafter "NUJ".

[11] This was following an exposé by the Sunday Independent based on documents requested under the FOI system. S Phelan, "€7.8m FAS programme 'a complete waste of space'", *Sunday Independent*, 11 February 2010. Available online at http://www.independent.ie/ irish-news/78m-fas-programme-a-complete-waste-of-space-26631347.html (date accessed 16 December 2013).

[12] The NUJ estimated that this has saved around €2 million annually. The exposé was produced largely by the *Sunday Tribune* but the story was also carried by many other newspapers. R Dwyer, "We have every right to be angry when politicians get golden parachutes", *Irish Independent*, 10 October 2009. Available online at http://www.irishexaminer.com/ viewpoints/columnists/ryle-dwyer/we-have-every-right-to-be-angry-when-politicians- get-golden-parachutes-102962.html (date accessed 16 December 2013).

expenditure exposed has already taken place but future savings occur because of the information revealed".[13]

The failure to quantify that benefit, or even engage with the idea of it at a governmental level reinforces the point that FOI appears not to be valued at that level, despite its positive impact.

[3–12]   Beyond the financial benefits, an effective FOI scheme should also increase public confidence in its Government, knowing that errors and problems are more likely to be both exposed and exposable. Similarly, citizens and civil society groups are given a tool by which they can exert information rights and gain access to information, whether directly related to them or of more general public interest. This is empowering to citizens and should, in principle, increase political participation. The availability of such processes should also result in an increase in effectiveness and operation of the public sector. Record keeping should become more systematic: the provision of reasons for decision more widespread; the exercise of discretion based on clearly stated and rational bases.[14]

[3–13]   The extent to which FOI delivers on these promises of improved accountability, transparency and citizen engagement is not easy to establish. Research undertaken by Hazell and Worthy in the UK regarding the impact of FOI on central Government offers some insight.[15] They found "little evidence that FOI improved Government decision-making", "little impact upon public understanding of Government decision-making" or evidence to support the argument that FOI had a positive impact on public participation or engagement in Government more generally.[16] Further they found that there had also been little impact on the public's trust in

---

[13] NUJ, above n 10. The reliance on this source supports our broader point regarding the failure to officially study the broader benefits of the system.

[14] These and other benefits were noted by Minister for State at Department of Finance, Martin Cullen TD at the commencement of the 1997 legislation: http://www.foi.gov.ie/speech-4 (date accessed 9 June 2014).

[15] R Hazell and B Worthy "The impact of Freedom of Information on central Government" (2009) End of award report to ESRC. Constitution Unit: UCL. RES 062 23 0164 available online at http://www.ucl.ac.uk/constitution-unit/research/foi/ESRC-end-of-award-report.pdf (date accessed 28 November 2013). Hereinafter "Hazell and Worthy". The research involved a variety of methods including interviews with central and local Government officials, MPs, peers and officials at Westminster as well as journalists, requesters and campaigners, an online survey of FOI requesters, analysis of press articles using FOI, analysis of relevant FOI case law and analysis of FOI disclosure logs.

[16] *ibid* at p 5.

Government as a result of FOI: they did note that this was likely because FOI generated stories generally highlighted negative and/or secretive behaviour of Government given that the "media report stories conform to poor expectations of politicians".[17]

In the Irish context McDonagh has also found that FOI has failed to produce **[3–14]** "direct engagement of citizens with the administration in regard to the securing of entitlements and benefits".[18] Her research on local government FOI decision makers revealed that although there had been some improvement on direct engagement between citizens and local government as a result of FOI, "patronage" has continued to be the primary method of interaction at the local government level.[19] We would content that it is likely that this clientelism has also persisted in relation to other public bodies.

Despite the well flagged benefits of FOI, it is also not without its **[3–15]** disadvantages and critics — whether that be its weaknesses or the inconveniences for public bodies operating under the system. There is a cost in having public sector workers commit time to processing FOI requests. In addition, it is generally believed, and there is some evidence to the effect, that FOI produces non-compliance and encourages a different type of secrecy.[20] In Ireland where the FOI legislation relates to written records[21] not the wider category of information, the effect is that verbal communications are not covered, falling as they do outside the definition of a record. It is difficult to establish the extent to which, as a result of this, communication in the public sector has moved to the medium of oral conversations, at least where the information is something the participants would not want to be "FOIable". However, there is plenty of anecdotal

---

[17] *ibid* at p 6.

[18] M McDonagh, "Access to local Government information in Ireland: attitudes of decision makers" (2010) 6(1) *Open Government: A Journal On Freedom of Information* 1 at p 14, hereinafter "McDonagh (2010)".

[19] *ibid.*

[20] C Hood, "Accountability and Transparency: Siamese Twins, Matching Parts, Awkward Couple?" (2007) 9(2) *Public Management Review* 191, at p 207; R Snell, "Administrative Compliance and Freedom of Information from three Jurisdictions: Australia, Canada and New Zealand", paper UCC conference, available online at http://www.ucc.ie/academic/law/foi/conference/snell99.html (date accessed 9 June 2014) in which Snell highlights destruction of documents, avoiding responding to FOI request and deletion of relevant information prior to disclosure.

[21] s 2(1) of the Freedom of Information Act 1997, hereinafter the "1997 Act". s 2(1) of the Freedom of Information Act 2014, hereinafter the "2014 Act".

evidence. Felle and Adshed recount testimony given to them by an Expert Focus Group to this effect "[a]n awful lot of what would otherwise have been committed to paper simply doesn't get committed to paper now any longer....".[22] McDonagh also found this to a limited extent at the local government level, at least in terms of some participants in her research expressing concern that "non-recording of information by officials" was taking place.[23]

[3–16]   There is also an oft raised concern that FOI prevents public sector workers from being forthright in their discussions and communications, particularly at central Government level, with the result that openness is stifled. This view is expressed by former UK Prime Minister Tony Blair:

> "Without the confidentiality, people are inhibited and the consideration of options is limited in a way that isn't conducive to good decision-making. In every system that goes down this path, what happens is that people watch what they put in writing and talk without committing to paper. It's a thoroughly bad way of analysing complex issues."[24]

[3–17]   This argument has historically been one of the main concerns voiced regarding the impact of FOI — the idea that firstly it will damage the work of Government by undermining the concept of collective cabinet responsibility and in turn, the ability of Parliament to hold ministers to account. The idea that discussions taking place at cabinet level might be exposed to public scrutiny clearly is in some tension with the idea that the cabinet should stand publicly unified on policy decisions while allowing internal debate to take place behind closed doors. In addition, the concern is also raised that civil servants will hold back on their advice to Ministers and/or that the neutrality of civil servants will be damaged.[25] Given these concerns it is interesting to refer again to the work carried out by Hazell

---

[22] T Felle and M Adshed "Democracy and the Right to Know – 10 Years of Freedom of Information in Ireland" (2009) No.4 Limerick Papers in Politics and Public Administration. Available at http://www.ul.ie/ppa/content/files/Felle_democracy.pdf (date accessed: 9 June 2014) quoting Brady at p 14, hereinafter "Felle and Adshed". The Expert Focus Group was made up of then Senator Dan Boyle, Joan Burton TD, Charlie Flanagan TD, Mark Hennessy of *The Irish Times* and Conor Keane formerly of *The Examiner*. Also present were the then Swedish Ambassador to Ireland His Excellency Claes Ljungdahl and former editor of *The Irish Times* Conor Brady.

[23] McDonagh (2010) above n 18 at p14.

[24] T Blair, *A Journey* (Arrow Books, London, 2011) at p 517, hereinafter "Blair".

[25] The significance of collective responsibility at Cabinet Government level is in fact recognised in the FOI legislation and is discussed in more detail below.

and Worthy on this point of the impact of FOI on central Government.[26] They found that there was no "'chilling effect' on frank advice and deliberation, or on the quality of Government records" as a result of FOI and they concluded that the "chilling effect" idea was a myth "albeit a pervasive one".[27]

At times, these concerns about the perceived, negative impact of FOI can result in outright hostility. The former UK Prime Minister Tony Blair embodies this position regarding FOI not as a force for good but instead operating, at least in practice, in an oppressive manner where it is utilised by opponents of the state to attack Government: [3–18]

> "Freedom of Information. Three harmless words. I look at those words
> as I write them, and feel like shaking my head till it drops off my
> shoulders. You idiot. You naive, foolish, irresponsible nincompoop.
> There is really no description of stupidity, no matter how vivid, that is
> adequate. I quake at the imbecility of it."[28]

Is there a Right to Freedom of Information?

Conceptualising FOI as a right may at first glance seem to be a matter of verbal semantics, but in doing so we are better able to transform transparency and access to information from something typically described as "being given" to citizens by the state into a positive right held by citizens. Thus, the development of a right of access to information would operate to counterbalance some of the historical orientation of administrative systems towards secrecy and opaque organisation. Indeed, the courts in Ireland have in recent times engaged directly with such concerns with the development of a right to reasons in part sustained by our FOI regime.[29]   [3–19]

Despite the fact that FOI can be understood to include a right to be informed of decisions and policy-making, and a right to participate,[30] it has not yet been fully developed as a core right at domestic, regional or international level, remaining largely a State response to the need for transparency. Indeed, information rights remain marginalised in that they are not   [3–20]

---

[26] Hazell and Worthy above at n 15.

[27] *ibid* at p 6.

[28] Tony Blair is on record as stating that his biggest regret as Prime Minister was the introduction of the Freedom of Information Act 2000, Blair, above n 24 at p 516-7.

[29] See discussion in chapter 10 at paras 10-27-10.48.

[30] A Roberts, "Structural pluralism and the right to information" (2001) 51 U. Toronto L.J. 262.

comprehended as "true rights". McDonagh highlights the fact that a right to information has been developed on an instrumentalist basis, operating "in the context of the realization of other rights".[31] However, as will be shown below, changes in attitudes can be identified in other jurisdictions and within regional level human rights systems.

[3–21] Information rights can be characterised as the part of the fourth wave of rights equivalent to civil, political and social rights.[32] In his discussion of information rights as they relate to citizenship, Bovens highlights that the understanding of freedom of information as a right means that it is something more than straightforward transparency:

> "The current rules on open government are for the most part mainly a question of *public hygiene*. Thus regulation is intended to increase the transparency of public administration, with a view to better democratic control and social accountability in government. By contrast, the information rights are most of all an element of *citizenship*. They concern first and foremost the social functioning of citizens, not only in relation to the public authorities, but also in their mutual relations and their relations with private legal entities. Information rights should be part of the civil rights chapter of constitutions, together with other individual rights."[33]

[3–22] Conceptually, information rights capture the idea of an active citizen, participating and engaging with Government decision and policy-making. To effectively engage with the State access to decision-making, improved accountability, and more transparent policy-making processes, are seen as essential. These are in principle easier to facilitate in an age of digital communications.[34]

[3–23] In practice, the idea of information sharing is difficult to establish given the long recognised competing rights of privacy, confidentiality and the public interest in matters such as security. As a result most freedom of information mechanisms tend to fall below the ideal. In addition, open Government and FOI alone are not capable of creating an informed citizenry without additional effective avenues and methods of facilitating public participation.

---

[31] M McDonagh, "The Right to Information in International Human Rights Law" (2013) 13(1) *Human Rights Law Review* 25 at p 26, hereinafter "McDonagh (2013)".

[32] M Bovens, "Information Rights: Citizenship in the Information Society" (2002) 10 J. Pol. Phil. 317.

[33] *ibid* at p 327.

[34] *ibid.* Bovens' article is centred on the idea of the *information society* and the impact this has on a changing conception of citizenship rights.

Thus, Hazell and Worthy found "little evidence" that FOI increased public participation or public "engagement" with Government in the UK. In fact they determined that most people making FOI requests were already politically active (campaigners) or professionally interested (journalists).[35] It is likely that a similar situation operates in Ireland.

We should also be caution about claims that open Government creates an [3–24] informed citizenship. There is a danger that, without clear systems to encourage and facilitate participation, it will ultimately be of limited value, simply providing a veneer of transparency. As we highlighted earlier, open Government ensures that citizens understand how decisions are made, have access to information about them and the wider public interest, and the State is held to account for its actions. An image of transparency merely lulls the public into the security of believing that if they need to know they can, but do not delve more deeply into the substance of State activities. In this context it is important to stress that FOI should be understood as one important component of a wider development regarding citizen engagement with the State and its related rights.

International and Regional Freedom of Information Standards

At the level of international law, the UN General Assembly first recognised [3–25] FOI as a fundamental right in 1946 at its first session. Adopting Resolution 59(I) it stated that:

> "Freedom of information is a fundamental human right and ... the touchstone of all the freedoms to which the United Nations is consecrated."[36]

Since then, the UN Special Rapporteur on Freedom of Opinion and Expression has taken an expansive view of FOI protection and has regularly stated in annual reports that the right to access to information held by

---

[35] Hazell and Worthy, *above* at n 15 at para 4.1.2.
[36] UN General Assembly, *Calling of an International Conference on Freedom of Information*, 14 December 1946, A/RES/59, available at: http://www.refworld.org/docid/3b00f0975f. html (date accessed 10 June 2013).

public bodies is safeguarded by Article 19[37] of the International Covenant on Civil and Political Rights.[38]

[3–26]　At a regional level, rights systems have regarded FOI as falling within the traditional freedom of expression framework.[39] Thus, the European Convention on Human Rights Article 10 includes the right to seek and receive information, the right to inform, and the right to be informed.[40] The Convention does not make direct reference to FOI and the ECtHR did not historically regard Article 10 as providing a general right of access to administrative information. Indeed, cases involving a denial of access to information have generally been dealt with under Article 8 right to private and family life.[41] There has, however, been a slow shift by the Court to

---

[37] Art 19 ICCPR states:

　　"Everyone has the right to freedom of opinion and expression; this right includes freedom to hold opinions without interference and to seek, receive and impart information and ideas through any media and regardless of frontiers."

　　In 2011 the UC Human Rights Committee published a new General Comment on this article which adopted a general right of access to information held by public bodies. For more discussion see McDonagh (2013) above n 31 at p 30-33.

[38] The UN Commission on Human Rights established the office of the Special Rapporteur in 1993. The office's mandate includes responsibility for clarifying the content of the right to freedom of opinion and expression: FOI being part of this.

[39] For example, the African Charter on Human and Peoples' Rights (Art 9) http://www.achpr.org/instruments/achpr/#a9 (date accessed 10 June 2014) and the American Convention on Human Rights (Art 13) http://www.oas.org/en/iachr/expression/showarticle.asp?artID=25& (date accessed 10 June 2014). The Inter-American Court of Human Rights has also made what can be described as a seminal decision in *Claude Reyes v Chile*, Order (IACtHR, 19 Sep 2006) establishing that traditional rights protections on free expression which include the right to "seek" and "receive" state information should be interpreted to mean that the public have a right of access to such information, and the State is under a duty to provide it. http://www.corteidh.or.cr/docs/casos/articulos/seriec_151_ing.pdf (date accessed 10 June 2014).

[40] Art 10 states:

　　1. "Everyone has the right to freedom of expression. This right shall include freedom to hold opinions and to receive and impart information and ideas without interference by public authority and regardless of frontiers....

　　2. The exercise of these freedoms, since it carries with it duties and responsibilities, may be subject to such formalities, conditions, restrictions or penalties as are prescribed by law and are necessary in a democratic society, in the interests of national security, territorial integrity or public safety, for the prevention of disorder or crime, for the protection of health or morals, for the protection of the reputation or rights of others, for preventing the disclosure of information received in confidence, or for maintaining the authority and impartiality of the judiciary."

[41] *Gaskin v UK* [1989] 12 EHRR PC concerning the refusal to grant the applicant access to his child-care records.

develop a limited recognition of FOI as a clearer component of Article 10[42] a journey McDonagh has described as "long and tortuous".[43]

In *Guerra v Italy*, despite a decision by the Commission endorsing a right of access to information, the Court restricted the idea under Article 10(2) to the concept of a negative duty placed on Government which "prohibits a Government from restricting a person from receiving information that others wish or may be willing to impart to him".[44] The Court went on to note that the right did not impose positive obligations on States to collect and disseminate information.[45]

[3–27]

However, more recent case law from the Court has indicated that Article 10 might include a right of access to documents held by public bodies. In *Sdruzeni Jiboceske v Czech Republic*[46] the Court recognised the refusal of a State to provide access to public information was an interference with Article 10 rights. This was further developed in *Társaság a Szabadságjogokért v Hungary*[47] when the Court took a broader interpretation of Article 10 and clearly recognized the right of access to official documents. In that case the court found that the refusal to provide information to the Hungarian Civil Liberties Union by Hungary's Constitutional Court was a "monopoly of information [that] thus amounted to a form of censorship".[48]

[3–28]

---

[42] Art 10:

    1. Everyone has the right to freedom of expression. This right shall include freedom to hold opinions and to receive and impart information and ideas without interference by public authority and regardless of frontiers. This article shall not prevent States from requiring the licensing of broadcasting, television or cinema enterprises.

    2. The exercise of these freedoms, since it carries with it duties and responsibilities, may be subject to such formalities, conditions, restrictions or penalties as are prescribed by law and are necessary in a democratic society, in the interests of national security, territorial integrity or public safety, for the prevention of disorder or crime, for the protection of health or morals, for the protection of the reputation or the rights of others, for preventing the disclosure of information received in confidence, or for maintaining the authority and impartiality of the judiciary.

    CJS knight, "Article 10 and a right of access to information" (2013) Public Law 468 and A O'Neill, "Freedom of Information as a Fundamental Right" available online at http://freedominfo.org/2014/10/test-test-be (date accessed 13 November 2014).

[43] McDonagh (2013) above n 31 at p 34.

[44] (1988) 26 EHRR 357 at para 53, quoting the judgment in *Leander v Sweden* [1987] 9 EHRR 433 at para 83.

[45] *ibid*.

[46] App No 19101/03, Eur CtHR (2006).

[47] [2009] ECHR 37374/05.

[48] *ibid* at para 28.

[3–29] Reverting to Article 8, the ECtHR has noted the significance of information in personal files held by public authorities and the need for people to have effective access to that information in *Haralambie v Romania*.[49] In that case the applicant had faced a series of obstacles that prevented effective access to a file on him drawn up by the former Communist Government's secret service.

[3–30] At the EU level there have also been developments regarding FOI: in particular as it has developed into a common area of "freedom, security and justice" as set out under the Treaty of the European Union.[50] The requirements of common policies in the policing, immigration and financial regulation arenas, amongst others, have necessitated the sharing of information between Member States.[51] This, in turn, has required a growth in the regulation of information sharing, including freedom of information and data protection regulations.

[3–31] Transparency of decision-making has also become more significant for the EU as its growth resulted in a perception of a disconnection between citizens of Europe and the EU's institutions. Access to information has therefore been considered as a key component of the move to strengthen "the democratic nature of the institutions and the public's confidence in the administration."[52] Thus the 1993 Code of Conduct on Access to Documents[53] had as a core principle the idea that the public would "have the widest possible access to documents held by the Commission and the Council". Although one must note that this is access to *documents* and not the wider concept of *information*.

[3–32] At the treaty level, Article 15(1) of the Treaty on the Functioning of the EU[54] established the principle that EU institutions "shall conduct their work as openly as possible" in order to promote good governance and participation.

---

[49] [2009] ECHR 21737/03.

[50] Art 3(2).

[51] For example the establishment of the border-free Schengen Area required the establishment of the Schengen Information System (II) and the Visa Information System to facilitate information sharing between member states, this latter system is, for example, monitored by the European Data Protection Supervisor.

[52] Code of Conduct Concerning Public Access to Council and Commission Documents, 1993 OJ L 340, 31.12.1993 (93/730/EC) Available online at http://eur-lex.europa.eu/LexUriServ/LexUriServ.do?uri=CELEX:31993X0730:en:HTML (date accessed 2 July 2014).

[53] *ibid.*

[54] 2008 OJ C 115/47, hereinafter "TFEU".

Article 16(1) also established that "everyone has the right to the protection of personal data concerning them".[55] Beyond these general requirements, there has been a specific move towards the creation of administrative rights under the European system including a right to FOI, within limits.[56] The Commission regarded this development as a necessary step, moving already existing protections into the category of "new rights". Thus the EU Charter of Fundamental Rights[57] (CFR) starts with a traditional approach to information in Article 11, combining the right to Freedom of Expression and Information:

> "Everyone has the right to freedom of expression. This right shall include freedom to hold opinions and to receive and impart information and ideas without interference by public authority and regardless of frontiers."

Article 41 of the CFR establishes a right to "good administration" based on the concept that in Article 41(1) "every person has the right to have his or her affairs handled impartially, fairly and within a reasonable time by the institutions and bodies of the Union."[58] While in addition Article 42 provides for a right of access to documents:

[3–33]

> "Any citizen of the Union, and any natural or legal person residing or having its registered office in a Member State, has a right of access to documents of the institutions, bodies, offices and agencies of the Union, whatever their medium."

However, once again, the right is confined to documents and not the broader concept of information.

Translating this general right into secondary legislation provides a more concrete framework for operation of the system. Thus Regulation 1049/2001 grants a right of access to documents held by the European Parliament, Council and Commission. This right is given to any citizen of the EU and all natural/legal persons residing or having a registered office in a Member State of the EU. The fact that the system is not in effect a freedom of

[3–34]

---

[55] Art 16(2) sets out that the need for data processing legislation at both the EU and Member State level.

[56] Other rights include access to justice, the right to good administration, the right to complain to the Ombudsman, and to complain to the Committee of Petitions.

[57] 2010 OJ C 83/02, hereinafter "CFR".

[58] *ibid* at Art 41(1).

information system has been reinforced by a decision by the Court of First Instance in *WWF European Policy Programme v Council:*

> "[T]he concept of a document must be distinguished from that of information. The public's right of access to the documents of the institutions covers only documents and not information in the wider meaning of the word and does not imply a duty on the part of the institutions to reply to any request for information from an individual."[59]

[3–35] It should also be noted, that even within this relatively narrow confines, Article 4 of the EU Regulation 1049 provides, as with most such systems, for limitations upon which a refusal to provide access can be established. These include security, defence, international relations and financial policy under Article 4(1)(a), privacy under Article 4(1)(b), and, subject to the public interest in disclosure, commercial interests, court proceedings and investigations under Article 4(2). In addition, the system allows for refusals where disclosure would "seriously undermine the institution's decision-making process".[60] The Regulations require that such exceptions are interpreted narrowly.[61]

[3–36] The 2001 Regulation, generally known as the Transparency Regulation, is now 12 years old and in recent years there have been attempts to reform it. In May 2013, the outgoing EU Ombudsman, Nikiforos Diamandouros, highlighted his view that there had been an erosion of a culture of secrecy amongst EU civil servants, but that the progress was ultimately too slow. Discussions to expand the regulation have made little progress in recent times and he noted that "the political climate at this point in the European Union is not favourable to in fact moving [the] frontiers [of openness] forward".[62]

[3–37] Finally, the Council of Europe Convention on Access to Official Documents 2008, is the first binding international legal instrument recognising a general right of access to official documents held by public bodies.[63]

---

[59] [2007] ECR II-911, at para 76.
[60] Art 4(3) Reg 1049/2001, subject to the overriding public interest in disclosure.
[61] Case C-506/08 P *Sweden v Commission* 21 July [2011] ECR I-nyr at para.75.
[62] http://euobserver.com/institutional/120261 (date accessed 13 November 2014).
[63] http://conventions.coe.int/Treaty/EN/Reports/Html/205.htm. Status as of July 2014 was that six stated had ratified the treaty and a further eight countries had signed it. It will only come into force after 10 states have ratified the convention: http://conventions.coe.int/

However, the Convention has been criticised for promoting limited standards of openness.[64] Ireland has not signed this Convention to date. While Transparency International has noted that the Department of Public Expenditure and Reform stated aim is to ratify the Convention "as soon as possible", the continued FOI fee system could be problematic in this regard.[65]

A Brief History of Freedom of Information

Although FOI as a fundamental right has taken some time to gain a toehold in courts, there has been a significant national legislative, and in some cases constitutional, recognition of its importance. FOI first emerged in Sweden in 1766 when it enacted its *Freedom of the Press and Right of Access to Public Records Act*.[66] In fact Sweden has "maintained a long and unbroken tradition of transparency"[67] with the current version of that law now one of four fundamental pieces of legislation that form part of its Constitution.[68] The idea of Freedom of Information took a while to take hold outside of Sweden however, but by the end of the twentieth century, it had been widely adopted in a range of legal and political systems.[69] At the time of writing,

[3–38]

Treaty/Commun/ChercheSig.asp?NT=205&CM=1&DF=&CL=ENG (date accessed 2 July 2014).

[64] A coalition of over 250 NGOs, information commissioners and some Governments published a response to the convention in 2008 expressing disappointment and noting in particular that "the treaty applies only to a narrow range of public bodies, does not impose maximum time-limits for responding to requests, and fails to establish that those requesting information have a right to appeal to an independent body or court." http://www.article19.org/data/files/pdfs/press/council-of-europe-adopts-second-rate-treaty-on-access-to-information.pdf (date accessed 27 November 2013).

[65] National Integrity systems, Country Study Addendum 2012, Transparency International, (2012) p.32, available online at http://transparency.ie/sites/default/files/TI%20Country%20Study%20Addendum2012.pdf (date accessed 25 November 2013).

[66] Tryckfrihetsförordningen, TF. Available online at http://www.riksdagen.se/en/Documents-and-laws/Laws/The-Constitution/ (date accessed 1 May 2013).

[67] McDonagh, *Freedom of Information Law*, (2nd ed) (Thomson Round Hall, Dublin, 2006) at p 4, hereinafter "McDonagh (2006)".

[68] The other key pieces of legislation are the Instrument of Government, the Act of Succession and the Fundamental Law on Freedom of Expression. For more information see http://www.government.se/sb/d/2853/a/16199 (date accessed 2 July 2014).

[69] There are a variety of organisations working on access to information that maintain data regarding the extent of FOI adoption. For example *Right2Info:* http://www.right2info.org/ and *Freedominfo.org* http://www.freedominfo.org/about-us/ — both have up to date information on their websites regarding developments in this area.

99 countries had legislation relating to FOI in place and over 50 protect it in their constitution.[70]

Ireland is, in many ways, typical in moving from a default position of secrecy regarding access to information. As secrecy in relation to official information was a key characteristic of the Westminster style Government it is not surprising that Ireland's position was in a large part sustained in legal form by official secrets legislation inherited from the British system, but cultivated by the Irish State. Irish legislation is modelled on the inherited British Official Secrets Act passed in 1911. Of particular note is s 2, which imposed an extensive prohibition on the dissemination of any information without prior authorisation. This ban was reinforced by the threat of prosecution.[71]

[3–39]   An opportunity to liberalise the system arose in 1963 when the legislation was reviewed by the then Justice Minister Charles Haughey TD; however it was not taken. Instead, the new Act prevented official documents being released without the express permission of the responsible Minister. Public officials could be prosecuted for the unauthorised sharing of information as per s 4.[72] The Act also made it an offence to receive information. Section 13 provided that it was an offence to "contravene" or "attempt to contravene" the Act, punishable on conviction by a fine and by a maximum of seven years imprisonment. This reinforced the policy of secrecy by not merely discouraging transparency, but criminalising it. The prevailing

---

[70] For information on this see http://home.broadpark.no/~wkeim/foi-list.htm (date accessed 2 July 2014).

[71] Birkinshaw highlights that this legislation was passed with virtually no debate in the UK Parliament, with the legislation being passed against a background of crisis when Germany sent a gunboat to Agadir in Morocco on the pretext of protecting a German Colony, this provoked a security scare and led politicians to believe war was imminent. P Birkinshaw, *Freedom of Information: The Law, the Practice and the Ideal*, (4th ed.) (Cambridge University Press, Cambridge, 2010) at p 83.

[72] Official Secrets Act 1963, hereinafter "OSA", s 4:

"A person shall not communicate any official information to any other person unless he is duly authorised to do so or does so in the course of and in accordance with his duties as the holder of a public office or when it is his duty in the interest of the State to communicate it."

Note that the FOI legislation softened this position with the inclusion of an amendment to OSA s 48 (1):

"A person who is, or reasonably believes that he or she is, authorised by this Act to communicate official information to another person shall be deemed for the purposes of s 4 of the Official Secrets Act, 1963, to be duly authorised to communicate that information."

attitude was expressed by the Minister as he introduced the legislation in the Dáil — "surely a minister or Government is entitled to decide whether a thing is secret or confidential and mark it as such".[73] The difficulty with the official secrets approach was, however, its potential for being abused. The 1963 Act allowed a Minister to designate any information as "secret", thus allowing information regarded as embarrassing to the Government to be deemed undisclosable.[74] However, although the legislation was extremely broad in scope, it was rarely used in practice. This was in part attributable to the manner in which an overall culture of secrecy had been successfully entrenched in the culture of public bodies.

The Development of Freedom of Information Legislation in Ireland

In the long run widespread secrecy could not be sustained and the secretive [3–40] nature of Government and the damage associated with it began to be exposed by the political scandals which emerged in the 1980s. At the same time, pressure for change emerged from Ireland's membership of the European Union. This required a decentralised decision-making system and operated rules of accountability in relation to regional funding and structural funds and later, access to environmental information.[75] The result was a slow change in culture from both external and internal forces which meant that adoption of FOI legislation was inevitable.

The first decisive step was in fact the establishment of the Office of the [3–41] Ombudsman in the early 1980s.[76] The setting up of a public complaint mechanism was the beginning of a significant change of culture that acknowledged, albeit reluctantly, the need for oversight. In addition, this general movement towards improved accountability was reflected in several public sector reforms during the 1990s.[77]

---

[73] 194 *Dáil Debates Col* 1493 (5 April 1962).

[74] J Doyle, "Freedom of Information: Lessons from the international experience" (1997) 44(4) *Administration* 64.

[75] Felle and Adshed, above at n 22. See McDonagh (2006) above n 67 generally for background information on access to documents of EU institutions at pp 19-37.

[76] Discussed in detail in chapter 4: The Ombudsman and Administrative Justice.

[77] The Comptroller and Auditor General (Amendment) Act 1993, the Ethics in Public Office Act 1995, and in 1997 the Electoral Reform Act, the Public Service Management Act and the Committees of the Houses of the Oireachtas (Compellability, Privileges and Immunities of Witnesses) Act 1997.

[3–42]   As we discuss in chapter 4, despite a slowly changing culture, the move to more open and accountable Government did not come easily. In the early days of the Ombudsman, civil servants displayed an unwillingness to accept the Ombudsman's jurisdiction to question their decisions. The first Ombudsman Report to the Oireachtas noted "some continuing tensions" with various Government departments[78]: those tensions have not completely disappeared. In the context of access to information, particular strains were evident when Ministerial and civil servant concerns regarding cabinet confidentiality were tested. It was this faultline which was to become an important trigger in the move to adopting a FOI system.

[3–43]   The specific issue arose out of the Beef Tribunal,[79] the first tribunal of inquiry to expose inappropriate relationships between business and politics in Ireland. The Tribunal was set up to investigate alleged wrongdoing in relation to beef exports including tax evasion, malpractice and regulatory weaknesses. The inquiry shone a light on the integrity of Government.[80] Ultimately, the report published by the Beef Tribunal found that there was a lack of documentation for decisions regarding the granting of export credits supporting the beef industry.

[3–44]   One specific incident within the investigation is often quoted as significantly adding to the pressure for FOI.[81] The tribunal had been presented with conflicting evidence as to whether a cabinet meeting had decided to limit the distribution of contracts regarding particular export licences to two named companies. The Attorney General objected to certain questions being put to the former Minister for Industry and Commerce Ray Burke TD on the grounds of cabinet confidentiality. A judicial review of a decision by the Tribunal to proceed with the questioning resulted. A majority of the Supreme Court in *Attorney General v Hamilton (No.1)*[82] held that cabinet

---

[78] Quoted in 109 *Dáil Debates Col* 481 (17 October 1985).
[79] The Beef Tribunal is discussed in more detail in the chapter 5: Public Inquiries and Administrative Justice.
[80] 445 *Dáil Debates Col* 190 (1 September 1994).
[81] References to this can be found in http://www.hiqa.ie/system/files/FOI_first_10_yearsen. pdf (date accessed 29 November 2013) and http://www.theirishstory.com/2010/07/25/ a-short-history-of-freedom-of-information-in-independent-ireland/ (date accessed 29 November 2013).
[82] [1993] 2 IR 250.

confidentiality was a necessary corollary to the principle of collective responsibility of Government laid down in Article 28.4.[83]

The result of this flashpoint, was a shift in public opinion, with a new public appetite for transparency emerging. By the November 1992 election freedom of information was part of the political agenda of some parties, although it was not until 1994 that a formal commitment was made by the Fine Gael/Labour Party/Democratic Left Programme for Government which stated that it would "reform ... institutions at a national and local level to provide service, accountability, transparency and freedom of information".[84] Responsibility for developing the necessary FOI legislation was given to Minister of State at the Department of the Tánaiste, Eithne Fitzgerald TD. It took two years to publish the Bill, which McDonagh notes was attributable to the "complexity of the legislation" and the need to engage in wide-ranging consultations with Government departments "not all of whom appear to have been wholehearted in their support of the proposals".[85] Minister Fitzgerald described the intended effect of the legislation as being to "turn the culture of Official Secrets Act on its head. It will replace the presumption of secrecy with a presumption of openness".[86] Although that shift amounted to a fundamental challenge to the existing workings of the civil service and Government, the Bill was ultimately largely uncontroversial in debate[87] and became law on 21 April 1997, coming into force 21 April 1998.

[3–45]

---

[83] The impact of this regarding public inquiries and the seventeenth amendment to the Constitution which provided that confidentiality could be limited in the public interest in relation to the administration of justice and public inquiries will be discussed in chapter 5: Public Inquiries and Administrative Justice.

[84] *A Government of Renewal: A Policy Agreement between Fine Gael, the Labour Party and Democratic Left* (December 1994). Available online at http://michaelpidgeon.com/manifestos/docs/pfgs/PfG%201994%20-%201997%20-%20FG-Lab-DL.pdf (date accessed 2 July 2014). The Government also committed itself to reviewing the 1963 Official Secrets Act. This was carried out by the Dáil Committee on Legislation and Security which published its report calling for repeal of the 1963 Act in February 1997, Select Committee on Legislation and Security, *Report on Review of the Official Secrets Act, 1963* (Irish Stationary Office, Dublin, 1997).

[85] McDonagh (2006) above n 67 at p 39.

[86] E Fitzgerald, "Freedom of Information: Building a New Culture of Openness", in R Lohan *et al* (eds) *For the Record: Data Archives, Electronic Records, Access to Information and the Needs of the Research Community* (Institute of Public Administration, Dublin, 1996) at p 8.

[87] McDonagh notes that most of the criticism related to the problem of the Bill not going far enough, McDonagh (2006) above n 67 at p 40.

[3–46]   The 1997 Act was ground breaking in changing the operation of Irish Government and providing citizens with a statutorily protected right of access to information for the first time, yet it was not a comparatively radical instance of FOI legislation. It was shaped by pre-existing legislation in other jurisdictions and the experience of implementing access to environmental information under the EU regulations.[88]

[3–47]   At the heart of the legislation are four fundamental features which provide for:

    i.   a right of access to particular Government records where a request for access is made;
    ii.   a requirement that information concerning the operation of Government departments and public bodies is published;
    iii. a right for citizens to request amendments to personal information held on them; and
    iv.   a statutory right to be given reasons for an administrative decision.

It is worth stressing that these include both the requirement of public bodies to respond to requests for information and include the imposition of positive obligations on public bodies to be more transparent. We will consider the first three of these components in this chapter. The right to reasons will be considered as part of the wider right to reasons in administrative law in chapter 10.

A Rights of Access to Records

Access to Records

[3–48]   Section 11 of the Freedom of Information Act 2014 provides for the right of access for citizens to records either held by or under the control of a public body. This is a broad right as the requesting person does not need to show an interest in the record. However, as the long title of the legislation makes clear, the right of access to information is not absolute and must be balanced against competing interests, those being "the public interest and the right

---

[88] See S Bugdahn, "Does the EU Stifle Voluntary Policy Transfer? A Study of the Introduction of Freedom of Information in Portugal and Ireland", (2007) 85 (1) *Public Administration* 123 for an analysis of the implementation of the Access to Environmental Information Directive 1990 in Ireland and Portugal.

to privacy".[89] We will consider how these competing interests operate as limitations on the right later in this chapter; firstly, we must examine limits as to the scope of the right of access. Before we do so, however, the reader should note that the title of the 2014 Act reflects the fact that it is not amending legislation but in fact imposes a new FOI regime replacing that first established in 1998.

At a fundamental level, access to information is limited by the fact that the legislation relates to "records" rather than to a wider idea of "information". Section 2 of the 1997 Act had provided a wide definition of a record: **[3–49]**

> "[A]ny memorandum, book, plan, map, drawing, diagram, pictorial or graphic work or other document, any photograph, film or recording (whether of sound or images or both), any form in which data (within the meaning of the Data Protection Act, 1988) are held, any other form (including machine-readable form) or thing in which information is held or stored manually, mechanically or electronically and anything that is a part or a copy, in any form, of any of the foregoing or is a combination of two or more of the foregoing."

This definition included emails, references, notes and decisions. It did not include unrecorded, verbal information or information which someone has knowledge of. The 2014 Act has updated this definition to include material in any electronic device or machine readable form. However, it is unclear whether it was really necessary to provide a more detailed definition given the breadth of the 1997 definition.[90] **[3–50]**

---

[89] The long title of the 2014 Act opens with the statement:
"An Act to enable members of the public to obtain access, to the greatest extent possible consistent with the public interest and the right to privacy, to information in the possession of public bodies, other bodies in receipt of funding from the State and certain other bodies ...."

[90] s 2(1) of the 2014 Act:
"record" includes—
(a) a book or other written or printed material in any form (including in any electronic device or in machine readable form),
(b) a map, plan or drawing,
(c) a disc, tape or other mechanical or electronic device in which data other than visual images are embodied so as to be capable, with or without the aid of some other mechanical or electronic equipment, of being reproduced from the disc, tape or other device,
(d) a film, disc, tape or other mechanical or electronic device in which visual images are embodied so as to be capable, with or without the aid of some other mechanical or electronic equipment, of being reproduced from the film, disc, tape or other device, and

Bodies Subject to Freedom of Information Requirements

[3–51]   A further limitation in the legislation relates to the types of bodies, specifically "public bodies" falling under the remit of the Act,[91] which includes all central Government departments, local authorities, the HSE, and a diverse range of public bodies. Since the 1997 Act, the Minister for Finance has also exercised the power to extend the remit of FOI to include Universities[92] and voluntary organisations in the health sector[93] amongst many others.

[3–52]   The 2014 reforms make a significant change to the operation of the system, adopting a starting position whereby all public bodies will be subject to FOI unless specifically exempted.[94] This partially answers concerns about bodies which had been exempt from the FOI regime, particularly An Garda Síochána[95] and financial institutions such as the National Assets Management Agency (NAMA)[96] and the National Treasury Management Agency (NTMA). An Garda Síochána's full exclusion from the FOI regime

---

(e) a copy or part of any thing which falls within *paragraph (a), (b), (c)* or *(d)*, and a copy, in any form, of a record shall be deemed, for the purposes of this Act, to have been created at the same time as the record;

[91] Part 2 of the 2014 Act provides for s 6 public bodies and s 7 prescribed bodies. In addition, Schedule 1 sets out "Partially Included Agencies" in Part 1 and "Exempt Agencies" in Part 2.

[92] SI No 475 of 2001: Freedom of Information Act, 1997 (Prescribed Bodies) (No. 4) Regulations, 2001.

[93] SI No 329 of 1999: Freedom of Information Act, 1997 (Prescribed Bodies) Regulations, 1999. As will be seen in the paragraph below this power is now unnecessary as there is a presumption that FOI is extended to all new public bodies. However, the reader should also note that the Minister with primary responsibility for FOI has changed under the 2014 Act and is now the Minister for Public Expenditure and Reform.

[94] However, the Minister for Public Expenditure and Reform has the power to make an Order to specifically exclude them in whole or in part if required, s 6(3). As noted in n 91 above Schedule 1 part 2 provides a list of these.

[95] The inclusion of An Garda Síochána would be subject to exemptions related to criminal investigations and security, and would primarily apply to the administrative arm of the organisation.

[96] NAMAs original exclusion from the FOI provisions was justified on the basis of "commercial sensitivity". Its resistance to FOI once established was illustrated by a challenge to a decision of the Information Commissioner that it was a public body and therefore subject to requests for access to environmental information under the EC (Access to Information on the Environment) Regulations 2007 (SI No 133 of 2007). The High Court in *NAMA v Commissioner for Environmental Information* [2013] IEHC 86 found that it was a public body and therefore subject to the Regulations, at the time of writing a Supreme Court decision is pending following an appeal by NAMA. The AIE regulations are a parallel system to Freedom of Information but cover a wider range of public bodies and operate solely in relation to environmental information.

has been out of step with most other jurisdictions.[97] The amending legislation extends FOI to the Gardaí for the first time, but this extension is extremely limited; including only administrative records relating to human resources, finance or procurement matters. This continues to be out of step with the rest of Europe.

Similarly, financial bodies are to be "partially covered" by the 2014 Act[98] with the result that operating activities of such organisations are generally not included in order to allow them space to deal with sensitive commercial issues. However, concerns have been raised that these protections are in reality too broad particularly in relation to the NTMA, with the result that the terms and conditions of staff employment are excluded from the FOI regime.[99]

[3–53]

Finally, some bodies continue to be excluded from the FOI regime even after the 2014 Act. Schedule 1 part 2 lists "exempt agencies" which includes most State-sponsored bodies such as ESB and Bord Gáis.[100] The primary justification for their exclusion is the

[3–54]

> "potential for negative commercial effects that could impact adversely on their competitive standing and commercial performance and to safeguard the State's economic and financial interests".[101]

Particular controversy has arisen in this area in relation to whether Irish Water should be subject to FOI. The draft legislation included Irish Water

---

[97] Research carried in 2009 on the right to know and policing in Europe found that only Ireland adopted a position of fully exempting the police from its FOI regime: Access Info Europe, *The Right to Know: Europe and the Police* (2009) available online at http://www. access-info.org/documents/Access_Docs/Using/Civil_Liberties/Europe_and_the_Police. pdf (date accessed 3 December 2013).

[98] 2014 Act, Schedule 1 lists a number of bodies which are to be "partially included". Other bodies include the Adoption Authority, Labour Relations Commission and the various Ombudsmen.

[99] As McDonagh points out this could "remove from the scope of FOI information relating to remuneration paid to staff members of the NTMA" which had previously been released following a decision of the Information Commissioner in 2010 that information on the salary of the former CEO of NTMA should be released in the public interest (http://www. oic.gov.ie/en/publications/annual-reports/2010-annual-report/online/chapter3.html#s5 (date accessed 12 December 2013), M.McDonagh "FOI bill concerns must be tackled" *Irish Examiner* 25 November 2013, available online at http://www.irishexaminer.com/analysis/ foi-bill-concerns-must-be-tackled-250591.html (date accessed 2 July 2014).

[100] Irish Rail is included, as it is the only rail provided in the state and there is therefore no issue of competition to consider regarding sensitive commercial material.

[101] Minister Brendan Howlin TD, *Dáil Debates* 2 October 2013 Freedom of Information Bill 2013: Second Stage.

as an exempt body despite it also operating as a monopoly provider and having previously been subject to FOI under local authority control. However, following pressure Irish Water was brought within the FOI regime as of 13 March 2014.[102]

[3–55]   In contrast, s 7 of the 2014 Act provides the Minister with a power to extend FOI to private bodies "significantly funded by the Exchequer" using ministerial orders. Minister Howlin TD informed the Dáil at the Second stage debate on the Bill that his "officials will consult relevant Departments regarding governing criteria to assess which bodies should be brought under the Freedom of Information Acts".[103] This is aimed at bringing voluntary sector organisations providing services to vulnerable groups into the scheme.

[3–56]   A final general limitation is included in the 1997 Act, that the scheme has prospective effect but allows access to retrospective information in two limited situations. Firstly, records pre-dating the commencement of the legislation can be requested, if it relates to the requester's personal information and secondly, if the granting of access to such historic records is considered necessary or expedient to the understanding of records post-dating the commencement of the legislation.

Refusal of Access to Records

[3–57]   Apart from the specified restrictions noted above, it is possible for a public body to refuse a request. There are a variety of administrative grounds for a refusal under s 15 of the 2014 Act. Grounds for refusal include where the record does not exist or cannot be found after all "reasonable steps" to find it have been taken[104]; where granting the request would "cause a substantial and unreasonable interference with, or disruption of, the other work of the public body" because of the number of records involved[105]; and where there is a failure to pay a fee.[106]

---

[102] See "Irish Water's details will be available under FOI", *Irish Independent*, 13 November 2013 available online at http://www.independent.ie/irish-news/irish-waters-details-will-be-available-under-foi-29749580.html (date accessed December 13 2013).

[103] Second style date, above n 101.

[104] s 15(1)(a) and s 7(1)(b).

[105] s 15(1)(c) – note that this provision extends the scope of this reason this to include a "particular functional area" of the public body in addition to the whole public body.

[106] s 15(1)(h).

The legislation also provides for restrictions characterised as *exclusions* and [3–58] *exemptions*. These seek to protect a variety of interests, both of the State and of third parties. The reasoning for the strategy was underlined in the first FOI report, delivered by the Department of Finance, under s 15(6) of the 1997 Act informing the Houses of the Oireachtas of the preparations carried out to implement FOI which noted it as being necessary "in order to allow Government business to be properly conducted".[107] The discussion below provides a brief summary of these mechanisms and is not intended to be an exhaustive treatment.[108]

Exclusions mean certain types of information are wholly excluded from [3–59] disclosure. Section 42 provides for restrictions and sets out the various types of record that the legislation does not apply to. Significant examples under the section would include court and tribunal records, certain records held by the Garda Síochána in relation to sensitive operations such as witness protection, records which would reveal sources in relation to criminal investigations, records held by the Attorney General and the DPP.[109]

Exemptions relate to types of records which are exempted under certain [3–60] conditions. Part Four of the 2014 Act requires the right of access to these records to be balanced with competing interests. Examples of these competing interests include the public goods of the maintenance of law and order and state security, and certain individual interests such as confidentiality, privacy and commercial concerns.

---

[107] http://foi.gov.ie/wp/files/2010/09/1st-report-by-minister-for-finance.pdf (date accessed 13 December 2013) at p 9.

[108] For a more detailed treatment of the operation of the system see McDonagh (2006) above n 67.

[109] s 42 also applies to records held by tribunals of inquiry, records relating to the President, a record held by the Central Bank of Ireland, the disclosure of which is prohibited by the Rome Treaty, the ESCB Statute, or any Supervisory Directives within the meaning of the Central Bank Act 1942, a record given by an FOI body to a member of the Government or a Minister of State for use by him or her for the purposes of any proceedings in either House of the Oireachtas or Oireachtas committee, a record relating to any of the private papers (within the meaning of Art 15.10 of the Constitution) of a member of either House of the Oireachtas or official documents of the Houses that is required by the rules or standing orders of either or both of such Houses to be treated as confidential, a record relating to information whose disclosure could reasonably be expected to reveal or lead to the revelation of the identity of a person who has provided information to an FOI body in confidence in relation to the enforcement of the criminal law.

[3–61]   Twelve grounds of exemptions are set out in Part II

i.	Meetings of the Government (s 28)	ii.	Deliberations of FOI bodies (s 29)
iii.	Functions and negotiations of public bodies (s 30)	iv.	Parliamentary, court and certain other matters (s 31)
v.	Law enforcement and public safety (s 32)	vi.	Security, defence and international relations (s 33)
vii.	Information obtained in confidence (s 35)	viii.	Commercially sensitive information (s 36)
ix.	Personal information (s 37)	x.	Research and natural resources (s 39)
xi.	Financial and economic interests of the State (s 40)	xii.	Enactments relating to non-disclosure of records (s 41)

[3–62]   Unlike the exclusions, most exemptions are not absolute. However, providing a straightforward account of their operation is somewhat difficult because they are not set out in a consistent language format. However, some clear elements can be identified, not least the fact that a number of significant tests operate in relation to some or all of the exemptions.

[3–63]   Firstly the scheme utilises an *injury test* which requires that an exemption can operate where some form of harm or injury would result from disclosure. For example, s 40(1)(a) states that a ground for refusal may be where

> "...if, in the opinion of the head, access to the record could reasonably be expected to have a serious, adverse effect on the ability of the Government to manage the national economy or on the financial interests of the State."[110]

[3–64]   However, there is no single definition of the ambit of the test, and its operation varies between the different sections and therefore requires individual application by decision-makers to the precise wording when implementing the test. For example, some sections refer to "prejudice" arising from disclosure, while others refer to adverse effects. In addition,

---

[110] The harm test can also be found in relation to commercially sensitive information under s 36(1)(b) where disclosure could cause financial loss or gain or prejudice a competitive position; defence, security and international relations under s 33(1); functions and negotiations of a public body under s 30(1); and law enforcement and public safety under s 32(1)(a) where harm would occur as a result of the disclosure of the record not the nature of the document.

different standards of proof of injury arise through the use of different words such as "could", "would be likely" and "could reasonably be expected to".[111] However, regardless of the exact wording, if the test is not satisfied, the record will have to be released to the applicant unless it comes under some other exemption.

Secondly, some exemptions operate on the basis of a *class* test. This means that a record can be exempt because it belongs to a particular class of records, for example Government records[112] or records covered by legal professional privilege.[113]   **[3–65]**

Finally, the scheme operates a *public interest test* which functions in relation to the specific operation of some exemptions. In practice this test applies to approximately half of the provisions and permits the head of a body to release a record if it is found to be in the public interest to do so. The reasoning of this approach is that the benefit of the information being in the public domain is found to outweigh any harm that might arise from disclosure. The Information Commissioner has advised decision-makers to   **[3–66]**

> "list the public interest arguments for and against the release of the records in question, apply a weighting to each, hone in on the most important and make a judgement as to where the balance of the public interest lies."[114]

Examples of this test can be found in s 29 (deliberations of FOI bodies) and s 36 (commercially sensitive information).[115] If no public interest test is included in the section, then the application of an exemption is conclusive and the record will not be released.

Exemptions can be either *mandatory* or *discretionary*. Mandatory exemptions oblige the head of a public body to refuse disclosure where their legal conditions for the exemption are met. This approach is adopted in relation to Government records[116] and records relation to international relations   **[3–67]**

---

[111] For a more detailed discussion of this see McDonagh (2006) above n 67 at p 124.

[112] Meetings of the Government, s 28, 2014 Act.

[113] Legal professional privilege, s 31(1)(a), 2014 Act.

[114] Office of the Information Commissioner, *Short Guide to the FOI Acts.* Available at http://foi.gov.ie/3-1-brief-introduction-to-exemptions/ (date accessed 11 July 2013).

[115] Other sections include the functions and negotiations of public bodies in s 30, information obtained in confidence in s 35, research and natural resources in s 39, financial and economic interests of the State and public bodies in s 40, 2014 Act.

[116] s 28, 2014 Act.

and security.[117] Discretionary exemptions, on the other hand, allow for the head of a public body to exercise her judgment as to whether to refuse a request, even though the terms of an exemption have been met.

[3–68] Unsurprisingly, the exercise of discretion under the FOI exemptions is an important administrative decision to be undertaken by a public body, and should be carried out according to normal administrative law requirements. Importantly, the Information Commissioner has stressed that the discretion awarded is not unfettered. In *The Sunday Times and Office of the Revenue Commissioners*[118] the Commissioner concluded that a public body should show that it had exercised its discretion "appropriately" under the then 1997 Act.[119] This requires the public body's refusal is in line with the "aims, principles and policies underpinning" the Act[120] and that a clear case be made out by the body in support of the use of the exemption.[121]

[3–69] A further requirement is that *third party interests* be considered as part of the process. Section 38 of the 2014 Act protects information given to public bodies which is of a personal, commercially sensitive or confidential nature. It does this by imposing a duty on the head of a public body, in some circumstances, to consult third parties before deciding whether a requested record should be disclosed. This is designed to provide third parties with an opportunity to contribute to the decision-making process regarding disclosure.[122] However, it does not provide a third party with an opportunity to make the final decision on disclosure. The process becomes pertinent where the record falls within one of three types of record and the head of the public body decides it is in the public interest to disclose it.

---

[117] s 33, 2014 Act.

[118] Letter Decision No. 030624, 11 August 2005.

[119] The issue related to s 22(1A), 1997 Act which applied at the time and which exempted records in relation to Tribunals. The same approach will be required in relation to the 2014 Act.

[120] *Deely v The Information Commissioner* [2001] 3 IR 439, per McKechnie J at para 1.

[121] *Irish Examiner and Department of Finance* Decision Information Commissioner, 23 February 2010. Available at http://www.oic.gov.ie/en/Decisions/Decisions/Irish-Examiner-Department-of-Finance.html (date accessed 11 July 2013). The case related to a request in relation to the Department of Finance's Risk Management Strategy 2006 and the operation of its s 20 refusal.

[122] s 38 sets out the procedure required where requests are made in relation to (a) material obtained in confidence (s 35), (b) commercially sensitive information (s 36), and (c) personal information (s 37).

The final method of preventing records being accessed is via a system of *certificates* which operates in relation to particularly sensitive records.[123] The certificate, once issued, conclusively affirms that a record is exempt from the FOI regime. This system includes a *Ministerial Certificate* which empowers the Minister to issue a certificate to the effect that a record to which access is requested is exempt under the legislation. These operate in relation to records in the area of law enforcement,[124] security and international relations.[125] The Minister's decision cannot be reviewed by the Information Commissioner but is subject to review by the Taoiseach and other members of the Government[126]; provision is also made for an appeal to the High Court on a point of law.[127] Certificates remain in force for two years, although there is a mechanism for renewal.[128] Each Minister is required to provide a report to the Information Commissioner annually regarding the number of certificates issued in the year which are then included in the Annual Report. This at a minimum provides a degree of transparency in the operation of the process, at least in terms of the number of certificates issued.

[3–70]

To date, the procedure has been used sparingly, although there has been a steady rise from two in 2000 and 2002 to five in 2009 and to twelve in 2011. In her 2012 Annual Report, the Information Commissioner reported five of the twelve certificates were issued by the Minister for Justice and Equality, three by the Minister for Foreign Affairs, three by the Minister for Trade and one by the Minister for Justice, Equality and Law Reform.[129] In 2013 three new certificates were issued by the Minister for Foreign Affairs and twelve existing certificates.[130]

[3–71]

---

[123] s 34(1)(ii), 2014 Act.

[124] s 32 and s 34(1)(ii), 2014 Act.

[125] s 33 and s 34(1)(ii), 2014 Act.

[126] s 34(7)(a) 2014 Act provides for the periodic review of the issuing of certificates.

[127] s 24(2), 2014 Act.

[128] s 34(13), 2014 Act.

[129] Office of the Information Commissioner, *Annual Report 2012*, (Office of the Information Commissioner, Dublin, 2012) http://www.oic.gov.ie/en/publications/annual-reports/2012-annual-report/online/media/information_commissioner_ar_english_web.pdf (date accessed 2 July 2014), hereinafter "2012 Annual Report".

[130] Office of the Information Commissioner, *Annual Report 2013*, (Office of the Information Commissioner, Dublin, 2013) http://www.oic.gov.ie/en/publications/annual-reports/2013-annual-report/online/media/oic_ar_2013_english.pdf (date accessed 11 June 2014).

Cabinet Papers

[3–72]   Section 28 of the 2014 Act operates to protect Cabinet records. This exemption supports the principle of cabinet confidentiality discussed in chapter 2 of this book. The concern regarding the publication of these documents is that public scrutiny could undermine collective ministerial responsibility for the decisions of Cabinet as protected by Article 28.4.2° of the Constitution. In addition, concern is often raised that access to such discussions will stifle frank policy discussions at the highest level of Government.

[3–73]   Access to cabinet papers has been critical in the debates around freedom of information and, as mentioned in relation to the Beef Tribunal, was one of the trigger points for the adoption of a freedom of information regime in Ireland.[131] The refusal by Government Ministers to provide answers to the Tribunal was on the basis of cabinet confidentiality which was subsequently upheld by the Supreme Court in the case of *Attorney General v Hamilton (No.1)*.[132] In a 3:2 majority decision, Finlay CJ found that the collective responsibility obligation on Government meant that there was a

> ... necessity for full, free and frank discussion between members of the Government prior to the making of decisions, something which would appear to be an inevitable adjunct to the obligation to meet collectively and to act collectively.... The obligation to accept collective responsibility for decisions and , presumably, for acts of government as well, involves, as a necessity, the non-disclosure of different or dissenting views held by members of the Government prior to the making of decisions.[133]

[3–74]   Unsurprisingly, the 1997 Act protected cabinet papers against disclosure with a class-based exemption in s 19. There is also no public interest test in this exemption so once a record falls within its scope, disclosure is denied.[134] Originally, s 19 included a time limit which functioned to prevent the exemption working in relation to records made more than five years before the receipt of the FOI request.[135] This was controversially amended in

---

[131] See discussion above at para [3.43].

[132] [1993] 2 IR 250.

[133] *ibid* at 266. G Hogan, "The Cabinet Confidentiality Case of 1992" (1993) *Irish Political Studies* 131.

[134] A detailed discussion of the operation of s 19 can be found in McDonagh (2006) above n 67 at ch 6.

[135] s 19(3)(b), 1997 Act.

2003,[136] extending the time limit to ten years. In explaining the change, then Minister for Finance Charlie McCreevy TD stated:

> "I do not believe that it's in the public interest that documents about Government decisions on important issues are released before a sufficient period of time has elapsed. Otherwise, the only effect is to undermine the workings of Government. Like all organisations which have the right to decide how to carry out their business, Government is no different. Our work is very complex. In taking decisions on important economic and social issues, the Government has to look at different alternatives and approaches. It has to debate these freely and reach a decision on behalf of the community. For this process to work effectively, records relating to Government business need to be properly protected."[137]

Indeed, one of the key justifications was the need to protect sensitive discussions around the Northern Ireland peace process. There was little dissent in Oireachtas debates on this issue at the time but criticism of the extension gained ground and the 2014 Act has returned the time limit to five years.[138]   [3–75]

The Application Process

Briefly, a person who wishes to exercise their rights under the 2014 Act can make a written request under s 12 of the 2014 Act to the head of a public body. The FOI body should provide "reasonable assistance" to a requester[139] and s 11(3) establishes that a FOI body should have regard to: [3–76]

(a) the need to achieve greater openness in the activities of FOI bodies and to promote adherence by them to the principle of transparency in Government and public affairs;

(b) the need to strengthen the accountability and improve the quality of decision making of FOI bodies; and

(c) the need to inform scrutiny, discussion, comment and review by the public of the activities of FOI bodies and facilitate more effective

---

[136] Freedom of Information (Amendment) Act 2003, s 14.
[137] http://foi.gov.ie/press-release-6 the change had been recommended by the High Level Review Group on the Freedom of Information Act 1997, *Report to the Government*, (December 2002).
[138] s 28(3)(b), 2014 Act.
[139] s 11(2), 2014 Act.

participation by the public in consultations relating to the role, responsibilities and performance of FOI bodies.

[3–77] The motives of the person requesting the information should not be taken into account in relation to the question of access; the idea being to allow open access and not to provide restrictions on the basis of an "interest" requirement. A request should be acknowledged within two weeks[140] and a decision as to whether to grant or refuse the request should be provided within four weeks.[141] An extension may be provided by up to a further 20 working days if the request relates to a large number of items.

[3–78] If a request is refused, s 13(2)(d)(i) of the 2014 Act requires that reasons be given along with findings on material issues which are relevant under s 13(2)(d)(ii). This allows the applicant to understand the reason for the refusal, to decide whether to appeal and to encourage public bodies only to use exemptions where they have a good reason to do so. As the Information Commissioner's manual makes clear, a statement of reasons needs to "show a connection, supported by a chain of reasoning, between the decision and the decision maker's findings on material issues".[142] If the Commissioner, upon review of the decision, considers the statement of reasons to be inadequate, s 23(1)(b) requires that she direct the head of the public body to provide a statement[143] "containing any further information".

Publication of Information on the Operation of Public Bodies

[3–79] While freedom of information is most often identified with the disclosure of information from public bodies, a central part of the process of achieving greater transparency is found in the requirement that bodies publish information about their operation and decision-making. As already

---

[140] s 12(2), 2014 Act.

[141] s 13(1), 2014 Act.

[142] Office of the Information Commissioner, *Guide to Rules Procedures Practices, Guidelines, and Interpretations used by the Office of the Information Commissioner,* para 5.4. Available online at http://www.oic.gov.ie/en/About-Us/Policies-and-Strategies/FOI-Manuals/Section-16-Manual/Section-16-Manual.pdf (date accessed 2 July 2014). This is the section 16 Manual required under the 1997 Act as amended, and will be replaced in due course following the full implementation of the 2014 Act. Hereinafter *OIC Guide to Rules.*

[143] To both the requester and the Information Commissioner.

discussed, public bodies were traditionally secretive in nature so imposing a positive obligation to publish such information has resulted in a significant practical change. The 1997 Act created a system whereby public bodies were required under s 15 to publish information regarding their activities in the form of a "reference book" and s 16 to publish what was known as their "internal law": that is their rules, guidelines and precedents. These dual obligations applied to public bodies defined by the 1997 Act, and as a result some key bodies were excluded.[144]

However, the development of information and communications technol-   **[3–80]**
ogy had led to a conclusion that the manuals are now an outdated approach to the publication of information in this area. As a result the above require-ments have been replaced in the 2014 Act by a requirement that public bodies prepare and publish a "publication scheme" under s 8. These schemes must detail the classes of information each body has published or intends to publish and how the information will be made available. The idea is to develop a more engaged and proactive approach by FOI bodies towards information sharing. Section 8(5) of the 2014 Act states that:

> In preparing, reviewing or revising a publication scheme under this section, an FOI body shall have regard to the public interest—
>
> (a) in allowing public access to information held by the FOI body,
> (b) in the publication of reasons for decisions made by the FOI body, and
> (c) in publishing information of relevance or interest to the general public in relation to its activities and functions generally.

As part of the process of assisting FOI bodies to develop this new approach, it is anticipated that a Code of Practice for FOI will be published alongside the new system and this is likely to include guidance as to how to carry out the process.[145]

---

[144] See discussion above at para 3.51 regarding state-sponsored bodies, An Garda Siochána and key financial organisations.

[145] This publication scheme approach is similar to that adopted in the UK, *Freedom of Information Act 2000* s 19. However, there is one significant difference; in the UK system the Information Commissioner must approve the scheme, whereas under the 2014 Act this is not required.

Right to Reasons

[3–81]   In brief, prior to the introduction of FOI legislation, the law had not provided a clear statement of the circumstances in which reasons for administrative decisions were required to be given. In particular, it had been suggested that a right to reasons for administrative decisions only applied to cases where a person affected by a decision displayed a serious intention to challenge it by judicial review or where an appeal was possible.[146] The 1997 Act clarified the position by providing in s 18 a right to a written statement of reasons and finding of fact in respect of any act of a public body concerning that individual, provided the individual has a material interest in a matter affected by the Act. This is now replaced by s 10 of the 2014 Act. This issue will be considered in more detail in chapter 10 of this book in the wider context of reasons with administrative law.

A Right to Amend Personal Information

[3–82]   Section 9 provides members of the public with a right to have personal information held on them by a public body amended. This legal right accompanies the right of access to information and is equivalent to the right under s 6 of the Data Protection Act 1988 which allows individuals to seek amendments of personal data. In addition to a personal application, the right can be exercised by parents and guardians of minors or other representatives under s 17.

[3–83]   Where the public body disagrees with the requester and believes that the information is in fact correct, it must attach a copy of the application to the relevant record. However, this does not apply where the application is construed to be defamatory or additions would be excessive. Details of amended records must be provided to any other public body or person to whom the record has been provided within the previous 12 months.

The Role of Information Commissioner — Review and Enforcement

[3–84]   As seen in our discussion of the Office of the Ombudsman in chapter 4, a normative system of administrative justice is ultimately only as effective as

---

[146] McDonagh (2006) above n 67 at p 58 referencing Hogan and Morgan *Administrative Law in Ireland* (3rd ed) (Round Hall, Dublin, 1998) at p 572 (4th ed, para 14-121).

its enforcement mechanisms. With the Freedom of Information Act process being dependent upon interactions between ordinary individuals and institutional actors, a system wide apparatus for ensuring that breaches of the law are investigated and resolved in an open and dependable manner was clearly needed. This reflected the fundamental inequality of arms between the parties, which was aggravated by the inherent control a freedom of information body has over its own workings and arrangements.

Typically, a freedom of information system operates through both internal and external review mechanisms: Ireland has also adopted such an approach. Firstly, there is an *internal review* process. This type of review is regarded as having a number of benefits in that it is generally quick and low cost. In addition, it frequently results in greater information release, reduces the number of external complaints and ultimately improves management within public bodies.[147] Chapter three of the 2014 Act provides for such a review in relation to a variety of decisions.[148] The process involves a review by the head of the public body[149] of the decision and may lead to the decision being affirmed, annulled or an alternative decision being provided.[150] An appeal to the Information Commissioner cannot proceed unless an internal review has first taken place.[151] **[3–85]**

Internal Review

Internal reviews are to be completed within three weeks of a request. The legislation does not direct how reviews should be carried out, so there is a degree of discretion as to how the process is conducted.[152] The internal review decision must be communicated to the applicant including reasons **[3–86]**

---

[147] *ibid* at p 495.

[148] s 21 of the 2014 Act allows for an internal review in a number of situations including where there has been a refusal regarding access (s 21(1)(a)), a refusal to amend personal information (s 21(1)(b), and regarding a decision to charge a fee (s 21(1)(g).

[149] Or a person who has been delegated the power under s 21(2) 2014 Act.

[150] s 21(2)(b) 2014 Act.

[151] s 22(1) 2014 Act.

[152] In *X and Health Service Executive North Eastern Area*, Letter Decision No. 040140, 2 December 2005, available online at http://www.oic.gov.ie/en/Decisions/Decisions/Ms-X-and-the-Health-Service-Executive-North-Eastern-Area.html (date accessed 16 July 2013) the Information Commissioner concluded that a scope of review to be carried out by a reviewer was limited by the grounds of appeal set out by the applicant.

and, where a request is refused, the relevant provisions of the legislation, relevant findings and details of public interest considerations.[153]

[3–87]   In a 2001 report on compliance by public bodies with the FOI system[154] the Information Commissioner reviewed the operation of the internal review system. The report noted that while the process generally operated in a satisfactory manner the biggest defect was a "widespread failure to give proper reasons" to meet the requirements of the legislation.[155] More than ten years later, it is to be expected that the system is well embedded and public bodies have taken on board the need to monitor and support this significant internal system. However, delays in processing internal reviews continue to be a problem, and this has been highlighted by the Information Commissioner as symptomatic of a continuing failure to prioritise FOI requests.[156]

External Review

[3–88]   While internal review systems are critical to the operation of FOI there is also a need for a stronger *external review* system. This is particularly so, given that, as McDonagh notes, the very operation of compulsory internal systems "prior to activation of avenues of external review, results in delays in the accessing of external review mechanisms".[157]

[3–89]   While there are a variety of models used globally to provide external review of FOI decisions, the one adopted by the Irish legislation relies upon an Information Commissioner.[158] The Office was established under the 1997 Act[159] and was in large part modelled on the Office of the Ombudsman which by the time the legislation was being drafted was already seen as a

---

[153] S 8(2)(d). Note that this information does not need to be provided where discovery of the existence or non-existence of a record is contrary to the public interest or damaging to certain interests.

[154] *Freedom of Information – Compliance by Public Bodies,* (2001) available at http://www.oic. gov.ie/en/Publications/Annual-Reports/Previous-Annual-Reports/2001-Annual-Report/Report-of-Compliance-by-Public-Bodies-with-Freedom-of-Information-Act.html (date accessed 16 July 2013).

[155] *ibid* at chapter 6.

[156] 2012 Annual Report above n 129 at chapter 1.

[157] McDonagh (2006) above n 67 at p 495.

[158] As McDonagh notes there are two other models – the courts as a primary review forum as used in the USA and a tribunal as used in Australia. *ibid* at 495-6.

[159] s 43 of the 2014 Act states that the office of the Information Commissioner will continue to operate despite the repeal of the 1997 Act.

major administrative justice success. As a result the Information Commissioner is appointed in the same way as the Ombudsman[160] and in the same way that independence from Government is critical in relation to the Ombudsman, it is reinforced in relation to the Information Commissioner. The relationship between the Ombudsman and Information Commissioner has been cemented through the adoption of a dual appointment system whereby the one person holds both offices simultaneously.[161] In recent times, with financial pressures increasingly affecting the administrative review systems of the State, this operational burden-sharing has become more and more attractive to Government. While a full scale merger of all "integrity branch" offices might have been proposed, however, legal and practical difficulties have prevented this development, particularly in relation to the Children's Ombudsman and Irish Language Commissioner.[162]

The Information Commissioner has the power to review decisions taken at the internal review stage and those exempt from internal review under s 22(1) of the 2014 Act. There are three key exclusions: **[3–90]**

a) A decision made by the Information Commissioner regarding a record held by the Commissioner, this decision is reviewable by the High Court[163];

b) A decision that has not been subject to an available internal review[164];

c) Where a conclusive certificate is made under the legislation or where a decision to refuse access is subject to such a certificate.[165] The High Court has jurisdiction in this area.[166]

---

[160] s 43, 2014 Act. See discussion of the appointment of the Ombudsman in chapter 4 relating to s 2(2) Ombudsman Act 1980.

[161] This dual role is not an essential feature of the offices but is permissible under the legislation and Ireland is not the only country to adopt such a system, for example the New Zealand Ombudsman is also responsible for freedom of information, see http://www.ombudsman.parliament.nz/ (date accessed 16 December 2013). Despite this dual operational system, it is important to note that the Information Commissioner has one key operational advantage over the Ombudsman — decisions of the Information Commissioner are legally binding, s 22(14)(b), 2014 Act.

[162] See discussion in chapter 4 at para [4.75].

[163] s 22(1)(i). Where the Information Commissioner is also the Ombudsman this also applies to records of the Office of the Ombudsman.

[164] s 22(1)(ii), 2014 Act.

[165] s 34(3)(b), 2014 Act.

[166] s 24(2), 2014 Act.

[3–91] It should also be noted that the Commissioner has the power to refuse to carry out, or to discontinue a review where he concludes that the application is frivolous or vexatious,[167] a decision not subject to review by the Commissioner[168] or where it is believed that the decision is subject to another review by the Commissioner.[169] The list of reasons for refusing a review have been expanded by the 2014 Act and now also includes where it would cause "substantial and unreasonable interference" to the work of the Commissioner's Office. In her 2012 Annual report,[170] the Information Commissioner noted that a total of 200 cases were reviewed by the Office.[171] The most likely outcome of complaints was that they were affirmed by the Commissioner,[172] 20% were resolved through settlement while a small number were annulled[173] or varied.[174]

[3–92] *The Office of the Information Commissioner's Guide to Rules* sets out its approach to reviewing decisions.[175] An initial assessment of the application is carried out by an investigator in order to assess the best approach to the application. The manual notes that a

> "… substantial proportion of reviews (about 50%) are decided otherwise than by way of binding decision of the Commissioner under section 34(2). In many cases, reviews are completed by way of settlement between the parties (as contemplated by section 34(7)), by withdrawal of the application for review or by discontinuance. In such cases, usually one or other of the parties or both modify their positions."[176]

There is a distinct advantage to avoiding the more formal binding process of resolving complaints. It provides a quicker resolution of the complaint for the applicant and allows the FOI body to avoid the time consuming process of being subject to a review. Finally, as with the Ombudsman, an informal resolution is cheaper for the Office of the Information Commissioner than a review.

---

[167] s 22(9)(a)(i), 2014 Act.
[168] s 22(9)(a)(ii), 2014 Act.
[169] s 22(9)(a)(iii), 2014 Act.
[170] 2012 Annual Report, above n 129.
[171] s 22(9)(a)(vii), 2014 Act.
[172] 81 out of 200.
[173] 11 of 200.
[174] 8 of 200.
[175] above, n 142.
[176] *ibid* para.5.1.

During the initial assessment, the investigator should consider whether another party should be notified, gauge whether adequate reasons have been given by the public body, identify whether a review can be resolved without a binding decision, and consider what other information is needed from the parties. The investigator will likely examine the records relevant to the dispute, although this will not always be absolutely necessary. Finally, the investigator is required to find out if the point at issue in a complaint has already been decided in another case or is being examined already.

[3–93]

Where a case is not resolvable without a binding decision or through a settlement, a review will be carried out. Section 22(12)(b) of the legislation states that a decision:

[3–94]

> "to refuse to grant an FOI request shall be presumed not to have been justified unless the head concerned shows to the satisfaction of the Commissioner that the decision was justified."

Thus, the public body has to establish that its decision was appropriate under the legislation. It will therefore be invited by the investigator to make a submission to this effect. The Information Commissioner has noted "[t]he importance of cogent, well-argued submissions, clearly identifying the basis for exemptions and harm and/or public interest considerations, where relevant".[177]

Section 45(6) of the 2014 Act provides that the Commissioner should operate a procedure which she considers "appropriate in all the circumstances of the case"[178] and that the procedure can be "as informal as is consistent with the due performance of the functions of the Commissioner".[179] These include powers:

[3–95]

- to require information to be provided on the basis that it is relevant to a review or investigation;
- to require witnesses to attend;
- to remove and retain records for a reasonable period; and
- to enter premises occupied by a public body.

---

[177] Information Commissioner, *Short Guide to the FOI Acts*, chapter 6, available online at http://foi.gov.ie/short-guide-to-the-foi-acts/ (date accessed 16 July 2013).
[178] s 45(6), 2014 Act.
[179] *ibid.*

Failure to comply with such requirements or the hindering of the Commissioner is a summary offence.[180]

[3–96] The powers provided in the 2014 Act reflect those in the original 1997 legislation[181] and allow for wide discretion. This was considered by McKechnie J in *Deely v Information Commissioner*[182]:

> "It seems to me that under Section 37 (6) of the Act [now s 45(6) of 2014 Act], the Commissioner, in conducting a review under Section 34 or an investigation under Section 36, has an extensive discretion as to the procedures which he may adopt or follow. Certainly, when dealing with a refusal the Commissioner can only be encouraged to pursue a solution to the joint satisfaction of the public body and the requester, and in so doing he must be free, in accordance with the underlying intention of the Act, to perform the preparatory work to his decision in whatever way he wishes, informally if that be his choice. It need hardly be said, however, that in so doing he must not compromise the due and proper performance of his function."[183]

[3–97] The courts have noted further that the discretion is extensive so long as the procedures adopted by the Information Commissioner do not breach the rules of constitutional justice. Thus, Quirke J in the High Court in *The National Maternity Hospital v The Information Commissioner and Parents for Justice*[184] concluded that:

> "The procedures to be adopted by the Commissioner in respect of such reviews are entirely within her discretion provided that they do not offend recognised principles of natural and constitutional justice. The procedures which she adopted in the review under appeal permitted all of the parties with an interest in the review to make full and detailed written submissions on every relevant aspect which affected their respective interests. Each of the parties who participated in the review was provided with full and equal access to the Commissioner and to her officials.

---

[180] Under s 45(7) it is an offence to refuse to comply with a request to supply information/records or to obstruct the Commissioner in the performance of her duties. If found guilty under this provision a person would be subject to a summary conviction and liable to a Class A Fine and/or imprisonment of up to six months. The 2014 Act has also now made it an offence to wilfully and without lawful excuse destroy or alter a record subject to an FOI request, s 52.

[181] s 45 of the 2014 Act replaces s 37 of the 1997 Act.

[182] [2001] 3 IR 439.

[183] *ibid* at para 4.

[184] [2007] IEHC 113.

I know of no principle of natural or constitutional law or justice which confers upon parties who make submissions to a decision-making body the right to respond to the submissions made by every other party who participates in the process. The review undertaken by the Commissioner was a statutory process which expressly envisaged and permitted the adoption of informal procedures."[185]

In relation to constitutional justice, there is no right to an oral hearing before the Commissioner, rather the Commissioner can determine in what form submissions can be made. Likewise, there is no requirement within the legislation that hearings be held in public nor that legal representation be provided. All such decisions would fall within the discretion of the Commissioner. Generally, the procedure would not require such hearings as the procedure set out in the current *Guide to Rules Procedures Practices, Guidelines, and Interpretations used by the Office of the Information Commissioner*[186] involves an investigation of the FOI bodies' decision based on the request for a review provided by the complainant. **[3–98]**

Review decisions are required to be made "in so far as is practicable" not later than four months after an application is received.[187] However, in the 2012 Annual Report of the Commissioner, it was noted with regret that only 19% of cases closed were done so within the statutory time frame.[188] The problem of timing has prompted the office to consider reforms of their procedures to improve "case turnaround times".[189] Upon completion, the decision must be communicated to the applicant, the public body and relevant third parties along with reasons.[190] **[3–99]**

Compliance

As we discuss in our chapter on the Ombudsman the issue of public body compliance is critical to the effective operation of the integrity institutions. **[3–100]**

---

[185] In *South West Area Health Board v Information Commissioner* [2005] 2 IR 547 the failure of the Information Commissioner to allow the birth mother in a case involved adoption records to be given an opportunity to make presentations before a decision was made was found to be a breach of constitutional justice. Available online at http://foi.gov.ie/Case-No-030830-The-National-Maternity-Hospital-and-the-Information-Commissioner (date accessed 2 July 2014).

[186] above n 142.

[187] s 22(3), 2014 Act.

[188] 2012 Annual Report above n 129 at p 30.

[189] *ibid* at p 31.

[190] s 22(10), 2014 Act.

The Information Commissioner has a distinct advantage over the Ombudsman system given that decisions are binding on public bodies. However, despite this, in her 2012 Annual Report, the Commissioner stressed the need to "foster better working relationships with public bodies", not least to improve efficiency in dealing with complex reviews.[191] Primary causes for concern in cooperation have been the questioning by public bodies as to whether information requested by the Information Commissioner under s 37 should be forwarded by them.[192] In response, the Commissioner stressed in her report that failure to cooperate is a criminal offence under s 37.[193]

[3–101]   Further, the Commissioner highlighted the tendency of public bodies to request deadline extensions on the basis of insufficient staff resources to process requests under the FOI system.[194] This was, in the Commissioner's view, indicative of a broader mindset where by such bodies may not regard FOI obligations as being on a par with other statutory duties:

> "It remains the fact that some public bodies fail to recognise that the administration of the FOI Act is one of their statutory functions which should be afforded as much weight as any other statutory function."[195]

[3–102]   This view is compounded by the failure of public bodies to provide cover where FOI staff are on leave. It appears then that even 16 years after the introduction of FOI legislation, some FOI bodies appear to continue to be at best indifferent to the need to provide an effective FOI mechanism. As the Commissioner herself noted in 2010 "in practice FOI is irksome and time consuming"[196] and it can be politically uncomfortable in terms of the exposure of controversial or embarrassing details about political and public

---

[191] 2012 Annual Report above n 129 at p 31.

[192] s 37, 1997 Act is now replaced by s 23, 2014 Act.

[193] *ibid.*

[194] "Information Commissioner: staff resources no excuse for FOI delays", *The Journal* May 14 2013 http://www.thejournal.ie/information-commissioner-staff-resources-no-excuse-for-foi-delays-908584-May2013/ (date accessed 13 December 2013).

[195] *ibid.*

[196] Emily O'Reilly, "Controlling Access: Responding to Political and Administrative Resistance to Access" (2011) CBA 2nd Annual Privacy and Access Law Symposium and 7th International Conference of Information Commissioners (ICIC). Available online at http://www.oic.gov.ie/en/news/speeches-articles/2011-speeches-articles/controlling-access-responding-to-political-and-administrative-resistance-to-access-.html (date accessed 16 December 2013).

administration activity.[197] For some, including the information Commissioner at the time, Emily O'Reilly, the 2003 Amendment Act was clear evidence of the politicians "falling out of love" with FOI.[198] Even the renewed political commitment to FOI by the Fine Gael/Labour coalition has been muted; with the detail of the 2014 Act revealing a number of limitations alongside liberalisations.

An effective information regime is ultimately dependent, to a significant [3–103] extent, upon the goodwill of those implementing it. It is clear that there are FOI bodies who have to some extent embraced the spirit of the Act and who have, as a result, adopted an efficient and proactive approach to it. Felle and Adshed note in particular positive instances of best practices emanating from the Department of Finance, the Department of Enterprise Trade and Employment and the Department of Foreign Affairs.[199] For example, the Department of Finance took a decision to publish the Tax Strategy Group Portfolio of documents after each budget "in the interests of open Government".[200]

Other departments have adopted a more "letter of the law" approach to [3–104] FOI: Felle and Adshed highlight the Department of Health as an example of this approach. The approach can be understood as neither hindering the operation of the legislation nor being enthusiastic about it.[201] Finally, some departments such as the Department of Justice have developed, or maintained, a reputation for secrecy.

McDonagh's research on the attitudes of decision makers in local [3–105] Government in relation to FOI illustrates clearly both the positive and negative potential of the Act. Her cohort of participants, taken from local Government FOI decision makers, voiced an "overwhelmingly positive" view of FOI.[202] This not only related to the benefit of FOI to the public generally but also included the idea that it had produced benefits for local Government itself. In particular, participants regarded it as having improved record keeping and produced better decision-making.[203]

---

[197] For example the disclosure of records concerning expenses of expenses of members of the Oireachtas. *Ibid.*
[198] *ibid.*
[199] Felle and Adshed above n 22 at 13.
[200] *ibid* – this decision followed a series of FOI requests.
[201] *ibid* at 14.
[202] *ibid* at 12.
[203] *ibid* at 7.

McDonagh also found that participants were troubled by the failure to provide adequate resources to effectively operate the system.[204] There were further concerns about record management systems in local Government and the need to adopt more ICT systems. This is, in fact, a problem not confined to the local Government sector but is a problem in many areas of the public sector. Investment in integrated records management systems was not a priority during the Celtic Tiger years and is now considered a costly improvement. What is perhaps most significant in McDonagh's research is the manner in which highlights the existence of a freedom of information constituency *within* freedom of information bodies, with individuals looking to promote a broader relationship between freedom of information and improved governance within their organisations.

Enforcement of Information Commissioner Decisions

[3–106]   As we have already noted, the decisions of the Information Commissioner are binding on a public body. However, the 1997 Act did not specify the manner in which this obligation could enforced in circumstances where a body refuses to follow a decision. Failure to comply might have fallen within s 37(7) of that Act, which created the offence of hindering or obstructing the Commissioner in the performance of her duty. In addition, the Commissioner had the power to apply to the High Court by way of judicial review for an order of mandamus requiring compliance by the body concerned with the decision.[205] The 2014 Act has subsequently clarified the previous statutory duty on the public body to comply with the Commissioner's decision. Section 45(8) allows the Office to apply for a court order to "oblige the FOI body to comply with [its] decision" where that body has failed to do so. While this new development is very welcomed in enhancing the enforcement powers of the Information Commissioner, the legislation does not make it clear how such orders are to be enforced.

---

[204] *ibid* at 9.

[205] McDonagh (2006) above n 67 at p 519. See discussion on the remedy of *mandamus* in chapter 13: Judicial Review Procedure and Remedies.

Appeals to the Courts from the Office of the Information Commissioner

An appeal can be made to the High Court under s 24(1) of the 2014 Act: [3–107]

> "A party to a review under section 22 or any other person affected by
> the decision of the Commissioner following such a review may appeal
> to the High Court
> - (a) on a point of law from the decision, or
> - (b) where the party or person concerned contends that the release
>   of a record concerned would contravene a requirement
>   imposed by the European Union, on a finding of fact set out or
>   inherent in the decision."

Subsection (b) is a new addition to the FOI regime; previously, only a right
of appeal on a point of law existed. Although generally, issues of fact will
not be subject to appeal, in practice issues of fact and law may be intertwined.

Fees and Their Impact on Freedom of Information

One point of controversy in the running of the FOI regime has been the   [3–108]
charging system introduced by the Freedom of Information (Amendment
Act) 2003.[206] The costs were €15 for a non-personal request, €75 for an
internal review and €150 for an appeal to the Information Commissioner.[207]
However, there was no fee when the request related exclusively to personal
information about the requester. The fee was imposed on top of any
administrative charge a public body might levy on a requester in relation
to the time spent searching and retrieving records. These charges were
€20.95 per hour for searching and four cent per sheet for photocopying. The
legislation required that an estimated cost of search and retrieval has to be
provided to the requester if it is likely to be in excess of €50.79.[208] In relation
to these retrieval costs the Office of the Information Commissioner
concluded that the "Oireachtas intended to confer some latitude on public
bodies in their estimation of the time to be spent on a search and retrieval
of records ..." and that it should be done on the basis of "efficient

---

[206] s 14 and SI No 264 of 2003 – Freedom of Information Act 1997 (Fees) Regulations 2003 s 3.
[207] In order to apply for an external review a requester must first have been through the
internal review system with the result that a total charge of €240 will have been paid in
fees before a request can come before the Information Commissioner.
[208] s 47(7), 1997 Act.

practices".[209] However, concerns have been expressed that high search and retrieval fees appear to have been used to dissuade people from pursuing requests[210] and a lack of overall transparency in the way the fees are calculated.

[3–109]   The charging of the up-front fee introduced by the 2003 Act appear to have a significant impact on FOI requests. Minister for Public Expenditure and Reform Brendan Howlin noted in 2013 that:

> "[t]he evidence is that the introduction of high appeal fee levels has acted as a very strong disincentive to applications for both internal reviews and appeals by requesters who are dissatisfied with the decision-making of public bodies.
>
> The consequent diminution in oversight and scrutiny by the Information Commissioner of the implementation of the legislation by public bodies is unlikely to have a positive effect on the quality of decision-making or the extent to which decision-makers would apply key balancing tests, in particular relating to the public interest favouring release."[211]

[3–110]   Indeed, the Information Commissioner found that "in 2002, the last full year before the introduction of fees, 7,936 non-personal requests were made; for 2011, this figure had dropped to 3,857 requests".[212] Felle and Adshed set out testimony from their expert focus group which included a variety of highly critical statements on the impact of the fee system including it being a "huge curtailment" and a view that "we do not have a *Freedom of Information Act* now".[213] In practice the view that the imposition

---

[209] *Mr ABW and the Department of Enterprise, Trade and Employment* (Case Number 99151) (2000) available online at http://www.oic.gov.ie/en/Decisions/Decisions/Mr-ABW-and-the-Department-of-Enterprise,-Trade-and-Employment.html (date accessed 16 December 2013).

[210] Felle and Adshed, above, n 22 at pp 18-19. They note that there is no direct evidence of this but they cite newspaper articles raising concerns including one by Shane Ross related to an alleged claim by FÁS for €1000 for access to documents related to expenses in that organisation.

[211] http://per.gov.ie/2013/02/11/speech-by-the-minister-for-public-expenditure-and-reform-mr-brendan-howlin-t-d-university-of-limerick-11-february-2013-the-right-to-know-examining-15-years-of-the-freedom-of-information-act-in-i/ (date accessed 26 November 2013).

[212] Emily O'Reilly, "Open Government: Where are we now?" http://www.oic.gov.ie/en/news/speeches-articles/2012-speeches-articles/open-government-where-are-we-now-.html (date accessed 26 November 2013).

[213] Felle and Adshed, above n 22 at p 16, quoting Charlie Flanagan and Mark Hennessy respectively.

of fees permanently damaged the number of applications has not been completely sustained given that the number of FOI applications recovered to its pre-2003 figure by 2012.[214] However, other factors do need to be noted in relation to these figures – the pre-2003 application numbers date from a time when FOI was new, high levels of use in the early days of the FOI system would be expected. In relation to more recent figures it should be recalled that more bodies have now been brought within the FOI regime. It is important to note that the level of appeals continue to be significantly depressed, this may relate to cost, but might also be a function of improved decision–making by FOI bodies prompting less need for appeals.[215] However, regardless of these figures the fact is that the charging of fees was a step that appeared to undermine the State's commitment to transparency and access to information.

On a practical side, the charging of fees also had a negative impact on public bodies. Between 2004 and 2009 the amount raised by fees was reported by O'Connor to be around €525,000.[216] However, for many public bodies the administrative cost of collecting the fee is likely to be higher than the revenue received.[217] Nonetheless, the data on this is not clear, not least because the Government has stated it is unable to provide estimates.[218]   [3–111]

Comparatively, charging has in recent years become rare in other jurisdictions – only Ireland, Canada and Israel impose up front charges for FOI requests.[219] Ideally, FOI should operate under free access — thus   [3–112]

---

[214] OIC figures indicate that in 2003 18,443 FOI requests were made, this dropped to 12, 597 in 2004 but had recovered to 18,985 in 2012. However, non-personal requests to which the fees attach were 7,216 in 2003, fell to 3,191 in 2004 and were only 3,980 in 2012. Figures are from Office of the Information Commissioner Annual Reports available online at http://www.oic.gov.ie/en/Publications/Annual-Reports/ (date accessed 14 October 2014).

[215] OIC figures indicate that the level of internal reviews in 2003 was 1580 while in 2012 it was 654 and the number of applications for review accepted by the Information Commissioner in 2003 was 922 compared with 335 in 2012, *ibid*.

[216] O'Connor, above at n 8 at p 6.

[217] O'Connor, *ibid* notes that a majority of public bodies process 20 or less non-personal requests per year, amounting to a maximum of €300 annually under the 2003 Act scheme "which seems unlikely to cover the administrative costs for one of those bodies in handling the fees" and that where the number of applications are as low as five the fee system costs system is counter-productive.

[218] *Through the Looking Glass, http://www.broadsheet.ie/tag/freedom-of-information/* 15 November 2013 (date accessed 26 November 2013)

[219] Transparency International, Money, Politics, Power: Corruption Risks in Europe (Transparency International, 2012) at p 31.

Article 7 of the Council of Europe Convention on Access to Official Documents states that:

> (1) Inspection of official documents on the premises of a public author-ity shall be free of charge....[220]
>
> (2) A fee may be charged to the applicant for a copy of the official docu-ment, which should be reasonable and not exceed the actual costs of reproduction and delivery of the document. Tariffs of charges shall be published.

[3–113] Following the change in the Irish legislation in 2003, there has been consistent calls by international bodies[221] for the abolition of, or at least reduction in, the fees. The OECD has stated that:

> "[t]he Government should reduce barriers to public information by making all requests under the *Freedom of Information Act 1997* free.... While user charges may limit frivolous requests (and thereby reduce burdens on the Public Service), they also serve as a disincentive to greater openness."[222]

[3–114] The Fine Gael/Labour Programme for Government in 2011 had made a commitment to "restore the Freedom of Information Act to what it was before it was undermined by the outgoing Government".[223] However, when the 2013 Bill was published it maintained a reduced fee regime — the application fee was to remain at €15 and reductions would be made for reviews so that the fees would be €30 for internal reviews and €50 for an application to the OIC.[224] In addition, the Government introduced a controversial amendment into the Bill at committee stage which would have allowed FOI bodies to impose multiple fees for what it considered to be multifaceted requests.[225] These are FOI requests that contain more

---

[220] Although note that museums and archive can charge under Art 7(1).

[221] Including the Council of Europe's anti-corruption body – the Groups of States against Corruption (GRECO) in the 2007 Compliance Report on Ireland, Greco RC-II (2007) 11E, available online at http://www.coe.int/t/dghl/monitoring/greco/evaluations/round2/GrecoRC2(2007)11_Ireland_EN.pdf (date accessed 17 July 2013).
and the Organisation for Economic Cooperation and Development (OECD)

[222] OECD, *Ireland: Towards an Integrated Public Service*, (OECD, 2008) at p 220. Available at

[223] http://www.merrionstreet.ie/wp-content/uploads/2010/05/Programme_for_Government_2011.pdf (date accessed 16 December 2013)

[224] s 27.

[225] The proposed s 27(9)(a) read as follows:
"Where a request to an FOI body under *subsection (1)* is made up of 2 or more parts seeking separate and distinct information relating to functions and responsibilities

than one part and have developed over the years since the introduction of the fee system in 2003. The proposed s 27(9)(a) would have allowed the FOI body to break down such a request into its component parts and impose a fee on each. Journalists highlighted, at the time, that such an approach would have further dissuaded the media from asking difficult questions of state bodies.[226] The Government countered with a position that "the current climate" made it necessary for fees to be charged.[227] However, having been faced with sustained criticism and well organised campaign by journalists and civil society organisations, the amendment, along with the upfront €15 application fee, were ultimately withdrawn by the Government in July 2014, a move that was widely approved.[228]

The explanatory memorandum to the 2013 Bill also stated that: [3–115]

> "The review of FOI which is ongoing is considering options for a reform of the search and retrieval fees regime which is not believed to operate properly or on a consistent basis across FOI bodies."[229]

The legislation now provides that the first five hours of a search are free and imposes a fee ceiling of €500 on a single request.[230] An upper limit of €700 also applies, above which a public body may refuse to process a request, though this is contingent upon the body co-operating with the requester to limit or break up their request for information. The FOI body may also decide to process a request which totals more than €700, though in such circumstances the requester may pay the full amount over the €500 cap.

---

carried out by different functional areas of the FOI body, the head of the FOI body concerned shall treat each part of the request as a separate FOI request. The requester shall be required to pay a further fee for each separate request under this paragraph, or the requester shall pay the fee for whichever request or requests he or she may specify or modify the request so that no further fee is payable."

[226] M Cooper, "Additional freedom of information charges would have cost us all dearly", *Irish Examiner*, 15 November 2013. Available online at http://www.irishexaminer.com/viewpoints/columnists/matt-cooper/additional-freedom-of-information-charges-would-have-cost-us-all-dearly-249696.html (date accessed 16 December 2013).

[227] "Minister Brendan Howlin describes FOI fee as a "token charge", *The Journal*, 12 November 2013, http://www.thejournal.ie/foi-bill-ireland-2-1172335-Nov2013/ (date accessed 16 December 2013).

[228] M Minihan, "Cabinet abolishes €15 Freedom of Information fee" *The Irish Times*, 1 July 2014.

[229] Explanatory memorandum Freedom of Information Bill. Available online at http://per.gov.ie/wp-content/uploads/FOI-Bill-2013-expl-memo.pdf (date accessed 16 December 2013).

[230] See s 27(3) of the 2014 Act. s 27(12) lays out the procedure for handling requests for information which would attract a fee of over €700.

Conclusion

[3–116]   It is generally acknowledged that the introduction of the 1997 Freedom of Information Act was a "watershed moment for the development of modern Ireland" indicating as it did a "commitment to openness and transparency" and a movement away from the deeply rooted tradition of secrecy.[231] As we have highlighted in this chapter, many public bodies have, in large part, integrated FOI into their activities and if not enthusiastically embracing transparency, have at least adopted new and more open practices.

[3–117]   However, the mere creation of legislation will not secure the effective functioning of a freedom of information system without adequate resources to ensure its day to day operation and a positive recognition of its value by both public officials and the general public alike. Regardless of cost, politicians and public servants often hold two key objections to the system. Firstly, as expressed by Tony Blair earlier in this chapter, the idea that freedom of information is used not to liberate citizens from secrecy but by journalists to punish those in power. This belief is fundamentally incorrect, with the reality being that by far the majority of FOI requests relate to personal information. In addition, while journalist and opposition politicians do make good use of the system, their motivations are by and largely primarily the exposure of problems. As we have noted above regarding cost, the governance benefits of freedom of information are often left uncalculated, with departmental actors fixating upon the direct staffing and administrative costs.

[3–118]   Secondly, there is the claim that only confidentiality will ensure effective decision-making — a suggestion that Justice Brandeis was incorrect when he wrote that

> "Publicity is justly commended as a remedy for social and industrial diseases. Sunlight is said to be the best of disinfectants; electric light the most efficient policeman."[232]

Again, this view does not hold up to scrutiny. Although it is clear that some information will not be written down under an FOI system, it remains the case that the systems of exemptions and balancing of competing interests

---

[231] Felle & Adshed above n 22 at p 17.

[232] Louis D Brandeis, *Other People's Money and How The Bankers Use It* (Martino Publishing, Eastford, 2009 (1932)) at p 92.

under FOI regimes offers strong protection for sensitive information protecting it from damaging disclosure.

Overall FOI is for the most part a positive, but ultimately relatively modest step towards transparency. However, FOI needs to be underpinned also by a modernisation of information systems. A key problem with progressing transparency in Ireland has been the ongoing poor record keeping and failure to engage with effective, integrated information management systems. The current economic climate will only result in a continued failure to systematically and strategically take up ICT developments.

[3–119]

Beyond that, a wider understanding of openness includes an adoption of an "open data" policy such as has been adopted by the Australian Government which provides a single location for the sharing of information related to public services.[233] The presumption is one of proactive information sharing, rather than waiting for information to be requested. For example, it would be normal within such a system to publish school inspection reports, something that is currently not permitted in Ireland even under the FOI regime. This requires not merely a grudging acceptance of sharing some information, but a positive engagement with the idea that the public should have access to large areas of information held by the public sector. To date we remain a long way from the shift, which as the Emily O'Reilly, the former Information Commissioner, noted

[3–120]

> "lies precisely in Governments seeing and harnessing the value of the proper collection and re-use of their data to improve the quality of life of all of those they govern."[234]

Ultimately FOI should become less central to accessing mainstream information as a culture of openness develops across the state. Its significance in the longer term is therefore in retrieving the information Government is less keen to share. Seen in this way FOI should not be regarded as a costly administrative burden but valued as an important cultural change in the public sector that supports accountability and transparency in conjunction with other core administrative justice mechanisms.

---

[233] See http://data.gov.au/ which is the Australian Government's data access website designed to "encourage public access to and reuse of Government data by providing it in useful formats under open licences."

[234] O'Reilly, above n 212.

CHAPTER FOUR

THE OMBUDSMAN AND ADMINISTRATIVE JUSTICE

Introduction

The institution of the Ombudsman enjoys a prominent place across the globe and has been employed as a core element of constitutional design, of legislative enforcement and in securing governmental accountability. The Ombudsman "brand" has been applied to both the public and private sectors, across a variety of thematic areas, in Ireland and the rest of the world. Common to all these schemes are its role in investigation and in providing a flexible and informal system of redress against public and private bodies. As indicated by these functions, its defining characteristic has been taken to be independence from those who it investigates.

[4–01]

When focussing upon the creation and functioning of Ombudsmen in Ireland, specific issues begin to emerge, many of which reflect overall regulatory philosophies in the Irish public sector and the State's constitutional order.[1] Throughout this chapter we will focus largely upon the main instance of ombudsmanry in Ireland — the Office of the Ombudsman — rather than other instances such as the Children's Ombudsman or private sector oriented applications of the concept.[2] In terms of Ireland's public sector, the prevalence of clientelism[3] had, historically, the potential to negate calls for the foundation of the Ombudsman and, more broadly, the need for dispute resolution procedures outside the courts. The potential for this was most directly witnessed in a speech by then Minister Charles Haughey in 1966:

[4–02]

> "Ireland is a small compact community. There is hardly anyone without a direct personal link with someone, be he Minister, T.D., clergyman, county or borough councillor or trade union official, who will interest himself in helping a citizen to have a grievance examined and, if

---

[1] Readers should note that some elements of this chapter were featured in F Donson and D O'Donovan, "Critical Junctures: Regulatory Failures, Ireland's Administrative State and the Office of the Ombudsman" (2014) *Public Law* 472.

[2] For an overview of the Financial Services Ombudsman see D Boyle, *Financial Services Ombudsman – An Overview* (2005) 23 ILT. The Office is enshrined legislatively in the Central Bank and Financial Services Authority of Ireland Act 2004—s 16 and schedules 6 and 7, and empowers the Ombudsman to act as an independent statutory officer, to arbitrate unresolved complaints from consumers of financial services. This superceded previously existing voluntary Ombudsman schemes within the banking and insurance industry.

[3] For a modern study of clientelism in Irish political life see Richard Sinnott, Niall O'Reilly, Sarah Jane Delany, *The extent of clientelism in Irish politics: Evidence from classifying Dáil questions on a local-national dimension. Proceedings of 21st Irish Conference on Artificial Intelligence and Cognitive Science*. Available at http://arrow.dit.ie/dmccon/31 (date accessed 9 October 2014).

possible, remedied....The basic reason therefore why we do not need an
official Ombudsman is because we already have so many unofficial but
nevertheless effective ones."[4]

[4–03] Professor John Kelly expressed disappointment that this statement could
be made by a senior Minister promoting as it did "the primitive system of
clientship and patronage". He noted that

> "This phenomenon was, in the distant past, a sure sign of a society
> where a weak man had no hope of justice without the aid of a strong
> one, and its general replacement in civilised countries by a regular,
> strong, and impartial process of law is a major social milestone."[5]

While this mindset has receded over time the underlying philosophies of
the Ombudsman were always likely to bring it into collision with some of
the traditional orientations of the Irish political culture.

[4–04] In this chapter, we will outline not just the day-to-day running and
legislative underpinnings of the institution, but also seek to locate it
within the broader context of the Irish system of parliamentary democracy
and the separation of powers. This reflects the growing tendency
internationally to regard the ombudsman as an essential supplement to
the classical branches of judiciary, legislature and executive. While
traditional accounts often reductively focus on the Ombudsman as a
form of alternative dispute resolution, we attempt to supplement this
with a consideration of its broader role as a public institution in producing
systematic standards of good governance and administration and in
aiding fundamental democratic oversight by the people, the parliament
and the executive in monitoring the implementation of legislation and
related administrative practice. This underlying purpose ideally secures
the "horizontal accountability" of un-elected officials, which in turn
leads to more concentrated democratic engagement with the intricacies

---

[4] The speech was to have been delivered by Finance Minister Charles Haughey to the
Solicitors' Apprentices Debating Society but was eventually given by the Secretary to the
Department of Finance TK Whitaker after Mr Haughey was unable to attend. "We do
not need an Ombudsman says Whitaker: T.D.s extremely assiduous" *The Irish Times*, 12
November 1966, 11. The delivery of a speech with a strong political element led to criticism
in the Dáil and rumours that TK Whitaker had later resigned because of a disagreement
between him and than Minister Haughey, 225 *Dáil Debates* Col 1123 (16 November 1966).

[5] As quoted by then Ombudsman, Emily O'Reilly at the Free Legal Advice Centres 2006
Conference, *Public Interest Law in Ireland – the Reality and the Potential*, Available at http://
www.flac.ie/download/pdf/flac_pil_proceedings_final.pdf (date accessed 8 October 2012).

of ever more bureaucratic and technocratic forms of modern administration. This has led some academic commentators to regard the Ombudsman as part of a reinvigorated doctrine of the separation of powers, which embraces an "integrity branch" to combat the gaps and inertia produced by traditional judiciary-executive-legislature divisions.[6]

The Ombudsman in Ireland: Legislative Underpinnings and History

The commonly understood origin of the Ombudsman institution is from the Swedish *Justitieombudsman* established in 1809. It was initially copied regionally[7] and then expanded globally.[8] As will be explored in the Irish context, while unities of nomenclature exist, many Ombudsmen remain oriented towards differing emphases, with some jurisdictions emerging from constitutional turmoil relying upon the office for human rights protection, others have sought to employ the institution to improve accessibility to justice. This flexibility and constitutional adaptability should demand reflection on the institution within the broader context of renewing Ireland's constitutionalism after recent failures of regulatory oversight. Within this spectrum, the Office of the Ombudsman in Ireland has combined a number of prominent functions:

[4–05]

- Standard setting for the civil service;
- Investigation power;
- Alternative dispute resolution between complainants and public sector bodies.

The Ombudsman thus plays an important and *distinctive* role in the Irish legal system — a body that is mandated to overcome the inaction that may result from the strict formalism of the doctrine of the separation of powers.

[4–06]

---

[6] The term "integrity branch" was first used by Professor Bruce Ackerman in the context of the US Constitution. See B Ackerman, "The New Separation of Powers" (2000) 113(3) *Harvard Law Review* 633 at pp 694-696.

[7] Danish Constitution 1953 incorporated an equivalent — an *Ombudsmand*, while Germany used similar techniques in a specified sector through the creation of an ombudsman for military affairs in 1954.

[8] Thus, it was established in New Zealand 1962 through the Parliamentary Commissioner (Ombudsman) Act 1962. That country established the first industry Ombudsman, the Banking Ombudsman, in 1992. The UK first created an Ombudsman office in 1967 with the establishment of the Parliamentary Commissioner for Administration 1967—Parliamentary Commissioner Act 1967.

The ability to supplement the separate spheres of legislative-executive-judiciary, and mediate engagement rather than inaction, is of critical import to the postmodern bureaucratic State.[9]

[4–07] The history of the Ombudsman in Ireland begins with the consideration of the system of administrative justice in the formative Devlin Report (Public Services Organisation Review Group) 1969.[10] The sub-group which considered this issue identified the possibility of establishing a *Commissioner for Administrative Justice*, but did not make an express recommendation for an Ombudsman to be created. The Committee regarded such a body as not matching the country's administrative tradition, which reflected the prevalent fear at that time that Ministerial authority and accountability over departmental affairs would be diluted.[11]

[4–08] However, as the Ombudsman model became more established globally during the 1970s, the idea also started to gain ground in Ireland. In 1977, an All-Party Committee on Administrative Justice[12] recommended the establishment of an Ombudsman. The drafting of the legislation began under a Fine Gael/Labour Party coalition Government but power quickly changed hands. In power, Fianna Fáil was less than enthusiastic about creating an Ombudsman, and thus, although the Ombudsman Act was passed in 1980, it was not activated until 1983 when a Fine Gael/Labour Party coalition returned to power. The legislation finally came into force in 1984 with Mr Michael Mills, a journalist, becoming the first occupant of the post.

[4–09] These underlying political tensions provide a background to the serious disjuncture between the original legislative framework and today's Ombudsman. The body was focused initially only upon central civil service administration — with jurisdiction over local authorities, State sponsored bodies and health boards only being earned in future years. Investigation of police and prison service functions, as well as clinical

---

[9] A Tran and A Stuhmcke "The Commonwealth Ombudsman: An integrity branch of Government?" 32(4) *Alternative Law Journal* 195 (2007) 233.

[10] Devlin Report, *Report of the Public Services Organisation Review Group*, (The Stationery Office, Dublin, 1969) (Prl. 792).

[11] The Review Group's preferred approach was to widen in-house semi-independent appeals and give the Commissioner a general oversight role over these, however, it was never adopted.

[12] This was established in response to a private members motion on the issue in the Dáil.

judgments in hospitals were excluded, reflecting a mistrust of the Office, despite long established international comparators.

This initial mistrust was also reflected by two early crises for the office.   **[4–10]** Firstly, when Fianna Fáil returned to office in 1987 it set about dramatically reducing the budget of the Ombudsman Office as part of wider public sector funding cuts.[13] For Michael Mills,[14] it was clear that the budget reduction was a political attack on the Office of the Ombudsman. Indeed, he wrote a special report to the Oireachtas attesting to the fact that further budget cuts would lead to the closure of the office.[15] Although the budget situation was resolved when the Department of Finance undertook a review of the financing of the Office,[16] a second crisis arose as the six-year term of Michael Mills drew to a close later in 1989. Only on the last day before the Dáil rose for the Christmas break did the Minister for Finance recommend that Mr Mills' appointment be extended for a second term. Had they failed to do this, his appointment would have lapsed at the start of 1990 and he would have been too old to fit within the legislative criteria for a new appointment.[17]

The resilience of the Ombudsman during these early years may   **[4–11]** ultimately be traced to a number of legislative provisions that enhanced the security and independence of the office. Appointment to the post is made by the President following the passage of a resolution recommending an individual by both the Dáil and the Seanad.[18] The term of office is six years,[19] though the Ombudsman may request that he or she be relieved of his or her post by the President. The President may

---

[13] In 1987 the office's budget was cut by 20% (IR£100,000) resulting in a loss of five staff members. In 1988, the cut was repeated — IR£100,000 removed from the budget with another five officers lost.

[14] M Mills, *Hurler on the Ditch: Memoir of a Journalist who Became Ireland's First Ombudsman*, (Currach Press, Dublin, 2006) at pp 142-47, hereinafter "Mills".

[15] Referenced in Mills, *ibid* at p 145. s 6(7) Ombudsman Act empowers the Ombudsman to submit a report to the Oireachtas with respect to the Offices functions.

[16] The review was announced by Minister for Finance, Ray MacSharry 382 *Dáil Deb.* col. 1797 (24 June 1988).

[17] The Ombudsman Act s 2(7) states that "A person shall be not more than 61 years of age upon first being appointed to the office of Ombudsman". See discussion of the incident in Mills, above n 14 at pp 147-50.

[18] Ombudsman Act 1980, s 2(2).

[19] *ibid*, s 2(4).

remove the Ombudsman, but only for stated misbehaviour, incapacity[20] or bankruptcy. Removal requires a supporting resolution passed by both Houses of the Oireachtas.[21] Section 4(1) of the Act enshrines as a general principle that "[t]he Ombudsman shall be independent in the performance of his functions".

[4–12]   The Ombudsman (Amendment) Act 2012 added an additional element to the appointment process whereby the appointment includes a hearing by an Oireachtas Committee.[22] Thus, when a new Ombudsman was being sought in 2013, the nominated candidate — Peter Tyndall — was referred to the Public Services Oversight and Petitions Committee prior to formal appointment.

Reviewing Maladministration

[4–13]   The first foundational question to consider in assessing the effectiveness and constitutional position of an Ombudsman is the yardstick that he or she is mandated to apply in investigating or hearing complaints. In Ireland this was defined in s 4(2) of the 1980 Act. This lists seven grounds for finding a "defect" in an administrative decision, namely where it is:

- Taken without proper authority (*ultra vires*);
- Taken on irrelevant grounds;
- The result of negligence or carelessness;
- Based on erroneous or irrelevant considerations;
- Improperly discriminatory (this was later linked with the Equal Status Act 2000);
- Based on undesirable administrative practice;
- Otherwise contrary to sound or fair administration.

[4–14]   There is, therefore, no definition of a defect. The legislation makes no reference to maladministration, as would be found in other jurisdictions, but as Hogan and Morgan note, the list covers the types of errors "that might be seen to fall into that wider category".[23] It should also be noted that

---

[20] Under current provisions he or she must vacate the office upon reaching 67 years of age.

[21] Ombudsman Act 1980, s 2(3)(b).

[22] s 2(2A) Ombudsman Act 1980, as amended by Ombudsman (Amendment) Act 2012.

[23] G Hogan and DG Morgan, *Administrative Law in Ireland*, (4th ed) (Round Hall, Dublin, 2010) at p 400, hereinafter "Hogan and Morgan".

the Ombudsman has proved to have a wide, implicit discretion as to the meaning and application of these grounds.

This echoes a feature of the initial Ombudsman creating legislation — the Parliamentary Commissioner Act 1967 — in the United Kingdom. While maladministration did appear in that Act (s 5(1)), it was not defined. The debate on the Bill within the House of Commons, however, featured a contribution by the Leader of the House of Commons, Richard Crossman, which became known as the "Crossman catalogue":   **[4–15]**

> "A positive definition of maladministration is far more difficult to achieve. We might have made an attempt in this Clause to define ... all the qualities which make up maladministration.... It would be a wonderful exercise – bias, neglect, inattention, delay, incompetence, inaptitude, perversity, turpitude, arbitratiness and so on. It would be a long and interesting list."[24]

Crossman ultimately concluded that the meaning of maladministration would be filled out organically by case-work. Thus, though his enumerated examples grew into conventional indicia, it was possible for Sir William Reid, in his 1993 Annual Report of the Ombudsman, to argue for a progressive interpretation of the idea of maladministration, to further include: **[4–16]**

> "...unwillingness to treat the complainant as a person with rights; refusal to answer reasonable questions; knowingly giving advice which is misleading or inadequate; offering no redress or manifestly disproportionate redress; and partiality."[25]

Maladministration therefore runs the spectrum from near duplication of judicial review[26] to more open-textured concepts of good governance of administration. The latter have been further elucidated by the   **[4–17]**

---

[24] HC Deb 18 October 1966, vol 734, col 51. Available online at http://hansard. millbanksystems.com/commons/1966/oct/18/parliamentary-commissioner-bill (date accessed 2 November 2012).

[25] Parliamentary Commissioner for Administration, "Third Report 1993-94", (HMSO, London, 1994). Mr Reid underlined the need for openness: "To define maladministration is to limit it. Such a limitation could work to the disadvantage of individual complainants with justified grievances which did not fit within a given definition." at para 7.

[26] These would include grounds such as *ultra vires* and review related to the control of discretionary powers including the taking into account irrelevant considerations and improper purpose. Their inclusion is justified on the basis that the complainant can have such errors addressed without the high cost of proceeding to court.

Ombudsman in *The Ombudsman's Guide to Best Practice for Public Servants.*[27] The guide consists of a checklist and provides that the public should be dealt with "properly, fairly and impartially". This striving for a development and understanding of good administration is a component of many Ombudsman Offices.[28]

[4–18] Though we see a tradition of openness and pragmatism in both the Irish and UK approaches, a broader question remains: the interaction of the Ombudsman's investigation power with the courts. Grounds for review by the Ombudsman often coincide with those of judicial review, so how distinct are the concepts of unreasonableness, for example, applied in the different fora? This issue arose for the Irish Office in the context of the *Redress for Taxpayers Special Report* where the Ombudsman defended the added value of her report despite the availability of judicial review. Responding to the possible interaction of her role with that of the courts, the Ombudsman noted that:

> "I must make my own decisions about what is "contrary to fair or sound administration" having regard to the general principles developed by the Irish courts as well as by, for example, the Court of Justice of the European Communities and the European Court of Human Rights. I also take into account the various principles of good administration developed by international bodies such as the Council of Europe which the State has accepted even though they may not be enshrined in domestic statutory law. These principles would, in any event, be most unlikely to conflict with any similar principles developed by the Irish courts. As Ombudsman, I am not therefore, precluded from developing incrementally, and on a case by case basis, rules of good practice the infringement of which by public bodies would be "contrary to fair or

---

[27] First published in the Ombudsman's 1996 Annual Report, an updated version was included in the 2002 Annual Report. Available online at http://www.ombudsman.gov.ie/en/Publications/Guidelines-for-Public-Bodies/The-Ombudsman's-Guide-to-Standards-of-Best-Practice-for-Public-Servants/ (date accessed 13 July 2014).

[28] For example the Parliamentary and Health Service Ombudsman in the UK published its *Principles of Good Administration* in 2007 after a public consultation process. In that document it was concluded that good administration "means 1. Getting it right, 2. Being customer focused, 3. Being open and accountable, 4. Acting fairly and proportionately, 5. Putting things right, and 6. Seeking continuous improvement." (PHSO 0188, London, 2009) Available online: http://www.ombudsman.org.uk/__data/assets/pdf_file/0013/1039/0188-Principles-of-Good-Administration-bookletweb.pdf (date accessed 3 November 2014).

sound administration", subject, of course to the avoidance of conflict with the courts."[29]

The Ombudsman clearly has more scope than a court to review the merits of a complaint, and has generally been willing "to push the boat out".[30] The statement above clearly reflects the fact that an Ombudsman can, and will, go further to expand the concept of maladministration.

Furthermore, the Ombudsman is able to animate areas in which administrative law has traditionally been deferential or non-invasive, such as in supervising discretionary judgments. For example, in making findings in relation to the Revenue Commissioners operating procedures, the Ombudsman has relied on the organisation's own internal best practices, stressing the importance of the Fifth Report of the Commission on Taxation 1985[31] to her work. In this Report, all relevant actors accepted the discretionary nature of the Revenue Commissioners' role in applying the relevant law, but also placed a general administrative duty of "care and management" to mitigate hardship upon the organisation. This received legislative recognition in s 849 of the Taxes Consolidation Act 1997, and is applied constructively and broadly by the Office of the Ombudsman in its deliberations.

[4–19]

The interplay between fair administration and human rights protections should also be noted as a significant and growing development in the area of Ombusmanry generally. Thus, the Council of Europe Human Rights Commissioner, Thomas Hammarberg, has exhorted national ombudsman institutions throughout Europe to work in partnership with their respective national human rights institutions as part of the "national human rights structures". The Commissioner has since been even more emphatic, describing ombudsmen as "the principal defenders of human rights", an "extra-judicial mechanism" guaranteeing independent

[4–20]

---

[29] Office of the Ombudsman, *Redress for Taxpayers (Special Report)* (Office of the Ombudsman, Dublin, 2002) at p 8. Available online: http://www.ombudsman.gov.ie/en/Publications/Investigation-Reports/Government-Departments-other-Public-bodies/Redress-for-Taxpayers-Special-Report-/ (date accessed 3 November 2012)

[30] A phrase used by Michael Mills in his reports in the early days of the Ombudsman Office. See Hogan and Morgan, above n 23 at p 401.

[31] Commission on Taxation, *Fifth Report of the Commission on Taxation* (Stationary Office, Dublin, 1985).

scrutiny and, in consequence, deserving enhanced encouragement and protection.[32]

[4–21]   Whilst the Ombudsman in this jurisdiction has been circumspect in the use of rights language, the values clearly come through the reports published by the Office.[33] Thus, in the Annual Report of 2000 the Ombudsman laid out the "background rights" that underlie the decision making powers of public bodies noted five "core values governing the state/citizen relationship [namely] the need to uphold the autonomy, dignity, respect, status and security of individuals".[34] The role of such values was noted as particularly significant as the public sector developed "a human rights approach to service provision",[35] and thus as human rights became internalised by the civil service itself the Ombudsman could claim a mandate for their use as legitimate expectation of the citizen. Finally, it is clear that the Ombudsman, as an organ of the state[36] is required to discharge its statutory duties and functions in a manner that is compatible with the requirements of the European Convention on Human Rights.

---

[32] T Hammarberg, *'Ombudsmen are Key Defenders of Human Rights – their independence must be respected'*, Viewpoint, published on 18 September 2006, Available at http://www.coe. int/t/commissioner/viewpoints/060918_en.asp (date accessed 9 October 2012). These exhortations followed a Council of Europe Assembly resolution in 2003 encouraging ombudsmen to become more actively engaged in human rights disputes: Parliamentary Assembly of the Council of Europe, Recommendation 1615 *adopted* on 8 September 2003. The resolution anticipated the recommendations of a report commissioned by the Secretary General of the Council of Europe and the President of the European Court of Human Rights on how to deal more efficiently with the unmanageable workload of the Court.

[33] Emily O'Reilly, as Ombudsman, provided the most structured reflection on the relationship between maladministration and human rights law in a 2007 speech to the British and Irish Ombudsman Association, available at: http://www. ombudsmanassociation.org/docs/HumanRightsOmbudsmanEmilyOReilly.pdf (date accessed 13 July 2014):

...Human rights are the legitimate business of an Ombudsman. This does not in any sense challenge the legitimate and vital role of other institutions in the vindication of human rights but, rather, suggests that the value system protected by international human rights norms binding states are perfectly reconcilable with the formal legal remit of an Ombudsman.

[34] Office of the Ombudsman, *Annual Report of the Ombudsman, 2000* (Office of the Ombudsman, Dublin, 2001), chapter 3, at p 13, quoting D Oliver in "The Underlying Values of Public and Private Law" in M Taggart (ed.) *The Province of Administrative Law* (Hart Publishing, Oxford, 1997).

[35] *ibid.*

[36] As defined by s 3 of the European Convention on Human Rights Act 2003.

Can the Ombudsman Review Law?

The shading of the Ombudsman Act standards from a legal through to an [4–22] administrative fairness orientation has been the source of tension between Government departments and the Office of the Ombudsman. In a 1997 Report issued following her investigation of three complaints involving late claims for contributory pensions, the Ombudsman noted that the Department of Finance's response to all communications "at all stages has been to say that the impugned decisions are taken in accordance with the law".[37] The Ombudsman noted that these submissions relied upon inferences from the civil service that "it is not open to the Ombudsman to be critical of decisions taken in accordance with law".[38] Section 4 however, is quite clear that the grounds can be applied independently of one another, thus as the report noted, "it is possible for an action to be taken with 'proper authority' but would ... be found to be 'contrary to fair and sound administration'".[39] The situation is slightly more complicated with regard to the ability of the Ombudsman to recommend redress in cases where the challenged decisions were prescribed by law. In a case where the relevant statutory arrangements provided the public body with no discretion or flexibility regarding redress, the Ombudsman has taken the position that its Annual Reports should draw the attention of the Minister and the Oireachtas "to the need to amend the law which was producing effects which were contrary to fair or sound administration".[40]

In the case of late claims for contributory pensions by insured people, the [4–23] Department had argued that it had no discretion, unless the Department itself was at fault for the delay. The relevant time limit for making claims had been laid down by Ministerial regulation. Nevertheless, the Ombudsman proceeded with the investigation. Firstly, this was due to the failure of the Department to take any action in relation to the issue which had been ongoing over an extended period of time — and because the

---

[37] Office of the Ombudsman, *Investigatory Report on the non-payment of arrears of contributory pensions*, para 12. Available at: http://www.ombudsman.gov.ie/en/Publications/Investigation-Reports/Government-Departments-other-Public-bodies/Investigation-Report-on-the-non-payment-of-arrears-of-contributory-pensions/Ombudsman's-Powers-and-Jurisdiction.html (date accessed 12 October 2012), hereinafter "Pensions report".

[38] *ibid* at para 12.

[39] *ibid* at para 13.

[40] *ibid*.

Ombudsman's Office had been receiving high numbers of complaints annually regarding the matter. Secondly, on the jurisdictional issue, the Ombudsman noted that s 4(2) of the Ombudsman Act 1980 referred to actions "taken in the performance of administrative functions", not enquiring into legislative actions. She defined a legislative action as "the making of a law; it is not the application of that law to individual cases or categories of cases".[41] Consequently, in responding to the question of whether she could "criticise in an investigation report the particular provisions of statutory regulations?" she concluded that she could certainly consider whether the regulations were *ultra vires* the primary legislation, as these would be "without proper authority." In relation to cases where the regulations were *intra vires* the Ombudsman also found that she could criticise regulations that were producing an adverse, i.e. unfair and unreasonable, effect where the result was "contrary to fair or sound administration".

[4–24] The Office of the Ombudsman included, in an appendix to the Pensions Report, a legal argument in favour of the appropriateness of it making redress recommendations which call for the amendment of regulations. The opinion argued that while traditionally statutory instruments are regarded as secondary legislation and their contents therefore, as a "law-making" event, "this may be an incomplete description".[42] Article 15.2.1° of Bunreacht na hÉireann confers "sole and exclusive power of making laws" upon the Oireachtas.[43] Regulations therefore are called into existence only by the primary Act, and the Minister may not therefore be a law-maker as such, particularly as the power to make a regulation is no more than the power to put into effect the Oireachtas' principles and policies.[44] The Minister is further bound by an obligation to act "with

---

[41] *ibid.*

[42] *ibid*, Appendix 2 – The Administrative Nature of Statutory Instruments.

[43] Art 15.2.1° states:

   1   The sole and exclusive power of making laws for the State is hereby vested in the Oireachtas: no other legislative authority has power to make laws for the State.

   2   Provision may however be made by law for the creation or recognition of subordinate legislatures and for the powers and functions of these legislatures.

[44] Pension Report, above n 37, Appendix 2. Where these principles and policies are not present to guide Ministerial discretion then the delegation of power by the Oireachtas is likely to be unconstitutional. The Supreme Court in *Cityview Press Ltd. v An Comhairle Oiliúna* [1980] IR 381 clearly laid out the test regarding "principles and policies" when it held that:

"the ultimate responsibility rests with the Courts to ensure that constitutional safeguards remain, and that the exclusive authority of the National Parliament in

basic fairness, reasonableness and good faith". The opinion then moves to note the argument of Wade that delegated legislation is a mixed action of both administrative and legislative functions.[45] To take away the power of recommending amendment from the Ombudsman would, regardless of the conceptual debate, have the effect of diminishing to ability to engage with entrenched, regulation-facilitated unfairness.[46] In the Irish context, such a role is, in our view, compatible with the overall purpose of the Ombudsman. As part of the "integrity branch", the Ombudsman, as an agent directly responsive to the people, can concentrate and mediate democratic oversight over technocratic instruments that are usually simply laid before the Dáil without any motion.[47] Ultimately with respect to the contributory pension

---

the field of law-making is not eroded by a delegation of power which is neither contemplated or permitted by the Constitution. In discharging that responsibility, the Courts will have regard to where and by what authority the law in question purports to have been made. In the view of this Court, the test is whether that which is challenged as an unauthorised delegation of parliamentary power is more than a mere giving effect to principles and policies which are contained in the statute itself If it be, then it is not authorised; for such would constitute a purported exercise of legislative power by an authority which is not permitted to do so under the Constitution. On the other hand, if it be within the permitted limits - if the law is laid down in the statute and details only are filled in or completed by the designated Minister or subordinate body - there is no unauthorised delegation of legislative power." (O'Higgins CJ at 398-9)

[45] W Wade and CF Forsyth, *Administrative Law*, (10th ed) (Oxford University Press, Oxford, 2009) at p 731 –

"there is only a hazy borderline between legislation and administration, and the assumption that they are two fundamentally different forms of power is misleading". There is a broader discussion of the democratic nature of regulations at 857-904. In the United Kingdom, the Parliamentary Commissioner was encouraged by the Standing Committee in Parliament to regard the content and potential amendment of regulations as within his jurisdiction.

[46] As Wade notes in the 5th edition of his *Administrative Law* book such unfairness is arguably more serious and systematic than errors in individualised discretion: "what was administration if done once apparently ceased to be so if done repeatedly under a rule". The UK Commissioner, he noted, had parked these "conceptual controversies" and treated maladministration "as any action or inaction by Government Departments which he feels ought to be criticised, including anything which is unreasonable, unjust or oppressive". W Wade, *Administrative Law*, (5th ed) (Oxford University Press, Oxford, 1982) at p 733.

[47] There is little legal authority on the impact of a failure to lay a statutory instrument before the Oireachtas. Historically there was limited authority to the effect that such a failure would not invalidate the legislation. However, Hogan and Morgan note that Houses of the Oireachtas (Laying of Documents) Act 1966, which requires statutory instruments to be laid before the houses of the Oireachtas within 21 sitting days was designed to enable the Houses to examine the delegated legislation with a view to possible annulment, and so the laying requirement might now be viewed as more "mandatory" than "discretionary". Hogan and Morgan, above n 23 at p 37.

investigation, the Ombudsman discovered that the Minister had substantial extra statutory discretion in the processing of claims, which obviated "the need to take a position on the legal standing of Ministerial regulations".

Bodies Subject to Review

[4–25]   The second plank of the jurisdiction of the Office refers to object-body jurisdiction: which public bodies fall inside and outside its purview? Since its creation, the number of bodies covered by the Ombudsman had remained largely stable, covering the Civil Service, local authorities, the public health services[48] and An Post. This was despite the fact that a need to expand and track the institutional creep within civil service structures had been reflected in draft legislation which proposed additional bodies be brought within the jurisdiction of the Ombudsman. These attempts at reform were first brought forward in 1985 and were thereafter regularly proposed,[49] however over time the need for reform had become more and more significant. In this regard, the Ombudsman had stressed the findings of an OECD report which had found that the reliance of the Irish State on semi-State agencies had "decreased the overall accountability of the public service while increasing fragmentation and complexity".[50]

[4–26]   In late 2012 the Ombudsman (Amendment) Act was finally piloted through the Oireachtas. This amending legislation implemented a major expansion of the jurisdiction of the office, adding over one hundred further named State agencies.[51] In addition to these named bodies the legislation also allows for the automatic inclusion of all public bodies, except those specifically excluded. As noted above, this expansion of jurisdiction cannot be regarded as necessarily proactive, as there has been a long established trend towards the creation of single-purpose

---

[48] Note the public voluntary hospitals were only added in 2007.

[49] A fact noted in the Office of the Ombudsman Annual Report 2011, Office of the Ombudsman, *Annual Report of the Ombudsman, 2011* (Office of the Ombudsman, Dublin, 2012), hereinafter "Ombudsman 2011 Report".

[50] OECD Report Ireland: Towards an Integrated Public Service, Published 6th June 2008, Available at http://www.oecd.org/gov/oecdpublicmanagementreviews-irelandtowar dsanintegratedpublicservice.htm (date accessed 9 October 2014). Cited in *Maintaining the accountability of a fast changing public service, The Irish Times,* 11 July 2008.

[51] Bodies within jurisdiction now include the Court Service, FÁS, third level institutions of education, the National Roads Authority and Vocational Education Committees.

agencies by Government, which had been recognised in the scope of the Freedom of Information Acts. The legislation is therefore an attempt to catch up with the expansion of semi-State bodies.

It should also be noted that the Ombudsman's jurisdiction remains **[4–27]** excluded in a number of instances. Firstly, not all public bodies are to be included with the remit of the Ombudsman, even after reform. Thus, commercial semi-State bodies[52] and regulatory bodies of a highly specialised nature[53] are not included; nor are decisions by independent complaint handling bodies.[54] In addition, the Ombudsman has no jurisdiction in cases where:

- The matter is, or has been, before the courts[55];
- Where the potential complainant has a statutory right of appeal to the courts[56];
- Where there is a right of appeal to an independent appeal body.[57]

These three exclusions are, however, subject to a further provision **[4–28]** allowing the Ombudsman to proceed with the investigation "where special circumstances make it proper to do so". The remaining exclusions are:

- Where the complaint is made outside the time limit, which is twelve months from the time of the action or the time when the complainant first became aware of the action, whichever is later[58];
- Complaints which relate to recruitment or terms and conditions of employment[59];
- Complaints relating to or affecting the terms or conditions of a contract for services[60];

---

[52] For example Aer Lingus and the newly created Irish Water. See N Baker, "Ombudsman: I should be able to receive Irish Water Complaints", *Irish Examiner*, 2 October 2014.
[53] For example the Commission for Aviation Regulation.
[54] For example the Office of the Ombudsman for Children.
[55] s 5(1)(a)(i).
[56] s 5(1)(a)(ii).
[57] s 5(1)(a)(iii).
[58] s 5(1)(f).
[59] s 5(1)(c).
[60] s 5(1)(d)(ii).

- Complaints relating to or affecting the terms or conditions upon and subject to which pensions, gratuities or other superannuation benefits are payable[61];
- Complaints regarding the administration of the law relating aliens and naturalisation procedures,[62] the administration of prisons, the actions of An Garda Síochána, actions which relate to national security or an action of the Defence Forces[63];
- Complaints concerning pardon or remission of prison sentences and other court penalties[64];
- Complaints regarding The Health Services Executive, from January 2007, go through a statutory complaints procedure. Unresolved complaints examined under this procedure can thereafter be referred to the Ombudsman.[65]

[4–29]   A notable consequence of the above exclusions has been that the Department of Justice has succeeded in remaining outside the Ombudsman's purview, a practice not mirrored in a large number of comparative jurisdictions. The Ombudsman (Amendment) Act 2012 continues this exclusion. In two key areas there has been some promise of the development of alternative complaint mechanisms, thus a new complaints system for prisoners is being developed[66] and a new statutory appeals system was promised under the Immigration, Residence and Protection Bill 2010. However, as the Ombudsman has made clear, the

---

[61] s 5(1)(d)(i).

[62] The exclusion of matters relating to immigration and residence has been highlighted as a major concern by the Ombudsman particularly because the Office receives high numbers of complaints in relation to these matters yet is prevented from investigating them despite being able to offer "an accessible cost free alternative to the courts". Office of the Ombudsman, *Submission to the Joint Committee on Justice, Equality, Defence and Women, Rights - Immigration, Residence and Protection Bill 2008* (2005). Available at: http://www.oireachtas. ie/documents/committees30thdail/j-justiceedwr/reports_2008/submission15.doc   (date accessed 3 November 2012).

[63] s 5(1)(e)(i) and s 5(1)(b).

[64] s 5(1)(e)(i) and (ii). All actions before the commencement of the Ombudsman Act (prior to 7 July 1983) apart from those relating to insurability and benefit entitlements under the Social Welfare Acts.

[65] The complaint mechanism for the HSE operates under the Health Act 2004, part 9. s 54(1) of that legislation allows for referral of complaints to the Ombudsman, or the Ombudsman for Children where someone is "dissatisfied with a recommendation made or step taken in response to a complaint under" the legislation.

[66] A complaint procedure has now been created under Rule 57A and Rule 57B, Prison Rules 2007 (SI No 11 of 2013). For further information see Irish Prison Service Policy for Prisoner Complaints.   http://www.irishprisons.ie/images/pdf/complaints-policy.pdf   (date accessed 5 November 2014).

processes that are developed in this area "must be robust and truly independent if they are to provide a genuine alternative to Ombudsman oversight".[67]

The exclusion of clinical judgments from the ambit of Office's health related inquiries has also come under the spotlight. The new Ombudsman, Peter Tyndall, has held discussions with Government to press for a change in the law to widen his remit to include complaints involving clinical matters. This comes alongside an announcement from his office that it is investigating the handling of complaints by public hospitals.[68]   [4–30]

Other limitations on jurisdiction arise which should be noted. The scope of the Ombudsman's jurisdiction is limited by s 5(1)(a)(iii) which disqualifies from investigation any action taken by a public body if the person affected by the action has a right of appeal, reference or review to a body not within the Ombusman's remit. Section 5, however, goes on to state that the Ombudsman may investigate actions within subsection 1(a)(iii) where, in the view of the Ombudsman, there are "special circumstances that make it proper to do so". Such circumstances arose in the context of the August 2001, *Passengers with Disabilities Report*, where the Ombudsman justified her examination because of, firstly, the limited scope of the available appeal but, also, secondly the significant difficulties faced by the carers in the specific cases. This section is a significant instance of the Act guarding against duplication of remedies and the focusing of the Ombudsman on distinctive ground.   [4–31]

There is, finally, a more broad-based Ministerial exclusion power contained in s 5(3) of the Ombudsman Act, which although available, has not yet been used. The subsection allows the Minister to request in writing that the Ombudsman not investigate an action, where it is part of the functions of that Minister's Department or an officer or body whose functions are related to that Department. The request must include full reasons as to why the request is being made. On receiving the request, the Ombudsman is under an obligation to cease investigation. The complainant and other persons deemed appropriate by the Ombudsman are entitled to a copy of the request and the statement of   [4–32]

---

[67] Ombudsman 2011 Report, above at n 49.
[68] P Cullen, "Ombudsman to investigate low levels of health complaints", *The Irish Times*, 13 June 2014.

reasons supplied with it. Furthermore the terms of any Ministerial requests received must be included in the Ombudsman's Annual Report to the Oireachtas.[69]

The Powers of the Office

[4–33] In this section we critically analyse the process of investigation undertaken by the Office, and the degree of compliance by the relevant public bodies. In setting out the powers of the Ombudsman, we rely both upon the Ombudsman Act 1980, but also the existing practice embodied by the s 16 manual issued by the Office under the Freedom of Information Acts 1997-2003. In an interesting synergy between two administrative justice rubrics, this manual collates "the rules, procedures, practices, guidelines and interpretations" used by the Office as well as an index of any precedents kept by it.

[4–34] Initially, we should note the measures taken by the Ombudsman to ensure that its complaint mechanisms operate to achieve effective access to justice for the public. Thus, in addition to offering a broad number of practical avenues for making complaints,[70] the Office has established the *Link* project with a number of Citizen Information Centres, whereby visitors to these centres are facilitated to making complaints. In addition, staff members from the Office make regular, well publicised regional visits.

[4–35] There are two gateways to Ombudsman investigation. Under s 4(3) the Ombudsman shall not investigate an action unless: (a) a complaint has been made in relation to the action by a person; or (b) it appears, having regard to all the circumstances, that an investigation into the action would be warranted. In relation to individuals' complaints, the Ombudsman, upon carrying out a preliminary examination, may refuse to carry out an investigation if it is vexatious, the complainant has insufficient interest in the matter or that the complainant has not taken reasonable steps to seek redress or has not has completed the redress process that is underway.

---

[69] Ombudsman Act 1980, s 6(7).

[70] The Ombudsman accepts complaints which are made by letter, telephone, e-mail, online through the Office's website, or by personal visits either to the office in Dublin or to temporary regional offices which are visited by staff on a monthly basis.

Section 4(3)(a) therefore requires there be a complainant who is a person affected, although in practice the Ombudsman has interpreted this widely to include family members and other "representatives".[71] Complaints must involve an "adverse" impact on some person although what is considered "adverse" is left undefined and is rarely discussed directly in the Ombudsmans' reports.[72] A complaint must relate to a public body listed by the Ombudsman Act 1980 for investigation, as discussed in the previous section, and specifically to an action "taken in the performance of administrative functions".[73]

[4–36]

A complaint proceeds from the Ombudsman Office with a letter of notification and a request for a report being addressed to the relevant public body. The letter represents a summary of the complaint, referring to all the points raised by the complainants. As an administrative practice, bodies are required to respond to a report request as soon as possible and not later than fourteen days after the request for information has been issued. Extensions of time for the preparation and submission of the report may be available, where the "complaint is complex, involves copious amounts of documentation or research, or where the body needs to obtain legal advice".[74]

[4–37]

Legally, the Ombudsman Act imposes a number of obligations of co-operation upon public bodies and officials. Section 7(1)(a) notes that the Ombudsman may:

[4–38]

> "...for the purposes of a preliminary examination ... require any person who in the opinion of the Ombudsman, is in possession of information ... that is relevant to the examination ... to furnish that information ... to the Ombudsman and, where appropriate, may require the person to attend before him for that purpose and the person shall comply with the requirements."

Although the 1980 Act did not provide a remedy where someone refuses to comply with a request of the Ombudsman, this has now been amended by

---

[71] See, for example, the discussion below at para [4-52] – [4-54] regarding the *Beaumont Hospital Cancer* case.

[72] The presumption here is that where a complaint is upheld there is some negative impact inherent in that judgment.

[73] s 4(2) Ombudsman Act 1980. See discussion above at paras **[4-13]** and **[4-23]**.

[74] s 16 manual, 9.

the 2012 Act, s 7(1) was updated to allow the Ombudsman to apply to the Circuit Court for an order directing a person to comply.

[4–39]   The legislation provides for some essential natural justice protections: thus a person to whom a requirement is addressed is entitled to the same immunities and privileges as belong to a witness before the High Court.[75] Those involved in an investigation:

> "shall not by act or omission obstruct or hinder the Ombudsman in the performance of his functions or do any other thing which would, if the Ombudsman were a court having the power to commit for contempt of court, be contempt of such court".[76]

[4–40]   In terms of administrative practice in interviewing complainants and officials, the Office of the Ombudsman has published its *Procedural Guidelines relating to the Conduct of Investigation Interviews*. The interview is designed to seek additional information relevant to the action/ decision: to obtain the views of officials concerning points made by the complainant; to evaluate administrative practice involved in the decision; and where the evidence indicates unfairness, to suggest that the body might consider a review of the case.[77]

[4–41]   The Office operates an Investigations Panel[78] which decides whether individual investigations should ultimately proceed or not. It then communicates the priority of the case to the Investigations Unit which then processes the complaint in a manner compatible with the legislative mandate. The Ombudsman Act establishes that an investigation is to be conducted "otherwise than in public",[79] and the body involved must be notified of the proposed investigation and be given the opportunity to respond.[80] Beyond these specifics, s 8(3) provides a broad discretion for the Ombudsman to decide the procedures for conducting an investigation.

---

[75] Ombudsman Act 1980, s 7(2). Further, under s 7(6) any statement or admission made by a person during the course of an Ombudsman investigation, including the preliminary examination phase, is inadmissible in criminal proceedings.

[76] *ibid* s 7(3).

[77] Office of the Ombudsman, *Section 16 Manual*, Appendix 6.

[78] This panel is comprised of the Ombudsman, the Director General, the Investigations Unit Senior Investigator and the Complaints Process Manager.

[79] Ombudsman Act 1980, s 8(1).

[80] s 8(2).

Finally, the question of whether legal representation would be appropriate will be decided by the Ombudsman.[81]

Once a finding, report or recommendation has been prepared, s 6(6) of the Act demands that the Ombudsman shall not complete any adverse findings until the person or body affected is given an opportunity to consider them and make representations to the Office regarding the matter. The results of the investigation are, under s 6(2), to be sent to the relevant body who was subject to complaint, their parent Government body, any person who is alleged to have taken or authorised the actions complained of, and any other person whom the Office views appropriate. The complainant will be notified of the result of the investigation, the recommendation of the Ombudsman and the response of the body to the recommendation.[82] Under the Ombudsman (Amendment) Act 2012 the Ombudsman is now empowered to request that a body inform the Office within a specified time period of their response to any recommendations made.[83] Finally it is important to note that there have been positive experiences of mediation which have supplemented the investigation process.[84]   **[4–42]**

Crucially, beyond the legislative underpinnings, the administrative practice of the Ombudsman must comport with common law principles of natural justice and reasonableness, the Constitution and the scrutiny of the public itself. Constitutionally, questions of procedural fairness in relation to the operations of the Office have not been directly tested in the courts. However, in the private realm, the Financial Services Ombudsman (FSO) has been the subject of judicial review on the basis of constitutional justice. It is as yet unclear how far there might be a cross over between the two areas, given that the operation of different Ombudsmen derives from their statutory powers, however, it is worth noting the approach being taken by the courts in the private realm.   **[4–43]**

In the cases of *J & E Davy v Financial Services Ombudsman & anor*[85] and *Lyons v Financial Services Ombudsman*[86] it was accepted by both courts   **[4–44]**

---

[81] s 8(4).

[82] s 6(4).

[83] Ombudsman Amendment Act, s 9(3A)(b)

[84] See discussion of the *Beaumont Hospital Cancer Case* below at paras [4.52]-[4.54], where mediation between the parties was successfully used.

[85] [2010] IESC 30, Supreme Court.

[86] [2011] IEHC 454, High Court.

that the Ombudsman's procedure were informal in nature. In *Davy* however this did not mean that the Ombudsman could deny a party discovery of documents "which may be necessary in the interests of fairness to enable a party to establish or answer a complaint".[87] The Supreme Court in that case also noted that whilst an oral hearing might be less than appropriate in an informal complaint mechanism, situations might arise where it may be necessary. This was further clarified in the *Lyons* decision where the High Court concluded on the facts that the "'essence of the appellants' case has not been properly evaluated in the absence of an oral hearing". The crucial issue highlighted by Hogan J that would tend towards an oral hearing being required, was the shift in the Ombudsman's role from the mediatory to the adjudicatory role. Thus he stressed that once

> "...the Ombudsman proceeds to adjudication, a legal Rubicon is thereby crossed, not least having regard to the potential legal consequences of such an adjudicatory decision".[88]

The question of whether an oral hearing should be provided has since been the focus of a number of cases before the High Court and the FSO has provided Guidelines on when it regards oral hearings to be necessary.[89]

[4–45]   As has already been noted, these cases do not relate to the public Ombudsman's office. Two critical differences arise between the public office and that of the financial services ombudsman. As the Office of the Ombudsman investigates public bodies as corporate entities, many actions are attributed to unnamed civil servants, and it is not clear whether the courts would be as active in enforcing fair procedure in such a context. However, should the office engage in naming individual decision makers, this may make it more susceptible to review. Secondly, the Ombudsman makes recommendations only, whereas the findings of the Financial Services Ombudsman are legally binding.[90] Nevertheless, Hogan and Morgan have observed[91] that "there is no reason why [the

---

[87] Davy, above n 85 at 39.

[88] Lyons, above n 86 at para 38.

[89] https://www.financialombudsman.ie/complaints-process/oral-hearing-guidelines.asp?m=4 (date accessed 14 July 2014).

[90] s 57 CI(9) of the Central Bank and Financial Services Authority of Ireland Act 2004.

[91] Hogan and Morgan, above n 23 at p 423.

courts] should not" apply the same standard of constitutional justice to a public Ombudsman should a case concerning a specific individual arise.[92]

Ombudsman Investigations and Public Body Compliance

The Ombudsman has a number of options available to it in relation to possible recommendations when a complaint is upheld. They may include, under s 6(3), that the matter complained of be further considered, that specific measures be taken to remedy, mitigate or alter the adverse effects of the action or that the reasons for taking the action be given to the Ombudsman. Subsections 6(5) and 6(7) allow the Ombudsman, if not satisfied with the response of a body to his or her recommendations to lay a special report before the Oireachtas. As to what measures might actually be taken, or remedies provided, the legislation is not specific and, as a result, a significant level of discretion has been left in the hands of the Ombudsman. Typical remedies would include financial payment,[93] an apology, or a change in administrative procedures. Some specific examples of the remedies provided will be offered below as we consider the operation of the complaint and reporting system in recent years. [4–46]

In terms of complaints received, there has been a consistent upward trend during the lifetime of the Office. Overall more than 90,000 people have had valid claims upheld by the Ombudsman over the past thirty years.[94] In 2013, 3,412 complaints were received[95]: this is a slight decrease [4–47]

---

[92] A grievance raised by Michael Healy-Rae TD on behalf of one of his constituents regarding a complaint against the Ombudsman and her officers over the handling of a planning complaint illustrates, however, that challenges may be limited. In this instance the complainant was informed of the internal complaint mechanisms and an internal investigation was initiated but the complainant remained dissatisfied. Dealing with the issue through a written answer, Minister for Public Expenditure and Reform Brendan Howlin endorsed the independence of the Office of the Ombudsman: "In view of the facts of the case and the statutory independence correctly bestowed upon the Ombudsman, it would be inappropriate for me to initiate an investigation into the conduct of the Ombudsman in this instance." Dáil Éireann Written Answers, Office of the Ombudsman, 8 May 2012. Available http://www.kildarestreet.com/wrans/?id=2012-05-08.727.0 (date accessed 15 October 2014).

[93] This may be, as a penalty, a back-payment, costs and/or compensation.

[94] *Ombudsman News Release on Publication* of the 2013 Annual Report, 28 May 2014. Available online at: http://www.ombudsman.gov.ie/en/News/Media-Releases/2014-Media-Releases/90-000-complaints-received-in-30-years.html (date accessed 13 July 2014).

[95] Office of the Ombudsman, *Annual Report of the Ombudsman*, 2013 (Office of the Ombudsman, Dublin, 2014) at p 16. Available online at https://www.ombudsman.gov.

on 2012 which had also seen a decrease from 2011. The record for the number of complaints was established in 2010.[96] However, even with two years of reductions the level is still far higher than it was a decade ago. Following a major organisational review, the Office has been able to improve its processing rates and closed 58% of cases within three months, 90% within 12 months.

[4–48]   The breakdown of complaints reflected the concerns of many people in recessionary times with the highest percentage of complaints — 46.5% — being made against the Department for Social Protection, while Local Government and the HSE were also significant sources of complaints at 27.5% and 17.3% respectively.[97] 16.4% of the complaints received were resolved or partially resolved and 24.7% were provided assistance by the Ombudsman Office, while 45.1% were not upheld and the remaining were either withdrawn or halted. Where the Office is unable to provide assistance, it plays a valuable role in directing people to more appropriate forms of assistance.

[4–49]   In 2008, the Ombudsman Office carried out their first user survey[98] which revealed that a majority of those surveyed (71%) had not contacted the Ombudsman Office until after the public body had actually made their decision. Indeed, 59% had already spent a significant amount of time[99] dealing with that public body in trying to resolve their complaint before they made contact with the Ombudsman. Only around one third (32%) indicated that they had been made aware of the relevant Code of Practice on complaint handling by the public body with whom they were in dispute, while few were informed that they could contact the Ombudsman Office regarding their complaint.[100]

---

ie/en/Publications/Annual-Reports/2013-Annual-Report/AnnualReport2013/media/ombudsman_annual_report_2013.pdf (date accessed 13 July 2014), hereinafter Ombudsman Report 2013.

[96] A record number of *enquiries* were received by the general public – 11,451, which was 23% increase on the previous year. Ombudsman Report 2011, above n 49.

[97] Ombudsman Report 2013, n 95 at p 16.

[98] The results of this were published in the 2009 Annual Report. The Office of the Ombudsman are in the process of organising a second user survey year for the period 1 June 2011 to 30 June 2012. http://www.ombudsman.gov.ie/en/Publications/Annual-Reports/2009-Annual-Report/AnnualReport2009/chapter3.html#s2, (date accessed 8 September 2012).

[99] More than six months.

[100] The level of information regarding referrals to the Ombudsman Office varied significantly with 35% of those complaining about the HSE reporting they had received information compared with only 8% of those complaining about local authorities.

The survey also highlighted the high expectations of those who used the **[4–50]** Ombudsman, particularly regarding a swift and positive resolution to their dispute. Over one third (36%) expected that their complaint would be resolved through the decision of the public body being reversed. However, as the 2009 Report notes, only 11% of cases resulted in that dramatic an outcome.[101] The impact of this level of high expectation can be seen more generally on users' sense of satisfaction with the Ombudsman service. 66% of those surveyed were satisfied with the handling of their complaint. However, when those figures are broken down by satisfaction with the outcome of a complaint, 97% of those who were satisfied with the result of their complaint reported that they were also satisfied with the Ombudsman Office. Where someone was not satisfied with the outcome the figure dropped to a low level of 37%. This is not surprising and indicates the strong role that outcomes of complaints make regarding the overall process.

As well as these systematic comments, it is beneficial to provide some **[4–51]** selected examples of the casework of the Ombudsman to illustrate the sometimes undervalued impact of the institution. We will focus here on two main categories of cases. In the first category of cases, complainants turn to the Ombudsman for more *distinctive forms of redress and a more informal process*. A case which illustrates the unique benefits of the Ombudsman procedure over court litigation in such circumstances is the *Beaumont Hospital Cancer Case*. This tragic case occurred in 2003 when a cancer patient was admitted to the hospital on a bank holiday weekend and was misdiagnosed, did not received adequate follow-up consultations and ultimately died 10 days after admission as a result of the failings in his medical treatment. In line with internal complaint procedures, an independent review team was appointed by the hospital, and in 2007 it produced a report; however the family did not view that report as going far enough in addressing the issues they had raised. They considered that it misrepresented the family's experience, and sought to have some changes incorporated, but their request was turned down. Following on from this decision the family instituted legal proceedings, but also made a complaint to the Ombudsman Office.

---

[101] Office of the Ombudsman, *Annual Report of the Ombudsman, 2009* (Office of the Ombudsman, Dublin, 2010) at p 44.

[4–52]   In her 2009 Annual Report, the Ombudsman noted that the complainant (the man's daughter) had no real desire to take legal action against the hospital, and withdrew legal proceedings so as to allow the Ombudsman to deal with the case. In doing so, she was motivated by the need to get

> "clear answers with regard to her late father's treatment, an apology for the shortcomings in his treatment and assurances that lessons had been learned within the hospital system."[102]

[4–53]   It appears the complainant's view was that the adversarial and costly nature of litigation endangered these outcomes.

[4–54]   The Office of the Ombudsman set up a number of meetings with senior personnel at the hospital, which led to the hospital CEO meeting with the family in order to apologise for the failures, a detailed written apology was also provided. In doing so, the hospital acknowledged that communication failures had occurred and that the father should have been medically reviewed when he first appeared at the Accident Emergency Unit on a Bank Holiday Monday. The complaint also resulted in Beaumont Hospital establishing a new system that sought to ensure a clearer division of responsibilities between consultants on duty. This case illustrates effectively, therefore, the valuable impact that can be achieved by the informal and flexible approach of the Ombudsman. A court case would have been unlikely to have drawn out the sort of detailed apology and reformed procedures that were achieved in this case. The impact beyond the specifics of the complaint were a significant matter for the complainant and the Ombudsman's report concludes that the changes brought about to Beaumont Hospital procedures represented "considerable progress and should ensure that patients receive continuous and consistent care, crucial to their health and wellbeing".[103]

[4–55]   A second category of successful cases which can be identified are instances where the Ombudsman displayed an ability to change administrative practice. The 2009 *Case on Delay in amending child's birth certificate to include natural father's name* is an example of this. In this case, a man complained about a prolonged delay by the General Registry Office in amending the birth certificate of his child. The change involved deleting the name of the man initially named as the child's father and replacing it with that of the

---

[102] *ibid* at p 62.
[103] *ibid*.

complainant. The child's mother and the man registered as the father failed to consent to the change; however the Registry Office made an initial decision to amend. The Office then delayed the amendment further to allow for the opportunity to make submissions or commence legal proceedings.

The complainant contacted the Ombudsman Office and it initiated an [4–56] investigation. During that investigation, the birth certificate was finally amended, over two and half years after this had been sought by the natural father. The Ombudsman found that the Registry Office had failed to strike a reasonable balance between the rights of the natural father, the child and the other parties. In a broad recommendation, the Ombudsman found that the Registry Office was to develop and publish clear guidelines covering all possible amendment scenarios. This was accepted by the Registry Office.[104]

A further instance of the challenging systemic administrative practice [4–57] occurred in 2011 when the Ombudsman launched an investigative report entitled *Too Old to Be Equal*.[105] This reported that the Mobility Allowance scheme run by the Department of Health to benefit those with a disability, had, since 2000, been in breach of the Equal Status Act because of a "bright line" age restriction of the benefit to those under 66 years old. Further, in an example of administrative inconsistency, the Report found that people who had been in receipt of Mobility Allowance before reaching the age of 66 did not have their allowance payments discontinued after they passed this age. The Ombudsman made very strong statements in her report that the Department of Health was aware of the illegality of the upper age limit, but that it had shown no "sense of urgency" to make the scheme compatible eleven years after the legislation had been passed, despite having received similar warnings from the Equality Authority. The particular applicant whose complaint triggered the broader report was awarded 6,000 euros in arrears. The Ombudsman further recommended that the Department complete

> "its review of the Mobility Allowance scheme and, arising from that review, revise the scheme so as to render it compliant with the Equal

---

[104] A written apology was also made, as well as an ex gratia payment.

[105] Office of the Ombudsman, *Too Old to be Equal – An Ombudsman investigation into the illegal refusal of Mobility Allowance to people over 66 years of age* (Office of the Ombudsman, Dublin, 2011). Available at: http://www.ombudsman.gov.ie/en/Publications/Investigation-Reports/Government-Departments-other-Public-bodies/Too-Old-to-be-Equal-/Too-Old-to-be-Equal-.pdf (date accessed 12 October 2014).

> Status Act 2000…this process … should be completed within six months of the date of the Investigation Report (that is, by October 2011)."[106]

[4–58] The Department accepted this recommendation, however, in her Annual Report for 2011, the Ombudsman made a formal report to the Oireachtas that the Department of Health had failed to comply with her recommendation. The Report included a very strongly worded condemnation, which represents the high point of the application of human rights norms by the Ombudsman:

> "In my original Investigation Report I observed that the apparent inability of the department to deal with issues, such as the inclusion of an illegal condition in the Mobility Allowance Scheme, leaves it open 'to the perception that it is unconcerned with the fact that it is operating a scheme which is at odds both with the law of the land and with human rights law more generally.' More than a year later, the department had not shown that this perception is unwarranted."[107]

[4–59] Following the 2011 report the Department once again failed to remedy the situation prompting the Ombudsman to issue a follow up report in 2012.[108] The report noted that the Department of Health had continued to allow the scheme to continue despite knowing of its illegality, and had rejected a further recommendation from the Ombudsman to remove the upper age limit.[109] In response, the Department had stated that it was unable to act on the advice because it "would create liabilities the State could not afford",[110] a position strongly criticised by the Ombudsman:

> "The Ombudsman rejects absolutely the attempt of the Department to represent its position as a commonsense response to an unfortunate situation in which, in order to target limited resources effectively, it is necessary to infringe on the law. There are options to be considered on how best to use scarce resources. Breaking the law is not one of those options."[111]

---

[106] *ibid* at p 3.

[107] Ombudsman Report 2011, *supra* n 49 at p 59. Accessible online http://www.ombudsman. gov.ie/en/Publications/Annual-Reports/2011-Annual-Report/AnnualReport2011/ media/ombudsman-ar-2011-eng.pdf (date accessed 3 October 2014).

[108] Office of the Ombudsman, *Too Old to be Equal? – A follow-up*, A report to the Dáil and Seanad under s 6(5) and (7) of the Ombudsman Act 1980, (Office of the Ombudsman, Dublin, 2012). Available online at: http://www.ombudsman.gov.ie/en/publications/ investigation-reports/government-departments-other-public-bodies/too-old-to-be- equal-%E2%80%93-a-follow-up/ (date accessed 5 November 2014).

[109] *ibid* at p 2.

[110] *ibid* at p 3.

[111] *ibid* at p 4.

In the interim, as the report notes, complaints regarding the operation of the scheme continue to be submitted to the Ombudsman Office and investigated accordingly. In responding in detail to the position of the Department, the Ombudsman relies on core accountability principles. Firstly, that there is an issue of trust relevant in the situation whereby the public should be able to trust the State to act with "integrity" in areas of complexity particularly against a background of scarce resources.[112] Secondly, that State agencies should act in an open and honest way: if there is a danger that a benefit such as the Mobility Allowance Scheme could be abolished or altered people affected should be given the necessary information. Finally, the report notes the question of the State's commitment to fundamental human rights norms. If the Department of Health is willing to override the fundamental principle of equality because of cost concerns this:

[4–60]

> "suggests that it has a very weak sense of the importance of supporting human rights principles and, indeed, a very weak sense of the rule of law and of its obligation to act in accordance with the law."[113]

The report was published the day after the Government had made its announcement on the expansion of the jurisdiction of the Ombudsman.[114] The endorsement of the Ombudsman as a champion of the people was therefore swiftly followed up with a high profile rebuke of a key State Department for failing to follow her recommendations and bring an important disability scheme into line with the law. This was a fine example of political leverage through what has been termed by one Ombudsman "the mobilisation of shame".[115] However, the response of the Government was to say it was "seeking further legal advice".[116]

[4–61]

It appears, however, that the follow-up report, and a later appearance by both Ministers and civil servants of the Department of Health before the

[4–62]

---

[112] *ibid* at p 17.

[113] *ibid* at p 18.

[114] The report was issued on the 24 October 2012. "Mobility Allowance Scheme –Ombudsman publishes special report to the Houses of the Oireachtas", Office of the Ombudsman Press Release, available http://www.ombudsman.gov.ie/en/news/media-releases/2012-media-releases/mobility-allowance-scheme-ombudsman-publishes-special-report-to-the-houses-of-the-oireachtas.html (date accessed 5 November 2014).

[115] M Oosting, former Netherlands Ombudsman, quoted in R Gregory and P Giddings, *Righting Wrongs: The Ombudsman in Six Continents*, (IOS Press, Amsterdam, 2000), at p 464.

[116] M Brennan, "Government Seeking legal advice on 'illegal' mobility allowance scheme", *Irish Independent*, 25 October 2012.

Joint Oireachtas Committee on Oversight and Petitions in February 2013, prompted the Department to impetuously cancel the scheme rather than make a considered attempt to bring it in line with the rule of law and accountability principles. Twenty days after the Committee hearing, the Mobility Allowance and the Motorised Transport Grant were closed to new applicants. The 5000 existing recipients would lose their benefits four months later. The Department restated that it had been unable to devise a lawful and effective mechanism within their €10.6 million budget. The unilateral decision was taken without notifying disability groups, the Ombudsman or the Joint Oireachtas Committee.

[4–63]   Unsurprisingly, disability groups were highly critical of this cut and as the four months came to an end the Department agreed payments to existing recipients should continue to "prevent hardship" and "alleviate stress, anxiety and uncertainty".[117] It indicated an intention to establish a new statutory regime in the area, but more than a year after the announced abolition of the schemes no alternative proposal has yet been published. The unlawful Mobility Allowance and the Motorised Transport Grant continue to operate.[118]

[4–64]   The boundaries and limitations of the Ombudsman's role are evident where the Office has not upheld complaints. For instance, in another 2009 case, a mother who was working full-time and caring for her son on a full-time basis was denied a respite care grant.[119] The Ombudsman, despite noting the "regrettable anomaly and potential social benefit poverty trap"[120] was unable to uphold her complaint regarding this decision, as the

---

[117] Department of Health Press Release, "Interim Report of the Review Group in relation to the Mobility Allowance and Motorised Transport Grant Schemes", 11 June 2013. Available at http://www.dohc.ie/press/releases/2013/20130611.html (date accessed, 23 April 2014).

[118] In an answer to a written question on the issue on 19 June 2014, then Minister of State Kathleen Lynch TD stated that the Review Group examining the Mobility Allowance was "nearing completion" and that for the present time those already in receipt of the payment would continue to do so "for a further number of months, pending establishment of new statutory provisions" but that the scheme remained closed to new applicants. Available online at http://www.thomaspringle.ie/written-question-on-mobility-allowance-and-motorised-transport-grant-update/ (date accessed, 13 July 2014).

[119] Annual Report 2009, *supra* n 95 at 51. Accessible online http://www.ombudsman.gov.ie/en/Publications/Annual-Reports/2009-Annual-Report/2009-Annual-Report.pdf (date accessed, 3 October 2012).

[120] *ibid.*

denial, regardless of its human consequences, reflected the primary legislation the administrators were applying.

As already indicated in our discussion of the Mobility Allowance Report, in attempting to secure the compliance of its addressee bodies and departments, there have been instances of tension and outright rejection of the Ombudsman's role and competence. Perhaps the most marked example of this arose in 2008, when the Ombudsman engaged in a wide-ranging report in relation to the administration of guardianship and foster parent schemes. The Report made systemic findings of maladministration in relation to allegations that the Health Services Executive was delaying payments under the scheme. The Health Services Executive contested the investigation report as beyond the powers of the Ombudsman and threatened legal action, including a threat to apply for an injunction to prevent the report being presented to the Oireachtas. Litigation was ultimately not pursued, however the Office of the Ombudsman did incur significant costs in requesting necessary legal opinions.[121]   [4–65]

Most concerningly, there have also been instances where the body rejecting the Ombudsman's competence over, and findings regarding, complaints, have been supported by the Government. This occurred in 2010, when the Department of Agriculture, Fisheries and the Marine was backed by the Government in refusing to accept the recommendations that a 200,000 euro payout be made to families of those fishermen lost at sea under the impugned compensation scheme. In February 2011, the Fianna Fáil/Green party Government vetoed an Oireachtas debate on the relevant Report by the Ombudsman, entitled *Lost at Sea*. A week later, an Oireachtas committee also voted to ignore it on instructions from the Government whip. In response, the Ombudsman delivered strident criticism, noting that reporting an uncooperative public body to parliament was "the final and most powerful weapon" in the Office's   [4–66]

---

[121] The cost to the Ombudsman Office was €52,000, with the total cost to all parties estimated in the Ombudsman Special report as amounting to €150,000. Office of the Ombudsman, *Gagging the Ombudsman? Aftermath of an Investigation by the Ombudsman of the Health Service Executive*, A Report to the Dáil and Seanad under s 6(7) of the Ombudsman Act 1980, (Office of the Ombudsman, Dublin, 2010). Available online at p 18: http://www.ombudsman.gov.ie/en/Publications/Investigation-Reports/Health-Service-Executive/Gagging-the-Ombudsman-/Gagging-the-Ombudsman-Aftermath-of-an-Investigation-of-the-HSE.pdf (date accessed, 5 November 2014).

armoury.[122] By failing to facilitate debate and recognise the significance of her Report, she claimed, the

> "[g]overnment were knowingly disempowering the office, potentially robbing it of its ability to make public bodies accountable and to secure redress for people badly served by the State".[123]

[4–67] In a speech shortly after the refusal to debate the matter, the Ombudsman heavily criticised Irish parliamentary culture. While she did not dispute the Government's right to reject the Report, she highlighted that such a rejection required a fair hearing.[124] In the event, media reaction was such that, an Oireachtas committee did eventually debate the report, with the findings and recommendations being somewhat predictably rejected by Government majority.

[4–68] Also in 2010, both the Health Services Executive and the Department of Health refused to co-operate with the Ombudsman's Report on the right to nursing home care in Ireland, denying her access to relevant information and documentation to assist the investigation. They submitted that the Ombudsman did not have the power to make broad systemic findings and that she was prejudicing ongoing legal actions. While the Government expressly backed this position, no legal action challenging the publication of the report was taken. In her Report, published at the end of 2010, the Ombudsman noted that the jurisdictional challenge put forward in response to her investigation was:

> "...the most serious mounted against the Ombudsman's Office since its establishment in 1984. The extent and nature of this challenge, occurring both at the outset of the investigation and at the stage of representations on the draft report, does raise serious issues for the Ombudsman as she goes about discharging her independent role."[125]

---

[122] E O'Reilly, "Watchdog needs State guarantee", *Sunday Times*, 5 June 2011, hereinafter "O'Reilly".

[123] *ibid.*

[124] E O'Reilly, "Relations between Ombudsmen and Parliaments", given at the eighth national seminar of the European Network of Ombudsmen, 20-21 October 2011, Copenhagen, Denmark.

[125] Office of the Ombudsman, *Who Cares? An investigation into the right to nursing home care in Ireland*, (Office of the Ombudsman, Dublin, 2010) at p 15. Available online at http://www.ombudsman.gov.ie/en/publications/investigation-reports/hse-nursing-homes/who-cares/ (date accessed, 5 November 2012).

The twin rejection of the Ombudsman's findings in 2010-2011 conflicted [4–69] with pre-existing practices. The most prominent instance of tension prior to this took place in 2002 when the Revenue Commissioners rejected the recommendations of the Ombudsman. This was, however, successfully resolved by the Oireachtas, who supported the Ombudsman report and directly engaged the Commissioners in complying with them. It is perhaps too early to suggest that there has been a shift in attitude by, at least, some public bodies in relation to cooperating with, and accepting the recommendations of, the Ombudsman Office. However, what is clear is that the relationship between the Government and the Ombudsman Office in 2010/11 had reached a low level, akin to that which existed in 1987 when the Fianna Fáil Government set about reducing the capacity of the office through serious budgetary cuts.

Resistance to findings of independent complaint bodies are not confined [4–70] to the Office of the Ombudsman. A more extreme example can be found in relation to a report published in 2011 by the Children's Ombudsman on the detention of children in St Patrick's Institution for Young Offenders in Dublin.[126] The report was based on work done by the Children's Ombudsman in St Patrick's over a number of years and primarily highlighted the concerns directly raised by the children detained in the institution. The report highlighted concerns regarding all areas of the operation of the institution and led the Ombudsman to call for the early closure of St Patrick's Institution. Crucially, in her introduction she noted the core aim of her work with the children concerned:

> "The aim of this consultation is in the first instance to make sure that their voices are heard. But there is little achieved if we do not convince those who come into contact with these young people that their views are legitimate, that the discrepancies that exist place a responsibility on them to communicate, to educate, to listen and to support these young people in understanding this world or regime as it is called."[127]

The calls for an early closure were met with little political enthusiasm, [4–71] and publicity of the report was muted. Eighteen months later, the publication of a damning report on the conditions in the institutions by

---

[126] Ombudsman for Children's Office, *Young People in St. Patrick's Institution*, (Ombudsman for Children's Office, Dublin, 2011). Available online at http://www.oco.ie/assets/files/St%20Pats%20Report.pdf (date accessed 5 November 2012).
[127] *ibid* at p 8.

the Inspector of Prisons, Michael Reilly, represented a further alarming indication of the attitude of the Ministry of Justice and the Prison Service to the consultation already carried out by the Children's Ombudsman.[128] As Emily Logan recalled recently:

> "people were sneering at the outcome of that report.... I was patronised somewhat and made fun of ... and made to feel that I was a bit naive in thinking that what the young people were saying was true."[129]

[4–72]   The view of officials was evidently that, a report by the Children's Ombudsman, based on the views of children within the system, was not credible as an *authoritative analysis* of the situation in the institution. The result of this was a refusal by those responsible for St Patrick's Institution at all levels to take notice of, and respond to, a coherent account of fundamental problems in relation to the detention of children.

[4–73]   The harm done by this type of rejection cannot be underestimated; with the experience indicating a lack of respect for the inquiry and fact-finding abilities of the Office of the Children's Ombudsman. The episodic rejection of Ombudsmen findings challenging administrative practice underline the prevailing selective commitment to their functioning, despite Government rhetoric surrounding the 2012 Amendment Act. It is worth contrasting the St Patrick's Report with the selection of the Children's Ombudsman to investigate the removal of Roma children from their families by Gardaí in October 2013. On that occasion, the Minister for Children identified the Children's Ombudsman as the preferred inquiry mechanism because she had "shown herself in the past to be well capable ... of doing this kind of independent report". [130]

[4–74]   Against this environment where administrative bodies can at times be resistant, uncooperative and ultimately even dismissive of the findings of Ombudsmen, we also find Government statements to the effect that the expansion of the remit of the Office of the Ombudsman is essential for

---

[128] Report on an Inspection of St Patrick's Institution by the Inspector of Prisons Judge Michael Reilly, Inspector of Prisons, 2012. Available online at http://www.justice.ie/en/ JELR/Appendix%20A%2005.10.pdf/Files/Appendix%20A%2005.10.pdf (date accessed 5 November 2014).

[129] C. Lally, "Concerns of children's Watchdog 'sneered at'", *The Irish Times*, 18 October 2012.

[130] "Children's Ombudsman has "trust of the public" needed for Roma cases probe", 26 October 2013, *thejournal.ie*. Available at http://www.thejournal.ie/emily-logan-trust-roma-garda-investigation-hse-1148755-Oct2013/ (date accessed 23 April 2014).

"ensuring that fair treatment is always provided" to the public and to achieve improved decision-making and greater accountability in public bodies. There is clearly a tension in Government between the acceptance of the need for an institution such as the Ombudsman and the episodic rejection of its findings on where they relate to challenging or inconvenient areas of administrative practice.

There has also, in recent times, been discussion of the need for a **[4–75]** consolidation of public Ombudsperson mechanisms. This occurred most prominently in the McCarthy Report[131] which stated that "[a]s a general principle, the Group advocates the bringing-together of related functions, with a concentration of resources and elimination of waste".[132] In relation to Ombudsman bodies this would involve an amalgamation of bodies which have complementary functions and would therefore reduce duplication of work in the area. The McCarthy Report argued that in most cases "this approach should yield back-office savings and/or provide scope for a more coherent and unified policy approach across similar sets of activities".[133] The result would be a rationalised "single Ombudsman Commission" which would incorporate the Office of the Ombudsman / Information Commissioner, the Children's Ombudsman, the Office of the Data Protection Commissioner and the Office of the Commission for Public Service Appointments.[134] In terms of the impact of the relationship between the Office of the Ombudsman and the Children's Ombudsman there is a limit as to how far that amalgamation can go. The current approach is to merge the back-office functions of the Children's Ombudsman into the Ombudsman's Office. The merger may go no further than that because of the specific remit the Children's Ombudsman possesses in relation to children's rights advocacy, and the position of United Nations Committee on the Rights of the Child on the importance of a dedicated ombudsman for children.[135]

---

[131] Report of the Special Group on Public Service Numbers and Expenditure Programmes,' published by the Department of Finance, 16 July 2009.

[132] *ibid* at p 14.

[133] *ibid* at p 18.

[134] *ibid* at p 51.

[135] UN Committee on the Rights of the Child, General Comment No 2, *The role of independent national human rights institutions in the promotion and protection of the rights of the child*, UN DOC CRC/GC/2002/2 (4 October 2002), paras 13-14.

[4–76]   It is interesting that these bodies are targeted, when there has so far been no mention of bodies such as the Office of the Appeal Commissioners for the purposes of the Tax Acts, the various Performance Verification Bodies, key appeals tribunals,[136] as well as the Garda and Defence Forces, Ombudsmen, probably on account of a greater valuing of their sectoral diversity.[137]

The Ombudsman, the Constitution and the Separation of Powers

[4–77]   As noted at the outset of this chapter, the Ombudsman is often regarded as a constitutional misfit, essential in practice but transgressive to traditional categories. Each of the branches of Government, executive, legislative and judicial, has to develop its own conception of the Office and how it interacts, and is reconciled, with the doctrine of the separation of powers. In the Irish context, this is further complicated by the lack of a secure anchor offered by constitutional recognition of the Office of the Ombudsman.

[4–78]   The question of constitutional recognition of the Ombudsman is not a new one within Ireland, but has, with the recent onset of recession and banking crises, received new energy given the dysfunction of many traditional forms of regulation. In this section, therefore, we must accompany a formalist analysis with a broader socio-legal query: how significant a role can the Ombudsman play in reinvigorating parliamentary democracy and administrative accountability in Ireland?

[4–79]   The Report of the Constitutional Review Group 1996 strongly endorsed the constitutional recognition of the Office. It noted that a majority of Western European democracies provide for an Ombudsman in their constitutions, as well as the European Union Ombudsman which oversees the European institutions. The Group noted that:

---

[136] For example the Refugee Appeals Tribunal.
[137] See T Murphy, "Is Ireland Ready for Droit Administratif?", part 7 available at: http://www.cpdseminars.ie/articles/is-ireland-ready-for-droit-administratif/ (date accessed 5 November 2014).

"in recent years a consensus has emerged in the two Houses of the Oireachtas about the desirability of not only maintaining the institution of Ombudsman but strengthening and developing it".[138]

While acknowledging the role of constitutional rights, it stressed that the additional protection by the Ombudsman "can be of particular advantage to those who are poor and without social position".[139] The trends of delegation and devolution within the public service also strengthened the need for a new provision. It also delivered a tacit endorsement of the systemic aspects of the Office's work: [4–80]

"The office has also developed a role in contributing to the elimination of the root causes of many of the complaints encountered, and to raising standards of public administration by identifying causes of maladministration and suggesting improvement."[140]

Constitutional recognition would further underline the independence and status of the Office:

"A constitutional guarantee for this independence would reinforce freedom from conflict of interest, from deference to the executive, from influence by special interest groups, and it would support to assemble facts and reach independent and impartial conclusions."[141]

The Review Group concluded by recommending that a new Article be inserted into the Constitution confirming the establishment of the Office. It would further provide for "an independent exercise of such investigative and other functions of the office in relation to administrative actions as may be determined by law…and consistent with the 1980 Act" in a manner similar to the protections which exist for the Comptroller and Auditor General. [4–81]

This recommendation is to be praised for its foresight, though it has ultimately lain unimplemented. The fact that the First Progress Report of the All-Party Oireachtas Committee on the Constitution endorsed the recommendation, and supplemented it with a specific text for inclusion in [4–82]

---

[138] First Progress Report, All Party Oireachtas Committee on the Constitution, 1997, Dublin, accessible http://www.constitution.ie/reports/1st-Report-APOCC.pdf at 165 (date accessed 5 November 2012).

[139] *ibid* at p 81.

[140] *ibid* at p 173.

[141] *ibid* at p 174.

the Constitution, confirmed widespread support for this, but inertia set in. Meanwhile, within the United Kingdom's (admittedly unwritten) constitutional system, there have been similar endorsements of the role of the Ombudsman in fulfilling the promise of parliamentary democracy. This is embodied by the statement of the Public Administration Select Committee of the UK Parliament in 2007:

> "There is now an extensive network of bodies concerned with the regulation of standards of conduct in public life. These constitutional watchdogs have different functions, and are organised in a variety of different ways. They cover the essential ground and generally work well in safeguarding high standards of conduct; but they have often been set up in response to particular problems and insufficient attention has been paid to their design features and the need for coherence in the system as a whole. The time has come to recognise that the machinery of ethical regulation is now an integral and permanent part of the constitutional landscape."[142]

[4–83]   In Ireland, however, the question of constitutional recognition remains unresolved. Following the banking crisis and the Government position on the *Lost at Sea* report, Emily O'Reilly underlined that constitutional recognition was of renewed relevance.[143] While it would not affect the daily conduct of the Office, it would deliver to it a standing similar to the Auditor and Comptroller General. Ultimately the most recent Programme of Government of the Labour/Fine Gael coalition did not contain an express commitment and the terms of reference of the Constitutional Convention did not identify it as a priority.[144]

[4–84]   The political torpor around the office reflects a recurring trend in the history of the Office. The dynamic of opposition referred to by Senator Maurice Hayes as seeking to "induce torpor through malnutrition" recurs in cyclical fashion.[145] Few institutions have received such glowing political

---

[142] Public Administration Select Committee, *Ethics and Standards: The Regulation of Conduct in Public Life*, (The Stationary Office, London, 2007) HC 121-I, at p 3.

[143] O'Reilly, above n 122.

[144] *ibid.* The Fine Gael election manifesto, did however, commit to constitutional recognition. However, the issue is not one of the eight listed issues for consideration by the Constitutional Convention. The list was provided by the Taoiseach in a Dáil debate moving the Constitutional Convention on 10 July 2012. 772 *Dáil Deb.* (10 July 2012)

[145] Quoted in K Murphy, *The Role of a National Ombudsman in respect of European Community Law*, speech given at "The Respective Role of the Community and National Institutes or Bodies in the Supervision of the Application of European Community Law", Strasbourg, 12-13 September 1996.

rhetoric as the Ombudsman, but this has failed to be transformed into more tangible support at the constitutional, and even governmental, level. This must be seen as a product both of the political marginality of administrative reform and the institutionalised clientelism within which many Irish politicians are habituated or strictured.

In conceptualising the interactions of the office with the branches of Government, Parliament is often seen as the key actor. This reflects the reality that in European States, the Office is frequently titled the "Parliamentary Ombudsman". In the Irish context, as we have noted in relation to the *Lost at Sea* debate, the Oireachtas, and its background parliamentary culture, are the final bulwark for the Ombudsman when the Office is faced with opposition. In addition, in an era of legislative hyperactivity, where the production of legal norms by parliaments has reached unprecedented levels, the Ombudsman's role in aiding the Parliamentary oversight function is critical. The Office represents a key node for ensuring that Parliament will not merely produce legislation, but see that it is faithfully implemented and engage with the institutional questions and practices it may well have itself produced. **[4–85]**

In view of these functions, successive Ombudsmen have been well placed to critique the quality of parliamentary debate and oversight since the establishment of the office. In a speech entitled *Executive Accountability and Parliamentary Democracy* delivered in 2011, Ms O'Reilly stressed the need for a deeper reflection on the quality of parliament: **[4–86]**

> "Both I, and my predecessor...have spoken and written on numerous occasions of the dangers inherent in accepting that parliament is, for the greater part, a charade, that parliamentarians have in many cases lost the sense of parliament as an independent entity acting in the public interest. While few will acknowledge this openly, senior civil servants working with Ministers and sitting in on Oireachtas debates must, in very many instances, become profoundly cynical; either that, or they too have lost the sense that a properly functioning parliament is fundamental to a properly functioning democracy."[146]

---

[146] E O'Reilly, *Executive Accountability and Parliamentary Democracy,* speech given at "Executive Accountability and Parliamentary Responsibility", NUIG, 26 March 2011. Available at: http://www.ombudsman.gov.ie/en/News/Speeches-Articles/2011/Executive-Accountability-and-Parliamentary-Democracy.html (date accessed 5 November 2012).

[4–87]   In placing these issues within the context of Ireland's recession and the arrival of the Troika, it is appropriate to highlight a statement of Brian Lenihan TD, in response to the Ombudsman's report to the All-Party Oireachtas Committee on the Constitution which he was the Chair:

> "The Ombudsman's opinion is that in the longer term, the relationship between the Oireachas and the Executive, as well as the relationships within the Executive may need to be thought through afresh in the context of a wider programme of constitutional reform. The All-Party Oireachtas Committee on the Constitution shares this view... Clearly the Ombudsman is a graphic example of the pressing need for effective oversight of Government and public administration. For a small country like Ireland, the committee is well aware of the need to ensure the Government has the capacity to respond speedily to challenges in the external environment. *Too sensitive a balance could lead to an enfeebled Executive....*" [147]

At the time of the above statement, Mr Lenihan was a backbench TD, but was, upon his ascension to the post of Minister for Finance, destined to oversee some of the most significant, and ultimately unsupervised, executive decisions ever taken by the Irish State.

[4–88]   In investigating the constitutional position of the Office, however, it is also important to note that some aspects would be occluded if we were to describe the Ombudsman as parliament's watchdog over an all-powerful executive. The Ombudsman can also be seen as acting *for* the Executive in ensuring Departments implement legislation. As referenced above, in the Irish context, the Ombudsman Act complicates this relationship by allowing a Minister to order the cessation of investigations.

[4–89]   In terms of *judicial* engagement with the Ombudsman mechanism, there would seem, at first glance, to be a conflict. As outlined elsewhere in this book, the Irish Courts have often prioritised a heavily judicialised model of tribunals and other forms of fact or error finding mechanisms. It is clear that the Courts and the Ombudsman adopt different methodologies to resolving disputes, and sensitivity to these differences is required within both institutions. One of the strongest endorsements of the distinct *and essential* constitutional role of Ombudsmanry is seen in the decision of the

---

[147] Emphasis added. 540 *Dáil Deb*. Col. 543 (13 February 2001).

Canadian Supreme Court in *Re British Columbia Development Corp. v Friedmann*

> "[t]he powers granted to the Ombudsman allow him to address administrative problems that the courts, the legislature and the executive cannot effectively resolve".[148]

The legislature can improve its engagement with the Ombudsman **[4–90]** however, although a question remains as to how that relationship works under the wider ambit of the separation of powers. Recent developments in relation to Oireachtas structures may shine a stronger light on this relationship — in 2012, the Oireachtas Joint Sub-committee on the Ombudsman was established, under the wider remit of the Joint Committee on Public Service Oversight and Petitions.[149] The terms of reference of the new sub-committee include a requirement that they consider the Reports of the Ombudsman as laid before the House under the terms of the Ombudsman legislation, consideration of motions related to appointment[150] and any other matters that might be referred to the sub-committee by the Houses of the Oireachtas.[151] This suggests that oversight and review of the activity of the Ombudsman is to be devolved in the first instance to the committee.

The terms of reference of the sub-committee require it to develop guidelines **[4–91]** to assist it to collaborate with the Ombudsman "including a right of initiative for the Joint sub-committee in bringing specific matters to the attention of the Ombudsman".[152] In addition the Joint Sub-Committee on Public Petitions can refer a petition to the Ombudsman where that might be appropriate.[153]

The creation of the subcommittee reflects the 2011 Programme for **[4–92]** Government. This stated that a "dedicated Ombudsman Committee" should be established which would create a formalised system for engagement between the legislature and the Ombudsman, offering:

---

[148] *Re British Columbia Development Corp. v Friedmann* (1984), 14 DLR (4th) 129, at 139-40.

[149] There is a second sub-committee on Public Petitions. http://www.oireachtas.ie/parliament/oireachtasbusiness/committees_list/psop-committee/ (date accessed 5 November 2014).

[150] Under s 2 of the 1980 Act.

[151] Dáil Standing Orders 165A allow for the establishment of the committee and its sub-committees.

[152] Dáil Standing Orders 165A (11) (a) (i).

[153] Dáil Standing Orders 165D (2)(a).

> "a formal channel of consultation and collaboration between the Oireachtas and the Ombudsman, responsible for receiving and debating her annual and special reports and for ensuring that her criticisms and recommendations are acted upon."[154]

[4–93] However, it also reflects the desire of the Office of the Ombudsman to ensure that the problems experienced in the relationship between the two bodies in 2010-2011 are not institutionalised into an ongoing rejection by the legislature of any Ombudsman criticism. Thus, in her 2011 Annual Report the Ombudsman welcomed the development of the sub-committee regarding it as being part of an "ongoing constructive engagement with the Government, the relevant Ministers and their officials".[155] It remains to be see whether the greater engagement between the Ombudsman and the Oireachtas can achieve the rebalancing of the relationship between the Ombudsman and the Government and further strengthen the office. It is interesting to note that as part of these reforms the question of the constitutional status is not being pursued.

[4–94] The importance of understanding the Ombudsman's place in institutional theory and in political culture has been stressed in this chapter and remains critical to the development of the office. However, there is no doubt that the personal profile and judgment of the Ombudsman are key variables in the institution's success. The recent election of Emily O'Reilly to the post of European Ombudsman by the European Parliament underlines the effectiveness of her response to the cultural resistance this chapter has analysed.[156]

Future Reforms

[4–95] Pressure for reform of the operation of Ombudsman machinery is currently being exerted by the EU following the adoption of the EU Alternative Dispute Resolution (ADR) Directive.[157] This places a

---

[154] Programme for Government, p 20, quoted in Report on Revised Orders of Reference for the Joint Committee, 2012, p 4.

[155] 2011 Annual report, above n 48 at p 17.

[156] European Ombudsman press release, "Emily O'Reilly begins work as European Ombudsman", 30 September 2013. Available at: http://www.ombudsman.europa.eu/en/press/release.faces/en/51921/html.bookmark (date accessed 23 April 2014).

[157] Directive 2013/11/EU of the European Parliament and of the Council, 21 May 2013 on alternative dispute resolution for consumer disputes and amending Regulation (EC) No

requirement on all EU Member States to provide effective access to ADR mechanisms by mid-2015, in order to resolve disagreements between businesses and consumers.

This has implication for services that were previously offered by the state but have in recent years been privatised. The Ombudsman in his 2013 report noted that privatisation and contracting out had significant implications for the access to redress mechanisms:

[4–96]

> "when services are privatised, then access to redress can be lost. This has recently happened in the case of Irish Water, where water services were formerly within jurisdiction when provided by local authorities. The removal of jurisdiction occurred without consultation with the Office and is a matter of considerable concern."[158]

Given that the EU directive will require the State to provide an effective ADR body to provide such redress the Ombudsman has already staked a claim to that space with the idea of the Ombudsman as a "one stop shop" redress mechanism offering a remedy to those affected by both private and public bodies in a "so-called hybrid model".[159] Clearly this would represent a shift in orientation, and the Office would have to be refined to discharge such a role. Of particular note is the issue of whether binding recommendations should be made in such a context, along the lines of the Financial Services Ombudsman. The assumption is that non-public bodies will not regard themselves as being obliged to follow non-binding recommendations and extra weight would therefore need to be attached to the Office. However, the longer term impact of this may be to increase the quasi-judicial nature of the Ombudsman adjudication process and encumber investigation processes with the complexities of constitutional justice obligations.[160]

[4–97]

Worryingly, the Ombudsman also noted the possibility that shifting the Ombudsman Office form a public domain into this hybrid model would require a shift in financing. While the Office of the Ombudsman is funded

[4–98]

2006/2004 and Directive 2009/22/EC. Available online at http://eur-lex.europa.eu/LexUriServ/LexUriServ.do?uri=OJ:L:2013:165:0063:0079:EN:PDF (date accessed, 13 July 2014).

[158] 2013 Annual Report, above n 95 at p 27.

[159] *ibid.*

[160] See discussion of this regarding the Financial Services Ombudsman, above at para [4.44].

from the public purse, private sector ombudsmen are usually funded by the sector they are operating in so

> "funding would ... need to come from the industry, whether through a levy, a charge per case, or a combination of both. The cost should not fall to the public purse. The cost can act as an incentive to get things right in the first place – the so-called "polluter pays" principle."[161]

This suggestion is not without its dangers.

[4–99]   The inclusion of private financing arrangements within the Office of the Ombudsman, albeit an office that would be operating in a new hybrid model, could have a significant impact on its perceived independence. The model of the Financial Services Ombudsman is one that we should not necessarily be quick to follow. The recent case of *O'Brien v Financial Services Ombudsman*[162] exposed tensions in the operation of the Financial Services Ombudsman and criticisms made of it by Free Legal Advice Centres (FLAC); in particular FLACs concerns that the FSO tended to take a "pro –industry attitude"[163] to complaints including that of Mr O'Brien.[164]

Conclusion

[4–100]   We began this chapter with a reference to the statements of former Taoiseach Charles J Haughey justifying his opposition to creation of an Irish Ombudsman. In describing the casework of the Office, we have shown that it represents a key, distinctive forum for complainants, offering accessible, informal and flexible solutions, often to those unable to afford litigation. Increasingly, it has supplied leadership in developing norms of proper administration and good governance, directly communicating with decision-makers and administrators. Without constitutional recognition however, the Ombudsman sits unsteadily on the fickle tides of our underlying political culture. An analysis of its strengths and weaknesses must ultimately move to a reflection upon the broader

---

[161] *ibid.*

[162] [2014] IEHC 268 High Court.

[163] *ibid* at 95.

[164] See also the issue of the FSO criticism of High Court decisions requiring oral hearings – R McMahon, "Financial Services Ombudsman: a preference for "talk" over rights?" A Clatter of Law blog, 3 February 2014, http://aclatterofthelaw.com/2014/02/03/financial-services-ombudsman-a-preference-for-talk-over-rights/ (date accessed 14 July 2014).

distortions within our parliamentary democracy and the institutional and regulatory patterns within the administrative state. While the rhetorical support of many politicians continues to arrive, their political and legislative actions have not borne out a deeper commitment to the Office and its underlying philosophies. While ultimately we must leave the causes of this to the political judgment of the reader, the words of another political figure, former Minister Noel Dempsey, provide an appropriate bookend:

> "The most important part of the job (of public representative) is ensuring, through our work, that the system works for every citizen, not just the ones who come to our clinics. Public representatives shouldn't be distracted from their national function by constant clientelism - by becoming a hero to one citizen through finding a way around a system when the real responsibility is to change the system to benefit all citizens... Any time public representatives abandon their judgment to serve a lobby group they don't believe in, they are betraying their calling. Our state and semi-state organisations are not scrutinised nearly enough by our national politicians, particularly in relation to their service delivery to citizens. Because the whole basis of what we do politically is adversarial competition, there's little opportunity for a collective approach to solving problems."[165]

---

[165] Quoted by E O'Reilly in her 2010 address "In the Public Interest: Lessons from the Ombudsman Experience" given to the Institute of Public Administration, Conference on Good Governance. Available at http://www.oic.gov.ie/en/news/speeches-articles/2010-speeches-articles/in-the-public-interest-lessons-from-the-ombudsman's-experience.html (date accessed March 17 2014).

PUBLIC INQUIRIES

Introduction

"We need a public inquiry" is a standard response to a crisis, scandal or disaster: some have even gone as far to call it "Pavlovian".[1] The demand is made by politicians, commentators, concerned citizens and victims alike. Indeed, these inquiries have become part of the political and legal landscape of Ireland, informing us on the background to disasters, corruption, governance or misconduct in our society.

[5–01]

As Hogan and Morgan note, public inquiries can be established on a variety of legal bases within Ireland[2] and are designed to achieve a variety of ends.[3] For the most part they are established under statute, under the Tribunals of Inquiry (Evidence) Act 1921, the Commissions of Investigation Act 2004, or specialised legislation.[4] For our purposes we will focus on the twin mechanisms of the more general public inquiry empowered by the 1921 Act (as amended) and the 2004 Act. The term public inquiry will be used to encompass both types of inquiry where their operation is being discussed in a wider, more general framework. These large scale public inquiries operate as a key mechanism for "finding out what really happened" or exposing the wrongdoers. This is because our administrative and political system has adopted a relatively narrow approach to the public inquiry and prioritised this particular form. That is not to say we have not had other types of inquiry, but rather that they are often less visible and underplayed in media and academic commentary.

[5–02]

It is important to consider from the start why the public inquiry is seen as a particularly good method of "finding the truth" regarding such large-scale controversies. In many ways we are similar to our near neighbour, the UK, in this respect. The appeal of the public inquiry may be in part due to the more fundamental flaws of our other accountability

[5–03]

---

[1] See comment by J O'Keefe TD in the second reading debate on the Commissions of Investigation Bill (as it then was) 581 *Dáil Debates* Col 935 4 March 2004.

[2] G Hogan and DG Morgan, *Administrative Law in Ireland* (4th ed) (Round Hall, Dublin, 2010) at para 8-08. Hereinafter "Hogan and Morgan".

[3] M Elliott "Ombudsman, Tribunals and Inquiries: Re-Fashioning Accountability Beyond the Courts", in N Bamford and P Leyland *Accountability in the Contemporary Constitution* (Oxford University Press, Oxford, 2013). Hereinafter "Elliott".

[4] For example, the recent investigation into the Cork Air crash which occurred in 2011 was carried out under SI No 460 of 2009 – Air Navigation (Notification and Investigation of Accidents, Serious Incidents and Incidents) Regulations 2009. Legislation also exists to allow for inquiries to be established after train accidents — Railway Safety Act 2005 s 64, and shipping accidents — Merchant Shipping Act 1894, s 465.

mechanisms, not least the traditional weaknesses inherent in the Oireachtas as an accountability mechanism.[5]

[5–04]   The forthcoming Oireachtas Committee Banking Inquiry will provide an important test of the Parliamentary forum as a fact-finder and accountability mechanism. In chapter 2 we noted that the Oireachtas has traditionally been seen as particularly feeble in this regard.[6] While there have been signs of a growing confidence and increased activity in and around some Oireachtas Committees such as the Public Accounts Committee, this has not been without its difficulties. Not least the fundamentally political nature of the Oireachtas and the fear that party politics cannot be fully removed from that forum. Reflecting this, O'Malley has raised concerns about the capacity of TDs and Senators to do an effective job:

> "TDs and Senators simply do not have the time to conduct many inquiries properly themselves and perform their roles as legislators/representatives fully. Even in normal committee proceedings TDs line up to ask the same question but often don't even hang around to listen to the answer."[7]

[5–05]   He instead argued that a public inquiry should be instituted whereby the TDs could "set the questions" and hire others to find the answers.[8] This in a sense is what the traditional public inquiry is doing — it can be seen as a contracted out, yet independent, mechanism for investigating a set of facts and circumstances, which can provide some specific answers along with lessons for avoiding similar future mistakes.

[5–06]   In this way although the public inquiry is independent, and often rather legalistic in its operation, it should be seen as "an outcrop of public administration, and is not within the legal system."[9] Despite this administrative character, it also fits well with the battle mentality of the

---

[5] See discussion in chapter 2.

[6] The failings are not simply as a result of the decision of the Supreme Court in *Maguire v Ardagh* [2002] 1 IR 385 but relate to fundamental difficulties around the ability of the Oireachtas to function effectively in this way. See discussion in chapter 2 at paras 2.85 - 2.124.

[7] E O'Malley, "An Oireachtas inquiry into the banking crisis would be a show trial", *The Journal.ie*, 9 July 2013, http://jrnl.ie/983727 (date accessed, 3 July 3014).

[8] *ibid*. O'Malley voiced a preference for a Commission of Investigation given the cost and speed problems of Tribunals of Inquiry which will be discussed below.

[9] L Blom-Cooper, "What went wrong on Bloody Sunday: a critique of the Saville Inquiry?" (2010) *Public Law* 61 at p 64.

political realm, something highlighted by Sir Stephen Sedley, speaking in the UK context, in his description of the public inquiry as "the organisation of controversy into a form more catholic than litigation but less anarchic than street fighting".[10]

The Public Inquiry As An Accountability Mechanism — Overarching Purposes

Primarily an inquiry performs a vital fact-finding role, being created to establish the particular facts of a situation or scandal. This is generally seen as the least difficult aspect of an inquiry and the mostly likely to be carried out successfully. However, even this relatively straightforward component has its difficulties and in fact may be more complex than is at first recognised. Thus the "facts" may well be contested, requiring a public inquiry to engage in fact adjudication. Indeed, it is clear that a public inquiry in Ireland is not without consequence even though it is:　　[5–07]

> "inquiring into these allegations and in reporting its opinion on them the Tribunal [it] is not imposing any liabilities or affecting any rights…
> It may come to the conclusion that some or all the allegations of wrongdoing are true, but this opinion is devoid of legal consequences."[11]

The power of the public inquiry to publicly investigate serious allegations and make findings of fact, albeit non-legally binding, has significant dangers for citizens' reputations. As we will see from the discussion in this chapter, those consequences for constitutionally protected rights to reputation, privacy and confidentiality have an important impact on the operation of public inquiries in practice.[12]　　[5–08]

Linked to this core fact-finding function, the inquiry also serves an accountability function. It is normally charged with investigating particular wrong doings and reporting on such errors or culpability whether by individuals or organisations. Fundamentally, in this regard, the initiation of a public inquiry is a feature of ministerial responsibility given that the decision to establish a public inquiry will often be done as part of the　　[5–09]

---

[10] S Sedley QC "Public Inquiries: A Cure or a Disease?" (1989) 52 MLR 469 at p 472. Hereinafter "Sedley".

[11] Per Costello J in *Goodman v Hamilton (No1)* [1991] 2 IR 542 at 556-7.

[12] See discussion below at paras [5.29]-[5.30] and paras [5.50]-[5.61].

Ministers accountability response to the Oireachtas.[13] Given this, there needs to be a recognition that

> "[Public Inquiries] are established and exist solely at the discretion of government. A government under pressure to review its policy or actions will often resist such an inquiry unless it becomes politically untenable not to establish one."[14]

[5–10]   In practice, the public inquiry needs to be understood as being of a different type than other accountability mechanisms.[15] Thus an inquiry will typically have a much wider frame of reference from other accountability mechanisms such as the courts — with a distinct advantage being that they can consider not only the specific legal questions set out before them but also broader questions of policy, implementation as well as political and historical frameworks. Importantly, an inquiry does not have to wait for a litigant to come along and initiate their case — it is a response by the Oireachtas and/or Government to wider public interest concerns. However, as we will see an inquiry does tend to mirror many of the characteristics of a court — it is usually public, transparent and engages with fair procedures. Borrowing from the positive traits of the courts, while avoiding having the process encrusted by legalism is central to the overall distinctiveness of the mechanism:

> "By being public it borrows one of the strengths of the legal system, funnelling the arguments away from the anarchy and subjectivity of public debate and into the apparently objective and orderly forum of a proceeding which the world can watch bit in which nobody speaks unless spoken to. By taking the form of an inquiry it escapes the constrictions of subject-matter and procedure which make litigation an inapt solution. There are now no parties, only those whose legitimate interest has gained them entry on sufferance; no isolated issue to be resolved; no predefined questions of fact to be answered or body of statue or common law to be applied to them

---

[13] J Beer QC, *Public Inquiries* (Oxford University Press, Oxford, 2011) at p 2, hereinafter "Beer". However, it should be noted that the decision to establish a Tribunal of Inquiry is ultimately one for the Oireachtas itself, whereas the decision to establish a commission of Investigation is one of the Minister. See discussions below at paras [5-43]-[5.44] and para [5.89].

[14] Law Commission, *The Role of Public Inquiries,* Issues Paper (Law Commission, Wellington, 2007) at para 37. Hereinafter "NZ Law Commission".

[15] Elliott above n 3 at p 250.

like acid to litmus paper. The matter, as lawyers like to say, is at large."[16]

Despite these characteristics inquiries remain "capable of supplying a more explicitly political (albeit non-partisan) form of accountability" than many other systems.[17]

One significant advantage public inquiries are often considered to have over other accountability mechanisms is increased levels of independence. A decision by the executive or the legislature to establish a public inquiry requires that the separation between the initial decision to create the inquiry and the ultimate outcome of the inquiry is unassailable. This should lead to better outcomes from the inquiry, particularly by making acceptance of recommendations and pronouncements more likely. In addition, the removal of party political components, should improve the level of information gathering and overall reflections on policy, implementation and reforms. Thus a public inquiry can serve as an accountability mechanism in a situation where "government or the public service is seen as incapable of giving an impartial response where one is needed."[18] This benefit is particularly evident when the investigation is into the workings of Government itself[19] or the political context of Government.[20]   **[5–11]**

Public inquiries are also able to produce positive outcomes such as policy and practice recommendations: although any such recommendations do not have to be followed by Government. Thus, an inquiry process is able to provide key messages regarding lessons to be learnt and guidance on how to prevent any reoccurrence of the problems being investigated. As   **[5–12]**

---

[16] Sedley above n 10 at p 470.

[17] Elliott above n 3 at p 251.

[18] NZ Law Commission above at n 14 para 37.

[19] The NZ Law Commission report highlights this and notes the examples from the UK context of the Hutton and Butler Inquiries both of which concerned issues around the decision to go to war with Iraq. *ibid* at para 40 and fns 42 and 43.

[20] In our own jurisdiction the Beef Tribunal into the Beef Processing Industry dealt with core issues of administrative accountability and the improper links between politicians and business people, http://thestory.ie/2012/04/02/the-beef-tribunal-report-1994/ (date accessed, 3 July 2014), while the Mahon Tribunal was set up to examine corrupt payments to politicians regarding political decisions, www.planningtribunal.ie/images/ SITECONTENT_700.pdf (date accessed, 3 July 2014). As

Beer notes in the UK context, this facet is often prioritised over blaming and punishing wrong doers.[21]

[5–13] Although not an accountability outcome, an important consequence of a public inquiry is its potential to restore confidence in Government, the State or the particular institution subject to the inquiry. It allows the body to draw a line under a particular crisis by having a clear account of the problem and then moving on with possible reforms and a renewed confidence.

[5–14] However, an inquiry can also have a negate impact on accountability particularly where it creates the impression that "something is being done" while in reality little change takes place. In addition, an inquiry can delay much needed action as Government waits for the inquiry to report. This can result in findings and recommendations being provided perhaps years after the events in question. If, as with recent large-scale Tribunals of Inquiry such as the Mahon Inquiry, the report takes well over ten years to be finalised, the public concern which initiated the process will likely have dissipated and the pressure for change will be much reduced.[22] In writing about the outcome of the Morris Inquiry into policing, Daly describes the "tribunal fatigue" evident from the manner in which "the build up to the establishment of relevant tribunals gains more attention and provokes more public outcry than the findings which are ultimately reached several years and several millions of euro later".[23]

[5–15] Ultimately, it is important for those involved in the design of inquiries to appreciate that the differing functions we have identified might not always sit well with each other. As the New Zealand Law Commission has stressed:

---

[21] Beer above n 13 at p 2 quoting evidence submitted by the UK Government to the House of Commons Public Administration Committee in 2004.

[22] The Mahon Tribunal ran from 1997-2012 and had wide ranging terms of reference. The inquiry did produce a series of findings and recommendations; although many of these have been accepted and acted on (see discussion in chapter 6 —Local Government and Planning) there remains a sense that change has not been as decisive as had been hoped, see T Hogan, "Mahon Tribunal's key recommendation still not introduced one year later" *Irish Independent,* 29 January 2013 available online at http://www.independent.ie/irish-news/mahon-tribunals-key-recommendation-still-not-introduced-one-year-later-29024344.html (date accessed, 4 July 2014).

[23] Y Daly, "Review: V. Conway, *The Blue Wall of Silence: The Morris Tribunal and Police Accountability in Ireland"* (2011) 26 (1) *Irish Political Studies* 119.

"The desire for public reassurance, which is often really about blame and retribution, can be at a variance with what Government considers to be a politically expedient outcome of an inquiry. Similarly, where accountability and blame is sought by an inquiry, that background is often ill matched to making broad and useful recommendations about procedures and policy to prevent a recurrence as policy decisions made on the basis of a one-off disaster are not necessarily the most pragmatic or rational. Finally, an inquiry that seeks to establish "what happened" may not deliver a therapeutic conclusion for those directly involved. Where public confidence is at issue, speed, openness and transparency may be required, but if the circumstances require that an inquiry be held in private, or that more time is taken, catharsis will not be achieved."[24]

A failing public inquiry can ultimately exacerbate the problems it was seeking to address and cause harm to the overall accountability system. As a result in a clear understanding of why an inquiry is taking place is needed to ensure corresponding and practicable terms of reference.

Finally, public inquiries may be legally required where a State is under an obligation to carry out an investigation under the European Convention on Human Rights. Under Articles 2 and 3 of the Convention[25] the State is required to hold effective and independent public investigations where its substantive obligations under those articles have been violated or where agents of the State are implicated in such violations. The inquiry is regarded as making the rights and protections in the convention meaningful. Thus, in *Jordan v UK* the European Court of Human Rights stated that an inquiry was a way of

[5–16]

"securing the effective implementation of the domestic laws which protect the right to life and, in those cases involving State agents or bodies, to ensure their accountability for deaths occurring under their responsibility...."[26]

In the Irish context, the inquiries set up by the State into the death of Savita Halappanavar in Galway University Hospital in 2013 raised compliance issues in this regard. In criticising the HSE, HIQA and inquest procedures,

---

[24] NZ Law Commission above at n 14 para 49.

[25] This has been implied into the Articles by the ECtHR on the basis that Art 1 of the ECHR requires a State to "secure to everyone within its jurisdiction the rights and freedoms defined in the Convention". Art 2 *McCann v UK* (1996) 21 EHRR 97; Art 3: *Assenov v Bulgaria* 28 October 1998, (1999) 28 EHRR 652.

[26] *Jordan v UK* (2001) 31 EHRR 6 at para 105.

it was argued that these investigations fell short of a full public inquiry, and could therefore have been held to be an ineffective remedy under Article 2 of the ECHR.[27]

[5–17] A reflection upon the above purposes, has underlined that, as Elliott highlights, "inquiries contribute to the diversity of, and so enrich, the accountability system".[28] A public inquiry can bring a number of distinct advantages to an investigation into accountability related matters. Firstly, there is a capacity benefit given that public inquiries normally have a clear legislative framework,[29] strong powers of compellability, published terms of reference[30] and resources to support their operation. However, in practice many of these are dependent on the willingness of Government to fund and support a particular inquiry.[31] While the influence of political actors may potentially result in any individual public inquiry having unique procedures, we will now provide an account of the most prevalent design features of high profile public inquiries.

Characteristics of Public Inquiries (Tribunals of Inquiry and Commissions of Investigation)

The Judge as Public Inquiry Chair

[5–18] Public inquiry independence, and the resulting credibility which flows from it, is reinforced by a certain level of judicial involvement in public inquiries through the appointment of a judge as chair. This has been a common element of Tribunals of Inquiries, and in many cases, of Commissions of Investigation. Having a judge chair an inquiry also brings specialist legal skills to an investigative and analytical process, not least the

---

[27] "The HSE, HIQA and inquest procedures that have begun do not satisfy the requirements of Article 2 of the European Convention on Human Rights. ... [S]hort of a full public inquiry, Mr Halappanavar may have no effective remedy in Ireland under Article 2". Mark Kelly, Director of the Irish Council for Civil Liberties quoted in "Savita's family may take a case to the European Court of Human Rights", 29 November 2013, *Thejournal.ie* http://www.thejournal.ie/savitas-family-may-take-a-case-to-the-european-court-of-human-rights-694279-Nov2012/ (date accessed, 20 June 2014).

[28] Elliot above n 3 at p 17.

[29] See discussion below at paras [5.43]-[5.80] regarding the Tribunals of Inquiry (Evidence) Act 1921 and paras [5.84]-[5.105] on the Commissions of Investigation Act 2004.

[30] See discussion below at of the importance and practical difficulties of delivering a clear terms of reference for Tribunals of Inquiry at paras [5.45]-[5.46], [5.72] and [5.82]. On establishing the legislative framework for Commissions of Investigation see para [5.91].

[31] See discussion below regarding resources and costs at paras [5.65]-[5.74] (on this aspect of Tribunals) and [5.85]-[5.86] (on Commissions).

forensic skills of examining both oral and written evidence. In many ways, the judge led inquiry has become, as Elliott puts it, the "Rolls Royce of the accountability system" bringing as it does the credibility of judicial independence.[32]

However, the appointment of a judge does not guarantee a public inquiry functions effectively, nor can it necessarily remove controversy and politics from the process. Beatson, writing about the UK experience, notes that it is wrong "to raise false expectations" in this regard.[33] Where an inquiry is examining issues where there are high stakes, whether political, financial or reputational, difficulties and controversy will likely arise. For example, the experience of the Mahon Tribunal illustrates both the vulnerability of an inquiry to concerted attack and the inability of a judicial chair to prevent this happening. The Mahon Tribunal Report directly acknowledged that a "sustained and virulent attack" was made on it by "senior Government ministers who questioned, *inter alia* the legality of its inquiries as well as the integrity of its members" in 2007-2008[34]:

[5–19]

> "It was entirely inappropriate for members of the Government to launch such unseemly and partisan attacks against a Tribunal of Inquiry appointed following a resolution passed by both Houses of the Oireachtas to inquire into serious concerns regarding corruption in public life. There appears little doubt but that the objective of these extraordinary and unprecedented attacks on the Tribunal was to undermine the efficient conduct of the Tribunal's inquiries, erode its independence and collapse its inquiry into that individual. They were as regrettable as they were ill-considered and unfounded."[35]

In the case of the Mahon inquiry the attacks failed to discredit the process but did contribute to the cost, delay and overall difficulties experienced by the Tribunal.

Given this context there are inherent dangers in placing a judge in a potentially politically sensitive environment. The danger may be that rather than the judge delivering independence to the tribunal, instead the political nature tribunal could undermine the independence of the

[5–20]

---

[32] Elliott above at n 3 at p 252.

[33] J Beatson, "Should Judges Conduct Public Inquiries?" (2005) LQR 221 at p 235.

[34] A Mahon, *Tribunal of Inquiry into certain Planning Matters and Payments* (The Stationary Office, Dublin, 2012) at p 22. Hereinafter "the Mahon Report".

[35] *ibid*.

judiciary.[36] Indeed, the US Supreme Court warned of these dangers when it stated that

> "the legitimacy of the judicial branch depends on its reputation for impartiality and nonpartisanship. That reputation may not be borrowed by the political branches to cloak their work in the neutral colors of judicial action."[37]

[5–21] The fact-finding nature of the public inquiry is also used to support judicial involvement: somehow it is supposed that judges have particular skills in this regard. Yet Elliott warns that the focus on evidence gathering and blameworthiness "invite an unduly narrow concept of accountability which borrows too heavily from the model adopted by the judicial system".[38] Thus, while courts engage in assigning responsibility for legal purposes from which liabilities and remedies can follow, the public inquiry is fulfilling a different purpose:

> Notions of fault, blame and responsibility are necessarily subtler in this sphere.... the ascription-of-responsibility function potentially served by inquiries, while not unimportant, shades into – in some senses, exists in the shadow of – [a] broader transparency function ... which serves to equip the public, politicians and the media to form their *own* views.[39]

[5–22] A clear set of rules as to when a public inquiry should be chaired by a judge cannot, however, be established and flexibility is required in this area. In our own jurisdiction, the large scale tribunals of inquiry have as a matter of practice been chaired by one or more judge. Smaller scale commissions of investigation have been chaired by legal personnel whether judges[40] or Senior Counsel.[41] The emphasis therefore remains on legally skilled chairs, which suggests that there remains a prioritisation of

---

[36] See Elliott above n 3 at p 252.

[37] Per Justice Blackmun, *Mistretta v United States* 488 US 348 at 261, 407 (1989), quoted by Beatson, above n 34 at p 235.

[38] Elliott above n 3 at p 254.

[39] *ibid.*

[40] The Commission of Investigation into the taping of phone calls at Garda stations is being chaired by Justice Niall Fennelly. http://www.merrionstreet.ie/index.php/2014/04/government-announces-terms-of-reference-for-commission-of-investigation-to-be-conducted-by-mr-justice-fennelly-2/ (date accessed, 4 July 2014).

[41] The Dean Lyons Commission of Investigation was chaired by George Birmingham SC (now a High Court Judge) http://www.justice.ie/en/JELR/Pages/Dean_Lyons_Commission_of_Investigation (date accessed, 4 July 2014).

a more legal form of accountability even in a non-legal accountability mechanism.[42]

Finally it needs to be clearly stated that public inquiries are not regarded   **[5–23]** as administering justice, even if they are chaired by a judge, for the purposes of Article 34.1 of the Constitution.[43] Thus, the Supreme Court in *Goodman International v Hamilton*[44] stated that "the critical factor [in the definition of the administration of justice] is trial and adjudication, not inquiry".[45]

The Public Nature of Public Inquiries

Unsurprisingly a public inquiry is expected to be held, for the most part, in   **[5–24]** open session with full public access. However, it is not clear that this is necessarily required. As we noted earlier, a lack of transparency may undermine its outcome at least in terms of reinforcing and achieving public trust and acceptance. However, in practice some issues will not be suitable for a public hearing, not least because publicity may damage the rights of participants. In addition, as we will see, the impact of holding hearings fully in public may also have a significant impact on the operation of a public inquiry in terms of increased procedural protections for participants, so much so that it undermines the efficient operation of the inquiry.

Section 2(a) of the Tribunals of Inquiry (Evidence) Act 1921 sets out the   **[5–25]** basic rule that proceedings of Tribunals of Inquiries should be held public:

> "A tribunal to which this Act is so applied as aforesaid-
>
> (a) shall not refuse to allow the public or any portion of the public to be present at any of the proceedings of the tribunal unless in the opinion of the tribunal it is in the public interest expedient so to do for reasons connected with the subject matter of the inquiry or the nature of the evidence to be given..."

However, this is not the default position for all inquiries. Commissions   **[5–26]** of Investigation, discussed in detail below, hold their hearings in private

---

[42] Elliott makes this point in relation to the UK model, above n 3 at p 256.

[43] Art 34.1 states that Justice shall be administered in courts established by law by judges appointed in the manner provided by this Constitution, and, save in such special and limited cases as may be prescribed by law, shall be administered in public.

[44] *Goodman International v Hamilton (No1)* [1992] 2 IR 542.

[45] *ibid* per McCarthy J at 607.

unless a witness requests that their evidence be given in public and the Commission of Investigation agree, or the Commission of Investigation is satisfied that it is in the interests of the investigation and fair procedure that a public hearing takes place.[46] This approach is adopted on the basis that a Commission of Investigation is a limited inquiry mechanism confined to fact finding only.

[5–27]   Public open hearings are generally seen as the most desirable approach to public inquiries because it is through that public access that the process gains legitimacy. However, there may be a difference between the public having access to a full and final report of an inquiry and access to all the hearings where evidence is aired. As the Law Reform Commission stated in its consultation paper on public inquiries, there is no constitutional requirement that an inquiry be held in public, so it is a matter for policy and implementation through legislation.[47] However, the judicial view of this has tended to come down on the side of public open hearings. Thus the chairman of the *Kerry Babies Tribunal* Lynch J asked a key question when he stated "[h]ow can an inquiry sitting in public, dispel public disquiet if crucial evidence is taken in private?"[48] Keane CJ commented in *Flood v Lawlor* that public hearings under s 2 of the 1921 Act were:

> "of paramount importance because the tribunal is established by a resolution of both Houses of the Oireachtas in order that matters of definite public concern should be investigated by an independent tribunal as a matter of urgency. As has been frequently pointed out, one of the objects and indeed probably the main object of an inquiry, is to seek to allay public concern arising from matters comprised in the terms of reference of the tribunal and affecting in general, although not exclusively, the conduct of public life at various levels and the conduct of public administration at various levels. That object of course will be defeated if the inquiry as a general rule is to be conducted in private rather than in public."[49]

---

[46] Section 11 2004 Act, see discussion below at para [5.93].

[47] Law Reform Commission, Consultation Paper on Public Inquiries Including Tribunals of Inquiry (LRC CP 22-2003) (LRC, Dublin, 2003) at para 8.01. Hereinafter "LRC CP". This contrasts of course with the constitutional requirement that court proceedings, save in exceptional/limited circumstances, be held in public under Art 34.1.

[48] Report of the Tribunal of Inquiry into "The Kerry Babies Case" (1985 Pl 3514) (The Stationary Office, Dublin, 1985) at p 142.

[49] Unreported, Supreme Court, 24 November 2000.

In the UK similar concerns have been raised and case law has teased out some of the issues. The decision to hold the *Harold Shipman Inquiry* in private[50] was challenged by the media and some of the families of the deceased in *R (Wagstaff) v Secretary of State for Health*.[51] The Divisional Court accepted the applicants' challenge to the legality of the decision of the Secretary of State for Health to hold a private inquiry. While the Secretary had argued that a private inquiry would encourage witnesses to speak freely and maximise efficiency, the Court found that these justifications were insufficient to justify an abrogation of the right of the public to receive information and ruled that the decision was irrational. The Court articulated some support for the idea that inquiries should generally be held in public; noting that there would need to be very strong reasons for moving an inquiry into a private sphere.[52] However, this view of openness as the default position for public inquiries has not been sustained through later English cases. In *Persey and others v Secretary of State for the Environment*[53] the Court found that there was no legal presumption that all public inquiries would be open. The Court distinguished *Wagstaff*, stating it turned on very particular facts and that the case was narrow in its focus. In *Persey* time was of the essence[54] and concerns about witness frankness were strong.

[5–28]

Irish experience has shown that, it is often difficult to sustain a public inquiry that is wholly public, particularly where constitutional justice issues arise. The Constitution protects a person's right to privacy and good name under Article 40.3.2° although these rights are not absolute and can

[5–29]

---

[50] The inquiry was set up after Harold Shipman was convicted at Preston crown court in January 2000 of the murder of fifteen of his elderly patients with lethal injections of morphine. It was begun in 2001 and investigated the extent of Shipman's crimes, why they were undetected for such a long period, and what systems could be developed to prevent a repeat of the tragedy. The inquiry was originally intended to be held under s 2 of the National Health Service Act 1977 with hearings in private and the final report to be made public.

[51] *R (Wagstaff) v Secretary of State for Health* [2001] 1 WLR 292.

[52] As a result of the decision the Secretary of State for Health announced the winding up of the previous inquiry and established a new public inquiry under the 1921 Tribunals of Inquiry Act.

[53] *Persey and others v Secretary of State for the Environment* [2002] EWHC 371 - the applicants challenged the decision of the Secretary of State to hold three private inquiries into the foot-and-mouth crisis of 2001. In particular they argued that the planned "Lessons Learned Inquiry" was a matter of public interest and should be held in public.

[54] In particular there were concerns that a recurrence of a foot-and-mouth outbreak was a real danger and that the inquiries were needed to understand how best to deal with the situation.

be qualified by the requirements of the common good. A public hearing can have a significant negative impact on a person in relation to their reputation, even where a report ultimately vindicates them. This has been recognised in relation to public inquiries in the case of *Redmond v Flood*[55] when the Court noted that while someone may be exposed to "distress and injury to their reputation":

> "[t]he right to privacy is, however, not an absolute right. The exigencies of the common good may outweigh the constitutional right to privacy. The exigencies of the common good require that matters considered by both Houses of the Oireachtas to be of urgent public importance be inquired into, particularly when such inquiries are necessary to preserve the purity and integrity of public life, without which a successful democracy is impossible."[56]

The result is that although the default position is that a Tribunal of Inquiry should be held in public, there is some recognition of the need for a flexible and balanced approach taking into account the competing issues of the public interest and a person's right to reputation and privacy.

[5–30]   The operation of Tribunals of Inquiries has therefore involved the use of a mixture of public and private hearings. Private hearings operate during the information gathering stages of these large-scale public inquiries during which the inquiry's lawyers sift through evidence relevant to the tribunal's line of investigation. Confidential hearings are held whereby witnesses attend, usually without their lawyers, and are interviewed by the inquiries' lawyers. The advantage of having a private information-gathering session is that the process does not harm those involved, as the information is not published. If it is to be used as evidence by the Inquiry, then it has to be given again in public and subjected to cross-examination by the person whose reputation may be damaged.[57] The courts have recognised the usefulness of this stage and provided Tribunals of Inquiry a significant amount of room for manoeuvre in managing the process

> "Tribunals of inquiry, however, necessarily have to conduct much of their initial investigations in private. This is both for practical reasons and to protect the interests and confidentiality of persons assisting the

---

[55] *Redmond v Flood* [1999] 3 IR 79.
[56] *ibid* at 88.
[57] Hogan and Morgan above n 2 at para 8-50 – 8-54.

Tribunal in its work. Furthermore, it enables the Tribunal to decide that a particular matter does not warrant a public hearing."[58]

To What Extent Do Public Inquiries Result in Positive Outcomes?

Sir Stephen Sedley's oft quoted statement that [5–31]

> "If public inquiries are to be known by their fruits, and if their proper fruits are reforms and improvements in law and practice, there is probably not a great deal to be said for them"[59]

This raises the prospect that public inquiries may in reality be ineffective in producing clear and discernable positive outcomes.

Public inquiries can be evaluated on a number of bases. There is the much [5–32] discussed easing of the public concern, something that can be rather difficult to evaluate in the aftermath of a public inquiry, not least because it is often the case that inquiries report long after the crisis that prompted the inquiry has subsided into the public memory and overtaken by more current concerns. However, there are some more tangible areas that can be considered, for example whether inquiries result in people being held to account and whether there is a recognisable impact from recommendations on policy and practice.

However, even where public inquiries are assessed in terms of whether [5–33] their recommendations are adopted, problems can arise. Recommendations may not be adopted for a wide variety of reasons, and a government's failure to implement them may not reflect the success or otherwise of the inquiry process. It should be recalled that there is no legal obligation on Government to accept the recommendations of a public inquiry nor a legal obligation to explain why they are not being implemented. However, at a minimum "an inquiry's report should present all the evidence, thus enabling others to make their own assessment of the way forward"[60] and an inquiry report should receive a "considered government response."[61]

---

[58] *O'Brien v Moriarty* [2005] IESC 32, judgment of Fennelly J, at 14.

[59] Sedley, above n 10 at p 469.

[60] NZ Law Commission Report, above n 14 at p 37 referencing G Rhodes, *Committees of Inquiry* (George Allen & Unwin, London, 1975) at p 205.

[61] *ibid* at p 37.

[5–34]   There is little empirical work carried out as to how far inquiries recommendations are implemented in Ireland.[62] The Department of Children and Youth Affairs published research carried out into the recommendations of family event inquiries[63] found that while some recommendations from the inquiries considered[64] were implemented or subsumed into wider policy, there was also an accompanying "recommendation fatigue" caused by "the succession of inquiries" resulting in diminishing returns from each subsequent inquiry.[65] In order to combat this, it was argued that recommendations would be improved by being informed by "all relevant sources of information, knowledge and expertise".[66] More generally, Beer offers some recommendations for improved practice in this area.[67] Firstly, that sufficient time and resources be allocated to the part of an inquiry that makes recommendations, noting that the focus is more often on the investigation phase. Secondly, that procedures are designed to uncover the right information and evidence which is used to develop recommendations. Thirdly, that proposed recommendations are discussed with those who will be responsible for implementation prior to their adoption. Finally that an audit system is developed in relation to them, for example an inquiry could be reconvened at a later stage to examine what has happened to its recommendations.

[5–35]   Ultimately the impact of a public inquiry revolves around the political will to act upon findings and implement recommendations. This is a recurring theme in relation to the operation of administrative justice accountability mechanisms that are not provided with a mechanism to enforce theirs decisions. We discuss this difficulty in chapter 4 on the Ombudsman where we reflect upon the need to ensure a strong and consistent commitment by the public sector to respect accountability findings. In Ireland, that commitment remains relatively weak at the present time in relation to systems that operate outside of the legal system.

---

[62] Internationally there is also little work done, see J Stutz, "What Gets Done and Why: Implementing the Recommendations of Public Inquiries" (2008) 51/3 *Canadian Public Administration* 501.

[63] H Buckley and C O'Nolan, *An Examination of Recommendations from Inquiries into events in families and their interactions with State services, and their impact on policy and practice* (DCYA, Dublin, 2013).

[64] Spanning 1993 – 2010, *ibid* at p 3.

[65] *ibid* at p 4.

[66] *ibid*.

[67] Beer, above n 13.

The History of the Modern Public Inquiry

Our public inquiry system was in large part inherited from the UK where [5–36] originally any public investigations into State problems and/or errors were carried out by Parliament[68]: these inquiries developed through the use of either Commissions of Investigation or Parliamentary Select Committees.[69] However, these methods were more often than not heavily affected by "party political motives"[70] which was a "characteristic defect" over the years,[71] a concern that continues to some extent today.

Perhaps the most well known example of the failure of this type of [5–37] inquiry was the 1912 *Marconi Scandal*. The affair concerned allegations that the acceptance by the then Government of a tender by the Marconi Company to build a series of wireless stations for the State was corrupt.[72] A Select Committee was established to investigate the matter but its report was split along party lines. The majority Liberal Party report cleared the Government, while the minority Conservative Party report found them guilty of "gross impropriety".[73] The subsequent Parliamentary debate adopted the same approach. GK Chesterton later described it as having "concluded as such affairs always conclude in modern England, with a formal verdict and a whitewashing committee".[74] The Marconi Select Committee Inquiry has since been regarded as the inquiry that "brought parliamentary inquiries into disrepute".[75]

---

[68] These inquiries were largely focused on the "mismanagement of war" and were generally held prior to any impeachment. *ibid* at p 4.

[69] A fairly comprehensive history of the development of public inquiries in the UK context can be found in the report of the Royal Commission on Tribunals of Inquiry (the Salmon Commission) 1966. Report of the Royal Commission on Tribunals of Inquiry, Cmnd. 3121 (Nov. 1966) hereinafter "Salmon Commission".

[70] As exemplified by the inquiry into allegations "that the Navy was riddled with Popery and that the Lord High Admiral ... had wantonly wasted public funds". The allegation was a political ploy but led a Select Committee of the House of Commons finding Samuel Pepys, who was Secretary to the Navy, guilty of Piracy, Popery and Treachery. When the case was referred to the Attorney General to consider prosecution it was found that the evidence relied on by the Committee was "tenuous and suspect" having been provided by professional informers. *ibid* at 11.

[71] *ibid.*

[72] Beer, above n 13 at p 6.

[73] *ibid.*

[74] GK Chesterton, *The Autobiography of GK Chesterton* (Sheed and Ward, New York, 1936) at 209.

[75] Public Administration Select Committee, *Parliamentary Commissions of Inquiry*, HoC 9th Report of session 2007-8 HC 473 (The Stationary Office, London, 2008), at p 7.

[5–38]   In response a new system of public inquiry was developed based on the Parnell Commission which had predated the Marconi inquiry. This Commission was established following allegations that Charles Stewart Parnell and others were responsible for the deaths of members of the British Government in Ireland. The investigation was established under the Special Commission Act 1888[76] and given special powers to inquire into the allegations and the powers and privileges of the High Court in order to conduct that investigation. These powers included compellability of people and documents, the power to punish for contempt and to issue warrants of arrest.[77] The legislation also provided protections for those appearing before the Commission. Thus, the commissioners could order a document in the possession of one party appearing before the inquiry be examined by another party,[78] witnesses could be cross-examined by another party[79] and evidence given by a party during the inquiry could not be used against them in any civil or criminal action.[80] The Parnell Commission was lauded as a success, its report was accepted by both pro- and anti-nationalist factions in Ireland and Parnell was vindicated.[81] It is therefore unsurprising that this model was later adopted as a solution to the politicisation of the Parliamentary inquiry system. As a result Westminster passed the Tribunal of Inquiry (Evidence) Act 1921[82] based in large part on the Parnell Commission.

[5–39]   However, despite this strong pedigree, the 1921 Act was in fact passed in haste through the UK Parliament[83] in response to another scandal needing a public inquiry.[84] The legislation provided that where both Houses of Parliament determined that a tribunal of inquiry was required to investigate a particular matter "of urgent public importance" then it should be established with all the relevant powers, rights and privileges of the High Court. Although the Bill originally intended that it would be Minsters who initiated inquiries this was rejected on the basis that the

---

[76] The Act was passed to deal specifically with the investigation.

[77] Special Commission Act 1888, s 2.

[78] *ibid* s 3.

[79] *ibid* s 6.

[80] Except for in relation perjury before the inquiry. *ibid* s 9.

[81] 35 volumes of evidence were published – Beer above at n 13 at p 5 fn 21.

[82] Hereinafter the "1921 Act".

[83] The Bill was introduced on 4 March 1921 and given Royal Assent just 20 days later on 24 March 1921. Beer, above n 13 at p 7.

[84] Allegations were made in 1921 that relevant papers concerning the awarding of contracts by the Ministry of Munitions had been destroyed by Departmental Officials. Beer *ibid* at p 6.

power to establish an inquiry was too great to be left solely in the hands of the Minister.[85] Thus it is Parliament who initiates a Tribunal of Inquiry, though the inquiry itself remains independent.

This legislation has formed the bedrock for the Irish system of Tribunals of Inquiry since the establishment of the State.[86] It remains in force today, although it has been amended on a number of occasions. It was also the main source of public inquiries in the UK until it was replaced by the Inquiries Act 2005 which consolidated and updated the law.[87] This updated framework has been criticised however, not least because it has involved a significant strengthening of ministerial control over statutory inquiries.[88] Nevertheless, refinement may still have been appropriate, given that the 1921 Act had not been widely used within UK public life, with only 24 Inquiries being established under its terms.[89]   **[5–40]**

The 1921 Act therefore has provided a framework for public inquiries in our and neighbouring jurisdictions. It has been subject to reviews over that time, one of the most significant being the Royal Commission on Tribunals of Inquiry. Although focused on the operation of the legislation in the UK, the report is worth noting in relation to the "cardinal principles" it set out when the report was published in 1966 which were to be followed in order to minimise the risk of harm or injustice to a person or their reputation: **[5–41]**

i.   Before any person becomes involved in an inquiry, the Tribunal must be satisfied that there are circumstances which affect him and which the Tribunal proposes to investigate;

---

[85] Note that a Commission of Investigation is initiated by a Minister or the Government. See discussion below at para [5.89].

[86] The operation of the 1921 Act is discussed in detail below at pars [5.43]-[5.61].

[87] The most high profile inquiry to be run under the *2005 Act* is the Leveson Inquiry: Culture, Practice and Ethics of the Press. Part 1 ran from 2011-12, Part 2 will commence after criminal prosecutions arising from phone tapping and related offences have been completed: http://webarchive.nationalarchives.gov.uk/20140122145147/http:/www.levesoninquiry.org.uk/ (date accessed, 6 July 2014).

[88] The Joint Committee on Human Rights noted that not only is the Minister now responsible for establishing Inquiries (as opposed to Parliament) but s/he can also close an Inquiry before publication of the report s 14, restrict attendance at an Inquiry or restrict disclosure of evidence s 19, and responsible for publishing the conclusions of an Inquiry s 25, Joint Committee on Human Rights, *Fourth report session 2004-05*, HC 224 2004-05.

[89] O Gay, *The Inquiries Act 2005*, SN/PC/06410 (House of Commons Library, London, 2012) p 3.

ii. Before any person who is involved in an inquiry is called as a witness, he should be informed in advance of allegations against him and the substance of the evidence in support of them;

iii. (a) He should have adequate opportunity of preparing his case and of being assisted by legal advisors;

(b) His legal expenses should normally be met out of public funds;

iv. He should have the opportunity of being examined by his own solicitor or counsel and of stating his own case in public at the inquiry;

v. Any material witnesses he wishes called at the inquiry should, if reasonably practicable, be heard;

vi. He should have the opportunity of testing by cross-examination conducted by his own solicitor or counsel any evidence which may affect him.[90]

[5–42]   These principles are cross jurisdictional given that they highlight the fundamental problem posed by public inquiries in relation to fair procedure. Unsurprisingly, given the significance of constitutional justice within our jurisdiction the operation of Tribunals of Inquiry in Ireland have in large part followed these six procedural safeguards.

Tribunals of Inquiry in Operation

Establishment of a Tribunal of Inquiry

[5–43]   A Tribunal of Inquiry can be established, to examine matters of "urgent public importance". Under s 1 of the 1921 Act, the executive branch shall establish a tribunal where the Houses of the Oireachtas call upon it to do so, and the power set out in the legislation will thereupon apply. It should be noted that the legislation does not expressly provide for the establishment of the tribunal of inquiry, but instead provides for the powers that such inquiries can use. The power to establish the inquiry rather derives from the Executive's inherent power to do so.[91] The practice is that the

---

[90] Salmon Commission above n 69 at p 17.

[91] *Goodman International v Hamilton (No1)* [1992] 2 IR 542 at 554:

"The Government or any Minister can inquire into matters of public interest as part of the exercise of its executive powers, but if this is done without reference to parliament then the inquiry will not have statutory powers which are to be found in the Tribunals of Inquiry (Evidence) Act 1921, and the Tribunals of Inquiry (Evidence) (Amendment) Act 1979."

Government establishes the inquiry under this inherent power and, where the 1921 Act is to apply a resolution of both Houses of the Oireachtas is required.[92]

Whether an issue falls within the definition of "urgent public importance" is a question for Government assessing both the political context of a particular crisis and the wider flow of public opinion. Whether the decision to establish a public inquiry is generally considered alongside the availability of possible alternative accountability mechanisms is unclear. However, in practice it seems that, given the costly and very public nature of this type of accountability mechanism, the choice of a tribunal of inquiry will likely be one of last resort adopted where a lower profile option is unavailable or deemed unsuitable. [5–44]

As we have discussed above, the purpose of a tribunal of inquiry is to

> "ascertain authoritatively the facts in relation to some matter of legitimate public interest which has been identified by its terms of reference and, where appropriate, to make recommendations as to how the future occurrence of the matter may be rendered less likely".[93]

The Terms of Reference of a Tribunal of Inquiry

The legislation does not deal directly with the establishment of terms of reference of the inquiry. Instead s 1(1) 1921 Act in effect leaves it to the Oireachtas and Government: [5–45]

> "Where it has been resolved (whether before or after the passing of this Act) by both Houses of [the Oireachtas] that it is expedient that a tribunal be established for inquiring into a definite matter described in the Resolution as of urgent public concern…"

The Law Reform Commission in their report on tribunals of inquiries argued that the legislation intended that the terms of reference should be "as clearly stated and precise as possible".[94] This is important, the tighter and more

---

[92] LRC CP above n 47 at para 2.24. The Law Reform Commission has recommended that the legislation be amended to expressly confer the power to establish Tribunals of Inquiry on the Executive. Para 2.37.

[93] *ibid* at para 2.05.

[94] Law Reform Commission, *Report on Public Inquiries Including Tribunals of Inquiries*, LRC 73-2005 at para 3.05. Hereinafter "LRC RP".

clearly defined the terms of reference, the better chance the tribunal has of carrying out the inquiry in a defined time and cost framework.

[5–46]   Experience, however, has found that maintaining control of the terms of reference can be difficult. Thus when the Office of the Attorney General undertook a comparative review of inquiries it found that there were nine clear drafting stages in preparing the terms of reference, and at each stage the terms of reference became wider.[95] The Law Reform Commission Report noted that drafting the terms of reference was in reality "one of the most important stages of the inquiry process"[96] and thus developing a system that would allow for precision in the process was essential. It therefore recommended that the tribunal of inquiry legislation be amended to require the inquiry to draft its terms of reference and that they should "set out the events, activities, circumstances, systems, practices or procedures to be inquired into as clearly and as accurately as possible".[97] In addition, it proposed that amendments to those terms of reference should be consented to and that a clear statement as to why amendment was necessary should accompany the request.[98]

Powers of Tribunals of Inquiry

[5–47]   Given that a public inquiry is a fact finding body, it requires a range of powers to successfully achieve that end. These are provided by the 1921 Act[99] s 1(1)[100] and s 4 of the Tribunals of Inquiry (Evidence) (Amendment)

---

[95] The nine stages were:
   1. Sponsoring department prepares a draft;
   2. Draft examined by OAG;
   3. Sponsoring department and OAG review draft;
   4. Chief Whips consider draft;
   5. Possible consultation with interest groups;
   6. Sponsoring department again considers draft and OAG gives legal clearance;
   7. Government makes decision on TOR;
   8. Draft put to both houses of Oireachtas – can be subject to amendment;
   9. Resolution passed by both houses containing TOR.
   Comparative Study into Parliamentary Inquiries and Tribunals of Inquiry (Pn 9796) at 26. See LRC CP *supra* n 47 at para 5.51.
[96] LRC RP above n 94 para 3.17.
[97] *ibid* at para 3.19.
[98] *ibid* at para 3.32 – amendment could be made by the sponsoring department or the tribunal.
[99] Note that the scope of the 1921 Act is limited, even with amendments, and many of the powers that are exercised are considered to be inherent powers. The Law Reform Commission Consultation Paper uses the example of the power of tribunals to retain counsel. See LRC CP *supra* at n 47 at para 6.02.
[100] s 1(1) provides Tribunals of Inquiry with the same "powers, rights and privileges as are vested in the High Court" including the power to summon a witness and enforce the

Act 1979.[101] The Supreme Court in *Lawlor v Flood*[102] held that s 4 of the 1979 Act needed to be read in conjunction with s 1(1) of the 1921 Act. The effect of this is that the tribunal of inquiry can make orders it considers appropriate for the purposes of its functions so long as they are powers the High Court holds.

These powers are supported by the creation of offences which operate to deal with those who obstruct the work of the tribunal of inquiry. Section 1(2) of the 1921 Act states that where someone fails to attend a tribunal of inquiry having been summoned to do so, or refuses otherwise to cooperate they are guilty of an offence, while s 4 of the 1979 Act provides that someone who fails to comply with an order of a tribunal will be in contempt of court. [5–48]

The 1921 Act s 1(3) provides that a person who gives evidence enjoys the privileges and immunities of High Court witnesses. This includes privilege against defamation, breach of confidence and offences under the Official Secrets Act 1963. As Hogan and Morgan note: [5–49]

> "there is a connection between these immunities and the obligations on witnesses to appear and answer, for it has always been accepted that it would be unfair to oblige a witness to answer questions truthfully and then to leave him exposed to the risk of defamation action if he does so".[103]

Procedures before Tribunals of Inquiries

A tribunal of inquiry is master of its own proceedings, having a wide discretion as to how the inquiry should generally be run: although as we will discuss below, it must operate under the rules of constitutional justice. [5–50]

> "the courts ... must afford a significant measure of discretion to the Tribunal as to the way in which it conducts these proceedings. It must, of course observe the constitutional rights of all persons who appear

---

attendance, examination of witnesses under oath, and the power to compel the production of documents.

[101] s 4 provides a tribunal "may make such orders as it considers necessary for the purposes of its functions, and it shall have, in relation to their making, all such powers, rights and privileges as are vested in the High Court or a judge of that Court in respect of the making of orders."

[102] [1999] 3 IR 107.

[103] Hogan and Morgan above n 2 at para 8-11.

before it or upon whom the decision of the Tribunal or the manner in which they conduct their business may impinge...."[104]

The legislation does not set out any clear guidance as to the specific procedures to be used other than requiring that hearings be held in public unless there is a good reason to exclude them.[105]

[5–51] In addition, it should be noted that the tribunal of inquiry is basically an inquisitorial body; something that was emphasised by Denham J when she noted that

> "[a] tribunal is not a court of law – either civil or criminal. It is a body – unusual in our legal system – an inquisitorial tribunal. It has not an adversary format".[106]

However, despite this, the practice of public inquiries can often descend into a more adversarial format with participants acting defensively in their approach to the process. This can be counterproductive to the fact and truth finding mission of the inquiry whereby the "need to be defensive and deny ... [gets] in the way of establishing the truth".[107]

[5–52] In practice, although there is no clear guidance on procedures the approach taken by recent inquiries has tended to follow a particular approach. These have naturally been informed by the rules of constitutional justice which we will consider below. Firstly, it is important to note that the rule against bias operates in relation to a public inquiry. Obviously, where a member of an inquiry has a pecuniary or other personal interest in proceedings before the inquiry then they should recuse themselves from being part of the proceedings or be liable to a judicial review challenge.[108] However, this point has not yet arisen in this context of a public inquiry, although

---

[104] *Flood v Lawlor* unreported, Supreme Court, November 24, 2000, quoted in LRC RP *supra* n 94 at para 8.22.
[105] s 2(a) 1921 Act.
[106] *Boyhan v Beef Tribunal* [1993] 1 IR 210 at 222.
[107] P McGrath, "Learning Within and Across Organizations: Investigating the Impact of Tribunals of Inquiry", Paper presented at the International Conference on Organizational Learning, Knowledge and Capabilities 26-28 April 2009 Amsterdam, the Netherlands at p 22 available online at http://www2.warwick.ac.uk/fac/soc/wbs/conf/olkc/archive/olkc4/papers/7dpaulmcgrath.pdf (date accessed, 8 July 2014).
[108] See chapter 11 - Natural Justice II: Bias in Decision-Making.

complaints that tribunals of inquiries have been biased against individuals do seem to be part of the public inquiry landscape.[109]

The rule against bias goes further than a direct interest and includes **[5–53]** situations where there is an appearance of bias. Subjective bias, as we discuss in more detail in chapter 11, is established where a "reasonable person in the circumstances would have a reasonable apprehension that the applicants would not have a fair hearing from an impartial judge on the issues".[110] Difficulties arise for inquiries because of the inquisitorial nature of the hearings whereby the Chairperson of the inquiry may be involved in questioning and therefore concerns may arise as to whether they are not perceived as being impartial.[111] As a result care must be taken to ensure that the Tribunal does not "descend into the forensic arena".[112] In practice, the procedure of public inquiries has evolved to ensure that in the main a Chairperson does not ask questions. Instead inquiries use their own Counsel to carry out relevant evidence gathering tasks including the carrying out of cross-examination at the public hearings.[113]

The Right to a Fair Hearing

The starting point in this area must be *In Re Haughey*[114] in which the **[5–54]** Supreme Court set out the minimum protections that should be afforded a "person of interest" (as opposed to a witness) before a hearing:

> "(a) that he should be furnished with a copy of the evidence which reflected on his good name; (b) that he should be allowed to cross-examine, by counsel, his accuser or accusers; (c) that he should be allowed to give rebutting evidence; and (d) that he should be permitted to address, again by counsel, the Committee in his own defence."[115]

---

[109] In *O'Callaghan v Mahon & Ors* [2008] 2 IR 514 the applicants alleged bias on the part of the Mahon Tribunal, the Supreme Court rejected the application noting that the applicants were asking the Court to conduct a "mini-tribunal".

[110] Per Denham J in *Bula Ltd. v Tara Mines Ltd. (No. 6)* [2000] 4 IR 412 at 441.

[111] Hogan and Morgan above n 2 at para 8-29.

[112] *Kiely v Minister for Social Welfare (No. 2)* [1977] IR 267 at 283.

[113] See LRC CP above n 47 at para 7.08

[114] *In Re Haughey* [1971] IR 217. This case is discussed in more detail in chapter 10: *Audi Alteram Partem*.

[115] *ibid* at 263-264.

The impact of this judgment in relation to the operation of tribunals of inquiry has been significant, and in many ways detrimental, at least in terms of the efficient running of an inquiry process. Although the Supreme Court in *Lawlor v Flood*[116] indicated that tribunals should not regard the *In Re Haughey* rights as "a ritual or a formula requiring a slavish adherence"[117] there has been a tendency to provide a high level of observance even where someone is merely a witness rather than a person of interest.

Right to Advance Notice

[5–55] The right to advance notice is the most basic right from *In Re Haughey* and has been understood by the courts to require a tribunal of inquiry to ensure that

> "witnesses ... know the subject matter of the inquiry and be advised as to the procedure to be adopted by it... [N]otice should be given to the witness of the area in respect of which it is intended to examine him."[118]

The result has been that a tribunal of inquiry will serve copies of evidence on parties who are likely to be affected by that evidence. In other jurisdictions procedural approaches have been adopted whereby prior notice of criticisms would be sent out to affected parties. In the UK an inquiry is under an obligation to send out "warning letters"[119] under the statutory regime.[120]

Right to Legal Representation

[5–56] Given the requirements of constitutional justice, and the danger to reputation, the issue of whether legal representation is available to those appearing before an inquiry is of significance. Normally, under the rules of constitutional justice, there is no right to legal representation and a number of factors such as the seriousness of the matter and the legislative

---

[116] *Lawlor v Flood* [1999] 3 IR 107.

[117] *ibid* at 143.

[118] *ibid.*

[119] Beer, above n 13 at p 161. The letters can also be called "salmon letters" and "Maxwell letters" if the inquiry is not operating under the Public Inquiries Act 2005 but is a non-statutory inquiry.

[120] The Inquiry Rules 2006 (SI No 1838) [United Kingdom] s 13(1) provides that the Chairman of an inquiry can send warning letters to (a) those he considers may be subject to criticism, (b) about whom criticism can be inferred from evidence, and (c) who may be subject to criticism in the report.

framework will be taken into consideration.[121] However, as noted above, public inquiries have tended to take the approach of applying the *In Re Haughey* rights widely and this trend is evident in the area of legal representation.

Section 2(b) of the 1921 Act gives a tribunal of inquiry discretion to grant legal representation to persons appearing before it. How far this extends relies in part on the rules of constitutional justice which would indicate that a "person of interest" be allowed legal representation given that their good name and related interests are at stake; such people are granted full representation by inquiries. Beyond "persons of interest", third parties can also make an application to an inquiry for authorisation of legal representation. If representation is granted they are generally given limited representation which relates to particular issues before the inquiry only.[122] **[5–57]**

However, in practice inquiries have often taken a wide approach to the granting of representation. The clearest example of this was the *Beef Inquiry* which allowed all witnesses to avail of legal representation (full and limited) during its proceedings. Representation was even extended to public representatives, along with the payment of legal costs, who had made allegations in relation to the inquiry[123] and were simply witnesses before the inquiry. This approach was far wider than would be provided in a court hearing[124] and wider than the rights as expressed in the *Haughey* decision where access to legal representation was predicated on the fact that the inquiry was investigating his misconduct. **[5–58]**

While inquiries have tended to take a wide approach to granting legal representation when a case has come before the courts they have not adopted the same position. In *Boyhan v Beef Tribunal*[125] the tribunal had granted limited representation to the United Farmers Association (UFA) which allowed them to have legal representation when their witnesses **[5–59]**

---

[121] See discussion in chapter 10: *Audi Alteram Partem*.

[122] LRC CP *supra* n 47 at paras 7.31-7.32.

[123] Thus, Deputies who had made statements in the Dáil based on information from constituents working in Goodman's factories that bad practices were going on there. They gave evidence to the Beef Tribunal and since they were making allegations they were dubbed "allegators" by Goodman. Deputies were represented before the Beef Tribunal and their costs were paid by the State.

[124] For a more extensive discussion see Hogan and Morgan above n 2 at para 8.40-1.

[125] *Boyhan v Beef Tribunal* above, n 106.

gave evidence, could examine those witnesses and participate in the part of the tribunal to which their evidence was relevant. The plaintiffs sought an injunction from the Court requiring that they be provided with full representation during relevant parts of the hearings on the basis that they represented the public interest and the interests of farmers. However, in the High Court Denham J rejected their application, basing her decision squarely on *In re Haughey*:

> "It is clear that the UFA is not an accused. Its conduct is not being investigated by the Tribunal. There are no allegations against the UFA or its members. It is a witness, which has proffered itself. As such, while its constitutional rights must at all times be protected it does not appear that its rights -- to good name, for example -- are in jeopardy in any way at all. The position of the UFA at this time in relation to the Tribunal is analogous to a witness in a trial and as such it is not entitled to the protection as set out at (a) and (d) by O Dálaigh CJ [in *In re Haughey*]. Its position, as a witness, is fully protected by the limited legal representation awarded by the Tribunal."[126]

Cross Examination

[5–60] The general approach adopted in inquiries is that a witness is examined by the inquiry counsel, cross-examined by interested parties, examined by their own lawyer and finally re-examined by the inquiry counsel. However, this is not to suggest that there is an automatic right to cross-examination, and this would of course fit with the general approach to cross-examination under the rules of constitutional justice. The lack of a right is supported by the general inquisitorial nature of the inquiry process.

[5–61] However, there are situations where cross-examination is appropriate where a person's good name or other rights are at stake:

> "Cross-examination adds considerably to the length of time which proceedings will take. But it is an essential, constitutionally guaranteed, right which has been the means of the vindication of innocent people... It must be firmly understood that, when a body decides to deal with matters as serious as those in question here, it cannot (apart from anything else) deny to persons whose reputations and livelihoods

---

[126] *ibid* at 222.

are thus brought into issue, the full power to cross-examine fully, as a matter of right and without unreasonable hindrances."[127]

Beyond this, the LRC has recommended that where evidence is uncontested it should be "read into" the record of the inquiry, parties should consent to this and the written account of the evidence made available. By ensuring that the evidence is published, for example on the inquiry website, the requirement of the inquiry operating in public under s 2(a) of the 1921 Act would be complied with.[128] However, the LRC did sound a note of caution in regard to this in that such an approach "should not be taken lightly" and in truth the report's preference appeared to be that evidence should be presented in person by a witness "rather than reading in an affidavit or document drafted with the aid of a solicitor or some other person".[129]

Standard of Proof

In terms of what standard of proof should be adopted in an inquiry, different tribunals of inquiry have adopted different standards depending on the terms of reference they had and the material they were investigating. Although it might be concluded that a criminal standard is not applicable to an inquisitorial fact finding process, conversely the consequences of an adverse finding by an inquiry might suggest that the balance of probability standard was also inappropriate. **[5–62]**

This question was considered in *Lawlor v Members of the Tribunal of Inquiry into certain planning matters and payments.*[130] Evidence was presented to the court of a diverse approach adopted by inquiries — the Kerry Babies tribunal applied "a 'sliding scale' employing at different times the standard of proof of beyond reasonable doubt, proof by way of "substantial probability" and proof "on the balance of probabilities" depending on the seriousness of the allegations".[131] While the Beef Tribunal adopted a criminal standard of proof, the Blood Transfusion tribunal used terminology consistent with the criminal requirement although not expressly adopting a "beyond reasonable doubt" standard. **[5–63]**

---

[127] *Maguire v Ardagh* [2002] 1 IR 385 at 707.
[128] LRC RP above n 94 at para 5.53.
[129] *ibid.*
[130] *Lawlor v Members of the Tribunal of Inquiry into certain planning matters and payments* [2009] IESC 50.
[131] *ibid* at 178.

[5–64]   In the *Lawlor* judgment Murray J adopted a position that generally a criminal standard would be unsuitable for a tribunal of inquiry because

> "no punitive sanctions or consequences attend the findings of a tribunal of inquiry. It is this fundamental distinction which differentiates the criminal law from the law applicable to tribunals."[132]

Nevertheless he also recognised that the impact of adverse findings on a person were serious and the civil standard might therefore be unsuitable too. Without wanting to develop an "intermediate standard of proof" he concluded that generally a civil standard should be adopted but that

> "[t]he findings made must clearly be proportionate to the evidence available. Any such findings of grave wrongdoing should in principle be grounded upon cogent evidence."[133]

Costs

[5–65]   Although there is no automatic right to costs, where legal representation has been granted, legal representation costs have in practice made up a substantial part of the overall costs of recent tribunals of inquiry.[134] In *McBrearty v Morris*[135] the applicants, as victims, had been granted the right to full legal representation before the tribunal but were seeking a costs order prior to their involvement because they could not afford to fund their own legal representation. Legal aid was not available to the applicants and the tribunal argued that it was not in a position to make a costs adjudication before it had made any findings in the investigation.

[5–66]   In the High Court Peart J held that there was no constitutional right under Article 40.3 (right to fair procedures) to have your costs paid for by the State and thus no requirement for the legislation to guarantee their costs in advance of the tribunal commencing.[136] The Court noted the overall difficulty in this area and the decision by the State to balance the competing

---

[132] *ibid* 185.

[133] *ibid* 184.

[134] The Comptroller and Auditor General Special Report on Tribunals of Inquiries found that these costs represented "between 63% and 85% of the total costs of three inquiries – the Mahon Tribunal, the Morris Tribunal and the Moriarty Tribunal. Comptroller and Auditor General, Special Report: Tribunals of Inquiry (Stationary Office, Dublin, 2008) at para.2.4. Hereinafter "CAG Report".

[135] *McBrearty v Morris* [2003] IEHC 154 High Court (13 May 2003).

[136] s 6(1) of the Tribunals of Inquiry (Evidence) (Amendment) Act 1979.

interests of those appearing before an inquiry and the wider expense to the public:

> "The legislature has revisited the question of costs of those appearing at tribunals and has decided how the matter is to be dealt with. It has decided to strike a balance between the right of some parties to whom representation has been granted to have their costs paid for, and the public's right to be protected from a situation where all witnesses who have been granted representation at the tribunal would have their costs discharged from public funds, regardless of whether they had co-operated or not, or given false or misleading information. In so deciding, due regard is had to the right of persons to have their costs paid, provided that they have cooperated."[137]

It is noteworthy that under s 6 of the Tribunals of Inquiry (Evidence) (Amendment) Act 1979 there is provision for recovery of costs where someone has not cooperated with the inquiry. However, the Minister for Finance in a submission to the Mahon Tribunal acknowledged that this power should "only be used in special circumstances and with due regard to the principle of proportionality".[138] He went on to note that where a party had been found to obstruct or hinder an inquiry or failed to cooperate with it then the inquiry could consider making an order that any additional payments incurred by the inquiry and/or third party as a result of that behaviour be payable by the offending party.   **[5–67]**

Tribunals of inquiry have utilised this power to refuse a person costs, in particular the Flood Tribunal. These actions came under scrutiny however in *Murphy v Flood*[139] where the applicant had been found by the Flood Tribunal to have obstructed and hindered the inquiry by failing to give a truthful account and as a result had been refused costs. The Supreme Court held that the Tribunal had acted *ultra vires* firstly in making findings of obstruction and hindrance — a criminal offence that the Tribunal had no power in relation to — and secondly in basing a decision to refuse costs on that finding. Hardiman J concluded that the   **[5–68]**

> "tribunal as constituted simply had no power to inquire into the question of 'obstruction and hindrance' and, even for the purpose of

---

[137] Above n 135 at p 83 of transcript.
[138] Quoted in the CAG Report above n 134 at para 2.56.
[139] *Murphy v Flood* [2010] IESC 21.

costs, could have discharged its function quite adequately by simply considering the question of cooperation."[140]

[5–69] A question arises however as to whether this type of decision-making goes beyond the typical fact finding of a Tribunal and brings it into the realm of administering justice; thus leading to a breach of Article 34.1.[141] Typically tribunals of inquiry have been found not to impose liabilities or affect rights and so therefore are constitutional. In *Murphy v Flood* the Supreme Court concluded that it did not have to decide whether the power under s 6 was unconstitutional because the Tribunal's decision in the case had in fact been *ultra vires* its power. This being said Hardiman J did sound a note of (*obiter*) caution:

> "It is certainly within the power of the legislature to make provision for an award of costs before a Tribunal of Inquiry. It did this in 1997 and had done so previously in 1979. But whether this new power, conferred on a tribunal which provides for the individual notably attenuated procedural safeguards by comparison with those available in a court is consistent with the Tribunal's established constitutional status which depends on its "findings" having the status merely of opinions and being "devoid of legal effect" is manifestly doubtful. But the issue does not, in my opinion, arise directly in the present case so I propose to abstain from expressing a concluded view on it."[142]

Previous case law has, however, indicated that the courts do not consider findings in relation to costs to be actions of administration of justice because that has to involve a ruling on substantive legal rights and not something tied up with procedure.[143]

[5–70] The wider question of whether tribunals of inquiries offer value for money and the thorny issue of the high cost of these institutions is one that has tended to dog large scale public inquiries. However, efficiency cannot be achieved at the expense of independence as the Comptroller and Auditor General's report stressed:

---

[140] *ibid* at 204.

[141] Article 34.1 states: Justice shall be administered in courts established by law by judges appointed in the manner provided by this Constitution, and, save in such special and limited cases as maybe prescribed by law, shall be administered in public.

[142] Above n 139 at 205.

[143] *State (Plunkett) v Registrar of Building Societies* [1998] 4 IR 1 involving a specialised investigation, under the Provident Societies (Am) Act 1978.

"The state faces a considerable challenge to achieve predictability and financial control in the case of tribunals of inquiry which operate under the authority of the legislature without compromising their independent investigations or the constitutional rights of witnesses."[144]

The cost of an inquiry is funded by the State and is the financial responsibility of the sponsoring Government Department. Thus, the Mahon Tribunal was funded by the Department of Environment, Heritage and Local Government. The primary costs arise out of the inquiries own administrative and legal staff, third party witness costs and the costs sustained by State bodies in supporting and participating in the inquiry. However, a significant factor in the costs has also arisen in many inquiries as a result of litigation brought against the inquiry. [5–71]

Concern as to costs and delay relating to inquiries prompted the Comptroller and Auditor General to carry out an examination of the costs and efficiencies of tribunals of inquiries which reported in 2008.[145] This looked at three high profile inquiries that had dominated the political landscape of the 2000s — the Mahon Tribunal, the Morris Tribunal and the Moriarty Tribunal. In terms of the time frames of inquiries, the report found that there were a number of contributing problems to this including: [5–72]

- The extended nature the investigations in these particular inquiries caused by wide terms of reference and a further extension of the scope of investigation once inquiries were underway;
- The largely adversarial procedures and practices that were adopted, including a large amount of time which was devoted to cross examination of witnesses during hearings;
- The legal challenges that the inquiries provoked;
- The difficulty in securing the attendance of some witnesses caused at times by the lack of cooperation and even obstruction by some witnesses;
- Procedural deficiencies in the inquiry process which meant that some orders were quashed.

As a result the report recommended reforms that would improve procedural efficiency in inquiries. It is interesting to note that these were [5–73]

---

[144] CAG Report, above n 134 at p 11.
[145] *ibid.*

along the lines of those previously set out by the Law Reform Commission report.[146] Foremost amongst the recommendations was the need to ensure focused terms of reference are adopted at the start of the process and limits on how far inquiries can extended once they have begun. In relation to procedures, the report noted that as the inquiry is not a body that can impose sanctions and is primarily a fact finding mechanism, there was significant scope for reducing cross-examination and instead allowing for the "reading-in" of evidence which is not contested or in written form. The report stressed that where a person's reputation is *not* at stake, a tribunal should adopt procedures that are less court like and more akin to an auditing process:

> "evidence gathering procedures that mirror those in auditing or other investigation work might be appropriate and efficient for much of this work".[147]

[5–74] The understanding of the role of the tribunal of inquiry informing the Comptroller & Auditor General's report was a fact finding-centric model, and there was an implicit subordination of its status as a wider accountability mechanism:

> "since a primary purpose of the tribunal is to establish facts designed to allow public administrations to mitigate risks to good governance and remedy shortcomings in control of public programmes rather than hold individual accountable (which is a matter for the courts) it would be worth considering whether efficiency could be improved by only proceeding to oral hearing in instances where a party after due notice asserts that their reputation or interests may be adversely affected."[148]

Even with this limited conception of the role of the tribunal of inquiry mechanism, such proposed reform steps would struggle to take hold given the potential impact on reputation that the hearings and report pose. Constitutional justice requirements have consistently pulled tribunals' procedures to a more judicial adjudicatory framework.

---

[146] LRC RP, above n 94 paras 11.23-11.36.
[147] CAG Report, above n 134 at p 9.
[148] *ibid* at p 11.

Challenging Tribunals of Inquiry

This chapter has already foreshadowed that judicial review proceedings   **[5–75]**
are available to challenge the operation of a tribunal of inquiry. Indeed
the Comptroller & Auditor General report noted that "[l]itigation has
been a feature of all the tribunals", with just over €4 million being spent
on court action up to 2007 in the three tribunals examined,[149] distributed
across 39 separate cases. For the most part those cases have involved
challenges to procedural rulings of the relevant Tribunals of Inquiry,
and more recently we have seen challenges to costs decisions.[150]

A more difficult question arises when considering how far the actual   **[5–76]**
findings of an inquiry can be challenged. The 1966 Salmon Commission
which considered the operation of the Tribunal of Inquiry system in the
UK, highlighted the fact that there was no right of appeal from a
Tribunal, nor did it think one was appropriate.[151] The main reasons put
forward in support of this were the fact that an appeal would effectively
require a rehearing of the evidence (something deeply impracticable
especially considering the often lengthy hearings involved in such
inquiries) and that a final resolution was important to the process
particularly to restore public confidence and draw a line under events.[152]
As Beer notes, there is also the significant point that public inquiries do
not make legally binding findings or determine liability under either
the civil or criminal law.[153]

Challenges to the findings of tribunals of inquiry have recently come   **[5–77]**
before the Courts in Ireland. In February 2014, Owen Corrigan was given
leave by the High Court to challenge the findings of the Smithwick
Tribunal into the killing by the IRA of two senior RUC officers in 1989. The
basis of the challenge however, is largely reliant on fair procedure claims,
in particular that he was not given advance notice in relation to contested
findings that were made against him.[154]

---

[149] *ibid* at p 33.
[150] See for example the discussion relating to *Murphy v Flood,* above at paras [5-68]-[5-69].
[151] Salmon Commission, above n 69 at para 134.
[152] See Beer, above n 13 at para 11.03.
[153] *ibid.*
[154] The Smithwick Tribunal also prompted strong criticism from three other retied Garda
Officers, who published a detailed critique of the findings although no report of a
judicial review of the findings had been reported. C Lally, "Three former senior gardaí
challenge tribunal findings", 28 January 2014, available online at http://www.irishtimes.

[5–78]   It must be stressed that judicial review challenges provide a very limited mechanism for grievances, and of course do not constitute an appeal. This was made clear by the High Court in *Richardson v Mahon*[155] when it refused to judicially review parts of the Mahon Tribunal report on the grounds that errors of fact had been made within jurisdiction. Thus, Dunne J stated:

> "It is a somewhat artificial exercise to break down the findings in the respective paragraphs complained of and to criticise elements of those paragraphs as being irrational or unreasonable findings. In truth, this is more in the nature of a challenge to "part findings" of the Tribunal. It seems to me that the manner in which this has been done by the applicant lends force to the argument that what is at the heart of this application is an error of fact and an error within jurisdiction which is not amenable to judicial review. It is not the function of the court in these proceedings to correct errors of fact made by the Tribunal and thus, I have concluded that the applicant is not entitled to the relief sought herein."[156]

[5–79]   As we noted in relation to this case in chapter 7 the Court would not permit a review of errors of fact that led to "part findings" of the Tribunal, holding that it was "not a court of appeal and does not engage in a rehearing to resolve conflicts of fact". Rather, in acknowledging that there was an error, the Court expressed confidence that the Tribunal would be "happy to correct the error".[157]

[5–80]   Judicial review remains available to quash a finding of fact from a tribunal of inquiry where it arises from a breach of fair procedures or because it falls within the test of unreasonableness, expressed by Dunne J in *Richardson v Mahon* in the traditional *The State (Keegan) v Stardust Compensation Tribunal*[158] that a finding "plainly and unambiguously flies in the face of fundamental reason and common sense". Judicial review proceedings therefore are available but very difficult to successfully argue.

---

com/news/crime-and-law/three-former-senior-garda%C3%AD-challenge-tribunal-findings-1.1670108 (date accessed, 8 July 2014).

[155] *Richardson v Mahon* [2013] IEHC 118.

[156] *ibid* at p 17 of transcript.

[157] This correction was duly made by the Mahon Tribunal, http://www.flood-tribunal.ie/asp/Index.asp?ObjectID=310&Mode=0&RecordID=451 (date accessed, 8 July 2014).

[158] *The State (Keegan) v Stardust Compensation Tribunal* [1986] 1R 642.

Reform

The operation of tribunals of inquiry has, as the discussion above **[5–81]** indicates, been subject to a variety of reviews and recommendations for reform. This chapter does not endeavour to provide a complete discussion of possible reforms: these can be found clearly expressed in the Law Reform Commission Report of 2005.[159] However, it is useful to note that the *Tribunals of Inquiry Bill* was brought before the Oireachtas in 2005 with the intention of consolidating and reforming the various pieces of legislation in this area.[160] Indeed, it was meant to put in place a modern and comprehensive statutory framework which would govern all aspects of a tribunal of inquiry from the time of its establishment to publication of its final report. The Bill was a product of the Law Reform Commission report but was also heavily modelled on the UK's Inquiries Act 2005[161] which was the source of the high profile Leveson Inquiry into the role of the press and the police into the infamous phone-hacking scandal.[162]

Significant proposed amendments include the clarification of the process **[5–82]** by which terms of reference are adopted and amended (s 6) and extensive powers in relation to cost (Part 9). In relation to the cost issue the Bill provides the Minister with the power to make regulations to set a maximum legal fee remuneration from the state (s 39) and the use of competitive tendering for the hiring of expert staff (s 5(3)). However, the Bill was abandoned, without explanation, by the former Government in 2009. It has been restored to the legislative agenda by the current Government and at time of writing is due to go to report stage.

---

[159] LRC RP, above n 94 at chapter 11.

[160] Tribunals of Inquiry (Evidence) Act 1921; the Tribunals of Inquiry (Evidence) (Amendment) Act 1979; the Tribunals of Inquiry (Evidence) (Amendment) Act 1997; the Tribunals of Inquiry (Evidence) (Amendment) Act 1998; the Tribunals of Inquiry (Evidence) (Amendment) (No. 2) Act 1998; the Tribunals of Inquiry (Evidence) (Amendment) Act 2002; the Tribunals of Inquiry (Evidence) (Amendment) Act 2004.

[161] The legislation can be accessed online at http://www.legislation.gov.uk/ukpga/2005/12/contents (date accessed, 8 July 2014). However, it should be noted that the Inquiries Act 2005 has not been a complete success. Costs remain a concern as does the lack of transparency regarding decision making as to when an inquiry should be held. In fact the data from the HL Select Committee which reported in 2014 was that only 14 public inquiries had been established under the legislation with other methods more often utilised such as alternative legislation or non-legislative inquiries. House of Lords Select Committee, *The Inquiries Act 2005: post-legislative scrutiny* (The Stationary Office, London, 2014).

[162] http://webarchive.nationalarchives.gov.uk/20140122145147/http://www.levesoninquiry.org.uk/ (date accessed, 8 July 2014).

[5–83]   In the meantime, however, reform of the operation of tribunals of inquiry has stalled and there is little appetite for their use so long as the perceived cost and timeframes of such bodies lead to a conclusion that they do not provide value for money as an accountability mechanism. It remains the case that, as the Mahon Tribunal Report notes, large scale, mostly judge led public inquiries "are typically only used as a last resort, when other agencies of investigation have failed to work or are unlikely to work".[163] In reality, their status as a failsafe on other accountability mechanisms seems well earned, with both their disadvantages and benefits seeming to point towards their targeted use on landmark governance crises.

Commissions of Investigation

[5–84]   The passing of the Commissions of Investigation Act 2004 came against a backdrop of deep dissatisfaction with the operation of Tribunals of Inquiries. Concerns about the cost and excessive length of tribunals led the Law Reform Commission to consider alternative inquiry models designed to minimise the impact of constitutional justice on such bodies. In furtherance of this objective, the Commission concluded that the best alternative would be to have an inquiry that was held in private:

> "The obvious advantage of this is that accusations against a person ... are not bruited forth to the world immediately. At most, if the inquiry finds the accusations to be substantiated, a version of them will appear in the final report, together with the inquiry's measured judgment."[164]

The Commission also noted that such a model could attract improved cooperation from participants. It is interesting to note that the report likened this approach to the work of the Ombudsman, at least in terms of emphasising institutional flaws over highlighting individual wrong doers.

[5–85]   Thus, when the legislation was put before the Dáil in 2004 then Minister for Justice, Michael McDowell TD, stressed the time and cost benefits of the new model which would still meet procedural justice requirements.[165] Speed and efficiency were key selling points, and although the legislation was largely welcomed, it is interesting to note that concerns were raised

---

[163] Mahon Report above n 34 at p 22.
[164] LRC CP above n 47 at para 10.07.
[165] 581 *Dáil Debates*, col 921, 4 March 2004.

from the start that the attempts to deal with costs were inadequate.[166] However, it was clearly stated that the proposed Commissions of investigation were intended to be a "lawyer free zone" where facts could be established without the need for cross-examination or comment.[167] This in turn led to some TDs voicing concern that the desire to reduce costs was perhaps being prioritised too much over the needs of constitutional justice.[168]

The legislation therefore established an additional method of investigation, a new type of public inquiry that was outside the Oireachtas and in the public realm, but which generally heard evidence in private and was focused on specific and manageable issues. Commissions of investigation were not meant to replace tribunals of inquiry, but instead would offer a more efficient fact finding inquiry which might be a precursor to a full tribunal of inquiry or an alternative where a large scale public inquiry was deemed unnecessary. The recent reluctance on the part of Ministers to establish tribunals of inquiry because of costs has meant that in practice commissions have been widely used since the legislation was passed.[169]   [5–86]

The legislation expressly notes the possible connection between a commission of investigation and a tribunal of inquiry in ss 44-46 of the 2004 Act. Thus where a tribunal of investigation is regarded as being necessary in an area already being dealt with by a commission of investigation the relevant Minister, or commission itself (if still in   [5–87]

---

[166] *ibid* at col 933 per O'Keeffe TD.

[167] F Sweeney, *Commissions of Investigation and Procedural Fairness: A Review from a legal perspective of the Commissions of Investigation Act 2004 and the Report into the Catholic Archdiocese of Dublin* (Dublin, 2013). Available online at http://www.bishop-accountability.org/reports/2013_10_29_Sweeney_ACP_Commissions_of_Investigation.pdf (date accessed, 8 July 2014) at para.1.4. This legal report by barrister Fergal Sweeney was commissioned by Association of Catholic Priests in Ireland. Hereinafter "Sweeney".

[168] *Supra* n 165, at col 934 per O'Keeffe TD.

[169] Recent inquiries set up under the Commission of Investigation model include the Mother and Baby Homes Inquiry, 11 June 2014 http://www.dcya.gov.ie/docs/11.06.14_Speech_by_Minister_for_Children_and_Youth_Affairs_C/3200.htm, (date accessed, 8 July 2014), the Commission of Investigation into telephone recordings in Garda Stations, 8 April 2014 http://www.merrionstreet.ie/index.php/2014/04/government-announces-terms-of-reference-for-commission-of-investigation-to-be-conducted-by-mr-justice-fennelly-2/ (date accessed, 8 July 2014), and the Commission of Investigation into the Banking Scandal, 19 January 2010 http://www.bankinginquiry.gov.ie/Documents/Misjuding%20Risk%20%20Causes%20of%20the%20Systemic%20Banking%20Crisis%20in%20Ireland.pdf (date accessed, 8 July 2014).

operation) will make all documents and material available to the Tribunal of Inquiry.[170] In this way it may be that a commission of investigation acts as a pre-inquiry information gathering exercise, reducing the amount of time and money needed for the full public investigation.[171]

[5–88]   An important limitation on this form of inquiry is that the commission of investigation is restricted to being a fact finding body only. It is generally stated therefore that a commission of investigation is not required to consider whether someone is culpable for an error. Indeed, the explanatory memorandum of the Bill noted that it would not be "the function of a Commission to adjudicate where there is a conflict or incomplete evidence"[172] which highlights the limitations of such bodies. Section 32(2) indicates how a commission should approach such evidence:

> If for any reason (including insufficient, conflicting or inconsistent evidence) a commission considers that the facts relating to a particular issue have not been established, the commission in its report –
>
> (a) shall identify the issue, and
>
> (b) may indicate its opinion as to the quality and weight to any evidence relating to the issue.

So the fact-finding remit only operates where the facts are settled; as Joe Costello TD noted in the debate on the Bill:

> "[t]his is presumably because the testing of conflicting accounts must involve due notice to the individuals likely to be adversely affected and the examination and cross-examination of witnesses, all areas where it is simply impossible to exclude legal participation."[173]

Given the surrounding media and political context however, it seems obvious that even this type of limited investigation can have significant repercussions for someone's reputation. This may result in either a

---

[170] s 45(1).

[171] The Nyberg Report on the Banking Crisis has been used in a slightly different way as a precursor to an inquiry to be carried out by an Oireachtas Committee. See http://www.bankinginquiry.gov.ie/ (date accessed 8 July 2014).

[172] Explanatory memorandum, p 2. Available online at http://www.oireachtas.ie/documents/bills28/bills/2003/2903/b2903d.pdf (date accessed, 8 July 2014).

[173] 581 *Dáil Debates* col. 941, 4 March 2004.

narrowing of the remit of commissions of investigation given that in practice uncontested facts will be rare; or the ever growing presence of constitutional justice in the proceedings of such inquiries.[174]

The 2004 Act allows for the establishment of commissions by Government not the Oireachtas. Approval of the Minister for Finance must also be provided. The express purpose of such establishment is to consider matters regarded by the Government as being of "significant public concern".[175] This term is not defined in the legislation but was described by Minister McDowell TD in the second reading debate on the Bill as being:

[5–89]

> "one that is of more than mere interest to the public; it must, instead, be an issue which has serious, including long-term, implications for public life. These implications could include the welfare and safety of a sector in society or the effective and safe operation of a significant public service."[176]

Although the Government initiates the inquiry, the Oireachtas must provide its consent to its creation,[177] so that the Minister is not able to act without parliamentary approval. In practice, however, the Government will hold the balance of power in the Oireachtas and consent is unlikely to be withheld. In any debate on the establishment of a commission of investigation a draft of the order and a related statement setting out the reasons for its creation must be laid before both Houses of the Oireachtas.

It should be recalled that when the original 1921 tribunal of inquiries legislation in was debated in the UK Parliament it was amended to ensure that the decision on establishment was given to Parliament and not the Minister. Although concerns were raised at the time the 2004 Act was passed that the public might "not have full confidence in a commission of investigation that has been set up by the Government of the day and which reports to Ministers of that Government", particularly where an investigation is into the actions of a Minister or related to a Government Department, this has not yet been apparent.[178]

[5–90]

---

[174] Concerns about the impact of the operation of Commissions of Investigation have been raised in relation to the Murphy Report: see Sweeney, above n 167.

[175] s 3(1).

[176] 581 *Dáil Debates* col. 922, 4 March 2004.

[177] s 3(2).

[178] See discussion below in relation to Alan Shatter TD and the Guerin Inquiry.

[5–91] However, Spencer, writing shortly after the legislation came into force, raised concerns about the fact that the process of establishing a commission of investigation is far more ministerial than Oireachtas based. [179] Section 3(1) provides the it is the Minister who proposes the establishment of a commission of investigation and s 3(2) only requires that the draft proposed order and related reasons be laid before the Houses of the Oireachtas. This in effect reduces the role of the Oireachtas from initiator of an inquiry, under the tribunal of inquiry system, to one of providing approval via the passing of a resolution on the draft order. The impact of the party whip on a vote to approve the establishment of a commission clearly means that that approval is largely guaranteed. The development of the terms of reference for a commission of investigation is also firmly placed with the Minister or the Government under s 4:

> 4(1) The order establishing a commission may authorise the specified Minister to set the commission's terms of reference.
>
> (2) If the order establishing a commission does not authorise the specified Minister to set its terms of reference, they may be set by the Government.

However, it should be noted that the legislation does not envisage the process of developing the terms of reference as being only the Minister's, it is to be done in consultation with affected and interested parties.[180] In order to ensure a focused, and therefore hopefully time limited, inquiry the terms of reference are to be set out as clearly as possible[181] and they must include a statement of estimated costs and the length of time the inquiry is expected to take.[182] Finally, s 6 places responsibility on the Minister in terms of any alterations to the terms of reference of a commission.

Commission of Investigation Procedure

[5–92] Part Three of the Act sets out the procedure to be adopted by the commission, although the specifics are vague with s 10 stating that:

---

[179] K Spencer, "A New Era of Tribunalism – The Commissions of Investigation Act 2004" (2005) *Bar Review* 80 at p 81.

[180] s 4(3): before setting a commission's terms of reference, the specified Minister or the Government, as the case may be, may consult with any persons.

[181] s 5(1) this includes referring to, as far as is possible "the events, activities, circumstances, systems, practices or procedures to be investigated".

[182] s 5(2)(i) and (ii).

"[a] commission may, subject to this Act and the commission's rules and procedures, conduct its investigation in the manner that it considers appropriate in the circumstances of the case."

Reflecting the underlying desire to avoid conflict and potentially costly litigation, the investigation is under a duty to seek the voluntary cooperation of those who might be able to assist the inquiry.[183]

While we have previously discussed the perceived need for inquiries to be conducted as far as possible in public, one significant aspect of commissions of investigation is that s 11 places it under an obligation to conduct its work in private unless:　　　　　　　　　　**[5–93]**

(a) a witness requests that all or part of his or her evidence be heard in public and the commission grants the request; or

(b) the commission is satisfied that it is desirable in the interests of both the investigation and fair procedures to hear all or part of the evidence of a witness in public.[184]

However, it should be noted that the Commission retains the discretion to refuse a request by a witness to a public hearing under s 11(a). In practice, given the requirements of constitutional justice, the operation of that discretion may be narrow.[185]

The advantage of private hearings is the reduced level of procedural safeguards that need to be implemented and the correlative reduction in cost and time of a public inquiry. Additionally it is often argued that witnesses are more likely to open up to an inquiry when not subject to the full scrutiny of publicity. Yet ultimately is it not difficult to square the idea of a primarily private process, with the need for ensure the fullest ventilation of issues of significant public importance? Proponents would argue that an important public element is restored by the publication of a commission's final report and the possibility that a full-scale public tribunal of inquiry might follow on if needed. However, it remains the case that private hearings are a significant change from the traditional　　**[5–94]**

---

[183] s 10(2).

[184] s 11(1)(a) and (b).

[185] Human Rights Commission, *Observations on the Commission of Investigation Bill*, February 2004, available online at http://www.ihrc.ie/publications/list/observations-on-the-commission-of-investigations-b/ (date accessed, 8 July 2014) at p 27.

public inquiry approach and this, together with the provisions on conflicting evidence, raises the question as to whether a commission of investigation can be understood to fall squarely into this general category of accountability mechanism.

[5–95]   Section 12 of the 2004 Act also provides that the commission must disclose to parties[186] to the proceedings

> "the substance of any evidence in its possession that, in its opinion, the person should be aware of for the purposes of the evidence that person may give or has given to the commission".[187]

The source of the information should not be disclosed unless the commission concludes that disclosure is needed "in view of the purposes of the investigation or in the interests of fair procedures".[188] The person to whom any information is disclosed must then be given the opportunity to comment on it either in writing or orally.[189]

[5–96]   Despite the private format of the commission of investigation, the legislation does place emphasise the procedural protections of those participating. Section 14 states that the commission can receive evidence in a variety of forms: orally, by affidavit or "as otherwise directed by the commission or allowed by its rules and procedures" including video and sound recordings and links.[190] Testimony is to be made under oath and where someone gives evidence remotely they must provide the commission with a sworn statement that the evidence was given voluntarily by them and that "to the best of his or her knowledge, the content is true and accurate".[191]

[5–97]   It nevertheless remains the case that each commission of investigation is master of its own procedure beyond these core requirements. Section 15 therefore states that the commission *may* establish or adopt certain rules and procedures in order to, *inter alia* ensure that it follows fair procedures in relation to receiving and recording evidence and submissions.[192]

---

[186] Whether as someone compelled to give evidence, voluntarily attending or about whom evidence is being given: s 12(1) (a)(b) and (c).

[187] s 12(1).

[188] s 12(2).

[189] s 12(3).

[190] s 14(1)(a) (b) and (c).

[191] s 14(2) (a)(b) and (c).

[192] s 15(1).

Despite the efforts of the creators of the 2004 Act, disputes regarding   **[5–98]**
constitutional justice have nonetheless arisen. Allegations of insufficient
procedural rights have been raised where individuals have been
identified, either directly in the report, or because of the nature of the
inquiry. Thus concern was raised in relation to the Murphy Report into
the institutional responses of the Church and State authorities to clerical
sex abuse.[193] In particular the perceived "naming and shaming" of those
clerics whom the Commission found wanting in child protection matters
was regarded by some as potentially belonging to the "adversarial
arena" and thereby inappropriate for a commission of investigation and
contrary to the principles of constitutional justice.[194] Similarly, former
Justice Minister Alan Shatter TD, responding to the findings of the
Guerin Report[195] accused the chair of the commission, Séan Guerin SC of
failing "to observe fair procedures in accordance with constitutional and
natural justice"[196] in particular noting that he had not been interviewed
as part of the inquiry. In a strident attack he raised concerns about the
operation of the inquiry under the 2004 Act:

> "I believe all of us should be entitled to know that we cannot, by way
> of any form of inquiry or review or other means, be secretly put on
> trial, have charges levied against us of which we have no knowledge,
> be prosecuted without being informed of the evidence, and convicted
> without being given the opportunity to speak or defend ourselves....
> I believe no one in the future requested to undertake such a task should
> be enabled to take to him or herself the role of investigator, prosecutor,
> judge, jury and executioner and entirely ignore fair procedures
> prescribed by our courts and which are specifically prescribed for
> the undertaking of a statutory inquiry under the provisions of the
> Commission of Inquiries Act 2004."[197]

---

[193] Sweeney, *supra* n 167.

[194] *ibid* at para 4.8. Concern was raised by Sweeney that lawyers are "by instinct adversarial, always needing to be on one side or the other, to have winners and losers." para 4.12.

[195] The Commission of Investigation was established in February 2014 to review the actions taken by An Garda Síochána in relation to allegations made by Sergeant McCabe concerning failures in investigating and prosecuting crimes. The report can be accessed online at http://www.merrionstreet.ie/wp-content/uploads/2014/05/Final-Redacted-Guerin-Report-OCR.pdf (date accessed, 8 July 2014) and led to the resignation of former Minister Alan Shatter on 7 May 2014.

[196] Statement of Alan Shatter TD reproduced in the *Irish Independent*, 19 June 2014 available online at http://www.independent.ie/irish-news/politics/alan-shatters-statement-in-full-on-the-publication-of-the-cooke-report-30368736.html (date accessed, 8 July 2014).

[197] *ibid.*

It may be that the courts will eventually evaluate this perspective, with judicial prouncements likely needed to make more tangible the delicate balance which the 2004 Act clearly attempted to chisel out.

Witnesses Privileges and Immunities Under the 2004 Act

[5–99]   As regards the compellability of witnesses, a commission is given similar powers to that of a tribunal of inquiry. Thus it can direct in writing persons to attend and to answer questions,[198] it can examine witnesses under oath and cross examine them "to the extent the commission thinks proper in order to elicit information relevant to a matter under investigation",[199] and it can direct them to produce documentation.[200] The making of a knowingly false statement to the Commission is made an offence under s 18.

[5–100]   Where the commission directs an interested party or witness to cooperate and they fail to comply with that direction, the commission can order compliance.[201] Failure to follow that order can in turn result in a person being liable to contempt of court proceedings[202] or charged with an offence.[203] A non-cooperating party can only be punished through one of these two options however.[204] An additional weapon in the commission's armoury, however, is that if a person is found to have failed to cooperate with s 16 directions or to have obstructed the commission they can be found liable under s 17 to pay the costs incurred by the commission that arise as a result of that non-cooperation; these can include legal costs.[205] Additionally, if another party has been negatively affected by the non-cooperation the commission may also order that their costs be paid.[206] Any order for costs under s 17 must be confirmed by the High Court on

---

[198] s 16(1)(a).

[199] s 16(1)(d).

[200] s 16(1)(e).

[201] s 16(6)(a).

[202] s 16(7) states:

"If a person against whom an order is made under *subsection (6)(a)* fails to comply with the direction specified in the order, the Court may deal with the matter as if it were a contempt of the Court."

[203] s 16(8) states:

"A person who, without reasonable excuse, fails to comply with a direction under *subsection (1)(a)* to attend before a commission is guilty of an offence."

[204] s 16(9).

[205] s 17(1).

[206] Including legal costs – s 17(2).

application by the chairperson of the commission.[207] This procedure may ensure that commissions of investigation do not face the problems encountered by tribunals of inquiry observed earlier in this chapter.

Costs, whether in terms of expenses or legal costs, are also provided for within the legislation. Section 16(3) states that a person attending before the commission is

    [5–101]

> "entitled to be paid by the specified Minister such amounts in respect of the expenses of his or her attendance as is determined in accordance with guidelines prepared by that Minister with the consent of the minister for Finance ...."[208]

In terms of efficiency, the commission of investigation model has generally been seen as more cost effective than the large scale tribunal of inquiry. However, where the terms of reference of a commission are large scale enough, or controversial (or both), costs can still be significant. For example, in relation to recent commissions of investigation into matters of public concern regarding An Garda Síochána, €2 million was provided in a supplementary estimate to meet the commission's costs.[209] This is a not insignificant amount of money, although the time frame set for completion of the report was six months. Mick Wallace TD voiced concerns in the Dáil regarding adequate resourcing in the context of the commission of investigation into the killing of Gary Douch in Mountjoy prison which only published its report over seven years after the incident:

    [5–102]

> "It appears that the State's conduct was a primary factor in that delay - there were delays in providing important documents, primary evidence was destroyed and there was a long delay in payment to Ms McMorrow for her work. Last June, it was noted that she had not been paid in more than three years, most of which time was during the lifetime of the current Government. It is a pity that under the 2004 Act any commission must be dependent on the Minister of the day to sanction its expenses."[210]

---

[207] s 17(3) and (4).

[208] s 16(3). s 16(10) makes it clear that expenses are not to be consider to include legal costs.

[209] http://www.kildarestreet.com/debates/?id=2014-05-07a.240 (date accessed, 19 June 2015).

[210] *Dáil Deb* 7 May 2014 Estimates for Public Services 2014 - Vote 2 - Department of the Taoiseach (Supplementary Estimate), Available online at http://www.kildarestreet.com/debates/?id=2014-05-07a.240 (date accessed, 19 June 2014).

Privilege

[5–103]   The 2004 Act provides under s 21 that the Act does not compel disclosure of information that an individual would be entitled to refuse to disclose under any rule of law or enactment on the grounds of any privilege or any duty of confidentiality. However, s 21(4) limits this protection as it provides that the commission must examine any document claimed to fall under this provision and "considered a written statement provided by the person concerned specifying the grounds for the claim, including the privilege or duty of confidentiality relied on". As Spencer notes, the danger of this provision is that a commission member will not be able to "disremember" information that they have examined, despite the fact it has been designated privileged.[211] As with other parts of the legislation, a balance is struck here in terms of efficiency, between preserving privilege and preventing unjustified claims which can frustrate the work of a commission.

[5–104]   Finally, s 19 provides a general exclusion of any evidence given before a commission of investigation from being used in subsequent "criminal or other" proceedings. However, there is a limit in relation to this protection, as s 19(2) prevents this exclusion operating in relation to s 45 which requires that where a tribunal of inquiry is established to examine matters covered in whole or part by a commission of investigation, then all evidence received as part of that commission shall be made available to the tribunal.

[5–105]   From this brief discussion it is clear that the approach taken in relation to commissions of investigation involves a more relaxed attitude towards constitutional justice.[212] It also involves an investigative approach that prioritises fact-finding efficiency, thus in part reducing its accountability capacity. However, despite these limitations it is clear that commissions of investigation are currently viewed as a credible accountability option. Nevertheless, it is important that the low key, fact finding nature of these inquiries is recognised and that commissions of investigation are should not be misused, leading to the false raising of accountability expectations in the public. As was noted earlier in this chapter a poorly designed public inquiry can ultimately do more harm than good in terms of both the problem being investigated and the wider accountability framework.

---

[211] Spencer, above n 179 at p 83.
[212] *ibid* at p 84.

Conclusion

Over the past few years we have seen a relatively high number of inquiries [5–106] which have engaged with fundamental instances of poor governance and scandal,, both in the form of tribunals of inquiries and more modest commissions of investigation. The reason for their prominence may well be in part because of a failure of the other systems of accountability, especially the traditional parliamentary mechanisms. We have already discussed these difficulties in chapter 2. However, it may also be because of a shift in attitudes towards the political and administrative systems of Government and a growing lack of trust generally. Indeed, in considering other accountability changes in the Irish State we can see that the period around the 1980s-1990s saw a significant shift in public understanding regarding the need for effective oversight of the State. In addition, as MacCarthaigh notes, the events that prompted many of the more recent inquiries took place during the 1980s; "a period of significant social and economic malaise in Ireland". [213] Or more recently the 1990s/2000s when Ireland moved into a period of rapid economic growth during which corruption and cronyism appeared to flourish, became more visible and ultimately less tolerable.

It is ultimately important to remember Wade and Forsyth's observation [5–107] that an inquiry

> "is often a procedure of last resort, to be used when nothing else will serve to ally public disquiet, usually based on sensational allegations, rumours or disasters".[214]

Indeed, for the most part this has been the case in Ireland. As the Mahon Tribunal Report stated — the large scale, mostly judge led public inquiry is "typically only used as a last resort, when other agencies of investigation have failed to work or are unlikely to work".[215] In reality, their use must be selective and targeted: recognising that they offer an accountability mechanism where all other systems are unsuitable and/or have already failed.

---

[213] M MacCarthaigh, *Accountability in Irish Parliamentary Politics*, (Institute of Public Administration, Dublin, 2005) at p 196.

[214] HW R. Wade and CF Forsyth, *Administrative law* (10th ed) (Oxford University Press, Oxford, 2009) at p 824.

[215] Mahon Report above n 34 at p 22.

[5–108]   The large scale public inquiry therefore can be understood almost as a set piece in the accountability system. It is useful where nothing else will do — whether because of the sensitivity of the subject matter, the fundamental public distrust of systems perhaps seen as closer to the state apparatus, or because of the scale of the concern. If we compare the operation of a public inquiry to one carried out by an Oireachtas committee, for example, the fear underlying the Oireachtas mechanism is its proximity the State: the fear of "gerrymandering", or of a lack of capacity to investigate. Public inquiries tend to satisfy the public concern element of a crisis or disaster (the two areas where they are most often held), but may not, in the end, have proved themselves effective in terms of practical outcomes or as triggers for broader reform movements.

LOCAL GOVERNMENT IN IRELAND

Introduction

The passage of the Local Government Act 2014 was heralded by Government   [6–01]
as the most radical reform to local government structures in the last one
hundred years:

> "This is the first time in over 100 years that we have attempted such a
> radical reform but it is necessary to bring our local government system
> up to date...."[1]

In this chapter, we will perhaps illustrate that this statement should be taken
as a commentary on the inaction and complacency of the past century, rather
than on the specific amendments offered by the 2014 Act. In terms of
summative statements regarding the actual reach and impact of local
government authorities in Ireland, we highlight two recent observations
made by international bodies in this area:

> "The report notes ... that the constitutional protection of local self-
> government is rather weak, that local governments only manage
> a modest amount of public affairs, and that the administrative
> supervision of their activities by the central level remains high."[2]

> "Local governments do not appear to be a significant source of fiscal risk
> in Ireland owing to their small size and lack of financial autonomy."[3]

While some points can be made to counterbalance such claims,[4] there is no   [6–02]
doubt that within the broader European context, Irish local government
structures are weak and lacking in overarching vision. The *sui generis*
character of Irish arrangements reflects the conflict which exists
domestically regarding the appropriate role of local government. These
inter-institutional tensions were correctly summarised by the above cited
Council of Europe Report, prior to the 2014 reforms:

---

[1] Minister for the Environment, Community and Local Government, Phil Hogan TD, Department of the Environment, Community and Local Government Press Release, 17 October 2013. Available online at http://www.environ.ie/en/LocalGovernment/LocalGovernmentReform/News/MainBody,34299,en.htm (date accessed 12 August 2014).

[2] The Congress of Local and Regional Authorities of the Council of Europe, *Report on Local Democracy in Ireland*, 30 October 2013. Available at: https://wcd.coe.int/ViewDoc.jsp?id=2113703 (date accessed 30 June 2014), at summary para 1.

[3] International Monetary Fund, *Ireland: Fiscal Transparency Assessment*, July 2013, IMF Country Report No. 13/209 (Washington D.C., International Monetary Fund) at page 60. Available at: http://www.imf.org/external/pubs/ft/scr/2013/cr13209.pdf (date accessed 30 June 2014).

[4] Not all additional points would be favourable: in terms of the IMF report, one would highlight the role local authorities played in creating planning policies which underwrote the Irish housing bubble.

"The rapporteurs had the impression that, at a national level, there is a strong tendency to keep the guidance of local government affairs in central government hands, with the argument that this is necessary in order to avoid mismanagement or clientelist tendencies and to guarantee efficiency. From the Government's point of view, systemic weaknesses in the structures, operational efficiency, governance and financing of the local government system as well as some instances of failure to perform certain functions adequately (resulting in the removal of certain functions from the elected councils) contributed to a lack of confidence and credibility in the local government system. This view of the situation is strongly contested by local authorities the rapporteurs had the opportunity to meet, who insisted on the fact that local authorities are efficient, reliable and willing to carry out functions that are within a local authority mandate in most European countries.... The two points of view are fully in opposition."[5]

[6–03] The 2014 Act did address some of the issues which have produced such institutional weakness, as well as attempting to prompt greater engagement with local government issues by Irish society.[6] The most significant aspects of the legislation:

-   Altered the territorial structure of Irish local government;
-   Refined the relationship between the democratically elected council and the council administration headed by the Chief Executive of the Council;
-   Contained some limited attempts to shift from a local administration model to a local *government* model;
-   Implemented some recommendations of the Mahon Tribunal into corruption in the planning system.

[6–04] As we shall see, however, these changes represented a highly targeted refinement and rebalancing rather than amounting to a reformed systemic vision. This was not due to a lack of policy reflection at central government level: a 2008 Green Paper[7] and the 2012 Action Programme for Effective

---

[5] Above n 2 at para 39.

[6] For an excellent discussion of how the weaknesses, and public perception of, local government has an adverse impact on the constituency work of *national* politicians see the 2013 paper published by Oireachtas Library and Research Service, Spotlight No 2 of 2013, *Localism in Irish Politics and Local Government Reform* (Stationery Office, Dublin).

[7] This was drafted following public consultation, see Department of Environment, *Green Paper on Local Government Reform*, April 2008 (Stationery Office, Dublin).

Local Government,[8] both attempted a holistic framing of the issues involved. Nevertheless, even the latter document ultimately adopted a qualified and incrementalist tone in discussing future action:

> "The role of local government in Ireland is narrow. Some traditional functions have moved to specialist organisations in recent years due to necessities of scale, resources and expertise. To make the most of its resources and capacities, the role of local government will be strengthened, having regard to relevant criteria, with a wider range of suitable functions. Its role will be refocused, particularly towards economic, social and community development. Central government involvement in operational details of local services will be further reduced and administrative controls and procedures streamlined. Local authority capacity to undertake services for a wider range of sectors will also be fully utilised."[9]

In this chapter, we will provide an analysis of the renewed structures of local government, and the reform philosophies which underpinned changes to major areas such as fiscal monitoring. Finally, in addressing planning and development enforcement, we provide a case study which highlights the recurring difficulties and tensions faced by local government decision-makers, political and administrative, in exercising their statutory functions and ensuring administrative justice in Ireland. [6–05]

Local Government in Ireland: Its Heritage, Status and Fundamentals

It is worth recalling that constitutional recognition of local government occurred only in the Twentieth Amendment to the Constitution in 1999, which inserted the new Article 28A, which *inter alia*, provided that: [6–06]

> "The State recognises the role of local government in providing a forum for the democratic representation of local communities, in exercising and performing at local level powers and functions conferred by law and in promoting by its initiatives the interests of such communities."[10]

---

[8] Department of Environment and Local Government, *Putting People First – An Action Programme for Effective Local Government*, October 2012 (Stationery Office, Dublin).

[9] *ibid* at p iv.

[10] This statement is echoed by s 63(1)(a) of the Local Government Act 2001, which provides that one of the functions of local authorities is "to provide a forum for the democratic representation of the local community".

[6–07]   This recognition, provides a welcome political acknowledgement of the role of local authorities, but through the phrase "conferred by law" underlined the prevailing requirement that local government functions must be expressly or impliedly conferred by primary legislation.[11] In the 2008 case of *Prendergast v Higher Education Authority*, Charleton J appeared reluctant to contemplate that Article 28A bestowed any additional, free-standing powers upon local government:

> "Every local authority is a creature of statute, the exercise of its powers is *enabled under the Constitution* but those powers do not arise out of the exercise of local government authority and history. Rather the powers of local government to raise funds, to spend them, or to set up schemes to disburse them appropriately arise from specific statutory provisions.... The doctrine of legal formalism is particularly apposite in the context of local government powers as those powers must firstly be granted by statute and, secondly, exercised in accordance with it."[12]

[6–08]   The resultant centrality of statutory interpretation to local government jurisdiction, has, somewhat inevitably, placed local decision-makers right in the cross-hairs of the *ultra vires* doctrine.[13] This, as Hogan and Morgan note, has produced some negative dynamics:

> "...prior to the enactment of the Local Government Act 1991 the doctrine of ultra vires applied quite rigidly in the case of all local authorities. This meant that enabling legislation has tended in the past to be very specific and even after the relaxation of the ultra vires rules the parliamentary draftsman has remained cautious".[14]

[6–09]   The 1991 Act, now refined and consolidated by the Local Government Act 2001, did moderate the application of the *ultra vires* rule against local government, with s 66(3) providing for a range of implied powers:

> "(a) Subject to this section, a local authority may take such measures... as it considers necessary or desirable to promote the interests of the local community.

---

[11] Through the prominent use of the phrase "conferred by law".

[12] *Prendergast v Higher Education Authority* [2009] 1 ILRM 47 at para 50.

[13] For readers as yet unfamiliar with this principle, it can at its most basic level be summarised as requiring that decision-makers' actions must be expressly or impliedly authorised by statute. The grounding "permissions" for local government conduct lie scattered across an enormous body of statute law, and the Constitution has not operated to fill in any gaps or oversights in statutory drafting.

[14] G Hogan and DG Morgan, *Administrative Law in Ireland*, (4th ed) (Round Hall, Dublin, 2010) at para 5-55.

(b) For the purposes of this section a measure, activity or thing is deemed to promote the interests of the community if it promotes, directly or indirectly, social inclusion or the social, economic, environmental, recreational, cultural, community or general development of the administrative area (or any part of it) of the local authority concerned or of the local community (or any group consisting of members of it)."[15]

The 2001 Act also provides a broad statement as to the implied powers of local authorities in relation to their statutory powers:

"[a] local authority may do anything ancillary, supplementary or incidental to or consequential on or necessary to give full effect to…a function conferred on it by this or any other enactment…"[16]

Finally, s 69 of the 2001 Act is a significant provision: setting out a number **[6–10]** of fundamental requirements a council must adhere to across all its actions. Its existence is particularly useful for elected members who, while often focussed upon their political mandates, are also required to act in a lawful manner:

"(1) Subject to *subsection (2)*, a local authority, in performing the functions conferred on it by or under any other enactment shall have regard to –
(a) the resources, wherever originating, that are available or likely to be available to it for the purpose of such performance and the

---

[15] Another provision which buttresses a whole range of everyday local authority activities is s 66(4) which allows a local authority in furthering the interests of local community to:
"(a) carry out and maintain works of any kind,
(b) provide, maintain, manage, preserve or restore land, structures of any kind or facilities,
(c) fit out, furnish or equip any building, structure or facility for particular purposes,
(d) provide utilities equipment or materials for particular purposes
(e) provide any service or other thing or engage in any activity that, in the opinion of the authority, is likely to benefit the community,
(f) upon and subject to such terms and conditions as the authority considers appropriate, provide assistance in money or in kind (including the provision of prizes and other incentives) in respect of the organisation or promotion of competitions, seminars, exhibitions, displays, festivals or other events, or organise or promote such events…
(g) upon and subject to such terms and conditions as the authority considers appropriate, provide assistance in money or in kind to persons engaging in any activity that, in the opinion of the authority, benefits the local community…
(i) enter into such contracts and make such other arrangements (including the incorporation of one or more than one company) as the authority considers necessary or expedient either alone or jointly with any other local authority or public authority or any other person."
[16] s 65(1).

> need to secure the most beneficial, effective and efficient use of such resources,
>
> (b) the need to maintain adequately those services provided by it which it considers to be essential and, in so far as practicable, to ensure a reasonable balance is achieved, taking account of all relevant factors, between its functional programmes,
>
> (c) the need for co-operation with, and the co-ordination of its activities with those of other local authorities, public authorities and bodies whose money is provided (directly or indirectly) either wholly or partly by a Minister of the Government the performance of whose functions affect or may affect the performance of those of the authority so as to ensure efficiency and economy in the performance of its functions,
>
> (d) the need for consultation with other local authorities, public authorities and bodies referred to in *paragraph (c)* in appropriate cases,
>
> (e) policies and objectives of the Government or any Minister of the Government in so far as they may affect or relate to its functions,
>
> (f) the need for a high standard of environmental and heritage protection and the need to promote sustainable development, and
>
> (g) the need to promote social inclusion.
>
> (2) A local authority shall perform those functions which it is required by law to perform and this section shall not be construed as affecting any such requirement.
>
> (3) Every enactment relating to a function of a local authority should be read and have effect subject to this section."

[6–11]   While this section, providing as it does a blueprint for cogent decision-making, should have a powerful educative effect on every employee and councillor within local government, judicial enforcement of this provision has not always been extensive. As will later be seen in the planning context, the obligation "to have regard to" is often discharged where one has informed oneself of the relevant issues and has given reasonable consideration to them.[17]

[6–12]   The above quoted provisions were aimed at reducing the complexity of the legal arrangements regulating local authority action. Such complexity was aggravated by the fragmented and incremental manner in which the basic functions of local authorities gradually sedimented into existence over the

---

[17] See *McEvoy v Meath County Council* [2003] 1 ILRM 431. As discussed later in this book, the increasing scope of the right to reasons (chapter 10) and the possible expansion of review to include proportionality analysis (chapter 9) may offer some small expansion of the justificatory burden placed on local authorities in the future.

years. Even today a statement of the "basic" functions of local authorities can only proceed by ticking off a number of broad categories; land use planning, waste management, water services (which are now to be transferred to Irish Water), building control, roads, some educational services and public libraries, fire services and public safety, social and affordable housing, recreational and social amenities, protection of local national heritage, flood protection and climate change adaptation. The specific competences and division of responsibilities in each of these areas varies, and each requires specific in-depth study by decision-makers.

Another aspect which added to the complexity of Irish local government arrangements was the presence of other local structures such as health boards, numerous town councils and local appointments commissioners. Their existence could be traced to the fact that until the Local Government Act 2001, the fundamental layout of Irish local government reflected the system created by the British Parliament through the Local Government (Ireland) Act 1898. The past twenty years have finally seen these historical bodies gradually removed from the landscape, with the Health Act 2004, for instance, abolishing regional health boards. The 2014 Act continued this process of institutional consolidation and administrative streamlining. [6–13]

Where a function is bestowed upon a local council, the Irish system features a further fundamental restriction on how it is to be exercised: the key distinction between executive and reserved functions. Executive functions are those which are carried out by a salaried city or county manager and her or his staff.[18] Reserved functions are those performed by the elected councillors. Clearly the most controversial of these functions in the Celtic Tiger years was the ability of the elected council to override certain planning decisions of the executive, a power which we discuss at paragraphs [6-23] and [6-29]. We will also analyse the legal relationship between the Chief Executive and the council and the expansion of reserved functions in the 2014 Act at paragraph [6-52]. It is worth noting at this point that the 2014 reforms changed the title of the office with the previously applicable title "Manager" now being replaced by "Chief Executive".[19] [6–14]

In terms of the make-up of elected representatives, we would remind the reader of recent reforms which removed the dual mandate permitting a [6–15]

---

[18] The system of management was created by the County Management Act 1940.
[19] s 144.

member of the Oireachtas to continue holding their local council seat.[20] This was viewed by advocates as an attempt to ensure a greater specialisation, but was met with strong opposition, including a failed constitutional challenge.[21] The debate regarding the dual mandate reflected the Ireland's status as "a country fascinated with the local dimension to national politics but without a properly functioning local government system".[22] In the context of this book as a whole, we would encourage the reader to reflect upon how a historically poorly functioning system of local government has distorted the role of the TD and the functioning of the national parliament as an accountability mechanism.

[6–16]   Considering the burdensome political heritage that can distort local government functioning in Ireland inevitably leads us to the recently controversial issue of territorial structure. The 2014 Act was perhaps at its most radical in its reorganisation of the institutional structures and territorial scope of local government in Ireland. The traditional town councils were abolished and replaced by municipal districts, which have more limited power.[23] The result of this was that the local elections of May 2014 elected 949 Councillors instead of 744 Town and 883 County Councillors. With the exception of those serving in major urban areas,[24] these newly elected councillors will become the first to serve simultaneously as County and Municipal District Councillors. As will also be seen,[25] the 2014 Act renders much of role of municipal districts dependent upon decisions taken at the county level. The selection of the county as the fundamental unit of local governance is of course, open to some criticism, as one can argue that they represent an intermediate unit between the local/municipal and the regional level. While the 2012 Action Programme featured a large number of arguments for the abolition of town councils, it

---

[20] Local Government (No 2) Act 2003 amended the 2001 Act inserting s 13A which disqualified members of the Oireachtas from being elected or co-opted to a local authority. The dual local authority and Parliamentary membership therefore ceased following the 2004 local elections.

[21] *Ring v Attorney General* [2004] 1 IR 185.

[22] This memorable statement was provided by Dermot Lacey, Dublin city councillor and former Lord Mayor of Dublin, in the review section of L Weeks and A Quinlivan, *All Politics is Local: A Guide to Local Elections in Ireland* (Collins' Press, Cork, 2009).

[23] Part 3 of the 2014 Act. One by-product of the changes is the abolition of the anomaly whereby those living in rural towns had two votes (one for the town council, one for the county council) whereas those in rural areas only voted for the county council.

[24] As mentioned later at para [6-32] a separate scheme operates within the major city councils of Dublin, Cork and Galway.

[25] At para [6-30] below.

failed to adequately consider arguments against the retention of county councils, which despite the cultural aura cast by GAA rivalries,[26] represents a geographic unit variable in size and unity. The new municipal district structure, it was hoped, would avoid the unsatisfactory separation of towns from their hinterlands which had marked the previous town council system, but there is evidence of continued artificiality in some local divisions.[27] This non-alignment with the actual spatial organisation of Irish society will continue to cause tensions and inefficiencies in local government and may impede the economies of scale which the 2014 reforms appeared to be pursuing.

Despite the obstacles created by historical hangovers, the 2012 reform document did attempt to frame a first principles account of the purposes a local government system should fulfil. This represented an unfortunately rare reflection on underlying values and represents an ideal point to end an historical overview. It generated a three line vision statement which can be used as a fundamental yardstick to evaluate current and past arrangements: **[6–17]**

> "Local government will be the main vehicle of governance and public service at local level — leading economic, social and community development, delivering efficient and good value services, and representing citizens and local communities effectively and accountably."[28]

In terms of how to achieve this, the expert group then stressed that reform initiatives should reflect framework principles, namely that they should: **[6–18]**

---

[26] Although GAA level competitions operate at the Parish level, the main organizational unit of the GAA is the county: "Inter-county competition, notably the provincial and all-Ireland championships that culminate every September in Croke Park, have kept county identity and county loyalties in nationalist Ireland viscerally strong, down to the present era of cable TV and sports commodification." D Dickson, "County histories, national narratives and missing pieces: A report from Ireland" (2009) Available online at www.victoriacountyhistory.ac.uk/sites/default/files/page-attachments/dickson_-_local_histories.doc (date accessed 12 August 2014).

[27] For example, Sinn Féin Senator Cullinane raised concerns about a decision to divide Carrigaline, Co Cork, along the Owenabue River which runs through the middle of the town: "having some 16 councillors from across two separate LEAs making decisions for the town is not prudent. Decisions will invariably lack the necessary focus, and confusion will arise in a situation in which neighbours living only a few hundred metres apart are obliged to make representations to different councillors." *Seanad Debs* 19 June 2013.

[28] Above n 8 at p 2.

- Recognise that local democracy is essential to representative democracy, given its ability to bring greater accountability and responsiveness to local needs;
- Acknowledge that the provision of more substantial functions was essential to encouraging public engagement and democratic accountability;
- Ensure "a more responsive, ethical and accountable representation and governance, with provision for appropriate participation by, and engagement with, communities",[29] together with a greater openness and transparency, including performance monitoring, involving external evaluation;
- Recognise that increasingly devolved decision-making could ensure greater accountability in local service delivery, by promoting closer relationships to the local citizen. A "rebalancing of responsibilities" could reduce "duplication and process associated with centralised supervision, by enabling central government to concentrate more on national issues and strategic policy matters"[30];
- Accompany any devolution with national policies and standards to ensure accountability, financial probity and capacity;
- Link local government structures to broader regional approaches to produce synergies and boost overall capacity;
- The reforms should also open up space for broader public service reform by ensuring "enhanced credibility so that Government can look confidently to local government for performance of existing and new functions consistent with national policy objectives".[31]

[6–19]   As we will see, the translation and implementation of this vision into concrete statutory reform was fettered heavily by political and historical factors. It is no accident that the above goals were presented in the form of a list, as ultimately the Action Programme struggled to order and balance the differing interests and values. Ultimately the reforms recalled the famous Irish anecdote where a hapless foreign tourist asks a rural dweller for directions and is advised: "if I were you, I wouldn't start from here". We will now analyse key dynamics, policy processes and relationships underpinning local government law following the 2014 Act.

---

[29] *ibid.*
[30] *ibid.*
[31] *ibid.*

Democracy Versus Administration: The Executive-Elected Council Relationship

The relationship between the executive of the local authority — the full   [6–20]
time staff led by the Chief Executive — and the local council — made up
of part time councillors — is a multi-faceted one, with many different
perspectives on the tensions and disputes which have accumulated over
the years. The reader may connect with this issue firstly through their
perceptions of planning issues, where the Mahon Tribunal criticised high
profile instances where the recommendations of city and county managers
were overruled by majority vote of the local councils. While it is clear that
such conduct was a crucial aspect of the ill-planned Celtic Tiger expansion,
we would encourage the reader to view the relationship holistically. The
arguments for an expanded role for elected councillors is that too extensive
a role for the executive results in a form of governance better described as
local administration than as local "government". One can argue that local
councillors have been subjected to administrative "training wheels" for
too long, resulting in a halfway house position: one that suffered from
both democratic deficits and an executive that could still have its judgment
defeated on a *once off* basis (using the infamous s 140 special resolution
described below). From this perspective, it was important to break the
staid nature of Irish local government — forcing its daily conduct into the
public limelight, by empowering the councillors, and thereby encouraging
the public to engage more actively than they have in the past. With the
2014 Act expanding the list of reserved powers, it appears that the
Government was persuaded by this latter desire. For those who remain
suspicious of the performance and capabilities of our local councillors,
however, the 2014 Act should be seen as the responsibilitisation of local
government. Councillors should find it more difficult to attribute poor
performance to the executive given the manner in which the new legislation
foregrounds their policy making and supervisory leadership. Furthermore,
the Act contains new national audit procedures for overseeing local
government, which we will outline after we analyse the changes at the
management/council interface.

The situation operating during the Celtic Tiger had been laid down in the   [6–21]
2001 Act. As mentioned earlier, this set out a number of reserved functions,
which were to be carried out by the local councillors.[32] These generally

---

[32] These are listed in Schedule 14 of the 2001 Act.

defined the policy setting role of the council, allowing them to set the parameters of the annual budget, the development plan and to pass bye laws. All functions not expressly included fall within the executive's purview.[33] These executive functions included the management of local authority employees and the day to day delivery of services. The most infamous provision in the 2001 Act, of course, was to be s 140, which permitted elected councillors to intervene in the executive affairs of the Manager if a special resolution was passed directing him to act in a particular way. In non-property related instances, such a resolution could be passed by a simple majority, for property related matters the agreement of three quarters of the council had to be obtained.[34]

[6–22]   The only restrictions on the passage of such resolutions were that the action prescribed had to be lawful and could not pertain to staff management and discipline. The requirement that the actions prescribed be lawful means that the executive is entitled to undertake, in effect, a quasi-judicial review of a resolution prior to it taking action to comply with it. Thus, if an executive forms the belief that the resolution was passed without taking relevant considerations into account or that it amounts to an unreasonable decision, it can refuse to implement the resolution.[35] The extent of this process however was questioned in the 2011 case of *Cullen v Wicklow County Council*, when O'Donnell J, in *obiter* comments, expressed concern that there was:

> "little to be gained by constituting the executive of the local authority as a shadow court of judicial review and much to be lost, in increased stress upon the executive and its advisors".[36]

[6–23]   In our view, however, it should be seen as quite common for administrative decision makers to carry out shadow judicial reviews[37] — the real question here is what legal supports are available to the executive. We believe that

---

[33] s 149(4) of the 2001 Act.

[34] The Act required that at least one third of council members be present and voting. s 34(7) Planning and Development Act 2000 set out the operation of s 140 in relation to property matters.

[35] This was recognised in the landmark case of *P & F Sharpe Ltd v Dublin Corporation* [1989] IR 701.

[36] *Cullen v Wicklow County Council* [2011] 1 IR 152 at para 3.

[37] We acknowledge that O'Donnell J's comments were rooted in the difficulties of doing so in the complex area of planning law.

in such circumstances provision should be made to turn to a legal officer[38] attached to the Department of Environment, Community and Local Government or even the National Audit Commission.[39] This would be cheaper than recourse to the courts or even an An Bord Pleanála appeal in the planning context. However, O'Donnell J's perspective may be preferred on grounds of realism — as we highlight throughout this book, the Irish administrative state has at times struggled to move from a reactive, court-centric view of administrative law to a culture of institutionally embedded, proactive legality.

In terms of power relations between the two sides of local government, **[6–24]** s 146 of the 2001 Act allowed the council to vote to suspend the city or county manager, by a 75% majority. A manager's eventual removal, however, required the consent of the Minister for Environment, Community and Local Government. In terms of everyday oversight, the council was able to require a manager to attend any meeting of the council or its related committees, to require the manager to submit breakdowns of forthcoming projects, to provide financial breakdowns and to publicise any orders made to councillors.[40] The manager was also required to advise and assist the council in the exercise of its reserved functions.[41] The 2014 Act has introduced a new range of supervisory tools. The renamed chief executive can be made to report to council on the implementation of any policy set-out by the council in furtherance of its reserved functions.[42] If the council is not satisfied that this report has answered their concerns or the conduct of the chief executive is viewed as unsatisfactory, it may adopt a statement setting out its objections. The Chief Executive is then required to provide a comprehensive response to these complaints, by either clarifying his or her actions or stating how the council's concerns will be addressed. The Chief Executive is furthermore, now obliged to provide a monthly management

---

[38] Though the use of s 140 in relation to specific planning matters is effectively cut down by the 2014 Act.

[39] One would at least hope that some form of agreed and cheap arbitration would not be opposed by two sides of the same organisation. The importance of the issue is at any rate reduced slightly by the fact that the 2014 Act removed the use of s 140 in planning related matters.

[40] 2001 Act, s 132(3) and s 152.

[41] *ibid.*

[42] This is done through inserting s 47 of the 2014 Act into subsections 132(5)-(8) of the 2001 Act. The report must include "actions already taken and planned to be taken to carry out the directions of the elected council in relation to the exercise and performance of its reserved functions."

report to the council, on a prescribed date.[43] Under the Act, these monthly reports must include an account of how the chief executive is implementing:

(i) The policy laid down by the elected council;

(ii) Service provision within the council area;

(iii) Any actions arising from the National Oversight and Audit Commission oversight reports.[44]

[6–25] The administration-policy strategic interface is also more integrated under the new procedure for drafting a Corporate Plan. These five year plans were required under s 134 of the 2001 Act, which mandated the local council, as a reserved function, to pass one within six months of a local election being held. Under the 2014 Act, the Corporate Plan must provide express policy statements, alongside overall management objectives. These include:

> "…the policy of the local authority in relation to its functions, services and priorities for expenditure in so far as this is not already set out in any other plan, statement, strategy or other document."[45]

The aim is to integrate in one plan all key policy objectives, key performance indicators and the staff and financial resourcing necessary for delivery. This process is clearly aimed at ensuring that no area of responsibility is allowed to drift as a result of the policy rudder being unmanned by the council, and to ensure that defined expectations are placed upon the administrative staff.

[6–26] The relationship between the executive and the council was also refined through the grant of additional reserved powers to the elected members. One of the most significant is the increased role granted to the councillors in the appointment of the chief executive alongside whom they will work. Prior to 2014 their role was limited to formal approval of the candidate

---

[43] The Act installs the seventh day of each month as the default for this, but this can be changed to another date by resolution. See s 51 of the 2014 Act, inserting a new s 136 into the 2001 Act.

[44] The monthly report also is the subject of possible Ministerial regulation (s 136(3)), with central government entitled to prescribe both the nature and the extent of information which must be covered. The Act expressly mentions, in s 136(5), the right of the Minister to require that responses and updates on the National Oversight and Audit Commission reports be reported on a quarterly basis. The Minister can also issue guidelines to ensure best practice is adhered to in the creation of the reports (s 136(4)). The operation of the National Oversight and Audit Commission is described below at paras [6–45] – [6–47].

[45] s 49(c) of the 2014 Act amending s 134(6)(e) of the 2001 Act.

selected by the Public Appointments Service.[46] Now, however, if the council fails to approve, by simple majority, the new Chief Executive, a fresh Public Appointments Service selection process must be carried out. Perhaps out of concern of the possible politicisation of employees, and the desire to ensure jobs remain attractive,[47] the government amended this provision in the Seanad to allow the Minister to issue regulations prescribing the manner in which the council proceed when responding to the Public Appointments Service's recommendation.[48]

Another new reserved function is created by the 2014 Act which inserts **[6–27]** s 134A allowing councils to adopt a draft Local Authority Service Delivery Plan. This plan will define the services the council will provide and the level of service it desires.[49] As well as institutional goal setting, it is hoped that creating such a document will underline the centrality of local council activities to citizens' everyday lives. Similar to the Corporate Plan, the Minister is again empowered to prescribe the content and form of the Service Delivery Plan. The Act requires the Service Delivery Plan to be created following the adoption of the yearly budget, with the plan being prepared in consultation with the elected members under the direction of the chief executive.

In terms of the substantive empowerment of local government, one **[6–28]** additional power that has been bundled in with the local government reforms in media coverage and the popular imagination is the right of the local council to vary (either increase or decrease) the property tax rate by 15%. This, however, is not laid down by the 2014 Act, but was rather introduced as part of the property tax legislation in 2012.[50] An amount equivalent to the overall property tax receipts is lodged by the Minister into the Local Government Fund, thereby establishing a defined and

---

[46] s 145(1) 2001 Act.
[47] This is the author's speculation, as there was no debate on this additional regulation making power during the Seanad debate.
[48] As per the new s 147 (4) of the 2001 Act.
[49] s 134 specifically provides for the mandatory inclusion of:
- A statement of the principle services to be provided in the area,
- Objectives and priorities in providing the services, and a plan for their delivery,
- Performance standards.
[50] s 20 of the Finance Local Property Tax Act 2012.

publicly recognisable funding base for local government. The equitable distribution of said funds remains the subject of much political debate.[51]

[6–29]   So far the 2014 Act appears to be travelling in the singular direction of increasing the power of the elected council. The changes made to the infamous s 140, modify this to some extent. Reflecting the Mahon Tribunal's strong condemnation that "[t]he use of s 140 in planning is a clear source of corruption risks",[52] Part VII of the 2014 Act removes the elected members' right to pass a s 140 resolution concerning any planning related matter or any matter involving financial or other benefit to an individual or single organisation. This represents an effort to tackle the "intercessionary" or "clientelist culture" which had distorted past local political activity. The hope is that rather than populist one-off interventions in executive decisions, councillors will focus, in the planning sphere in any rate, upon designing generally applicable policies which reflect the consolidated best interests of the entire community. Outside of decisions involving a benefit to an identifiable individual or organisation, s 140 continues to apply.[53]

New Municipal and Regional Bodies

[6–30]   The transition to the larger county and city council structures has been accompanied by the creation of a smaller unit of local government: the municipal district.[54] Most local representatives under the 2014 Act, serve simultaneously as county councillors and municipal district members. The Act designates a number of reserved functions for municipal district members, the most significant of which are likely the ability to adopt a *draft* budget for the municipal district[55] and to schedule district maintenance

---

[51] One Government proposal mooted at the time of the Local Government Act debates was that eighty per cent of the property tax received in a particular council area would be given to that council area. As noted by the Oireachtas Library and Research Service, however, no mechanisms to achieve this are included in the 2014 Act. See Oireachtas Library and Research Service, *Note: Local Government Reform Act: A Changing Role for Councillors?* 28 February 2014 (Stationery Office, Dublin).

[52] Final Report of the Tribunal of Inquiry into Certain Planning Matters and Payments (the Mahon Tribunal), available at: http://www.planningtribunal.ie/ (date accessed 12 August 2014) at p 2560. Hereinafter "Mahon Report".

[53] In fact the Act now requires two rather than three proposers of the resolution, and requires a resolution to be considered five days after it is lodged with the Chief Executive.

[54] We would also note at this point the possible creation of local area committees within city councils. See discussion below in para 6-33 regarding the creation of "area committees".

[55] s 102(4A)(c).

and repair works.[56] In terms of budgetary process, the Chief Executive is required to ("shall") consult with the members for each district for the purposes of preparing a "draft budgetary plan for the municipal district".[57] The chief executive shall present this draft to the Committee, which may adopt it by resolution. The Chief Executive "shall take account of this" draft plan in drafting the budget for the full council area, which will then be voted on by the full council. Clearly, therefore, there is some difficulty in evaluating the ability of the municipal district to secure its objectives. If the council budget does not reflect the wishes of the district members, the mechanism may come to be regarded as process chasing. There are some early signs of multi-party pacts being signed to secure control of both the council and municipal districts.[58] If so, party discipline may lead to municipal district members' budgets being accepted in a gesture of party solidarity. It is possible however, for some municipal districts to be controlled by parties who are in a minority on the council — which may raise the probability that their draft budgets are amended by the majority parties in the council. The two tiered system may thus make visible the manner in which party political considerations influence local government decision-making. As we shall see, one may query also if the municipal district differs sufficiently from a sub-committee of a local council in terms of substantive powers. There is, in short, potential for the districts to become the lost sock in the laundromat of Irish local governance.

The scheduling of district works is a significant function of the districts, but even in this area, it remains possible for local and national Government actors to limit their impact. Section 58(i) of 2014 Act,[59] allows district members to amend, by resolution, the draft schedule of municipal works proposed by the Chief Executive following the adoption of the council area budget. In exercising this power of amendment, the district members must pay "due regard" to the local authority budget and act in accordance with such conditions and requirements as may be prescribed by the regulations made by the Minister. **[6–31]**

---

[56] s 103A(1).

[57] Under the new s 102(4A)(a). The Minister may prescribe the manner and format in which the draft budgetary plan is prepared for submission to the district members.

[58] See for example, *Irish Examiner*, 5 June 2014, Fianna Fáil and Fine Gael Sign Pact to Control Councils: http://www.irishexaminer.com/ireland/ff-and-fg-to-sign-pact-to-control-councils-270971.html (date accessed 30 August 2014).

[59] Inserting the new s 103A into the 2001 Act.

[6–32]   Schedule 3 of the Act prescribes further local powers which are to be reserved functions of the Municipal District members. The following is a non-exhaustive sampling:

- Adopting statements regarding the economic elements of the local economic and community plan for consideration by council;
- Establishing a community fund to support initiatives to benefit for the community[60];
- Adopting a scheme whereby residents in an area make annual contributions towards community initiatives;
- Orders extinguishing a public right of way, designating or abandoning a public road, maintaining parking laws and fees;
- Traffic calming measures, designating taxi stands, tree preservation orders, casual trading, litter management and control;
- Bye-laws in the respect of the use of temporary dwellings and orders in relation to the creation and retention of temporary dwellings[61];
- Administering charges for local authority amenities, facilities and services;
- The municipal district may vote to give back the performance of their functions to the local council, but such decisions are subject to the approval of the Minister.

[6–33]   Municipal districts have been created in all but six local council areas: the four Dublin council areas, Cork City Council and Galway City Council. Instead of the district structure, the Act confers on these councils the ability to create Area Committees (or bodies bearing another title of their choosing). These bodies will not attract the reserved powers allocated to municipal districts.

[6–34]   The 2014 Act provides for the establishment of regional assemblies intended to cover areas larger than the city and county councils. The use of the phrase "provides for" reflects the fact that the Act permits the Minister to establish regional assemblies by Order.[62] Prior to this, there were eight regional authorities in existence, tasked with the promoting the co-ordination and cohesion of services. Two regional *assemblies* had also been established in 1999, to facilitate the distribution of EU structural

---

[60] Contributions to this fund may be accepted by any individual, business, community group or public authority.

[61] This power could be a matter of great importance to the Irish Travelling Community.

[62] s 62 of the 2014 Act, inserting a new s 43 into the Local Government Act 1991.

funds, which had been allocated on a regional basis.[63] The 2014 Act has abolished these bodies and the Minister has proceeded to establish two regional assemblies with a designated number of elected local councillors within the regional area constituting the members. The purpose of the regional assemblies is identified in the Act as "co-ordinating, promoting or supporting strategic planning and sustainable development, and promoting effectiveness in local government and public services".[64]

The statutory establishment orders permitted under the 2014 amendments allow for a range of interventions by the Minister in the creation and ongoing operation of regional assemblies, essentially deferring many of the design choices which stand to be made. Section 43(3) provides that an establishment order:

[6–35]

> "...shall contain such provisions as the Minister considers appropriate in relation to the membership of the assembly (including provisions in relation to the number of members of the assembly, the method, terms and conditions of their appointment and their tenure of office".

The Minister is also given further expansive powers to set out the jurisdiction and regulate the functioning of the assembly under s 43(4)(a), which provides that an establishment order:

[6–36]

> "... may contain provisions relating to any matter whatsoever arising in relation to such declaration, establishment or dissolution or in relation to the functions of the regional assembly concerned."[65]

The Minister is also expressly permitted to specify "matters to which the assembly shall have regard" in exercising its powers and may give directions in relation to their functioning.[66] An establishment order can also regulate the provision of grants from central Government to cover the

---

[63] These were the Southern and Eastern Regional Assembly and the Border, Midland and Western Regional Assembly and were established under the Local Government Act, 1991 (Regional Authorities)(Establishment) Order 1999, (SI No 226 of 1999).

[64] Local Government Act 1991 (Regional Authorities) (Amendment) Order 2014 (SI No 228 of 2014).

[65] The Act then supplements this extremely general provision by instancing a number of specific matters which the Minister may address in the order, including defining the assemblies' functions in relation to "regional spatial and economic strategy under the Planning and Development Acts 2000 to 2014" and "functions in connection with assistance from the European Union, with national investment programmes, or with the role of the National Oversight and Audit Commission".

[66] *ibid.*

expenses of the assembly and require the local authorities to contribute to the expenditure and expenses of the assembly.

[6–37] On the 29 May 2014, the Minister put in place the Local Government Act 1991 (Regional Authorities) Amendment Order 2014,[67] creating two regional assemblies: the Southern and Eastern Regional Assembly covers all council areas within Munster, as well as within Wicklow, Wexford, Kilkenny, Carlow as well as the Dublin council areas (Dun Laoighaire-Rathdown, Dublin City, Fingal and South Dublin). The Border, Midland and Western Regional Assembly, covers the rest of Leinster, Ulster and Connacht. The Southern and Eastern Assembly is to have 52 members with Border, Midlands and Western Assembly to have 31. Dublin City Council is allocated seven members, Cork County Council is allocated five, Donegal, Dun Laoighaire-Rathdown, Fingal, Galway, Kerry, Kildare, Mayo, Meath, South Dublin, Tipperary, Wexford and Wicklow and the council of the city and county of Limerick receive three seats and all other member councils receive two.

[6–38] As was signalled by the parent Act, the Order provides for the following functions:

> "It shall be the general function of a regional assembly to co-ordinate, promote or support strategic planning and sustainable development, and promote effectiveness in local government and public services in the assembly's region."[68]

and

> "To perform functions under Chapter I of Part II and Chapter III of the Part II of the Planning and Development Act 2000 (as inserted by the Local Government Reform Act 2014)."[69]

[6–39] We will return to this latter planning and development role later in this chapter. The Order also provides for the inheritance of the structural funds functions of the regional authorities by the regional assemblies. Further additions to the assemblies' functions remain, of course, possible under s 43.

---

[67] Above n 64.
[68] s 6(a) *ibid*.
[69] s 6(b) *ibid*.

In addition to the foregoing regional and municipal structures, the [6–40] Government has also radically reformed the bodies involved in the local economic and community development, which we deal with in a later thematic section of this chapter. Given these numerous changes there must be some concern at the sheer amount of structures and processes at play under the Local Government Act 2014. It is interesting to consider how the elected members (who are often part time, after all) will divide their time and prioritise their efforts. Considerable energy and resources will be expended on acclimatising to the new municipal district structure yet the extent of its practical import is dependent on a number of political variables. One overarching concern is that the public has limited time to track all these governance processes and media coverage may prove patchy given the sprawl of bodies and procedures. The fact that all this must be underpinned by additional circulars and Ministerial regulation underline the extent of the burdensome shuffling of organisational structures and planning processes involved.

Supervision of Local Government under the 2014 Act

Central Government

Central Government oversight of local government has always been [6–41] strong, even from the birth of the Irish State, when civil war concerns prompted the passage of s 12 of the Local Government (Temporary Provisions) Act 1923. This permitted the Minister for Local Government to "dissolve [councils] and transfer functions to any body or persons or person he shall think fit". The creation of the local management system in 1940, splitting reserved and executive functions between councillors and the Manager, (now Chief Executive), represented another significant indicator of a broader pattern of centralisation.[70] Financial dependence has also been a key lever ensuring central Government bears a powerful influence over local authorities. The abolition of domestic rates under the Local Government (Financial Provisions) Act 1978 resulted in a reduction in the revenue raising capacity of local government. Since that date, various attempts have been made to designate solid funding streams, including the assignment of motor tax revenue to local government in the Local Government (Financial Provisions) Act 1997. Under the 2001 Act

---

[70] City and County Management Act 1940.

further consolidation of the Local Government Fund took place, with an equalisation formula for distributing it eventually emerging. What resulted was the following average situation, which prevailed prior to the introduction of the property tax in 2012:

- *Commercial Rates*[71] (34% of revenue), levied annually by local authorities following the creation of a valuation list of local properties by the independent Commissioner of Valuation. This valuation centres upon the net annual value of the property, which is the hypothetical rental value of a property assessed by reference to a specified date. Once this rateable valuation is obtained, the local council then passes the annual rate on valuation, a multiplier figure which indicates the percentage of the total rateable valuation to be paid in commercial rates;
- *Sectoral Government Grants and Subsidies* (22%): Government Department funding of local initiatives within their subject area;
- *Receipts from Service Charges* (27%): This includes planning fees, household waste charges and household rents;
- *General Purpose Grants* (17%): this funding stream included motor tax receipts and the new household charge.[72]

[6–42] With the introduction of the property tax this funding landscape is shifting, with the desire of central Government that local government be funded

---

[71] Following the 1984 judgment in *Brennan v Attorney General* [1984] ILRM 355, agricultural rates are no longer collected. The court held that the existing collection system was based upon entirely outdated (1952) Griffiths poor law valuations and did not include sufficient review mechanisms to ensure that an unjust attack on individuals' property rights was avoided. The current commercial rates system, created by the Valuation Act 2001, contains extensive appeal mechanisms, which reflects the balancing process required when inhibiting constitutionally protected property rights. Following the receipt of a proposed valuation certificate, the individual or business is invited to make representations to the revision officer in Valuation Office, which he or she is obliged to consider and which may result in amendment. Thereafter appeal (within forty days) lies to the Commissioner, in practice a fresh revision occupier. Following the determination of this, an individual or business can obtain merits review from the Valuation Tribunal, provided that the application and the grounds for such an appeal are lodged within 28 days. Under s 39 of the Valuation Act, appeal on a point of law can be taken to the High Court, which is given the power to reverse, affirm or amend the valuation or to remit the matter to the Tribunal. Clearly, given the technical and expert nature of the valuation process, a significant amount of deference will be shown by the Courts, which are reluctant to intervene absent glaring factual error or error of law.

[72] These figures were supplied by the Department of Finance within the 2012 National Budget, and are quoted by the Council of Europe, above n 2 at para 74.

solely[73] by service charges and a property tax. It is currently not possible to describe the property tax revenue as a direct source of finance — the government has not required that a portion of this new tax be directly lodged into local budgets. The funds which will be collected will continue to be lodged into the local government fund. Thus the debate regarding equalisation seems set to continue to rage, with central Government decision-making regarding distribution persistently opaque:

> "...the system of distribution of grants of local governments from the Local Government Fund is not transparent and the rules have been set without consultation with local authorities. The equalisation formula existed for a short period only, because it included about 800 parameters and was not operable in reality. From 2008 onwards, equalisation has been done on the basis of an administrative assessment of needs and resources. The Government informed the rapporteurs that while equalisation does not operate through a single formula or model, it does involve a process using real current data. Developed on the basis of a "needs and resources" study of local government financing, it takes into account the individual circumstances of local authorities in determining annual funding allocations."[74]

It appears that further political engagement is necessary if this situation is to be reformed.

Apart from central government's financial role, the Minister also possesses **[6–43]** a range of powers to potentially intervene in the functioning of local authorities. It is perhaps telling that the Local Government Act 2001 employed the word "Minister" 461 times. The most extraordinary provision is s 216(1) of the 2001 Act which permitted the Minister to remove elected members from office whenever:

> "(a) the Minister, after holding a public local inquiry into the performance by a local authority of its functions, is satisfied that such functions are not being duly and effectually performed, or;
>
> (b) a local authority refuses or neglects to comply with a judgment, order, or decree of any court, or
>
> (c) a local authority fails to comply with a requirement made by notification under subsection (1) of section 10A [which allows a

---

[73] Though subsidies will continue to be available for local implementation of central Government programmes.

[74] Council of Europe report, above n 2 at paras 81 and 82. The division is achieved by reference to quarterly financial reports and specific submissions covering, inter alia, demographic, social, economic factors.

Minister to order modifications be made to budget or the council's activities due to the fact that projections for expenditure are not sustainable in the light of the authorities financial needs] within 14 days."[75]

[6–44] Where the Minister dismisses an elected member, he or she may appoint one or more person to act as commissioners for the local authority, who may exercise the reserved functions of the elected members until the next election is held. Clearly this power has been used only sparingly and not within the past 20 years.[76] The Minister also possesses, under s 199(8a) of the 2001 Act, the power to revoke any local bye law which she views as "objectionable".

National Oversight and Audit Commission

[6–45] Section 61 of the 2014 Act inserted into the 2001 Act the new s 126B, creating the National Oversight and Audit Commission (NOAC), an expert group tasked, under s 126C(1) with the following functions:

(a) "to scrutinise the performance of any local government body against or in comparison with any indicative matter…that:
(i) the Commission considers it appropriate to refer to (which shall include indicative matters relating to customer service), or
(ii) the Minister may prescribe by regulations for the purposes of this paragraph;

(b) to scrutinise the financial performance, including in relation to value for money, of any local government body, in respect of the financial resources, available to it;

(c) to support the development and enhancement of best practice in the performance by local government bodies of their respective functions;

(d) to monitor and evaluate adherence to any agreement in the nature of a service level agreement entered into by one or more local government bodies, whether or not all parties to such an agreement are local government bodies;

(e) to oversee how national policy in relation to local government is implemented by local government bodies;

---

[75] s 222 of the 2001 Act also provides an ancillary power giving the Minister the right to demand a report or obtain information from the local authority "he may consider necessary or desirable".

[76] Perhaps the most high profile instance of its use was the dismissal of the elected members of Dublin Corporation in 1969 when the Council set the rates to be collected at a level lower than that needed to cover the bill for health services. D Roche, *Local Government in Ireland*, (Institute of Public Administration, Dublin, 1982) at p 123.

(f) to monitor and evaluate the implementation of public service reform (including enhanced efficiencies) by local government bodies either generally or in respect of any local government body or class of such bodies;

(g) to monitor the adequacy of the corporate plan prepared-

    (i) by a regional assembly pursuant to section 44 (as amended by the Local Government Reform Act 2014) of the Local Government Act 1991, and

    (ii) by a council pursuant to section 134

and to evaluate implementation of such plans either generally or in respect of any local government body or class of such bodies;

(h) To take such steps as are appropriate under its other functions for the purposes of any request under section 126D [under which a Minister may request the Commission investigate a local authorities actions in relation any matter within their thematic area] and to furnish reports or other information in relation to that request to the Minister or the appropriate Minister, as the case may be;

(i) In addition to reports or other information furnished under section 126D and to its annual reports under section 126K, to prepare on its own initiative such other reports or information on matters relating to its functions as the Commission considers appropriate."

The Commission will therefore audit a wide range of local authority actions against national, regional and local yardsticks. Significantly, this extends beyond the financial, to *legality*, social inclusion and other bedrock principles. Its key contribution will arguably be to present a unified and holistic vision of best practice in local administration, as well as securing compliance with national objectives. In terms of mechanisms for implementing the findings of audits, the elected council is given a new reserved function to adopt an implementation plan which can prescribe measures to comply with NOAC findings. Thus, it is hoped that national oversight can disseminate normative standards which elected councillors can invoke when engaging with management. [6–46]

At the time of writing, the interaction of the national commission with the already functioning Local Government Audit Service (LGAS) was not wholly defined.[77] This latter body is a unit of the Department of Environment [6–47]

---

[77] In terms of its future interaction with NOAC, the 2014 Activity Report of the Local Government Audit Service merely states:

"This committee [*sic* – this should read "Commission"], in the course of carrying out its remit, can take account of the reports prepared by the LGAS. The LGAS will have engagement with this committee in the future which may impact on the national value for money work currently undertaken."

and Local Government, and was already tasked under s 117 and s 118 of the 2001 Act with drawing up a Code of Audit Practice. This Code of Practice prescribes key metrics and procedures to be followed by local government auditors who are tasked with assessing the financial position of local authorities.[78] The 2014 Act does heighten LGAS' role by providing for increased engagement by its auditor with local authority audit committees. The latter committees are tasked with reviewing any audited financial statements or reports concerning the local authority and to supervise the response of the Chief Executive to such findings. The 2014 Act allows the Minister to pass regulations concerning the composition of the audit committees and their functions. The local government auditor will also now attend a meeting of the local audit committee to explain her findings and respond to any queries.[79]

Community and Local Development as a Core Policy Area

New Community and Local Development Structures

[6–48]   As mentioned earlier, the 2014 Act makes radical changes to the existing framework for local development. Under it, the city and county development boards established in 2000 are abolished.[80] These had been made up of local government representatives, social partners, State agencies, community development organisations and county and city development boards. Their remit had been to draw up an overall strategy for economic, social and cultural development for their area.[81] To replace this structure, a new reserved function was created which require the elected council to create a Local Community Development Committee (LCDC),[82] whose purpose is broadly to develop, co-ordinate and implement a coherent integrated approach to local and community development. A more specific

---

Local Government Audit Service, *Activity Report 2014*, Department of Environment and Local Government, at p 25.

[78] In terms of financial efficiency, further supervision is also exercised through a Local Government (Value for Money) Unit established under the Local Government (Financial Provisions) Act 1997, s 14(4).

[79] Following this meeting, the local audit committee will prepare a report to the full council.

[80] s 35.

[81] They did not possess any funding for this purpose, and existed to co-ordinate efforts amongst the participating agencies.

[82] s 36 of the 2014 Act inserting a new s 49A into the 2001 Act. They may establish more than one, subject to ministerial approval (s 49A(3)).

range of tasks are set out in the new s 128B of the Local Government Act 2001[83]:

- To prepare the community elements of the new six year Local Economic and Community Plan [we will explain this new plan shortly]:
- To implement or arrange for the implementation of the community elements of the Plan:
- To review the community elements of the Plan at least once within the six years, and to if necessary amend the community elements;
- To consider and adopt a statement for consideration of the Council in respect of the economic elements of the draft plan;
- To provide ongoing monitoring and review of the implementation of local and community development programmes adopted by local councils;
- To seek to ensure effectiveness, consistency, co-ordination and avoidance of duplication between public funded local and community development programmes.[84]

The Ministerial guidelines encourage LCDCs to "drive meaningful citizen and community engagement in the scoping, planning, delivery and evaluation of local and community development programmes" in executing their functions.[85] **[6–49]**

The membership of the Committee is to be made up of members of the council, staff from the council executive, representatives of public bodies involved in the provision of services, representatives of local community interests and groups, and representatives of publicly funded or supported local development bodies. Despite this wide range of eligible organisations, however, the relevant Ministerial Guidelines provide that LCDCs have a "tightly defined membership, consisting of no more than 17 members".[86] The guidelines also distinguish between statutory and non-statutory representatives, and require that the maximum number of statutory representatives is eight, with a minimum of nine non-statutory representatives. Statutory representatives, under **[6–50]**

---

[83] Inserted by s 36 of the 2014 Act.

[84] It will also prepare an annual report on its own activities.

[85] Department of Environment, Community and Local Government, *Guidelines for the Establishment of Local Community Development Committees*, April 2014 at p 5.

[86] *ibid* at p 8.

the guidelines, are made up of elected councillors,[87] local authority officials[88] and State agencies,[89] whereas non-statutory representatives are defined as those individuals involved in community and voluntary interests,[90] social inclusion interests,[91] environmental interests,[92] representatives of local development and community development bodies, farming/agricultural interests, business/employer interests, trade union interests. This clearly aims to activate new and more diverse "publics" beyond elected representatives. The Act also provides an expansive definition of community development.[93] The LCDC is tasked not just with creating and exploring possible amendment of the community development limb of the plan, but also with managing its implementation.

---

[87] There must be a minimum of three elected councillors on the LCDC, and they may be selected through the 'grouping system or through the local authority's Corporate Policy Group.

[88] A minimum of two is required by the guidelines: specifically, the Chief Executive or a nominee of the Chief Executive and the local authority official in charge of managing the Local Enterprise Office, should be included.

[89] A minimum of two.

[90] Minimum of two members.

[91] Minimum of two members.

[92] Minimum of one member.

[93] s 66(3)(e) of the 2001 Act provides that:

"The promotion of local and community development includes, but is not limited to—

(a) promoting and supporting the interests of local communities, or any part of a community or group within a local community, including measures to enhance quality of life and well-being of communities and measures aimed at—

(i) tackling poverty, disadvantage and social exclusion through support for basic services and other initiatives,

(ii) supporting training and up-skilling, creating and sustaining employment and self-employment opportunities, and investing in local development through community-focused supports and services, and

(iii) the provision of infrastructure and community facilities and investment in physical regeneration and environmental improvements,

(b) supporting the capacity of local communities to improve their quality of life,

(c) supporting social enterprise, social capital, volunteering and active citizenship,

(d) developing integrated and evidenced-based approaches to local service planning and delivery,

(e) identifying the needs and priorities of local communities to enhance their well-being, and developing sustainable solutions that make the best use of local assets, strengths and opportunities to address those needs and priorities,

(f) exploiting and co-ordinating funding sources from the public, private and community and voluntary sectors to stimulate and support local development and sustainability, and

(g) promoting, supporting and facilitating community involvement in policy development and decision-making processes related to the planning, development and delivery of services."

Separate structures have been established pursuing local economic   [6–51]
development policy. Section 48 of the 2001 Act had already provided for
the creation of Strategic Policy Committees. The 2014 Act provides for the
creation of a new Strategic Policy Committee for economic development
and the supporting of local enterprise.[94] This, like other SPCs, will have a
membership of two thirds local councillors, one third sectoral interests. The
role of the economic development SPC is linked to other statutory reforms
contained in the County Enterprise Board (Dissolution) Act 2014. This
dissolves the thirty five City and County Enterprise Boards which had
been established as limited companies in 1993.[95] These boards supported
local business with seed grants and training with funding originating from
Enterprise Ireland. The Dissolution Act transferred their functions to
Enterprise Ireland, and created Local Enterprise Offices (LEOs) within each
local council area. These LEOs will support enterprise initiative under the
umbrella of Enterprise Ireland and central Government. In order to secure
local oversight, however, it is envisaged that the new Strategic Policy
Committees for economic development and enterprise will monitor the
activities of the LEOs.[96]

Local Economic and Community Development Plans

The 2014 Act makes it a reserved function of the council to approve the   [6–52]
Economic and Community Development Plan which will run for six
years.[97] As already mentioned, the LCDC is tasked with drafting the
community portions of the Plan. Under the statute, the SPC on economic
development does not yet have that role, which as a matter of default is
assigned to the local authority, but the Act allows the Minister to pass
regulations assigning the role of drafting the economic elements to the
SPC.[98] The local authority is also tasked with managing the implementation
of the economic elements of the final plan. Clearly the distinction between
economic and community development is key to the division of labour

---

[94] s 41 of the 2014 Act inserts s 48(1A) into the 2001 Act.
[95] They were given statutory status in 1995 under the Industrial Development Act.
[96] The minister supported this idea in the Seanad Debate on the Bill, on the 15 January 2014,
cited by the Oireachtas Library and Research Service Note, above n 52 at p 14.
[97] s 44 inserts s 66B into the 2001 Act.
[98] *ibid.*

between the relevant actors. In this regard, the 2014 Amendments introduce an extensive definition of economic development.[99]

In creating and passing the Plan, the local council and committees must have regard to the following factors under the new s 66C(1):

> "(a) the need to integrate sustainable development considerations into the Plan,
>
> (b) the resources, wherever originating from, that are available or likely to become available to it for the purpose of the Plan and the need to secure the most beneficial, effective and efficient use of such resources,
>
> (c) the need for co-operation with, and the co-ordination of its activities with those of other local authorities, public authorities and publicly funded bodies, the performance of some of whose functions affect or may affect the local authority and the Committee,

---

[99] The newly inserted s 66(B)(2) provides that economic development includes but is not limited to:

> "(a) creating and sustaining jobs,
>
> (b) promoting the interests of the community, including—
> > (i) enterprise and economic development across economic sectors,
> > (ii) foreign direct investment,
> > (iii) indigenous industry,
> > (iv) micro-enterprises and small and medium sized enterprises,
> > (v) tourism, and
> > (vi) agriculture, forestry and the marine sectors, and other natural resource sectors,
>
> (c) identifying local attributes that are essential
> > (i) to enhancing local economic performance, such as the quality of the environment and the qualities of cities, towns and rural areas, including—
> > > (I) accessibility, physical character, and infrastructure,
> > > (II) employment opportunities and quality of life,
> > > and the means by which these may be utilised to enhance competitiveness, and be supported by investment decisions relating to economic infrastructure (including transportation, water services, energy, communications and waste management), together with social and cultural facilities, and
> > (ii) to promoting local economic activities,
>
> (d) supporting enhancement of local innovation capacity, including investment in research and development capacity, technology transfer, up-skilling and re-skilling,
>
> (e) identifying, for existing and prospective businesses, opportunities to engage with local government on relevant matters in setting up and managing their businesses and to ensure speedy and coordinated access and response,
>
> (f) identifying local strengths and opportunities, weaknesses and deficiencies relevant to economic performance and —
> > (i) in relation to such strengths and opportunities having regard to economic and employment trends, the means of maintaining and augmenting them, and
> > (ii) in relation to such weaknesses and deficiencies, the means of addressing or rectifying them, and
>
> (g) identifying economic potential and the requirements to realise it."

(d) the need for consistency with the policies and objectives of the Government or any Minister of the Government or other public authority in so far as they may affect or relate to the promotion of economic and community development...and

(e) the need to integrate the economic and community elements...into the Plan."

Prior to adoption, the local council must obtain statements from each **[6–53]** municipal district and from the regional assembly regarding the consistency of the proposed plan with the council's own development plan, the regional and spatial strategy and the degree to which the economic and community development portions of the proposed plan are consistent with each other. The Minister retains a powerful supervisory role over the format and content of Economic and Community Development Plan with the new s 66H[100] of the 2001 Act, which grants expansive regulatory power to central Government:

"66H(1) The Minister may, following consultation with such public authorities as he or she considers appropriate, make regulations for the purposes of the relevant sections and sections 128B to 128F either generally or in relation to a regional assembly or a local authority or a Committee or to a particular class or classes of regional assemblies or local authorities or Committees and each regional assembly, local authority and Committee shall, to the extent that those regulations apply to it, comply with those regulations."[101]

---

[100] Inserted by s 44 of the 2014 Act.

[101] s 66H(2) then instances a number of examples of such regulations [without prejudice to the generality of s 66(H)(1)], such as regulations concerning:

"(a) the preparation of a Plan,

(b) the co-ordination of the preparation of the economic and community elements of a Plan,

(c) the integration of the economic and community elements into a Plan,

(d) the timing of the preparation of a Plan,

(e) the role of the strategic policy committee established pursuant to section 48(1A),

(f) extending or shortening the period of a Plan for the purposes of synchronising the time period for a Plan with other relevant plans and strategies,

(g) the format and content of a Plan,

(h) the procedures and processes to ensure consistency with the core strategy and objectives of the development plan of a local authority,

   (i) the procedures and processes to ensure consistency with the regional spatial and economic strategy and any regional planning guidelines referred to in subsections (2)(c)(ii), (3)(c)(ii) and (4)(a)

   (ii) of section 66C for the purposes of Chapter III of Part II of the Act of 2000,

(j) engagement and consultation with the local community in the preparation of a Plan,

[6–54] Clearly there remains enormous detail to be added to the economic and community pillars through the adoption of regulations, but the 2014 Act is a landmark reform in the area of community and economic development. In the former area, community actors have obtained the ability to drive the direction of local initiatives in their sectors, while the latter benefits from more defined structures and relationships to address local economic growth than the loose arrangements that existed during the Celtic Tiger.

Planning and Development and Local Government

[6–55] In any book on administrative justice and regulatory failures in Ireland, the issue of planning and development must receive some treatment. Clearly, at various points throughout this book, we address aspects of the planning and development system and the failures of Celtic Tiger Ireland. In the remainder of this chapter, we propose, without prejudice to the enormously detailed and specialized planning framework, to provide an analysis of prevailing decision-making structures and reform initiatives in the planning and development area. We hope that what follows therefore, will be seen as a critical case study on a priority area for local government in the aftermath of the collapse of the Irish economy rather than a bare bones, legalistic account of what is ultimately a vast area of law.

[6–56] As already discussed, the 2014 Act attempts to remove the clientelism which had marred the planning system, by removing the use of s 140. The 2014 local government reforms also attempt to implement a key recommendation of the Final Report of the Mahon Tribunal, by strengthening the role of regional assemblies to ensure the valuing of regional spatial strategies within local development plans. It is something of a disappointment, however, that the members of regional assemblies are not directly elected as the Tribunal recommended,[102] but rather consist of a

---

(k) public consultation when a Plan is being prepared or reviewed, effective participation by the public concerned,

(l) developing performance indicators and arrangements for measuring performance of a Plan,

(m) publication of a Plan,

(n) implementation of a Plan, including the preparation, review and updating of the implementation strategies provided for in section 66E(2) and the arrangements for implementation provided for in section 128B(1), and

(o) the review and amendment of a Plan."

[102] The Mahon Report noted that the Regional Authorities were "insufficiently accountable given the importance of their role in the planning system and that their role is insufficiently

number of local councillors. This may be a barrier to the new legislation's effort to mediate regional standards into local development plans.

The drafting of the local development plan is one of the most significant **[6–57]** roles belonging to a local council. This represents "an overall strategy for the proper planning and sustainable development" of the area, and must be created for each council area every six years.[103] Section 10 of the Planning and Development Act 2000 (as amended)[104] sets out the mandatory planning objectives which the development plan must include.[105]

---

transparent." The election of members was seen as a way of combating this problem. Mahon Report, above n 52 at p 2518.

[103] A development plan shall consist of a "written statement" and a plan or plans indicating the development objectives for the area in question.

[104] Hereinafter referred to as the PDA 2000.

[105] The objectives specified in s 10(2) are:
- "the zoning of land for exclusive or primary use for particular purposes" (*i.e.* residential, commercial, industrial, agricultural, recreational, *etc.*) [s 10(2)(a)]. It is expressly provided that there shall be no presumption in law that land remains so zoned in a subsequent development plan. Under s 95, sufficient land must be zoned for housing.
- "the provision, or facilitation of the provision of, infrastructure including transport, energy and communication facilities, water supplies, waste facilities," and waste water services [s.10(2)(b)]. Under the Waste Management Acts 1996-2003, the development plan is deemed to include the objectives contained in any waste management plan in force for the area.
- "the conservation and protection of the environment", especially the archaeological and natural heritage, and European sites and other prescribed sites [s 10(2)(c)].
- the integration of the proper planning and sustainable development of the area with the social, community and cultural requirements of the area and its population [s 10(2)(d)]. For example, section 94 requires that the plan provides for the housing of the present and future population of the area, by ensuring that sufficient and suitable land is zoned for residential use [s 95(1)] and by provisions in the Act in respect of social and affordable housing [s 96].
- the preservation of the character of the landscape, including preservation of views and prospects and the amenities of places and features of natural beauty or interest [s 10(2)(e); EC Habitats Directive; Council of Europe Landscape Convention].
- the protection of structures which are of special architectural, historical, archaeological, artistic, cultural, scientific, social or technical interest [s 10(2)(f) and (g)]. The development plan must contain a record of all protected structures of such interest within its functional area. This record continues to be part of any new plan.
- the preservation of the character of architectural conservation areas as defined in s 81 PDA 2000.
- "the development and renewal of areas in need of regeneration" [s 10(2)(h)].
- "the provision of accommodation for travellers, and the use of particular areas for that purpose" [s 10(2)(i)].
- "the preservation, improvement and extension of amenities and recreational amenities" [s 10(2)(j)].
- giving effect to the Major Accidents Directive in order to control.
- the siting of establishments.

Schedule 1 sets out discretionary objectives which it may contain.[106] The Minister may also prescribe further mandatory and discretionary planning objectives by regulation.[107] Unfortunately, reflecting the complex nature of Irish planning and local government law, these lists of objectives are not absolutely exhaustive, as other mandatory objectives include those contained under a waste management plan, under a planning scheme in a strategic development zone,[108] or under a local authority housing strategy.[109] These objectives supersede any contrary provisions in the development plan. Under s 22(10A) of the Waste Management Act 1996,[110] the waste management objectives prevail over another objective in the development plan in the case of conflict, even where the development plan was made later than the waste management plan. Given the structure of the 2000 Act, and the manner in which it provides a mechanism for listing all mandatory and discretionary objectives, Scannell argues that the council itself is not entitled to include objectives that do not trace back to those issued under statutory authority.[111] The document should address any

---

- the modification of existing establishments.
- development in the vicinity of such establishments [s 10(2)(k)].
- the provision of community services in particular schools, crèches, and other education and childcare facilities [s 10(2)(l)].
- "the protection of the linguistic and cultural heritage of the Gaeltacht" where there is a Gaeltacht in the area of the development plan [s 10(2)(m)].
- the promotion of sustainable settlement and transportation strategies in urban and rural areas including the promotion of measures to reduce carbon emissions and adapt to climate change [s 10(2)(n)]
- the protection of public rights of way [s 10(2)(o)].
- the protection, management and planning of landscapes and developed having regard to the European Landscape Convention.

[106] Schedule 1 to PDA 2000 list five categories of discretionary objectives which may be included in the development plan:
  (i) location and pattern of development;
  (ii) control of areas and structures;
  (iii) community facilities;
  (iv) environment and amenities; and
  (v) infrastructure and transport.

[107] Under s 22 of the Roads Act 1993, the National Roads Authority may request that the planning authority include its proposals within the plan. In passing their development plan, a local authority must not include an objective where the responsibility for achieving that objective would rest with another local authority, absent consultation with this second authority. s 11(3) requires consultation with the infrastructure and service providers, who must supply certain information where the council requests.

[108] As created under part IX PDA 2000 [s 169(9)].

[109] PDA 2000 s 94(1).

[110] As amended by s 4 of the Waste Management (Amendment) Act 2001.

[111] Y Scannell, *Environmental and Land Use Law* (Thomson Round Hall, Dublin, 2005) at p 46.

matters which will have a material impact on the pursuit of all objectives, as it effectively represents:

> "...an environmental contract between the planning authority, the Council and the community, embodying a promise by the Council that ... it shall not effect any development which would contravene the plan materially"[112]

The Planning and Development (Amendment) Act 2010 represented a first **[6–58]** reaction to the onset of the economic crisis by the then Fianna Fáil/Green Government. This strengthened the existing requirement that the relevant plan must be consistent with such national plans, policies and strategies as laid down by the Minister. The 2010 Act inserted a new s 10(1A) which requires the inclusion of:

> "a core strategy which shows that the development objectives in the development are consistent, as far as practicable, with national and regional development objectives set out in the National Spatial Strategy and regional planning guidelines."

Section 10(1B) requires the preparation of a core strategy statement not less **[6–59]** than one year after the revision of regional planning guidelines which affect the council area.[113] This must be accompanied by necessary variations to the development plan.

In addition to the general requirements of s 10(1)A, a core strategy must also *inter alia*:

> "10(2)(A)(a) Provide relevant information to show that the development plan and housing strategy are consistent with the National Spatial Strategy and regional planning guidelines.
> (b) Take account of any policies of the Minister in relation to national and regional population targets".[114]

---

[112] Per McCarthy J in *Attorney General (McGarry) v. Sligo County Council* [1991] 1 IR 99 at 113. See also *Keogh v Galway Corporation* [1995] 3 IR 457.

[113] s 10(1)D requires the inclusion of a "separate statement" showing how the development objectives contained in the plan "are consistent, as far as practicable, with the conservation and protection of the environment".

[114] The new s 10(2)B also specifically requires the core strategy to:
> (c) in respect of the area in the development plan already zoned for residential use or a mixture of residential and other uses, provide details of —
> (i) the size of the area in hectares, and (ii) the proposed number of housing units to be included in the area,

[6–60]   The 2010 Act was therefore the forerunner of efforts to incorporate a regional perspective on planning, which following the Local Government Act 2014, is now inherited by the regional assemblies. The preparation of a core strategy provides a mechanism for the practical integration of the specifics of local development plans with the express provisions of national and regional plans and guidelines and ministerial policy. In particular it provides core overall data which may trigger further action by the Department (or a future independent planning regulator) to secure compliance.

(*d*) in respect of the area in the development plan proposed to be zoned for residential use or a mixture of residential and other uses, provide details of—

(i)   the size of the area in hectares,

(ii) how the zoning proposals accord with national policy that development of land shall take place on a phased basis,

(*e*) provide relevant information to show that, in setting out objectives regarding retail development contained in the development plan, the planning authority has had regard to any guidelines that relate to retail development issued by the Minister under section 28,

(*f*) in respect of the area of the development plan of a county council, set out a settlement hierarchy and provide details of—

(i)   whether a city or town referred to in the hierarchy is designated as a gateway or hub for the purposes of the National Spatial Strategy,

(ii) other towns referred to in the hierarchy,

(iii) any policies or objectives for the time being of the Government or any Minister of the Government in relation to national and regional population targets that apply to towns and cities referred to in the hierarchy,

(iv) any policies or objectives for the time being of the Government or any Minister of the Government in relation to national and regional population targets that apply to the areas or classes of areas not included in the hierarchy,

(v)   projected population growth of cities and towns in the hierarchy,

(vi) aggregate projected population, other than population referred to in subparagraph (v), in—

(I)   villages and smaller towns with a population of under 1,500 persons, and

(II)   open countryside outside of villages and towns,

(vii) relevant roads that have been classified as national primary or secondary roads under section 10 of the Roads Act 1993 and relevant regional and local roads within the meaning of section 2 of that Act,

(viii) relevant inter-urban and commuter rail routes, and

(ix) where appropriate, rural areas in respect of which planning guidelines relating to sustainable rural housing issued by the Minister under section 28 apply,

(*g*) in respect of the development plan of a city or a town council, provide details of—

(i)   the city or town centre concerned,

(ii) the areas designated for significant development during the period of the development plan, particularly areas for which it is intended to prepare a local area plan,

(iii) the availability of public transport within the catchment of residential or commercial development, and

(iv) retail centres in that city or town centre.

Enforcement and Oversight of Development Plans

The Minister

The Minister enjoys a powerful macro policy-setting function and can influence the general direction proposed by a development plan. This function includes a power to issue directions under s 31 of the 2000 Act[115] to ensure the development plan is of the requisite quality[116]:   **[6–61]**

> "(1) Where the Minister considers that any draft development plan fails to set out an overall strategy for the proper planning and sustainable development of the area of a planning authority or otherwise significantly fails to comply with [the] Act, the Minister may, for stated reasons, direct the authority to take such specified measures as he or she may require to ensure ... compliance with this Act and...the authority shall comply with any such direction."

In practice, this power represents something of a final backstop on other mechanisms which the Minister has to supervise the quality of the plan. These include the ability to issue general guidelines and policy directives under s 28 and s 29 respectively. Local councils are placed under an obligation to "have regard to" any guidelines issued and "shall comply" with any policy directives. The Minister may not, in exercising these powers, involve himself or herself in particular planning applications or individual situations, the oversight of which is the function of An Bord Pleanála.   **[6–62]**

The main authority examining the nature and scope of s 31 directions is *Tristor Ltd v Minister for the Environment, Heritage and Local Government and ors.*[117] This case concerned a decision by Dun Laoighaire-Rathdown County Council to designate lands owned by the applicant company as a district centre for retail purposes in its development plan. The Minister had made submissions opposing the proposed designation, and when the elected members voted to incorporate it in the draft development plan he issued a s 31 direction instructing the Council to delete it.[118] According to its terms, the direction was grounded in the determination of the Minister that as a   **[6–63]**

---

[115] Part 2, Chapter IV.

[116] Hereinafter referred to as s 31 directions.

[117] *Tristor Ltd v Minister for the Environment, Heritage and Local Government and ors* [2010] IEHC 397.

[118] Two directions were in fact issued over the course of five days by the Minister; the second superseded the initial one and was the focus of the litigation.

result of the designation, the draft Development Plan was unsatisfactory in that it did not set out an appropriate strategy for proper planning and sustainable development of the area, and did not comply with the Planning and Development Act 2000 in three specific respects:

- – It did not accord with the Dun-Laoighaire-Rathdown portions of the Retail Strategy for the Greater Dublin Area 2008-2016 as prepared by the relevant Regional Authority;
- – It would be likely to damage the vitality of existing town centres and other proposed town centres in a manner contrary to the 2005 Guidelines for Planning Authorities on Retail Planning;
- – The proposed designation would be contrary to traffic and transport principles included in the 2005 Guidelines.[119]

[6–64] The applicant company argued that the objective existence of "a failure to set out an overall strategy for the proper planning and sustainable development of the area" was a condition precedent[120] to the exercise of the Minister's discretion and his claims were therefore liable to close scrutiny by the Court. Clarke J rejected this submission, finding that the Minister could wield the power where he considered that there had been such a failure. This discretionary decision of the Minister could only be judicially reviewed under ordinary principles of judicial review.[121] The applicant company then argued that the direction was invalid as it exceeded the scope of the statute. This was due to the fact that the disputed direction stated that the draft Development Plan failed to set out a "proper" strategy, whereas the statutory provision referred instead to an "overall" strategy. However, Clarke J refused to interpret the section as requiring the exact use of statute's language where the substance of the direction fell within the scope and purpose of the relevant section.

[6–65] Having found for the Minister on these questions of statutory interpretation however, Clarke J then ruled that the use of the term "proper" rather than "overall" was in fact indicative of a broader flaw in the Minister's direction. The Minister had failed to appreciate the fact that a s 31 direction should be

---

[119] The direction is published in full at para 2.8 of Clarke J's judgment, above n 117.

[120] For an explanation of the operation of "condition precedent" in judicial review see chapter 7 - Narrow *Ultra Vires*: Unauthorised Decision-Making.

[121] For instance where the applicant believed the Minister's decision was irrational or had failed to take into account relevant considerations.

issued to combat a failure to set out *any* strategy or *substantial failures* to comply with the 2000 Act. Clarke J held that:

> "It can hardly be doubted that there are many strategies which could be adopted.... It seems to me that, on a proper construction of the combined effect of s. 31(1) and s. 10, it is a matter for the planning authority to determine which of the range of possible strategies that could be pursued are to be included in a development plan. Provided that there is a strategy set out, and that it is reasonably described as an overall strategy for the proper planning and sustainable development of the relevant area, then it does not seem to me that the Minister is entitled to impose an alternative strategy simply because the Minister may prefer it. If it were the intention of the Oireachtas to give the Minister the widespread powers which the Minister asserts, it seems to me that the language of the section would have been expressed in very different terms."[122]

In terms of the specific reasons invoked by the Minister in the direction, **[6–66]** Clarke J held that the guidelines and strategies relied upon possessed no formal legal status. The Council was merely obliged to have regard to them, but was not bound to apply them. His Honour held that the council had had regard for the guidelines but had departed from them for *bona fide* reasons. No breach of the 2000 Act had therefore occurred, and the direction was invalid. In making these findings, Clarke J stressed the importance of s 27(2) of the 2000 Act in understanding the Oireachtas underlying intent. This subsection permitted the Minister to order that planning authorities comply with regional planning guidelines, but no order had been made in this case.[123] The Court proceeded to quash the Ministerial direction.

The *Tristor* case underlined the need to reflect further on the role of the **[6–67]** Minister in overseeing planning. The ambiguous, soft law nature of many of the planning guidelines prior to the introduction of the 2010 Act and the light touch nature of the obligation of "to have regard" was at the centre of the case. The Court in *Tristor* highlighted the fact that the Minister did possess deeper powers, but had not chosen to use them. The lack of a

---

[122] Above at n 117 para 6.14. Clarke J went on to comment in the same paragraph that:
> "I see no reason in principle why the Oireachtas might not give such powers to the Minister. It is fundamentally a matter of policy to determine the relative roles of the elected representatives at local level on the one hand, and the Minister on the other hand."

[123] Note also the *obiter* comments of Clarke J that person or company potentially affected by a s 31 direction had the right to make submissions to the Minister at para 8.3.

sustained and consolidated national vision of planning standards and enforcement shines through. The "half-in-half-out" nature of the national executive's use of the statutory framework reflects a broader regulatory confusion. This underlying dynamic of inconsistency perhaps motivated the core recommendation of the Mahon Tribunal that:

> "The Minister for the Environment's enforcement powers should be transferred to an Independent Planning Regulator who should also be charged with carrying out investigations into systemic problems in the planning system as well as being conferred with educational and research functions."[124]

[6–68] This recommendation has been accepted and the cabinet approved the establishment of the Regulator in May 2013 leaving the "appropriate modalities under consideration." [125] At time of publication, the Government is preparing the draft scheme for establishing such an independent regulator and the heads of the proposed Bill is due for publication.[126] There are, however, as we shall see later on, some signs that a full transfer of enforcement may not occur.

Local Authority Enforcement

[6–69] The local authority itself is under an obligation to comply with the development plan. The Planning and Development Acts 2000-2011, s 15(1) imposes a general duty on the local authorities to:

> "...take such steps within its powers as may be necessary for securing the objectives of the development plan."

[6–70] Section 178(1) further prohibits the planning authorities from effecting any development within its functional area which contravenes materially the development plan. The courts have also firmly responded to any political temptation to omit the location of controversial developments such as landfills or, in a disappointing reflection of Irish society, Traveller halting

---

[124] Mahon Report, above n 52, ch 18 Recommendations at p 2545.

[125] Department of the Environment, Community and Local Government, *Response to the Recommendations of the Final Report of the Mahon Tribunal*. Available at: http://www.environ. ie/en/Publications/DevelopmentandHousing/Planning/FileDownLoad,30749,en.pdf (date accessed 30 June 2014) at p 3.

[126] O Kelly, "Legislation to establish planning regulator to be introduced in months", *The Irish Times*, 18 February 2014.

sites, in development plans. In *Roughan v Clare County Council*,[127] the High Court stressed that if a local authority intended to use particular locations for set purposes, these should be indicated in development plans, lest the public's right to participate be endangered.

A further question relating to s 178 is what might represent a 'material **[6–71]** contravention'. Reluctant to leave open too much space for local authority interpretations, the courts have viewed this as a question of law for their determination.[128] In *Roughan* Barron J stated that local decision-makers should consider:

> "...in the light of the substance of the proposed development; whether or not any change of use would be significant; the location of the proposed development; the planning history of the site or area and the objectives of the development plan."[129]

More specifically, he added that:

> "What is material depends upon the grounds upon which the proposed development is being, or might reasonably be expected to be, opposed by local interests. If there are no real or substantial grounds in the context of planning law for opposing the development then it is unlikely to be a material contravention."[130]

It is worth noting that as a result of difficulties in getting controversial **[6–72]** developments through, specific regimes have now been designed under the Housing (Traveller Accommodation) Act 1998 and the Waste Management Act 1996. These are exempt actions[131] undertaken for the purpose of implementing a Traveller accommodation programme and the relevant area waste management plan from the material contravention prohibition.

Securing Compliance: The Enforcement Notice

Apart from regulating its own conduct, the planning authority must also **[6–73]** prevent material contravention and unauthorised development on the part

---

[127] *Roughan v Clare County Council,* unreported, High Court, 18 December 1998.
[128] *Wicklow Heritage Trust v Wicklow County Council* [1994] 4 IR 571.
[129] *ibid.*
[130] *ibid.*
[131] An exempt action is one that is exempt from the main planning system. In relation to this type of activity the normal planning system is replaced by a separate specialist planning arrangement, requiring prior consultation, under the specific legislation.

of other actors. There are two main weapons in the armoury of the local authority in doing so: the enforcement notice procedure and the s 160 planning injunction. Under s 153(7) of the Planning and Development Acts[132]:

> "Where a planning authority establishes, following an investigation under this section that unauthorised development (other than development that is of a trivial or minor nature) has been or is being carried out and the person who has carried out or is carrying out the development has not proceeded to remedy the position, then the authority shall issue an enforcement notice under section 154 or make an application pursuant to section 160, or shall both issue such a notice and make such an application, unless there are compelling reasons for not doing so."[133]

[6–74]   Under s 151 of the Planning and Development Act 2000, a person who carries out unauthorised development (i.e. carrying out development which is without or in contravention of planning permission) may also be guilty of a criminal offence with a maximum fine of approximately 12 million euros and two years' imprisonment.

[6–75]   The enforcement notice procedure commences with the issuing of a warning letter. This letter may be precipitated by either a complaint by any person that unauthorised development is occurring or has occurred[134] or by the authority itself where it believes an unauthorised development has been carried out or is ongoing.[135] The main function of the warning letter is that it requires the planning authority to consider whether to issue an enforcement notice. Where a complaint has been received, the authority is required to issue a warning letter no later than six weeks after receipt.

---

[132] Inserted by the Environment (Miscellaneous Provisions) Act 2011, s 27(b).

[133] s 153(8) states that:

> "Nothing in this section shall operate to prevent or shall be construed as preventing a planning authority, in relation to an unauthorised development which has been or is being carried out, from both issuing an enforcement notice under section 154 and making an application pursuant to section 160."

[134] Providing it appears that the representation is not vexatious, frivolous or without substance, s 152(1)(a).

[135] s 152(1)(b). Under s 157(4)(a) of the 2000 Act, an enforcement notice (or an enforcement proceeding) cannot be taken against a person where the relevant unauthorised development took place over seven years after planning permission should have been obtained or, where planning permission was obtained but not complied with, seven years have elapsed since the expiration of the relevant planning permission.

Section 152(4) sets out the following prescribed elements for a valid warning letter, which must:

- state that it has come to the attention of the authority that unauthorised development may have been or is being carried out;
- notify the owner/occupier that he or she may make a submission to the planning authority regarding the allegation no later than four weeks following the date of the warning letter;
- inform the owner/occupier that planning authority officials may enter on the land for inspection purposes;
- identify the possible penalties if an offence is found to have occurred;
- explain that the costs of the authority in relation to enforcement proceedings may be recovered in the event a s 160 injunction is sought or an enforcement notice issued.

Despite these requirements, it is important to note that in urgent cases **[6–76]** (urgency is assessed according to the nature of the unauthorised development and other relevant factors) the planning authority can immediately issue an enforcement notice without a prior warning letter or investigation. Barring this, in the ordinary course of affairs, following the letter, the planning authority proceeds to make a decision on whether to issue an enforcement notice. This is to be made as expeditiously as possible, and no later than twelve weeks following the issuing of the warning letter. Significantly, the decision to issue an enforcement notice falls within the discretion of the planning authority and is liable to challenge only by way of judicial review. In his 2007 work, *Planning and Development Law*, Simons expressed concern regarding the compatibility of the enforcement notice procedure with the European Convention on Human Rights[136] and we would encourage readers to consider the process in the light of our later chapter on that Convention.

It is important to note the existence of a declaration process under s 5(1) of **[6–77]** the Planning and Development Act 2000 whereby:

> "If any question arises as to what, in any particular case, is or is not development or is or is not exempted development within the meaning of this Act, any person may, on payment of the prescribed fee, request

---

[136] G Simons, *Planning and Development Law*, (2nd ed) (Thomson Round Hall, Dublin, 2007) at pp 299-300.

in writing from the relevant planning authority a declaration on that question...."[137]

[6–78]   This declaration does not operate to suspend the execution of an enforcement notice however, and a person who fails to comply with the notice may still be liable to enforcement proceedings. These enforcement proceedings may allow for a fuller ventilation of the relevant issues and the clarifying of crucial issues of fact, but it may in practice be unwise for an individual to risk exposure to criminal sanction and possible interim reputational damage in order to contest the planning authority's view of things. Where judicial review is employed to contest the substantive justification for issuing of the enforcement notice, it is only where the decision to issue an enforcement notice was so unreasonable that no local authority could have made it that an order of certiorari could be granted.[138]

[6–79]   In terms of its detailed contents, an enforcement notice can, where no planning permission has been granted, require work to stop, and where planning permission has been granted, order work to conform with that the permission. Specifically, under s 154(5)(b) the enforcement notice may:

> "...require such steps as may be specified in the notice to be taken within a specified period, including, where appropriate, the removal, demolition or alteration of any structure and the discontinuance of any use and, in so far as is practicable, the restoration of the land to its condition prior to the commencement of the development."

The notice must be complied with within a maximum of six months, but a notice may prescribe a shorter time period.

[6–80]   As the failure to comply with an enforcement notice is a criminal offence, the courts have been anxious to require that precise language be employed in their drafting. Two significant cases on this issue are *Dundalk Town Council v Lawlor*[139] and *Flynn Machine & Crane Hire Limited v Wicklow County Council*.[140] In the former case, O'Neill J quashed an enforcement notice where elements of it were not written with sufficient clarity and precision.

---

[137] A person must provide all the information necessary for the authority to make the relevant determination.

[138] A principle specifically laid down by Costello J in *O'Connor v Kerry County Council* [1988] ILRM 660.

[139] *Dundalk Town Council v Lawlor* [2005] IEHC 73, judgment delivered 18 March 2005.

[140] *Flynn Machine & Crane Hire Ltd v Wicklow County Council* [2009] IEHC 285.

In relation to the specified time limit for the remediating actions to be carried out, the notice merely stated that the prescribed time should be taken as "immediately commencing on the date of the service of this notice",[141] but did not indicate when the time allocated would elapse. Secondly, the remedial action prescribed by the order was uncertain and vague as the enforcement notice merely stated that the addressee should stop excavating and return the site to its previous condition. The *Flynn Machine & Crane Hire Ltd* case also examined the level of precision required. The enforcement notice in this case required the applicant to cease the use of its depot and associated offices and remove vehicles, machinery and temporary structures from the site. No commercial activities were to be carried out on the site. The notice specified a time period of six weeks for full compliance, but it prescribed separate time limits for certain individual actions. No time period had been set for compliance with the prohibition on all commercial activities. The applicant argued that the notice lacked precision as it was not possible to comply where a notice failed to identify the site or the portion of the site to which the notice applied. Furthermore, the steps prescribed were over-general, and the ban on all commercial activities, in particular, went further than was necessary to prevent alleged unauthorised development. In response to these claims, the respondent authority initially submitted that an enforcement notice could not be challenged where the planning authority had acted in a bona fide manner and had not taken irrelevant considerations into account.

O'Keefe J set out the general principles of review in applications such as the one before him: [6–81]

> "The decisions, the subject matter of this application are in general not amenable to judicial review unless the person attacking the decisions can demonstrate a clear departure by the decision maker from his statutory remit. Furthermore the onus lies on an applicant to establish that the respondent had no relevant material before it to support its decision, and in default of the applicant so establishing, this court can not reach a conclusion that the decision is irrational."[142]

On the facts, his Honour held that the notice identified the alleged   [6–82]
unauthorised development sufficiently, and any dispute over the description of the lands was not to be dealt with during judicial review

---

[141] Above n 139.
[142] Above n 140 at para 37, citing *O'Keeffe v An Bord Pleanála* [1993] 1 IR 38.

proceedings, but could be plead in enforcement proceedings in the event of non-compliance. As regards the time periods however, O'Keefe J held that the use of an overall time limit *and* other subsidiary time limits produced an intolerable lack of clarity along the lines identified by O'Neill J in *Lawlor*. O'Keefe J also found that the condition banning the future commercial use of the site was invalid as the terms of an enforcement order must address the alleged unauthorised development which has taken place, rather than seeking to restrain possible future uses of the property. In the event, the Court, in considering the appropriate remedial orders, elected to sever this future oriented requirement from the notice.

Securing Compliance: The Section 160 Planning Injunction

[6–83] The second central plank of planning enforcement is s 160(1) of the 2000 Act, which authorises the Circuit Court or the High Court to issue an injunction "where an unauthorised development has been, is being or is likely to be carried out or continued". An application may be made by "a planning authority or any other person, whether or not the person has an interest in the land". The powers available to the court are extensive and include the ability to "require any person to do or not to do, or to cease to do…anything that the Court considers necessary" to ensure:

> "(a) that the unauthorised development is not carried out or continued;
> (b) in so far as is practicable, that any land is restored to its condition prior to the commencement of any unauthorised development;
> (c) that any development is carried out in conformity with the permission pertaining to that development or any condition to which the permission is subject."

[6–84] The application of s 160 to the established homes of particular individuals was bound to attract some constitutional controversy given the guarantee of inviolability of dwelling provided for in Article 40.5.[143] This came to a head in the somewhat sprawling matter of *Wicklow County Council v Fortune* which across three separate editions, considered how s 160 was to operate in cases where the unauthorised developments constituted dwellings. In the original hearing,[144] the respondent had attempted to object to the

---

[143] "The dwelling of every citizen is inviolable and shall not be forcibly entered save in accordance with law."

[144] *Wicklow County Council v Fortune* [2012] IEHC 406, *Wicklow County Council v Fortune (No. 2)* [2013] 255, these judgments dealt with the chalet discussed above. *Wicklow County Council v Fortune (No. 3)* [2013] IEHC 397 concerned inter alia, the presence of additional caravans

granting of a s 160 injunction on grounds that the chalet in question constituted a dwelling and attracted the protection of Article 40.5. Hogan J held that Article 40.5 was applicable as it constituted:

> "...a free-standing, self-executing guarantee which applies to both civil and criminal proceedings and to both State and non-State actors alike."[145]

Despite its superficially absolutist connotations however, the word **[6–85]** "inviolable" did not preclude the use of s 160 against personal dwellings, and could not operate to allow individuals to "profit from their own deliberate and conscious wrongful actions by asserting an immunity from legal action and appropriate enforcement".[146] Nevertheless, the section had to be read in a manner which reflected the desire to ensure that any interference with a personal dwelling was objectively justified. Specifically, Hogan J held that in addition to establishing that a dwelling constituted unauthorised development:

> "It would be necessary to go further and show, for example, that the continued occupation and retention of the dwelling would be so manifestly at odds with important public policy objectives that demolition was the only fair, realistic and proportionate response... [Hogan J noted this justificatory burden could be discharged where]... the dwelling jeopardized or threatened the rights or amenities or others or visibly detracted from an area of high natural beauty or presented a real and immediate traffic or fire hazard or the structure in question so manifestly violated the appropriate development plan that the homeowner had no realistic prospect of ever securing permission in respect of the dwelling".[147]

Having established this principle, Hogan J then adjourned the matter to **[6–86]** allow the parties to adduce further evidence on whether the chalet should be demolished. In the resultant case of *Wicklow County Council v Fortune*

---

on the site. These had actually been removed by the time Hogan J delivered judgment, however. A final cessation of hostilities only arrived with *Wicklow County Council v Fortune (No. 4)* [2014] IEHC 267 where Hogan J granted a declaration that the house, which would not be demolished, did represent an unauthorised development. For those intrepid readers still reading this footnote, and in the interests of etymological accuracy, we note that one should refer to the Fortune matter as a tetralogy and not, as Hollywood studios are wont to do, as a quadrilogy.

[145] *ibid* at para 35. Art 40.5 is obviously most prominent in jurisprudence regarding the approval and execution of police warrants for searching dwellings or arresting individuals.

[146] *ibid* at para 40.

[147] *ibid* at para 42.

(No. 2),[148] the applicants advanced three justifications as to why, in the light of Hogan J's earlier finding, a s 160 order was nevertheless appropriate. Firstly, it was submitted that the failure to grant an injunction would undermine the effective protection of the environment. Secondly, that permitting the continued existence of the chalet would set a precedent and undermine planning controls in what was a scenic tourist area. Finally, they argued that a Natura 2000 site[149] located 240 metres from the chalet could be compromised by sewerage emanating from the respondent's property.

[6–87]   In order to determine these questions, Hogan J himself visited the chalet.[150] He ruled that it was well constructed and did not impinge in any way on the surrounding amenities or on neighbouring property owners. On the first point, he held that as the chalet had been held to represent an unauthorized dwelling, it would not be possible to sell it on or use it as collateral on a loan. On the second, he ruled that the existence of the chalet could not be relied upon by An Bord Pleanála when making a decision under s 37(2)(b)(iv) the Planning and Development Act.[151] On the third and final submission by the applicants, Hogan J ruled that despite the ongoing existence of the chalet no evidence of damage to the Natura 2000 site had been presented to the court. In order to alleviate any concerns, Hogan J elected to issue an order requiring Miss Forture to operate her effluent system in a manner compatible with existing Environmental Protection Agency guidelines.[152] Hogan J concluded by underlining the nature of the precedent set by this case:

---

[148] Above n 144.

[149] The Natura 2000 system is an EU network of nature protection areas created under the 1992 Habitats Directive: Council Directive 92/43/EEC of 21 May 1992 on the conservation of natural habitats and of wild fauna and flora.

[150] The memorable combination of high constitutional principle and everyday common sense in this case may put some readers in mind of the famous legally themed Australian film "The Castle" (1997).

[151] Above n 144. This provision allowed An Bord Pleanála to grant planning permission when the planning authority had refused permission on grounds of material contravention of the development plan in circumstances where:

"(iv) permission for the proposed development should be granted having regard to the pattern of development, and permissions granted, in the area since the making of the development plan".

Hogan J ruled that "permissions granted" extended only to lawfully authorized developments.

[152] *ibid* at para 32.

"None of this is to suggest that the arguments advanced by the Council are not important and weighty. In other cases, arguments of this kind might well prevail. But in the end I cannot ignore the solemn words of Article 40.5 which this Court is committed to uphold. The making of a s. 160 order on the particular facts of the present case would represent a drastic interference with the inviolability of the dwelling and with Ms. Fortune's property rights. If I may re-echo that which I already said in *Fortune (No.1)*, such an order could only be justified if compelling evidence requiring such a step had been advanced by the Council."[153]

The case of *Wicklow County Council v Jessup and Smith*[154] underlines the role which proportionality may play in s 160 applications. In *Jessup and Smith*, the planning authority applied for a s 160 injunction to compel the reconstruction of a building. While the development which had been undertaken by the respondents was clearly unauthorised, Edwards J refused to make a s 160 order as he was of the view that this would be a disproportionate response to the unauthorised actions. The case belongs to a number of post Celtic Tiger cases cited throughout this book as Edwards J stressed that: **[6–88]**

"The Court has been partly influenced in arriving at its view by the fact that the respondents are persons of relatively modest means. Further, although it has no direct evidence of it in the particular circumstances of this case, the Court takes judicial notice of the general downturn in the economy, the hardships that people in all walks of life are facing at this time, and of the fact that times are particularly hard for persons associated with the construction industry. It is presumed that the first named respondent as a project manager and architectural technician is affected in this way."[155]

The judgment therefore incorporates the financial means of the individual as a consideration in the approval and drafting of s 160 injunctions.[156]

Another recent case which provides an extensive analysis of when a s 160 injunction might be viewed as imposing disproportionate hardship on the addressee is *William Bailey v Kilvinane Wind Farm*.[157] The respondent in this   **[6–89]**

---

[153] *ibid.*

[154] *Wicklow County Council v Jessup and Smith* [2011] IEHC 81. The need to consider whether the granting of an injunction represents a proportionate response was first identified in *Morris v Garvey* [1983] IR 319.

[155] *ibid* at para 6.30.

[156] The Court granted a declaration ruling that the respondents had engaged in unauthorized development of the property in question.

[157] *William Bailey v Kilvinane Wind Farm* [2013] IEHC 509.

case was a wind turbine operator who having obtained a general planning permission for a project, obtained the planning authority's written approval for certain deviations from the precise specifications which had attached to the original planning permission. The deviations allowed, inter alia, the expansion of rotor blades on the turbines from thirty five metres to forty metres, reduced the number of turbines from four to three, and allowed for the positioning of the turbines to be altered "within a twenty metre tolerance of the grid positions identified in the planning application".[158] The wind farm was then constructed and operated from October 2006 to November 2010, at which point the operator applied for permission to replace two currently operating turbines and to construct a fourth. At this point, the deviations from the original permission came to the attention of local residents who submitted an application for a declaration under s 5 of the Planning and Development Act as to whether the development was authorized or unauthorized. The planning authority decided the deviations constituted exempted developments, however, upon appeal to An Bord Pleanála, the relevant inspector concluded that the deviations were materially outside the scope of the original permission and did not constitute exempted development. The residents lodged a s 160 application to close down the wind farm and return the land to its original condition. At the same time that this fell to be determined, the operator had ongoing judicial review actions against the s 5 determination of An Bord Pleanála. In addition, the operator was taking a review of a subsequent decision of the planning authority to refuse his expansion and replacement application, a decision based on the fact that the site had been found by An Bord Pleanála to be an unauthorized development.

[6–90]   Justice Peart refused to grant the injunction ruling that the use of the "draconian machinery"[159] represented by s 160 was not appropriate on the facts before the Court. As the operator had received the green light from the planning authority before taking any actions, he had acted in good faith throughout the process. The planning authority had not brought enforcement proceedings against him and had not supported the local residents' initiatives. An injunction would, in the circumstances of the case, impose disproportionate hardship on the operator. Peart J was fortified in this finding by his view that the applicant was not seriously and directly

---

[158] *ibid* at para 7.

[159] *ibid* at paras 44-45, quoting the phrase first used by Keane J as he then was in *Dublin Corporation v McGowan* [1993] 1 IR 405.

affected by the wind farm,[160] and his main objection was to the farm as a whole rather than the particular deviations. Furthermore, to grant an injunction would arguably represent the pre-determination of the competing judicial review actions, which should be permitted, in the Court's view, to run their course. The question of what action should be taken was best determined following the resolution of the judicial review of the s 5 declaration.

Individual Planning Permissions and An Bord Pleanála

The final aspect of planning enforcement or regulation is the individual   **[6–91]** planning permission, decided upon by the local authority, and through appeal, by An Bord Pleanála. A planning permission decision can be: (a) to simply grant it; (b) to grant it with conditions; or (c) to refuse it. Individual planning permissions are placed within the macro-planning framework we have already discussed by virtue of s 34(2)(a). This provides that in considering whether to grant permission the planning authority shall *only* have regard to the provisions of the development plan, any special amenity order relating to the area, any environmental or European designation applying to the site, the requirements of the Act itself and "where relevant, the policy of the government and the Minister".[161] While subsection 1 gives a general power to impose conditions, this is attenuated by a more extensive list of categories of condition provided in s 34(4) of the Act. A condition must be drafted in a clear fashion, and reasons must be provided for it.

In *Ashbourne Holdings plc v An Bord Pleanála*,[162] Hardiman J stressed that   **[6–92]** the power to impose conditions should be strictly construed and that the benefits of a condition should be "to the proposed development and not to any wider area".[163] The case concerned a condition whereby a golf club on the Old Head of Kinsale would have to permit public access through their course. At the time of the case s 34(4)(a) permitted the imposition of conditions on land controlled by an applicant adjacent to a planned development (in this case the clubhouse), where the planning authority viewed the condition as "expedient" for the purposes of or in connection

---

[160] This finding was due to there being forestry between the turbines and his home. The court did acknowledge that the turbines did impede the enjoyment of his farm and of the surrounding area. *ibid* at para 26.

[161] s 34 (2)(a).

[162] *Ashbourne Holdings plc v An Bord Pleanála* [2003] 2 IR 114.

[163] *ibid* at 129.

in the development authorised by the permission. The Supreme Court held that the word "expedient" meant that the benefits of the any condition should be "to the proposed development and not to any wider area". This reflected a broader, established principle that the power to impose conditions, which by their nature restrict property rights, should be construed narrowly. The condition requiring public access through the course could not be said to be advantageous to the construction of the clubhouse. In response to the judgment, s 8 of the Planning and Development (Strategic Infrastructure) Act 2006 amended s 34(4)(a) to allow for the imposition of conditions in such circumstances where the condition is:

> "...appropriate where any aspect or feature of that adjoining, abutting or adjacent land constitutes an amenity for the public or a section of the public for the purpose of conserving that amenity for the public or that section of the public."

A condition may not, however, "unduly burden" a developer.

[6–93] An appeal against a permission decision may be taken by the applicants or by any person who made written observations or submissions relating to the application. The matters under consideration at the appeal stage will mirror those at the initial stage. The main exception to this is where the planning authority rejected an application on the grounds that it would amount to a material contravention of its development plan. In such a circumstance, An Bord Pleanála may proceed to overturn only if the proposed development is of national or strategic importance, there are conflicting objectives in the development plan, the development should be authorised based on the contents of regional or national planning guidelines, the policy of the Minister or government or finally, where the pre-existing pattern of development and permissions granted in the area supports the grant.

[6–94] Given the deeply rooted nature of property rights within the Irish Constitution, it is little surprise that An Bord Pleanála procedures have often proven cumbersome. Nevertheless, s 126 PDA 2000 requires An Bord Pleanála "to ensure that appeals...are disposed of as expeditiously as may be", with the baseline statutory term being eighteen weeks. An Bord Pleanála has a discretion to hold an oral hearing of an appeal under s 134, but written submissions from parties directly involved and by persons other than these other than these parties often suffice. An Bord Pleanála is also able under s 50 of the 2000 Act to refer any point of law to the High Court, an innovation inserted by the Planning and Development (Strategic Infrastructure) Act 2006.[164]

Judicial review action represents, as we have already indirectly seen, the **[6–95]** last pillar of the enforcement and compliance framework. In terms of *locus standi*, Irish planning law has often been quite relaxed as we have seen in the context of s 160 injunction applications, and the right to make submissions before the Board. The procedure attaching to review applications is different from that under Order 84 (outlined later in this book). The time limit for a review of a decision under the 2000 Act is eight weeks from the date of the decision or the doing of an act by the planning authority or An Bord Pleanála. This may be extended where there is good and sufficient reason, and the circumstances which caused the time limit to be exceeded were outside the control of the applicant. Following a significant amendment in 2011,[165] leave to review will generally be granted in the following circumstances:

> "(a) there are substantial grounds for contending that the decision or act concerned is invalid or ought to be quashed, and
> (b) (i) the applicant has a sufficient interest in the matter which is the subject of the application."

Section 50A(4) states that "a sufficient interest for the purposes of subsection (3)(*b*)(i) is not limited to an interest in land or other financial interest".

The "sufficient interest" requirement may not easily be discharged by **[6–96]** publicly minded individuals or groups. Thankfully, however, amendments made to the Act in 2006, did move to make special dispensation for environmental NGOs where they are attempting to review a decision or act concerned "with a development which may have significant effects on the

---

[164] s 13.

[165] These amendments were a relief to many advocates for an inclusive approach to leave for planning reviews. Prior to this, the relevant requirement had been "substantial interest" In *Harding v Cork County Council* [2008] 4 IR 318 the Supreme Court endorsed a narrow construing of the term "substantial interest", taking it to require the establishment of the following by an applicant:
> (a) that he has an interest in the development of the subject of the proceedings which is 'peculiar and personal' to him
> (b) that the nature and level of his interest is significant and weighty
> (c) That his interest is affected by or connected with the proposed development.
The 2011 amendment has removed the impact of this ruling, and placed the position back towards the ordinary standard for leave, discussed in chapter 13.

environment".[166] In order to challenge the act or decision, the applicant will have to be a body or organisation with aims or objectives which relate to the promotion of environmental protection, to have pursued such aims or objectives for twelve months prior to the date of the application and satisfy such requirements (if any) that it would have to satisfy under s 37(4)(d)(iii) of the Act in order to be entitled to appeal to An Bord Pleanála pursuant to s 37(4)9c.[167] This latter precondition no doubt appears confusing to the reader, but refers to the ability of the Minister to lay down additional requirements which an environmental NGO must satisfy in order to make an appeal (or a review). These requirements may include matters relating to its membership, that the pursuit of its objectives be non-profit, that it possess a certain specified legal personality or internal constitution or ordering and that its application relate to an area of environmental protection to which the organisation's own aims or objectives relate.

[6–97] The provisions of the Act relating to environmental NGOs survived a significant potential qualification in *Sandymount and Merrion Residents Association v An Bord Pleanála and Others*.[168] In this case the Supreme Court addressed whether the applicant residents association possessed the necessary legal capacity to participate in judicial review proceedings under the Planning and Development Acts 2000-2011. It was not disputed that the associations satisfied the three statutory criteria specified above. The central issue was, even if the residents associations satisfied the three requirements under the statute, they did not possess the necessary *capacity* to take part in a judicial review action. This was because of the traditional general rule that "an unincorporated association cannot sue or be sued in its own name". The question was whether the statutory provisions manifested an intent to create an exception to this position. Clarke J held in favour of the applicants:

> "It is true, of course, that, in the ordinary way, for the reasons already identified, an unincorporated association or body does not have the legal capacity to bring or defend court proceedings.... However, it is also

---

[166] PDA 2000, s 50A(3)(b). The definition of such projects is elaborated on in the subsection wording: "where the decision or act concerned relates to a development identified in or under regulations made under section 176, for the time being in force, as being development which may have significant effects on the environment".

[167] *ibid.*

[168] *Sandymount and Merrion Residents Association v An Bord Pleanála & Others* [2013] IESC 51.

clear that there can be, whether by legislation or otherwise, exceptions to that general rule. The first question which arose was, therefore, as to whether s. 50A must be said to have created such an exception. It was argued on behalf of Dublin City Council and the State that any such exception must be clear and not arise simply by inference. I was satisfied that the true test is as to whether a statutory provision (in the absence of expressly conferring capacity) carried with it a necessary implication that capacity was being conferred. Against that test it seemed to me that the position was clear. It would be extraordinary if the legislature went to the considerable trouble of conferring standing to commence relevant environmental judicial review proceedings on environmental NGOs (subject to meeting the relevant statutory criteria) but at the same time intended that any such environmental NGOs not having legal personality would nonetheless be unable to bring such proceedings by virtue of a lack of capacity."[169]

Such a finding was supported by the fact that the Minister retained the ability to intervene by regulation to ensure any organisations of doubtful capacity could be excluded from taking reviews, but had not done so.[170] Furthermore an expansive approach to capacity was supported by key international legal instruments and agreements such as the EU Public Participation Directive and the Aarhus Convention.[171] The European Union   [6–98]

---

[169] *ibid* at para 5.2.

[170] Clarke J ruled at para 5.4:

"In addition it is clear that the Public Participation Directive allows national law, at a minimum, to regulate the rules by which associations or other bodies not having separate legal personality can be entitled to bring proceedings. It would, for example, be open to the Minister to make regulations requiring that any such bodies be registered prior to their having capacity. It is of interest that another jurisdiction having similar common law traditions to our own, that is Malta, now allows associations to participate in legal proceedings provided that they comply with the relevant Maltese legislation (see the Second Schedule to the Maltese Civil Code). Whether such a measure finds favour in this jurisdiction is, of course, a matter for the Oireachtas. However, at least so far as environmental litigation covered by European Union law is concerned, it is clear that the legislative regime both at the European and Irish level does not, necessarily, require that associations do not have to go through any formalities prior to having capacity. The Minister can regulate capacity both under the Irish legislation and the Public Participation Directive. However, the Minister has chosen, to date, not to make any appropriate regulations."

[171] This is the more common name for the United Nations Economic Commission for Europe Convention on Access to Information, Public Participation in Decision-making and Access to Justice in Environmental Matters ("the Aarhus Convention"). Ireland signed this upon its initial creation on the 25 June 1998, but only ratified on 20 June 2012. The European Union is also itself a signatory to the Convention. Article 2(4) of the Convention the "the public" as:

"The public" means one or more natural or legal persons, and, in accordance with national legislation or practice, their associations, organizations or groups"

legal order will, into the future, continue to have a powerful influence upon the intensity of judicial review, particularly as the European Union has itself ratified the Aarhus Convention. This Convention requires that review procedures allow individuals and groups to challenge certain acts or decisions on grounds of "substantive or procedural legality".[172] Thus, where planning decisions fall within the scope of European directives, the courts' scrutiny of them may be of greater intensity, and apply a standard more exacting than that manifest irrationality.

While Art 2(5) defines the public concerned as:

"the public affected or likely to be affected by, or having an interest in, the environmental decision-making; for the purposes of this definition, non-governmental organizations promoting environmental protection and meeting any requirements under national law shall be deemed to have an interest."

Art 9 is titled "Access to Justice" and provides:

"2. Each Party shall, within the framework of its national legislation, ensure that members of the public concerned

(a) Having a sufficient interest or, alternatively,

(b) Maintaining impairment of a right, where the administrative procedural law of a Party requires this as a precondition, have access to a review procedure before a court of law and/or another independent and impartial body established by law, to challenge the substantive and procedural legality of any decision, act or omission subject to the provisions of article 6 and, where so provided for under national law and without prejudice to paragraph 3 below, of other relevant provisions of this Convention.

What constitutes a sufficient interest and impairment of a right shall be determined in accordance with the requirements of national law and consistently with the objective of giving the public concerned wide access to justice within the scope of this Convention. To this end, the interest of any non-governmental organization meeting the requirements referred to in article 2, paragraph 5, shall be deemed sufficient for the purpose of subparagraph (a) above. Such organizations shall also be deemed to have rights capable of being impaired for the purpose of subparagraph (b) above. The provisions of this paragraph 2 shall not exclude the possibility of a preliminary review procedure before an administrative authority and shall not affect the requirement of exhaustion of administrative review procedures prior to recourse to judicial review procedures, where such a requirement exists under national law.

3. In addition and without prejudice to the review procedures referred to in paragraphs 1 and 2 above, each Party shall ensure that, where they meet the criteria, if any, laid down in its national law, members of the public have access to administrative or judicial procedures to challenge acts and omissions by private persons and public authorities which contravene provisions of its national law relating to the environment.

4. In addition and without prejudice to paragraph 1 above, the procedures referred to in paragraphs 1, 2 and 3 above shall provide adequate and effective remedies, including injunctive relief as appropriate, and be fair, equitable, timely and not prohibitively expensive. Decisions under this article shall be given or recorded in writing. Decisions of courts, and whenever possible of other bodies, shall be publicly accessible."

[172] Art 2(2).

The Failure of the Irish Planning System: Lessons for Governance

Having outlined this array of enforcement powers, we must pause to reflect   [6–99]
upon where the imbalances arose in a system featuring extensive
enforcement possibilities. The use of the planning system as a case study for
the broader failures of local government in Ireland is not without its potential
distortions. Nevertheless, in the public imagination, planning has become
the signature issue on which local government is assessed. The system
certainly reflected broader recurring debates regarding the executive/
political interface, the role of national political leadership, the potential
benefits of regional bodies and independent regulation. It also remains one
of the few real areas of power still remaining in the hands of local government.

The first key variable in evaluating the failings of the system was the lack of   [6–100]
normative clarity and leadership. This is clearly evidenced by the fact that there
are no official consolidations of the Planning and Development Acts 2000-
2011.[173] The prevailing methodology for amending the Acts has been described
by Scannell as "arcane" and "extremely difficult for practitioners to understand,
not to mind the ordinary members of the public".[174] Essentially amendments
involve the insertion of elliptical phrases into pre-existing statutes, requiring
the reader to continually cross-reference and piece together complex strands
of statutory expression.[175] Where amending legislation has been brought
forward it has suffered enormously from the flaws in parliamentary culture,
an issue we discuss in our chapters on parliamentary inquiries (chapter 2) and
the Office of the Ombudsman (chapter 4). The rushed process surrounding
the passing of the 2010 Act in particular was marked by a remarkable
insensitivity to the complexity of European legal norms.

Alongside the need for clarity and proper process, there were failures of   [6–101]
substantive leadership. As we have seen throughout this chapter, successive

---

[173] Both the Law Reform Commission and the Department of the Environment have issued
unofficial consolidations. See http://www.lawreform.ie/_fileupload/RevisedActs/
WithAnnotations/EN_ACT_2000_0030.PDF (date accessed 13 August 2014).

[174] Y Scannell, "The Catastrophic Failure of the Irish Planning System", (2011) 33 DULJ 396 at
p 396. Hereinafter "Scannell".

[175] This was judicially acknowledged by Fennelly J in *O'Connell v Environmental Protection
Agency* [2003] 1 IR 530 at 533.
   "it is necessary to steer through what counsel has aptly described as a statutory maze in
   order to uncover the effect of the regulations implementing the State's European Union
   obligations"

Ministers have been selective in their invocation of their legislative powers and have, even where flaws are identified, assumed a limited, reactive posture rather than a sustained defence of planning standards. This was seen for instance in the *Tristor Ltd* case,[176] where a s 31 direction was used to defend the relevant strategy documents, when an alternative course of action would have been the firmer, more systemic and principled use of s 29. This would have transformed the light touch obligation of having "due regard" to regional guidelines into an obligation of compliance. This is reflective of the manner in which "soft law" forms have given the appearance of regulation, but have rarely hardened into secure practical outcomes.[177] While readers may be tempted to blame political factors above all else, the broader administrative culture must also be subjected to critique, particularly when one considers the failure to appreciate Ireland's legislative frameworks non-compliance with EU legal norms. This resulted in successful infringement proceedings being brought by the European Commission to the Court of Justice of the European Union in relation to default planning permissions in 2008.[178]

[6–102]   The failure of the planning system also therefore reflects a crucial issue in the Irish administrative State: the need to ensure that legal knowledge is socialised within organisations which are dominated by non-lawyers. This extraordinary lacuna is highlighted by Scannell, who writing in 2011, delivered an outstanding peroration of prevailing bureaucratic culture:

> "There is only one lawyer in the Department and she is seconded from another Department. There are no senior Planning Law or EU law specialists in the Department itself. Administrators with no specialist expertise outnumber professionally qualified planners and environmental specialists...Outmoded practices ensure that bright administrators who develop an expertise in planning are rotated

---

[176] Above n 117.

[177] Scannell notes the department's attempts to ensure compliance with the ECJ's judgment *Commission v Ireland* (Case C-215/06) [2008] ECR I-491 through administrative circular as another example of such "defective governance". Above n 174 at p 403.

[178] *Commission v Ireland* Case C-210/06 [2008] ECR I-4911. As Scannell notes the division of labour between An Bord Pleanála and Environmental Protection Agency in considering major development projects was found to be an insufficient transposition of the relevant EU law directive in 2011. Case C-50/09 *Commission v Ireland*, 3 March 2011. She further instances the 2008 case of *Commission v Ireland* Case C-66/06 [2008] ECR I-158 finding the incompatibility of Irish law on exempted development with European environmental impact assessment directives. Relevant actors in the Department had been forewarned of the each of these instances of non-compliance but had waited for direct censure by the European Court. Above n 174 at 304-5.

to other divisions in the department or elsewhere. There does not appear to be any structured career planning for staff in environmental management or an expectation that they should acquire qualifications relevant to their work."[179]

These day to day dynamics were also exacerbated by a failure to ensure oversight of the planning system as a *system*. The widespread acceptance of the need for an independent regulator reflects the fact that Ireland has never conducted a full scale audit or review of its planning system.

In terms of local authorities' role, we have already canvassed the abuse of [6–103] the s 140 process, the failure to install anti-corruption protections and a tendency towards privileging certain sectors in line with broader Irish political clientelism and brokerage. The evaluation of local authority conduct should not be limited to the more extreme end of the continuum, but should focus on everyday incompetence such as the ignoring of expert advice and the tendency to collapse broader development principles in favour of political convenience.[180] The impacts of this upon the zoning of land are clear, as Kitchin *et al* argue:

> "a number of local authorities have essentially ignored good planning guidelines and regional and national objectives; sensible demographic profiling of potential demand; and the fact that much of the land zoned lacks essential services such as water and sewerage treatment plants, energy supply, public transport and roads. Instead permissions and zoning have been driven by the demands of local people, developers and speculators, the abandonment of basic planning principles by elected representatives; and ambitious, localised growth plans framed within a zero sum game of potentially being left behind with respect of development. Further, central government actively encouraged its excesses through tax incentive schemes and failed to adequately oversee, regulate and direct local planning"[181]

---

[179] *ibid* at 409. Clearly the transformation of these dynamics are uppermost in the Department's strategic planning.

[180] An An Taisce report in 2012 found that Donegal county had 2,250 hectares of residential zoned land in 2010, enough for an additional 180,000 people. In the years 2000-2010, approximately 50% of all residential planning permissions in the county had been granted on unzoned land. See An Taisce, *State of the Nation: Ireland's Planning System 2000-2011*, Available at: http://www.antaisce.org/sites/antaisce.org/files/an_taisce_2012_state_of_ the_nation.pdf (date accessed 30 June 2014).

[181] R Kitchin *et al, A Haunted Landscape: Housing and Ghost Estates in Post Celtic Tiger Ireland* (National Institute for Regional and Spatial Analysis, 2010), at p 2.

At the core of the above quote is in effect, "the prisoners' dilemma", whereby even a local authority who might have preferred to abide by proper planning principles would have their commitment to expertise crowded out by a realistic fear. This race to the bottom sets in where levels of trust in a national system decline and the regulatory tiller is unoccupied.

[6–104]   Turning to the putative bulwark for the system of individual applications, *An Bord Pleanála*, it is clear that even an independent regulator's role is heavily conditioned by surrounding political and legal contexts. Former Chairperson of the Board Mr Brian O'Connor has expressed some regret regarding his term of office:

> "While we did refuse permission for many developments we regarded as unacceptable, my greatest regret is that the Board did not take a stronger stand against residential developments that were based on bad zoning, remotely located and of poor design quality. I did realise at the time that some of the developments coming before the Board, particularly residential schemes, were questionable and indeed at publication of various annual reports I referred to concerns about the poor standard of some of the developments in tax incentive areas, the appropriateness of the suburban type schemes being attached to towns and villages around the country and to the sustainability of the zoning policies of many local authorities. However, the Board often found itself in a difficult position because in our planning system if the land is properly zoned in the development plan and serviced there is a presumption in principle that development will be permitted and to refuse could mean local authorities being faced with claims for compensation by landowners. While it is a fact that the Board did refuse many schemes that fell short of adequate planning or design standards, often in the teeth of local and media criticism, it did permit some which with hindsight it might have refused."[182]

[6–105]   As we move into the future, these criticisms must now transform into practical action. Much remains unclear about the possible future role to be played by the independent planning regulator, and many variables will affect Government's decision-making. On 7 May 2013, the government approved the creation of the Office of the Planning Regulator (OPR). Then Junior Minister Jan O'Sullivan TD provided a basic definition of its function:

---

[182] J O'Connor, *Closing Address to the Irish Planning Institute Annual Conference 2011* at p 8. Paper available at: http://www.pleanala.ie/news/chairpersonipi.doc (date accessed 30 June 2014).

"The OPR, which will be established with an independent corporate identity, will have three core functions. It will carry out independent appraisal of regional and local level statutory plans prepared and adopted under the Planning and Development Act 2000, as amended, including development plans, local area plans and regional planning guidelines. The Planning regulator will advise the Minister on the content of the plans, and, where appropriate, provide advice that all or part of a plan should be amended or rejected (through a ministerial direction). The advice of the OPR will be published. The OPR will also have investigate powers to examine, *inter alia*, possible systemic failings in the planning system...the OPR will also be mandated to carry out the research, training and education roles identified by the Mahon Tribunal."[183]

This would seem to indicate that the Government has chosen not to fully transfer the Minister's powers to the regulator. Instead, it seems the OPR will function in a supervisory or advisory capacity, in order that, as the Minister put it, "the final forward planning decisions remain political in nature".[184] This latter framing perhaps reflects a fundamental distrust of independent regulators within the Irish State. Even if a "full" transfer occurred, the Oireachtas (and by extension the Minister) would still control the fundamental norms to be applied by the regulator. Flexibility can be built into the relevant statute to ensure that the OPR is responsive, with an override power, for instance, being given to the Minister with appropriate legislative oversight. In parliamentary discussion however, the Government presented two options for the forthcoming legislation. Either a "full transfer" which it associated with relinquishing accountability and political ownership or, alternatively, adapting existing arrangements to provide for more oversight. The former "option" represented a reductive vision of the potential of the regulator — in fact such a regulator would do no more than make politicians abide by the development plans and legislative norms which politicians themselves created. We are concerned that this may reflect the already identified tendency of Irish politicians that the application of legislative standards should remain subject to political finessing.[185] The draft Scheme for the regulator was not released prior to this book going to

[6–106]

---

[183] Minister Jan O'Sullivan, "Written Answer to Question regarding planning issues", *Dail Debates* Thursday, 13 February 2014, [7215/14], Question 168.

[184] Quoted in the Irish Independent, *Mahon Tribunal's key recommendation still not implemented one year later*, 28 January 2013.

[185] We discuss this tendency in our chapter on the Office of the Ombudsman, Chapter 4.

press, but we encourage the reader, upon its issuance, to reflect upon whether it responds fully to the lessons learned from the property crash.

Conclusion

[6–107]   As this book was being written, the Irish media was dominated by one story: the cancellation of the five Garth Brooks concerts which were due to be held at Croke Park in 2014. The extraordinary pressure from members of the public, politicians and media for an act of political intercession to secure the go-ahead for concerts underline the subsisting scepticism of systemic regulation.[186] The importance of adopting a publicly minded approach to planning design, of agreeing visions for development based on objective criteria must be defended by planning legislation. The intrinsic value and disciplinary function of agreed rules and independent oversight must be validated in forthcoming regulatory interventions in both planning and broader local government contexts. The question for lawyers, regulators and administrators is how to ensure legislation and institutional design can help secure this change in the underlying political climate.

---

[186] A freedom of information request revealed that the Taoiseach had received over 1000 emails on the matter including requests that he intervene to "do everything in [his] power to make an exception for these concerts" And to change the law to "bring great happiness to many and the country as a whole". C O'Sullivan, "Kenny was sent 1,000 emails on Garth gigs", *Irish Examiner*, 13 August 2014.

CHAPTER SEVEN

Narrow *Ultra Vires*:
Unauthorised Decision-Making

Introduction

A key principle of constitutional governance — and many republican political theories — is the principle of legality. This, in synergy with the idea of the rule of law and constitutionalism more generally, demands that governmental agencies have legal authority for any action they undertake. This chapter focuses upon *ultra vires* in *the narrow sense*, namely where an administrator or decision maker operates "beyond the powers" granted by the substantive terms of the statute or delegated legislation. Chapters 8 and 9 of this book will address *ultra vires* in the *broad sense* — where the power granted by the statute is misapplied during the reasoning process — in such circumstances as bad faith, unreasonableness and the failure to exercise discretion. Such a distinction is largely one for the convenience of students, but also highlights the centrality of statutory interpretation as the starting point for administrative law analysis. The cases and scenarios here described, were not taken by lawyers enfeebled by overreliance on secondary legal sources, but rather those empowered with what must remain a core, primary legal skill: the construing of statutes. [7–01]

As a result, the doctrine of *ultra vires* should provoke reflection upon the parliamentary process in Ireland. The notion of parliamentary consent is tied to the predictability of future actions taken under the statute and the resulting consciousness of the pros and cons of its passage. For administrators, the wish is for predictability in statutory interpretation, as setting the range of permissible actions represents the first step to integrating administrative law standards. In the era of the legislative guillotine, strong executive capture of the legislative branch and a strong tendency towards legislation of an enabling rather than directive quality, the notion of a distinct and measured grant of legal authority by a supervising parliament must be reviewed for elements of fiction. [7–02]

In this chapter we will outline the first subset of instances where a decision maker may operate in "excess of power", these are: [7–03]

1) Delegation;
2) Error of Law;
3) Errors of Mixed Law and Fact.

All of these grounds, and indeed all the grounds of review discussed in the next chapter, are dependent upon construing the relevant legislation being used by the decision-maker. As a result we must begin with an account of both the principles of statutory interpretation and their implications underpinning administrative law practice.

The Need for Legislation: Executive Power as a Source of Legal Authority

[7–04]   The degree to which the executive enjoys an inherent ability to pursue certain actions is a preliminary issue in measuring the centrality of statutory authorisation to administrative law. Article 28.2 of Bunreacht na hÈireann acknowledges the existence of such abilities, stating, as it does that, "the executive power of the state shall, subject to the provisions of this constitution, be exercised by or on the authority of the Government". The residual nature of this power leads to it generally being described as the power to implement and administer laws and policy. Given the fused nature of the executive-legislative power in Ireland, the ability of the executive to equip itself of power through parliament has led to a paucity of case law defining the executive branch.[1]

[7–05]   It is clear that the diminished status of prerogatives in Irish law means that statutory authority has a greater role than in Britain or even other common law jurisdictions such as Australia or Canada. In the cases of *Byrne v Ireland*[2] and *Webb v Ireland*,[3] the Irish Supreme Court found that large aspects of the royal prerogative power did not survive the Irish Free State's creation. It is important to note, however, that while this led some to announce the non-survival of the royal prerogatives, such unqualified statements were questioned in *Geoghegan v Institute of Chartered Accountants*.[4]

---

[1] An early judicial recognition of the distinctive nature of executive power occurred in the case of *State (C) v Minister for Justice* [1967] IR 106.

[2] *Byrne v Ireland* [1972] IR 241.

[3] *Webb v Ireland* [1988] 1 IR 353.

[4] *Geoghegan v Institute of Chartered Accountants* [1995] 3 IR 86. O'Flaherty J resisted such a conclusion at 106 of the judgment:

"[a]s regards the decisions in *Byrne v. Ireland* and *Webb v. Ireland*, since each was concerned with a single question in respect of the royal prerogative (whether the State was immune from civil suit in the one case and the State's entitlement to treasure trove

The possible existence of freestanding prerogative power was explored   **[7–06]**
most fully in *Howard v Commissioner for Public Works*.[5] The majority, led
by Finlay CJ, rejected an argument that a general planning statute did not
apply to the State, finding that to embrace such would be contrary to the
republican quality of the constitution. Finlay CJ traced the notion of a
State exemption to the particular position of the crown in English
constitutional history.[6] The strong dissent of Justice O'Flaherty in the case
continues to subsist however, and it may, again, not be correct to simply
state that the 1922, and the later 1937 Constitution expunged all
prerogatives.[7] Cahillane argues the existing case-law permits an
interpretation that

> "the feudal prerogative powers, which were created because the
> 'personal pre-eminence' of the King would not have survived the
> creation of the Irish Free State but those that are based on public interest
> could have".[8]

Pragmatically, in terms of Government administration, prerogatives,   **[7–07]**
rather than an abstract historical concept, could also be "positively
useful".[9] Cahillane identifies a number of modern instances where such a
power could be helpful to a central Government in emergency scenarios
including:

---

in the other), it may be that if in a future case a wider question is raised concerning
the royal prerogative, the parameters of the judgments in these cases may need to be
delineated."

[5] *Howard v Commissioner for Public Works* [1994] 1 IR101.

[6] In ruling for the non-application of such an exemption, he cited the case of *The State of West
Bengal v Calcutta Corporation* 1967 AIR 997, Subba Rao CJ:

"There is therefore no justification for this court to accept the English canon of
construction for it brings about diverse results and conflicting decisions. On the other
hand, the normal construction that the general act applies to citizens as well as to
the State, unless it expressly or by necessary implication exempts the State from its
operations, steers clear of all the said anomaly. It prima facie applies to all states and
subjects alike, a construction consistent with the philosophy of equality enshrined in
our Constitution. This natural approach avoids the archaic rule and moves with the
modern trends. This will not cause any hardship to the state. The State can make an act if
it chooses, providing its exemption from its operation, though the State is not expressly
exempted from the operation of an act under certain circumstances, such an exemption
may necessarily be implied. Such an act, provided it does not infringe fundamental
rights, will give the necessary relief to the State."

[7] See L Cahillane, "The Prerogative and its Survival in Ireland: Dusty Antique or Positively
Useful?" (2010) 1(2) IJLS 1 at p 25.

[8] *ibid.*

[9] *ibid.*

> "...the power to keep the peace, the prerogative power which comes into play in the event of a grave national emergency, and includes the power to enter upon, take and destroy private property".[10]

[7–08] Generally in Ireland, any executive action that may affect constitutional or legal rights and interests will have to be buttressed by a legislative authorisation. A relatively rare judicial examination of an executive scheme, which was created entirely separately from a legislative rubric occurred in *Bode v Minister for Justice*.[11] The case concerned the Irish Born Child 05 Scheme,[12] which allowed a number of foreign national parents of children born in the State prior to 1 January 2005 to apply for leave to remain.[13] When called upon to examine a decision taken under the scheme, the Supreme Court refused to apply constitutional or European Convention on Human Rights principles to its application, characterising it as *ex gratia* and regarding it as a situation where the state was exercising its powers generously. The Court ruled that those who had been unsuccessful under the scheme were in the same legal position as they had been prior to their application. Thus they were regarded as remaining entitled to have the Minister consider all relevant constitutional and ECHR rights. The negative decision under the scheme could not affect any substantive claim that they could make for permission to remain in the State. The case showed that where an executive scheme does not dispose with legal rights or obligations, but rather directs decision-makers on how to undertake an existing discretionary decision making process, judicial review examination of procedural fairness or other grounds may be minimal. This is similar to the manner in which the executive's conduct of foreign policy has received significant deference from the judicial arm.[14] Some contrast can be drawn between the effusive constitutional republicanism expounded in relation to prerogatives and the freedom of action granted to the executive arm by

---

[10] *ibid* at p 26.

[11] *Bode v Minister for Justice* [2008] 3 IR 663.

[12] Irish Born Child Administrative Scheme for Immigrant Residency 2005 (IBC/05) created by the Department of Justice, Equality and Law Reform.

[13] The scheme continues to function through updated iterations which provide for conditional extensions in leave to remain for this group of people. See the current arrangement at: http://www.inis.gov.ie/en/INIS/Pages/WP07000030 (date accessed 19 March 2013).

[14] See the statement of Fitzgerald CJ in *Boland v An Taoiseach* [1974] IR 338 at 362:
"In my opinion, the courts have no power, either express or implied, to supervise or interfere with the exercise by the Government of its executive functions, unless the circumstances are such as to amount to a clear disregard by the Government of the powers and duties conferred upon it by the Constitution."

the *Bode* judgment, particularly in conceiving first principles in the relationship between Government and citizen. The reviewability of executive schemes has been the subject of great debate in other jurisdictions.[15] It is certainly possible to imagine justifiable concerns with the administration of funding schemes following natural disasters such as flooding if these were implemented without being put on a statutory footing. Regardless, the case underlined the presumption that powers not explicitly bestowed upon non-executive organs are taken to fall into the remit of the Government.

The case of *Prendergast v Higher Education Authority & Ors* provided a more extensive reflection on the ambit of executive power.[16] The plaintiff in this case was a student who had failed to gain a place in an Irish medical school. He challenged the Government cap set upon the number of European students, and the related failure to allow him to pay the enhanced fees required of foreign (non-EU) medical students. The decision to preserve a number of spaces for non-EU students, paying higher fees had been made by the Minister for Education, in conjunction with the Higher Education Authority in 1988. In the run-up to the case, expert recommendations —which proposed cutting the number of non-EU places and increasing the EU ones — were in the process of being implemented, also through Executive power.

[7–09]

In giving judgment, Charleton J ruled that the applicant was seeking the overturn of the entire admission system,[17] and summarised the case as asking the question: "Does the Executive, therefore, have the power to give money for higher education based on a settled policy?"[18] In response, his Honour stressed that the courts should not imply that constitutional drafters of 1922 and 1933 "somehow did not know what they were doing and mistakenly created a Government without any traditional powers in executive matters".[19] Hogan and Whyte had identified a number of instances since the foundation of the State where Government actions were, on balance, best characterized as taken under the mandate of

[7–10]

---

[15] For example the landmark report on such schemes by the Federal Ombudsman in Australia: available at: http://www.ombudsman.gov.au/files/investigation_2009_12.pdf (date accessed 1 September 2014).

[16] *Prendergast v Higher Education Authority & Ors* [2009] 1 ILRM 47.

[17] *ibid* at para 45. "the applicant asks that the entire system should be overturned"

[18] *ibid* at para 46.

[19] *ibid* at para 52.

prerogatives.[20] Charleton J further added to the track record of acting upon freestanding executive power, adding that the State had

> "set up a civil legal aid scheme based on specific administrative measures as to competence and qualification, prior to legislation; has decided on the disbursement of funds in aid of developing countries; and, in large measure prior to specific enabling legislation, has directed the civil service, the army and the police force of the State."[21]

His Honour cited in further support the statement of Hogan and Whyte that:

> "It is also the case that it is not always necessary for the Government to have to rely on statutory authority in order to exercise executive power. The Government frequently exercises the executive power of the State in relation to foreign affairs, and specifically the conclusion of international agreements, without having to have recourse to legislation and in the domestic arena, successive Governments have used extra-statutory schemes to provide benefits to citizens. Governments may also enter into contracts and acquire and dispose of property without statutory authority and on a number of occasions, companies have been established by the executive in the absence of statutory authorisation. *On the other hand, legislation is required before the executive may impose any obligation or burden on citizens.*"[22]

---

[20] As Hogan and Whyte state:
> "For instance, by what authority could the Government – in the absence of specific legislative authority – establish an extra-statutory scheme such as the Criminal Injuries Compensation Tribunal? What about the State's power to create corporations by letters patent? Did the prerogative power to grant such letters patent; the power to grant patents of precedent for counsel or, indeed, the right to grant passports, vanish with the enactment of the Constitution of 1922? One might argue, perhaps, that the Government could discharge such powers by virtue of the executive powers granted to it by Article 28. The fact remains, however, that were it not for the very existence of the prerogative in the first place – and its supposed survival after 1922 – no one would have ever sought to argue that the Government could have discharged such functions in the absence of appropriate enabling legislation"

Hogan and Whyte, *JM Kelly: The Irish Constitution* (4th ed) (Butterworths, Dublin, 2003) at para 8.2.10. Hereinafter "G Hogan & G Whyte".

[21] Above n 16 at para 54 of the judgment. He continued:
> "Now, in 2008, there may be acts providing for those bodies to obey lawful orders, but these are relatively recent. The army personnel were hardly entitled to refuse to serve in, or to logistically support, peacekeeping missions in Congo, for instance or in other places where the army has greatly advanced Ireland's stature as a country committed to the pacific settlement of disputes. To organise the civil service and the army and the Gardaí, the Government through its ministers needs to hire people and to dispense with their services."

[22] Hogan and Whyte above n 20 at para. 5.1.18.

Having quoted this passage, however, Charleton J took a more expansive view of executive power, expressing doubts as to the validity of Hogan and Whyte's position that statutory authorization was required to impose any obligation or burden on citizens".[23] His Honour adopted the view that the examples instanced earlier in his judgment had affected citizens' rights and obligations in far reaching ways. His Honour then stressed the *Sinnott* branch[24] of constitutional case law on the proper role of the courts in reviewing Government action, and strongly defended the right of the executive to create policy.[25] It is submitted that *Prendergast* underlines the unclear nature and foundations of executive power in Ireland.[26]

---

[23] Above n 16 at para 56 of the judgment he continued:

"Central to the exercise of government power is the establishment of policies for the proper governance of Ireland. Taxation of the people, which can only be carried out by legislation in specific terms, provides the funds that are necessary to implement policy. No doubt, in deciding upon a policy the Government will have regard to the directive principles of social policy as set out under Article 45 of the Constitution, which are not ... cognisable by any Court under any of the provisions of the Constitution. The fundamental function of Government is to keep order, to decide the direction in which the country is to go and to disburse the funds collected through taxation from the people in aid of their objective. In a democracy, the people are entitled, in the event of disagreement with the Government on issues, large and small, to vote accordingly."

[24] *Sinnott v Minister for Education* [2001] 2 IR 545 in which the court found that they should not adopt a policy making role in relation to socio-economic rights and issues.

[25] Above n 16 at para 57 he stated:

"There is no doubt that the Government is not entitled to rely on aspects of the prerogative inherited from our rule by another power, that relate to the dignity of the monarch and which are inconsistent with the Christian and democratic nature of the State under the Constitution. That does not mean that the Government has no residue of inherited powers that are not provided for by statute. Actions of Government which have, for instance, the result of imposing a tax; or of increasing police powers, or similar powers by departmental officials, whereby people may be arrested or dwellings searched or compelled to undergo interrogation; or which go outside the specific terms of the statutory scheme passed by the Oireachtas to regulate a particular area of administration are, in the history and tradition of the Irish people, outside the realm of any constitutional construction of powers that are capable of being exercised by the Government. The full extent and the limit of those powers are not to be decided by me in this case. I am satisfied, however, on the authorities cited, that the government is entitled: to set a policy for the training of a specific number of medical graduates to meet the needs of the State; to decide what funds are appropriate to be disbursed in that regard; to decide that particular forms of education should be free, or should be contributed to by fees; and to decide that foreign students can take up spare places at an economic cost to the benefit of the economy."

[26] A final point to note is that the Equal Status Acts supplement the Constitution, by injecting a new layer of oversight over non-statutory schemes, as was best seen in the case of the non-statutory scheme for mobility grants for those with a disability in our chapter on the Ombudsman. This of course did not avail the applicants in *Bode*, to whom in the circumstances, as non-nationals, the Equal Status Act was disapplied. In *Prendergast* a similar exemption s 3(d)(i) applied in relation to fees charged to non-nationals, and his claim based on constitutional inequality failed.

Construing the Power: Relevant Principles of Statutory Construction

[7–11]   The centrality of statutory interpretation to the practice of administrative law is hard to overstate, indeed as de Smith and Brazier have claimed: "to a large extent judicial review of administrative action is a specialised branch of statutory interpretation".[27] The creation of a legislative guide to Irish statutory interpretation - the Interpretation Act 2005 — consolidated many aspects, and sought to bring about some curtailing certainties to issues which had long preoccupied the Irish judiciary — particularly the use of extrinsic materials and the status of purposive interpretation. In this section we will consider the key principles in this area.

The Primacy of the Literal Method of Interpretation

[7–12]   This method involves giving the words of the statute their literal, plain, or ordinary meaning. This can be distinguished from the purposive method whereby the courts interpret the provision in the light of the purpose for which it was enacted. It is important, however, to avoid attempts to force the dichotomy of literal and purposive, as it is ultimately the holistic perspective set out by Bennion which continues to best capture the practice of the courts:

> "The so called literal rule of interpretation nowadays dissolves into a rule that the text is the primary indication of legislative intention, but that the enactment is to be given a literal meaning only where this is not outweighed by more powerful interpretative factors."[28]

This also reflects the positivist concept of the "open texture" of language.[29]

[7–13]   The Interpretation Act 2005 allows for the use of internal aids, defined as "any material which is published with an Act, but is not a substantive provision of the Act".[30] External aids continue to be used in judicial

---

[27] SA de Smith and R Brazier, *Constitutional and Administrative Law* (8th ed) (Penguin, London, 1998) at p 516.

[28] He refers to this as the "global method" of interpretation. FAR Bennion, *Understanding Common Law Legislation* (Oxford University Press, Oxford, 2001) at p 41 and on the "Global method" of common law interpretation, see p 84.

[29] HLA Hart, *The Concept of Law* (2nd ed) (Oxford University Press, Oxford, 1994), p 128. See also pp 127-136.

[30] The 2005 Act includes long and short titles, the preamble, but does not mention material added by the draftsman such as the cross-headings or marginal notes – despite the recommendation of a Law Reform Commission report that this be permitted.

practice, but it is important to note the continued application of the exclusionary rule, which restricts recourse to construing the "subjective" intention of parliament through reference to debates.[31] Irish interpretive practice has regularly fused both elements.[32] According to s 5 of the 2005 Act, where the plain intention of the Oireachtas is not reflected by the literal interpretation or it produces "ambiguous or obscure" interpretation, the purposive method of interpretation is now to be employed. The status of extrinsic aids was not addressed by the Act which neither permits nor prohibits reliance upon them.

Incidental or Complementary Powers

A key part of administrative decisions is that the public body has the ability to undertake those acts necessary to carry them out. As laid down by the 1880 case of *Attorney General v Great Eastern Railway* powers conferred by statute can include, by implication, a right to take any steps reasonably necessary to achieve the statutory purpose.[33] The most recent restatement of the law relating to implied powers by the Supreme Court occurred in the conjoined cases of *Magee v Inspector Murray & Superintendent Roche* and *McVeigh v Minister for Justice, Equality & Law Reform.*[34] Magee alleged that the relevant Garda Superintendent did not have the power under the Firearms Act 1925 to attach conditions to a certificate beyond those instances expressly specified by the Acts. In finding against Magee

[7–14]

---

[31] *Crilly v Farrington* [2001] 3 IR 251 at 283, Denham J argued: "[t]o hold that parliamentary debates are admissible would be an alteration in the law and an alteration which would have a profound effect". Significantly Murray J argued for a distinction between legislative history and parliamentary history, at 292.

[32] The literal approach is often embodied through the citation of *Rahill v Brady* [1971] IR 69. This case concerned the question of whether a cattle mart, held twice weekly throughout the year, was entitled to a "special event" licence under the Intoxicating Liquor Act 1962. Budd J in the Supreme Court stated, at 86, that "the ordinary meaning of words should not be departed from unless adequate grounds can be found in the context in which the words are used to indicate that a literal interpretation would not give the real intention of the legislature". In *Nestor v Murphy* [1979] IR 326, the Supreme Court held that a literal reading of the Family Home Protection Act 1976 to prevent the sale of a family home where the wife had not given her consent in advance but (because she was a joint tenant of the property) she was joining in the conveyance was "outside the spirit and purpose of the Act".

[33] *Attorney General v Great Eastern Railway Company* (1880) 5 App.Cas. 473. Lord Selbourne LC provided the statement of principle that "whatever may fairly be regarded as incidental to, or consequential upon, those things which the Legislature has authorised, ought not (unless expressly prohibited) to be held, by judicial construction, to be ultra vires." at 478.

[34] *Magee v Inspector Murray & Superintendent Roche* and *McVeigh v Minister for Justice, Equality & Law Reform* [2011] 1 ILRM 237.

in the High Court, Birmingham J found that the "statutory context here is one of control and restriction", and

> "there are elements within the Act which seem consistent only with belief on the part of the legislators that they were providing for certification which could be subject to conditions".[35]

The Supreme Court endorsed such an approach noting that the test laid down in *Attorney General v Great Eastern Railway Company*, "has stood the test of time", and had received unanimous support before the Supreme Court in *Keane v An Bord Pleanala*.[36]

Statutory Presumptions: Strict Construction of Particular Statutes

[7–15]   In unpacking the central principles of statutory interpretation it is also important to have regard to traditional presumptions which apply to statutory language. These operate in certain spheres where a piece of legislation seeks to achieve certain ends. Where such presumptions apply, any ambiguity in the wording will be applied strictly against the drafter.

Presumption Against Interference with Common Law Rights

[7–16]   The most recent authority discussing this principle is *BUPA Ireland v Health Insurance Authority (No 2)*.[37] Where parliament elects to interfere with legal rights of persons or corporations, "one must expect that the intended ambit or application of such provisions will be expressed in the legislation with reasonable clarity".[38] This "reasonable clarity" requirement has been used by the Office of the Ombudsman in its analysis of the Nursing Homes Support Scheme Act 2009. Sections 52

---

[35] *Magee v Murray & Anor* [2008] IEHC 371 at para 33. Birmingham J placed reliance particularly upon the fact that "…section 2(2) of the Act of 1925 makes it an offence to fail 'to comply with any conditions subject to which a firearms certificate was granted' [emphasis added]. Moreover, s 5(d) provides for the revocation of a certificate in a situation where the firearms certificate limits the purpose for which the firearm to which it relates is used but is in fact used for non authorised purposes. The combined effect of these sections is to indicate that at least some conditions can be imposed and some limitations placed on the extent of the authorisation".

[36] *Keane v An Bord Pleanala* [1997] IR 184. This case featured the following statement by Hamilton CJ encapsulating the relevant principle:
"The powers of the Commissioners, being a body created by statute, are limited by the statute which created it and extend no further than is expressly stated therein or is necessarily and properly required for carrying into effect the purposes of incorporation or may fairly be regarded as incidental to or consequential upon those things which the legislator has authorised."

[37] *Bupa Ireland v Health Insurance Authority (No 2)* [2009] 1 ILRM 81.

[38] *ibid* at 99-100.

and 53 of that Act, created, through amendment, a new category of service, separate from in-patient services, which would be charged for:

> "...one would expect this to be provided for in a stand-alone section or sections. Furthermore, if it was the intention of the Legislature to curtail an existing statutory entitlement, and particularly one of such importance to a vulnerable though sizeable group within society, then one would expect this to be set out explicitly."[39]

Interference with Property Rights

In general, an Act must be "construed on the basis that it was not the intention of the legislature to deprive the plaintiffs of their property or interfere with it save and in so far as that was necessary for the common good and was in accordance with the Constitution".[40] [7–17]

Presumption Against Taxing or Revenue Raising Powers

Express, clear words are required to ground governmental taxation powers. The implications of this were seen in the recent case of *Glenkirren Homes v The Revenue Commissioners*, which concerned the meaning of s 40(2) of the Stamp Duties Consolidation Act 1999, in particular, the meaning of the phrase 'amount due'.[41] In finding that the phrase included all sums in respect of which there was a legal liability, including monies payable in the future, Laffoy J reiterated the words of Rowlatt J in *Cape Brandy Syndicate v Commissioners of Inland Revenue*: [7–18]

> "It is urged that in a taxing Act, clear words are necessary in order to tax the subject. Too wide and fanciful a construction is often sought to be given to that maxim, which does not mean that words are to be unduly restricted against the Crown, or that there is to be any discrimination against the Crown in those Acts. It simply means that in a taxing Act one has to look merely at what is clearly said. There is no room for any intendment. There is no equity about a tax. There is no presumption as to a tax. Nothing is to be read in, nothing is to be implied. One can only look fairly at the language used."[42]

---

[39] Office of the Ombudsman, *Who Cares? An Investigation into the Right to Nursing Home Care in Ireland*, Report published on 9 November 2010 (Office of the Ombudsman, Dublin, 2010) at p 99.

[40] *Dunraven Estates Ltd v Commissioners of Public Works* [1974] IR 113 at 134.

[41] *Glenkirren Homes v The Revenue Commissioners* [2007] ITR 119.

[42] *Cape Brandy Syndicate v Commissioners of Inland Revenue* [1921] 1 KB 64 (at 71). The Irish approach was also summarized by Geoghegan J in *Harris v Quigley* [2006] 1 IR 165 at 183:

[7–19]   Another recent case, *Keogh v Criminal Assets Bureau* underlined the non-application of purposive methods of interpretation to such statutes.[43] However, the provisions of the Taxes Consolidation Act 1997 which lay to be examined in *Keogh*, did not impose any tax but set out the machinery by which the taxpayer is to be assessed and the appropriate tax recovered, leading to the application of normal principles of statutory construction.

The Strict Construction of Penal Statutes

[7–20]   This presumption provides that, per Kearns J in *DPP v Moorehouse*, "in construing a penal statute, the court should lean against the creation or extension of penal liability by implication".[44] In *DPP v Tivola Cinema Ltd*,[45] which concerned s 20 of the Intoxicating Liquor Act 1927, Barron J noted the obligations of parliament to provide "clear and unambiguous language" in drafting such provisions. Section 20 prohibited the sale of alcohol to persons who had not pre-booked a "seat" for the night's event and had arrived at the premises after 9.30pm. The question before the court was whether the location, which did not have seating, had breached s 20. As s 1(1) defined "theatre" in a manner broad enough to cover such venues, an offence was found to have occurred. [46]

"While as far as possible, a taxing statute should be interpreted in the same way as any other statute and should not be interpreted, if at all possible, as to create an absurdity, nevertheless there is a countervailing principle that where there is an ambiguity a taxing statute will be interpreted in favour of the taxpayer."

[43] *Keogh v Criminal Assets Bureau* [2004] 2 IR 159, Keane CJ stated at 170 that "its sole task is to determine whether, having regard to the language used, the tax has been expressly imposed: the court cannot have regard, as might be possible in other contexts, to what might be assumed to be the intention or governing purpose of the Act, other than an intention to levy such tax as the statute imposes."

[44] *DPP v Moorehouse* [2006] 1 IR 421.

[45] *DPP v Tivoli Cinema Ltd* [1999] 2 IR 260.

[46] In the case of *Dunnes Stores v Director of Consumer Affairs* [2006] 1 IR 355, the definition of grocery goods offered under the 1987 Grocery Order was strictly construed in relation to a penal statute provision:

"...the court must construe the phrase 'household necessaries...ordinarily sold in grocery shops' strictly and in seeking to determine whether or not that phrase...includes disposable nappies would have to be satisfied that it has a meaning which demonstrates by clear and unambiguous language that it includes disposable nappies." (at 361)

Justice Finlay Geoghegan relied heavily upon the Enquiry Reports issued by the Restrictive Practices Commission under s 5 of the Restrictive Practices Act 1972, an approach justified by s 8(1) of the 1972 Act which allowed the Minister to make orders only in respect of goods which have been considered in such reports. Accordingly, her honour was not satisfied that disposable nappies qualified as goods which were necessary for the running of a household, and commonly used for such by all members of the household. They were instead only used for very young children for their personal care and fell outside the statute's purview.

A case that underlined the centrality of literal interpretation, irrespective   **[7–21]**
of counter-veiling public policy factors, was *Kadri v Governor of Wheatfield*
Prison.[47] The individual in question had violently resisted deportation,
yet the Supreme Court quashed his purported continued detention as
ultra vires the statutory detention power.[48] In his concurring judgment,
Clarke J reflected more broadly on the jurisdiction of the courts, under s 5
of the Interpretation Act 2005, to correct mistaken construction:

> "It not only is necessary that it be obvious that there was a mistake
> in the sense that a literal reading of the legislation would give rise
> to an absurdity or would be contrary to the obvious intention of the
> legislation in question, but also that the true legislative intention can be
> ascertained. There may well be cases where it may be obvious enough
> that the legislature has made a mistake but it may not be at all so easy
> to ascertain what the legislature might have done in the event that the
> mistake had not occurred."[49]

A perhaps overly rigid application of the literal approach to statutory   **[7–22]**
interpretation in relation to penal statutes occurred in *Minister of Justice,*
Equality and Law Reform v Dolny.[50] O'Sullivan has heavily criticised the
approach taken, which arguably converted the offence of assault under the
Offences against the Person Act 1997 from a strict liability to an absolute
liability offence.[51] The better approach was to view s 2 and s 3 of the Act as
interconnected, an argument supported by extrinsic materials such as the
Explanatory Memorandum, prior statutory instances of the crime, the
overall context of the Act. Furthermore, the counter-veiling presumption of
constitutionality should have been taken into account.

Strict construction must be triggered by the existence of ambiguity, and in   **[7–23]**
making this initial finding the courts will eschew an overly flexible
approach, as indicated by O'Flaherty J in *DPP v Cormack*:

> "Unfortunately, there is I think a certain mythology abroad that some
> onus rests on the prosecution to prove cases to an impossible extent so

---

[47] *Kadri v Governor of Wheatfield Prison* [2012] IESC 27, judgment of 10 May 2012.
[48] Per Fennelly J:
> "The Court cannot adopt a flexible or purposive interpretation of a provision designed to
> protect personal liberty, all the more so when such an interpretation would do violence
> to the clear language of the Oireachtas", *ibid* at para 31.
[49] *ibid*, judgment of Clarke J, at para 3.7.
[50] *Minister of Justice, Equality and Law Reform v Dolny* [2009] IESC 48.
[51] C O'Sullivan, "The Importance of Correct Statutory Interpretation Technique: The case of
Minister for Justice, Equality and Law Reform v Dolny", (2010) 45(1) *Irish Jurist* 146.

as to exclude every hypothesis that might occur to the most ingenious mind. That is not the law."[52]

[7–24] This was further underlined in the recent case of *Delaney v Judge Coughlan*,[53] where the Supreme Court signaled resistance to any *compulsion* to adopt a rigidly literal approach in such situations. This case concerned the ability of a District Court, as a result of a 2005 legislative amendment, to extend the period of seizure of monies suspected to be the proceeds of crime by Gardai. McMenamin J writing on behalf of the Court stated:

> "Seen in the round, to construe the provisions in question as suggested by the appellant would defeat the objective of the legislation itself; it would negate the intention of the Oireachtas; it would run counter to the forfeiture provisions actually contained elsewhere in the Act which reflect the legislative intention; it would give rise to absurdity; it would suggest the legislature acts in vain, it lacks logic. This is not a situation where the statute "catches" conduct not intended by the legislature. Of course, in interpreting a statute a court must take the greatest care to lean against the possibility of doubtful penalisation, but this is not such a case. If there is an issue here, it is simply one of unhappy drafting; the error is very minor and the legislative purpose is clear."[54]

[7–25] This underlines that in determining the existence of ambiguity the Court will continue to approach the process holistically, as encapsulated by Bennion's statement we provided at the start of this section. While presumptions and legislative restatements provide the structure through principles of emphasis, one should bear in mind the continued suppleness at the level of application.

Improper Delegation of Decision-Making Powers

[7–26] This principle holds that when a statutory power is vested in a certain individual — the delegate of the legislature — it is that person who must exercise the power. There may be no further delegation of it to other people or bodies unless there is authorisation. It is important to note the prima facie nature of this principle; it is complicated by the nature of the power and the context in which it is used. This was acknowledged in

---

[52] *DPP v Cormack* [1999] 1 ILRM 398 at 400.
[53] *Thomas Delaney v Judge John Coughlan & Others* [2012] IESC 40.
[54] *ibid* at para 46.

the case of *O'Neill v Beaumont Hospital Board*,[55] where the Board of the hospital had unlawfully delegated to their Chief Executive a decision on whether the plaintiff a consultant surgeon had properly completed a period of probation:

> "...power has to be considered in the context in which it was conferred and the nature of the functions which the hospital board was seeking to fulfil."[56]

It is also important to remember that court will not enquire into the improper nature of a delegation where it is authorized by statute, even if the statute's provision is a wide, unfocused authorizing provision.[57]

Improper delegation can also occur when an individual or body relies [7–27] entirely upon the assessment of someone lower down in the operational hierarchy or simply upon someone who has been granted no statutory role in the matter. This is best described by the facts in *Dunne v Donohue*.[58] The Firearms Act 1925 provided that a Garda superintendent was required to assess the public safety implications of the issuing of gun ownership certificates. The Garda Commissioner introduced a directive requiring that certificates for certain guns had to be tied to the ownership of a "properly constructed and locked firearms cabinet". The Supreme Court ruled that in making a decision, the Garda superintendent, as the vested power-holder, could not be tied to any directive of the Commissioner. This area of law heavily interacts with the application of an inflexible policy in cases of discretion, which is outlined in chapter 8 of this book.

Heavy reliance on expert advice can cross the line here, as described by [7–28] the decision in *Genmark Pharma v Minister for Health*.[59] Carroll J stressed that "while the Minister was entitled to seek advice, he was not entitled to rely on advice in the form of conclusions without reference to the basic material on which those conclusion were based".[60] In *Genmark Pharma*, the evidential burden of proving inappropriate delegation was discharged by the failure to forward exhaustively all relevant

---

[55] *O'Neill v Beaumont Hospital Board* [1990] ILRM 419.
[56] *ibid* at 423.
[57] *Brennan v Donnellan & Ors* [2003] IEHC 58.
[58] *Dunne v Donohoe* [2002] IESC 35.
[59] *Genmark Pharma v Minister for Health* [1998] 3 IR 111.
[60] *ibid* at 127-128.

documentation for the forming of an opinion.[61] In a non-governmental context, such impermissible delegation also occurred in *Flanagan v University College Dublin*, where a committee of discipline relied entirely upon the recommendation of an outside, independent expert regarding the extent of plagiarism.[62]

[7–29]   The principle against delegation, otherwise known as the *delegatus* principle, has clearly had to be adapted to meet the realities of modern day Government — it is seldom practical for the nominated principal (person authorised to exercise the power) to make all the decisions personally. The English wartime case of *Carltona v Commissioner of Works*[63] laid down the principle that a statutory power conferred on a Government minister can ordinarily be exercised on the minister's behalf by another officer, even absent formal delegation:

> "In the administration of government in this country the functions which are given to ministers...are functions so multifarious that no minister could ever personally attend to them. To take the example of the present case, no doubt there have been thousands of requisitions in this country. It cannot be supposed that this regulation meant that, in each case, the minister in question should direct his mind to the matter. The duties imposed upon ministers and the powers given to ministers, are normally exercised under the authority of ministers by responsible officials of the department. Public business could not be carried on if that were not the case."[64]

As Hamilton CJ acknowledged in *Devanney v District Judge Shields & Ors*, this can be viewed as "a common law constitutional power".[65] Thus it is important to note, as Wade points out, "strictly speaking, there is not even delegation in these cases".[66]

[7–30]   In terms of exceptions to the *Carltona* doctrine, the judiciary have preserved a possible right of intervention, where, as Denham J expressed

---

[61] At the practical level, Carroll J stressed "that the Minister should have been sent whatever documentation was relevant to enable him to evaluate the advice and the submissions." *ibid* at 128.

[62] *Flanagan v University College Dublin* [1988] IR 724.

[63] *Carltona v Commissioner of Works* [1943] 2 All ER 560.

[64] *ibid*, Greene MR at 563.

[65] *Devanney v District Judge Shields & Ors* [1998] 1 ILRM 81.

[66] HWR Wade and C Forsyth, *Administrative Law* (10th ed) (Oxford University Press, Oxford, 2009) at p 267.

it *Devanney v District Judge Shields,* "exceptions in matters of significant importance where the Minister is expected to make the decision personally".[67] *Devanney* concerned the decision to appoint a District court clerk, which was legislatively vested in the Minister for Justice. The Court nevertheless found that the role of the Minister was a solely formal one, to give effect to a recommendation by officials.[68]

In recent years, the *Carltona* principle has been heavily relied upon in immigration and refugee law cases. The reliance placed on it within the immigration system has largely been uncontroversial in the eyes of the courts — with one exception — which is the possible need for the Minister to personally address the applicability of the non-refoulement[69] prohibition in s 5 of the Refugee Act 1996 to deportations conducted under s 3 of the Immigration Act 1999. Arguments for leave to review the non-involvement of the Minister were further energised by the case of *Meadows,*[70] discussed extensively in chapter 9. There, Murray CJ in discussing the concept of deference, appeared to implicitly rely upon the personal engagement of the Minister with the issues at hand: [7–31]

> "...If such material has been presented to him by or on behalf of the proposed deportee...the Minister must specifically address that issue and form an opinion. Views or conclusions on such issues have already been arrived at by officers who considered a proposed deportee's application for asylum, at the initial or appeal stages, and their conclusions or views may be before the Minister but it remains at this stage for the Minister and the Minister alone in the light of all the material before him to form an opinion in accordance with s.5 as to the nature or extent of the risk, if any, to which a proposed deportee might be exposed...The fact that certain decisions have been made by officers at an earlier stage in the course of the application for refugee status does not absolve him from making that decision himself."[71]

Cases then emerged regarding the compatibility of this statement with the reality that under the *Carltona* principle, a high level civil servant, and not the Minister, has made the majority of s 5 decisions. In *LAT v Minister* [7–32]

---

[67] Hogan J in *L v Minister for Justice and Equality,* para 8.
[68] *Devanney v District Judge Shields* [1998] 1 IR 230 at 263.
[69] Non-refoulement is the principle that an asylum applicant must not be returned to a country where there is a serious risk of torture.
[70.] *Meadows v Minister for Justice* [2010] 2 IR 701.
[71] *ibid* at 729.

for Justice,[72] Hogan J acknowledged that the decision to deport was one involving the weighing facts, policy and law. Furthermore, the Minister for Justice had, in debating the introduction of the relevant Act, given a reassurance to the Dáil that "the ultimate step, that of deportation, is undertaken…only with the express authority of the Minister in the form of a signed deportation order".[73] Despite this, Hogan J noted that "the usage of statute can only be of limited assistance in construing the vires of the Minister".[74] The Immigration Act 1999 had multiple sections devolving responsibility upon the Minister, leading Hogan J to find that nothing in "the structure, the context and the nature of the powers thereby conferred impliedly limit the scope of the Carltona doctrine".[75] Counsel for the applicant attempted to rely on the fact that s 5 of the Illegal Immigrants (Trafficking) Act 2004 allowed the Minister to appoint Immigration Officers, thereby underlining that the legislature had, where necessary, engaged with the issue of division of labour within the Department. Hogan J ruled out reliance on this Act, finding that it and Refugee Act 1996 were to be regarded as separate frameworks absent any clause calling for collective construal. In regard to Murray CJ's comments in *Meadows*, Hogan J stressed in his ruling in the factually similar case *FL v Minister for Justice* that the Chief Justice was seeking merely:

> "…to emphasise that the Minister could not be absolved from making a decision concerning the applicant's status (and specifically, whether she should have been deported) simply by reason of the fact that these issues had already been addressed by the Office of the Refugee Applications Commissioner or the Refugee Appeal Tribunal."[76]

[7–33] Finally, the possible application of the exceptional instance of *Devanney v District Judge Shields & Ors* was also ruled out:

> "While I accept that the decision to deport is often a complex one which has significant implications for the individual who is the subject matter of the order, I am not satisfied that it is of such intrinsic importance to the community at large that the decision can be made only by the Minister personally. It must also be recalled that the Minister for Justice has many onerous obligations. It cannot

---

[72] *LAT v Minister for Justice* [2011] IEHC 404. Hereinafter *"LAT"*.
[73] 600 *Dáil Debates* at Col. 750 (12 April 2005).
[74] *ibid* para 11.
[75] *ibid* at para 11.
[76] *FL v Minister for Justice and Equality* [2012] IEHC at para 15.

be suggested that the Oireachtas must have intended that he alone should personally take the decision to deport a given individual in every single case, since this would mean that he had responsibility for potentially hundreds of such decisions in any given year."[77]

In a decision initially seeming to go in the opposite direction, *Afolabi v Minister for Justice and Equality & Ors*, Cooke J did grant leave for review on this ground, finding that:

[7–34]

> "...the issue which is raised is undecided and clearly of considerable importance, particularly in view of the recent apparent change in practice within the Department to delegate to his officers entirely the functions of analysis and assessment, the formulation of the recommendations in the "Examination of File" note, the approval of deportation and the formal signing and sealing of the deportation order. There is thus no personal involvement on the part of the Minister in any aspect of the deportation process under s. 3 of the 1999 Act, in these cases."[78]

However, Hogan J's approach has received support in *PUO v Minister for Justice*.[79] There McDermott J refused leave to review, on the basis that as *Meadows* had been delivered "before a change in administrative practice occurred" he was satisfied that the comments in *Meadows* did not contemplate the non-applicability of *Carltona*.[80]

[7–35]

The formalism of the Carltona doctrine results in another instance of the characteristic inertia of Irish administrative law. Thus the legislature needs to make itself clearer by minimising the enabling tone of much of its legislation; however, judges remain reluctant to demand this change through striking down an entire corpus of decisions. Given the *jus cogens* (fundamental) status of non-refoulement in international law, for example, it is possible to argue that the *LAT* case is overly pragmatic and projects too much into the intention of a legislature, which has itself acknowledged the centrality of non-refoulement in its incorporation into domestic law of the UN Convention against Torture. If the decision is

[7–36]

---

[77] Per Hogan J quoting his decision in *LAT* (above n 72 at para 15) *ibid* at para 19.

[78] *Afolabi v Minister for Justice and Equality & Ors*, unreported, High Court, 17 May 2012 at para 31.

[79] *PUO v Minister for Justice* [2012] IEHC 458 (McDermott J, 6 November 2012).

[80] The judge also found that further factor was that the applicant in *PUO* had made no personal submissions to the Minister, and had chosen to "take no part" in the decision making process.

pragmatic and rooted in the realities of Government, one might argue that even requiring the Minister to participate would hardly prohibit reliance upon earlier materials. The ideal position is to take an approach that mediates between the constructed extremities of a conscientious minister burdened by caseloads and a civil servant making a decision that engages one of Ireland's most serious international legal obligations.

[7–37]   Of course, the Carltona principle can also be over-diluted — the greater the dispersal of power, the more difficult to ensure consistency and political control in a Government Department. At the policy level, the interchangeability of the Minister with his civil servants may not be suitable in all contexts. In pursuing such an approach, it is important to note the historical difficulties in distinguishing the political/administrative interface between Ministers and their civil servants discussed earlier in chapter 2 of this book. The Minister remains liable for the actions of their Department. As a signalling mechanism and normative stimulus, one cannot claim that the Carltona doctrine challenges Ministers to actively reflect on appropriate division of labour.[81] Regardless, it is more suitable for the legislature itself to affirm the appropriate emphasis in responsibility, as it has done in the National Treasury Management Agency (Amendment) Act 2000, s 9(3)(f) which stated:

> "the delegation or declaration shall not remove or derogate from the responsibility of any Minister of the Government to Dáil Éireann or as a member of the Government for the performance of functions of that Minister of the Government thereby delegated or to which the declaration relates."

In order to avoid practical constitutional imbalance, invocations of the Carltona doctrine should not diminish the Minister's responsibility to give

---

[81] Indeed the small nature of the country's administration has often led to calls for greater practical permissiveness. As Hogan and Morgan outline, in 1961, it was uncovered that the required permissions of the Minister for Health authorising involuntary detention of mental health patients had not been renewed. This oversight was attributed to the ill health of a civil servant, resulting in over three hundred instances of unlawful detention. In response to opposition criticism, Minister Sean McEntee argued:
> "[I]n these matters there must be some realism. It is all very well to say that constitutional justice theory requires that the Minister should accept full responsibility for everything the Department does ... Am I to accept responsibility for the fact that an officer of my Department suffers a breakdown? ... Is there anything I could possibly have done to ensure that this would not have occurred?"
G Hogan and DG Morgan, *Administrative Law in Ireland* (4th ed) (Round Hall, Dublin, 2010) at para 3-18fn.

a full account of actions, and thus functionally, this may well require individual civil servants' testimony before Oireachtas committees.

Certainly, administrative law doctrines should not permit easy confidence [7–38] that Ministerial accountability exists "as a matter of political theory *and reality*".[82] The Travers Report on the illegal charging of patients long-stay care in health board institutions represented a high point in poor division of responsibility. In defending the failure of his Department to take into account legal advice, then Minister Micheál Martin argued:

> "Ministers can only bear responsibility for issues in respect of which they are properly and adequately briefed and where they have knowledge of something. If they do not take action, then they bear responsibility. However, they cannot be held responsible for something of which they were unaware."[83]

This further underlines the organizational realities which condition [7–39] constitutional responsibilities across multiple levels. Further statutory intervention in this area would befit the seriousness of the issues involved, which common law doctrines have only highlighted rather than confronted.

Elusive Principles: Identifying Jurisdictional Errors

If statutory interpretation represents the core principle in defining the [7–40] decision-making power available, the judiciary has throughout the history of administrative law, sought to identify a principled account when their right to intervene is triggered. In identifying the boundaries of judicial intervention, there exist two key distinctions. Firstly there is a distinction between jurisdictional and non-jurisdictional errors which, on balance, seems to be sliding in importance. Secondly, there is the distinction between errors of law and errors of fact, which remains centre stage. Throughout this book we will meet difficult, abstract concepts such as these, and will take a functional approach to fixing their content. So, rather than initially defining what a jurisdictional error is, it is more useful as a starting point to consider what the professed functions of the

---

[82] Per Hogan J in *LAT* above n 72 at para 16.
[83] Joint Committee on Health and Children, Travers Report: Presentations, 21 April 2005, Statement by Minister for Health, Micheál Martin. Available at: http://debates.oireachtas. ie/HEJ/2005/04/21/00003.asp (date accessed 20 April 2014).

concept of jurisdictional error are? What anxieties prompt judges to invest so heavily in muddy distinctions between errors of law, errors of fact, errors of law and fact?

[7–41]   The decision to initially focus judicial review upon errors of law reflects the principle of legality/doctrine of *ultra vires*. The court's role was to check the authority of the body taking the decision — to ask whether the decision was legally permitted, rather than whether it was the correct one. This distinguishes judicial review from merits review (appeal). The distinction satisfies, in the formal sense, the doctrine of the separation of powers. Substantively, however, the difficulty lies in distinguishing flawed factual determinations from incorrect legal interpretations. To take a practical example, let us take a hypothetical scenario where a statute allows a local council to prohibit political protests in public places on weekends. A local council decides to ban a Gay Pride parade. The first thing we can ask is was there an error of law by deciding the Gay Pride parade was political? This is decided by the specific statutory context and the rules of statutory interpretation and is a decision that the courts view themselves as being well positioned to take.[84] Yet, the situation can easily be characterised in a different way: that is that any error on the part of the council was simply one of fact; it erred by its *application* of the term 'political' to the facts known about the Gay Pride parade.

[7–42]   The second key structuring principle was traditionally founded on the basis of judicial review for errors being mandated by the principle of legality and by the substantive provisions of the Constitution (including, of course, the rights provisions). On the other side of the balance sheet, however, the judiciary has sought to defend the possibility that some errors made by administrators must have been contemplated by the legislature — meaning that part of the statutory grant of powers embraces the right of public bodies to make errors.

[7–43]   Perhaps the clearest summary of the traditional position was provided by the Australian judge Hayne J in *re Refugee Review Tribunal; ex parte Aala*:

> "There is a jurisdictional error if the decision maker makes a decision outside the limits of the functions and powers conferred on him or her, or does something which he or she lacks power to do. By contrast,

---

[84] In contrast to the US courts, who under the so-called Chevron doctrine, are deferential to statutory interpretations undertaken by specialised agencies of the their 'home' statutes.

incorrectly deciding something which the decision maker is authorised
to do is an error within jurisdiction."[85]

This idea that decisions can occur outside the 'walls' of the power, and **[7–44]**
within the 'walls' of the power became a powerful category within judicial
review. Jurisdictional error was thus another traditional device to
distinguish between merits review (appeal) and judicial review. This
separation of powers function, has led various countries to effectively
constitutionalise the concept, which given its indeterminate, chameleon
nature has not proved altogether successful.[86] The imprecision of the term
"jurisdictional" has spanned borders and time, eliciting the condemnation
of United States Justice Felix Frankfurter, who described the idea of
jurisdiction as "a verbal coat of too many colours" as well as "a morass' in
which one can be led by "loose talk about jurisdiction" with the term being
one of "the most deceptive legal pitfalls".[87] It is now commonly agreed that
in the pursuit of what may be legitimate policy concerns, generations of
judges have adopted a rigid, formalistic approach to the categories, which
can embrace instances of considerable injustice. As one of the leading
figures of the 20th century administrative law commented, "no satisfactory
test has ever been formulated for distinguishing findings which go to
jurisdiction from findings which go to merits".[88]

Respecting the Right to Make Errors: Jurisdictional Error Emerges

In England and Wales, the law begins with a departure point, and an arrival **[7–45]**
point. The doctrine of jurisdictional error was expressly born in *R (Martin) v
Mahoney*,[89] and placed within clear boundaries some sixty years later in
Anisminic v Foreign Compensation Tribunal.[90] The rule prior to *Anisminic* is
best summarised by the judgment of the Court of Appeal in that very
matter, where the lower court defended the applicable review as:

> "...the test on jurisdiction, in the only sense in which it is relevant
> here, is whether the Commission had power to enter upon the inquiry

---

[85] *Re Refugee Review Tribunal; ex parte Aala* (2000) 204 CLR 82 at 141.
[86] Australia has recently moved to establish the ability to correct for jurisdictional error as
the unalterable core of judicial power. The concept has played a central role in Canadian
constitutional jurisprudence since the 1970s.
[87] *City of Yonkers v United States* 320 US 685 [1944] at 695.
[88] SA de Smith *et al, Judicial Review of Administrative Action* (5th ed) (Sweet and Maxwell,
London, 1995) at p 255.
[89] *R (Martin) v Mahoney* [1910] 2 IR 695. Hereinafter "*R (Martin)*".
[90] *Anisminic v Foreign Compensation Tribunal* [1969] 2 AC 147. Hereinafter "*Anisminic*".

and make a determination; and not whether the determination was right or wrong in fact or in law".[91]

[7–46] This category of jurisdictional error had derived from the early judgment in *R (Martin) v Mahoney*.[92] In this case it was held that a lack of sufficient evidence for a conviction under s 1 of the Betting House Act 1853 could not be quashed. Despite the fact that the magistrate in the original trial had failed to apply an earlier judgment of the House of Lords, the original court could not lose its original jurisdiction through the error:

> "...the contention that mere want of evidence to authorise a conviction creates a cesser of jurisdiction involves the unwarrantable proposition that a magistrate has...jurisdiction only to go right."[93]

[7–47] The judgment in *R (Martin)* was given by all eight judges of the King's Bench Division, sitting in April and June 1910. It effectively created the category of "error of law within jurisdiction", or, put another way, a forgivable, or authorised, error of law. The compliance pull of the judgment proved so strong, that Morgan describes a generation of judges as having been "almost hypnotised" by it.[94]

Moderation Through Exception

Conditions Precedent to Jurisdiction

[7–48] With *R (Martin) v Mahoney* enshrined as precedent, judges moderated its "pure jurisdiction" doctrine slightly by placing a hurdle in front of administrative bodies at the entrance door to the walls of their jurisdiction. This established that the decision of a body in *determining its own jurisdiction could not be conclusive* and had to be open to review, in order to ensure effect was given to the intentions of the Oireachtas in passing the empowering legislation. Identifying which conditions are *precedent* to jurisdiction and which are merely passed down from the legislature to the body for determination by the body itself is a matter of statutory

---

[91] Court of Appeal judgment, per Sellers LJ [1968] 2 QB 862 at 884.

[92] Above n 89.

[93] *ibid* at 707.

[94] Morgan, *Hogan and Morgan's Administrative* Law, (4th ed, Student Version) (Round Hall, Dublin, 2012) at para 10.57 hereinafter "DG Morgan". The compatibility of this traditional doctrine with injustice was arguably most clearly seen in the *State (Keegan) v Stardust Victims Compensation Tribunal* [1986] IR 642.

interpretation. Conditions precedent are also described as collateral facts or facts collateral to jurisdiction in the case-law.

However, even here we see the ability of statutory interpretation to defeat the condition precedent exception. This can be seen, for example, in *State (Davidson) v Farrell*,[95] where Kingsmill Moore J ruled that the Oireachtas, in passing the Rent Restrictions Act 1946, had intended to give the District Court jurisdiction to determine the term 'premises'. Were the District Court to make an error of law in interpreting this word, it was not reviewable, even as a condition precedent. He noted that:

[7–49]

> "The [District] Court may make an error in law in interpreting the word 'premises', or an error in fact in determining that money has been expended when it has not, but these are errors within the jurisdiction conferred...It is regrettable to have to give a decision which may effect an injustice. The Court in *Mahony's Case* were faced with the same unpleasant prospect but they decided that, even though it was admitted that the conviction was wrongful, yet the limited jurisdiction of the Court in certiorari prevented it from quashing the order of the magistrates. I must do the same."[96]

Beyond this type of limiting decision, the most powerful authority embodying the idea that the correct interpretation of statutory terms constitutes a reviewable condition precedent is *Ryanair v Labour Court*.[97] The Court held that the Labour Court was required to correctly define the four statutory elements of a "trade dispute" before it had jurisdiction to proceed with an investigation, and that this definition was subject to judicial review. Furthermore in *Foley v Judge Murphy*,[98] a community service order made by a District Court judge was challenged on the basis that the judge did not inquire into the appropriateness of a sentence of imprisonment.[99] Dunne J found that this duty to inquire was a condition precedent to the giving of community service, and such an inquiry had to be manifested through a "clear indication of what the appropriate term of imprisonment would be",[100] not merely through a statement that the

[7–50]

---

[95] *State (Davidson) v Farrell* [1960] IR 438.

[96] *ibid* at 455.

[97] *Ryanair v Labour Court* [2007] 4 IR 199.

[98] *Foley v Judge Murphy* [2005] 3 IR 574.

[99] As required under s 2 of the Criminal Justice (Community Service) Act 1983, which allowed for community service where "the appropriate sentence would but for this Act be one of penal servitude".

[100] Above n 98 at 584.

appropriate penal sentence would be zero days. The community service order was quashed.

[7–51] The unsettled nature of the designations in these cases was underlined by the statement decision of the Supreme Court in *Killeen v Director of Public Prosecutions*,[101] where the Supreme Court again employed the category of error within jurisdiction:

> "It may be that an error of law committed by a tribunal acting within its jurisdiction is not capable of being set aside on certiorari: see the *State (Davidson) v Farrell* 1960 I.R. 438. It is otherwise where the error of law has as its consequence the making of an order which the tribunal had no jurisdiction to make."[102]

[7–52] O'Reilly argues that *Killeen* embodies "the uneven manner in which the Superior Courts have dealt with error of law within the jurisdiction of the tribunal or court of limited and local jurisdiction".[103] He also notes the obiter comments of Keane CJ, in *Slatterys Limited v Commissioner of Valuation*[104]:

> "I am satisfied that, even if it could be said that the decision of the first respondent [the Commissioner of Valuation] on the facts of this particular case was that it was a case to which Article 5(b) [of the Urban Renewal Act 1986 (Remission of Rates) Scheme 2011] applied was erroneous – and I am very far from saying it was - it was nonetheless an error made within his jurisdiction and, accordingly, was not amenable to being set aside by way of certiorari'."[105]

Error of Law on the Face of the Record

[7–53] A further traditional exemption that moderated the exclusionary operation of the non-jurisdictional error category was *error of law on the face of the record*. This category has a long heritage tied to the specific history of the common law system which resulted in there being no

---

[101] *Killeen v DPP* [1998] 1 ILRM 1.
[102] *ibid* at 8.
[103] J O'Reilly SC, "Errors of Law and Errors of Fact as Grounds for Judicial Review" (2012) 47 (1) *Irish Jurist* 1 at p 8. Hereinafter "O'Reilly".
[104] *Slatterys Limited v Commissioner of Valuation* [2001] 4 IR 91. This case had already been disposed of under the separate review ground of unreasonableness.
[105] *ibid* at 100.

method by which a matter before a superior reviewing court could be reheard. The sole record was that which was entered on the roll of court and which the parties could seek to impeach before a superior court by showing that a conclusion featured in it was an error. In reviewing the lower court, the superior court would assess that physical record which was the sole resource placed before it.[106]

Clearly, the "record" is the key parameter for this ground, with the [7–54] landmark definition of it provided by Lord Denning, which has been judicially approved in Ireland:

> "The Record must contain at least the document which initiates the proceedings; the pleadings, if any; and the adjudication; but not the evidence, nor the reasons, unless the tribunal chooses to incorporate them. If the tribunal does state its reasons, and the reasons are wrong in law, certiorari lies to quash the decision."[107]

In approving this statement in *Ryan v Compensation Tribunal*,[108] Costello [7–55] nevertheless stressed that an isolated mis-description in an extensive statement of reasons would not represent an error on the face of the record.[109] The reader should note, however, that this category has been used very rarely in modern times. Examples of recent unsuccessful invocations are *Dunnes Stores v Holtglen Ltd*,[110] *L v Refugee Appeals Tribunal*,[111] and *SK v Minister for Justice*.[112]

Both the error of law on the face of the record and the condition precedent [7–56] to jurisdiction approaches were of great utility to judges seeking a practical resolution. They allowed judicial review to be pursued without the duty to tend to the increasingly tangled conceptual garden of jurisdictional error. In Ireland, the pragmatic use of these categories has persisted. The pressure on Irish judges to develop a freshly consolidated,

---

[106] Discussed in more depth by A Radcliffe and A Cross, *The English Legal System* (2nd ed) (Butterworth & Co, London, 1946).

[107] *R v Northumberland Compensation Appeal Tribunal Ex p. Shaw* [1952] 1 KB 338 at 352.

[108] *Ryan v Compensation Tribunal* [1997] 1 ILRM 194 at 200.

[109] A statement recently underlined by Hogan J in *SK v Minister for Justice* [2011] IEHC 371 at para 15.

[110] *Dunnes Stores v Holtglen Ltd* [2012] IEHC 93.

[111] [2010] IEHC 362.

[112] Above n 106, *L v Refugee Appeals Tribunal*. A successful example was *Bannon v EAT* [1993] 1 IR 500 where the error in question related to the applicability of the European Communities (Safeguarding of Employees' Rights on Transfer of Undertakings) Regulations 1980.

modern conception of judicial review continued to build, however, particularly given the sweeping redesign undertaken by the judiciary in England and Wales.

The *Anisminic* Abolition

[7–57] Despite the ability to use the condition precedent device to moderate unfairness, the principle of legality seems to make a demand for a broader culture of compliance with administrative and judicial bodies. Modern case law, particularly in England and Wales, has now shifted to evaluating their actions to ensure they are congruent, through judicial supervision and correct statutory interpretation, with the wishes of the legislature. The landmark case of *Anisminic* marked the commencement of a process whereby the category of jurisdictional error was eased out of use in favour of rendering all errors of law reviewable. While the actual judgment in *Anisminic* was open to interpretation, later cases derived a ratio which was to produce a striking impact. This was best summed up by Lord Diplock in *O'Reilly v Mackman*:

> "...the breakthrough that the *Anisminic* case made was the recognition by the majority of this House that if a tribunal whose jurisdiction was limited by statute or subordinate legislation mistook the law applicable to the facts as it had found them, it must have asked itself the wrong question, i.e. one into which it was not empowered to inquire and so had no jurisdiction to determine. Its purported 'determination' not being a 'determination' within the meaning of the empowering legislation was, accordingly, a nullity."[113]

Lord Browne-Wilkinson in *R v Hull University Visitor, ex parte Page*, simply stated:

> "In general, any error of law made by an administrative tribunal or inferior court in reaching its decision can be quashed for error of law".[114]

---

[113] The case also contained the famous statement by Lord Diplock in *O'Reilly v Mackman* [1982] 2 AC 237 (at 278):
  "...the landmark decision of this House in *Anisminic Ltd. v. Foreign Compensation Commission* [1969] 2 A.C. 147, and particularly the leading speech of Lord Reid, which has liberated English public law from the fetters that the courts had theretofore imposed upon themselves so far as determinations of inferior courts and statutory tribunals were concerned, by drawing esoteric distinctions between errors of law committed by such tribunals that went to their jurisdiction, and errors of law committed by them within their jurisdiction."
[114] *R v Hull University Visitor, ex parte Page* [1993] AC 682 at 702.

The abiding impact of the *Anisminic* abolition was confirmed recently in **[7–58]**
the judgment of Lord Dyson JSC in *Lumba v Secretary of State for the Home Department*:

> "A purported lawful authority to detain may be impugned either
> because the defendant acted in excess of jurisdiction (in the narrow
> sense of jurisdiction) or because such jurisdiction was wrongly
> exercised. *Anisminic Ltd v Foreign Compensation Commission....*
> established that both species of error render an executive act ultra
> vires, unlawful and a nullity. In the present context, there is in
> principle no difference between (i) a detention which is unlawful
> because there was no statutory power to detain and (ii) a detention
> which is unlawful because the decision to detain, although authorised
> by statute, was made in breach of a rule of public law…the importance
> of *Anisminic* is that it established that there was a single category of
> errors of law all of which rendered a decision ultra vires."[115]

For the student today, the simple statement that all errors of law are **[7–59]**
reviewable represents an alluring lifebuoy amidst the confusing currents
moving within the term "jurisdiction". Existing Irish authorities,
however, underline the fact that the relative clarity of English law still
remains out of reach, bringing into a sharper light the failure of normative
leadership in this area by the Irish Supreme Court.

Rather than the clean cut approach offered by the post *Anisminic* UK case- **[7–60]**
law, the Irish case of *State (Holland) v Kennedy*, delivered only a glancing
blow to the doctrine of jurisdictional error.[116] The immediate facts of *State
(Holland) v Kennedy* concerned the conviction and imposition of a prison
sentence upon a minor between the ages of 15 and 17. The Children Act
1908 forbade imprisonment absent evidence showing that the individual
was of such "unruly character" that it was not possible to detain him or
her in detention centre. The District Judge had here certified Mr Holland
on grounds of the bare fact of his having been guilty of a particularly
serious assault, without any further evidence that he was of "unruly
character". The majority of the Supreme Court held that the Judge had
erred, and the Act required previous evidence of a behavioural pattern;
not just an individual crime. This error, furthermore, was "not made
within jurisdiction".[117] The precise ground for this determination is

---

[115] *Lumba v Secretary of State for the Home Department* [2012] 1 AC 245 at para 66.
[116] *State (Holland) v Kennedy* [1977] IR 193.
[117] *ibid* at 201 (judgment of Henchy J).

unclear, however, with Henchy J's judgment resisting clear characterisation. At times, it can be classified both as an expansionist case along the lines of *Anisminic* or alternatively a condition precedent decision in line with *State (Davidson v Farrell)*.

[7–61] Henchy J's approach in the later case of *State (Abenglen Property) v Dublin Corporation*[118] crossed back towards the older approach of condition precedent in finding that a failure by the respondent to apply the relevant development plan in attaching conditions to a grant of planning permission would not ground *certiorari*. However, it is important to note the less than optimal fit of these cases with *Anisminic*, as pointed out by O'Reilly, who stresses that

> "the Supreme Court was not presented during his [Henchy J]'s tenure with an appeal squarely raising the issues determined by the House of Lords in *Anisminic*".[119]

Nevertheless, the practical reality after *Abenglen* is well summarised by de Blacam:

> "Nonetheless the Irish courts have, in the aftermath of Abenglen, quashed decisions affected by errors of law as if it were received doctrine that such errors give rise to a general right to review."[120]

[7–62] Justice McKechnie did provide a rejoinder to any bright line approach in the unreported High Court judgment of *Rita Leonard v District Judge John Garavan*, where his Honour cautioned that:

> "[*Abenglen*] would appear to preserve intact a court or tribunal's power to err provided that the error was within jurisdiction…However even in such circumstances if the error was responsible for a failure to uphold a person's rights, either under natural or constitutional justice, then, it is said that an extra flaw exists which flaw would result in an order of *certiorari*. This and similar statements on the issue of jurisdiction must continuously be reviewed in the light of a judicial tendency to enlarge the occasions upon which the decision of an inferior court could be susceptible to High Court challenge."[121]

---

[118] *State (Abenglen Property) v Dublin Corporation* [1984] IR 381.

[119] O'Reilly, above n 103. Hereinafter *"Abenglen"* at p 4.

[120] M de Blacam, *Judicial Review* (2nd Ed) (Butterworths, Dublin, 2009), at p 81.

[121] *Rita Leonard v District Judge John Garavan*, unreported, High Court, 30 April 2002 at para 24.

We can only surmise that the reluctance of the Irish judges to *Anisminic* is tied to Irish courts tendency towards pragmatism, as well as a commitment to contextual rather than conceptual reasoning.

A further example of such a pragmatic, contextual approach to these [7–63] questions was seen in the judgment of Hogan J in *CE v Minister for Justice, Equality and Law Reform*.[122] In *CE*, the member of Refugee Applications Commission had failed to put it to the applicant during the course of the hearing that an internet search revealed no relevant local news reporting of a murder which the applicant had claimed to have occurred in Nigeria. This was a breach of the statutory requirement in s 13(10) of the Refugee Act 1996 that the applicant was to be provided with a description of the sources and nature of the information which the decision-maker was taking notice of. Hogan J however, noted that while this was an error of law, this error fell within "the middle range"[123]:

> "…the error in question – non-compliance with the requirements of s. 13(10) of the 1996 Act – is a technical one. It would be unrealistic to say that the error goes to the very heart of the Tribunal's jurisdiction, even if it could otherwise be characterized as a jurisdictional error in the sense understood by the modern doctrine of jurisdictional error which has evolved since the seminal decision of the House of Lords in *Anisminic v Foreign Compensation Commission* [1969] 2 A.C. 147."[124]

The two more recent cases of *Shackleton* and *McKernan* appeared to open [7–64] up some new avenues of resolving the now forty year debate, by shifting the focus away from jurisdictional errors of law towards "serious" or "unreasonable" errors of law, which the court must intervene to quash. In *Cork County Council v Shackleton*,[125] an arbitrator had incorrectly interpreted the social and affordable housing requirements laid down by s 96 of the Planning and Development Act 2000. Clarke J held:

> "…where there has been a *significant error in the interpretation of a material statutory provision* leading to a decision of the property

---

[122] *CE v Minister for Justice, Equality and Law Reform* [2012] IEHC 3 (Judgment of Hogan J, 11 January 2012).

[123] His Honour therefore viewed the error as quite far removed from that disclosed in *Stefan v Minister for Justice* [2001] 4 IR 203 where material information had been withheld from the Commission member by reason of a translation error. This omission was found to go to the very essence of a fair adjudication before the Commission and, further, that it was one which could not be safely cured by means of an administrative appeal. *ibid* at para 29.

[124] *ibid* at para 30.

[125] *Cork County Council v Shackleton* [2007] IEHC 241.

> arbitrator being wrong in law, any such decision should, prima facie, be quashed."[126]

His Honour anchored his right to correct for error of law in the fundamental nature of the legal question before the arbitrator.

[7–65] In *McKernan v Employment Appeals Tribunal*,[127] which concerned a challenge to the refusal of an unfair dismissal claim by the Tribunal, Feeney J relied on the *Shackleton* approach in stating that in review the court:

> "...must consider whether or not the decision of the Tribunal was grounded on an erroneous view of the law and whether the decision turned on an incorrect and wrong determination of a legal issue."[128]

[7–66] A decision based on such an error, in his view, was unreasonable, under the then applicable *Keegan* reasonableness standard.[129] It is clear that a seriousness of an error of law is measured by its materiality to the result. The ability to sever or detach the error from the result evidentially is deeply contextual and particular to the reasoning process at hand. Furthermore, the seriousness of the error should also be measured against legislative intent: if the parliament has created an imperative duty, surely this must be carried out, independent of any judicial receptiveness to encouraging administrative expediency. Otherwise, a pragmatic focus on "preserving the uncontaminated result" does not trace back adequately to the principle of legality.

[7–67] Echoing the Supreme Court decision of *Stefan v Minister for Justice, Equality and Law Reform*,[130] Hogan J stressed that those seeking to take action to correct jurisdictional errors can, in some circumstances, be justifiably directed towards administrative avenues of appeal, which represent the ideal fora for correction:

> "...many of these errors can be characterized as jurisdictional, but in truth they often register in the middle of a spectrum which ranges from a pure appeal point on the one hand to that to which goes to the very essence of the jurisdiction on the other. Save where the error

---

[126] Emphasis added at 215.
[127] *McKernan v Employment Appeals Tribunal* [2008] IEHC 40.
[128] *ibid* at para 4.6.
[129] The judicial review ground of "reasonableness" is discussed later in chapter 9 of this book.
[130] Above n 123.

registers at the upper end of this spectrum or where the facts disclose a clear injustice, the judicial preference for exhaustion of administrative remedies tends to prevail."[131]

Thus an error of a more minor or 'technical' character may not be quashed, and an exhaustion of appeals is essential. Of course, what happens if the appeal fails to resolve a "middle of the spectrum" error is where the ambiguity has now been transferred.

Errors of Fact, Mixed Questions of Fact and Law

The traditional position in this area is best summarised by Hogan and [7–68] Morgan who highlight the imperviousness of a factual error to review as being "among the most definite rocks of the island of immunity impregnable to judicial review".[132] This can be attributed to legitimate judicial defence of the line between merits appeal and judicial review. Nevertheless, it is possible to identify some exceptional cases, instances of what may be called "jurisdictional facts" or facts which are sufficiently entwined with the law that the courts may intervene.

The case of *Ryanair v Flynn* established that "a very high threshold must be [7–69] met" before the courts will intervene against a factual error.[133] The case centred on the determination that Ryanair's baggage handling staff were paid below the industry norm. Ryanair sought to review errors of fact it alleged had been made by the industrial experts making the decision. They argued that the experts had erred even at the departure point for the analysis: which companies were comparable to Ryanair. Furthermore it claimed they had failed to accurately identify the relevant working arrangements in Ryanair. Kearns J noted the extensiveness and specialised nature of the dispute:

> "In the instant case, not merely are the facts in dispute, but differences of opinion exist as to the appropriate methodology for establishing the facts and as to the inferences to be drawn therefrom."[134]

---

[131] *ibid*, at para 28.
[132] Above n 81 at p 305.
[133] *Ryanair v Flynn* [2000] IEHC 36 at 264.
[134] *ibid*, at 266-7.

The difficult process of even isolating the variables involved suggested that the courts should be slow to engage in review.

[7–70]   In the later decision of *Aer Rianta v Commissioner for Aviation Regulation* O'Sullivan J appeared to signal the shutting down of any lingering openness to factual error in any context.[135] Hogan and Morgan conclude that this default position still represents the enforced reality, but also perceive a "significant blurring around the edges".[136] The slight loosening of the orthodoxy has been seen in a particularly demanding context: refugee law. This is an area of law that relies heavily upon subjective inferences from the facts. In the Irish context, the failings of the Refugee Tribunal and its closed administrative culture of fact finding, have led to some successful challenges in the courts.

[7–71]   The traditional, exclusionary approach is embodied by the case of *VP and Another v Refugee Appeals Tribunal*.[137] There the Tribunal had decided that the feared mistreatment of the applicants was unlikely, given both the prevailing political circumstances in Moldova and the involvement in Government of the political party supported by one of the applicants. The error of fact occurred in a mistranslation of the relevant criminal provision of the Moldovan Criminal Code, which had to some extent adversely affected the determination.[138] Feeney J subsumed a potential intervention based on an error of fact into the separate ground of irrationality and unreasonableness.[139] His Honour reiterated the basic rule of administrative law that bodies entrusted with executive tasks are entitled to error within jurisdiction. Furthermore, the alleged error in

---

[135] *Aer Rianta v Commissioner for Aviation Regulation* [2003] IEHC 707.

[136] Morgan, above n 94 at para 10.135.

[137] *VP and Another v Refugee Appeals Tribunal* [2007] IEHC 415 at 7–8.

[138] This was derived from a translation of the relevant provision of the Moldovan Criminal Code which suggested that insult to a police co-worker was required to constitute the offence. The Tribunal concluded that because the applicant was clearly not a police worker, he could not be guilty of a criminal offence which was defined as involving a "police co-worker". A further translation of the relevant criminal provision was then requested, and it identified the offence as dealing with the harassment of a police informer rather than an insult to a police co-worker. If the latter translation was correct, it would mean that the applicant did not have to be a co-worker of a police worker in order to commit an offence under the relevant provision. The applicants claimed that the earlier mistranslation had resulted in an error of fact going to jurisdiction.

[139] This standard at the time of this case was the *Keegan* test of irrationality discussed later in the chapter.

this case was not central to the ultimate conclusion, and did not therefore render the decision irrational.

The case of *AMT v Refugee Appeals Tribunal*[140] was one where the material   **[7–72]**
significance of the error of fact overpowered the deferential concerns of the court. In making its decision, the Tribunal had relied on an incorrect fact: that the applicant had travelled from France to Germany by bus. The application was ultimately rejected for lack of credibility, grounded partly in the implausible nature of his travel movements. Reliance on the *Ryanair* and *Aer Rianta* cases was rejected by Finlay Geoghegan:

> "I have concluded that a different principle arises in relation to the error in this case to that at issue in the above cases. The question of how the applicant travelled between France and Germany was not a factual issue in dispute upon which the Tribunal member was adjudicating. Rather, the Tribunal member was required to adjudicate upon the credibility of the applicant and his story. As part of that adjudication, in accordance with the above principles, she was required to assess the story of the applicant as disclosed in the course of his application, either at interview or in writing or at the oral hearing before the Tribunal member. The error of fact made is as to what was the story told or the evidence given…Whether one considers the legal principles applicable to the assessment of credibility in claims for refugee status or the principles of constitutional justice, I have concluded that the obligation of the Tribunal member is to assess the credibility of the applicant in relation to the story as told or evidence given by him/her. This did not happen in this case. In assessing the credibility of the applicant, the Tribunal member has included as part of his story a fact for which she had no relevant material and, further, placed reliance upon such fact in a manner adverse to the applicant in reaching a conclusion against the credibility of his story. Such error renders the decision invalid."[141]

Justice Finlay Geoghegan reiterated that the courts had limited entitlement to intervene, which is dependent upon the "materiality of the error to the decision reached".[142]

---

[140] *AMT v Refugee Appeals Tribunal* [2004] 2 IR 607.
[141] *ibid* at 615.
[142] *ibid*.

[7–73]   In the later case of *HR v Refugee Appeals Tribunal*,[143] the mistaken error of fact was found to be of a grave nature and potentially had, sufficient linkage to *both* jurisdiction and the ultimate result, that *certiorari* was issued. The Tribunal member in this case had mistakenly claimed that the plaintiff had not referred to her brother's detention in a psychiatric hospital at Belarus at her s 11 application interview, when in fact this had been discussed. It had, in fact, been at the preliminary hearing under s 8 of the Refugee Act 1996 that she had failed to mention her brother.[144] Justice Cooke stressed that it was "an important mistake because the Tribunal member himself emphasises that the passage relates to a 'fundamental piece of information'". In responding to counsel for the Tribunal's argument that the mistake was one of fact, was not material when the decision was read as a whole, and alternatively that it should be regarded as an error within jurisdiction, Cooke J acknowledged *Ryanair v Flynn*. Nevertheless, he found:

> "without in any way dissenting from that as a correct statement of law, the Court would express doubt as to whether what has happened in this case is either a mere mistake of fact as such, or a mistake of fact made within jurisdiction."[145]

In identifying the line which was crossed, he stated that the mistake was not one where "for example, the decision-maker mistakenly treats some events of past persecution as having taken place on a wrong date or in the wrong place".[146] Rather the mistake was as to "the course and content of the asylum procedure in which the Tribunal member is exercising jurisdiction".[147] In addition, the error was heightened in significance by the extensive reliance on the demeanour of the applicant by the decision-maker:

---

[143] *HR v Refugee Appeals Tribunal* [2011] IEHC 151, 15 April 2011, hereinafter *"HR"*.

[144] This was proven on the face of the Commissioner's s 13 decision, the notes from the s 11 interview and within, Part 3, 'Summary of the Applicant's Claim' in the Tribunal decision itself. Para 14 of the judgment:
"Whether the explanation lies in the lapse of ten months between the oral hearing and the date of the decision or in some other factor which is not immediately apparent, there can be no doubt but that when the Tribunal member came to write the findings upon which the conclusion of the Contested Decision rests, he was under the impression that what he describes as "a fundamental piece of information" had been overlooked and, in effect, withheld during the asylum process up to and including the s. 11 interview."

[145] *HR* above n 143 at para 16.

[146] *ibid* at para 17.

[147] *ibid*.

> "before a decision maker in the asylum process bases a rejection of a claim upon lack of credibility based mainly on the personal appearance and demeanour of the claimant, the decision-maker ought to be fully confident that the basis of the claim and all relevant facts and circumstances recounted have been fully and correctly understood and that there is no possibility that the decision-maker and claimant have been at cross purposes on any material point."[148]

These decisions are, however, clearly set within the bounds identified by Hogan J in the case of *SK (Ethiopia) v Minister for Justice, Equality and Law Reform*: [7–74]

> "This Court can quash an administrative decision on this ground only where there have been serious errors of fact such that, taken cumulatively, they amount to an error of law, or where the administrative body thereby effectively assumes a jurisdiction which it does not otherwise have."[149]

In *SK*, the Tribunal member had found that a questionnaire filled out by the applicant had failed to mention her medical condition, however it contained an answer regarding her health issues. Furthermore, the applicant had mentioned a heart condition upon her arrival in the state but her communication of this had been complicated by the absence of an interpreter. The Tribunal's finding of inconsistency, which was based on these errors, had fed into an adverse assessment of her credibility. Consequently, due to these inaccurate factual premises, Hogan J concluded that "the negative credibility inference drawn by the Tribunal member cannot be regarded as a reasonable one".[150] Thus where certain facts are central, the courts will bridge between any factual error and the legal task the decision-maker is required to perform and review their actions. Underneath this bridge however lies the "even more difficult marshland"[151] of mixed law and fact. [7–75]

Questions of Mixed Fact and Law

A question of mixed fact and law arises where a legal determination is welded onto, or necessarily attaches to, the determination of relevant facts. Where an interpretation of law grounds incorrect inferences of fact, [7–76]

---

[148] *ibid* at para 7.
[149] *SK (Ethiopia) v Minister for Justice, Equality and Law Reform* [2011] IEHC 301 at para 7.
[150] *ibid* at para 19.
[151] Morgan, above n 94 at [10-93].

cumulatively leading to a material result, intervention may be perceived as appropriate. Perhaps the most accessible explanation of this category was given by the US Federal Circuit Judge Thomas Ambro in *Interfaith Community Org v Honeywell Intl inc*:

> "A question of fact can be answered solely by determining the facts of a case (without any need to know the law relevant to the case). A question of law can be answered solely by determining what relevant law means (without any need to determine the facts of a case). A mixed question of fact and law can only be answered by both determining the facts of a case and determining what the relevant law means. For example, imagine that a man is appealing his conviction under a law that states "it is a crime to be tall." What kind of question is: "Was the trial court correct to find the man 'tall'?" Can we answer it solely by determining the facts of the case? No, because even if we know the fact that the man is five feet ten inches, we do not know if he is "tall" in the sense that Congress intended the word "tall" to mean. Can we answer it solely by determining what the relevant law means without knowing the man's height? No, because even if we know that the statute defines "tall" as "six feet or taller," we do not know how tall the man is. Thus, we have a mixed question of fact and law. Once we know the facts of the case (that the man is five feet ten inches tall), and what the relevant law means (it is a crime to be six feet tall or taller), we can answer "no" to the question "Was the trial court correct to find the man 'tall'?"[152]

[7–77] This statement highlights the importance of statutory context. We have already seen that there is a stronger possibility of a lapse into jurisdictional error where the statute lays down a structured definition — in such cases one can at least argue the existence of certain facts is intertwined, as a matter of statutory design, with the satisfaction of a legal test. Statutes can also, however, constitute more an enabling of discretionary, expert judgment, permitting recourse to an enormous variety of factual matters. A statute can also lie somewhere in between those two extremes, which is arguably where the (still judicially unrecognised) category of mixed fact and law finds its root. The leading discussion of this category in Irish law occurred in the 2007 case of *Ashford Castle Ltd v SIPTU* where Clark J discussed the nature of the tasks given to administrative bodies under statute.[153] It is important to note that the division of "fact" and "law" in this

---

[152] *Interfaith Community Org. v Honeywell Intl. inc* 399 F.3d 248 United State Court of Appeals, Third Circuit at para 77-78.
[153] *Ashford Castle Ltd v SIPTU* [2007] 4 IR 70.

context, often represent a policy judgment regarding the proper role of administrative bodies and the courts. This was recognized in the recent UK Supreme Court judgment in *Jones (by Caldwell) v First-tier Tribunal* where Lord Hope stressed that:

> "…a pragmatic approach should be taken to the dividing line between law and fact, so that the expertise of tribunals at the first tier and that of the Upper Tribunal can be used to best effect. An appeal court should not venture too readily into this area by classifying issues as issues of law which are really best left for determination by the specialist appellate tribunals."[154]

The subtle continuum between the extremes of factual and legal analysis received a sensitive treatment by Edwards J in considering "an appeal on a point of law" against the Employment Appeals Tribunal in *Minister for Agriculture and Food v Barry and Others*.[155] In considering the meaning of "point of law", the Court noted statement of McCracken J in *National University of Ireland Cork v Ahern*[156]:   **[7–78]**

> "The respondents submit that the matters determined by the Labour Court were largely questions of fact and that matters of fact as found by the Labour Court must be accepted by the High Court in any appeal from its findings. As a statement of principle, this is certainly correct. However, this is not to say that the High Court or this court cannot examine the basis upon which the Labour Court found certain facts. The relevance, or indeed admissibility, of the matters relied on by the Labour Court in determining the facts is a question of law. In particular the question of whether certain matters ought or ought not to have been considered by the Labour Court and ought or ought not to have been taken into account by it in determining the facts, is clearly a question of law, and can be considered on an appeal under s8(3)."[157]

---

[154] *Jones (by Caldwell) v First-tier Tribunal* [2013] UKSC 19 at para 16.

[155] *Minister for Agriculture and Food v Barry and Others* [2008] IEHC 216.

[156] *National University of Ireland Cork v Ahern* [2005] 2 IR 577.

[157] It also cited Donaldson MR in the English case of *O'Kelly and others v Trusthouse Forte PLC* [1983] ICR 728 at 761:
> "The judgment of the appeal tribunal in this case suggests that there is a difference of judicial view as to whether the question 'Is a contract a contract of employment or a contract for services?' is a mixed question of fact and law or a question of law, but I do rather doubt whether the triple categorisation of issues as 'fact' 'law' and 'mixed fact and law' is very helpful in the context of the jurisdiction of the appeal tribunal… Whilst it may be convenient for some purposes to refer to questions of "pure" law as contrasted with "mixed" questions of fact and la, the fact is that the appeal tribunal has no jurisdiction to consider any question of mixed fact and law until it has purified or distilled the mixture and extracted a question of pure law."

[7–79]   At this point, we must signpost the inevitable crossing over to the content of other chapters. As well as the exceptional errors of fact cases we cite here, the errors involved in many of these cases can, and have been, absorbed into other grounds of review. For instance an error of fact which leads to an irrelevant consideration being taken into account may be attacked: likewise an omission of a fact may constitute a failure to take account a relevant consideration.[158] The potential correction of errors of law through a test for unreasonableness has always existed; part of finding a decision reasonable being that it is factually sustainable.[159]

[7–80]   The growth of a potential separate head of error of fact within the England and Wales continues to be debated. In the case of *E v Home Secretary*,[160] Carnwarth LJ gave specific treatment to the boundaries and mandate for judicial intervention where an error of fact occurred:

> "In our view, the time has now come to accept that a mistake of fact giving rise to unfairness is a *separate head of challenge* in an appeal on a point of law, at least in those statutory contexts where the parties share an interest in co-operating to achieve the correct result. Asylum law is undoubtedly such an area. Without seeking to lay down a precise code, the ordinary requirements for a finding of unfairness are apparent…First, there must have been a mistake as to an existing fact, including a mistake as to the availability of evidence on a particular matter. Secondly, the fact or evidence must have been "established" in the sense that it was uncontentious and objectively verifiable. Thirdly, the appellant (or his advisers) must not have been responsible for the mistake. Fourthly, the mistake must have played a material (not necessarily decisive) part in the tribunal's reasoning."[161]

---

[158] See discussion in chapter 8 regarding irrelevant and relevant considerations.

[159] The task of an advising lawyer is to present the category most likely to lead to success for their client, which, often lies with other grounds. This strategic landscape has led to some distorted understanding. De Smith distils the reality of how to respond to mistakes of fact:

> "taking into account of a mistaken fact can just as easily be absorbed into a traditional ground of review by referring to the taking into account of an irrelevant consideration, or the failure to provide reasons that are adequate or intelligible or the failure to base the decision on any evidence. In this limited context, material error of fact has always been a recognized ground for judicial intervention."

De Smith, Woolf and Jowell, *Judicial Review of Administrative Action*, (5th ed) (Sweet & Maxwell, London, 1995) at p 297.

[160] *E v Home Secretary* [2004] QB 1044.

[161] *ibid* at 1071.

While, these tests seem to catch much of the emphasis of existing Irish **[7–81]** cases, we agree with Daly[162] that if the Irish courts ever formalize a doctrine, it will likely deal with these scenarios under the more traditional grounds of review such as the obligation to take into account relevant considerations or reasonableness.

The recent case of *Richardson v Judge Alan Mahon & Others* provided a **[7–82]** mention of *E* in an Irish context.[163] Here Dunne J refused to correct errors of fact in a Tribunal of Inquiry report. The tribunal had made incorrect findings regarding Mr Richardson's fundraising activities, including that he had, in testimony, claimed to have no knowledge of the source of a donation of IR£39,000, which the tribunal was investigating. The Tribunal found it "incredible" that he was unable to so account, and, based on his access to relevant bank accounts, found that he had intentionally refused to disclose matters to the tribunal. This finding was clearly in error: Mr Richardson had never been called upon to account for source of money by the tribunal. Having quoted the above statement from *E*, Dunne J ruled on the use of the case by counsel for the applicant:

> "The approach in that case does appear to be somewhat at variance
> with the decision in the case of *Ryanair Ltd. v Flynn* but the key to the
> difference in approach is almost certainly to be found in the nature of
> the case before the court in the Court of Appeal, namely, a decision in
> an asylum/immigration case, where there is, as pointed out, a shared
> interest in cooperating to achieve the correct result. I do not think
> that the case of *E* is of assistance to the court in these proceedings."[164]

Dunne J then proceeded to dispose of the issues under the heading: **[7–83]** *"Decision on fair procedures and unreasonableness/irrationality and error of fact within jurisdiction"*. This heading again underlined the multiplicity of ways a court can characterize these cases. Certainly her Honour ruled out any separate head of review for error of fact based on *Ryanair v Flynn*. Furthermore, her Honour rejected the centrality of the errors to the overall findings of the Tribunal, noting that if anything the conclusions were merely "part findings". The applicant had selected those portions of the tribunal's reasoning which were in error, while excluding others which were correct:

---

[162] P Daly, "Judicial Review of Factual Error in Ireland", (2008) 30(1) DULJ 187.

[163] *Richardson v Judge Alan Mahon & Ors* [2013] IEHC 118.

[164] *ibid* at para 41.

> "It is a somewhat artificial exercise to break down the findings in the respective paragraphs complained of and to criticise elements of those paragraphs as being irrational or unreasonable findings. In truth, this is more in the nature of a challenge to "part findings" of the Tribunal. It seems to me that the manner in which this has been done by the applicant lends force to the argument that what is at the heart of this application is an error of fact and an error within jurisdiction which is not amenable to judicial review. It is not the function of the court in these proceedings to correct errors of fact made by the Tribunal and thus, I have concluded that the applicant is not entitled to the relief sought herein."[165]

[7–84]   The Court would not permit review of errors of fact that led to "part findings" of the Tribunal. This sits comfortably with the refugee law case-law, where any determination on credibility is directly and immediately connected, as a matter of law, with the overall determination. Materiality and centrality appear to increasingly provide the baseline for intervention.

Conclusion

[7–85]   In addition to the specific issues of law considered in this chapter, we would like the reader to emerge with two immediate themes to carry forward. The first is the centrality of statutory interpretation to the exercise of administrative powers, a theme which naturally suffers when the subject is given a systemic, analytic treatment in a classroom rather than when it is experienced in practice. In terms of trends in Irish statutory interpretation, it is important to note a number of ways in which the judiciary have heightened the need for accurate construing of language. First of all, Irish executive power, in general, has not operated as an expansive failsafe reservoir to fill out any gaps in jurisdiction. Secondly, the literal method of interpretation requires high quality drafting as recourse to extrinsic aids to bear out parliamentary intent is limited. The fact that many prevailing models of Irish legal education do not include a unified course on statutory drafting or interpretation is something liable to change in the era of legislative hyperactivity. Until such reform takes place, administrative law will continue as the primary

---

[165] *ibid* at para 53.

site for raising these issues. Students and administrators should not be blinded as to their importance.

Our analysis of jurisdictional error also featured a number of elements   **[7–86]**
which will recur throughout the various heads or grounds of judicial review. Firstly, it is important, when embarking on a judicial review action or merely studying administrative law, to understand the *function* and *values* which underpin a particular ground of challenge. Jurisdictional error is clearly one of the most complex topics in administrative law, and the temptation is to read it like a chain novel of cases, constantly seeking the underlying progressions of plot. Yet when confronted by untidiness, it is important to note that the technicalities and lines which are drawn by the concept of jurisdictional error, foreshadow many of the anxieties and values which affect other grounds of review. There is a sense in which jurisdictional error was developed as part of a need to express concerns regarding levels of appropriate deference to the judgment of decision makers and the proper role of law and legal actors. This actor or spatial approach which centred on separate spheres of "law" and "fact", has come under pressure from a more contextual approach, which rejects the rigidity of bright line categories, and seeks to exercise contextual judgment based on the materiality of the error to the final decision and the rights and natural justice entitlements of the individual. This contextual emphasis ideally prioritises the continuum over the bright line distinction, values and function over artificially categorising errors. As will be seen throughout this book however, such contextualism can also take the form of a more regressive tendency to cast the result in each case as fact-specific. An increasing pragmatism in resolving cases, as witnessed in our courts, can leave conceptual issues under-addressed and actually result in a failure to provide systematic or principled accounts of how a particular ground of review is evolving.

CHAPTER EIGHT

LEGISLATIVE PURPOSE, DISCRETION AND THE REASONING PROCESS

Introduction

In this chapter we will look at how three traditional grounds of review aim [8–01] to achieve one basic purpose: ensuring that administrative decision-makers wield their power in line with the purpose underlying the statute. Conceptually, therefore, it is clear that much of this material in this chapter "calls back" to the preceding chapter on *ultra vires*. The aim of ensuring that Government power is not exercised for improper purposes and that all relevant considerations are taken into account is part of the same overall approach which requires that the decision-making, acting under statute, should match the parliament's objective expectations. This, of course, includes an expectation of constitutionality: that the administrator will recognise that a statutory framework should be applied in a manner cognisant of the constitution. In this sense while the discussion in chapter 7 of narrow *ultra vires* focussed upon the need to comply with express language of the primary Act, in this chapter we begin to progress into "broad *ultra vires*", where decisions may be struck down for a failure to comply with what can be extremely loosely termed as the underlying framework of rationality, intention or purpose of the statute.

While administrative law might appear to centre on judicial cases, its actual [8–02] subject matter remains the daily activities and the decisions issued by those exercising public power. Thus, at this point we would like to express two hopes for the reader. Firstly, as much as we are discussing technical concepts, these cases are also about everyday stories and time pressured actors who fumble decisions. Any administrative law book which looks to generate core principles and legal tests should not blind us to the fact that judgments are made up of the interaction of facts and law. We would urge the reader to read full judicial review judgments. Secondly, we would like at this point in the book to urge readers to place themselves on the receiving end of the cases: what is the practical impact on Government decision-makers? The reader, whether ordinary citizen, lawyer or Government decision-maker, should be able to pick up a decision-letter they have received, or recount past dealings with Government actors, and assess the degree to which they reflected the legal principles we are discussing.

In recent years much of the discussion has pertained to the *intensity* of [8–03] review undertaken by the courts. This is reflected in the extensive nature of chapter 9 examining reasonableness and proportionality. Yet, this debate was only possible once the common law had constructed the *grounds* of review: these traditional categories represent traditional waypoints for a judge to intervene with decision-making. In our discussion of judicial review procedure in chapter 13 we observe that their diversity is sometimes not respected by legal counsel, who often adopt a somewhat scattershot approach in submissions, leading with a primary argument and then attempting a range of more stretched claims. In carrying out our primary research for this book, we were disappointed by this tendency, and also by a related emphasis upon reasonableness and proportionality. The obligation to take into account all relevant considerations should be respected as a ground which looks at how decision-makers treat evidence and structure their reasoning. In our view, before we rush to argue that a decision was substantively disproportionate, we must reflect more fully on the how judges should oversee the *construction* of the relevant interests and of evidence bases for decisions.

Bad Faith/Improper Purpose

[8–04]   One long established ground of challenge is that of bad faith or improper purpose. Most attempts to make out this ground will have to prove deliberate or malicious misconduct rather than a simple error. Instances which do not involve dishonesty, but rather actions radically incompatible with the purposes and terms of the statute can also be framed under other grounds of review such as irrelevant considerations or unreasonableness. Consequently, it remains a residual ground, with only a few successful cases.

[8–05]   The *locus classicus* for the bad faith category in Ireland is *State (O'Mahony) v South Cork Board of Public Health*.[1] The applicant was a tenant who sought to purchase her cottage from the respondent as provided for by statute. Maguire P found that her application had been refused due to "mere pique" which was attributable to past clashes between her and the respondent. The Court therefore quashed the decision and required the Board to reconsider her application according to the law. Such instances of bad faith are bound to be rare: as the burden of proving malice or dishonesty on the part of public officials is a heavy one.

---

[1] *State (O'Mahony) v South Cork Board of Public Health* [1941] Ir Jur Rep 79.

One of the earliest cases involving improper purpose is *Hoey v Minister for Justice*.[2] There, the applicants had sought an order requiring the minister to require Louth County Council to supply courthouse accommodation for the Circuit Court to sit in Drogheda. The holding of Circuit Court hearings in Drogheda had been discontinued by legislative order under s 31 of the Civil Bill Courts (Ireland) Act 1851 which provided that the use of Drogheda as a Circuit Court venue should be discontinued. The applicants argued that the latter order had been made for an improper purpose, namely to head off the threat of their legal action. While holding that s 31 had not survived the creation of the modern court system, Lynch J stated that even if it had, he would have found that the main purpose of the closure orders had been to stave off litigation rather than to regulate the functioning of the court system.

[8–06]

The courts may also be confronted with a situation where a permissible purpose co-exists with an impermissible purpose. In *Cassidy v Minister for Industry and Commerce*,[3] the Supreme Court upheld a ministerial order which set maximum prices for the sale of alcoholic beverages on the basis that they were following the legitimate purpose, the controlling of price increases. While the applicants alleged that the orders were passed at least in part to ensure they obeyed voluntary arrangements in the future, the Court held that this was "merely subsidiary and consequential to the dominant and permitted purpose".[4] In the more recent case of *Kennedy v Law Society of Ireland (No.3)*,[5] Fennelly J stated that the improper purpose had been present as an equal motivation to the proper purpose from the outset of the case. The trial judge had found that "the pursuit of the impermissible objective was as important to the first respondent as the permissible one".[6] *Kennedy* concerned the appointment, by the respondent body, of an accountant to investigate the affairs of a solicitor. The applicant argued that in appointing an accountant, the Society was seeking not merely to investigate his compliance with relevant professional legislation, but also his possible involvement in fraud. Importantly, when it came to providing the relevant test, Fennelly J held that where the improper

[8–07]

---

[2] *Hoey v Minister for Justice* [1994] 1 ILRM 334.
[3] *Cassidy v Minister for Industry and Commerce* [1978] IR 297.
[4] *ibid* at 309.
[5] *Kennedy v Law Society of Ireland (No.3)* [2002] 2 IR 458.
[6] *ibid* at 489.

purpose "materially influenced" the decision-maker, its decision was rendered void.

Uncertainty

[8–08]   A decision may also be quashed where its meaning cannot be reasonably ascertained. The primary examples of this in the Irish context have occurred in the specifying of conditions in planning permissions. In *Ashbourne Holdings v An Bord Pleanála*,[7] where a condition which would have required the operators of a golf club on the Old Head of Kinsale "access to the cliff path and cliff edges for interest groups". This was quashed by Kearns J on the grounds that the phrase "interest groups" was not properly defined, and no allowance appeared to have been made for the time and manner of such access, and how it would be practically delivered.[8]

[8–09]   It is important to note, that just as a decision can be uncertain, similarly its underlying reasoning can be found to have been too vague and uncertain. This may, logically, be viewed as a form of unreasonableness or a failure to take a relevant consideration into account. Yet, regardless of categorisation, it is, in some ways an area for possible development particularly given the growing obligations to provide reasons and undertake some sort of proportionality analysis. It may be that the failure to make a certain determination of intermediate issues, for example, is a ground for quashing the main decision. One instance of this may be *Ali v Minister for Justice, Equality & Law Reform*,[9] where the applicant successfully challenged a departmental decision to refuse his family reunification application. Despite the fact the applicant had been sending money transfers the decision-maker controversially found that "the frequency and amount of money transfers do not satisfactorily establish that the four subjects are financially dependent upon the refugee".[10] The official then immediately progressed to make a broader finding: that the applicant did not have sufficient income and resources to support and maintain the subjects of the application in the State, and recommended refusal. The Court ruled that the manner in which the decision was expressed made it difficult to identify the role which the first finding had played in reaching the second finding:

---

[7] *Ashbourne Holdings v An Bord Pleanála* [2003] 2 IR 114.

[8] *ibid* at 345.

[9] *Ali v Minister for Justice, Equality & Law Reform* [2011] IEHC 115.

[10] *ibid* at para 15.

"...Given the meagre resources of the applicant in this country, is it rational to suppose that he would part with the sums in question if he did not feel that the recipients were depending upon him to do so?...the uncertainty created by this conclusion is enhanced by the following finding that the refugee does not 'have sufficient income and resources to support and maintain the subject of the application in the State'. Had that been clearly identified as a factor considered in the exercise of the discretion to refuse, no problem would arise. However, because it is expressed in effective support of the consideration of dependency as 'financial dependency' there is sufficient ambiguity or lack of clarity in the decision to warrant it being reconsidered. It has been argued on behalf of the respondent that even if there was held to have been an error or ambiguity in the manner in which the issue as to the ability to support the subjects of the application was treated or expressed in the Contested Decision it ought not to be quashed because the Minister was in any event entitled to exercise his discretion to refuse on the basis of that factor. The Court cannot agree. It is not inconceivable that a different view of the application might have been taken if the author of the Consideration memorandum had first concluded that the sister and three children were in fact dependent family members."[11]

The uncertainty created by the muddled reasoning of the advisor could not be cured by the defence that there were other broader determinations which would have permitted the Minister to reach his decision. This is a significant case, underlying that an error on a subsidiary matter may taint an entire decision, if its role in the overall finding is not sufficiently explained. There may be opportunities to frame cases in terms of uncertainty, rather than attempting to argue that the entire decision being unreasonable or disproportionate as a result of the flawed sub-finding. **[8–10]**

The taint of uncertainty was also identified in *Meadows v Minister for Justice*, where Murray CJ found that the recommendation with which the memorandum submitted to the Minister with the file was "not helpful and adds to the opaqueness of the decision".[12] The memorandum merely stated that "refoulement was not found to be an issue in this case", a statement which was found to be singularly unwelcome by the Chief Justice: **[8–11]**

"This decision is open to multiple interpretations which would include one that refoulement was not an issue and therefore it did not require

---

[11] *ibid* at para 22.
[12] *Meadows v Minister for Justice* [2010] 2 IR 701 at 733.

any discretionary consideration. On the other hand it may well be that the Minister did consider refoulement an issue and that there was evidence of the appellant in this case being subject to some risk of being exposed to FGM but a risk that was so remote that being subject to FGM was unlikely: alternatively he may have considered that while there was evidence to put forward to suggest that the appellant might be subjected to FGM that evidence could be rejected as not being of sufficient weight or credibility to establish that there was any risk."[13]

What these cases illustrate is how the failure to clearly resolve points and state their implications as you move through a discretionary decision can create uncertainty which requires reconsideration.

Taking Irrelevant Considerations into Account/Failure to Take Relevant Considerations into Account

[8–12]   In reaching a decision, the considerations which a decision-maker legally should or should not take into account are dependent upon the statutory provisions applying, as well as the overarching purpose to those provisions. In addition to the four corners of the primary statute, however, recent years have underlined the European Convention on Human Rights Act 2003 or the EU Charter of Fundamental Rights often produce a powerful undertow of relevant considerations which may surprise a decision-maker unaccustomed to such frameworks. As we discuss in chapters 14 and 15, judges continue to debate the appropriate degree to which these generalist legal instruments need to be expressly invoked and reasoned through by decision-makers across the civil service. The restated requirement of proportionality would seem to require that they be weighed in balance in some way, even if they do not alter the overall result. In such a context, and more generally, mapping this ground of review accurately requires two questions to be answered:

1.   What are the relevant considerations for the decision-maker, particularly in the light of the purpose for which the statutory power was granted? Relatedly, what matters should be viewed as irrelevant?

2.   What does it mean to take a particular consideration into account?

---

[13] *ibid.*

Identifying Relevant and Irrelevant Considerations

Individual Rights

The constitutional rights of a person affected by the decision exert a **[8–13]** powerful influence on the generation of relevant considerations — as laid down in *State (Lynch) v Cooney*:

> "It is to be presumed that, when it conferred a statutory power, parliament intended the power to be exercised only in a manner that would be in conformity with the constitution and within the limitations of the power as they are to be gathered from the statutory scheme or design."[14]

The process of statutory interpretation in such instances of seemingly **[8–14]** vague and broad discretions was laid out most extensively in the landmark case of *East Donegal Co-operative Ltd v Attorney General*.[15] The primary Act in this case, the Livestock Marts Act 1967, gave broad discretion to the Minister to revoke or grant licences for the operation of marts. Walsh J laid down a powerful statement of the gravitational pull of the presumption of constitutionality and the broad context or purpose of an Act over such provisions:

> "The words of the Act, and in particular the general words, cannot be read in isolation and their content is to be derived from their context. Therefore words or phrases which at first sight might appear to be wide and general may be cut down in their construction when examined against the objects of the Act which are to be derived from a study of the Act as a whole including the long title."[16]

In examining the Act's provisions, Walsh J found that the statutory power **[8–15]** was anchored in considerations implicit in the surrounding provisions and context. Particularly useful was the statute's statement of conditions which could be attached to licences — logically these provisions signalled the grounds for the exercise of the Minister's broader power to refuse or grant. They included the right to ensure the mart was not too close to a place of worship, was not hazardous to traffic, to ensure the regulation of opening hours to avoid disruption to the local economy as well as conditions to ensure the interests of users and other members of the local economy were

---

[14] *State (Lynch) v Cooney* [1982] IR 337 at 380-381.

[15] *East Donegal Co-operative Livestock Marts Ltd v Attorney General* [1970] IR 317.

[16] *ibid* at 341.

protected. This was also supported by the regulation-making powers granted to the Minister under the Act which were anchored in the

> "proper conduct of the businesses concerned, the standards in relation to such places and to the provision of adequate and suitable accommodation and facilities for such auctions.".[17]

Thus a grant of a discretion to a Minister should be understood as follows:

> "All powers granted to the Minister by s. 3 which are prefaced or followed by the words "at his discretion" or "as he shall think proper" or "if he so thinks fit" are powers which may be exercised only within the boundaries of the stated objects of the Act; they are powers which cast upon the Minister the duty of acting fairly and judicial in accordance with the principles of constitutional justice, and they do not give an absolute or an unqualified or an arbitrary power to grant or refuse at his will…"[18]

[8–16] There is no doubt that since the *East Donegal* case was decided in 1970, the process of legislative drafting has undergone enormous changes. Ireland, in line with other jurisdictions, has more recently, seen a trend towards legislative hyperactivity — often linked to a desire to confine decision-makers to an exhaustively stated set of considerations which covers as many scenarios as possible. There are many possible reasons for this including the growing dominance of the executive arm in the creation of laws allows a greater receptivity to lobbying on the basis of bureaucratic convenience, as well as a logical desire to litigation proof statutes. Furthermore the influence of the civil law mindset — as manifested in its codified approach to legislation — has increased as the role of European Union instruments has expanded.

[8–17] The creation of National Asset Management Agency Act 2009 resulted in a considerable amount of commentary and case-law regarding how this crucial agency would go about wielding its extensive statutory powers. In *Dellway Investments v NAMA*,[19] which, as we see in chapter 10 of this book was a case centred on the constitutional implication of procedural fairness,[20]

---

[17] *ibid* at 342.

[18] *ibid* at 343-344.

[19] *Dellway Investments Ltd. v National Asset Management Agency* [2011] 4 IR 1. Hereinafter "*Dellway*".

[20] Another significant aspect of the case was the question of whether the Agency had in fact made a decision regarding the applicant's assets at all.

there was some significant discussion also of the nature of the statutory power granted to the Agency. Fennelly J noted that in order to find a right to procedural fairness, it was first necessary to analyse whether when acquiring an asset under the legislation, NAMA was "bound to consider" the interests of the borrower.[21] NAMA had submitted that the text of s 84, which gave the power to acquire assets, made the power exercisable exclusively in the interests of NAMA, with regard to the objectives of the Act. Section 84(1), it was argued, in effect rendered the interests of the borrower irrelevant, as it provided that:

"NAMA may acquire an eligible bank asset of a participating institution if NAMA considers it necessary or desirable to do so having regard to the purposes of this Act and in particular the resources available to the Minister. NAMA is not obliged to acquire any particular, or any, eligible bank asset of such an institution on any grounds."

The High Court judgment in the matter had appeared to accept NAMA's view that subsection rendered the interests of the borrower are irrelevant: **[8–18]**

"That NAMA has a discretion which it can exercise so as not to acquire an eligible bank asset is not doubted. It is necessary to analyse the Act to determine the factors that can or must properly be taken into account by NAMA in the exercise of that discretion. The Court has concluded that the purpose of the discretion, as a matter of statutory construction, is not one which is designed as a means of protecting customers of a participating credit institution. Rather, the discretion is designed to give to NAMA the possibility, at its own discretion, not to acquire assets where there is some good reason (consistent with the overall objectives and purpose of the Act) for not so doing".[22]

In the Supreme Court, NAMA argued that it was neither obligated, *nor* **[8–19]** *empowered*, to consider the interests of the borrower. This, it argued, was supported by the statement of discretionary considerations provided by s 84(4) of the Act, which it was submitted displayed

"an intention on the part of the Oireachtas that the discretion to exclude eligible assets be exercised for the benefit of NAMA".[23]

---

[21] Above n 19 at 314.
[22] [2010] IEHC 364, reported alongside the Supreme Court judgment at [2011] 4 IR 23 *et seq*. The cited statement appears at 51.
[23] Above n 19 at 318-319.

It is important at this juncture to cite s 84(4), which reads:'

> "Without prejudice to the generality of the subsection (1), NAMA may, in deciding whether to acquire a particular eligible bank asset, take into account –
>
> (a) whether any security that is part of the bank asset is adequate,
>
> (b) whether any security that is part of the bank asset has been perfected,
>
> (c) the value of that security,
>
> (d) whether the relevant credit facility documentation is defective or incomplete,
>
> (e) whether the participating institution concerned or any other person has engaged in conduct concerning the bank asset that is or could be prejudicial to the position of NAMA,
>
> (f) whether the participating institution has complied with its contractual and legal obligations and its obligations under this Act in relation to the bank asset, or its eligible bank assets generally,
>
> (g) whether in NAMA's opinion the participating institution has advanced a sufficient quantum of the credit facility concerned,
>
> (h) the quality of the title to any property held as security that is part of the bank asset,
>
> (i) any applicable legal, regulatory or planning requirement that has not been complied with in relation to development land held as security that is part of the bank asset,
>
> (j) any association with another bank asset of a participating institution,
>
> (k) the performance of the bank asset,
>
> (l) any matter disclosed in any due diligence carried out by the participating institution or NAMA,
>
> (m) the type of other eligible bank assets (whether of the participating institution or any other participating institution) that NAMA has acquired or proposes to acquire, and whether not acquiring the particular eligible bank asset concerned would contribute to the achievement of the purposes of this Act, and
>
> (n) any other matter that NAMA considers relevant."

[8–20] In perhaps the clearest example of the restrictive statutory interpretation technique NAMA advocated, it submitted that s 84(4)(n) did not permit it to consider the interests of the borrower, as the overarching context of the Act's purposes and provisions curtailed the apparent openness of the language. For the Agency to consider the interests of the borrower, would:

"...be fundamentally at odds with, and indeed undermine, the manner in which the Act must work in order to achieve its objectives and the ultimate goal of ridding the banks' balance sheets of problematic loans thereby addressing the systemic risk to the financial system".[24]

Fennelly J noted that by adopting such a position, whereby the interests of the borrower were not merely not a mandatory consideration, but were in fact an impermissible consideration, NAMA had "set itself a very high threshold".[25] Citing the landmark statements of law from *East Donegal* already outlined in this chapter, he concluded: [8–21]

> "...NAMA is incorrect in submitting that the Act, as a matter of statutory construction, precludes consideration by NAMA of the interests of a borrower whose loans are being acquired from the financial institution which made the loans.
>
> The Attorney General also argued that, by reason especially of the national economic emergency and the urgency of NAMA's work, the exclusion of the right to a hearing was justified. Nobody, of course, doubts the extreme seriousness of the burst of the property bubble, the financial crisis, the crisis in the public finances and the drastic effects of all these on the lives of citizens. However, we do not reach and do not need to consider, and I have not considered, whether the exclusion of the appellants' right to be heard would be justified, if it is not, in fact and in law, excluded. It is not necessary to justify an exclusion, if as here, there is no exclusion. For that reason, it is not necessary to consider whether the national financial emergency justifies it."[26]

Contradictory Material

In addition to considering the rights of the individual, another general category of relevant consideration that may arise is the obligation, in factual matters, to consider flatly contradictory material which is placed before the decision-maker. This arose in the case of *D.V.T.S. v Minister for Justice, Equality and Law Reform*,[27] where Edwards J held that information which directly contradicted the basis upon which an asylum refusal decision had issued ought to have been referred to by the decision-maker. [8–22]

---

[24] *ibid* at 320.
[25] *ibid*.
[26] *ibid* at 322-323.
[27] *DVTS v Minister for Justice, Equality and Law Reform* [2008] 3 IR 476.

Political Considerations

[8–23]   Another issue that has often arisen is the role of political considerations in the planning sphere. A fertile source for litigation has been the failure of local council to act judiciously in considering whether to vote to direct the Manager to grant Planning permission for a particular development under s 4 of the City and County Management Act 1955. In *Flanagan v Galway County Council*,[28] the elected members of the council had ordered the County Manager to provide planning permission on grounds of the special circumstances of the applicant. When the Manager refused to do this, the applicants sought a grant of mandamus from the High Court. Blayney J held that this could not be done, as the resolution of the elected members had taken into account irrelevant considerations — namely the submission that the applicant would have to emigrate if the permission was not forthcoming, when the statute permitted consideration of proper planning and development within the area.[29]

Consideration of Relevant Material Must Occur

[8–24]   Once relevant considerations have been identified, it is important to note that, generally, they must be taken into account. This imperative exists regardless of overall weakness of a party's case. In *AMSJ (Somalia) [No 2]*,[30] Clark J, held that even where a Tribunal Member disbelieved claims of past persecution, it was necessary to consider all relevant considerations exhaustively:

> "The decision simply states that the Tribunal Member was not satisfied as to the appellant's credibility in relation to the claim advanced by him. The reader is thus left wondering…whether [the Tribunal Member] was so unimpressed by the claim made that he simply did not address his mind to the question of ethnicity at all."[31]

[8–25]   Negative findings in relation to credibility could not be allowed to crowd out other relevant considerations which the decision-maker was bound to take into account:

---

[28] *Flanagan v Galway County Council* [1990] 2 IR 66.

[29] Similar cases include *P & F Sharpe Limited v County Manager* [1989] IR 701 and *Griffin v Galway County Manager* (Unreported judgment, 31 October 1990, Blayney J.)

[30] *AMSJ (Somalia) [No 2]* [2012] IEHC 453.

[31] *ibid* at para 13.

> "While it is very important for an asylum seeker to tell the truth, it is also important for the protection decision-maker to separate those aspects of an applicant's narrative which have been found not to be plausible or credible from those aspects of the case which are accepted. Thus, a decision-maker may be satisfied as to the origin of the applicant but might reach the conclusion that the narrative of past persecution is implausible and lacking credibility. The decision-maker must provide a reasoned determination on the issue that notwithstanding the accepted origins of the applicant, the claim is not sustainable."[32]

Aside from enforcing the relevant statutory requirements, the Court in requiring a determination of ethnicity in this case, was also preventing possible negative consequences for the applicant at the humanitarian stage, where the Minister for Justice would rely upon the facts determined by the Tribunal to consider whether to deport the applicant. It is worth stressing that while this judgment stresses the importance of considering relevant considerations, the courts still retain a discretion to rule that an omission or error is truly insignificant; and therefore deny a remedy while severing the irrelevant consideration from the record of the decision.   [8–26]

Inflexible Application of a Policy/Fettering a Discretion

One particular instance of failing to take into account relevant considerations occurs where a decision-maker allows a departmental or organizational policy to crowd out consideration of other relevant matters. This ground balances two underlying imperatives of public administration: the need for consistency (particularly in high volume decision-making areas); and the requirement of individualized justice. For the purposes of judicial review, it is clear that the former aim is ascendant — a Minister may create policy rules which guide the exercise of discretion in his Department, and indeed these internal "soft law" documents have come to effectively dominate many Government decision-makers' working lives. Nevertheless, decision-makers remain under an obligation to maintain an "open mind" about varying a policy where individual circumstances or the interests of justice require it.[33] As Keane CJ commented in *Glencar Explorations plc v Mayo County Council (No. 2)*:   [8–27]

---

[32] *ibid* at para 16.
[33] The dueling requirements were well summarized by Keane J in *Carrigaline Community Television Broadcasting Company Ltd v Minister for Transport, Energy and Communications* [1997] 1 ILRM 241 at 284:

"... The fact that it [the respondent] is obliged to have regard to policies and objectives of the Government or a particular minister does not mean that, in every case, it is obliged to implement the policies and objectives in question. If the Oireachtas had intended such an obligation to rest on the planning authority in a case such as the present, it would have said so."[34]

[8–28] The landmark statement of the fundamentals of this ground of review remains that provided by Kelly J in *Mishra v The Minister for Justice*:

"In my view there is nothing in law which forbids the Minister upon whom the discretionary power...is conferred to guide the implementation of that discretion by means of a policy or set of rules. However, care must be taken to ensure that the application of this policy or rules does not disable the Minister from exercising her discretion in individual cases. In other words, the use of a policy or set of fixed rules does not fetter the discretion which is conferred by the Act. Neither, in my view, must the application of those rules produce a result which is fundamentally at variance with the evidence placed before the Minister by an applicant."[35]

[8–29] In *McVeigh v Minister for Justice, Equality and Law Reform*,[36] the applicants had been refused permission to import a high caliber rifle into the State on the basis that this was contrary to established policy. The High Court had ruled that an inflexible approach had not been proved on the facts.[37] The Supreme Court however, held that the Minister's discretion had been fettered by inappropriate policy considerations. The Minister had indicated

---

"In the case of this and similar licensing regimes, the adoption by the licensing authority of a policy could have the advantage of ensuring some degree of consistency in the operation of the regime, thus making less likely decisions that might be categorized as capricious or arbitrary. But it is also clear that inflexible adherence to such a policy may result in a countervailing injustice. The case law in both this jurisdiction and the United Kingdom illustrates the difficulties in balancing these competing values."

[34] *Glencar Explorations plc v Mayo County Council (No. 2)* [2002] 1 IR 84 at 142.

[35] *Mishra v The Minister for Justice* [1996] 1 IR 189 at 205.

[36] *McVeigh v Minister for Justice, Equality and Law Reform* [2010] IESC 28. The appeal involved three separate applicants, with only Mr McVeigh being successful; the other two cases were dismissed on the facts.

[37] *McCarron v Kearney* [2008] IEHC 195 per Charleton J at para 19:
"An individual superintendent ..., retains authority over his own discretion. That must be respected unless there is evidence of improper conduct. I am not satisfied that the respondent in any way fettered his discretion as to the issue of firearm certificates. Rather, it seems to me, that he exercised a sensible policy through an individual decision which is within the terms of legislation concerned with the public good. It is a reasonable, lawful and sensible practice for those who have to decide on applications to exercise privileges at law to have regard to a set of guiding principles."

that any licence to import would not be granted without a firearm certificate for the weapon being granted by a local superintendent. His letter then noted that the current policy was that firearm certificates would only be given for certain rifles, and the applicants' weapon fell outside these categories. Inflexible application was evidenced firstly by the fact that the Minister had referred to a single unified policy in relation to such firearms when:

> "...the Minister had no function in the grant of firearms certificates and, a fortiori, in formulating such policies. Moreover, there could not, at that time, be a single policy. The function was allotted to Garda Superintendents in their own individual districts. I do not say that it was impermissible for the Minister to have regard to the need for any person possessing or using a firearm to have a firearms certificate, granted by his local superintendent. If the Minister had formulated the matter differently by referring, for example, to the unlikelihood of being granted a certificate, his decision might have been defensible. Since that situation did no arise, it is unnecessary to decide a hypothetical case."[38]

Evidence before the court which was suggestive of inflexibility included the failure to afford the applicant the chance to make submissions, as such an omission can infer a lack of openness: **[8–30]**

> 'The Minister offered the applicant no opportunity to address the possibility of any exception to the policy or the merits of the particular firearm. Indeed, it could be said that the communications between the appellant and the Minister had some of the character of a dialogue of the deaf. The appellant surprisingly made no effort to explain his need to import a Westley Richards double barrel .470 calibre rifle. On all the evidence in these cases, this was a high calibre weapon. Indeed Mr. Kelly's affidavit suggests that it was a weapon for use primarily for the shooting of heavy game, such as elephants. The Minister, for his part, did not propose to open any dialogue with the appellant. In any event it is quite clear that the Minister's decision as communicated was infected by the vice of inflexibility."[39]

---

[38] Above n 36 at para 70.

[39] *ibid* at paras 71-73. Similarly in *Ezenwaka v Minister for Justice, Equality and Law Reform,* [2011] IEHC 328, Hogan J found the Minister had unduly fettered his discretion in rigidly applying the policy that the Irish Born Child Scheme could not apply to second and subsequent families, but was focused only on immediate families. Crucially, immigration officials viewed this Ministerial position as dispositive and "[t]he Ezenwakas were given no effective opportunity to address the possibility that an exception should have been made in their case" (at para 19).

[8–31]   This notion of a 'dialogue of the deaf' is supported by a much older UK authority, the statement of Bankes LJ in *R v Port of London Authority, ex parte Kynoch*:

> "There are on the one hand cases where a tribunal in the honest exercise of its discretion has adopted a policy, and, without refusing to hear an applicant, intimates to him what its policy is, and that after hearing him it will in accordance with its policy decide against him, unless there is something exceptional in his case. I think counsel for the applicants would admit that, if the policy has been adopted for reasons which the tribunal may legitimately entertain, no objection could be taken to such a course. On the other hand there are cases where a tribunal has passed a rule, or come to a determination, not to hear any application of a particular character by whomsoever made. There is a wide distinction to be drawn between these two classes."[40]

[8–32]   The mere willingness to hear submissions on a matter does not however rule out a fettering of discretion. In the case of *Whelan v Fitzpatrick & Anor*,[41] a District Court judge had, in rejecting an application for legal aid certification, stressed that he did not give legal aid in driving cases. Counsel for the respondent submitted that this comment should be interpreted as a general view that legal aid would not be granted automatically, and relied on the fact that the judge had embarked on a process of considering the matter, which was an indicator of an open mind. Budd J refused to accept this stance on the facts:

> "The simple and clear meaning of the pronouncement that the first named respondent did not give legal aid in driving cases, is that he meant what he said and so had made his mind up to refuse the application for legal aid. A judge is expected (and obliged by law as decided by the Supreme Court), to give reasons for his decision. The learned District Court Judge in this case gave no other reason for his decision. He did explore the means of the applicant to the extent that he said that if the applicant could afford a car, he could afford a solicitor. However, this misconception on his part was cleared up by counsel informing the court of his instructions that the applicant did not own the car in question and from the context of the statement of means the court must have been well aware that the applicant, who may be jeopardy of a custodial sentence if convicted, was relatively impecunious. Furthermore it was clear that he was facing a grave offence of a nature that there may be technical defences available or

---

[40] *R v Port of London Authority, ex parte Kynoch* [1919] 1 KB 176 at 184.
[41] *Whelan v Fitzpatrick & Anor* [2008] 2 IR 678.

even defences on the merits which an experienced lawyer would be able to draw to the court's attention. The tenor of the proceedings as outlined in the affidavit is that the learned District Court Judge did improperly fetter his discretion at the threshold by asserting and imposing a fourth criterion namely that 'being charged in a driving case was a bar to receiving legal aid.'"[42]

An approach which can be characterized as more receptive to a decision-makers perspective was seen in *Crofton v Minister for the Environment, Heritage and Local Government*.[43] Here, the applicants alleged that the Minister had inflexibly applied a no-shooting policy on State lands, including those lands which the State had recently acquired which had been used for shooting up until their transfer into State hands. This policy was legally permissible under s 11(2) of the State Property Act 1954.[44] The question before the Court was whether the Minister had accompanied his invocation of the policy with an openness to making a possible exception. Hedigan J held that the fact that the Minister had held a single meeting with the applicant (the Director of the National Association of Regional Games Council) was sufficient evidence of engagement with the possibility of making an exception. The meeting had been called to discuss a report of a Scientific Review Group on Hunting, which recommended the varying of the policy. Yet, the Minister, at the meeting, had indicated that he had not considered the report in any detail, and would not be engaged further on whether the policy would be changed. Care needs to be exercised with the use of this judgment in the future, as it raises the prospect that mere pro forma steps can signal an open mind — the applicant here clearly believed that "a dialogue of the deaf" was all the meeting ultimately represented. Formal consultations may not be accompanied by the relevant mental state of "considering" the making of an exception, and the reasoning of the eventual decision should also be analysed by reference to the expectations of the relevant statute.

[8–33]

---

[42] *ibid* at 704-5.
[43] *Crofton v Minister for the Environment, Heritage and Local Government* [2009] IEHC 114, Judgment of Hedigan J, 10 March 2009.
[44] This allows the Minister to determine whether and to what extent, access to and activities on State lands should be restricted.

Unwritten Policy and Organisational Cultures

[8–34]   Cases in this area are largely driven by factual inquiry, and as Judge J stated
in the UK case of *R v London Borough of Harrow ex parte Collymore* the
question for the Court is not whether the authority has an absolute policy
on paper but whether it operates a fettered discretion in fact.[45] The possible
role of requests under freedom of information legislation in overcoming
the burden of proof in proving more inchoate forms of inflexible policy was
seen most prominently in the recent case of *B v Minister for Social Protection*.[46]
The applicant in this case was the mother of an autistic child who had had
their application for a domiciliary care allowance rejected.[47] In deciding
whether the child's disability rose to the necessary level of severity to
qualify for the payment, the deciding officer was required to have regard
to the opinion of the medical assessor on the issue of severity.[48] In the
applicant's case, the deciding officer followed the finding of the medical
assessor that the child did not, as required by the statute, need "continuous
care and attention substantially in excess of the care and attention normally
required by a child of the same age".[49] On review, the applicant contended
that the Department "in effect operates a policy whereby the opinions of its
medical assessors are following slavishly by Department deciding officers,
irrespective of the evidence submitted by claimants".[50] This alleged policy
represented an abdication of statutory duty.[51] In support, the applicant's
solicitors undertook freedom of information requests, submitting by
affidavit that the officer believed to have taken the decision to reject the
application had, over the course of 3,806 decisions, never departed "from
the Medical Assessor's opinion in any of the decisions nor did any of the
other Deciding officers referred to in that Freedom of Information

---

[45] *R v London Borough of Harrow ex parte Collymore* [1995] ELR 217 at 227.

[46] *B v Minister for Social Protection* [2014] IEHC 186.

[47] This payment is administered under s 186C(1) of the Social Welfare Consolidation Act 2005.
The qualification requirements are, inter alia, that:
   (a) the applicant child has a severe disability requiring continual or continuous care
        and attention substantially in excess of the care and attention normally required by
        a child of the same age,
   (b) the level of disability caused by that severe disability is such that the child is likely
        to require full-time care and attention for at least 12 consecutive months.

[48] Under s 186C(3)

[49] Social Welfare (Miscellaneous Provisions) Act 2010, s 186C(1)(a).

[50] Above n 46 at para 8.

[51] s 300 of the Social Welfare Consolidation Act 2005 provided that "Subject to this Act, every
question to which this section refers [which includes domcilliary care allowance decisions]
shall, save where the context otherwise requires, be decided by a deciding officer."

request".[52] A later freedom of information request resulted in the Department stating that:

> "Notwithstanding that accurate statistics on this issue are not readily available; the Department considers that it would be highly unusual for a deciding officer to decide against a medical assessor's opinion on the question of medical eligibility."[53]

In addition to this information, aspects of an affidavit sworn by the assistant principal of the department was also found by the Court to support the application's contention of an unreflective culture within the Department. In particular, the affidavit commented that, in the applicant's case: **[8–35]**

> "There is in fact no conflict of medical evidence — rather there is a difference between the opinion formed by the Applicant's doctors *who understandably are advocating on behalf of the Applicant* and her son and the opinion of the Medical Assessor whose function is to provide to the Deciding Officer an independent medical opinion having assessed the information and facts provided."[54]

Barrett J strongly condemned this statement, pausing "to note just how remarkable the underlined averment is", in light of the fact that the applicant's documentation included testimony from a GP and a specialist multidisciplinary HSE team who had all met the child personally, and whom the court stressed were offering *"bona fide,* properly reasoned professional opinions".[55] In response to such submissions, it appeared to Barrett J that the: "Department apparently adopts a disdainful mind-set and prefers instead the desk-top reviews of its own medical assessors who have no personal knowledge of the individual case at hand."[56]   **[8–36]**

The deputy principal's affidavit also sought to justify why it would be unusual for a Deciding Officer to differ from the medical assessor. Medical assessors were doctors of at least six years practice and the statute required deciding officers to have regard to their opinions. Furthermore reliance was placed upon the fact that: **[8–37]**

---

[52] Affidavit of solicitor Gareth Noble cited at para 9 in the judgment, above n 46.

[53] *ibid* at para 10.

[54] *ibid* at para 11 (emphasis in the original judgment).

[55] *ibid* at para 12.

[56] *ibid.*

> "Deciding officers in any given case have the option of discussing the matter with the Medical Assessor involved before any individual decision is made. Therefore if a Deciding Officer has any issue with the Medical Assessor' opinion…the Deciding Officer can discuss and clarify the basis for their opinion with the Medical Assessor. This may and can lead to the Medical Assessor revising their opinion or satisfying the Deciding Officer with regard to his/her concerns. Alternatively, a deciding Officer can refer the case to another medical assessor for a second opinion if desired."[57]

[8–38]   Barrett J, in response to this submission, stated that "it might perhaps be queried how competent non-medically qualified deciding officers are to assess and/or test the views of medically qualified assessors".[58] His Honour ultimately found that one would expect to see some disparity of views, and was fortified by the freedom of information request finding adherence by the particular initial deciding officer with the medical assesser in 3,806 out of 3,806 cases. The "almost disdainful" reference to the applicant's medical evidence in the deputy principal's affidavit was also cited by Barrett J in ruling that not all relevant considerations were taken into account. In concluding his judgment, his Honour elected to supplement the finding of an inflexible policy with a more serious finding that, in fact, the deference shown towards the medical assessors constituted an abdication of the Deciding Officers' statutory duty, not merely an inflexible exercise of it. In so finding, his Honour ruled that the medical assessor's opinion had been entirely determinative in B's application. The case clearly stands as a powerful instance where a judicial review action has critically examined the prevailing culture and institutional arrangements of first instance decision-making in Irish Government departments.

What Does it Mean to Consider? Issues of Weight and Depth

A Question of Fact

[8–39]   In order to bring this chapter to a close, we will now analyse the depth of the obligation to "consider". Will merely mentioning a matter suffice? What indicates adequate consideration? In commencing this analysis, it is important to first signal that the question of whether the decision-maker took a relevant factor into account is often a factual one — and is often linked to the right to reasons. An example of a basic instance of a failure to

---

[57] *ibid* at para 13.
[58] *ibid* at para 14.

take into account a relevant matter is *Butcher v The Minister for Justice and Equality.*[59] In this case, a convicted murderer imprisoned in an Irish jail applied, as permitted by statute, to serve the balance of his sentence in the UK. The Department took the view that the decision to transfer was a discretionary one which did not engage the applicant's right to family life under Article 8 ECHR. This position may have been based on the earlier Irish High Court case of *Nash* where Kearns J had held:

> "…the court is quite satisfied that no issue of fundamental human rights arises in the instant case. The applicant is serving two life sentences for two different murders in respect of which he was convicted after a trial in the Central Criminal Court and in respect of which no appeal was brought. It has not been suggested that any issue of fundamental rights or constitutional rights would arise in any situation where the applicant was required to serve out his sentence in one location rather than another in this jurisdiction".[60]

Crucially, however, since the judgment in *Nash*, European Court on Human   **[8–40]** Rights' decisions, *Dickson v UK*[61] and *Hirst v UK (No 2)*,[62] had established that decisions regarding prisoners did engage Article 8 rights, which had to be considered and then balanced against the public interest. This had not occurred in the Department's decision in *Butcher*, where the High Court ruled:

> "In this case the respondent has not stated, either to the applicant or to his solicitor, or by way of affidavit, whether he gave consideration to the applicant's family rights and if so, how he balanced them against the public interest identified by him in upholding the full term of the sentence imposed by the Irish Court…The Statement of Opposition specifically pleads that the evidence placed before the respondent in the application for transfer was tenuous and not sufficient to engage a consideration by the respondent of Article 8. This leads almost inevitably to an inference that consideration was not given to this aspect. That, in turn, quite apart from Convention considerations, leads to the conclusion that the decision was not made 'within the spirit and intent of the Act'."[63]

---

[59] *Butcher v The Minister for Justice and Equality* [2012] IEHC 347.
[60] *Nash v Minister for Justice. Equality and Law Reform* [2004] 3 IR 296 at 310.
[61] *Dickson v UK* (2008) 46 EHRR 41.
[62] *Hirst v UK (No 2)* (2006) 42 EHRR 849.
[63] Above n 59 at para 42.

[8–41]   Interestingly, the Court also rejected the contention that the discounting of the relevance of Article 8 was down to the conduct of the applicant:

> "It is indeed true that the information given in the application form was scant — however, the form itself does not allow space for much more. There is no suggestion on the face of the form that, for example, it could be accompanied by a letter setting out the applicant's circumstances in more detail. The only reference to additional material is in relation to official documents such as birth certificates and passports. Since it is likely that prisoners in the position of the applicant will be filling out the form without the assistance of a lawyer it is important that they be given the chance to make their case properly. In any event, it would have been open to the respondent to ask for more information if he felt that what was provided was insufficient."[64]

Its Relationship with Proportionality/Reasonableness

[8–42]   The question of what actually amounts to "considering" a matter is so context and fact specific that it is perhaps best only to note its centrality, and how the extent of the obligation to take something into account is influenced by the overarching standard of review e.g. be it intensive proportionality analysis or deference based reasonableness. Such a dynamic was seen in the deportation context in *Oguekwe v Minister for Justice*,[65] where Denham J mapped the obligation to consider all relevant factors in deporting the parents of an Irish citizen child, who is likely to be forced to relocate outside the country as a result:

> "I would affirm the decision that the consideration of the Minister should be fact specific to the individual child, his or her age, current educational progress, development and opportunities. This consideration not only to educational issues but also involves the consideration of the attachment of the child to the community, and other matters referred to in section 3 of the [Immigration Act 1999].
>
> The extent of the consideration will depend on the facts of the case, including the age of the child, the length of time he or she has been in the State, and the part, if any, he or she has taken in the community. Thus, his or her education, and development within the State, within the context of his or her family circumstances, may be relevant. If the child has been in the State for many years, and in the school system for

---

[64] *ibid* at para 43.
[65] *Oguekwe v Minister for Justice* [2008] 3 IR 795.

several years, and taken part in the community, then these and related facts may be very pertinent. However, if the child is an infant then such considerations will not arise.

However, I respectfully disagree with the learned High Court judge and I believe the High Court erred, in holding that the Minister was required to inquire into and take into account the educational facilities and other conditions available to the Irish born child of a proposed deportee in the country of return, in the event that the child accompany the deportee. I am satisfied that while the Minister should consider in a general fashion the situation in the country where the child's parent may be deported, it is not necessary to do a specific analysis of the educational and development opportunities that would be available to the child in the country of return. The Minister is not required to inquire in detail into the educational facilities of the country of the deportee. This general approach does not exclude a more detailed analysis in an exceptional case. The decision of the Minister is required to be proportionate and reasonable on the application as a whole, and not on the specific factor of comparative educational systems."[66]

Thus, the review of the reasoning process is shaped by the reasonableness **[8–43]** ground — one could summarise the requirement as not being the taking into account of all relevant factors, but the requirement to take into account all relevant factors necessary to justify a decision as proportionate or reasonable, together with those factors which are required by the statute. This underlines the systemic impact of any recalibration of the reasonableness ground and why we later use the term "setting the frame" to describe recent battles over the meaning of reasonableness and proportionality in Irish law. The obligation to take all relevant factors into account is a processual safeguard which ensures that the substantive requirement of proportionality or reasonableness is enforced. Yet, it is clear from Denham J's statement above, that the courts will take care not to micromanage proportionality analysis by examining each intermediate conclusion featured in a decision. Such an approach could lead to an encrusting of administrative decision-making with required matters — leading decision-makers to chase a box-ticking compliance with judicially required elements of analysis. Yet, we would argue that how the decision-maker considers the evidence should raise or lower the deference to be shown by the court. When looking at proportionality as a whole — instead of deferring to the expertise of the decision-maker because of *who* they are,

---

[66] *ibid* at 818.

the courts should set the level of deference according to *skill and sensitivity to context* that the decision-maker has manifested in the particular case before the court. This would help ensure that decisions are well-supported and encourage the supply of extensive justifications within the public service.

[8–44] Returning to the deportation context, which is of course an area which attracts significant judicial scrutiny, the judgment of Cooke J in *AO v Minister for Justice, Equality and Law Reform* perhaps generated an indication of possible instances where a decision-maker might *fail to consider* a matter:

> "No factor pertinent [to the daughter's] personal or family rights under the Constitution or her right to respect for private and family life under the Constitution has been *distorted, exaggerated or omitted* from consideration in the Court's judgment. Having regard to those circumstances and to the personal history of the family members it cannot be tenably maintained that the contested decision is either unreasonable or disproportionate."[67]

[8–45] The notion of the court assessing whether a consideration has been *exaggerated or distorted* might have struck one as quite rare under the old *O'Keeffe* standard of reasonableness. We submit however, that post-*Meadows* the spotlighting of the requirement of proportionality should alert practitioners to the fact that such findings may be more common. In order to balance competing interests, the decision-maker must not just acknowledge a consideration but must, to some extent, also weigh them adequately. Clearly a court will identify the detail required according to the seriousness of the matter and the statutory language applying. This reflects the fact that whereas *Keegan* and *O'Keeffe* required merely that all relevant matters be considered and that *a reason* for the overall decision be identified, proportionality may require a reasoning process which constructs a basic 'balance sheet' of interests. This would identify in some, if minimal, way the *value of or weight attached* to the relevant pros and cons of a decision. We will return to such possible implications of proportionality balancing later in the next chapter.

[8–46] Yet, until the issue of how *Meadows* interacts with the obligation to take all relevant considerations into account is determined, reliance can be placed upon earlier cases which appear to urge judges to avoid getting into issues

---

[67] [2010] IEHC 89 at para 57, emphasis added.

of weight. The clearest example of this is the 2006 case of *Kildare County Council v An Bord Pleanála*, where McMenamin J stated that the question of weight, other than a perverse inflation or deflation of a particular consideration that tipped the entire decision into irrationality,[68] was a question for the decision-maker:

> "The weight which ought to be attached to the objectives in the context of the Board's assessment of the proposed road development plan is a matter for the Board. Thus while relevance is a matter of law for the court, weight is a matter of discretion for the decision-maker."[69]

In making this statement, McMenamin J relied on UK authorities, many of which were decided prior to the introduction of the UK Human Rights Act 1998. Foremost amongst these was the then House of Lords judgment in *Tesco Stores Limited v Secretary of State for the Environment*: **[8–47]**

> "It is for the courts, if the matter is brought before them, to decide what is a relevant consideration. If the decision maker wrongly takes the view that some consideration is not relevant, and therefore has no regard to it, the decision cannot stand and must be required to think again. But it is entirely for the decision maker to attribute to the relevant consideration such weight as he thinks fit, and the courts will not interfere unless he has acted unreasonably in the *Wednesbury* sense... regard must be had to (material considerations)...but the extent, if any, to which it should effect the decision is a matter entirely within the discretion of the decision maker."[70]

---

[68] This principle was established in the context of environmental impact assessment by McKechnie J in *Kenny v An Bord Pleanála (No. 2)* [2001] 1 IR 407 which approved judgments of the courts of England and Wales such as *R v Rochdale Metropolitan Borough Council ex parte Millne* [2001] 81 P & CR 27, where it was stated by Pill and Chadwick LJ:

> "In my judgment what is sufficient is a matter of fact and degree. There is no blue print which requires a particular amount of information to be supplied. What is necessary depends on the nature of the project and whether, given the wording of (article 2 of the Directive), enough information is supplied to enable the decision making body to assess the effect of the particular project on the environment. I agree with Sullivan J. that the court cannot place itself in the position of reconsidering the detailed factual matters considered by the planning authority. Equally I accept that the court does have a role and there may be cases where the court can and should intervene and hold that *no reasonable local authority could have been satisfied with the amount of information which it was supplied in the circumstances of the particular case.'"

[69] *Kildare County Council v An Bord Pleanála* [2006] IEHC 173 at para 49.

[70] *Tesco Stores Limited v Secretary of State for the Environment* [1995] 1 WLR 759 per Lord Keith at 769. He also quoted Lord Hoffman's statement that:

> "the law has always made a clear distinction between the question of whether something is a material consideration and the weight which it should be given. The former is a question of law and the latter is a question of proper judgment which is entirely a matter

[8–48]   The fact that these authorities emanate from planning law must of course be underlined — the *O'Keeffe* case has long designated the area as one of the most inappropriate contexts for judicial intervention. In addition to citing the United Kingdom authority above, McMenamin J stressed the specific context of planning as entirely unsuited to any assessment of weight, an approach which likely prevails after the Supreme Court judgment in *Meadows*.

The Role of the Statutory Language

[8–49]   The statutory language which applies to the decision will also play a role — for instance, does the statute require the Minister to have regard, to give "due regard", to take matters into account? Or does it require compelling public interests or that the aim being pursued by the decision-maker be of sufficient importance to override other interests? In the latter contexts, the courts may require a more extensive consideration of how to construe and value the interests in question. Once these contextual factors are taken into account, and the relevant factors are considered, the court will then ask the question, would a reasonable authority, required to carry out a proportionality analysis of the interests involved, have been satisfied with the information before it or would it have devoted more time to analysing the factor?

[8–50]   Perhaps the most developed example of this reasoning process in action is *McCallig v An Bord Pleanála*.[71] While this case provides a developed account of how to recognise whether a relevant consideration has been taken into account, the authors would stress that the case overly emphasises a narrow interpretation of *Keegan/O'Keeffe* reasonableness and not the *Meadows* restatement. While a narrow approach to reasonableness might be appropriate in the planning context, it would be welcome to see the *Meadows* case referenced in such cases.

[8–51]   *McCallig* concerned the adequacy of information contained in an environmental impact assessment of a proposed wind farm prepared for the notice party, Donegal County Council. The applicant argued that a bird survey and report in the environmental impact statement were

---

for the planning authority…(provided it does not lapse into Wednesbury irrationality)."
ibid at 779.
[71] *McCallig v An Bord Pleanála* [2013] IEHC 60. Hereinafter "*McCallig*".

"not sufficiently comprehensive as regards the presence on the area of the proposed development of breeding birds and raptors, and that no assessment had been carried out as to the impact of the wind-farm, including aviation warning lights, on birds in the vicinity".[72]

The argument that this approach was insufficient was further supported, the applicant argued, by the requirement of EU Council Directive 85/337/E.E.C as amended by Council Directive 97/11/EC, that an actual assessment be undertaken on foot of sufficient information. Where insufficient information for that purpose was provided in the environmental impact statement, (EIS) the situation should not be remedied by imposing mitigatory planning permission conditions. The applicant pointed to the admission of the Planning Inspector that:

[8–52]

> "The inadequacy of the bird surveys has been extensively criticised in the submissions. I accept that the surveys are far from robust due to their limited duration, taken outside the recommended times etc. The Board will note that there is no information on migratory species, flight paths etc. and no reference to the recently reintroduced Golden Eagle. I accept that an all year round survey provides a greater level of detail and provides confidence that all significant features have been identified. Whilst the lack of detail on avifauna is noted by the Department of Environment, Heritage and Local Government, no issues with regard to particular species were raised. It was considered sufficient that a management plan for land/habitat be agreed prior to the commencement of development on the site. I note that the imposition of this type of condition has been considered acceptable in the past by the Board."[73]

The applicant argued that "the sufficiency of the information" contained in the EIS was an issue that went to jurisdiction.[74] It was acknowledged that "a question of quantitative assessment of information in the environmental

[8–53]

---

[72] *ibid* at para 47.

[73] *ibid* at para 92.

[74] "Article 94 of the Planning and Development Regulations 2001, set out the mandatory requirements for an environmental impact statement by reference to the provisions of the Sixth Schedule of those Regulations. Para 1(c) of the Sixth Schedule provides that an environmental impact statement must contain, 'data required to identify and assess the main effects which the proposed development is likely to have on the environment'. At para. 2(b) of the Schedule there is a further requirement that information by way of explanation or amplification of this information must also be furnished providing a description of the aspects of the environment likely to be significantly affected by the proposed development, including, in particular fauna and cultural heritage." *ibid* at para 97.

impact of statement" was not a matter for judicial intervention.[75] Here, however, Article 111(i) of the Planning and Development Regulations 2001, provided that An Bord Pleanála shall consider whether an environmental impact statement received by it in connection with an appeal complies with Article 94 and if not so satisfied may issue a notice under s 132 of the Planning and Development Act 2000, requiring an applicant to, "submit such further information as may be necessary to comply with the relevant Article". Such a request had not been made in this case.

[8–54]   Herbert J relied upon the ruling of MacMenamin J in the *Kildare County Council v An Bord Pleanála* case, that for a court to intervene on grounds of insufficiency of information it would have to find that the failure to seek new information "plainly and unambiguously flew in the face of fundamental reason and common sense".[76] The applicant would have to show that the failure to seek further information was one "which no rational or sane decision maker, no matter how misguided", would have made.[77] In the circumstances of the *McCallig* case, Herbert J ruled that this burden had not been met.

[8–55]   More positively, *RMK v Refugee Appeals Tribunal & Anor*, seems to indicate that courts will assess the decision to reject an item of evidence for reasonableness.[78] The review in question was the second taken, with an earlier review having quashed the first tribunal decision in the matter for a failure to adequately consider three medical reports created by doctors and the NGO group SPIRASI. These found, inter alia, physical scarring "highly consistent or typical of" abuse the applicant alleged had taken place.[79] The matter was remitted to the Tribunal for a fresh decision, which the applicant now challenged, again, for failure to consider the reports adequately. On this occasion it was alleged that the report was not adequately considered due to the fact that the Tribunal member had rejected them in the light of other factors, namely the applicant's overall credibility and the probability that the jail he claimed to have been housed in, may have in fact been

---

[75] *Kenny v An Bord Pleanála (No. 1)* [2001] 1 IR 565 and *Kenny v An Bord Pleanála (No. 2)* [2001] 1 IR 704.

[76] Above n 69 referencing *The State (Keegan) v Stardust Compensation Tribunal* [1986] IR 642 at 658 and *O'Keeffe v An Bord Pleanála* [1993] 1 IR 39.

[77] *ibid* at para 100.

[78] *RMK v Refugee Appeals Tribunal & Anor* [2010] IEHC 367.

[79] *ibid* at para 11.

closed. The Court considered whether the emphasis upon these negative findings justified the failure to value the medical evidence:

> "Ultimately the Court has found this a difficult case and has been particularly mindful that the assessment of credibility and the weight to be attached to documents is a matter entirely for the Tribunal Member…if the [jail] had in fact been closed in 2001, the applicant's account would fall apart. The Tribunal Member did not come down on either side in relation to the closure of the detention facility and expressly allowed for the possibility that it remained partially open in secret despite the Presidential Decree. He did not in fact prefer one COI report over another. That being so, he allowed for the possibility that the applicant was a prisoner in the [jail] and for his torture and ill treatment there. There can be no doubt that the closure is inextricably linked to the importance and weight of the SPIRASI report when all the evidence is viewed as a whole. It seems to the Court that if the applicant could in fact have been a prisoner in 2003, then the countervailing evidence rationalising a rejection of the SPIRASI report is simply not strong enough to outweigh its acceptance. With some hesitation, the Court is obliged to find that the decision to reject the medical evidence in the manner expressed by the Tribunal member is irrational. The Court concludes that the Tribunal Member failed to adequately consider the medical evidence and that his decision on the GLM *lacks the strength and clarity required* to reject the contents of the SPIRASI medical reports."[80]

Thus, it appears that a justificatory burden may arise where evidence that is objectively quite central to the overall claim is rejected.

The Impact of Incorrect Findings on the Overall Decision

There are instances where the courts have adopted a pragmatic approach to reviewing instances where a decision-maker picks up a "red-herring" as part of an otherwise unimpeachable decision. In such instances, the flexible nature of judicial review remedies allows judges to avoid what they might view as disproportionate reactions. Such an approach was seen *SIA (Sudan) v Refugee Appeals Tribunal*.[81] In this case, the Tribunal Member had made a number of very adverse findings in relation to the applicant's credibility, which the court upheld on review. Despite the fact that this overarching justification for rejection could not be impugned, the Court was critical of the inconsistency in the later finding that the applicant could

[8–56]

---

[80] *ibid* at paras 26-28.
[81] *SIA (Sudan) v Refugee Appeals Tribunal* [2012] IEHC 488.

internally relocate in the Port Sudan area. It was illogical, following a finding that a person did not have a well-founded fear of persecution, to then proceed to find that she could relocate elsewhere in Sudan to avoid (the supposedly non-existent) persecution. Clark J criticised "the tendency among protection decision-makers to consider the availability of internal relocation even when the applicant's narrative is found implausible".[82] We would argue that this error was indicative of an intellectual rigidity and poor dissemination of legal knowledge within the Tribunal. The judgment of Justice Clark, however, decided that such systemic considerations should not push the court into quashing the entire decision.

[8–57]   Nevertheless, her Honour's judgment represented a sharp rap on the knuckles for the Tribunal, stressing the need for greater care by decision-makers:

> "...such abundance of caution [in considering internal relocation even where persecution has not been found to exist] which emanates from the EC's (Eligibility for Protection) Regulations 2006 (S.I. No. 518 of 2006) and Regulation 7(1) thereof, only works if the decision maker also adds words to the effect ...'*even if I had not made adverse credibility findings and I accepted all that she says...*' Without words to that effect, the exercise is illogical in a claim which has been rejected on credibility grounds. No such qualifying words were used in this case...When the Tribunal Member was coming to her decision in this case, the Protection Regulations had been in force for more than two years. The terms of Regulation 7 should have been well known to her. In the view of this Court, internal relocation has no logical part to play in a decision on protection if the claim is rejected on credibility grounds."[83]

Despite this, however, "in view of the extensive negative credibility findings" Clark J elected to sever the reference to internal relocation "which was an ill-considered afterthought"[84] and refused leave for review.

[8–58]   It is important to note, however, that in the later case *of SR [Pakistan] v Refugee Appeals Tribunal*,[85] Clark J found that the flawed internal relocation findings at issue in the case could not, in the particular circumstances of that case, be severed:

---

[82] *ibid* at para 18.
[83] *ibid*.
[84] *ibid* at para 21.
[85] *SR [Pakistan] v Refugee Appeals Tribunal* [2013] IEHC 26.

"The Court is not prepared to support this approach as all the findings are interwoven and part of a holistic assessment of the claim. The credibility findings, the failure to state protection and the option of [internal relocation] all fuelled the negative recommendation."[86]

The Displacement of "Failure to take into Account a Relevant Consideration" as a Ground of Review

The operation of failure to take into account a relevant consideration as a ground of review has often failed to attract the type of sustained analysis given to procedural fairness and unreasonableness. This is no doubt due in part to the fact that each case involving the ground necessitates a differing statutory interpretation of the specific constellation of legislation applying. More broadly, however, the ground has, in recent years, been eclipsed by the alternative framing devices offered by unreasonableness or the right to reasons. Many instances of failure to take into account a relevant factor are now presented instead as a violation of procedural fairness, with judges finding a breach in the failure to give reasons for rejecting a particular item of evidence. This is seen, for instance, in the High Court case of *NM (Togo) v Lenihan*, where Clark J criticised the failure to take into account corroborative documentation as a breach of procedural fairness:

[8–59]

"While the Court is satisfied that the appeal lacked basic fairness, it will nevertheless deal with the applicant's submission that the Tribunal relied excessively on the applicant's answers in response to the Commissioner rather than on the evidence presented at the appeal. As a general principle of law, there is no doubt that the Tribunal is entitled, indeed obliged, to have regard to the entire asylum file and to the section 13 report. However, as a matter of general fairness, a tribunal member may not ignore the evidence given at the appeal in favour of the evidence provided at the earlier Section 11 interview without some discussion of the reasons for doing so."[87]

Clark J also found that there was "an uncomfortable absence of any assurance" from the Tribunal that it had evaluated all the evidence.[88] This was provoked in part from the failure to outline the applicant's submissions on appeal to the Tribunal, leading her honour to conclude that "while it was certainly open to the Tribunal to attach low weight to

[8–60]

---

[86] *ibid* at para 34.
[87] *NM (Togo) v Lenihan* [2013] IEHC 436 at para 33.
[88] *ibid* at para 37.

some of the documents, they seem to have instead simply been ignored".[89] The case is interesting, as Clark J refers to "basic fairness" throughout the judgment and heads the relevant section of the judgment "excessive reliance on section 11 interviews/failure to outline appeal submissions". This seems to indicate that a perverse weighting married with the failure to properly outline the applicant's argument combined to produce unfairness. It is unclear however, whether this is best framed as a failure to take relevant considerations into account or, as is more likely, a breach of procedural fairness. It may be that counsel in future cases, choose to apply the language of procedural fairness rather than relevant considerations.

Conclusion

[8–61]   Alongside the specific analysis of the grounds of improper purpose, uncertainty and taking into account relevant/irrelevant considerations, this chapter has also functioned as something of a transition between Chapter 7 on ultra vires and Chapter 9 on reasonableness and proportionality. This reflects the fact that the first step in making a case under the grounds of review set out in this chapter is the generation of permitted purposes or relevant considerations. This initially seems to be a matter of statutory interpretation, but is also influenced by constitutional implications, and increasingly, fundamental rights as protected at European level. As this chapter progressed we began to ask more searching questions of the reasoning process. What is meant by "considering" or "taking into account" is a question that had not presented much difficulty until the recent cases we outlined. Our discussion of this has clearly foreshadowed the influence of the developments outlined in the next chapter on reasonableness and proportionality. We have sought to highlight that more searching review for reasonableness or proportionality could generate greater obligations to reason through particular aspects of evidence. While we cannot ultimately identify any set outcome, we believe we have shown an emerging trend whereby judges are, at a minimum, having to increasingly confront how a decision maker should identify and balance relevant interests, avoid uncertainty of their reasoning and ensure that interests are not weighted in an overly distorted manner.

---

[89] *ibid.*

CHAPTER NINE

UNREASONABLENESS, PROPORTIONALITY AND ADMINISTRATIVE DECISIONS

Introduction

The "unreasonableness" ground represents the most debated judicial [9–01] review ground; it has attracted enormous controversy, particularly over the last decade. For some, recent judicial rulings, which form the basis of much of this chapter, threaten to unduly modify the long-established position that judicial review is concerned merely with the procedural aspects of a decision, not the correctness of its ultimate answer (merits review). It is important to note, however, that even the conventional understanding of unreasonableness standard of review contaminated the simplified division between process and substance. This chapter will show that the Irish courts have traditionally been willing to quash a decision due to a lack of rationality or where there is no evidence to support it. Nevertheless, more searching standards, such as requiring that a decision be "factually sustainable" or "proportionate" have often been marginalised due to judicial disquiet regarding their role in intervening with primary decision-makers.

There are two main reasons as to why unreasonableness as a ground of [9–02] review has undergone such sustained critical debate and evolution in the past few years. Firstly, we argue that judicial decision-making under this ground of review was traditionally subjective and impressionistic, with few judges tending to the upkeep of fundamental concepts and tests at the heart of its operation. As a result of the untidiness of the precedents, there was an unjustifiable drift away from necessary conceptual mapping in judicial decision-making. As we will set out in this chapter, recent decisions have provided a much needed corrective to this. Secondly, the growing role of the European Convention on Human Rights and EU law has had a significant impact in this area. Both systems make extensive use of the requirement of proportionality in decisions which invade the personal rights of the individual. Furthermore, these European obligations require that an effective remedy be available for any breaches of rights. This has provoked a crisis of sorts in raising the question — does the availability of judicial review for unreasonableness discharge the government's obligations to provide a forum to repair breaches of EU law and the ECHR? We give direct consideration to this European angle in chapters 14 and 15. Nevertheless, it exerts a gravitational pull on our general discussion in this chapter, which seeks to outline the test for reasonableness across *all* decisions, including those involving constitutional rights. The increased recourse to both ECHR and EU law standards in the Irish courts has served to shine a light on both the underlying normative drift in this area and the underexplored nature of the concept of reasonableness generally.

[9–03]   In considering these themes, this chapter focuses firmly upon the landmark Supreme Court judgments in *Meadows v Minister for Justice*,[1] which reaffirmed reasonableness' central role in judicial review, particularly in cases involving fundamental rights. In addition, as part of the majority judgments in *Meadows*, we have seen clear judicial recognition of the concept of proportionality in judicial review of administrative decision-making. Despite the controversy raging around this finding, and claims that it destroys the distinction between process and merits in judicial review, we argue that *Meadows* does not mark an unprecedented first intervention into merits balancing by the courts. Instead we view the decision as representing a new point of emphasis in long established judicial tasks. However, it is important to note, even at this early stage in the chapter, that due to the fragmentation of the *Meadow's* majority judgments, we are still in search of an agreed definition and any consistent practice in assessing proportionality. Within this uncertainty, it is clear, nevertheless, that judges (and by extension decision-makers) are now tasked with investigating whether a decision may be said to be disproportionate in its effects. This chapter, therefore, represents an early attempt to identify emergent trends in judicial review post *Meadows*.

The Test for Unreasonableness

Wednesbury Unreasonableness

[9–04]   The landmark case laying down the ground of unreasonableness is, of course, the English case of *Associated Provincial Picture Houses Ltd v Wednesbury Corporation*.[2] Despite innumerable later cases having arguably extended the notion of reasonableness, it remains popular to refer to *Wednesbury unreasonableness* in describing traditional approaches. Lord Greene MR ruled:

> "We have heard in this case a great deal about the meaning of the word 'unreasonable.'...It has frequently been used and is frequently used as a general description of the things that must not be done. For

---

[1] *Meadows v Minister for Justice* [2010] 2 IR 701. Hereinafter "*Meadows*".
[2] *Associated Provincial Picture Houses Ltd v Wednesbury Corporation* [1948] 1 KB 223.

instance, a person entrusted with a discretion must, so to speak, direct himself properly in law. He must call his own attention to the matters which he is bound to consider. He must exclude from his consideration matters which are irrelevant to what he has to consider. If he does not obey those rules, he may truly be said, and often is said, to be acting 'unreasonably'. Similarly, there may be something so absurd that no sensible person could ever dream that it lay within the powers of the authority. Warrington LJ in *Short v Poole Corporation* [1926] Ch. 66, 90, 91 gave the example of the red-haired teacher, dismissed because she has red hair."[3]

While these various elements of unreasonableness could operate together, Lord Greene also stressed their individuality: [9–05]

"The court is entitled to investigate the action of the local authority with a view to seeing whether they have taken into account matters which they ought not to take into account, or, conversely, have refused to take into account or neglected to take into account matters which they ought to take into account. Once that question is answered in favour of the local authority, it may still be possible to say that, although the local authority have kept within the four corners of the matters which they ought to consider, they have nevertheless come to a conclusion so unreasonable that no reasonable authority could ever have come to it."[4]

In the first quote above we see that a number of judicial review grounds can fall within the term unreasonable. Yet, as the second quote indicates, Lord Greene also contemplated instances of a free standing unreasonableness ground in instances where the "conclusion is so unreasonable that no reasonable authority could ever have come to it". [9–06]

The *Wednesbury* approach was restated in the 1985 case of *Council of Civil Service Unions v Minister for the Civil Service*[5] by Diplock LJ. He found that it applied to any [9–07]

"decision which is so outrageous in its defiance of logic or of accepted moral standards that no sensible person who had applied his mind to the question to be decided could have arrived at it."[6]

---

[3] *ibid* at 229.
[4] *ibid*.
[5] *Council of Civil Service Unions v Minister for the Civil Service* [1985] AC 374.
[6] *ibid* at 410.

The *Keegan* Test for Unreasonableness

[9–08] In considering the Irish position in relation to *Wednesbury* in the case of *State (Keegan) v The Stardust Victims Compensation Tribunal*,[7] Henchy J rejected some elements of Diplock's reworked approach to unreasonableness. In particular, he expressed concern with the idea of anchoring unreasonableness in the concept of "accepted moral standards" or "logic". In relation to the latter concept of logic, he stressed that "many examples could be given of reputable decisions and of substantive laws which reject logic in favour of other considerations".[8] Henchy J described the former concept of "accepted moral standards" as being "a vague, elusive and changing body of standards",[9] which ought not to be relied upon. He therefore regarded the true heritage of *Wednesbury* as lying:

> "…in considering whether the impugned decision plainly and unambiguously flies in the face of fundamental reasons and common sense…the necessarily implied constitutional limitation of jurisdiction in all decision-making which affects rights or duties requires, *inter alia*, that the decision-maker must not flagrantly reject or disregard fundamental reason or common sense in reaching his decision."[10]

[9–09] It is important to note that the judgment links the test to matters affecting constitutional rights or duties. The Constitution may therefore also play a powerful role in defining what is meant by common sense and reason. Furthermore, it is significant that unreasonableness may be triggered by failing to give *regard* to reason — i.e. failing to weigh in balance reasonable considerations — as this underlines that some sort of balancing process is contemplated. This is an important point to note in relation to our later discussion of proportionality; in particularly the claim that the insertion of proportionality balancing in Irish judicial review is a "revolutionary" step.

A Narrowing of the Unreasonableness Ground: *O'Keeffe v An Bord Pleanála*

[9–10] The *dicta* of Henchy J in *Keegan* was quickly installed as the approved standard by a generation of Irish judges. This declared consensus however,

---

[7] *State (Keegan) v The Stardust Victims Compensation Tribunal* [1986] IR 642. Hereinafter "Keegan".
[8] *ibid* at 657.
[9] *ibid* at 658.
[10] *ibid*.

arguably obscured some sharpening of the underlying language attaching to the test of reasonableness. A number of decisions stressed the need to defer to the decisions of tribunals and sought to further signal the reluctance of judges to disturb decisions using the ground. In *O'Keeffe v An Bord Pleanála*, Finlay CJ emphasised the rarity of a decision being overturned on the basis of unreasonableness:

> "The circumstances under which the court can intervene on the basis of irrationality with the decision maker involved in an administrative function are limited and rare....it is necessary that the Applicant should establish to the satisfaction of the Court that the decision making authority had before it *no relevant material which would support its decision*".[11]

The judgments in *O'Keeffe* represented a winnowing, even of Henchy J's [9–11] criteria.[12] This was influenced by a desire to respect the expertise of a particular respondent authority in question, but Finlay CJ seemed also to feel that such a standard should be applied to all administrative decisions. The term *relevant* was inserted instead of the more open textured "reason and common sense". "Irrational" was taken as an unproblematic synonym for reasonable — despite the fact that its literal meaning is linked more closely to absurdity. This narrowing of unreasonableness was reinforced by the later contribution of Hamilton CJ in *Denny v Minister for Social Welfare*,[13] who, in *obiter* comments, was invoked with approval in the statement of O'Sullivan J in *Aer Rianta v Commissioner for Aviation Regulation*:

> "...to be reviewable [as irrational] it is not sufficient that a decision-maker goes wrong or even hopelessly and fundamentally wrong: he must have gone completely and inexplicably mad; taken leave of his senses and come to an absurd conclusion."[14]

---

[11] *O'Keeffe v An Bord Pleanála* [1993] 1 IR 39 at 72. Hereinafter "*O'Keeffe*".

[12] In this regard, it is instructive to read the judgment of Costello J in the High Court prior to the Supreme Court appeal, which forms part of the report cited above n 11. At 56, having reviewed the evidence on the planning matter at hand — the erection of a transmitting station mast — his Honour found:

> "it was a development which would lead to 'excessive' levels of nuisance which would require 'repetitive' remedial action to eliminate it, a nuisance which would be both 'widespread' and 'chronic'."

The disregarding of relevant technical expert evidence, together with the poverty of justification for doing so led to Costello J concluding that no reasonable local authority would have taken the course of action.

[13] *Denny v Minister for Social Welfare* [1998] IR 34 at 37-38. Hereinafter "*Denny*".

[14] *Aer Rianta Cpt v Commissioner for Aviation Regulation*, [2003] IEHC 12. As Morgan notes at p 517 of DG Morgan, *Administrative Law in Ireland* (Student edition) (Round Hall, Dublin, 2012) McKechnie J, warned of the non-compatibility of this statement with the fundamental

[9–12]   The manner in which these statements were derived, without extensive examination of the core terms, or of developments in comparative jurisdictions, led to an unfocused treatment of reasonableness, which is centred on whether the error could be characterised as extreme enough. Many of the judgments from this period displayed the tendency of Irish judges to act reflexively — to invoke a general philosophy of deference to the decision-maker and then not accompany this with a layered and structured reasonableness analysis. *O'Keeffe* reduced a process which should involve recourse to logic and due regard to reason to a mere headnote appraisal of the sources of the decision. When a more considered treatment did arrive in *Meadows*, it surprisingly made no mention of the "relevant material" standard and focused instead on *Keegan*.[15] Greater up-front reflection on the judicial values which produced *O'Keeffe* would have produced a more historical accurate account of how reasonableness has operated in the Irish legal context.

The Role of Deference in Unreasonableness

[9–13]   It is clear that a philosophy (if not a doctrine) of deference to the executive underlay much of this movement, but was not conceptually unpacked. The most advanced statement of principle was supplied by Hamilton CJ in *Denny*:

> "...I believe it would be desirable to take this opportunity of expressing the view that courts should be slow to interfere with the decisions of expert administrative tribunals. Where conclusions are based upon an identifiable error of law or an unsustainable finding of fact by a tribunal such conclusions must be corrected. Otherwise it should be recognised that tribunals which have been given statutory tasks to perform and exercise their functions, as is now usually the case, with a high degree of expertise and provide coherent and balanced judgments on the evidence and arguments heard by them it should not be necessary for the courts to review their decisions by way of appeal or judicial review."[16]

[9–14]   The pragmatism of judicial decisions in the period between *Keegan* and *Meadows* served to deprive Irish administrative law of normative leadership.

---

requirements of relevant EU law in *Neurendale Ltd (t/a Panda Waste Services) v Dublin City Council* [2009] IEHC 588 at para 181.

[15] See P Daly, "Standards of review in Irish administrative law after *Meadows v Minister for Justice, Equality and Law Reform*", (2010) 17(1) DULJ 379 at p 381. Hereinafter "*Daly*".

[16] *Denny* above n 13 at 37.

The Supreme Court decision in *Meadows* did not wholly renounce such proclivities, and while it developed a new test, it is clear that, as we discuss at para [9-21], at least one member of the Court doubted that technical formulae could capture the nature of judicial decision-making in the area. The case law prior to *Meadows* therefore remains significant, as it captures an Irish judicial mindset that may not ultimately be overruled by the heavily qualified and highly technical reworking of the reasonableness test represented by *Meadows*.

To conclude our historical account, it must be noted that even prior to **[9–15]** *Meadows*, the reasonableness ground has had a defined core that has been of practical utility for Irish practitioners and judges. It is therefore valuable to reflect on how the test operated in relation to the specifics of cases coming before the courts. We can start this process by studying, not only Henchy J's formulation of the test in *Keegan*, but also its immediate and practical consequences in relation to the case before him. The matter concerned the death of the applicant's two children in the Stardust nightclub fire.[17] The applicant was seeking to recover damages for nervous shock as a result, but was rejected by the relevant compensation tribunal, despite his wife's claim being successful. The Supreme Court ruled in *Keegan* that it was not possible to set aside the finding on grounds of it being unreasonable. Nevertheless, in the later case of *State (Creedon) v Criminal Injuries Compensation Tribunal* a decision to deny compensation was overturned where no substantive reason had been advanced for it.[18]

In *Ashbourne v An Bord Pleanála*,[19] the High Court condemned as **[9–16]** unreasonable two planning conditions attached to the construction of the new golf course at the Old Head of Kinsale. These required public access to the lighthouse and coastal lookout, and interest group access to the cliff face during all daylight hours. Kearns J condemned the imposition of these conditions, where no pre-existing right of way had been recognised. By seeking to allow access to the land at any time during the day, and not prescribing any particular route, the condition:

> "...has the capacity to completely frustrate and/or render inoperable the use of the headland as a golf course...Furthermore, the terms of the condition as imposed obliges the golf course operator to keep this

---

[17] Another child survived suffering serious injury.
[18] *State (Creedon) v Criminal Injuries Compensation Tribunal* [1988] IR 51.
[19] *Ashbourne Holdings Ltd v An Bord Pleanála* [2003] 2 IR 114.

facility open, regardless of weather conditions, regardless of whether the course is open or closed and regardless of whether or not the golf development continues. I do not believe that any reasonable authority would have attached such a condition to a development of this nature."[20]

[9–17]   In *Matthews v Irish Coursing Club*, the High Court overturned a decision to fine the owner of the winning dog in a major competition, when it emerged that it had been doped.[21] O'Hanlon J commented that it was fundamentally at variance with common sense (as was statutorily embodied by the statutory objectives of the Greyhound Industry Act 1958) to fine the owner without removing the cup or prize money.

[9–18]   In *White v Dublin City Council*[22] the applicants successfully challenged as unreasonable a failure to advertise significant changes to the planning permission granted to their neighbour. The changes had been made at the respondent's behest, and reversing the initial plans shared with the applicants, meant that the new house would overlook their property. Fennelly J held that the decision-maker should have appreciated that the applicants would likely wish to object and that this objection would need to be considered.

Meadows: Restatement or Evolution?

Meadows v Minister for Justice: Background

[9–19]   The immediate facts of *Meadows* concerned a deportation order which had been issued against a Nigerian woman who claimed that her life would be endangered and she would be subject to female genital mutilation were she returned.[23] In the High Court, Gilligan J had applied the *Keegan* standard in holding that there had been relevant supporting material before the Minister to justify the decision he had taken. As a result no substantial grounds for review existed, but he nevertheless certified a point of law to

---

[20] *ibid* at 344-45.

[21] *Matthews v Irish Coursing Club* [1993] 1 IR 346.

[22] *White v Dublin City Council* [2004] 1 IR 545.

[23] Ms Meadows claims that she be entitled to remain were based upon (i) s 5 of the Refugee Act 1996, which prohibited expulsion where "in the opinion of the Minister, the life or freedom of that person would be threatened on account of his or her race, religion or nationality, membership of particular social group or political opinion". She also made an application to remain on humanitarian grounds under s 3(6) of the Immigration Act 1999, this latter claim the Supreme Court characterized as a prerogative of mercy claim.

the Supreme Court on the relevant standard that ought to be applied to such a decision, namely an administrative decision which affects or concerns constitutional or fundamental rights.[24] Crucially, the circumscribed nature of the proceeding, as a point of law matter, affected the clarity of the case: whatever formulation the Supreme Court produced, it would not have to accompany its principled reasoning with a practical application to a case in front of it. Thus, even if a role for proportionality was recognised, it would not be embodied through a worked example.

While we have explained the need for clarity, it is important at this point to explain why the question of what role proportionality could or should play in reasonableness review is one of enormous currency and debate within the Irish legal system. Firstly, the UK had begun itself to reconsider the heritage of *Wednesbury* review and the degree to which it could embrace proportionality analysis. This process has continued even to the time of writing, with the 2014 decision in *Kennedy v The Charity Commission* arguing for a close connection between reasonableness and proportionality.[25] Clearly, the Irish Supreme Court could be expected to engage with the question of whether reasonableness contained the flexibility to permit proportionality review or whether the latter was in fact transgressive to traditional approaches. Secondly, there was the question as to why proportionality had come to play such a central role in evaluating the constitutionality of legislation, but not in the review of administrative action. Finally, there was the increasing use of proportionality by the Irish Courts in the context of both EU law and the European Convention on Human Rights Act 2003, which we discuss more fully in chapters 14 and 15. Against this background, many looked to the Supreme Court to address whether the approaches to proportionality in those spheres were confined to their particular legal contexts. In effect this queried whether courts undertaking review should continually "swap lenses" between proportionality and reasonableness when reviewing administrative action under the Constitution, European law or the ECHR. **[9–20]**

In addition to the gateway question of whether proportionality analysis was permitted and in what context, a further question emerged as to what model of proportionality the Supreme Court might endorse. Would the Court adopt the approach of approving what might be termed the default **[9–21]**

---

[24] *Meadows v Minister for Justice* (Unreported, High Court, Gilligan J, 4 November, 2003).

[25] *Kennedy v The Charity Commission*, [2014] UKSC 20, Judgment of 24 March 2014, at para 54.

four step proportionality test for ECHR rights? Or would it approve another, more restricted form of proportionality? In order to proceed we need a working definition of the former "structured" version of proportionality, with the most comprehensive Irish example being that adopted by Irvine J in applying the European Convention on Human Rights Act 2003 in *Pullen (No 1)*. His Honour stated that, in the context of the European Convention on Human Rights, an action would be found proportionate where:

> "(a) ... the objective of restricting the right is so pressing and substantial that it is sufficiently important to justify interfering with a fundamental right;
>
> (b) ... the restriction is suitable: it must be rationally connected to the objective in mind so that the limitation is not arbitrary, unfair or based on irrational considerations;
>
> (c) ... the restriction is necessary to accomplish the objective intended. In this respect the public authority must adopt the least drastic means of attaining the objective in mind, provided the means suggested are not fanciful; and
>
> (d) ... the restriction is not disproportionate. The restriction must not impose burdens or cause harm which is excessive when compared to the importance of the objective to be achieved."[26]

A core question in *Meadows* was thus whether the court would generally adopt such a structured proportionality analysis, or would fashion an alternative approach omitting some of, or modifying, the four steps of legitimate aim, rational connection, minimal impairment and overall balance.

[9–22] Six and a half years after the High Court ruling, the Supreme Court confronted the broad question submitted to it by Gilligan J. Isolating the precise *ratio* of the majority in *Meadows* requires close reading, as overlaying each judgment reveals distinct emphases that fragment the formation of unified principles. Furthermore, many of the judges' own statements seem to doubt the idea that any forms of words could have the impact of assuring genuine uniformity of approach given the multitude of legal contexts in which reasonableness would be pleaded. This is seen in the statement of Fennelly J that "at one level all this is no more than semantics; what is

---

[26] *Pullen v Dublin City Council (no 1)* [2008] IEHC 379 at para 39.

irrational or unreasonable depends on the subject matter and the context".[27] Fennelly J also seemed to narrow the precedential value of his own contribution by expressly stating that the principle of proportionality was "more fully developed" by the other members of the majority (Denham J and Murray CJ) than in his own judgment.[28]

Rejection of Anxious Scrutiny

Firstly, one may conclude that the Court rejected the idea of "anxious scrutiny" or a sliding scale of review which varies according to the nature of legal rights in question. The majority on this point (Murray CJ, Hardiman and Fennelly JJ), justified this on the basis that its practical application was very impressionistic and did not add anything concrete to the process of review: [9–23]

> "...it is neither appropriate nor necessary to have a different standard of review for cases involving an interference with fundamental, constitutional or other personal rights. For example, it would be wrong and confusing to have two different standards of judicial review for planning decisions depending on whether the review was being sought by the applicant for permission (the owner of the land with constitutionally-protected rights) or a third party objector (with a merely legal right to object)...."[29]

Hardiman J argued that it hardly represented an advance to say the Court should always give matters before it careful scrutiny.[30] Its emergence in the UK reflected that jurisdiction's unwritten constitutional order, which prioritised the supremacy of parliament and as a partial step towards harmonizing its judicial review traditions with the requirements of the UK Human Rights Act.[31] [9–24]

---

[27] *Meadows*, above n 1 at 825.

[28] *ibid* at 826.

[29] *Per* Fennelly J, *ibid*.

[30] Hardiman J appeared entirely nonplussed by the descriptor anxious, noting that "it is to be hoped and assumed that the judiciary will be undeviatingly careful in any case where there is an entitlement to apply for judicial review", *ibid* at 782.

[31] Indeed it is important to point out that the pre Human Rights Act statements had already recognized the basic principle that intensity of review could vary according to the interests affected by the decision. See *Bugdacay v Secretary of State for the Home Department* [1987] 1 AC 514 and *R v Ministry of Defence, ex parte Smith* [1996] QB 517 where Bingham MR stated at 554: "The more substantial the interference with human rights, the more the court will require by way of justification before it is satisfied that the decision is reasonable."

Proportionality as an Element of Reasonableness

[9–25]   Secondly, a majority recognised that reasonableness, properly understood, contains an element of proportionality. However, beyond this recognition they failed to reach a consensus as to the extent to which proportionality amounts to a free-standing element within the review process: i.e. that finding a decision to be disproportionate means it *must* be quashed. Of the majority, arguably only Denham J adopted this latter position (though even she at times noted the "inherent similarity" between the two analyses for reasonableness and proportionality).[32] Fennelly J argued that a decision would only be quashed if it were *sufficiently* disproportionate to draw it into the category of unreasonable.[33] Murray CJ merely referred to proportionality as an element in the overall analysis without identifying its weight:

> "In examining whether a decision properly flows from the premises on which it is based and whether it might be considered at variance with reason and common sense I see no reason why the Court should not have recourse to the principle of proportionality."[34]

[9–26]   This latter quote underlines that for Murray CJ and Fennelly J, in particular, the proportionality analysis could be accommodated within the pre-existing *Keegan* unreasonableness standard.[35] This expansion of the ground is underlined by the fact that, as Hogan and Morgan note, this "infusion of Keegan by the principle of proportionality", appears to occur regardless of whether constitutional rights are involved.[36] Thus, it is clear that the traditional grounds of judicial review have been expanded, but does this apply across all cases, whether they affect fundamental rights or not? Denham J tied the new standard to the expectation that

---

[32] There is a potential inconsistency with her earlier statement in passing that a reviewing judge should assess "whether the effect on the rights of the applicant would be so disproportionate as to justify the court in setting it aside on the ground of manifest unreasonableness". *ibid* at 743.

[33] If the decision were to "affect fundamental rights to such a disproportionate degree, having regard to the public objectives it seeks to achieve, as to cross a threshold, and to be justifiably labeled as so unreasonable that no reasonable decision-maker could justifiably have made it". *ibid* at 825-6.

[34] *ibid* at 723.

[35] Murray CJ expressly followed the statement of Keane J in *Radio Limerick One Limited v IRTC* [1997] 2 IR 291, where the latter held that a decision can be quashed where it is so disproportionate as to be manifestly unreasonable.

[36] Hogan and Morgan, *Administrative Law in Ireland*, (4th ed) (Round Hall, Dublin, 2010), at para 15.135.

"the reviewing court bear in mind the principles of the Constitution of Ireland, 1937, the European Convention on Human Rights Act, 2003, and the rule of law, while applying the principles of judicial review."[37]

The reference in this quote to the "rule of law", is taken by Daly as suggesting that the reformed standard of review should apply outside the confines of fundamental rights.[38] There are pragmatic arguments in favour of non-restricted approach, as any attempt to restrict the application of the new approach would encourage forced efforts to recast general legal interests enjoyed by an applicant as reviews relating to fundamental rights — an eminently achievable semantic task, as Hardiman J indicated in his dissent.[39] Justice Hardiman also directly criticised the expansion of the test as rupturing the traditional principles of review as it:

[9–27]

"...looks for explanation and justification from the decision maker [which is]...inconsistent with the proper principles of judicial review, and with the view that the onus of proof remains on the applicant."[40]

The other dissentient, Justice Kearns, similarly would not endorse the new approach in the context of Ministerial discretion though he did comment that it "may serve well as a test for assessing first instance decisions".[41]

What Form of Proportionality is the Supreme Court Referring to in *Meadows*?

Thirdly, it is by no means clear that the "element" of proportionality recognised by the majority in *Meadows* is the full, and not somehow attenuated, version of the steps described above. Both Fennelly J and Murray CJ seemed to focus on proportionality as balancing, rather than as a reasoning process. The failure to do so is frustrating and leaves many unresolved questions, as accurately argued by Brady:

[9–28]

---

[37] *ibid* at 741.

[38] See Daly, above n 15 at p 387. Murray CJ also referred to "administrative decisions" without express restriction in his judgment.

[39] His Honour stated:

"[A] great many such applications arise in areas where there can be little doubt that a constitutional right is implicated. A review of the disposition of a criminal matter by the District Court would almost certainly be in this category as would the great majority of, if not all, asylum cases. The great bulk of litigation arising from Tribunals and Commissions of Inquiry also deals with constitutional rights to good name and otherwise which are said to be implicated".

ibid at 784.

[40] *ibid* at 794.

[41] *ibid* at 735.

> "[T]he connecting of reasonableness to proportionality in this manner is not enough to explain how proportionality is to be applied in administrative law cases involving fundamental rights. While proportionality may be linked to reasonableness, that bare fact does not explain how proportionality is to be measured. If it is merely the case that the word proportionality needs to be dropped into judgments at opportune moments, then there is no meaningful guidance for future courts. The word, of itself, does not explain what is to be done, apart from the fact that "proportionality" gives the impression of generally being a good thing".[42]

[9–29] Brady then proceeds to argue for an expanded interpretation of Justice Fennelly and Murray's judgments to embrace the structured analysis argued for by Denham J, as outlined in paragraph [9-30]. While we support the overall aim of his piece, the underlying difficulty that the other members of the majority did not seem to expressly approve of Denham J's test remains to be confronted by the Irish courts. The sense that judicial review is a deeply contextual and pragmatic exercise and simply not controllable through a form of words, seems to be an inchoate factor shaping the reticence of Murray CJ and Fennelly J. As we noted earlier in this chapter, Irish judges have been content to reason without structure in this area, so we must not approach *Meadows* with the presumption that it *must* provide an answer or a consolidated test. Rather both judges supply merely a framework endorsement of the concept of proportionality as requiring sufficiently weighty considerations to be present to justify limitations upon rights.[43]

[9–30] Denham J, in contrast, set out a more developed conception, whereby proportionality requires that:

> "...(a) the means must be rationally connected to the objective of the legislation and not arbitrary, unfair or based on irrational considerations; (b) the rights of the person must be impaired as little as possible (c) the effect on rights should be proportional to the objective".[44]

---

[42] A Brady, "Proportionality, Defence and Fundamental Rights in Irish Administrative Law: The Aftermath of Meadows" (2010) 17(1) DULJ 136 at p142. Hereinafter "Brady".

[43] Though Fennelly J preferred the idea that the scope of encroachment must be commensurate with the justification for it, see *Meadows* above n 1 at 827.

[44] *ibid* at 753. This formulation was expressly adopted from the Canadian case of *Chaulk v R* [1990] 3 SCR 1303.

This is quite an inelegant expression of the proportionality analysis, as Biehler argues the last step is "circular", in relying upon the concept of "proportion" which the test itself is meant to embody. In addition, step (c) does not expressly embrace the idea of balancing the interests of society with those of the individual, which features in the jurisprudence of England and Wales.[45] It is important to note that this conception is already established in the constitutional review of legislation, as developed by Costello J in *Heaney v Ireland*.[46]

[9–31]

In assessing whether Denham J's test represents the law in this jurisdiction, Brady correctly identifies a critical gap in the judgments of Fennelly J and Murray CJ: both expressly fail to recognise the second step — the idea that the rights of the person must be impaired as little as possible — and through their statements appear only to endorse steps one and three. As Brady concludes, "it is worth noting, that while Murray CJ does not endorse minimal impairment, he does not expressly reject it either".[47]

[9–32]

How do we go about construing such silence? It is arguable that the refusal to recognise the second step is a product of the traditional approach to review in this area. The minimal impairment step requires judges to define alternative courses of delivering or constructing a policy and this can be viewed as rupturing the old reasonableness approach by requiring a more polycentric analysis. Without it, the enhanced proportionality test would settle merely on a proportionality balance of the government's chosen policy. Once it is rationally connected with the overall objective, the legal content of the right will be identified and the two balanced in an analysis closed to any reference to alternative courses of action. This latter balancing would be substantive, not procedural. As a result of the separation of powers and the long established judicial discomfort with intervening in the merits, the circumstances where a judge will find such disproportion between the means and ends would remain rare. Yet we have already seen that such a narrow, "is this a sledgehammer to crack a nut" proportionality test has already featured in older cases under the reasonableness standard.[48]

[9–33]

---

[45] See on this point, H Biehler and C Donnelly, "The Irish Supreme Court inches towards proportionality review", (2011) 1 *Public Law* 9.

[46] *Heaney v Ireland* [1994] 3 IR 593, Denham J expressly stated that she "would adopt the approach to the proportionality test similar to that of Costello J", *Meadows* above n 1 at 743.

[47] Brady, above n 42 at p 141.

[48] Brady does also acknowledge this alternative, "much looser" approach, *ibid* at p 149. He cites the case of *Tuohy v Courtney* [1994] 3 IR 1, where the court inquired as to "whether the

While the test can be justifiably criticised as undisciplined, disorganised and subjective, its selective, targeted invocation in limited contexts may strike Irish judges as more respectful of the separation of powers than a uniform application of the minimal impairment test inherent in a full proportionality approach.

[9–34]   The authors would, like many commentators, prefer the courts to adopt the structured approach. However, to date, its endorsement has only come in cases involving the proportionality of *legislation* and in assessing compliance with European Convention on Human Rights provisions.[49] Murray CJ may also have been influenced in not extensively discussing minimal impairment due to the nature of a deportation decision — which had previously been characterised as "a stark choice to make, either to deport or not to deport. There is no halfway house".[50] Such a scenario may occur in practice, and it could be argued that when taking decisions an administrative decision-maker will have more limited freedom than parliament has in passing legislation. Yet fundamental rights consist not merely of existence (or non-existence) of an entitlement, but also affect the *constructing of the interests* involved in the decision. These procedural aspects of the individual's rights can always be defended, even if the ultimate answer is a yes or a no. It may be that the refusal to recognise the minimal impairment step is attributable to a desire to avoid 'process chasing' in the protection of rights: the focus is not upon getting the decision-maker to consider whether additional options for obtaining the policy goal of a decision were available but upon evaluation of whether the decision-maker chose an option which represents a fair limitation on the individual's rights. Under this understanding proportionality is about whether the answer is legally justifiable, not whether it is the one outcome that optimises rights protection.[51]

---

balance contained in the impugned legislation is so contrary to reason and fairness as to constitute an unjust attack on some individual's constitutional right" (at 47).

[49] *Pullen v Dublin City Council (No 1)* [2008] IEHC 379.

[50] *AO & DL v Minister for Justice* [2003] 1 IR 1 at 92.

[51] We discuss this debate between the optimizing and state limiting understandings of proportionality in chapter 1 at paras [1-60]-[1-63]. We would associate mistrust of the minimal impairment rule with a mistrust of proportionality balancing as a whole – ultimately, it seems to rely upon the idea that it is better for a court to identify the core content of a fundamental right, and outside of this leave a discretionary area of policy judgment on which of rights limiting (or protecting) options is preferable. This ultimately may be traced back to anxieties about the separation of the powers, or the desire to leave space for a dialogue or contestation around the meaning of rights amongst the political and judicial branches.

The *Meadows* Decision and Deference

Fourthly, the Court failed, ultimately, to assign a defined role and position **[9–35]** to the notion of curial deference. This is not to say that deference is not instrumental, but rather that in Ireland, it has not yet been formally incorporated as a distinct step or independent doctrine to be applied in judicial review. It is implicitly everywhere and yet formally nowhere. Clearly, considerations of deference were guiding Denham J in her preference for a bifurcated standard of review whereby the new *Meadows* standard would be used in cases involving fundamental rights, but the traditional "relevant material" standard of *Keegan* could be employed elsewhere. Denham J saw the idea of deference as having had a strong impact on Irish standards of review, despite the fact that there had not been much abstract judicial reflection on the term. For instance, her Honour tied the heavily restricted "no relevant material" *O'Keeffe* test to "areas of special skill and knowledge, such as planning and development".[52] Thus it was deference to context that accounts for the restricting of the initial *Keegan* standard. In cases involving fundamental rights, a similar process was to occur — but in the opposite direction — requiring a closer examination of the decision in question. In *Meadows*, the decision was "not an area of technical skill in the sense of the decision in *O'Keefe*".[53] Denham J was the only member of the Court to claim that the level of deference could be set at the outset, by categorising the type of decision being dealt with.

Such deference doctrines have been described as "non-justiciablity in pastel **[9–36]** colours",[54] by which is meant that they can allegedly result in the watering down of the role of judicial actors based on the malleable characterisations of particular areas. It is interesting that Denham J's approach could be described as defensive: her Honour expressly recognises only one area — planning and development — which had *already* received deferential treatment by the courts. It may be, that her discussion in this area can be conceived as a response to the stinging dissent of Hardiman J, who described the majority's approach as revolutionary. Denham J's judgment illustrated that just as deference had been used to narrow Keegan, it could be used to expand it — a similar logic, if different application.

---

[52] *Meadows* above n 1 at 738.

[53] *ibid* at 744.

[54] TRS Allan, "Human Rights and Judicial Review: A Critique of 'Due Deference'" (2006) 65 CLJ 671 at p 689.

[9–37]   In contrast, Fennelly J's approach to deference rejects the deployment of broad "spatial" categories. His Honour seemed to indicate that, there appears to be little to gain from engaging with a decision on such an abstract basis, rather:

> "It is natural…for any decision maker to be the more hesitant, the more deliberate, the more cautious as the decision he or she is considering will the more gravely trench on the rights or interests of those likely to be affected."[55]

[9–38]   One of the benefits of the *Meadows* judgment is the linking of deference with expertise, rather than other vaguer notions that appear in comparative jurisdictions.[56] The need for decision-makers to anchor their right to act undisturbed on the basis of their expertise, and not their mere identity as executive actors, should provide an indirect stimulus to construct such expertise on the ground. Above all, Irish judicial review of administrative decisions can at last avoid impressionistic deference based upon selective and aridly conceptual invocations of the separation of powers doctrine. Daly, in a memorable contribution, succinctly sums up the contradictions between judicial review of *legislation* and of *administrative decisions*:

> "If proportionality is the appropriate standard of review where legislation is said to infringe constitutional rights, there "seems to be no reason" that it should not be the standard of review where administrative action is said to infringe constitutional rights. Indeed, holding otherwise would lead to the perverse conclusion that what could not be accomplished by the democratically-elected Oireachtas, could nevertheless be done by an unelected administrative official. Moreover, if courts apply the presumption of constitutionality so as to save legislation from constitutional challenge by presuming that administrative decision-makers will act constitutionally, those decision makers must surely be required to act constitutionally."[57]

[9–39]   Yet, in his dissent in *Meadows*, Hardiman J continued to attempt to separate the interpretation of legislation affecting constitutional rights, where proportionality already occurs,[58] from any proportionality analysis of whether *individual decisions* were justified:

---

[55] *Meadows* above n 1 at 824.

[56] We discuss debates around such approaches in the UK in chapter 1 at paras [1-56]-[1-59].

[57] Above n 15 at p 386.

[58] Readers will recall that the landmark case of *Heaney v Ireland* [1994] 3 IR 593 installed proportionality as the core standard for the constitutionality review of legislation.

"Questions such as proportionality in my view apply to an assessment of the laws and procedures established by law whereby decisions of a particular kind are made, rather than to the individual decisions themselves".[59]

This approach relies upon a heavily foreclosed vision of the proper role of judges as lying in the identification of legal standards, while removing themselves to a significant extent from their application. Brady, in critiquing such a viewpoint — highlights that proportionality review is arguably more appropriate for administrative law than for challenges to legislation: **[9–40]**

"Legislation is debated in public and enacted by the democratically elected Oireachtas. Legislation is prospective and potentially affects every citizen. In such circumstances, the normal political processes may provide a means of remedying any fundamental rights difficulties... The same is not true of administrative action. The number of people directly affected by a specific administrative decision is often very narrow, indeed administrative decisions are often directed at a single individual. Furthermore, executive decision-makers have substantially less democratic accountability than does the Oireachtas and their decision-making process is not necessarily transparent and open. In such circumstances, violations of fundamental rights can be expected to arise just as often in cases involving administrative decisions as in cases involving legislation; arguably even more often."[60]

As we conclude our discussion of the judgments in *Meadows*, it is interesting to consider the competing visions of law, policy and administration which lie underneath the judgments and resultant commentary upon them. The question of how, precisely, authorities "earn" deference from the court is an important one. It is perhaps, an emerging site of green light administrative law,[61] and may result in judicial review decisions carrying a broader regulatory content rather than only focusing on the resolution of single cases. Such a model of deference, despite its potential downsides,[62] is more facilitative of Government action, in that it allows for the positive valuing of expertise in judicial review. It is clear that taking a spatial approach to deference, whereby the authority is merely dubbed an expert in the factual and technical underpinnings of the decision, and the judge as expert in the law, does little to resolve the dilemma of when to intervene — most **[9–41]**

---

[59] *Meadows* above n 1 at 791.

[60] Above n 42 at p 138.

[61] This school of thought was discussed in chapter 1 at paras [1-48]-[1-52]

[62] See chapter 1 at paras [1-55]-[1-59]

decisions relate to the interface between the two. Even in the case of wholly discretionary decisions, which the judges in the Supreme Court described as unlikely to be interfered with — the protection of rights still provides a subsisting mandate for judicial intervention.

Refinement or Revolution? A Survey of Post-*Meadows* Case-Law

McSorley v Minister for Education: Embracing Proportionality

[9–42]   Given the lack of clarity we have highlighted in the *Meadows* decisions, we must now move on to reflect on the impact of the Supreme Court decision through a review of recent case law on unreasonableness and proportionality. In doing so we start with a decision that most clearly embodies the core practical impact of *Meadows* — *McSorley v Minister for Education*.[63] This case, perhaps, underlines that while confusion continues regarding the nature and scale of proportionality analysis, *Meadows* has created a discernible judicial comfort level for intervention where an action is manifestly disproportionate. The applicant in *McSorley* had been a school principal at Kilkenny City Vocational School for thirteen years. The school had been in turmoil upon her arrival and in the period 2001-2003, three complaints were upheld against her. In December 2005, the Minister for Education established an enquiry into the matters, which eventually reported in April 2011. Following submissions from the applicant on the matter, the Minister found her unfit to hold office based on the earlier errors, despite eight years having passed since the last upheld complaint against her. The Court heard extensive evidence as to her performance in the meantime, instancing her as a successful agent of change in the school. As a result of the delay in taking action, and her more than adequate performance in the meantime, the High Court was satisfied that the decision to remove her was manifestly disproportionate. Hedigan J noted that the High Court will apply the doctrines of unreasonableness and proportionality "together", even in instances "involving a Minister's exercise of near absolute discretion".[64] Invoking Denham J's summary of the core principles, Hedigan J ruled the decision to remove her as principal was disproportionate:

---

[63] *McSorley v Minister for Education* [2012] IEHC 201.
[64] *ibid* at para 5.8.

"Clearly the circumstances under which the Court can intervene with a decision maker involved in an administrative function such as herein are limited. However as stated above the Court must have regard to the implied constitutional limitation of jurisdiction in all decision-making which affects rights. Any effect on rights should be within constitutional limitations and should be proportionate to the objective to be achieved. If the effect is disproportionate this justifies the court setting aside the decision. Clearly the Ministers decision has a profound effect upon the applicant's rights. Thus the Court must ask was the decision reached in this case disproportionate? The objective of the inquiry into Ms. McSorley performance must ultimately have been to determine whether her continuance in the role was consistent with the provision of a proper functioning school where she worked. In this regard it must be noted that Ms. McSorley has served as principal of the school for 12 years. Her appointment in 1999 was to an extremely challenging role. The previous incumbent had resigned and the school was facing falling enrolment numbers. There was unrest between various parties at the school. The three complaints upheld against her involved events that occurred between 2001 and 2003. The incidents occurred when she was relatively new to her role. The complaints upheld were eight to ten years old when the decision to dismiss her was made. In the meantime all the evidence that this Court has heard is to the effect that she was doing a very good job. Mr O'Connor described her as "a very considerable force for good in the school" and found that: "there is no doubting her commitment to the school and her efforts to 'turn around' a school which, when she took over as Principal was in serious decline as a consequence of both internal and external pressures. It seems to me that bearing in mind the inordinate length of time since the events in question and balancing that with her apparently very satisfactory performance of her duties as principal in the time between, there is in the decision to now remove her from her post, a manifest disproportionality that requires the Court to intervene. There must be an order to quash the decision of the Minister to dismiss the applicant from her post."[65]

The respondent's attempt to rely upon the "fundamentally at variance with reason and common sense" standard did not succeed in such a case of manifest disproportionality.

---

[65] *ibid* at para 7.6.

[9–43]   Other, similar examples of such findings of manifest disproportionality can be found.[66] However, post-*Meadows* case-law has continued to differ over the scope of the Supreme Court's decision, and in the absence of clarity, an unstructured, impressionistic approach to proportionality analysis has predominated as the discussion below will make clear.

O(O) & A(O) v Refugee Appeals Tribunal: A Limited Approach to Proportionality

[9–44]   The high point for those who favour of a narrow reading of *Meadows* is the judgment of Clark J in *O(O) & A(O) v Refugee Appeals Tribunal*,[67] a case which concerned the Minister for Justice's assessment of whether a deportation would result in "insurmountable obstacles" to the enjoyment of family life. Such Ministerial decisions had already been assessed for reasonableness prior to the *Meadows* decision, in cases such as *Alli*[68] and *Asibor*.[69] Counsel for the applicants, however, argued:

> "...that the legal landscape has changed since the decision of the Supreme Court in *Meadows*.... In particular, it is argued that proportionality is now an issue which must be addressed by the Court when judicially reviewing the lawfulness of any decision which affects fundamental rights. It was submitted that had the *Meadows* decision been available to this Court, *Alli and Asibor* would have been differently decided. It was argued that those decisions cannot now stand as the law has fundamentally changed. This new argument has resulted in many of the *"insurmountable obstacles"* cases being further adjourned pending the determination in this case."[70]

[9–45]   In her ruling, Clark J, firstly held that the Minister had failed to provide adequate reasons so as to allow the applicants to properly discern the rationale and basis for his determination concerning their constitutional rights. In particular, the Minister failed to provide any reason for ignoring submissions made relating to the conditions in Nigeria. Having disposed of the case at hand, Clark J then embarked on a consideration of the

---

[66] In *S (P) & E (B) v Minister for Justice* [2011] IEHC 1, Hogan J struck down a decision of the Minister for Justice because the Court found "that the decision was both disproportionate and unreasonable."

[67] *O(O) & A(O) v Minister for Justice, Equality and Law Reform* [2011] IEHC 78. Hereinafter "*O(O) & A(O)*".

[68] *Alli (a minor) v Minister for Justice* [2009] IEHC 595, (Unreported, High Court, Clark J, 2 December 2009).

[69] *Asibor (a minor) v Minister for Justice & Ors* [2009] IEHC 594.

[70] *O(O) & A(O)* above n 67 at para 4.

standard of review post-*Meadows*. Counsel for the applicants had relied upon the statement of Murray CJ in *Meadows*:

> "In examining whether a decision properly flows from the premises on which it is based and whether it might be considered at variance with reason and common sense I see no reason why the Court should not have recourse to the principle of proportionality in determining those issues. It is already well established that the Court may do so when considering whether the Oireachtas has exceeded its constitutional powers in the enactment of legislation.
>
> The principle requires that the effects on or prejudice to an individual's rights by an administrative decision be proportional to the legitimate objective or purpose of that decision. Application of the principle of proportionality is in my view a means of examining whether the decision meets the test of reasonableness."[71]

For Clark J, however, this passage did not expand pre-existing *Keegan* test, **[9–46]** in fact, her Honour found "no substance" to that argument:

> "The passage quoted from the Chief Justice's decision does not contain any new principle, neither is it possible to infer that the *Meadows* decision effected any change to the application of the principle of proportionality, either under the ECHR or the Constitution. The three judges of the Supreme Court who formed the majority, who held that proportionality was part of the assessment of reasonableness appropriate to the judicial review of all administrative decisions affecting fundamental rights, were individually at pains to state that the concept of proportionality was not new in Irish law."[72]

Since the *Meadows* judgment Clark J noted, arguments had been made as to effects "including that all previous deportation decisions must now be considered frail and that the legal landscape pertaining to the applicable test in judicial review has been redrawn."[73] Clark J rejected this however, arguing that the case bore a narrow *ratio*:

> "The key guidance to be derived from *Meadows* is not its discussion on the inclusion of the concept of proportionality in the test of reasonableness, but rather the unanimous determination by the Court that no new standard of review such as *anxious scrutiny* as applied in

---

[71] *ibid* at para 70.
[72] *ibid* at para 71.
[73] *ibid* at para 72.

the UK forms part of Irish law. The majority determined that the test of reasonableness which has been applied since *The State (Keegan) v. Stardust Victims Compensation Tribunal* [1986] I.R. 642 (*'Keegan'*) was adequate to provide an effective remedy in judicial review, even where the decision under review has the potential to affect a person's fundamental."[74]

[9–47] Crucially, in her discussion of Denham J's judgment, Clark J did not centre her analysis upon her Honour's endorsement of the structured approach to proportionality, but rather focused upon statements tying proportionality to the reasoning in *Keegan*.[75] The examination of Murray CJ's judgments,

---

[74] *ibid* at para 73. Clark J went on to quote Fennelly J in *Meadows*, above n 1 at 826, with added emphasis:

"It seems to me that the principle of proportionality, more fully developed in the judgments which have been delivered by the Chief Justice and of Denham J, can provide a sufficient and more consistent standard of review, without resort to vaguer notions of anxious scrutiny. The underlying facts and circumstances of cases can and do vary infinitely. The single standard of review laid down in Keegan and O'Keeffe is sufficiently responsive to the needs of any particular case. [...] *This does not involve a modification of the existing test as properly understood. Rather it is an explanation of principles that were already implicit in our law.*"

ibid at para 74.

[75] The relevant extracts cited by Clark (*ibid* at paras 75-76) were as follows:

"In her judgment, Denham J. reiterated her position, at para. 18, on the appropriate test to be applied in judicial review a number of times. That determination was:-

'[...] Where fundamental rights and freedoms are factors in a review, they are relevant in analysing the reasonableness of a decision. This is inherent in the test of whether a decision is reasonable.'

Adopting the reasoning of Henchy in Keegan, she stated:-

"25. [...] Any effect on rights should be within constitutional limitations, should be proportionate to the objective to be achieved. f the effect is disproportionate it would justify the court setting aside the decision.

26. [...] I am satisfied that the test applied by Henchy J., and agreed to by all of the members of the Court, is the correct test. It should be applied in all the circumstances of each case. In a case where the decision maker has a special technical skill, such as in *O'Keeffe v. An Bord Pleanála*, the test should be applied strictly. In a case where fundamental rights are in issue, such rights form part of the constitutional jurisdiction of the Court in which a reasonable decision is required to be made and, if made, analysed. [...]

38. The *test as stated by Henchy J. in The State (Keegan) v. Stardust Victims' Compensation Tribunal is sufficiently general when construed broadly in relevant circumstances to be applied so that fundamental rights may be protected.*

39. The term "irrational" is less relevant in that it relates to situations which are alleged to be perverse and arise less frequently in litigation.

40. The term "unreasonable" is the key, it is broader and essentially the basis of this type of scrutiny. A decision which interferes with constitutional rights, if it is to be considered reasonable, should be proportionate. If such an approach is not taken then the remedy may not be effective. This is relevant especially when access to the courts has been limited by the legislature.'"

(Emphasis added by Clark J, judgment of Denham J above n 1).

similarly stressed the manner in which all reasoning regarding proportionality had called back to *Keegan* as a foregoing authority.[76] Clark J, therefore goes on to state:

> "Contrary to the extraordinary arguments made that proportionality is a new and defining principle in judicial review…. Clearly the inclusion of proportionality as part of reasonableness did not have its origins in *Meadows*."[77]

Apart from these general statements of principle, Clark J relied upon portions of Murray CJ's judgment which have been less prominent in academic considerations of *Meadows*. In particular, she highlights Murray CJ's examination of deportation cases, which followed his statements of general principle, and strongly indicated that the impact of his general statements of principle on the prevailing approach to taking such decisions would be minimal. In particular in referring to his previous decision in *AO and DL*, his Honour noted that he had applied a proportionality analysis, and concluded. [9–48]

> "It seems to me entirely reasonable to conclude that the circumstances relating to the applicants are not unique but on the contrary it is a situation that could apply or would apply to a substantial proportion of applicants for asylum. In these circumstances it seems to me entirely reasonable that the Minister would consider whether a refusal to make a deportation order in such circumstances could call in question the integrity of the immigration and asylum systems including their effective functions. This is a matter for him…."[78]

---

[76] For example, at para 78 of *O(O) & A(O)* above n 67 , Clark J cites Murray CJ's statement that "The foregoing citations set out the essence of the principles which were applied in those two cases by this Court when judicially reviewing the administrative decisions in question." *Meadows* above n 1 at 721.

[77] *ibid* at paras 81-82. Clark J cited as immediate support for this position, the statement of Murray CJ in *Meadows* that:

> "The principle requires that the effects on or prejudice to an individual's rights by an administrative decision be proportional to the legitimate objective or purpose of that decision. Application of the principle of proportionality is in my view a means of examining whether the decision meets the test of reasonableness. I do not find anything in the dicta of the Court in Keegan or O'Keeffe which would exclude the Court from applying the principle of proportionality in cases where it could be considered to be relevant. Indeed in *Fajujonu v. Minister for Justice* [1992] I.R. 151 to which I will refer in more detail shortly, this Court made express reference to the need of the Minister to observe the principle of proportionality when deciding whether to permit the immigrants in that case reside in the State."

Meadows above n 1 at 723.

[78] *ibid* at 726. Referencing the earlier case of *AO and DL v The Minister for Justice* [2003] 1 IR 1.

[9–49]   Clark J argued that Murray CJ had a foreclosed vision of the impact of his general analysis on the particular area of deportation, and "was clearly restating the law relating to the deportation of the parents of citizen children and not changing that law"[79]:

> "On the other hand I did not exclude that there may be cases where, in exceptional circumstances, the Court might require evidence of the manner in which the integrity of the immigration and asylum systems could be called in question but that was not required in that particular case. What I had in mind there was that a purely formulaic decision of the Minister may not in particular circumstances be a sufficient statement of the rationale or reasons underlying the decision."[80]

[9–50]   There was nothing new injected but a re-emphasis of existing approaches and Clark J rejected any claims of disjuncture between the pre- and post-*Meadows* era:

> "Proportionality then, and long before that, formed part of a sound evaluation of the reasonableness of an administrative decision. A decision could not be reasonable if its effect were disproportionate to the objective pursued."[81]

[9–51]   Clark J's approach to *Meadows* is to view it as an emanation rather than an advancement of *Keegan*. That the judgment does not seem to fully address the status of Denham J's structured proportionality definition presents difficulties for those who construe *Meadows* as a deeper, more substantial reflection on an existing principle. The judgment in *O(O) & A(O)* adopts the view that a preexisting proportionality analysis has been applied regularly in Irish law, but does not evaluate the extent to which it has been applied in a structured manner. To some, writing such a history of the operation of *Keegan/O'Keeffe* standard represents an appeal to formal legal standards rather than actual applications. It may be that the reality of the use of proportionality in Irish administrative law is not to be found in the healing metaphor of the inclusive nature of language of *Keegan*, but rather in evaluating existing case-law with a sharp eye for the tendency towards exclusionary applications of the concept. While our tone here may appear critical, we wish to stress Clark J's approach simply underlines the reservoir of conflicting principles emerging from *Meadows* and the legitimate

---

[79] *O(O) & A(O)* above n 67 at para 86.
[80] *Meadows* above n 1 at 727.
[81] *O(O) & A(O)* above n 67 at para 89.

entitlement of future judges to query how these may interact and be ranked, especially in particular statutory contexts. Finally, it is important to remember that Clark J's comments were strictly *obiter*, and it is arguable, given her emphasis on Murray CJ's findings in *AO and DL*, that the majority of her conclusions were specific to the deportation context.

Efe v Minister for Justice, Equality and Law Reform: Protecting Rights Through Proportionality

A contrasting approach to *Meadows*, was seen in the admirably direct and extensive examination provided by Hogan J in *Efe v Minister for Justice, Equality and Law Reform*.[82] While, cautioning that it was "perhaps, too early to evaluate the precise significance of the decision", two central points were clear. Firstly, Hogan J held that "a majority in the Supreme Court was prepared to apply a general proportionality test in respect of all decisions affecting fundamental rights…".[83] Therefore: [9–52]

> "…it can no longer be said that the courts are constrained to apply some artificially restricted test for review for administrative decisions affecting fundamental rights on reasonableness and rationality grounds. This test is broad enough to ensure that the substance and essence of constitutional rights will always be protected against unfair attack, if necessary through the application of a *Meadows*-style proportionality analysis."[84]

This latter quote does contain some ambiguity on the *trigger* for the application of a *Meadows*-style proportionality analysis. When will it be necessary to do so? What are the sharpening factors in a case which call for its employment? A mere permission does not automatically translate into action. Secondly, Hogan J argued that following the decision in *Meadows*: [9–53]

> "…it is equally clear that the *O'Keeffe* test has been reinterpreted and clarified to take fuller account of the earlier judgment of Henchy J in *Keegan*".[85]

Our analysis of the case-law since *Meadows* has however, found numerous instances where the *O'Keeffe* standard has been invoked. Furthermore, the

---

[82] *Efe v Minister for Justice, Equality and Law Reform* [2011] 2 IR 798. Hereinafter "*Efe*".
[83] *ibid* at 815.
[84] *ibid* at 827.
[85] *ibid* at 815, referring to the cases of *O'Keefe v An Bord Pleanála* and The *State (Keegan) v Stardust Compensation Tribunal*.

judgment of Fennelly J in *Meadows* continued to claim that proportionality "can operate within the confines of the *Keegan* or *O'Keeffe* test".[86]

[9–54]   Yet beyond these two core claims, the judgment of Hogan offers an erudite appraisal of the history of judicial invocations of reasonableness and proportionality in Ireland. He notes that "it would be churlish not to acknowledge that judicial attitudes to this question in this jurisdiction have waxed and waned over the last fifty years or so".[87] In a useful consideration of past cases, he clearly regarded *The State (Lynch) v Cooney* as a core precedent, with its test requiring a reason for a decision to be "*bona fide* held and factually sustainable and not unreasonable".[88] The failure to invoke this precedent in *O'Keeffe* was clearly viewed by Hogan J as a contributory factor in the confused landscape which followed:

> "For some reason *Lynch* was not referred to in *O'Keefe*, despite the former's seminal status as an absolutely critical decision dealing with the reviewability of ministerial and, by extension, administrative decisions. Perhaps it is for this reason that in some respects these two decisions cannot be easily aligned. If the former decision required that a ministerial decision must be shown to be factually sustainable before the opinion of the Minister could be upheld, this seems at odds with the latter decision inasmuch as it decided that the courts could not interfere – at least in the specialist sphere of planning law – with an administrative decision save in the "no evidence" type cases."[89]

[9–55]   Hogan J cited *Neurendale Ltd v Dublin City Council,*[90] a case held in the weeks leading up to the *Meadows* judgments where McKechnie J held that *O'Keeffe* had indeed qualified *Keegan*. It was clear, for Hogan J, that simply referring to the *Keegan-O'Keeffe* standard somewhat obscured the fact that the latter decision had inspired two fresh trends in the case-law. Firstly, it had stimulated the tendency to claim that "courts could only quash for unreasonableness or irrationality in quite special — or perhaps it would be more accurate to say — extraordinary cases".[91] The second was an

---

[86] *Meadows* above n 1 at 827. Emphasis added.

[87] *Efe*, above n 82 at 808.

[88] *The State (Lynch) v Cooney* [1982] IR 337, Judgment of O'Higgins CJ at 361.

[89] *ibid* at 809.

[90] *Nurendale Ltd. v Dublin City Council* [2009] IEHC 588

[91] *Efe* above n 82 at 809. This was reflected by the decision in *Aer Rianta v Commissioner for Aviation Regulation* [2003] IEHC 12 in particular.

increased reliance upon deference in review standards.[92] Hogan J stressed that the *Meadows* decision "did not simply drop out of the sky" but was rather anchored in "increasing judicial unease with the manner in which *O'Keeffe* had come to be applied in practice".[93] He then identified three cases which embodied such uneasiness; *Holland v Governor of Portlaoise Prison*,[94] *I v Minister for Justice, Equality and Law Reform*,[95] and *Clinton v An Bord Pleanála (No.2).*[96]

Reflecting on the development of judicial review in this area, Hogan J stressed the underlying judicial responsibility for identifying standards of review as amounting to something more than mere semantics, but instead as a matter of great impact: [9–56]

> "...there is nonetheless a clear difference in principle between saying on the one hand that a decision is unreasonable because there is "no evidence" for the conclusion reached, while on the other quashing a decision because it does not flow from the original premises of the decision maker...It will be a rare case indeed where there is absolutely no evidence to support a particular proposition. By contrast, there may well be many instances where there is *some* evidence to justify a particular decision, but where the ultimate conclusion simply does not flow from the original premise (*Keegan*) or but nonetheless falls to be quashed for lack of proportionality (*Meadows*).'[97]

Hogan J then provided what is perhaps the most developed judicial consideration of the idea of deference. Noting that the question of deferring to technical expertise was well established before *Meadows*,[98] the judgment then moved to a broader consideration of the factors which may lead a Court to defer: [9–57]

> "Quite independently of questions of technical expertise, there are naturally certain types of issues which do not admit of easy resolution if ordinary legal standards and principles or even conventional legal reasoning are to be employed. Thus, in the sphere of planning

---

[92] Stressing that deference "is far from a relatively new concept" Hogan J cited *Philadelphia Storage Battery Co. v Controller of Industrial and Commercial Property* [1935] IR 575 as an example of early judicial discussion of the idea.

[93] *Efe*, above n 82 at 813.

[94] *Holland v Governor of Portlaoise Prison* [2004] 2 IR 573.

[95] *I v Minister for Justice, Equality and Law Reform* [2008] 1 IR 208.

[96] *Clinton v An Bord Pleanála (No.2)* [2007] 4 IR 701.

[97] *Efe*, above n 82 at 816.

[98] Citing in support *M & J Gleeson Ltd v Competition Authority* [1999] 1 ILRM 401.

and development, the resolution of questions involving technical engineering assessments, sustainability, aesthetics and even taste probably admit of limited judicial involvement...But this approach would have a much more limited (if, indeed, any) application in many other spheres of the planning process. At the other end of this spectrum, for example, the question of whether the compulsory acquisition of land was objectively necessary in the public interest squarely engages the substantive protection of property rights, and as Geoghegan J. so carefully explained in *Clinton (no. 2)* [2007] 4 I.R. 701), these rights would not be adequately protected by a test which was satisfied by showing that there was a reasonable basis for the decision."[99]

[9–58]   In the particular context of immigration and asylum, which was the subject matter of the case at hand, Hogan J stressed that "much might depend...on the experience and expertise of the particular decision-maker in the context of the decision at hand".[100] Where an asylum claim, for example, involved "complex societal and group behaviour", its resolution:

> "...would undoubtedly benefit from decision-makers possessing specialist knowledge of the understanding of the society and behaviour in question. If, in this sort of unusual case, the decision maker were shown to have this type of expertise, then, of course, the courts should generally defer to it...But where, as in the general run of things, the decision maker has not even visited the country in question and is, for example, entirely reliant on country of origin information to assist with a credibility assessment, any doctrine of curial deference would seem misplaced. If, for example an African administrator, was to claim a specialist knowledge of contemporary Irish political, social and cultural history based solely on his or her having read or consulted US State Department country of origin information regarding Ireland, this would be justly viewed her with some scepticism, not to speak of outright incredulity. Why should the position be viewed any differently in the case of those Irish decision-makers whose knowledge of the political and social affairs of specific African countries is derived almost exclusively from similar sources?"[101]

[9–59]   In the case before the Court, the task before the decision-maker was to assess the impacts on the applicant's family of his proposed deportation, and also to examine whether it was realistic to expect them to follow him to Nigeria. Hogan J stressed that no deference should be applied when reviewing such

---

[99] *Efe*, above n 82 at 812.
[100] *ibid*.
[101] *ibid* at 812-3.

tasks — firstly, the decision-makers could not claim any specialist knowledge or expertise, and secondly, the decision engaged fundamental rights, "the protection of which is the solemn duty of the Court".[102] Hogan J therefore found that "whatever be the parameters of the curial deference doctrine, it has no relevance to the present case".[103] Somewhat confusingly, however, in the next sentence, he found that "it cannot be said that any doctrine of *heightened* deference is applicable",[104] which seems to carry the connotation that an ordinary form of deference may underlie it.

MEO (Nigeria) v Minister for Justice, Equality and Law Reform: Sledgehammers and Nuts

Despite the clearly defined alternatives offered by Clark J and Hogan J, the overwhelming sense upon surveying the emerging case law is one of confusion, and a tendency to cite the exceptional nature of proportionality rather than its general application. Furthermore, the use of proportionality is impressionistic, as judges, rather than running a distinct structured analysis, appear to take an overarching view of whether the matter is clearly or manifestly disproportionate. Perhaps the strongest example of this is the decision of Cooke J in *MEO (Nigeria) v Minister for Justice, Equality & Law Reform*.[105] In this case Cooke J rejected a submission that a decision to deport was deficient "in the *Meadows* sense": **[9–60]**

> "It is not immediately clear to this Court what the "requisite reasoning standard" of the *Meadows v Minister for Justice* [2010] 2 I.R. 701 case requires. In this Court's understanding, the ratio of the majority judgment of the Supreme Court in that case is that a *clear disproportionality* in the impact of an administrative decision can constitute "manifest unreasonableness" for the purposes of administrative law and is thus to be taken as coming within the bounds of the Court's jurisdiction to annul an administrative decision on grounds of unreasonabless [as per *Keegan*]. The essential consideration in *Meadows v Minister for Justice*, it seems to the Court, was not so much the establishment of a particular standard of reasoning, as a finding that there had been a total absence of reasoning in the sense that the decision maker had been presented with evidence of a risk of subjection to female genital mutilation

---

[102] *ibid* at 813.
[103] *ibid*.
[104] *ibid*.
[105] *MEO (Nigeria) v Minister for Justice, Equality & Law Reform* [2012] IEHC 394.

upon repatriation and had rejected the representation with a simple statement that "refoulement" was not found to be an issue…"[106]

[9–61]   Such an attempt to apply a narrow, factual reading on the *Meadows* judgments neglects the character of the *Meadows* action as a point of law reference. The requirement of a *clear* disproportionality in the result represents a continuation of the pragmatic nature of the Irish judicial reasoning. Rather than commencing with a standard of proportionality which is applied in each specific context, its meaning is reverse engineered from the factual presumption that its use to quash discretionary decisions must be rare.

[9–62]   The impressionistic, sledgehammer to crack nuts approach was expressly endorsed as lying at the core of *Meadows* by Cooke J in *Afolabi v Minister for Justice and Equality & Ors*.[107] He noted that Murray CJ had cited with approval a passage from Keane J in *Radio Limerick One Ltd v IRTC*, where he stated that regardless, it was clear that the disproportion in a decision could be "so gross" as to render it unreasonable.[108] For Cooke J the result this merely underlined that:

> "…an administrative measure or decision may be unlawful as manifestly unreasonable if an administrative sledge-hammer is employed to crack a legislative or policy nut."[109]

Minister for Justice v Ostrowski: **Proportionality as a Signaling Device**

[9–63]   The confused nature of the High Court jurisprudence relating to *Meadows*, makes the brief (and entirely *obiter*) return to the *Meadows* judgments by the Supreme Court in a European Arrest Warrant matter, *Minister for Justice v Ostrowski*,[110] somewhat puzzling. McKechnie J delivering the joint judgment of the Court which provided a brief overview of the functions of the proportionality principle in Irish law, noting that it "is now clearly

---

[106] *ibid* at para 88, emphasis added

[107] *Afolabi v Minister for Justice and Equality & Ors* [2012] IEHC 192, hereinafter "*Afolabi*".

[108] *Radio Limerick One Ltd v IRTC* [1997] 2 ILRM 1 at 20:
"Whatever the view may be taken as to the desirability of that approach, it can be said with confidence that, in some cases at least, the disproportion between the gravity or otherwise of a breach of a condition attached to a statutory privilege and the permanent withdrawal of the privilege would be so gross as to render the revocation unreasonable within the *Wednesbury* or *Keegan* formulation."

[109] *Afolabi* above n 107 at para 19.

[110] *Minister for Justice v Ostrowski* [2013] IESC 24.

discernable in a multitude of circumstances" and "is an established rule of domestic jurisprudence".[111] He noted further that:

> "...a core objective which motivated its creation was the establishment of a criteria, whose structure and use is more rational and more objectively verifiable than the more subjective concept of reasonableness, by which a measured balance could be had and retained between the public benefit of a given decision and the harmful effects of that decision on the affected individual. Proportion is key in such regard."[112]

Interestingly, his Honour also stressed the need to consider the relationship [9–64] of rights to the public interest, rather than the traditional and simplistic division of rights versus the public interest. Thus the latter should be understood as lying within the former, providing the judiciary with a clear mandate to intervene:

> "The test in a sense is both permissive and restrictive. Action by a variety of bodies on behalf of the public is of course both an inherent and an indispensable feature of modern society. When such impacts on fundamental rights however, a principle value of democracy (freedom) is diminished. It is essentially as important to the citizen that such diminution is as minimal as possible, as it is to have the measure activated in the first instance. Means, at judicial level, are required to evaluate and to achieve this balance. One measure and one of increasing importance in this armoury is, as I have said, proportionality."[113]

Despite the way proportionality was often transmuted into other words in [9–65] the course of judicial reasoning (such as "appropriate" or "suitable") and the manner in which its meaning may shift according to context, it remained:

> "...quite a valuable assessment method and should be so treated. Furthermore, there is a powerful value in its name, identity and recognition which adds to its intrinsic impact, and therefore, even where readily interchangeable with other expressions, I would be quite slow in dropping its nomenclature. Whilst such may lack the impressive ancestry of the epithet "natural" in the phrase "natural justice", nonetheless it has a particular signification, and thus its widespread use should be maintained. Provided its meaning is properly understood in a given context, any misunderstanding can be avoided."[114]

---

[111] *ibid* at para 31.
[112] *ibid* at para 32.
[113] *ibid* at para 33.
[114] *ibid* at para 34.

[9–66]   This is a valuable affirmation of proportionality as a signaling device to administrators, with its use carrying an expressive value in registering the importance of rights. Warning that *Meadows* had not been expressly pleaded by either party, McKechnie J contributed a general statement of the principle of proportionality, without specifying whether it applied in the context of constitutional law, administrative law or EU law:

> "Therefore, may I say that the principle examines the objectives (and their legitimacy) of a given decision and the impact on the rights which it affects, and measures the correlation between both. If the result, having correctly valued the competing interests, lacks balance, the measure may be condemned. At a more formal level it can be said that this assessment review, involves the following four elements: legitimate objective, rational connection, minimal impairment, and overall balance (Brady, "Proportionality, Defence and Fundamental Rights in Irish Administrative Law: The Aftermath of Meadows 2010 1 D.U.L.J 136-171). When correctly applied, the justification for the conclusion preferred, should be both evident and transparent."[115]

[9–67]   This comment was clearly *obiter* but underlines the chameleon-like nature of *Meadows* as a precedent. While we would largely support Brady's consolidated proportionality test, his article, as discussed above, explored the possible meanings of *Meadows*. Of course, McKechnie J was discussing the concept of proportionality generally, rather than proportionality as it operates in the judicial review of administrative decisions. Nevertheless, given the fragmentary nature of the majority judgments in *Meadows*, it remains debatable as to whether such a structured approach to proportionality is to be employed in the administrative context. While Denham J (as she then was) expressly recognized it, as we have outlined, there have been few applications of this four step approach in the post-*Meadows* case-law.

Conclusion

[9–68]   We have described the use of proportionality post *Meadows* as impressionistic. Perhaps a more sympathetic descriptor would be "contextual".[116] As we have seen, it is possible to say that proportionality is available, but we do not yet know the trigger for such an analysis. Shifts in

---

[115] *ibid* at para 36.

[116] One reason we chose "impressionistic" over "contextual" is due to the underdevelopment of idea of deference which makes the exact role of context difficult to map.

approach and episodes of uncertainty are not new in relation to this area of judicial review. Indeed, reasonableness as a ground has often undergone periods of dormancy,[117] but the current phase, freed as it now is from the excesses of the "no evidence" standard, may yield more positive results for litigants. *Meadows* is a decision which extols the flexibility of reasonableness analysis, but the foregoing case-law should also serve to remind us of how that flexibility can be shaped to match an individual judicial assessment of a particular case at hand. This statement is not meant as a stinging (and frankly irresponsible) rebuke carrying the suggestion that High Court judges "do their own thing", but rather an objective comment drawn from the reality that the Supreme Court precedent in this matter remains open-textured and in need of finessing. Perhaps what we see in all this discussion is an implicit sense that for many judges, semantics — the selection of a particular form of words — simply cannot operate to systemically order the practical assessment of reasonableness. In many ways, the experiences of judging — something which the authors do not share — seem to point Irish judges towards pragmatism. Further dialogue regarding this is necessary. Our own sense is that sensitivity to context is to be celebrated, but context deserves a structured treatment.

Later in this book in chapters 14 and 15, we will see what is in many ways, **[9–69]** the next iteration of the proportionality debate. This arises because having provided a renewed and more flexible statement of reasonableness and proportionality in *Meadows*, many Irish judges now hold that this allows judicial review to constitute an effective remedy for those seeking vindication of their ECHR and EU law rights. The result is that, having arguably only just untangled the threads of unreasonableness analysis in Irish law, the *Meadows* approach is prima facie viewed as accommodative of the traditionally more searching international balancing processes. For the critics of *Meadows*, there is a deep irony in this position — that being that a review process which became encrusted with non-interventionist logic through *O'Keeffe* is now being pointed to as an adaptive remedy. As we will see, this question ultimately has a powerful effect upon an individual's ability to rely upon European norms to overturn decisions.

---

[117] In an Australian context, one of the authors would note that an undergraduate class in Australia would feature approximately four or five authorities, following which discussion would shift to relevant and irrelevant considerations as a more invoked ground of review. Yet Australia recently stirred out of this dormancy with the landmark decision in *Li v Department of Immigration and Citizenship* [2013] HCA 18, which has seen the reasonableness lecture expand to three hours.

Audi Alteram Partem

Introduction

Who ought decrees, nor heares both sides discust,

Does but unjustly though his Doome be just.[1]

The idea of natural justice involves two primary principles: *audi alteram partem* (the right to a fair hearing) and bias. Unlike other jurisdictions, which apply natural justice as a rebuttable common law presumption, in Ireland these two principles are placed upon a constitutional footing. Constitutional justice is rooted in the Article 40.3.1° injunction that the state "protect...from unjust attack" the personal rights of the citizen.[2] Statutes purporting to remove this kernel of procedural protection are thus held to be unconstitutional. The interchangeability of labels in this area namely, "natural justice", "constitutional justice" and "procedural fairness" reflects the differing sources which have constructed the requirements — both statutory, constitutional and common law. Largely however, the lack of consistency in the terminology used suggests that these differing sources work in synergy rather than as heavily differentiated obligations. We also must note at the outset that further procedural fairness obligations arise under Article 6 of the European Convention on Human Rights and the right to fair procedure under European Union law; these are discussed later in the book in chapters 14 and 15.

[10–01]

In asking what sharpens the requirements of fairness and what might reduce it, we see a range of policy factors mapped out. For lawyers, in particular, the formality of the court is a powerful heritage which exerts a significant gravitational pull and is often installed as the apogee of procedural protection. In Ireland, natural justice is, as we have already noted, also installed as a constitutional right. Such centripetal influences operate to centre the area upon the rights of the citizen. However, as Professor John McMillan has noted "excess can be as damaging as deficiency", and centrifugal forces of administrative pressures can also act upon the area.[3] Fair procedures can frustrate aims such as finality, efficiency and flexibility in decision-making. As a result McMillan calls on us to recall

[10–02]

---

[1] Seneca, *Medea: A Tragedie*, Translated by ES Esq (1648).

[2] Constitutional justice, specifically a duty to observe "basic fairness of procedures" applies even where aliens are involved. Barrington J in *State (McFadden) v The Governor of Mountjoy Prison (No. 1)* [1981] ILRM 113 at 122.

[3] J McMillan, "Natural justice: too much, too little or just rights?", (2008) 58 AIAL Forum, paper delivered to the Australian Institute of Administrative Law, National Administrative Law Forum, Canberra, 2007. Available online at http://www.ombudsman.gov.au/files/

the need to balance: "natural justice is a doctrine of law, but it must develop sensibly as a doctrine of administrative law".[4]

[10–03] Taking on this message, we should not elevate procedural fairness to a position of being an unimpeachable good, but instead debate its practical impacts. In this way we can reflect more clearly on its benefits and limitations. It can be associated with a legalism that projects judges as narrow experts in fair decision-making, or which encourages a tendency to chase process rather than engage with the contents of the administrator's reasoning. This point has been argued most vociferously by Professor Julian Disney:

> "When pursued with obsessive legalistic vigour, 'natural justice' is often the enemy of real justice. ... [A]doption of complex procedures to comply with traditional principles of 'natural justice' has meant that many people are effectively prevented from getting any form of justice at all. Well-meaning lawyers, and others who are involved in the administrative review system, should be very careful not to encrust the system at the lower levels with a whole range of apparent safeguards which, in practice, will harm many people in great need and may be of largely illusory benefit for many other people."[5]

[10–04] Many commentators critical of the core operating assumptions of natural justice allege such a lack of connection between process and substance — arguing that, for all its classical taproots, procedural justice can often represent the "last meal before a hanging". One can counter this view, however, by arguing that procedural fairness is often connected to the judiciary's perception of an overarching substantive unfairness. De Blacam argues that Irish courts have often indirectly tackled substantively unjust results through forced procedural fairness reasoning:

> "First the [natural justice] terminology may be used loosely; secondly, procedural fairness sometimes embraces substantive fairness; and finally, any unwillingness to make explicit reference to a want of

---

August_2007_Natural_justice_too_much_too_little_or_just_right.pdf (date accessed 14 October 2014) at p 1.

[4] *ibid.*

[5] J Disney, "Access, Equity and the Dominant Paradigm" In J McMillan (ed), *Administrative Law: Does The Public Benefit?* (AIAL Administrative Law Forum, 1992) 1 at p 7. We would also note in this context the comment of Hogan and Morgan "there is no sign that any Irish judge has questioned the view that what is good for a court is (in a somewhat modified way) good for a public administrator." G Hogan and DG Morgan, *Administrative Law in Ireland* (4th ed) (Round Hall, Dublin, 2010) at para 12-04, hereinafter "Hogan and Morgan".

substantive fairness is not to be confused with an unwillingness, when the occasion arise, to condemn a decision for that very reason."[6]

It is clear that procedural fairness is a deeply contextual matter, with judges varying its content along a continuum based upon diverse considerations such as statutory provisions, efficiencies and the perceived seriousness of the subject matter. This in itself raises challenges and frustrations for administrative bodies in trying to identify its content. It is important to consider the diversity of situations as obligations can vary according to where the administrative process in question falls on the inquisitorial to adversarial range. **[10–05]**

We noted in chapter 1 of this book some administrative law theorists are critical of legal actors' tendency to overvalue the practical worth of their traditional doctrines. These green light theorists argue that law is just one way of regulating administrative decision-making — and is often a very inefficient tool, imposing high costs in terms of efficiency and actual substantive outcomes. Such arguments may be responded to with the argument that participation ensures more accurate decision-making, by requiring engagement with the affected individual's perspective. More broadly, one can argue that democracy, as manifested through the individual's right to participation, represents the motive force for the imposition of procedural fairness obligations. As we will now see, the pursuit of participation as an end in and of itself is a powerful motive force in Irish natural justice jurisprudence. **[10–06]**

Flexibility and Specificity: The Interactions of Context and Content

While students, practitioners and administrators will be eager to identify a clear checklist of requirements in reaching a decision, we have already noted the significance of the fact that many judgments in this area are deeply contextual. An important piece of advice is, therefore, to unpack the context and the various public policy and individual interest aspects. The Australian case of *Mobil Oil Australia Pty Ltd v Federal Commissioner of Taxation* best summarises this: **[10–07]**

> "Notwithstanding what Lord Loreburn said in *Board of Education v Rice* 1911 AC 179 about 'always giving a fair opportunity to those who

---

[6] M de Blacam, *Judicial Review* (2nd ed) (Tottel Publishing, Dublin, 2012) at para 11-05.

were parties in the controversy to correct or contradict any relevant statement prejudicial to their view', the books are full of cases which illustrate both the impossibility of laying a universally valid test by which to ascertain what may constitute such an opportunity in the infinite variety of circumstances that may exist, and the necessity of allowing full effect in every case to the particular statutory framework within which the proceedings take place...what the law requires in the discharge of a quasi-judicial function is fairness. That is not a label for any fixed body of rules. What is fair in a given situation depends upon the circumstances."[7]

[10–08]   Procedural fairness is also significant in that it is a component of judicial review where the traditional separation of public and private law are, if not completely crossed, then at least sidestepped. It is clear in cases of the termination of employment for misconduct, for example, that often high standards of natural justice apply, as Henchy J noted in *State (Gleeson) v Minister for Defence*:

"Where..... the discharge is for a reason that is discreditable, the fundamentals of justice require that the man shall have an opportunity of meeting the case for discharging him for that reason. That is the minimum that is needed to guard against injustice.....It would be an affront to justice if the law were to hold that a decision with such drastic consequences for the man involved, and possibly for his dependants could be made behind his back."[8]

[10–09]   Findings impacting upon the professional reputation of individuals also attract high standards.[9] Nevertheless, students would do well to avoid reasoning by category or checklist. As we shall see over the course of this chapter, procedural fairness requirements require practical balancing and an attentiveness to context. What follows is an overview of the major recurring themes as to when, and to what extent, procedural fairness will apply.

---

[7] [1963] 113 CLR 475 at 504.

[8] *State (Gleeson) v Minister for Defence* [1976] IR 280 at 295.

[9] *Prendiville v Medical Council* [2008] 3 IR 122 at para 131.
    "....I am satisfied the high standards of natural justice must apply.....The applicants were entitled to expect that there would be strict adherence to the rules of natural justice and that justice would not only be done but be seen to be done in their dealings with the Council."

Contract Versus Administrative Law: Which Organisations are Subject to Procedural Fairness Frameworks?

The question of which bodies are amendable to judicial review, is a persistent question across multiple jurisdictions. Ireland boasts case-law going in many different directions, and often dependent upon context. The factors weighing on such a decision were admirably fused into one test by Finlay CJ: [10–10]

> "The principle which, in general, excludes from the ambit of judicial review decisions made in the realm of private law by persons or tribunals whose authority derives from contract is ... confined to cases or instances where the duty being performed by the decision making authority is manifestly a private duty and where his right to make it derives solely from contract or solely from consent or the agreement of the parties affected. Where the duty being carried out by a decision making authority ... is of a nature which might ordinarily be seen as coming within the public domain, that decision can only be excluded from the reach of the jurisdiction in judicial review if it can be shown that it solely and exclusively derived from an individual contract made in private law."[10]

The onus of proving non-amenability to judicial review is on the respondent. A more recent Supreme Court case, *O'Donnell v Tipperary (South Riding) County Council*,[11] concerned an application to review the termination of the employment of a station officer of a fire station. Denham J ruled that on the facts, the matter was within the public domain, and while there was a contract between the applicant and the council, it had a significant public element. She reiterated the two pronged test of *Beirne* that the decision-maker should be performing a private duty and its right to make the decision must derive solely from contract or consent of the parties. [10–11]

---

[10] *Beirne v Commissioner of An Garda Siochana* [1993] ILRM 1 at 2. See also *Eogan v University College Dublin* [1996] IR 390. There the applicant, who was the holder of a statutory professorship in the University sought to quash a decision requiring him to retire at the age of 65 years and abolishing a previous practice under which there had been an entitlement to continue until the age of 70 years. The respondent sought to resist the application for judicial review upon the ground that the University was a private body which did not derive powers from statute and had made its decision on the basis of its private contract of employment with the professor. Shanley J applied the principle enunciated by Finlay CJ in the *Beirne* case, emphasising particularly that a decision which will ordinarily be seen as coming within the public domain will be excluded from judicial review only "if it can be shown that it is solely and exclusively derived from an individual contract made in private law".

[11] *O'Donnell v Tipperary (South Riding) County Council* [2005] 2 IR 483.

[10–12]   The reviewability of certain decisions taken by the National Asset Management Agency was endorsed by Finlay Geoghegan J in *Treasury Holdings v National Asset Management Agency*.[12] In the case, counsel for NAMA relied heavily the British precedent of *R (Birmingham and Solihull Taxi Association) v Birmingham International Airport*, to argue that enforcement by public bodies of rights rooted in commercial contractual arrangements are not amenable to judicial review, outside of instances of fraud, corruption or bad faith.[13] Finlay Geoghegan J concluded that any differences of approach there might be within the UK jurisprudence were "minimal, and may be more one of nomenclature than of substance".[14] NAMA was found to fail both limbs of the Irish test: its function was bestowed by statute and, while taking a commercial decision in relation to scheduling repayments, it was enjoined to consider the public interest.[15] On the second limb, the right to make such decisions did not derive *solely* from contract, as NAMA's right to initially purchase the loans derive from statute.[16] Further, any decision to enforce the loans for non-payment would have to take into account public interests defined by statute.[17]

[10–13]   In *Geoghegan v Institute of Chartered Accountants in Ireland*,[18] the applicant, a professional member of the Institute of Chartered Accountants sought to quash proceedings taken against him by the institute's disciplinary committee. The Institute was a professional body incorporated by royal charter, endowed with functions of representation of its members as well as disciplinary functions. It did not have the sole right to admit members to the accountancy profession, but being an institute member allowed one to carry out certain statutory tasks, such as auditing, under the Companies Acts. The observations of Denham J in this case are strictly *obiter* but have exerted some influence on the boundaries of Irish law.[19] In finding the

---

[12] *Treasury Holdings v National Asset Management Agency* [2012] IEHC 297.

[13] *ibid* at para 76. See *R (Birmingham and Solihull Taxi Association) v Birmingham International Airport* [2009] EWHC 1913 (Admin.).

[14] *ibid* at para 78.

[15] *ibid* at para 80.

[16] *ibid* at para 81.

[17] *ibid* at para 82.

[18] *Geoghegan v Institute of Chartered Accountants in Ireland* [1995] 3 IR 86. Hereinafter "*Geoghegan*".

[19] In *Rafferty v Bus Eireann* [1997] 2 IR 424. Kelly J (at 441) identified certain factors in that case by reference to these factors identified by Denham J in *Geoghegan*, in finding that the case involved a sufficient public law element to justify judicial review:

   "1. This case relates to a major method of public transport and to persons employed in that operation. Public transport is important to the community. Disputes

matter susceptible to review she stressed that the case related to a major profession, which was important in the community, with a special connection to the judicial organ of Government in the courts in areas such as receivership, liquidation, examinership, as well as special auditing responsibilities. The royal charter, as well as legislation affecting the institute, had "a nexus with two branches of the Government". Given the consequences she found that the disciplinary committee was required to act in accordance with the principles of natural justice.

There are instances, however, where the courts will refuse to find a **[10–14]** sufficiently public interest subsisting in the overall relationship. For example, in the case of *Bloxham v Irish Stock Exchange plc*[20] an attempt to rely upon the *Geoghegan* principles and review the actions of the Irish Stock Exchange failed. The High Court ruled that the revocation of membership in the Stock Exchange was not a matter of public law. The applicants' submissions, in seeking to satisfy the amenability test, had relied heavily on the introduction of new regulations, the European Communities (Markets in Financial Instruments) Regulations 2007 (SI No 60 of 2007) which gave the Stock Exchange a regulatory role. Traditionally the relationship between the Stock Exchange and its members, including the applicant, had been governed by private contract. The applicant submitted that as the Stock Exchange was the sole authorised body which could operate a "regulated market" for trading activities, its decisions were of such importance to the State that it bore a public dimension. The 2007 regulations charged the Stock Exchange with monitoring compliance of members with trading conditions, the reporting of market abuse and the

---

concerning persons employed therein which might give rise to industrial action have consequences of hardship, particularly for members of the community who are entirely dependant upon it.

2. The original provider of the service now being given by the respondent, was the statutory corporation, C.I.E. The respondent itself owes its existence to the Act of 1986. Furthermore, it is the Act which places restrictions upon it concerning its employees through section 14.

3. The functions of the respondent and its employees come within the public domain of the State. Although a company formed by registration, I cannot ignore its statutory genesis.

4. The method by which the contractual relationship between the respondent and its employees is regulated, is subject to the statutory intervention which is contained in s. 14 of the Act of 1986.

5. The consequences of an unlawful interference with the contractual rights of the respondent's employees may be very serious for them."

[20] *Bloxham v Irish Stock Exchange plc* [2013] IEHC 301.

creation of the necessary arrangements and procedures for ensuring adequate supervision. Crucially, however, it did not grant the Stock Exchange the ability to discipline; rather the role was limited to reporting on possible abuse to the Central Bank. As a result, Cooke J refused to hold that the regulations "can be viewed as having created a form of nexus between the ISE and the Central Bank as a public authority".[21] This finding was heavily supported by the reality that although the Stock Exchange had a monopoly in operating a "regulated market", full membership in it was not an absolute pre-requisite for companies to participate in the exchange.

[10–15]   Two of the most prominent decisions construing the relationship between an applicant and the institution as a contractual, and not a public law one, are *Rajah v The Royal College of Surgeons*[22] and *Quinn v The Honourable Society of Kings Inns*.[23] *Rajah* concerned an application for judicial review by a medical student who, having sat two sittings of an exam, had not been readmitted. The Student Progress Committee was granted discretion to refuse a right to repeat the year, having considered the student's academic record and any mitigating circumstances. This decision was then sent to be ratified by the Academic Board. The applicant wished to review the Board's ratification as *ultra vires*: it had previously readmitted other students with inferior results to her own. Furthermore, she had not received any reasons for the decision. Keane J held that in enrolling, the student had consented to a contract which involved an agreement to be bound by the university regulations and appeals process. Consequently the issue was not a public law matter and not subject to review. *Rajah* was endorsed in the case of *Quinn*, where Smyth J ruled that:

> "The Examination Board's jurisdiction derives from the Education Rules of the Respondent. The Applicant was accepted as an applicant in the Entrance Examination on the basis of those rules. Accordingly insofar as the decision involved in those proceedings is concerned, the Applicant's rights are determined by a contract and the matter is essentially a private one relating to the rights of a student with respect to the Respondent. The fact that the Respondent's powers may initially derive from a charter is removed and indirect to the consideration of the instant case – as was made clear in re Malone's Application, it is necessary to consider the nature of the power as well as its source.

---

[21] *ibid* at para 53.

[22] *Rajah v The Royal College of Surgeons* [1994] 1 1R 384. Hereinafter "*Rajah*".

[23] *Quinn v The Honourable Society of Kings Inns* [2004] 4 IR 344. Hereinafter "*Quinn*".

The Examination Board when deciding to fail the Applicant was not exercising a disciplinary function and so is clearly distinguishable from [*Geoghegan v. Institute of Chartered Accountants in Ireland* [1995] 3 IR 86]...."[24]

In the more recent case of *Zhang v Athlone Institute of Technology*,[25] discussed below, however, Dunne J held that a decision to penalise a student for breach of examination rules was amenable to review. Her Honour stressed that unlike in *Quinn* and *Rajah*, the respondent was "exercising a disciplinary function", which derived from regulations made under the Regional Technical Colleges Act 1992. She stated that *Quinn/Rajah* findings would have had a bearing "if this was a case in which what was at issue was not a disciplinary matter".[26] In making this finding, Dunne J stressed that:

[10–16]

> "As a general proposition, the Courts should not be the place in which to deal with questions of discipline arising in academic institutions but there may be cases in which the nature of a breach of the right to fair procedures is such that recourse to the Courts is unavoidable."[27]

Clearly, there are also a range of bodies which lie in between private contractual relationships and statutorily regulated institutions. In the case of sports organisations, judicial review is available where it involves the imposition of a substantial sanction such as a suspension which bars a person from all competition.[28] Similarly the claim of a right to a livelihood grounds an entitlement to review in the case of licensing and regulatory decisions, despite any commercial characterisation which could be made.[29] Furthermore review where there is an interference with an individual's property rights is unproblematic in the Irish context, given the presence of constitutional protections. Recently the area of inquests, once viewed as inquisitorial and immune to natural justice review, was placed within its ambit. In *Ramsever v Mahon*, Fennelly J held that while there was no entitlement to "the full panoply of natural justice requirements of disclosure in advance of the hearing",[30] families may have the right to call

[10–17]

---

[24] *ibid* at 364. Malone's Application refers to a decision of the Northern Ireland Court of Appeal in *Re Malone's Application* [1988] NI 67.

[25] *Zhang v Athlone Institute of Technology* [2013] IEHC 390.

[26] *ibid* at para 34.

[27] *ibid* at para 35.

[28] *Quirke v Bord Lúthchleas na hÉireann* [1988] IR 83.

[29] For example, *East Donegal Co-Operative Ltd v Attorney General* [1976] IR 400 relating to the licensing of agricultural marts.

[30] *Ramsever v Mahon* [2006] 1 IR 216 at 219.

evidence, witness and cross examine, as might be appropriate in a fact finding, rather than adversarial process.

Emergency and the Pressures of the Administration

[10–18]   Recent years have seen a number of cases where the judiciary have endorsed Ireland's heritage of vindicating the individual's right to fair procedures, despite the possible practical impact upon administrative decision makers. McMahon J's statement in *Khan v Health Service Executive*, for example, underlines the value traditionally attached to natural justice by the Irish judiciary:

> "... [the HSE] must comply with rules which adhere to fair procedure/ standards. The [HSE] might like it to be otherwise. To those involved in administration, adherence to fair procedure standards may appear cumbersome, irritating and even irksome on some occasions. Undoubtedly, the necessary adherence may slow down the administrators and may not be conducive to efficiency. But that is the way it is. The battle between fair procedures and efficiency has long since been fought and fair procedures have won out. The insistence on fair procedures governs all decision makers in public administration."[31]

[10–19]   Clearly, one should not characterise these comments as absolute and, outside of core well defined case-law there is still room for a court to have regard to the needs of efficiency. McMahon J's statement was prominently cited by Hardiman J in his sustained examination of the prominence of fair procedures in Irish jurisprudence in *Dellway Investments v National Asset Management Agency*.[32] This case concerned the procedures for acquiring loans from developers, whereby the Government would meet with the banks to decide those most in need of being taken over by NAMA. The evidence from the Attorney General stated:

> "So, there is no interaction with the borrowers in the process, that is correct, but the bank has an obligation of utmost good faith to provide information, not just information relating to whether an asset is an eligible bank asset or not, but the broader issue of whether the asset might be acquired by NAMA, to enable NAMA to make a decision on acquisition. And key to the structure of the Act and understanding of the position is the legislature thought it appropriate that NAMA's interaction should be the bank that would in the ordinary course [have]

---

[31] *Khan v Health Service Executive* [2008] IEHC 234 at 7.
[32] *Dellway Investments v National Asset Management Agency* [2011] 4 IR 1, hereinafter "*Dellway*".

all of the relevant information concerning the borrower as that was an efficient way of dealing with this and, of course, the whole purpose was to take the assets, the loan assets from the bank."[33]

Hardiman J was unimpressed by a system which did not provide for any input or notification of the developer. He noted the expansion of natural justice protections led to the abandonment of

[10–20]

> "previous limitations, such as those based on whether the decision is of a *quasi* judicial or of an administrative nature, or whether the decision making body has 'the trappings of a court'".[34]

He emphasised the conclusion of Woolf *et al*, that across the common law world:

> "The law has moved on; not to the state where the entitlement to procedural protection can be extracted with certainty from a computer, but to where the Courts are able to insist upon some degree of participation in reaching most official decisions by those whom the decisions will affect in widely different situations".[35]

Justice Hardiman endorsed this statement as applying in Ireland, ruling that a decision could not be taken under a statute if a person affected by it would have no input in it.[36] This reflected the progressive elevation of the right to fair procedures to constitutional status. Given this status, it was only the most serious exception which could effectively oust a person affected's rights. Such counterfailing imperatives did exist, but were limited:

[10–21]

---

[33] *ibid at* 277.

[34] *ibid at* 279.

[35] *ibid*. H Woolf, J Jowell and A Le Sueur, *Judicial Review of Administrative Action* (6th ed) (Sweet & Maxwell, London, 2009) at p 356.

[36] *ibid*. He also endorsed the conclusion of G Whyte and G Hogan, *JM Kelly: The Irish Constitution* (4th ed) (Tottel, Dublin, 2003) at para 6.1.52:

> "(a)… a person affected by, or with an interest in the outcome of an administrative decision has the right to have an adequate notice of this decision and to be given an adequate opportunity to make his case before that administrative body. What the courts will require as an "adequate opportunity' will very much depend on the circumstances since the requirements of natural justice are not fixed and unchanging".

Furthermore, while Hardiman J did not undertake a full survey of relevant ECHR jurisprudence, his Honour did note Justice Macken's reference to *Fazenda Publica v Ministerio Publico (Case C - 349/07)* delivered on the 18 December 2008. There the Court held that the need for "observance of the rights of the defence" inheres in "the addressees of decisions which significantly affect their interests". Justice Hardiman stressed that "the similarity in language and scope with the Irish jurisprudence is striking."

"A property owner has a clear right to have his property respected by the State and safeguarded from trespass or seizure by others; but there may be imperatives arising from a state of war or armed rebellion, an accident, or an acute emergency created by fire, natural disaster or other sudden and extreme circumstances which justify transient trespass upon his property without his consent or without taking the time to see if he, as owner, wishes to urge any reason against it. Thus, the placing of a fireman's ladder in one's garden, to save imperilled life and property, does not require *audi alteram partem* if the garden's owner's is absent."[37]

[10–22]   In perhaps the most memorable passage of the judgment, Hardiman J cautioned against allowing claims of emergency to extinguish well established rights, noting:

"the cry of 'emergency' would be sufficient to set all rights aside at the whim of the Executive. Our Constitution makes specific provision for 'war or armed rebellion'. It is not for the courts to extend those provisions to a situation which is not one of war or armed rebellion. That would require a decision of the people in a referendum, if they thought it necessary or prudent to confer such unreviewable powers on the state. The cry of 'emergency' is an intoxicating one, producing an exhilarating freedom from the need to consider the rights of others and productive of a desire to repeat it again and again."[38]

[10–23]   His Honour then proceeded to examine cases where attempts had been made to justify a failure to observe *audi alteram partem*. He described "extreme urgency" as the "dominant countervailing factor", seen in cases such as *O'Callaghan v Commissioners of Public Works*,[39] *O'Ceallaigh v An Bord Altranais*[40] and *DK v Crowley*.[41] In *O'Callaghan*, the Court rejected the argument that a farmer should have been heard before an ancient fort on his land was listed as a national monument. The farmer had created a situation of emergency through his own actions, and had the Commissioners not acted the fort would have suffered serious damage.[42] In *O'Ceallaigh*, Justice Hardiman himself had acknowledged the possibility that the Board's ability to temporarily suspend a person from practicing could be exercised

---

[37] *Dellway*, above n 32 at 289.

[38] *ibid*.

[39] *O'Callaghan v Commissioners of Public Works* [1985] ILRM 364. Hereinafter "*O'Callaghan*".

[40] *O'Ceallaigh v An Bord Altranais* [2000] 4 IR 54. Hereinafter "*O'Ceallaigh*".

[41] *DK v Crowley* [2002] IR 744. Hereinafter "*DK*".

[42] Additionally it had not been possible for the Commissioners to contact the plaintiff as his address was not known them.

without notice to the person affected, if it had "to act so rapidly that it is not a practical possibility to give notification of the complaints".[43] In *DK*[44] the Supreme Court struck down the system for interim barring orders under s 4(3) of the Domestic Violence Act 1996 as unconstitutional. The statute had failed to prescribe a fixed period of short duration for operation of an *ex parte* barring order, once it was obtained. As a result, respondents to such applications were denied audi alteram partem in a manner which was disproportionate and unnecessary.

In *Dellway*, Hardiman J found no reason to apply such reasoning to the statutory framework underpinning the NAMA decision. It was not an interlocutory step, but a final decision for which there was no provision for reconsideration or for appeal, with NAMA also enjoying considerable legal immunity in respect of its actions. He also found there was "no proof nor even any convincing suggestion of urgency, much less of impossibility" of performing the Act's functions were the right to be heard given the borrowers.[45] Most significantly of all perhaps, was the fact that banks enjoyed the right to contribute to the decision-making process, which to Hardiman J seemed "logically and realistically to exclude any considerations of urgency or efficiency".[46] **[10–24]**

Other Recognised Exceptions and Restrictions

A number of other exceptional categories to the *audi alteram partem* rule have also emerged.[47] These include legislative decisions which affect large categories of people. Clearly the concept of representative democracy frustrates any attempt to seek court intervention in this area, but delegated legislation has prompted a number of cases. In *Cassidy v Minister for Industry*[48] the High Court found that industry specific statutory instruments were not subject to review for fair procedure, when it refused to require consultation with a vintners' association prior to an order affecting maximum prices for the sale of alcohol in Dundalk. Hogan and Morgan note that the situation has been muddled, however, by a number of cases **[10–25]**

---

[43] Above n 40 at 130.

[44] Above n 41.

[45] *Dellway*, above n 32 at 293.

[46] *ibid* at 294.

[47] Though Hardiman J ultimately ruled they were non-applicable to the case before him in *Dellway*.

[48] *Cassidy v Minister for Industry* [1978] IR 297.

which have held natural justice applied to the making of bye laws.[49] Whether the rules of *audi alteram partem* apply in the formation of *policy* is a further, distinct question. The creation of a general policy to be applied to a distinct group is not subject to *audi alteram partem*. It must be remembered, however, that when the Minister comes to implement such a policy in particular cases, it is generally recognised that the individual has the right to plead exigent circumstances.

[10–26]   Finally, where the matter under challenge is trivial,[50] or if it is merely a decision to make an initial investigation of a person, which due to its private nature, cannot be viewed as carrying with it a sanction or harmful consequence, *audi alteram partem* cannot be said to apply. However, we should note that such "pure" investigations, involving only the obtaining of facts without any express or implied pronouncement on them, are rare in practice, as we discuss later in this chapter at para [10–76]. In addition to these categories, a further exception applies to Garda investigations.[51] Beyond these limitations, it is also important that the reader understand that a free-floating resource for decision-makers may lie in the discretion granted to them to determine particular procedures. This discretion can result in the court showing some deference for experience and practical knowledge of the decision-making body in how they proceed with their application of fair procedures. Having highlighted particular contextual and policy factors bearing upon the extent and content of constitutional justice, we will now move to consider particular aspects of natural justice.

The Right to Reasons

[10–27]   The right to reasons represents the key starting point for fair procedures, as the presence or absence of the grounds for a decision can frustrate or animate the other requirements of *audi alteram partem*, such as prior notice, construction of an appeal and a fair hearing. In this key area then, the recent landmark judgment of the Supreme Court in *Mallak v Minister for Justice,*

---

[49] Hogan and Morgan, above n 5 at para 14-220. See *Re South Western Fisheries Region (No 7), Kerry District Conservation of Salmon and Sea Trout Bye-Law, Teahen v Minister for Communications, Energy and Natural Resources (No 1)* [2008] IEHC 194 (Laffoy J) and *Teahen v Minister for Communications, Energy and Natural Resources (No 2)* [2009] IEHC 399.

[50] *Dunnes Stores Ireland Company v Maloney* [1999] 3 IR 542.

[51] *Brady v Haughton* [2006] IR 1.

Equality and Law Reform[52] seemed, after thirty years of somewhat ad-hoc and contradictory case-law, to have clarified the obligation of decision-makers to give reasons for the decisions.

The idea that the right to reasons is a primary gateway to ensuring the rule of law was seen in the earlier case of *State (Daly) v Minister for Agriculture*, where a civil servant on probation was fired without any notice, reasons or dialogue regarding his performance.[53] Barron J stressed that: **[10–28]**

> "Such powers may only be exercised in conformity with the Constitution. The view of the Minister must be seen to be bona fide held, to be factually sustainable and not unreasonable. If no reasons have been given for the exercise of the power, then this court cannot review the exercise of the power in the light of these criteria. The court must ensure that the material upon which the Minister acted is capable of supporting his decision. Since the Minister has failed to disclose the material upon which he acted or the reasons for his action there is no matter from which the court can determine whether or not such material was capable of supporting his decision. Since the Minister continues to refuse to supply this material, it must be presumed that there was no such material."[54]

Similarly in *International Fishing Vessels Ltd v Minister for the Marine*,[55] Blayney J stressed that in refusing to give reasons "the Minister places a serious obstacle in the way of the exercise of that right [to judicial review]."[56] The Court was willing to find a breach of fair procedures particularly due to the possibility of overcoming the adverse finding in reapplying for the licence in question and the serious consequences for the appellant. While both of these cases found that reasons must be provided, it is important to remember that the reliance upon an "access to justice" justification was pragmatic. Both Barron and Blayney JJ linked the provision of reasons to the possibility of an appeal or reapplication. In circumstances where such mechanisms were unavailable, the precedential value of the findings was unclear. It is arguable that such pragmatism on the part of judges   **[10–29]**

---

[52] *Mallak v Minister for Justice, Equality and Law Reform* [2012] 3 IR 297, hereinafter "*Mallak* [2012]".

[53] *The State (Daly) v Minister for Agriculture* [1987] IR 165. His letter of termination merely stated that "the conditions of probation attaching to the probationary position [had] not been satisfied".

[54] *ibid* at 172.

[55] *International Fishing Vessels Ltd v Minister for the Marine* [1989] IR 149.

[56] *ibid* at 155.

undervalued the interlinkage of the provision of reasons with the broader functioning of the Constitution: such as the citizen's own confidence in the rule of law and facilitating democratic oversight.

Mallak and the Presumption of a Right to Reasons

[10–30]   Despite some positive judgments, therefore, prior to *Mallak v Minister for Justice*, there had been "a persistent view…that there is no general obligation at common law to give reasons for administrative decisions".[57] In favour of this, it is important to note that unmodulated, literal requirements may not fit with the deeply contextual nature of designing fair procedures. Each aspect of fair procedures falls to be evaluated through a holistic judgment — the degree to which the procedures in place, *as a whole*, facilitate access to justice. This was seen in the statement of Fennelly J in *Mallak*:

> "…The obligation to give fair notice and, possibly, to provide access to information or, in some cases, to have a hearing are intimately interrelated and the obligation to give reasons is sometimes merely one part of the process. The overarching principle is that persons affected by administrative decisions should have access to justice, that they should have the right to seek the protection of the courts in order to see that the rule of law has been observed, that fair procedures have been applied and their rights are not unfairly infringed."[58]

Thus, judicial interventions in this area have tried to eschew a monolithic requirement. Nevertheless *Mallak* seemed to strengthen the position of those who have called for the provision of reasons be instituted as a default requirement.

[10–31]   The appellant in *Mallak* was a Syrian refugee, who had lived and worked in Ireland and who made an application for naturalisation in 2005.[59] After a

---

[57] *Mallak* [2012] above n 52 at para 3.

[58] *ibid* at para 52.

[59] He had made at least one application prior to this, and was told throughout that each application would take a year to a year and half to be examined. s 15 states that:
"The Minister may, in his absolute discretion, grant the application, if satisfied that the applicant – (a)(i) is of full age, or (ii) is a minor born in the State; (b) is of good character; (c) has had a period of one year's continuous residence in the State immediately before the date of the application and, during the eight years immediately preceding that period, has had a total residence in the State amounting to four years; (d) intends in good faith to continue to reside in the State after naturalisation (e) has, before a judge of the District Court in open court, in a citizenship ceremony or in such manner as the

two and a half year delay, in November 2008, he received a letter refusing his application.[60] This stated that "the Minister has exercised his absolute discretion, as provided for by Irish Nationality and Citizenship Acts 1956 and 1986" and stating that there was no appeals process under the legislation. In response the appellant requested access to documents under the Freedom of Information Acts 1997 and 2003, as well as a s 18(1) request for reasons for the decision. As noted in chapter 3, this imposes a general obligation on every public body head to provide written statement of reasons. The Department refused this under s 18(2)(b), stating that non-disclosure of reasons was contemplated by the citizenship statute.[61]

The appellant had lost the preceeding High Court action, which dealt with three core issues. Firstly, whether the Minister, irrespective of the statutory wording, could be compelled to state reasons for the refusal. Secondly, whether the 1956 Act was unconstitutional if the Minister was able to refuse to give reasons. The final issue was whether principles of European Union law applied to benefit the appellant. Cooke J, on the first issue, stressed that the term "absolute discretion" which was used in s 15, evidenced an unambiguous intention of the Oireachtas to rule out the need to provide reasons. This made it impossible, therefore, to draw a common law implication to create such an obligation. This position was strengthened by the nature of the decision which Cooke J characterised as involving the bestowal of a discretionary privilege or benefit rather than a decision grounded in legal rights:

[10–32]

> "While it might be said that the evolution of the principle of fair procedures and the obligation to state reasons over the last 25 years would have reduced the occasions when neither obligation arose

---

Minister, for special reasons, allows – (i) made a declaration, in the prescribed manner, of fidelity to the nation and loyalty to the State, and (ii) undertaken to faithfully observe the laws of the State and to respect its democratic values."

[60] He had initially written to complain regarding the delay in September 2008, and received a reply stating no decision had yet been made. His wife was granted a certificate of naturalisation and was an Irish citizen at the time of the action.

[61] In July 2010 in *Abuissa v Minister for Justice, Equality and Law Reform* [2011] 1 IR 123, Clark J had held that Ministerial discretion was absolute and there was no obligation to furnish reasons. Cooke J similarly held in *Jiad v Minister for Justice* [2010] IR 187. In the Supreme Court hearing, counsel for the applicant identified a number of instances where the Minister had in practice, disclosed reasons. These included *Mishra v Minister for Justice* [1996] 1 IR 189 (Kelly J), *LGH v Minister for Justice, Equality and Law Reform*, Unreported, 31 January 2009 (Edwards J), and *Hussain v Minister for Justice, Equality and Law Reform* [2011] IEHC 171 (per Hogan J), where the Minister provided reasons in the course of orders being made quashing decisions refusing to grant certificates of naturalisation.

in respect of a decision with adverse consequences, it remains the position, in the view of this Court, that the principle of fair procedures and the requirement to state reasons can have no application where an administrative decision is wholly devoid of any detrimental or disadvantageous consequence for its addressee."[62]

[10–33] Cooke J, in making the latter point, also displayed an affinity with the "makes no difference" principle, ruling that "the refusal of the certificate in no way alters the position or status of the applicant", and as a result "the need for an effective remedy only arises where there is some wrong to be made good".[63] The final argument, that in determining an Irish citizenship application, the Minister was, in effect, determining European Union citizenship entitlement was also rejected.[64] Cooke J ruled that neither Treaties nor EU legislation "sought to encroach in any respect upon the sovereign entitlement of the Member States to determine the basis upon which national citizenship will be accorded",[65] and the Charter of Fundamental Rights could only apply to Member States when they are implementing Union law.

[10–34] Mr Mallak appealed to the Supreme Court which began its analysis by attempting to interpret s 15 so as to conform with the Constitution. In setting the context for this, it tackled two underlying presumptions of the Minister: firstly where a matter is left to the absolute discretion of the decision-maker, it followed automatically no reasons need be given; secondly, that the grant of naturalisation was a matter of benefit or privilege rather than of right. On the first matter, Fennelly J stressed that a statute cannot grant arbitrary power, such that the Minister does not need to have a reason.[66] A grant of "absolute discretion", would however, render a challenge on grounds of unreasonableness or irrelevant considerations

---

[62] *Mallak v Minister for Justice* [2011] IEHC 306 at para 15, hereinafter "*Mallak* [2011]".

[63] *ibid* at para 22. He stressed:

> "the refusal of the certificate of naturalisation is a refusal to accord a privilege in respect of which there is no right or entitlement to qualify. It has no effect upon the personal status in law or on the legal rights of the disappointed applicant. Thus, neither French nor European law in relation to judicial review of administrative decisions affords any basis for departing from the approach of Costello J. to the entitlement to judicially review a measure devoid of legal effects upon its addressee or to the entitlement to a statement of reasons from the decision-maker for that purpose".

[64] Reliance was placed upon the Court of Justice judgment in C-135/08 *Rottmann v Freistaat Bayern* [2010] ECR I-01449.

[65] *Mallak* [2011] above n 62 at para 24.

[66] The necessarily implied constitutional limitation of jurisdiction in all decision-making which affects duties requires *inter alia*, that the decision maker must not "flagrantly reject or

extremely difficult. Once a reason was required for the exercise of the power however,

> "the characterisation of the Minister's discretion as absolute provides no justification for the suggestion that he is dispensed from observance of such requirements of the rules of natural and constitutional justice as would otherwise apply."[67]

On the second issue, the Court accepted that the grant or refusal of a certificate of naturalisation was "at least in one sense, a matter of privilege rather than of right".[68] Nevertheless   **[10–35]**

> "the mere fact that a person in the position of the appellant is seeking access to a privilege does not affect the extent of his right to have his application considered in accordance with law or to apply to the court for redress".[69]

Where the Minister was rejecting an application on the basis of one of the enumerated statutory conditions, in particular the assessment of good character issue, previous rulings had stressed these actions were amenable to judicial review.[70] Fennelly J now extended this to the broader, general discretion which the Minister enjoyed under the section.[71]

Moving to an evaluation of existing case law, Fennelly J considered the previous judgment of Costello J in *Pok Sun Shum v Ireland*,[72] where his   **[10–36]**

---

    disregard fundamental reason or common sense in reaching his decision" as per Henchy J *State (Keegan) v Stardust Victims' Compensation Tribunal* [1986] IR 642 at 658.

[67] *Mallak* [2012] above n 52 at para 45, Fennelly J cited in support the decision of Hogan J in *Hussain v Minister for Justice* [2011] IEHC 171 at para 17:

    "This description nevertheless cannot mean, for example, that the Minister is freed from the obligations of adherence to the rule of law, which is the 'very cornerstone of the Irish legal system': *Maguire v Ardagh* [2002] 1 I.R. 385, at 567, per Hardiman J. Nor can these words mean that the Minister is free to act in an autocratic and arbitrary fashion, since this would not only be inconsistent with the rule of law, but it would be at odds with the guarantee of democratic government contained in Article 5 of the Constitution."

[68] *ibid* at para 46. This was 'undoubtedly a major reason' for Costello J's conclusion in *Pok Sun Shum v Ireland* [1986] IR 593 that no reasons were required to be given.

[69] *ibid* at para 47.

[70] Edwards J in *LGH v Minister for Justice, Equality and Law Reform* [2009] IEHC 78 held that the Minister had been wrong to take into account the minor traffic offenses of the applicant's two adult sons in assessing character.

[71] *Mallak* [2012] above n 52 at para 50. This was further supported by the UK Court of Appeal decision of *R v Secretary of State ex parte Fayed* [1998] 1 WLR 763 where the court refused to view the applicants were deserving of any diminished standard of review because they were, in effect, seeking the privilege of UK citizenship.

[72] *Pok Sun Shum v Ireland* [1986] ILRM 593.

Honour had stated that: "there is no general rule of natural justice that reasons for the decisions of an administrative authority must be given". This statement could, however, shift "in the case of exercise of a particular statutory power", with Costello J attaching importance "to the presence or absence from the statutory scheme of a right of appeal. The absence of a statement of reasons may render such a right nugatory". While in the case of naturalisation, there was no provision for appeal, the letter to Mr Mallak invited him to "reapply for the grant of a certificate of naturalisation at any time", which seemed to represent that the Minister's concerns could be cured in future applications. Fennelly J stressed that:

> "While, therefore, the invitation is, to some extent, in ease of the appellant, it is impossible for the appellant to address the Minister's concerns and thus to make an effective application when he is in complete ignorance of the Minister's concerns.
>
> More fundamentally, and for the same reason, it is not possible for the appellant, without knowing the Minister's reason for refusal, to ascertain whether he has a ground for applying for judicial review, and by extension, not possible for the courts effectively to exercise their power of judicial review".[73]

[10–37]   In this finding, Fennelly J was fortified by the comments of Finlay CJ in *The State (Creedon) v Criminal Injuries Compensation Tribunal*[74]:

> "Once the courts have a jurisdiction and if that jurisdiction is invoked, an obligation to enquire into and, if necessary, correct the decisions and activities of a tribunal of this description, it would appear necessary for the proper carrying out of that jurisdiction that the courts should be able to ascertain the reasons by which the tribunal came to its determination. Apart from that, I am satisfied that the requirement which applies to this Tribunal, as it would to a court, that justice should appear to be done, necessitates that the unsuccessful applicant before it should be made aware in general and broad terms of the grounds on which he or she has failed. Merely, as was done in this case, to reject the application and when that rejection was challenged subsequently to maintain a silence as to the reason for it, does not appear to me to be consistent with the proper administration of functions which are of a quasi-judicial nature."[75]

---

[73] *Mallak* [2012] above n 52 at paras 64-65.
[74] *The State (Creedon) v Criminal Injuries Compensation Tribunal* [1988] IR 51.
[75] *ibid* at 55.

While this statement was *obiter dicta*, Fennelly J stressed that it was "logically [10–38] closely related to the earlier holding of irrationality, which was in turn, closely connected with the refusal of the Tribunal to elaborate the reason for its decision", and was therefore "worthy of considerable respect".[76]

His Honour also referred to "an emerging commonly held" view that [10–39] persons are entitled to reasons. Firstly there was s 18 (1) of the Freedom of Information Act 1997 and Article 296 of the Treaty on the Functioning of the European Union which provides that "legal acts shall state the reasons on which they are based…". Article 41 of the Charter of Fundamental Rights of the European Union provides that every person benefits from what is called in the heading the "Right to Good Administration", which includes the "the obligation of the administration to give reasons for its decisions".[77] His Honour therefore concluded:

> "The developing jurisprudence of our own courts provides compelling evidence that, at this point, it must be unusual for a decision maker to be permitted to refuse to give reasons. The reason is obvious. In the absence of any reasons, it is simply not possible to make a judgment as to whether he has a ground for applying for a judicial review of the substance of the decision and, for the same reason, for the court to exercise its power. At the very least, the decision maker must be able to justify the refusal. No attempt has been made to do so in the present case and I believe it would be wrong to speculate about cases in which courts might be persuaded to accept such justification."[78]

The Minister had supplied only a general submission "that there are issues [10–40] of public policy that lean against the giving of reasons" which were "apparent from the nature of the Minister's decision" and the Information Commissioner's finding that reasons were not available under s 18 of the Freedom of Information Act. The Court found, however, that "no reasons

---

[76] *Mallak* [2012] above n 52 at para 62.
[77] Case C-417/11 *Council v Bamba* was cited by the Supreme Court at para 69. Furthermore, the UK Court of Appeal decision of *R v Secretary of State ex parte Fayed* [1998] 1 WLR 763. Lord Woolf had stated that:
> "I have already indicated that at commonlaw there is no universal obligation to give reasons but despite this I would certainly regard this as a case where reasons should be given but for section 44(2). However, in the light of the express prohibition on requiring the Secretary of State to give reasons I would not myself regard this as a case where the need for reasons is so essential that fairness cannot be achieved without reasons as long as an applicant has been given sufficient information as to the subject matter of the decision to make such submissions as he wishes." (at 773).
[78] *Mallak* [2012] above n 52 at para 74.

related to the public interest have been disclosed even in the most general terms".[79] Fennelly J sought to recentre the Court's evaluation not on specific demands, but anchored against the overall benchmark of fairness:

> "In the present state of evolution of our law, it is not easy to conceive of a decision-maker being dispensed from giving an explanation either of the decision or of the decision-making process at some stage. The most obvious means of achieving fairness is for reasons to accompany the decision. However, it is not a matter of complying with a formal rule: the underlying objective is the attainment of fairness in the process. If the process is fair, open and transparent and the affected person has been enabled to respond to the concerns of the decision-maker, there may be situations where the reasons for the decision are obvious and that effective judicial review is not precluded."[80]

[10–41] The Court refused to infer that the Minister had no reasons, noting that Minister would have had power, pursuant to s 17(2) of the Refugee Act 1996 to restrict the rights otherwise enjoyed by the appellant, if, "in the interest of national security or public policy ('ordre public'), it is necessary to do so".[81] Yet the non-invocation of such provisions clearly vexed Fennelly J ("one can understand the appellant being mystified"),[82] particularly given that Mr Mallak's wife had a certificate of naturalisation. Given the very small and extraordinary subset of possible justifications which subsisted, the Court clearly felt comfortable in quashing the decisions. If reasons had been provided, it might well have been possible for the appellant to make relevant representations when making a new application. That might have rendered the decision fair and made it inappropriate to quash it.[83] Into the future, the Court would only focus on the matter in front of it:

> "Following the making of the order, it will be a matter for the Minister to consider the application afresh. It will be a matter for him to decide what procedures to adopt in order to comply with the requirements of fairness. It is not a matter for the Court to prescribe whether he will give notice of his concerns to the appellant or disclose information on which they may be based or whether he will continue to refuse to disclose his reasons but to provide justification for doing so. Any question of

---

[79] *ibid* at para 75.
[80] *ibid* at para 66.
[81] *ibid* at para 75.
[82] *ibid* at para 76.
[83] *ibid*.

the adequacy of reasons he may actually decide to provide or any justification provided for declining to disclose them can be considered only when they have been given."[84]

Given its expansive discussion of the requirement to give reasons, beyond the particular statutory context in which the decision had been taken, it appeared that *Mallak* had installed the provision of reasons as the default setting in public administration. Nevertheless, this default could be varied by Government: firstly where a powerful public policy justification for non-provision is present, or where the process as a whole has given sufficient insight to the bases for the decision at the information, application or hearing stage. [10–42]

Murphy v DPP: A Roll Back from a General Right?

It was something of a surprise therefore, that the Supreme Court "stuck an oar in the riverbed" and appeared to backtrack from the *Mallak* approach in the 2014 case of *Murphy v Director of Public Prosecutions*.[85] O'Donnell J described the judgment in *Mallak* as "nuanced", and stressed that the case turned, to a significant extent, on the existence of a statutory obligations to give reasons under freedom of information legislation: [10–43]

> "Mallak undoubtedly brings the common law on the duty to give reasons into line with the obligations of statute, but it does not address the question whether the common law requires decision-makers to go further than the statutory requirement."[86]

This characterisation of the judgment in *Mallak* was unexpected, as while the existence of statutory duty to provide under the freedom of information legislation was expressly referenced in that judgment, the court in *Mallak* appeared to push off from that observation into a more broadly framed discussion of the right to reasons in common law. *Murphy* has therefore cast some doubt over the argument that *Mallak* grounds a baseline expectation, across a variety of statutory contexts, that reasons will be given. [10–44]

On the other hand, by stressing the importance of statutory context the court is adopting a position in line with the fact that a decision-maker may deny reasons where there is compelling justification for doing so. It may be [10–45]

---

[84] *ibid* at para 77.
[85] *Murphy v Ireland, The Attorney General and the Director of Public Prosecutions* [2014] IESC 19.
[86] *ibid* at para 40.

that the warning of O'Donnell J is a reminder that *Mallak* merely creates a default position which is dependent upon context. The *Murphy* action itself was a challenge whereby the applicant argued that the Director of Public Prosecutions was under a duty to provide reasons for the decision to send him for a non-jury trial at the Special Criminal Court in relation to a number of alleged taxation offences. Intervention into the realm of criminal prosecutions has long been sensitive for the Irish judiciary, with the area traditionally regarded as non-justiciable. The Supreme Court in *Murphy* ruled that a kernel of procedural fairness could apply, but given the public interests at play in such decisions, this was of a very limited scope:

> "The question in any case is whether the Director of Public Prosecutions was entitled to consider that the ordinary courts were inadequate to secure the administration of justice in a particular case. Review of such a decision should be the exception and never the routine, and only when an accused person can put forward a substantial case that the decision making process has miscarried. The legal position outlined above balances the desirability of reasoned decision making to strengthen the administration of justice with the necessity to ensure that the process is tightly controlled to avoid routine disclosure and review which could undermine it."[87]

It would clearly be difficult to satisfy the bar of "substantial case" of miscarriage of justice applying to reviews for procedural fairness.

[10–46] The emphasis upon balance in the above passage, in our view, was the recurrent concern throughout the *Murphy* judgment, and was central to the resolution of the case. This is why, even when presenting a broad interpretation of the *Mallak* decision, we have used the term "default" or "presumption" to describe the duty to give reasons. It is clear that the *Mallak* requirement must be balanced against other public interest factors, in the case of *Murphy*, anti-terrorism and security. This balancing process was of course, evident from the judgment in *Mallak* itself.

[10–47] The earlier comment of O'Donnell J regarding the centrality of freedom of information legislation to the *Mallak* judgment, may, however display a potentially separate discomfort on the part of the judiciary with imposing a general common law requirement alongside the relevant statutory provisions. This may be attributed to traditional fears regarding judicial

---

[87] *ibid* at para 43.

activism, but also reflect an anxiety regarding the practical invasiveness of requiring a Government decision-maker to take notice of two separate streams of obligation — the specific scheme of procedural fairness set out in the primary statute and some sort of general common law requirement to give reasons. Clearly, in terms of practical efficiency, it would be better for the two streams to be reconciled and harmonized. It seems clear that the Irish judiciary in *Mallak* sent a message to the legislature that a failure to give of reasons — absent strong public interest justification — can be cured by the courts using common law principles. Yet the Supreme Court may doubt the efficacy of it becoming the primary institutional actor in the defence of the right to reasons. In short, *Mallak* was clearly a message to the legislature and the administrative State to view the denial of reasons with great seriousness, to address the issue by statute and to affirm its centrality to appeal and review mechanisms in their actions. Predicting what may follow forces us to confront an overarching issue of Irish constitutional culture: the need for the legislature to integrate the court's reasoning into its law-making role. Without a revaluing of the right to reasons by the executive and legislature, the Court will be forced to assess whether post *Mallak* case-law should be shaped by institutional restraint (deferring to terms of, and interests set out, in the relevant statute) or principled intervention to affirm the fundamental entitlement to reasons.

Circumstances Where a Fresh Statement of Reasons May be Unnecessary

In assessing the right to reasons, an issue which arises is whether some **[10–48]** decisions are of such a nature that the reasons underlying them can be viewed as identifiable without the need for the applicant to receive a fresh, direct statement of them. This was evaluated in the recent case of *EMI v Data Protection Commissioner*.[88] This case concerned a settlement entered into by an internet service provider and several music companies, to facilitate the application of a "three strikes and you're out" rule to individuals illegally downloading copyrighted material. The Data Protection Commissioner, concerned that this would involve the inappropriate sharing of personal information, issued an enforcement notice against the internet provider. Seeing their arrangement endangered, the music

---

[88] *EMI v Data Protection Commissioner* [2013] IESC 34, hereinafter "*EMI*".

companies took an action arguing that the reasons supplied by the Commissioner in the enforcement notice were inadequate.

[10–49]   In commencing his judgment, Clarke J noted that the provision of the reasons was required by s 10(4)(a) of the Data Protection Acts, which states that:

> "An Enforcement Notice shall—(a) specify any provision of this Act that, in the opinion of the Commissioner, has been or is being contravened and the reasons for his having formed that opinion..."[89]

Clarke J provided a direct statement of the *substantive content* of the right to reasons in the aftermath of *Mallak*:

> "It follows that a party is entitled to sufficient information to enable it to assess whether the decision is lawful and, if there be a right of appeal, to enable it to assess the chances of success and to adequately present its case on the appeal. The reasons given must be sufficient to meet those ends."[90]

[10–50]   The Court then moved to analyse the circumstances where the reasons for the decision can be reconstructed or inferred from the prior process or additional documents. Clarke J noted his prior, High Court, decision in *Sister Mary Christian v Dublin City Council*,[91] in which it was alleged that Dublin City Council had failed to provide adequate reasons for parts of the Dublin City Development Plan. In that case, his Honour stressed that where secondary documents were relied upon as evidence of the reasons for the relevant decisions, these should have been internalised by direct reference in the development plan:

---

[89] *ibid* at para 6.1.

[90] *ibid* at para 6.5. Clarke J, in para 6.4, cited in support his comments in the Supreme Court's ruling in *Rawson v Minister for Defence* [2012] IESC 26 at para 6.8:

> "While the primary focus of a number of the judgments cited, and indeed aspects of the decision in Meadows itself, were on the need to give reasons as such, there is, perhaps, an even more general principle involved. As pointed out by Murray C.J. in Meadows a right of judicial review is pointless unless the party has access to sufficient information to enable that party to assess whether the decision sought to be questioned is lawful and unless the courts, in the event of a challenge, have sufficient information to determine that lawfulness. How that general principle may impact on the facts of an individual case can be dependant on a whole range of factors, not least the type of decision under question, but also, in the context of the issues with which this Court is concerned on this appeal, the particular basis of challenge."

[91] *Sister Mary Christian v Dublin City Council* [2012] IEHC 163, hereinafter "*Sister Mary Christian*".

"It does not seem to me that it necessarily follows from the above analysis that the reasons have to be included in the development plan itself. It is, for example, possible that there may be documents referred to in the development plan which can provide the rationale for aspects of the measures incorporated into the development plan. In addition, documents prepared in the context of the adoption process may, depending on the content, also be capable of being relied on as an authoritative statement of the rationale. However, the requirement of reasonable certainty as to the reasons seems to me to necessitate that any documentation said to represent the reasons must be either expressly referred to in the development plan or be, by necessary implication, from the terms of the development plan, clearly adopted by those voting in favour of the development plan as part of the reasoning concerned."[92]

Clarke J acknowledged that this decision predated that of the Supreme Court in *Mallak*, which recognised that "there may be circumstances where it is not necessary for the reasons to accompany the decision itself".[93] Despite the fact that his *Christian* judgment had derived from the context of a development plan, Clarke J held that there was "a more general principle at play".[94] He held that it may be possible to construe reasons by the surrounding documents and prior process:

[10–51]

"Legal certainty requires, as was pointed out in *Christian*, that it must be possible to accurately determine what the reasons were. There should not be doubt as to where the reasons can be found. Clearly, an express reference in the decision itself to some other source outside of the decision document meets that test. Where, however, it is suggested that the reasons can be found in materials outside both of the decision itself together with materials expressly referred to in the decision, then care needs to be taken to ensure that any person affected by the decision in question can readily determine what the reasons are notwithstanding the fact that those reasons do not appear in the decision itself or in materials expressly referred to in the decision."[95]

Furthermore, Clarke J held that the exceptional case envisaged by Fennelly J in *Mallak* was likely to occur only in the *adjudicative context*:

---

[92] *Sister Mary Christian, ibid* at para 9.2.
[93] *EMI*, above n 88 at para 6.7.
[94] *ibid* at para 6.8.
[95] *ibid*.

> "Where, for example, an adjudicator makes a decision after a process in which both sides have made detailed submissions it may well, as Fennelly J. pointed out in *Mallak*, be that the reasons will be obvious by reference to the process which has led to the decision such that neither of the parties could be in any reasonable doubt as to what the reasons were. But it seems to me that, in a case where any party affected by a decision could be in any reasonable doubt as to what the reasons actually were, it must follow that adequate reasons have not been given."[96]

[10–52]   His Honour further stressed that in assessing whether reasons were ascertainable, the courts should not overly rely upon the ability of the party affected to infer them. This was especially so where there was an express statutory provision requiring reasons to be included. The probability that the party affected could gain a working knowledge of the underlying rationale could not discharge the legal obligations of the statutory decision maker to supply adequate reasons. This aspect of the ruling is welcome, as it should avoid any undue weight being attached to cases such as *Orange v Director of Telecoms (No. 2)*[97] and *O'Keeffe v An Bord Pleanála*,[98] cases in which the court appeared more willing to place the onus on the applicant to deduce reasons from disparate surrounding sources.

[10–53]   Where a statement of reasons should be given, the question of when it must be provided also arises. Sensitivity to administrators was shown by the High Court in *McAlister v Minister for Justice and Law Reform*, where the provision of reasons in an affidavit upon the commencing of High Court

---

[96] *ibid* at para 6.9. On the facts, at para 7.4, Clarke J found:

"The reasons must be adequate to meet the record companies' needs in that regard. As pointed out, it may well be obvious to the parties involved in an adversarial process as to what the reasons for the decision of an adjudicator were in the light of the case made to that adjudicator and the adjudicator's decision. However, where a legally binding measure is sought to be put in place which affects parties beyond those who were part of the process leading to the adoption of the measure concerned, then there is a greater onus on the decision-maker to ensure that the reasons are transparent not just to those who were involved in the process, but to anyone else who might be affected as well. In the planning process, for example, all documents relevant to that process would normally be available to any interested party. If the reasons for a planning decision require reference to the process leading to that planning decision, then it is reference to a process which is transparently open to all. However, where, as here, the process affected the record companies but only directly involved Eircom and the Commissioner, it will inevitably be more difficult to satisfy the requirement for reasons from a consideration of the process."

[97] *Orange v Director of Telecoms (No. 2)* [2000] 4 IR 159.
[98] *O'Keeffe v An Bord Pleanála* [1993] 1 IR 39.

action was held to suffice.[99] It can be argued that accepting such a late trigger point displayed a court-centric view as regards access to justice. Judicial review is merely one forum a plaintiff may pursue, and is the most financially onerous. In this regard, the recognition of the importance of the possibility of re-application in *Mallak* may open up an expectation that reasons will be supplied earlier is the relevant timeline.[100]

How Extensive Should Reasons Be?

Giving the Gist of the Decision

The degree of specificity required in an account of reasons, is a key variable in the likely success of any future challenge to the decision. Section 10(1) of the Freedom of Information Act 2014[101] represents, of course, a powerful intervention in this area, conferring a right on a person who is affected by an act of the public body, and has a material interest in a matter affected by the act or to which it relates, to apply and be given a statement of the reasons for the act, and any findings on any material issues of fact made for the purposes of the Act. As we saw in the *Mallak* case, however, it is important to note that s 10, does not impose any obligation to provide a statement of reasons where such was never created previously. **[10–54]**

The level of generality which normally applies to the provision of reasons was laid down by the Supreme Court in *Faulkner v Minister for Industry and Commerce*,[102] where the applicant was challenging her failed application for promotion in the Department. The Labour Court ruled that **[10–55]**

> "having examined in detailed the claimant's assessment records, the Court is satisfied that the Department had reasonable grounds other than sex or marital status for her non-promotion in April 1989".

O'Flaherty J upheld this disclosure as sufficient:

> "…administrative tribunals…should be required only to give the broad gist of the basis for their decisions. We do no service to the public in

---

[99] *McAlister v Minister for Justice and Law Reform* [2003] 4 IR 35. The case concerned the refusal to provide reasons for the refusal of temporary release.

[100] This would match developments in the European sphere, see *Michel v European Parliament* (Case 195/80) [1981] ECR 2861.

[101] Replacing s 18(1) of the Freedom of Information Act 1997.

[102] *Faulkner v Minister for Industry and Commerce* [1997] ELR 107.

general, or to particular individuals, if we subject every decision of every administrative tribunal to minute analysis."[103]

[10–56]   Hogan and Morgan have noted however, that

"while...the general judicial consensus has been to set a rather low standard for the cogency of reasons, this approach has been challenged by some judges and commentators".[104]

The leading decision in this regard, is that of Kelly J in *Deerland Construction v Aquatic Licensing Appeals Board*,[105] where in finding the reasons provided to be inadequate, reliance was placed upon the following statement of Brown LJ in *South Bucks County Council v Porter*:

"The reasons for a decision must be intelligible and they must be adequate. They must enable the reader to understand why the matter was decided as it was and what conclusions were reached on 'the principal important controversial issues', disclosing how any issue of law or fact was resolved...The reasoning must not give rise to a substantial doubt as to whether the decision maker erred in law, for example, by misunderstanding some relevant policy or some other important matter, or by failing to reach a rational decision on relevant grounds. But such adverse inference will not readily be drawn. The reasons need refer only to the main issues in dispute, not to every material consideration. They should enable disappointed developers to assess their proposals of obtaining some alternative development permission, or, as the case may be, their unsuccessful opponents to understand how the policy or approach underlying the grant of permission may impact upon future such applications. Decision letters must be read in a straightforward manner, recognising that they are addressed to parties well aware of the issues involved and the arguments advanced. A reasons challenge will only succeed if the party aggrieved can satisfy the court that he has genuinely been substantially prejudiced by the failure to provide an adequately reasoned decision."[106]

---

[103] *ibid* at 111.

[104] Hogan and Morgan, above n 5 at para 14-141.

[105] *Deerland Construction v Aquatic Licensing Appeals Board* [2009] 1 IR 673. Hereinafter "*Deerland*".

[106] *South Bucks County Council v Porter* [2004] 1 WLR 1953 at para 36. This "proper, intelligible and adequate" standard had already been recognised in Ireland see *Ní Éili v The Environmental Protection Agency*, Unreported, Supreme Court, 30 July 1999: "the reasons must be 'proper, intelligible and adequate,' as had been held. What degree of particularity is required must depend on the circumstances of each case...".

Considering the Context: When Should More Detail be Provided?

We would caution however, against unmooring this quote and applying it as a general principle. The obligation to provide reasons must be reconciled with the context of the decision at hand, in particular the seriousness of the matter or the relevant statutory framework. The introduction of the concept of proportionality balancing also complicates matters: in order to facilitate effective access to judicial review there may need to be some evidence that the decision-maker genuinely considered all factors in balance.[107] In *Kikumbi v The Office of the Refugee Applications Commissioner, et al*,[108] Herbert J stressed the distinction between complex, multifaceted decisions and those which are more clearly defined:

[10–57]

> "Moreover, it seems clear that the question of the degree to which a decision must be supported by reasons stated in detail will vary with the nature of the decision itself. In a case such as *International Fishing Vessels Ltd. v. Minister for the Marine* [1989] I.R. 149, or *Dunnes Stores Ireland Company v. Maloney* [1999] 3 I.R. 542, there was a multiplicity of possible reasons, some capable of being unknown even in their general nature to the person affected. This situation may require a more ample statement of reasons than in a simpler case where the issues are more defined."[109]

In the immigration context, Hardiman J's judgment in *FP v Minister for Justice, Equality and Law Reform*,[110] stressed that:

[10–58]

> "Where an administrative decision must address only a single issue, its formulation will often be succinct. Where a large number of

---

[107] It is of little surprise, therefore, that Murray CJ made obiter comments regarding the provisions of reasons in *Meadows v Minister for Justice* [2010] 2 IR 701:

"An administrative decision affecting the rights and obligations of persons should at least disclose the essential rationale on foot of which the decision is taken. That rationale should be patent from the terms of the decision or capable of being inferred from its terms and its context.

Unless that is so then the constitutional right of access to the courts to have the legality of an administrative decision judicially reviewed could be rendered either pointless or so circumscribed as to be unacceptably ineffective."

[108] *Kikumbi v The Office of the Refugee Applications Commissioner et al* [2007] IEHC 11.

[109] *ibid.* at p 8. See also the comments of Murphy J in *O'Donogue v An Bord Pleanála* [1991] ILRM 751, at 757. "It has never been suggested that an administrative body is bound to provide a discursive judgment ... but on the other hand the need for providing the grounds of the decision... could not be satisfied by recourse to an uninformative if technically correct formula... it would be necessary ... to indicate in its decision that it had addressed its mind to the substantive issue...".

[110] *FP v Minister for Justice, Equality and Law Reform* [2002] 1 IR 164.

persons apply, on individual facts, for the same relief, the nature of the authorities' consideration and the form of grant or refusal may be similar or identical. An adequate statement of reasons in one case may thus be equally adequate in others. This does not diminish the statements essential validity or convert it into a mere administrative formula."[111]

[10–59]   One recent judgment which testifies to the differential applications of the standard according to context was *RO v Minister for Justice*.[112] This case concerned adverse credibility findings made against the applicant in a Refugee Tribunal decision. The decision of the Tribunal identified seven specific instances where the applicant's account was found not to be credible. On the facts, Mac Eochaidh J found "a reason was stated or was patent in respect to each finding".[113] In the course of making this finding, Justice Mac Eochaidh proceeded to provide an overview of the case-law, particularly in the context of refugee credibility findings. The applicant had placed heavily reliance upon *Deerland Construction v Aquatic Licensing Appeals Board*.[114] His Honour combined this with a survey of cases specific to credibility findings. He noted firstly the judgment of Peart J in *Memishi v The Refugee Appeals Tribunal*, which quoted with approval the United States Court of Appeal in *Diaz-Marroquin v Immigration and Naturalisation Service*.[115] Peart J concluded that:

---

[111] *ibid* at 175.

[112] *RO v Minister for Justice* [2012] IEHC 573, hereinafter *"RO"*.

[113] *ibid* at para 17. His Honour underlined that:

"I need hardly add that the duty to give reasons on credibility findings is not automatically breached where the reason for the incredulity is patent and is therefore not expressly stated. In this case for example, the fifth reason given for disbelieving the applicant related to her claim that she walked to the next village in an hour. When it was put to her that the next village was some 70 kilometres distant, she said that she ran. That the Tribunal does make the obvious comment that no human being could run much less walk 70 kilometres in an hour and that for this reason she is disbelieved, does not offend the rules on giving reasons for credibility findings)."

[114] *Deerland* above n 105.

[115] *Diaz-Marroquin v Immigration and Naturalisation Service* (2001) U.S. App. Lexis 2352:

"...adverse credibility determinations must be (1) supported by specific, cogent reasons and (2) the reasons set forth must be substantial and must bear a legitimate nexus to the finding...The inconsistencies in Diaz's testimony do not provide adequate support for finding that Diaz lacked credibility. The inconsistencies were minor...they did not enhance Diaz's asylum application... Also they were communicated through an interpreter...The second reason that the IJ used to justify her adverse credibility finding was that she found parts of Diaz's testimony implausible. Without more, personal conjecture is an insufficient basis for an adverse credibility determination".

"The principles which emerge…are that a Tribunal is not entitled to make adverse credibility findings against an applicant without cogent reasons bearing a nexus to the decision, that the reasons for any such adverse finding on credibility must be substantial and not relating only to minor matters, that the fact that some important detail is not included in the application form completed by the applicant when he/she first arrives is not of itself sufficient to form the basis of an adverse credibility finding, and finally, that the fact that the authority finds the applicant's story inherently implausible or unbelievable is not sufficient. Mere conjecture on the part of the authority is insufficient, and that corroboration is not essential to establish an applicant's credibility. As general principles, I agree."[116]

Nevertheless, in *RO* Justice Mac Eochaidh cautioned that in applying these principles, judges should remember that: **[10–60]**

"…when a court is reviewing the adequacy of reasons for credibility findings, it is not conducting the same level of scrutiny of the adequacy of reasons as it might undertake if it were reviewing a substantive decision, such as a decision to grant a planning permission or grant a mobile phone licence. As I have observed earlier, credibility findings in an asylum application are subordinate decisions on the pathway to the substantive decision - to grant or withhold international protection."[117]

It is submitted that a proper characterisation of credibility assessment is that of a powerful, floating variable rather than mere subordinate aspect or step. It is well documented that credibility can leak out across the ultimate analysis of the objective criteria of the refugee definition. In such a context, the materiality of the finding is arguably not fully captured by the label "subordinate decision". If the latter category is invoked in future cases, this could run the danger of encouraging abstractness in the provision of reasons. Nevertheless, Mac Eochaidh J concluded his analysis by providing a helpful checklist in such cases, which may be summarised here: **[10–61]**

---

[116] *Memishi v The Refugee Appeals Tribunal* (Unreported, Peart J, 25 June 2003). This was further developed by Cooke J in *IR v Minister for Justice, Equality and Law Reform* [2009] IEHC 353, who ruled, at para 11, that

"A finding of lack of credibility must be based on correct facts, untainted by conjecture or speculation and the reasons drawn from such facts must be cogent and bear a legitimate connection to the adverse finding.

The reasons must relate to the substantive basis of the claim made and not to minor matters or to facts which are merely incidental in the account given."

[117] *RO*, above n 112 at para 28.

(i)   Were reasons given or discernible for the credibility findings?

(ii) If so, were the reasons intelligible in the sense that the reader/addressee could understand why the finding was made?

(iii) Were the reasons specific, cogent and substantial?

(iv) Were they based on correct facts?

(v) Were they rational?[118]

[10–62]   The role which UK and US case-law, in particular the *South Bucks County Council v Porter*[119] judgment, have played before the Irish courts suggests that given the contextual nature of the judgments involved, decision-makers should seek out comparative approaches in their areas. Furthermore, the reasoning process contemplated by the legislation, together with any provisions specifying the disclosure of a decision is also very significant. For example, s 34 (10) of the Planning Acts 2000-2011 clearly shapes the provisions of reasons for planning decisions:

> "A decision ... shall state the main reasons and considerations on which the decision is based, and where conditions are imposed ... the main reasons for the imposition of any such conditions, provided that where a condition imposed is a condition described in subsection (4), a reference to the paragraph of subsection (4) in which the condition is described shall be sufficient..."

[10–63]   As Hogan and Morgan note,[120] the requirement in s 3(3) of the Immigration Act 1999, provides that in making a deportation order, the Minister must give reasons for it. In *Dimbo v Minister for Justice, Equality and Law Reform*,[121] this obligation was interpreted to require "grave and substantial reason[s]". Hogan and Morgan state that the "formulation sounds that it was intended to go beyond the normal standard",[122] with the result that the reasoning supplied to the individual may need to be more extensive than in other fields. Such examples underline the need for the legislature to engage with the question when creating legislation, as absent direct regulation, the extent of the reasons to be supplied will have to match the emphasis of the overall Act.

---

[118] *ibid* at para 30. This last question will clearly, as a practical matter, fall to be considered under the unreasonableness ground in a judicial review action.

[119] *South Bucks County Council v Porter* [2004] 1 WLR 1953.

[120] Hogan and Morgan, above n 5 at para 14-129.

[121] *Dimbo v Minister for Justice, Equality and Law Reform* [2008] 2 ILRM 481.

[122] Hogan and Morgan, above n 5 at para 14-129.

The Right to Adequate Notice of a Decision

The Basic Right to Notice

The right to notice of a forthcoming act directly affecting one's rights is well established, particularly in the employment context. In the case of *Gallagher v Corrigan*,[123] disciplinary action against four prison officers was rendered void, by the fact that no charge had been made against them, even though they were asked to respond to adverse report findings made in relation to them. In *State (Gleeson) v Minister for Defence*,[124] the discharge of an individual from the defence forces was quashed due to the failure to inform him of the grounds prior to the decision or to facilitate him making a reply. The obligation extends beyond mere notice of the reason, but as was held in *State (Gleeson)*, the applicant should have prior notice of the essential facts and findings. Furthermore, the possible consequences of a negative decision for the individual should be identified. **[10–64]**

Outside of these core obligations, the measures required lie along a continuum. In deciding whether to share further detail, such as witness statements, the determining factors, according to the Supreme Court in *Director of Public Prosecution v Doyle*[125] are: **[10–65]**

(i) The seriousness of the charge;
(ii) The centrality of the evidence;
(iii) The adequacy of the existing notice already provided;
(iv) The risk of injustice.

The Obligation to Investigate and Declare Evidence

A related aspect is the obligation to investigate and declare evidence, particularly if the decision-maker is well placed to do so. In *Braddish v DPP*, Hardiman J stressed that Gardaí owe an obligation **[10–66]**

> "arising from their unique investigative role, to seek out and preserve all evidence having a bearing or potential bearing on the issue of guilt or innocence".[126]

---

[123] *Gallagher v Corrigan* Unreported, High Court, Blayney J, 1 February 1988.
[124] *State (Gleeson) v Minister for Defence* [1976] IR 280.
[125] *Director of Public Prosecution v Doyle* [1994] 2 IR 286.
[126] *Braddish v Director of Public Prosecutions* [2001] 3 IR 127. De Blacam provides an excellent account of notice and proper prior investigation, above n 6 at paras 13.12-13.16.

Relatedly, the more serious the matter the greater the obligation to declare the rights and entitlements of the person affected during the process. This was seen in *Flanagan v University College Dublin*,[127] where the university's committee of discipline was, in the eyes of Barron J, under a duty to inform the applicant of her rights under the hearing procedure. The limits of this obligation were explored in *Keogh v Criminal Assets Bureau*, Keane CJ held that "it is manifestly not the function of the second respondents…to give gratuitous advice, in all circumstances, to members of the public as to their legal position".[128] This is an area that will need to be further explored by the courts, particularly in sharpening the obligations of authorities towards more vulnerable people. Certainly judicial interventions should reference any prior findings of the Ombudsman and the customer service commitments of public authorities as relevant to expectations in this area. While these cannot be elevated to full legal requirements, the goal must be to ensure organisations are engaging with the issues involved, rather than simply adopting a reactive posture to judicial review actions.

[10–67]   A recent case where adequate notice was not provided was *Atlantean Ltd v Minister for Communications & Natural Resources*.[129] This involved a challenge to the Minister's reduction of a mackerel quota enjoyed by the applicant fishing company. The decision was made on the basis of the Minister's apparent belief that Atlantean had been responsible for widespread failures to declare the landing of fish.[130] Clarke J stated that while the circumstances of each case can influence the content of procedural fairness, including notice, the allocation of fishing quotas was not too dissimilar from situations involving the termination of employment. He held that the Minister had failed to disclose what evidence officials[131] had to justify their accusations that Atlantean had violated the requirements of the quota scheme. Without such disclosure the Minister's notification constituted an unfair "bare accusation".

---

[127] *Flanagan v University College Dublin* [1988] IR 724.
[128] *Keogh v Criminal Assets Bureau* [2004] 2 IR 159 at 176.
[129] *Atlantean Ltd v Minister for Communications & Natural Resources* [2007] IEHC 233.
[130] The European Commission had reduced Ireland's national quota under Regulation (EC) No. 742/2006 of the 17 May, 2006, as a result of what it regarded as widespread non-declaration. In redesigning the quotas, the Minister was attempting to allocate responsibility. *ibid* at paras 3.7 – 3.9.
[131] Scottish officials had been behind the allegations, *ibid* at para 3.11.

An area in which courts have been especially conscious of notice has been [10–68] in procedures applying to fitness to work and sickness absence, when employers send employee for a medical assessment. In *Delaney v Central Bank of Ireland*,[132] the High Court held that the employee was entitled to the briefing provided to the doctor prior to the examination, as well as a copy of the doctor's report.[133]

The Level of Notice

The question of whether all justifications and factors influencing the [10–69] decisions need to be identified in prior notice was discussed in *International Fishing Vessels v Minister for Marine (No. 2)*, where the Minister set forth a number, but not all, grounds for refusing a fishing licence renewal application. McCarthy J adopted a permissive stance:

> "If he fails to notify the applicant of a matter which, on its own, causes him to make his decision, then his decision must be quashed. If however, there are valid reasons for his decision based upon matters of which he has notified the applicants and given them ample opportunity to make representations, the fact that there are other reasons of which he had not given them notice, does not, in my view, invalidate his decisions."[134]

Judicial review in Ireland, still shaped as it is by reasonableness standards, may be unlikely to unpack the substantive balancing of the relevant factors undertaken by the decision-maker. The result of this precedent may be, therefore, that in most cases partial omissions of relevant, but not determinative, issues may not lead to adverse court findings.

The Obligation to Give Notice in an Emergency Situation

The Courts have had to consider whether notice is required when the [10–70] decision-maker needs to implement a decision rapidly in an emergency context. Where the decision seriously affects the constitutional rights, notice must still be given in order to facilitate representations by the

---

[132] *Delaney v Central Bank of Ireland* [2011] IEHC 212 at para 9.6.
[133] The failure to do so appeared largely due to legal advice that the briefing given to the doctor would be subject to legal professional privilege, to prepare for personal injuries at work assessment or related litigation. It is correct that the correspondence with the doctor will be covered by privilege where the briefing is done for the dominant purpose of actual or contemplated litigation, however, where it is done to determine fitness to work, it must be shared.
[134] *International Fishing Vessels Ltd v Minister for the Marine* [1991] 2 IR 93 at p 103.

affected party. This requirement was made clear in *Dellway v National Asset Management Agency*[135] where the prominent developer Mr Paddy McKillen challenged the entitlement of the NAMA to acquire what it claimed to be distressed loans from the balance sheets of financial institutions. NAMA had made the decision to acquire the loans belonging to Mr McKillen's various corporate entities based on the argument that they represented a systemic risk to the banking system.[136] The acquisition was made under s 84 of the National Management Agency Act 2009 without any notice being given to Mr McKillen. Counsel for NAMA invoked the extraordinary economic circumstances in justifying this, claiming that even a banking customer who was not in arrears was not entitled to any notice or hearing before compulsory acquisition of their loans. As we discussed above, the Supreme Court refused to accept such restrictions of constitutional justice. Hardiman J perhaps indicated the degree to which notice lies at the core of the right to a fair hearing in Ireland:

> "It is trite law to say that a right to a hearing carries with it a right to notification of the proposed decision and to sufficient detailed information, including criteria, as may be necessary to allow the person to be affected to make the best case he can against the decision which he fears."[137]

Decision-Making Steps: How Early is it Before Fair Hearing Rights Apply?

[10–71] One of the trickiest aspects of designing organisational procedures is dividing a decision-making process into distinct steps, from investigation to determination of facts through to a final decision. Clearly the obligation to respect the rights of the person affected takes it strength from the practical consequences that result from the step taken. Yet there are circumstances where the launching of an investigation, where it is linked to a decision to suspend the person pending the final outcome, cannot be saved by procedural fairness later in the process.

[10–72] The strongest recent example of a poorly designed organisational process was seen in the case of *Zhang v Athlone Institute of Technology*.[138] This case

---

[135] *Dellway Investments v National Asset Management Agency* [2011] 4 IR 1.
[136] The level of exposure was estimated at 2 billion euros.
[137] *Dellway*, above n 135 at 296.
[138] Above n 25.

involved a foreign student studying at the respondent institute, who was alleged to have breached examination regulations. The examination in question started late and following a twenty minute delay a standard announcement warning students to place all notes and bags at the top of the examination hall, and all phones on the floor by their desks, was made. The applicant claimed that she did not hear this announcement being made, "as a result of noise, confusion caused by the late commencement of the exam and her 'somewhat limited English'".[139] She therefore kept her notes and other belongings on the floor with her mobile phone. Upon completing the examination she was informed by the invigilator that she was in breach of the examination rules. A breach of rules form was completed and the applicant completed a section outlining her defence. Following a hearing involving herself, the invigilator and the Academic Registrar, the Institute informed Ms Zhang that her marks in the relevant subject were quashed and she was required to repeat the module no earlier than Autumn 2013. At this stage, solicitors' for Ms Zhang wrote a letter complaining that the hearing and decision which had been conducted was inappropriate given the fact that the invigilator and the Academic Registrar were married. A fortnight later, the Institute informed them that it had agreed to set aside the initial decision and would shortly commence a new decision-making process chaired by an independent person not connected with the institution.

Three days before the new hearing was scheduled to be held the applicants' solicitors were still seeking information as to whether the hearing was a full appeal against the invigilator's initial decision that Ms Zhang had breached the examination rules and what procedures the hearing would have, as well as a list of witnesses. The day before the hearing, the Institute informed them that the meeting would merely determine if there was a prima facie case for the applicant to answer. It stated that a full hearing "may or may not be held"[140] in the event there was a prima facie case, and until then the Institute ruled out the involvement of witnesses, saying that only the applicant and the invigilator would have the opportunity to speak. The Institute stated that the applicant and her lawyers "either misunderstood the process or [were] jumping the gun and your client cannot be prejudiced in any way by the process now being undertaken".[141]

[10–73]

---

[139] *ibid* at para 2.
[140] *ibid* at para 7.
[141] *ibid.*

[10–74]   Having outlined these facts, Dunne J turned to the Institute's regulations which provided that:

> "If a case is considered to exist, the Registrar shall report the case in writing to the Director. The Registrar's office informs the candidate and invites him/her to a formal meeting to discuss the alleged incident. The candidate is informed of the date, place and time of the meeting and that he/she shall have the right to have legal and/or other representation for the discussion of the matter, and to review all relevant material presented. This meeting of the Registrar with the candidate is minuted."[142]

What was envisaged was a two-step process, with the Registrar's full hearing following an initial determination that a prima facie case arose.

[10–75]   The scheduled hearing went ahead, its professed purpose being the determination of whether a prima facie case existed. At one point in the hearing, the applicants' solicitor requested the right to ask the invigilator a number of questions. The Chair rejected this saying, "not today. It adds to the confusion rather than clears it up".[143] When the solicitor inquired as to whether the Chair found the invigilator's account persuasive, he replied "I don't want to comment at the moment."[144] Despite this, a number of days later, the applicant received a letter informing her that the acting Registrar had found her in breach of examination rules, and issued a penalty on her mark. The applicant sought judicial review of this decision. The Institute attempted to defend its conduct on the basis that full appeal rights were present and also by stating that at the hearing the applicant had in effect admitted to breaching the regulations. Dunne J rejected these submissions finding:

> "What is manifestly clear is that the applicant together with her legal adviser going into that meeting could not have anticipated that as a result of what occurred on that date, there would be a finding or adjudication that she had in fact breached the examination regulations and that a penalty would be imposed on her without having given her any opportunity at all to be heard in relation to the issue of penalty."[145]

---

[142] *ibid* at para 9.
[143] *ibid* at para 16.
[144] *ibid*.
[145] *ibid* at para 30.

The area of employment law has increasingly emerged as an area where a [10–76] phased process is to be preferred. Where a distinct investigation phase is used, with diminished procedural rights accompanying it, the courts have been anxious to require that the investigator not stray into the subject of sanction. In the case of *Minnock v Casing Co Ltd and Stewart*, Clarke J identified a typology of preliminary investigations.[146] At one extreme was the "pure" investigation, which involved obtaining the relevant facts but not pronouncing upon them, this did not attract the rules of procedural fairness. The opposite extreme is an investigation where the investigator gathers the facts and makes formal findings. This latter process is covered by the rules of natural justice, and where there is a serious flaw the court will intervene. The term "finding" however, is probably best viewed as involving some element of a sanction such as suspension, which Clarke J himself had implied in the earlier case of *O'Brien v AON Insurance Managers*.[147] The practical result of these cases, nevertheless, is that companies should preserve a clear separation between investigation and disciplinary phases.

Obligation to Share Relevant Information

In *O'Callaghan v Mahon (No. 1)*,[148] the Supreme Court found that regardless [10–77] of what the Tribunal saw as the need for confidentiality, materials created during its investigative phase should have been shared with the applicant in order to facilitate cross examination of witnesses.

The need to provide access to relevant precedents and policy statements [10–78] has also provoked some controversy, particularly in the refugee context. While previous tribunal or administrative decisions may not be strictly binding in the manner of a court, consistency is often a goal to be pursued by such bodies. In *PPA v Refugee Appeals Tribunal*, the Supreme Court stressed that in a context where there are strongly linked, policy determinations to be made across individual decisions[149]:

> "…fair procedures require some reasonable mechanisms for achieving consistency in both the interpretation and the application of the law in

---

[146] *Minnock v Casing Co Ltd and Stewart* [2007] ELR 229.
[147] *O'Brien v AON Insurance Managers* [2005] IEHC 3.
[148] *O'Callaghan v Mahon (No. 1)* [2006] 2 IR 32.
[149] Such as whether a LGBTI person may face threats within country X, or there is insufficient protection from domestic violence afforded by the institutions of the State Y.

cases like this of a similar category. Yet, if relevant provisions are not available to an appellant, he or she has no way of knowing whether there is such consistency."[150]

[10–79]   Geoghegan J noted that the appellant had "no guarantee that the member of the tribunal has any personal knowledge of the previous decisions made by different colleagues". He stressed also an inequality between the sides, whereby advocates for the Office of the Refugee Commissioner had access to all previous decisions when appearing before the Tribunal. Nevertheless, there was clear concern for the potential financial implications of the Court's findings, with Geoghegan J underlining that he would not support the idea that an "open library containing redacted previous decisions" must be available.[151] A proportionate obligation was rather "reasonable access, in whatever form the tribunal considers fit, to previous decisions which are being reasonably required for legal relevance…".[152]

[10–80]   In the case of *OOC v The Minister for Justice Equality and Law Reform*,[153] the parents of the first named minor applicant alleged a lack of procedural fairness on the part of the Refugee Tribunal in its rejection as forgeries of two letters submitted in evidence.[154] The applicant argued that the Tribunal relied upon undisclosed country of origin information in making this determination. Furthermore, it had failed to investigate the potential that the two letters were genuine. In finding for the applicant, McDermott J noted the obligation within s 18(6) of the Refugee Act 1996 (as amended) was that:

> "The Appeal Board shall furnish the applicant concerned and his or her solicitor (if known) with copies of any reports, observations or representations in writing or any other document, furnished to the Appeal Board by the Commissioner copies of which have not been

---

[150] *PPA v Refugee Appeals Tribunal* [2007] 4 IR 94 at 105.

[151] *ibid* at 106.

[152] *ibid* at 110.

[153] *OOC v The Minister for Justice Equality and Law Reform* [2013] IEHC 278.

[154] The Court did not impugn the tribunal's rejection of an alleged threatening letter which was handwritten, but ultimately found for the applicant on the basis of a second letter which had been apparently sent from a Nigerian solicitor's office. The Tribunal decision is quoted at para 10 of the judgment:
"Two letters have been sent from Nigeria and these are exhibited on file. There is no objective evidence to suggest that either of these two letters is objectively reliable. Country of origin reports indicate that forging documents in Nigeria is very easy to do, such is the level of corruption. The letter from Chief Toye Coker & Company cannot therefore be relied upon as genuine".

previously furnished to the applicant pursuant to section 11(6) and an indication in writing of the nature and source of any other information relating to the appeal which has come to the notice of the Appeal Board in the course of an appeal under this section."

The main difficulty was the reliance upon unshared, general country of origin information in rejecting the letter; had the tribunal "confined itself to a finding that the letter was not verifiable or that it did not put much weight on its contents",[155] this would not have raised any procedural fairness issues. In the circumstances, however, where the country of origin information was directly linked to the discounting of the letter, and had knock on effects for the credibility of the applicant's father, McDermott J held that: [10–81]

> "...the Tribunal should have furnished the applicant with a copy of this information, indicated to the applicant in writing that there was a serious issue in relation to the authenticity of the letter and given the applicant an opportunity to address any allegation or suggestion that it was forged. At the very least the country of origin information and the issue should have been raised directly with the applicant at the oral hearing."[156]

It is important to note, however, that a right to relevant facts or materials does not represent a right to advance receipt of the arguments of the other side.[157] Where the matter involves only a decision-maker and the person affected, however, this facts versus arguments distinction has not yet been upheld. [10–82]

External Information Relied Upon by the Decision-Maker

Two further areas of difficulty have arisen in relation to whether information requested should be provided or withheld where it is not obtained directly through the hearing but comes from some external source. These are (i) where the information is a legal opinion; and (ii) where the information relates more to the general expertise and skill of the decision-maker. The status of the first category remains in need of clarification, with diverging High Court authorities. The oldest authority is *State (Polymark* [10–83]

---

[155] *ibid* at para 18.

[156] *ibid* at para 27.

[157] See *Davy v Financial Services Ombudsman* [2008] IEHC 256, where Charleton J held: "Where submissions [are] requested of the argument as to right and wrong, there is no need to exchange" at para 50.

Ltd) v ITGWU,[158] where Blayney J made an *obiter* comment that in seeking legal advice from its registrar, the Labour Court should have notified both parties, and given them an opportunity to make submissions on it. An opposite emphasis was chosen in *Georgopolous v Beaumont Hospital*,[159] where in electing to terminate a contract of employment no access to the advice of the legal assessor was provided to the complainant. On balance, this latter decision is not to be preferred, and in *Prendiville v Medical Council*,[160] Kelly J followed the decision in *Polymark* due to the closer factual fit with the case before the Court. Arguably, further support for the need to disclose legal advice was supplied in an indirect manner in *McManus v Fitness to Practice Committee*.[161] There the failure of the Committee to provide reasons for rejecting the advice of its legal assessor was held to breach fair procedures. While none of the prior three cases were mentioned in *McManus*, the thrust is that legal issues may be subject to contention and submissions regarding it may need to be facilitated.

[10–84] The second category noted above, relates to the situation where, in judging any case before her, an administrator is likely to bring to bear many background value preferences, methodologies and experiences. The stand out case in this area remains *Kiely v Minister for Social Welfare (No.2)*.[162] The core matter in dispute was whether it was possible for depression to trigger a heart attack — the answer to this question would in turn determine the pension entitlement of a widow following her husband's death. Differing conclusions were proffered by medical experts for the appellant and for the Minister of Social Welfare respectively. In the period of time between the hearing and the notification of decision to the applicant, the departmental medical assessor wrote a letter to the Appeals Officer enclosing fresh academic evidence as to why depression could not cause a heart attack. Having lost her case before the Appeals Officer, Kiely successfully appealed to the Supreme Court which found a breach of fair procedures in the failure to disclose the exchange of additional information. In a statement often invoked to define the obligations of expert testimony in decision-making,

---

[158] *State (Polymark Ltd) v ITGWU* [1987] ILRM 357.
[159] *Georgopoulous v Beaumont Hospital Board* [1998] 3 IR 132.
[160] *Prendiville v Medical Council* [2008] 3 IR 122.
[161] *McManus v Fitness to Practice Committee* [2012] IEHC 350.
[162] *Kiely v Minister for Social Welfare (No.2)* [1977] IR 267.

Henchy J ruled that the assessor's function was "to act as a medical dictionary and not as a medical report".[163]

The debate regarding the formation of general expertise and judgment **[10–85]** within departments and tribunals must be aired. For instance where training days or professional development events are ongoing, and address issues relevant to a case, should these be declared as influencing the decision-maker? If such processes are not rendered visible and declared, may allegations of institutional bias in the formation of departmental expertise appear?[164]

Finally, once the decision-maker has provided notice as to all the relevant **[10–86]** issues, and proceeds to making a finding, there is no obligation to circulate that finding for comment. This was seen in the recent case of *O'Callaghan v Judge Alan Mahon & Others*.[165] Here Mr O'Callaghan claimed that the failure to forewarn him of findings of corruption made against him in the Tribunal's final report constituted a breach of fair procedures. The applicant argued that the purpose of his appearance before the Tribunal had not been made clear to him as no direct allegations of corruption had been furnished to him by it when he appeared before it. He argued that the elements of the definition of "corruption" and "attempts to influence" should have been put to him. He argued that upon him making statements before the Tribunal denying any wrongdoing, counsel for the tribunal should have declared that it did not believe he was telling the truth. Endorsing a similar finding in the earlier case of *O'Callaghan v Mahon*,[166] Hedigan J found that:

> "I am satisfied that all payments referred to in its report as forming the basis of the Tribunal's finding of corruption were put to the applicant in such a way as to alert him and his legal advisers to the possibility they might be found to be corrupt and so as to allow him fully explain and answer. There were no new allegations and there could have been no doubt that the applicant was aware that the payments were being investigated to determine whether they were corrupt."[167]

---

[163] *ibid* at 284.
[164] This issue is discussed further in chapter 11 – Bias and Decision-making.
[165] *O'Callaghan v Judge Alan Mahon & Others* [2012] IEHC 603.
[166] *O'Callaghan v Mahon* [2009] IEHC 428.
[167] Above n 165 at para 5.6.

The Obligation to Hear the Other Side

[10–87] Having provided notice, the administrative body must then shift its focus towards facilitating the person affected to make their case to the decision-maker. The foundational case of *Re Haughey*[168] laid down the core requirements of *audi alteram partem* in cases where fundamental rights are affected. In circumstances where a Garda had made allegations against Mr Haughey which impugned his good name, the Oireachtas Committee hearing the matter it was required to ensure the following procedural protections:

> "(a) that he should be furnished with a copy of the evidence which reflected on his good name (b) that he should be allowed to cross-examine, by counsel, his accuser or accusers (c) that he should be allowed to give rebutting evidence; and (d) that he should be permitted to address, again by counsel, the Committee in his own defence."[169]

[10–88] As has been discussed in previous chapters, the Irish judiciary have strongly defended the right to fair procedure in parliamentary and tribunal contexts, with the formalities of the hearing often heavily legalised and shaped by the conventional ideal of court procedures. Such models have also been applied in matters affecting the right to earn a livelihood and where a student is alleged to have committed plagiarism. Clearly the seriousness of the subject, together with the nature of the body, shape the extent of the procedural steps which must be taken. As argued at the start of this chapter, it is difficult to overestimate the profound impacts, organisational and fiscal, individual natural justice rulings can have upon public administration in Ireland.

[10–89] As will be discussed extensively in chapter 15, Article 6 of the European Convention on Human Rights also foregrounds the right to hearing:

> "In the determination of his civil rights and obligations or of any criminal charge against him, everyone is entitled to a fair and public hearing within a reasonable time by an independent and impartial tribunal established by law."

---

[168] *Re Haughey* [1971] IR 217.
[169] *ibid* at 262-263.

Is An Oral Hearing Required?

The so called "Haughey rights" have featured heavily in judicial efforts to identify when the right to a fair hearing is triggered. Attempts by applicants to claim them during the information gathering stage have often been unsuccessful. In *Re National Irish Bank (No 2)*,[170] financial institutions under investigation by Inspectors appointed under Companies Act 1990 sought an order to compel those Inspectors to furnish them with copies of interviews with staff and customers, Kelly J held that:

[10–90]

> "What brings that [accusation triggering an entitlement to a hearing]
> about is a determination by the inspectors (a) that they will admit such
> an allegation as evidence and (b) that the admission of it may give rise
> to adverse conclusions being drawn against the party accused. It is
> then and only then that the rights identified by the Supreme Court in
> *In re Haughey* come into play."[171]

Nevertheless, a simple distinction cannot be drawn between the investigative and the examination of evidence phases, as was seen in *O'Ceallaigh v An Bord Altranais*.[172] This case considered the question of whether a nurse had the right to be notified before the establishment of a formal inquiry under s 38 of the Nurses Act 1985. The Supreme Court held that reading such an obligation into the statute would not overly impede the process and was justified in the light of the possible effects upon the applicant. The ruling of Barron J in *State (Murphy) v Kielt*,[173] offers an excellent baseline on the circumstances in which a hearing is required, as being those where:

[10–91]

> "...the rights of an individual are seriously threatened and he would
> not otherwise have any means either of seeking to vindicate himself or
> to alleviate the hardship which he might suffer."[174]

Thus, a hearing is required where the "rights" of an individual are threatened. While unpacking the term "rights" at the conceptual level is a complicated matter, in practice Irish law has opted for a pragmatic, case by case approach. There is a heavy overlay, with the second element noted by

[10–92]

---

[170] *Re National Irish Bank (No 2)* [1999] 3 IR 190.
[171] *ibid* at 216.
[172] *O'Ceallaigh v An Bord Altranais* [2000] 4 IR 54.
[173] *State (Murphy) v Kielt* [1984] 1 IR 458.
[174] *ibid* at 464.

Barron J in the quote above — the seriousness of the consequences for the applicant.[175]

[10–93] The final factor in the decision to hold a hearing relates to the subject matter of the dispute — an oral hearing must represent the sole method for examining the truth of the matter. A contested factual element has been viewed as a characteristic requirement for such an entitlement.[176] As Costello J noted in *Doupe v Limerick County Council*, the right to fair procedures:

> "...does not require that every administrative order which may adversely affect rights must be preceded by a judicial-type hearing involving the examination and cross-examination of hearing...it is clear that the requirements of the rule may be fully satisfied by the adoption of quite informal procedures. In some cases an applicant may be entitled to make his submissions orally, in others a written submission will meet the requirements of the rule."[177]

[10–94] As an area dominated by subjective assessment of personal credibility, decisions affecting asylum seekers have led to prominent judicial analyses of the need for an oral hearing. In the case of *SUN v Refugee Applications Commissioner*,[178] the applicant's asylum application had been rejected largely on the basis of a negative assessment of his personal credibility. In addition, however, his case had been adversely affected by the fact that his country of nationality (South Africa) had been designated as a safe country of origin under s 13(5) and s 13(6)(e) of the Refugee Act 1996.[179] This latter finding was held by the Court to have been included at the discretion of the decision-maker; it was not mandatorily required by the Act and could have

---

[175] The case of *Quirke v Bord Lúthchleas na hÉireann* [1988] IR 83, was an example of where, because of the substantial penalty involved, a decision was quashed for a failure to hear the applicant.

[176] Seen in *Mooney v An Post* [1998] 4 IR 288. There Barrington J stressed that the person affected by a disciplinary process "had raised no issue of fact which needed to be referred to a civil tribunal" at 263.

[177] *Doupe v Limerick County Council* [1981] ILRM 456 at 464.

[178] *SUN v Refugee Applications Commissioner* [2012] IEHC 338.

[179] s 12 of the 1996 Act provided for prioritisation of certain classes of application, including where the country of nationality had been designated as safe. The Minister designated South Africa as a safe country of origin by Refugee Act 1996 (Safe Countries of Origin) Order 2004 (SI No 714 of 2004). Where such a designation is in operation, an applicant is presumed not to be a refugee unless reasonable grounds for the contention are shown to exist. (See s 11A(1) Refugee Act 1996).

been waived by the Commissioner.[180] With the safe country designation in place, an oral hearing at the appeal stage was excluded, despite the fact that an oral hearing was the only effective way to examine the subjective credibility of his account. Clarke J had in the earlier case of *Moyosola v Refugee Applications Commissioner* noted the danger inherent in this approach:

"If the Refugee Appeals Tribunal feels, for example, that such a finding [of a safe country of origin] was not justified but nonetheless has doubts as to the credibility of the applicant, the RAT cannot, apparently, conduct an oral hearing to satisfy itself on credibility. How should it then act?"[181]

Confronted with this exact possibility in *SUN*, Cooke J concluded that the denial of an oral hearing based on the mere fact of nationality was a breach of natural justice: [10–95]

"The denial of an oral hearing which is otherwise available to asylum seekers as part of a statutory appeal remedy in a case where assessment of personal credibility is the sole or central issue challenged in the s.13 report, by reason only of a factor (nationality), which has no rational connection to role of a hearing in the appeal, renders the procedure, in the judgment of the Court, unfair to a degree which is incompatible with the guarantee in Article 40.3 of the Constitution.... [W]here the key issue in the appeal is the fact that an account of facts given personally at first instance has been disbelieved, the primary, if not the exclusive, possibility of successfully reversing that result lies in the appellant's prospect of persuading a second decision-maker that he can and should be believed. To remove that possibility when it is not rationally necessary to do so having regard to the fact that the appellant already faces the procedural disadvantage of the s.11A(1)(a) presumption is to render the appeal procedure unfair in the sense of the Constitutional guarantee."[182]

This case underlines the irreplaceability of an oral hearing in serious disputes centred upon personal credibility and also that in such circumstances, the courts will be reluctant, in cases affecting fundamental   [10–96]

---

[180] This was significant as the stress upon the fact that the applicant was a national of a safe third country had a number of statutory implications including raising a rebuttable presumption that he was not a refugee as well as limiting appeal rights as facilitated by the operation of s 11B, s 12(1)(m) and s 13(8)(a) of the 1996 Act.

[181] *Moyosola v Refugee Applications Commissioner* [2005] IEHC 218.

[182] Above n 178 at paras 46-48.

rights, to permit the removal of an oral hearing entitlement on the basis of mere efficiency.[183] The knock-on implication of *SUN*, is that, where a first instance decision relies upon a safe third country designation alongside other grounds, any attempt to limit the applicant to a written appeal should be quickly challenged. If it is not challenged before an appeal proceeds to the Tribunal, however, a recent High Court case, *TES & Ors v Minister for Justice, Equality and Law Reform & Ors* shows that courts may not grant leave for judicial review on the ground that an oral hearing was not provided.[184] The lack of a hearing may result in closer scrutiny of the Tribunal reasoning on other grounds however.[185] We will return to the

---

[183] The utility of an oral hearing must of course be proved in the circumstances of the case. See Mac Eochaidh J in *AW v The Office of the Refugee Applications Commissioner* [2013] IEHC 71 at para 26 of the judgment:

"The principle I discern from the authorities cited is that there is no right to an oral hearing at the RAT but where demeanour-type or personal credibility findings underpin the first instance decision, then the applicant may require the opportunity to give oral evidence again on appeal. For example, if ORAC refused protection because it disbelieved an applicant and did so exclusively on grounds of evasiveness, or memory failure or the manner in which evidence was uttered, then fairness would seem to require that such applicant be permitted to speak again. I have not been able to discern what possible advantage would accrue to the applicant by an oral hearing, assuming that he recounts the same evidence which was given to ORAC. I have read the judgment of Birmingham J. in *S. v. RAC* [2008] IEHC 399 where complaint was made about the absence of an oral appeal where credibility findings had been made. The learned trial judge examined each such finding and concluded that written submissions would suffice to express complaint about such findings. I have conducted a similar exercise in this case and reach the same conclusion."

[184] *TES & Ors v Minister for Justice, Equality and Law Reform & Ors* [2012] IEHC 554. Clark J (at para 14 of her judgment) found that:

"Had the challenge been brought [before the Refugee Appeal Tribunal examined the matter], it is unlikely in light of the decision of Cooke J. in *S.U.N. [South Africa] v. The Refugee Applications Commissioner & Others* [2012] IEHC 338 (30th March 2012) that the application of s. 13(6) (e) would have survived the challenge. While the Court is generally critical of reliance on the application of s. 13(6) and therefore paper based appeals in cases which are not manifestly unfounded, it remains the responsibility of an applicant, who is under the present procedures always legally represented, to challenge such a decision at the earliest opportunity and not after the appeal has been considered. Leave on these grounds is refused."

[185] See para 21, *VM v Refugee Appeal Tribunal & anor* [2013] IEHC 24 (Judgment of Clark J):

"One further aspect of this case of serious concern to the Court is that the appeal was conducted without an oral hearing. The Court is powerless at this remove to review or amend the Commissioner's finding that s. 13(6) of the Refugee Act 1996 applied on the facts relied on in the applicant's claim. The Court therefore looks with heightened vigilance at the process of the documentary appeal in circumstances where an appellant has no opportunity to appear and explain or expand on any perceived inconsistencies or deficits in his / her claim. Unlike when the appeal is conducted orally, the Tribunal had no particular advantage over the Court in the assessment of credibility of an appellant as the same papers are before the Court as were considered by the Tribunal...".

issue of oral hearings in the asylum system in our discussion of recent cases regarding the right to an effective remedy in European Union law in chapter 14.

Oral Hearings in the Context of Expertise: Complexity and Contested Facts

Instances where the Financial Services Ombudsman has elected not to hold an oral hearing, have also produced a number of high profile recent cases. These show that the courts will attach importance to the aims of the governing statute and the expertise of the body, but that they will also require an oral hearing where a dispute is complex or dominated by contestable facts. A case in this latter category is *Davy v Financial Services Ombudsman*,[186] where the Supreme Court found against the Ombudsman, ruling that an oral hearing should have been afforded. Despite the statutory aim of accessible justice, and the expertise of the Ombudsman, Finnegan P held that written submissions were insufficient in circumstances where there was a conflict of material fact: namely the degree of the investment expertise of committee members of a Credit Union.[187] In *Hyde v Financial Services Ombudsman*,[188] Cross J held that the respondent could not have fairly determined the issue without a hearing where there was a dispute as to whether certain oral statements had been made to the complainant.

[10–97]

Two cases which, on the facts, endorsed the non-holding of a hearing were *Molloy v Financial Services Ombudsman*[189] and *Carr v Financial Services Ombudsman*.[190] In the former case, the bank in question argued that the complainant had misidentified the relevant bank official with whom he had interacted when signing a form. The official, who the bank contended had been present, did not remember the applicant, but would testify that her usual practice was to clarify the content of the form with the customer before signature. In such circumstances, McMenamin J held that an oral hearing would not have resolved the divergence between the sides and would not have affected the ultimate outcome. He also stressed that where

[10–98]

---

[186] *Davy v Financial Services Ombudsman* [2008] IEHC 256.
[187] In so holding he adopted the test referred to in the judgment of Costello P in *Galvin v Chief Appeals Officer* [1997] 3 IR 240.
[188] *Hyde v Financial Services Ombudsman* [2011] IEHC 422.
[189] *Molloy v Financial Services Ombudsman* Unreported, High Court, MacMenamin J, 15 April, 2011.
[190] *Carr v Financial Services Ombudsman* [2013] IEHC 182.

a party is legally represented during the complaint process, it should not be permitted to raise the issue on appeal, in the absence of any objection at first instance. In *Carr*, O'Malley J also concluded in favour of the Ombudsman on the facts:

> "I do not consider that he erred in his assessment that there was no dispute such as would require the holding of an oral hearing. Further, there was no direct request for such a hearing, merely the statement that medical information would be available "on request" or at a "face to face meeting". There was no attack on the credibility of the appellant. Alternative views on how the evidence should be interpreted were put forward but there was no real dispute as to what the evidence was. The core issue, that of the conduct of EBS, was, on the facts of this case, always going to be determined on the correspondence."[191]

Can a Hearing be Delegated?

[10–99]   One final matter needs to be consider in this area of oral hearings — whether the conduct of the hearing may be delegated to a lower level official or whether all members of the decision-making body would be present. This is context-dependent, with delegation often permitted in statutorily defined areas such as planning legislation.[192] In contexts which are regulated by common law standards or where the number of proceedings being carried out are less voluminous, the decision-maker may not delegate the function.

Right to Legal Representation and Related Rights

[10–100]   A good starting point in considering the right to legal representation is *O'Brien v Personal Injuries Assessment Board*.[193] This case concerned a challenge to the practice of the board whereby it barred an applicant from communicating with it through a solicitor. The Supreme Court provided a baseline statement of the circumstances where legal representation should be permitted, per Denham J:

> "Legal representation is a right of special importance in common law jurisdictions where the legal system is adversarial. This right is referable to court proceedings, prior to court proceedings, and in situations where there may be serious consequences for a person and

---

[191] *ibid* at para 92.

[192] *Murphy v Dublin Corporation (No. 2)* [1972] IR 215.

[193] *O'Brien v Personal Injuries Assessment Board* [2009] 3 IR 243, hereinafter "*O'Brien*".

the Oireachtas has not exercised a constitutional balance excluding legal representation. The applicant has a right to access the courts and to litigate to recover damages for personal injuries. To advance these rights the applicant is entitled to legal representation. This right does not apply solely to litigation in court. While the process in the respondent is not a court, it may conclude the claim with an assessment, or it may be a process preliminary to court proceedings. Thus the process before the respondent is a critical part of the applicant's claim."[194]

In such circumstances, any attempt to restrict the right to legal representation would have to be clearly expressed in legislation. The PIAB Act 2003 did not expressly exclude lawyers and while the aims of the Act included efficiency and alternative resolution of disputes, such an exclusion could not be inferred.[195] Macken J stressed[196] that the nature of the scheme was sufficiently similar to court proceedings to justify the High Court's finding that legal representation was sufficiently important "even outside the sphere of the administration of justice proper".[197]   **[10–101]**

Nevertheless, where the courts form the belief that legal representation was not contemplated by the legislature, they have not been willing to challenge any characterisation of the area as unsuited to lawyers. The High Court has held that a prisoner does not have a right to legal *representation* before a sentence review group.[198] This was rejected as legal presence at the hearing would be "disproportionate and would have the effect of changing the whole character of the procedure" involved.[199]   **[10–102]**

---

[194] *ibid* at 255.

[195] The exact provisions are found in s 7 of the Act of 2003 which provides:
"(1) Nothing in this Act is to be read as affecting the right of any person to seek legal advice in respect of his or her relevant claim and no rule shall be made under section 46 that affects that right.
(2) Subsection (1) shall not be read as requiring any procedure to be followed by the Board or hearing to be conducted by it that would be required to be followed or conducted by a court were the relevant claim concerned to be the subject of proceedings."
s 54(2) of the Act of 2003 provides:-
"The Board shall have all such powers as are necessary or expedient for, or incidental to, the performance of its functions under this Act."

[196] *O'Brien* above n 193 at p 278.

[197] *O'Brien ibid*. McMenamin J in the High Court had relied upon *re Haughey* [1971] IR 217, *Maguire v Ardagh* [2002] 1 IR 385, *Mosley et al v St. Louis Sough Western Railway* (1981) 634 F.2d 942 and *Powell v Alabama* (1932) 287 US 45 in making this finding (at p 35 of the judgment).

[198] *Barry v Sentence Review Group* [2001] 4 IR 167.

[199] *ibid* at 170.

[10–103] In forming a judgment on the legal representation requirement, the seriousness of the matter may not be the sole criterion. This was discussed extensively by the Supreme Court in *Burns & Hartigan v Governor of Castlerea Prison*,[200] where two prison officers claimed a breach of fair procedures due to their lack of a lawyer during a disciplinary process. The internal oral proceedings in question had been held under delegated legislation,[201] which, the Governor had found, did not provide for legal representation. The alleged professional misconduct related to an invalid overtime claim for escorting a prisoner to hospital. Upon finding the officers guilty, the Governor entered a reprimand on their records, restricted them to in-prison duties for a year and took steps to deny them a salary increment.

[10–104] The Supreme Court found firstly, that as the delegated legislation did not preclude legal representation, it remained possible for the Constitution to require it. Geoghegan J determined, that on balance, "legal representation was clearly unnecessary in this case". The need for a lawyer was to be judged in the particular circumstances of the case:

> "...the issues were factual issues connected with the day to day running of the prison. It is difficult to see why a lawyer would be required. The rules specify who is to be an advocate and, therefore, subject to the overall obligation of fairness they should be followed. The cases for which the Governor would be obliged to exercise a discretion in favour of permitting legal representation would be exceptional."[202]

[10–105] Thus, even though the matter had serious consequences,

> "the issues of proof were purely ones of simple fact and could safely be disposed of without a lawyer".

He drew force for this finding from the UK case of *R v Secretary of State for the Home Department, ex parte Tarrant*.[203] This case laid down six criteria which should be taken into account when exercising discretion to permit legal representation in a prison context:

1. The seriousness of the matter, and the likely consequences flowing from it;

---

[200] *Burns & Hartigan v Governor of Castlerea Prison* [2009] 3 IR 682, hereinafter "*Burns*".
[201] Prison (Disciplinary Code for Officers) Rules, 1996 (SI No 289 of 1996).
[202] *Burns* above n 200 at 688.
[203] *R v Secretary of State for the Home Department, ex parte Tarrant* [1985] 1 QB 251.

2. The likelihood that points of law will arise during the proceedings;
3. The capacity of the individual to represent herself/himself;
4. Complexity of the procedures employed;
5. The need for reasonable speed;
6. The need for fairness as between prisoners and as between prisoners and prison officers.

The Supreme Court stressed that this list was "merely of the kind of factors which might be relevant in the consideration of whether legal representation is desirable".[204] The Court stressed that the relevant Governor had to consider whether "from the accused's point of view legal representation is needed in the particular circumstances of the case".[205] Nevertheless, Geoghegan J reiterated that "in most cases" the provisions of the rules would apply, and that "legal representation should be the exception rather than the rule". **[10–106]**

Finally, we should note the anecdotal embodiment of the need for representation in many Irish students' examination answers has traditionally been the case of *Flanagan v UCD*.[206] There, the High Court held a student was entitled to be represented by a lawyer in a disciplinary hearing determining a plagiarism application, despite the relevant internal rules only allowing for an academic dean or student union officer.[207] **[10–107]**

The nature or quality of the legal representation has also been the subject of debate. The High Court has generally endorsed the freedom of a person to choose their own specific lawyer, noting that instances where "a choice of legal representative being an obstacle to the proper conduct of the proceedings will be rare indeed".[208] The greatest obstruction to availing of counsel is the potential cost, a difficulty which may be compounded by Ireland's lack of civil legal aid.[209] Government assistance is not available outside of limited recognised instances such as wardship applications,[210] **[10–108]**

---

[204] *Burns* above n 200 at 688.

[205] *ibid.*

[206] *Flanagan v UCD* [1988] IR 724.

[207] Under the regulations the student could be represented by the Dean of Women's Studies and/or the President of the Students' Union.

[208] *Law Society of Ireland v Competition Authority* [2006] 2 IR 262 at 282.

[209] Though the right to a lawyer in a criminal trial is constitutionally protected.

[210] *Kirwan v Minister for Justice, Equality and Law Reform* [1994] 2 IR 417.

inquests[211] and challenges to involuntary mental health detention.[212] In a recent High Court case, *Health Service Executive v OA*,[213] O'Malley J awarded full legal costs to a mother, whose income was so low as to ground an entitlement of legal aid, but who had availed of private representation before the Family Court. This was despite submissions by the Health Service Executive, who argued that to allow persons who were manifestly eligible for legal aid to choose private counsel was contrary to public policy and catastrophic for its finances.[214] O'Malley J rejected this by noting such an approach would constitute invidious discrimination, distinguishing the applicant from other people who chose private representation based solely on the proposition that she was poor.[215]

Cross Examination

[10–109]   While the *Tarrant* criteria set out in paragraph [10-105] above may be used to assess the necessity of the presence of a lawyer, a further issue is the need for cross-examination during a hearing. The Supreme Court in *Kiely v Minister for Social Welfare (No. 2)*,[216] provided "a classic statement of why it may be unfair to refuse an opportunity for cross-examination to a person whose own evidence is subject to cross-examination".[217] The Appeals Officer in *Kiely*, in deciding on entitlement to widows' benefit, had used the written opinion of one doctor to rebut the oral testimony of two others. Henchy J stressed the need for equality of arms in the administrative context:

> "...Any lawyer of experience could readily recall cases where injustice would certainly have been done if a party or a witness who had committed his evidence to writing had been allowed to stay away from the hearing, and the opposing party had been confined to controverting him simply by adducing his own evidence... Where essential facts are in controversy, a hearing which is required to be oral and confrontational for one side but which is allowed to be based on written and, therefore, effectively unquestionable evidence on

---

[211] *Stevenson v Laney* Unreported, High Court, Lardner J, 10 February 1993.

[212] *Magee v Farrell*, Unreported, High Court, Gilligan J, 26 October 2005.

[213] *Health Service Executive v OA* [2013] IEHC 172.

[214] *ibid* at paras 48-50.

[215] *ibid* at para 65.

[216] *Kiely v Minister for Social Welfare (No.2)* [1977] IR 267, hereinafter *"Kiely"*.

[217] Quote from the United Kingdom High Court in *R (on the application of Bonhoeffer) v General Medical Council* [2012] IRLR 37.

the other side has neither the semblance nor the substance of a fair hearing".[218]

The case of *Borges v Fitness to Practice Committee*[219] provided a similar endorsement of the need for cross-examination in the context of allegations of professional misconduct. There the applicant had been struck off the British medical register for inappropriate touching of female patients. The Irish Medical Council then began proceedings to strike out his registration in this country. In doing so, it sought to rely upon the transcript of the British proceedings. The applicant successfully claimed that such reliance significantly reduced the ability of the Committee to arrive at a different conclusion to the British body. As a result, the admission of such evidence, without the ability to cross-examine the decision-makers was a denial of constitutional justice. It would be incorrect to characterise the cross-examination requirement as absolute, however, as was seen in *State (Boyle) v General Medical Services (Payment) Board*.[220] There the Board relied upon statistical data concerning the average number of home visits conducted by doctors under a particular scheme, in finding that the applicant's claims were excessive. Keane J held that it was not required for the expert who had compiled the data to be cross-examined, as the applicant had received the breakdown, and had not raised a specific objection to it which need to be resolved.

[10–110]

Both *Kiely* and *Borges* were considered by the United Kingdom Court in a recent case, *R (on the application of Bonhoeffer) v General Medical Council*.[221] The High Court provided a number of factors which decision-makers should have regard to. The disciplinary matter in this case involved an allegation of serious sexual misconduct by a consultant of international repute. The case against the consultant relied upon the testimony of one witness, a male, Witness A, who was resident in Kenya, where the misconduct was alleged to have occurred. While Witness A had offered to testify in person in the UK, the Council elected to rely upon hearsay evidence, due to the risks of local reprisals against Witness A in Kenya were he to testify in person or by video link. The likelihood of harm to the witness came from two groups: homophobic elements in Kenyan society

[10–111]

---

[218] *Kiely* above n 216 at 281-282.
[219] *Borges v Fitness to Practice Committee* [2004] 1 IR 103.
[220] *State (Boyle) v General Medical Services (Payment) Board* [1981] ILRM 242.
[221] *R (on the application of Bonhoeffer) v General Medical Council* [2012] IRLR 37.

and local residents who were loyal to the applicant consultant. The decision to proceed on the basis of hearsay was justified by reference to the public interest, including the protection of patients, maintenance of public confidence and the need to uphold proper standards of behaviour.

[10–112] Upon review, the High Court held that there was no absolute entitlement, whether under Article 6 of the European Convention on Human Rights or in the common law, to cross examine core witnesses in disciplinary proceedings. The fact that Witness A was the sole witness did not immediately disallow hearsay evidence — the question was to be addressed with multiple factors in mind. Firstly, the seriousness of the allegations, in this case they would have grave effects on the career and reputation of the accused party. Additional factors were the centrality of the witness to the case against the accused party and the practical difficulties in securing attendance. The Court was not persuaded by the public interest factors cited by the Council, noting that ultimately the decision not to allow oral testimony was due to the particular facts of the case. It was not reasonable for the Council to conclude that the threat to Witness A would be greater if he gave in person or video testimony than if his hearsay evidence was admitted.

Conclusion: The Values and Goals of Procedural Justice

[10–113] Professor Ian Holloway in his comparative work on the status of natural justice in common law systems, has provided a taxonomy of rationales for its centrality.[222] Firstly, one may cite its *instrumental* value to public administration, as hearing the other side is seen as improving decision making. Secondly, it also complements the *rule of law* by increasing public confidence in decision-making. Thirdly, it has deep constitutional tap-roots, reflecting *libertarian* visions of justice. Finally, fair procedures relates also to respecting the *dignity* of the individual, or, if one prefers, a deliberative democratic orientation towards citizen participation.

[10–114] Claims regarding the *instrumental value* of procedural fairness has traditionally met with resistance from administrators. As Australian Chief Justice French has commented

---

[222] Taxonomy provided by I Holloway, *Natural Justice and the High Court of Australia: A Study of Common Law Constitutionalism* (Ashgate, Aldershot, 2002) at pp 286-294.

"there is a tendency in some quarters to regard procedural fairness as a species of ethical ornamentation, a moral luxury which is a drag on efficient decision-making".[223]

This is a question that can only be settled at the empirical level, though Irish administrative law is sadly lacking such investigations. What is clear is that the tendency to conflate the dignity oriented, libertarian and deliberative democratic justifications together deletes the subtleties and ambiguities in each category. In many respects there is an anti-critical spirit regarding procedural fairness in the Irish legal system. Clearly it is viewed as a classical civil and political right by its judicial proponents, but the accompanying socio-economic and polycentric impacts on administrative design must also be weighed. The judiciary, with the court system installed as its paradigm of justice, have at times slipped into a comfortable, activism around the concept. As we discuss in chapter 5 on public inquiries and chapter 2 on Parliamentary oversight, the decision in *Re Haughey* installed a heavy premium upon the right to a good name and a fear of parliament's ability to impugn an individual's reputation. It is somewhat ironic that the right to reasons — a key gateway right which renders the ultimate decision visible to those affected, lagged somewhat behind the Haughey protections.

Ultimately, where *audi alteram partem* is most valuable is where it leads to increased reasoning on the part of the decision-maker and increased information for the person affected. Despite this however, the traditionally forgiving nature of reasonableness standards in Irish law has meant that information submitted and evidence advanced could be easily submerged by other considerations. As was argued in chapter 9, even marginal shifts in overall review standards can prevent the "islanding" of Ireland's assertive procedural fairness protections. Rather than allegations that it merely chases process, the right to a fair hearing can become more identified with a positive culture of administrative justification. Procedural rights in areas such as planning did little to uncover the distorted and misguided practices of local government in the run up to the crash. There is something ironically paternalistic in linking fair hearing rights to democracy or the rule of law if they do not yield outcomes for the individual. If the proverb says living well is the best revenge, getting it right is the best form of justice.

[10–115]

---

[223] Chief Justice Robert S French, Sir Anthony Mason Lecture, 7 October 2010, *Procedural Fairness – Indispensable to Justice?* at p 2.

BIAS AND DECISION-MAKING

Introduction

The second limb of procedural fairness is the principle of *nemo iudex in*   [11–01]
causa sua, namely the fundamental principle "no man should be a judge in
his own cause". The deep roots of this prohibition against bias in Irish law,
was reflected upon by Murray J (as he then was) in *Maguire v Ardagh*.[1] In
that case, which related to the obligation of Oireachtas Committee to abide
by procedural fairness, his Honour stressed that the principle against bias
constituted "fully half of that irreducible essence of natural justice".[2] This
was evident for instance, in 17th century England, the great diarist Samuel
Pepys had been without a remedy against "a committee composed of his
bitterest enemies and chaired by a man who did not conceal that he wished
to enjoy Pepys office". Since then, for "upwards of two hundred years" the
courts had "excluded a person with a bias or interest, subjective and
objective, from sitting in judgment on another".[3] This has led one Irish
judge to comment that the principle of bias "is probably ... as old as the
common law itself ...".[4] Beyond these strong judicial pronouncements, the
Irish Constitution is expressly oriented against such practices with its
injunction to "defend and vindicate" the personal rights of the citizen, with
express recognition of the citizens' right to good name.[5]

In introducing the principle against bias, it is first necessary to outline a   [11–02]
number of core distinctions. We may first distinguish between *actual* bias
and *apparent* bias. The former is, of course, quite rare, as even at the
pragmatic level, a case will often be framed as apparent bias even where a
party might suspect that "the adjudicator...was deliberately setting out to
mark or hold against a particular party".[6] Actual bias depends upon a
subjective evaluation in order to reach a particular conclusion based solely
on the facts at hand. Apparent bias, however, can arise where a reasonable
person might have perceived bias due to the relationship or conduct of a
decision-maker. The central test is therefore objective with the question
being asked whether the reasonable observer would have apprehended
bias. This reflects an underlying need to preserve public confidence in

---

[1] *Maguire v Ardagh & Ors* [2002] 1 IR 385.
[2] *ibid* at 703.
[3] *ibid*.
[4] *O'Reilly v His Honour Judge Cassidy and Others*, [1995] 1 ILRM 306, O'Flaherty J.
[5] Bunreacht na hÉireann, Art. 40.3.1°.
[6] *Orange Communications v Director of Telecom* (No. 2) [2000] 4 IR 159 at 251 *per* Geoghegan J.
Hereinafter "*Orange Communications*".

decision-making. As Denham J (as she then was) commented in *Dublin Wellwoman Centre Ltd & Ors v Ireland & Ors*:

> "With the development of the modern communications media and an increasingly educated and enquiring society the public perception of the impartiality of the courts is a cornerstone of the administration of justice in our constitutional democracy."[7]

[11–03] Apparent bias will be *presumed* in a number of traditionally sensitive instances: such as where the decision-maker has a financial or other personal interest in the matter before her. This presumption has not, as yet, crossed the line to automatic disqualification of the decision-maker, with flexibility preserved for instances of minimal financial involvement, for example. The judgment of Denham J in *Dublin Wellwoman* identified four separate factual contexts in which a claim of bias may often arise. This reflected the reality that the current concept of bias developed largely through cases falling within these four areas of material interest, pre-judgment, prior involvement in a matter, and the existence of personal attitudes and beliefs. We will deal with each of these in turn before we turn to more general principles applicable across all categories, such as reasonable suspicion and the reasonable observer test.

[11–04] We will also conclude the chapter by considering another category which may exist in the minds of public; that of *structural* or organizational bias. Some litigants have sought to invoke the bias principle to criticize the lack of independent appeal in certain Government decisions. As we will see, such allegations of institutional bias have not generally succeeded before the Irish Courts.

Material Interest

[11–05] The involvement of financial or material interest in a decision has long been held as destructive of procedural fairness. In *Doyle v Croke*,[8] a strike committee had received an industrial dispute settlement of IR£360,000 from a liquidated company. The strike committee, who were all former employees of the company in question, elected to have these monies

---

[7] *Dublin Wellwoman Centre Ltd & Ors. v Ireland & Ors.* [1995] 1 ILRM 408 at 422. Hereinafter "*Dublin Wellwoman*".

[8] Unreported, High Court, 6 May 1988.

divided equally amongst those who had participated fully in the picket.[9] A number of employees excluded from any share successfully challenged the decision on grounds of bias. All members of the strike committee had had a financial interest in the division of the monies.

The case which perhaps sets the borderline in this category is *Dublin and County Broadcasting Ltd v Independent Radio and Television Commission*.[10] The respondent body was responsible for allocating sound broadcasting contracts. The Commission was made up of multiple members and chaired by a former Supreme Court judge. The decision was challenged, however, by the applicant company on grounds of financial interest of one ordinary member, Mr O'Donovan. He had owned approximately £30,000 worth of shares in the dominant shareholding company of the successful applicant for the contract in question. About a year beforehand, he had attempted unsuccessfully, to fully transfer the shares. Crucially, however, Murphy J ruled that Mr O'Donovan had attempted to divest himself of shares, and had "bona fide believed he had successfully done so". The fact that he had, technically, retained some legal rights in the shareholding did not affect the overarching sense that "he could not as a matter of law or honour resile from the action he had taken".[11] Consequently, the "vast majority of people" would have believed that no financial interest existed to taint the decision.

[11–06]

The treatment of financial interests in *Dublin and County Broadcasting* suggests that Irish courts prefer to avoid automatic disqualification — whereby the objective existence of a pecuniary interest immediately impugns the decision.[12] While the *obiter* comments of Geoghegan J and Keane J in *Orange Communications* did not condemn the amenability of British courts to automatic disqualification, they did not stretch so far as to install it in Irish law. Rather, the comments should perhaps be read as underlining the seriousness of the issues involved for maintaining public confidence in the judicial system. O'Brien has argued persuasively for the

[11–07]

---

[9] This resulted in a proposal which would benefit 150 employees out of a total workforce of 270.

[10] *Dublin and County Broadcasting Ltd v Independent Radio and Television Commission*, Unreported, Murphy J, High Court, 12 May 1989. Hereinafter *"Dublin and County Broadcasting"*.

[11] *ibid* at 16.

[12] See generally, F O'Brien, *"Nemo Iudex in Causa Sua*: Aspects of the No-Bias Rule of Constitutional Justice in Courts and Administrative Bodies", (2011) 2(2) *Irish Journal of Legal Studies* 26. Hereinafter *"O'Brien"*.

approach adopted by the Australian Federal Court of Appeal in *Ebner*, where the majority of the Court doubted that the "confidence of fair-minded people in the administration of justice would be shaken by the existence of a direct pecuniary interest of no tangible value".[13] This *de minimis* exception should be taken as existing in Irish law.

[11–08] While it maybe obvious to the reader, it is worth stating that the material interest category would also cover circumstances where there is no separation of prosecutorial and decision making functions. This occurred for example in *Heneghan v Western Regional Fisheries Board*, where a decision was set aside as the person who initiated the dismissal proceedings, had acted as "witness, prosecutor, judge, jury and appeal court".[14]

Personal Attitudes, Family and Social Relationships

[11–09] Due to its geographical size, Ireland might be viewed as liable to produce a body of case-law under this heading. Yet, it has become clear that this is a remarkably stable category of bias, with few cases succeeding outside of the context of immediate family relationships. The leading authority is *O'Reilly v Judge Cassidy (No. 2)*, in which a challenge was made to a liquor licence decision where counsel for the objecting party was the daughter of the relevant Circuit Court judge.[15] Flood J noted firstly that the fact that a judge's daughter was presenting a case before him was not sufficient to give rise to the possibility of a reasonable man considering that bias could follow, as the public could be assumed in such circumstances to have faith that the judge would be bound by his oath of office. In this particular case, however, there was sufficient evidence outlining the respondent judge's favourable treatment of the case at hand, to give rise to a reasonable apprehension.

[11–10] A more modern instance of family relationships potentially giving rise to a reasonable apprehension of bias arose in *Kenny v Trinity College Dublin*.[16] The applicant was objecting to plans by the College to create new student accommodation at Trinity Hall and the university applied to have the matter struck out as frivolous. One of the central witnesses for the university

---

[13] *Ebner v Official Trustee in Bankruptcy* (2001) 176 ALR 644 at para 38. *O'Brien*, n 12 at p 38.
[14] *Heneghan v Western Regional Fisheries Board* [1986] ILRM 225.
[15] *O'Reilly v Cassidy (No.2)* [1995] 1 ILRM 311.
[16] *Kenny v Trinity College Dublin* [2008] 2 IR 40.

was an employee of Murray O'Laoire architects. The brother of Murray J, who was presiding, was a partner in the aforementioned architecture firm. The Supreme Court found that the test for apprehension of bias was satisfied in such circumstances. Fennelly J noted that a personal relationship with a witness could suffice, citing in support the UK decision of *Locabail*.[17] There the Court had recognized that personal friendship or animosity or close acquaintance between the judge and any member involved of the public involved in the case could give rise to a reasonable apprehension. On the particular facts in *Kenny*, Fennelly J noted that the brother in question was based in Limerick, not in Dublin and had had no involvement whatsoever in the particular project. The applicant had, however, alleged that the firm had concealed documents from the Court and thus, the integrity and conduct of the firm as a whole was being impugned. In such circumstances, and especially as the Court was reviewing its own procedures. Fennelly J held that a reasonable apprehension had been raised.

The overlapping business relationships and personal interactions which featured in the above mentioned case of *Dublin & County Broadcasting Ltd v Independent Radio and Television Commission*[18] are not uncommon in Irish society. The allocation on contracts by the respondent Commission was challenged on grounds of bias due to the close relationship between a Commission member, a Mr O'Donovan and the Denis O'Brien controlled company E-Sat Television Ltd. Mr O'Donovan had been chairman and a director of E-Sat, but he resigned six months before the contract was awarded due to a dispute with Mr O'Brien, who had previously been engaged to his daughter. Murphy J held that these close personal and business ties raised no real likelihood of bias and "no right-minded man would have thought so".[19] Clearly, practical considerations were an overarching factor in the Court's assessment of the case: Mr O'Donovan had disclosed that he knew the promoters of twelve of the thirteen applicants to the commission. In addition to this professional reality, he had fully disclosed these relationships to the chairman of the respondent Commission.

The idea that underlying personal views can ground a reasonable apprehension of bias is supported by the case of *Dublin Wellwoman Centre*

[11–11]

[11–12]

---

[17] *Locabail Ltd v Bayfield Properties Ltd* [2000] QB 451.

[18] Above n 10.

[19] *ibid* at 15.

Ltd v Ireland.[20] There, the notice party successfully appealed to the Supreme Court for Carroll J to discharge herself from hearing a High Court action concerning an injunction to prohibit the publication of abortion information due to a reasonable perception of bias. As Chairwoman of the Commission for the Status of Women, a statutory body, Carroll J had made a written submission concerning the availability of such information. A bulwark against such actions is now provided by the possibility of adopting the approach proposed by Keane CJ in *Rooney v Minister for Agriculture*,[21] whereby the judge may request the senior available judge of the court, of which he or she is a member, to determine whether recusal is appropriate. This avoids not merely bias but the countervailing concern that

> "a judge cannot permit a scrupulous approach by him to be used to permit parties to engage in a form of shopping under the guise of challenging the partiality of the Court".[22]

Nevertheless, Keane CJ expressed confidence in the standard approach, and stressed that the referral to the senior member should occur in cases of particular difficulty.

[11–13]   While it has so far yet to arise in Ireland, the question of how to treat judicial involvement in academia arose in the UK case of *Timmins v Gormley*.[23] In this case, the ruling of a trial judge was invalidated as academic articles and books which he had authored had made trenchant criticisms of the insurance industry's conduct in fostering delays and refusing to deal fairly with claimants. The Court stressed that extra-judicial publications would give rise to bias only if the views were expressed in unqualified terms or in an extremely strong manner, so that a reasonable observer would view the judge as not being able to hear the case with an open mind. Another

---

[20] Above n 7.

[21] *Rooney v Minister for Agriculture*, Unreported, Supreme Court, 23 October 2000.

[22] *ibid* at 2.

[23] *Timmins v Gormley* [2000] 1 All ER 65. The matter has received some consideration in Australia, see In *Re Minister for Immigration and Multicultural Affairs; Ex parte Epeabaka* [2001] HCA 23; 206 CLR 128 at 133 [12] (*"Epeabaka"*), Gleeson CJ, McHugh, Gummow and Hayne JJ observed (in the context of a member of the Refugee Review Tribunal who published material on the Internet to tell the public about how he approached his position):

> "For people who hold judicial, or quasi-judicial, office to set out to give the public 'some idea of where [they are] coming from' might be regarded by some as reflecting a commendable spirit of openness; but it has dangers. It may compromise the appearance of impartiality which is vital to public confidence in the administration of justice. It is the recognition of such a danger that has traditionally caused judges to exercise caution in their public conduct and statements."

instructive example from the UK is *Re Medicaments and Related Classes of Goods (No. 2)*,[24] where the fact that the expert economist attached to the Restrictive Practices Tribunal had applied for a job with a consultancy firm, one of whose directors was an expert witness in a case in which she was involved, was found to raise a reasonable apprehension of bias.

Professional Ties

In the landmark case of *Bula Ltd v Tara Mines Limited and others (No. 6)*,[25]   **[11–14]**
discussed further below,[26] the Supreme Court rejected as unfounded a
challenge to one of its previous decisions on grounds that two of the judges
had, while barristers, provided advice and representation to one or more
parties in the litigation. In the case of *Kenny v Trinity College Dublin*,[27] the
applicant argued that the decision should be quashed due to presence on a
University committee of the Pro Vice Chancellor, whose "career and
background" as well as oath of office, meant that she would "be naturally
biassed [*sic*] in favour of the college".[28] Fennelly J rejected this argument,
stressing that

> "it would need a considerable and, in my view, unjustified step to
> disqualify a qualified person from performing the valuable service
> of adjudicating on disputes merely because of past professional
> associations or social links or background".[29]

He noted the practical impacts of adopting such a course, as a vast number   **[11–15]**
of administrative and adjudicative bodies draw on a pool of persons
qualified by their experience, including past and present professional or
career links, to bring balanced judgment and common sense to the
resolution of disputes. Fennelly J also invoked the statements of Lord
Bingham, Lord Woolf and Sir Richard Schott, (VC) in *Locabail (UK) Ltd v
Bayfield Properties Ltd*:

> "It would be dangerous and futile to attempt to define or list the factors
> which may or may not give rise to a real danger of bias. Everything
> will depend on the facts, which may include the nature of the issue to
> be decided. We cannot, however, conceive of circumstances in which

---

[24] *Re Medicaments and Related Classes of Goods (No. 2)* [2001] 1 WLR 700.
[25] *Bula Ltd v Tara Mines Ltd & others (No. 6)* [2000] 4 IR 412. Hereinafter "*Bula Ltd*".
[26] See paras [11-28] – [11-30].
[27] *Kenny v Trinity College Dublin* [2007] IESC 671.
[28] *ibid* at 5.
[29] *ibid.*

> an objection could be soundly based on the religion, ethnic or national origin, gender, age, class, means or sexual orientation of the judge. Nor, at any rate ordinarily, could an objection be soundly based on the judge's social or educational or service or employment background or history, nor that of any member of the judge's family; or previous political associations; or membership of social or sporting or charitable bodies; or Masonic associations; or previous judicial decisions; or extra-curricular utterances (whether in textbooks, lectures, speeches, articles, interviews, reports or responses to consultation papers); or previous receipt of instructions to act for or against any party, solicitor or advocate engaged in a case before him; or membership of the same Inn, circuit, local Law Society or chambers."[30]

[11–16]   The recent case of *Keegan v District Judge Kilrane*,[31] represents an exception to these generally applicable principles, however, though its reasoning should be viewed as specific to its facts. There, a reasonable apprehension of bias was held to arise where a District Court judge who heard a trial involving multiple road traffic offences had, as a local solicitor, represented the applicant on a number of occasions in court. These included a number of instances which related to alcohol consumption, a fact which was highly relevant to the matter at hand, which related to drink driving. In ruling for the applicant the High Court stressed the public perception of the state of affairs was the primary consideration in its reasoning. While clearly not authority for widespread recusal where a judge has acted on behalf of a party to the proceedings, the case should prompt reflection upon where the boundaries of recusal lie in the case of a judge who dealt with a locally concentrated and large body of casework as a local practitioner.

Prior Involvement and Pre-Judgment

[11–17]   One the most important lines to define in addressing these type of cases, is that between prejudgment and predisposition. Murphy J in the course of his judgment in *Orange Communications*[32] approved the statement of US Justice Frank *In Re JP Lenihan*:

> "Democracy must, indeed, fail unless our courts try cases fairly, and there can be no trial before a judge lacking in impartiality and disinterestedness. If, however, 'bias' and 'partiality' be defined to

---

[30] Above n 17 at para 25.
[31] *Keegan v District Judge Kilrane* [2011] IEHC 516.
[32] Above n 6 at 242.

mean the total absence of preconceptions in the mind of the judge, then no one has ever had a fair trial and no one ever will. The human mind, even in infancy is no blank piece of paper. We are born with predispositions; and the process of education, formal and informal, creates attitudes in all men which affect them in judging situations, attitudes which precede reasoning in particular instances and which, therefore, by definition are prejudices."[33]

One of the more interesting recent cases, *Kelly v National University of Ireland*   **[11–18]**
(UCD)[34] discussed whether a judge's comments condemning the personal conduct of a party during a case could give rise to an appearance of bias. The plaintiff in the case had sought the recusal of Hedigan J, based on comments made during an earlier and separate case, and upon conduct in the hearing of the matter at hand. In the prior matter, Hedigan J had ruled against the applicant, stressing that "the waste of public money expended upon this all but pointless set of proceedings is also scandalous".[35] Furthermore, the applicant alleged that the criticism of him during the hearing of the second matter also raised a reasonable suspicion of bias. Hedigan J had strongly condemned the applicant as having behaved like a "petulant child" in having posted "material online which was scandalously abusive of Mr Justice Kechnie".[36] Hedigan J refused to recuse himself from this latest matter:

> "...it seems to me that the reasonable observer would be outraged by the abusive material placed on the internet by the plaintiff concerning the judge who had given a decision unfavourable to him, and would very likely be of the view that the Court did not go nearly far enough in comparing his actions to those of a petulant child. The applicant is not the first party to be rebuked from the bench and he will not be the last. Judges should not lightly recuse themselves of their responsibility to hear cases that come before them. It is noteworthy that this is the third such application made by the plaintiff for a judge to recuse himself or herself. In my view the applicant has not advanced grounds capable of supporting the proposition that the reasonable man have an apprehension that there would not be a fair hearing."[37]

---

[33] In *Re JP Lenihan* [1943] 138F (2d) 650 at para 1.
[34] *Kelly v National University of Ireland (UCD)* [2012] IEHC 169.
[35] *ibid* at para 2.
[36] *ibid*.
[37] *ibid* at para 3.

[11–19]   The existence of possible ill will towards one of the parties on the part of a committee member was successfully negotiated on the facts of *Radio Limerick One Ltd v Independent Radio and Television Commission*.[38] The respondent body had terminated the applicant's broadcasting contract. One member of the Commission was a former head of news at the station who, following an incident where a news report was redacted by management, had commenced proceedings before the Employment Appeals Tribunal. The Supreme Court found no apprehension of bias arose as the individual in question had absented herself from its meetings at which the instance of redaction was discussed, and where the Commission made its final decision. This underlines that organisations should take all practical steps possible to vitiate the appearance of bias.

[11–20]   In the case of *JJ Rhatigan & Company Ltd v Paragon Contracting Ltd & Anor*, the applicants argued that an arbitrator had given rise to a reasonable suspicion of bias by, *inter alia*, taking into account privileged information and by his treatment of the applicant's witnesses.[39] In relation to the former, Murphy J stressed that the issue of wrongful disclosure had been adequately addressed by the arbitrator declaring it. The latter claim revolved, *inter alia*, around a comment the arbitrator had made regarding an applicant witness, namely that "judging by what we have been saying in the last few minutes I would nearly be ready to christen her Margaret Thatcher but however".[40] Murphy J held that this comment could not ground a real likelihood of bias, as while "the arbitrator's reference to the plaintiff's witness as Mrs. Thatcher may have given cause for concern", the matter had been raised by the applicant at the time and "it was duly clarified by the arbitrator that he should not have made the remark and did not intend it to be disparaging".[41]

The Pitfalls of the Media Interview

[11–21]   The case of *O'Driscoll v Law Society & Anor*[42] represents an important warning to decision-makers should they choose to publicly comment on an ongoing investigation. This was a challenge to a Law Society Disciplinary Committee decision concerning the alleged charging of excessive fees by a law firm in Residential Institutions Redress Act 2002. The applicant relied

---

[38] *Radio Limerick One Ltd v Independent Radio and Television Commission* [1997] 2 IR 291.
[39] *JJ Rhatigan & Company Ltd v Paragon Contracting Ltd & Anor* [2009] IEHC 117 at para 10.1.
[40] *ibid* at para 10.2.
[41] *ibid* at para 10.5.
[42] *O'Driscoll v Law Society & Anor* [2007] IEHC 352.

upon a number of comments made by one member of the Committee, in a newspaper article concerning the controversy of how abuse survivors were being billed by some solicitors. In the piece entitled *"Double-Charging abuse case solicitors may be struck off"*,[43] it was reported that the committee member had called an emergency meeting of the Law Society to discuss the issue. Furthermore she was quoted as saying:

> "I think it is nothing less than scandalous if solicitors are taking money over and above the fees which they are also getting. It must be remembered that their costs are being paid separately and to actually take money from a claimant's award is a very serious offence in my books."[44]

The Court rejected the contention that this comment was general in nature: [11–22]

> "I do not accept that her comments were truly general in the sense in which that word is normally understood. The issue here was one of overcharging. Whilst it may have involved more than one firm of solicitors, nonetheless it was in reality a discrete and confined issue, affecting a particular group of clients who were together bonded by their former experience and by a common tribunal to which their applications were made. The fact that she did not target any single firm of solicitors is in my view of little value. I therefore reject each of these suggestions as in any way establishing a position of neutrality on the part of Ms. Foley. In my opinion, she used strong language and gave the appearance of declaring a definite position on the issue. No qualifications were offered to meet circumstances in which a solicitor and client charge would be entirely lawful. Her views covered solicitors "taking money over and above the fees which they are getting". Such money was at the core of the allegation. I therefore think that a reasonable person could believe that she had firmly established a view and placed that view on public record. In my opinion, to publicly so declare was highly regrettable and whatever the motivation, her judgment in so acting was both inappropriate and unwise."[45]

McKechnie J stressed that the contention that Ms Foley was only one   [11–23]
member of the Committee would not avail the respondents, and was, in the particular circumstances of the case, "irrelevant". This position was supported by the ruling of Murphy J in *Dublin and County Broadcasting Limited v Independent Radio and Television Commission*, where his Honour

---

[43] A Sheehan, "Double-Charging abuse case solicitors may be struck off", *Irish Independent* October 10 2005.

[44] *O'Driscoll v Law Society*, above n 42 at para 54. Hereinafter *"O'Driscoll"*.

[45] *ibid* at para 58.

had ruled that the fact that a person accused of bias might be outvoted or may not have been the dominant material would be immaterial.[46]

[11–24] Ms Foley was unlikely to have taken a backseat in the decision due to her status as the Director of Consumer Affairs, a statutory office under the Consumer Information Act 1978:

> "As a statutory office holder, she had particular responsibility for consumer affairs and consumers. Her position therefore on such matters was particularly striking. She was no ordinary member of the public. She was quite unlike a spokesperson for a lobby or pressure group. She bears no comparison to other public figures who offer views on matters of general or particular public interest. She was quite clearly distinguishable from members of the Executive or members of the Legislature who frequently express views on various topics e.g. the level of sentencing appropriate to particular crimes. Her position was totally dissimilar from all of the above; this not only because of her statutory appointment but also, and particularly so, because of her membership of the actual CCR Committee which sat in these cases. *Given her specific area of interest, it would be difficult to believe that she did not carry into the discussions of such committee, the views as previously expressed by her on this topic.*"[47]

[11–25] This case matches the Supreme Court's approach in the earlier case of *O'Neill v Beaumont Hospital Board*,[48] where three members of a hospital board were barred from participating in assessing the applicant's probationary period performance, as they had been critical of him in the run up to the hearing. In *McGrath v Trustees of Maynooth College*,[49] the Court held that prior knowledge of the relevant facts, or the existence of strongly held general belief concerning the matter did not impugn a decision-maker provided that full hearing rights were provided to the applicant and there was a commitment to reserving final judgment until all relevant issues were agitated.

Judicial Criticism During Cases

[11–26] An interesting debate regarding prejudgment of evidence arose in *Fogarty v Judge O'Donnell*.[50] In the course of a District Court criminal matter, the

---

[46] Above n 10.
[47] *O'Driscoll* above n 44 at para 57, emphasis added.
[48] *O'Neill v Beaumont Hospital Board* [1990] ILRM 419.
[49] *McGrath v Trustees of Maynooth College* [1979] ILRM 166.
[50] *Fogarty v Judge O'Donnell* [2008] IEHC 198.

Judge had used the word 'irrefutable' to describe some of the prosecution's evidence, prior to the defence having completed its case. McMahon J ruled that:

> "What is important, indeed vital, however, is that the judge does not in such circumstances make a definitive determination before all the evidence has been heard…Moreover, it is important also that the judge does not give the appearance that he has prejudged a decision and in this respect he should take great care when expressing himself during the course of the trial that he does not express himself in language which would suggest that he has come to a hasty decision in the matter. Whether the language used by a judge during the course of a trial is such that it indicates bias in the sense that it shows that the judge has made up his mind before he has heard all the evidence, depends on the facts and circumstances of each case. The use of an infelicitous word or phrase during the trial by the judge should not always compel such a conclusion. To define bias one must look at the overall picture and in the present case one must contrast the use of that single word with the action of the respondent."[51]

The District Judge in this case had clearly signalled that he was not impressed with the applicant's evidence, but had listened to the argument and decided to avoid making a final determination until he had heard from a further witness on the relevant issue (involving the sequencing of traffic lights). Thus, no apprehension of bias was raised when a holistic view was taken. It is also clear from *Minister for Justice and Law Reform v McGuiness*, that an isolated comment from a decision-maker may not be cured by overall conduct.[52] The case concerned a challenge to a surrender on foot of a European Arrest Warrant. Counsel for the respondent had sought certification of a point of law of exceptional public importance to enable an appeal to the Supreme Court. Counsel for respondent also requested that Edwards J, who was presiding, recuse himself based on comments made during the initial hearing. In particular she claimed that the Court had made a suggestion that she had an "agenda" in respect of the Attorney General's policy for executing the warrants, in a tone which seemed to imply there was an ulterior motive beyond that of defending the respondent. Significantly, Edwards J was in a position to review the digital audio recordings of the proceedings, which was helpful given the reference to the "tone". Reflecting upon these, Edwards J recused himself on the basis of a

[11–27]

---

[51] *ibid* at para 6.
[52] *Minister for Justice and Law Reform v McGuiness* [2011] IEHC 313.

possible perception of bias, while defending the broader manner in which he had approached the case:

> "[the Court's] suggestion that the issue raised…was being raised in pursuit of an "agenda" was unfortunate and may have created the incorrect impression in the mind of the respondent that the Court regarded the point being raised as being inappropriate and/or unmeritorious and that it had prejudged the substantive argument." [53]

The case underlines the reality that the rise of technology may make the evidential burden of proving a reasonable apprehension of bias easier to discharge.

The Test for Bias: Reasonable Apprehension in the Eyes of the Reasonable Observer

[11–28] The foregoing analysis represented a summary of the main factual contexts in which claims of bias have arisen before the Irish courts. It should not, however, be taken as endorsing a categorical approach. As noted throughout this chapter, the question of bias is highly context specific. While the facts may vary, the Courts have, however, generated a general frame for analyzing if objective bias exists. The relevant test in Ireland was laid down in *Bula Ltd v Tara Mines Ltd. (No. 6)*,[54] where Denham J (as she then was) and McGuiness J endorsed the reasonable apprehension test. Denham J offered perhaps the authoritative version of the test:

> "…it is well established that the test to be applied is objective, it is whether a reasonable person in the circumstances would have a reasonable apprehension that the applicants would not have a fair hearing from an impartial judge on the issues. The test does not invoke the apprehension of judge or judges. Nor does it invoke the apprehension of any part. It is an objective test – it invokes the apprehension of the reasonable person".[55]

---

[53] *ibid* at para 9. In particular Edwards J had suggested a possible referral to the Bar Council/ Law Society for professional misconduct in response to manner in which the challenge was being presented.

[54] Above n 25.

[55] *ibid* at 441.

This is supported by the earlier test propounded by Keane CJ in *Orange*   **[11–29]**
Communications Ltd. v Director of Telecoms (No 2),[56] whereby a decision will
be set aside

> "where there is a reasonable apprehension of suspicion that the decision
> maker might have been biased, i.e. where it is found that, although
> there was no actual bias, there is an appearance of bias".[57]

The sole distinction between the *Bula Ltd* and that in *Orange Communications*   **[11–30]**
(No. 2) is the substitution of the word "suspicion" for the term
"apprehension". This was, Denham J stated, necessary as even though
suspicion was used throughout the existing case law, she preferred to
avoid using "suspicion of bias" as it sometimes carried broader
connotations and "unintended nuances of meaning".[58] This finessing
and the broader underlying concepts have been expressly reaffirmed
in recent cases concerning bias.[59] A final element in the analysis
which should be noted is the observation of Finlay CJ in *O'Neill v
Beaumont Hospital*,[60] where he noted that in analyzing the facts, the
court should "take the interpretation more favourable where there is
ambiguity to the plaintiff than to the defendant."

The Attributes and Knowledge of the Reasonable Observer

The element of the test which has perhaps attracted the most reflection is   **[11–31]**
that of the 'reasonable observer', particularly what attributes and
knowledge should be attributed to him or her. The centrality of the observer
to the functioning of the test is indicated by the *O'Callaghan v Mahon*
judgment:

> "[the test is] …whether a reasonable hypothetical person, who was
> not unduly sensitive and had knowledge of all the relevant facts and
> circumstances, would have a reasonable apprehension that the decision
> maker would not be fair and impartial."[61]

---

[56] Above n 6.

[57] *ibid* at 186.

[58] Denham J noted that this point had been made by the Australian High Court in *Livesey v
New South Wales Bar Association* (1983) 151 CLR 288 at 293.

[59] See for instance *Kelly v Visitors of Trinity College Dublin* [2007] IESC 61, *O'Reilly v Lee* [2008]
4 IR 269.

[60] Above n 46 at 439.

[61] *O'Callaghan v Mahon* [2008] 2 IR 514 at 515.

[11–32]   Irish reflections on the nature of the reasonable observer are perhaps not as systemic as other jurisdictions (to whom we will also briefly turn). In *Dublin and County Broadcasting v Independent Radio and Television Commission*, discussed above, Murphy J held that bias analysis should be approached "on the basis of what a right-minded person might think", in particular that the court should disregard the perception of a person who is "ill-informed and did not seek to direct his mind properly to the facts".[62] Based on the already outlined facts of the case, Murphy J was finding that the observer should be taken as being able to understand the technical equity doctrine under which the individual in case retained a residual interest in otherwise divested shares. The imputing of factual knowledge to a reasonable observer also occurred in *Kenny v TCD*, where Fennelly J described him or her as "an independent observer, who is not overly sensitive, and who has knowledge of the facts".[63] In *Kenny*, therefore, the observer would not make a snap judgment based on the relationship between the presiding judge and the architecture firm of which his brother was partner, but would also reflect upon the fact that the brother had had no direct involvement in the project at the centre of the court dispute. The decision, as already outlined, reflected a cautious approach given that the Supreme Court was reviewing one of its own decisions.

[11–33]   For further reflection upon the reasonable observer we must turn to other common law jurisdictions, which ultimately produce a welter of contradictory and impressionistic case law.[64] In *Locabail*, the House of Lords held that "matters outside the ken of the ordinary, reasonably well informed member of the public", should be excluded from the mind of reasonable observer.[65] A particularly memorable contribution to the jurisprudence is the judgment of Kirby J in the Australian High Court case of *Johnson v Johnson*. He stressed that the observer should not be regarded as unduly neurotic or "complacent nor unduly sensitive or suspicious".[66] Kirby J went on to state that the courts should also avoid the attribution of any detailed knowledge of the law, and avoid the overarching tendency to "impute all that was eventually known to the court to an imaginary reasonable person' as to do so 'would be only to hold up a mirror

---

[62] Above n 10 at 16.
[63] Above n 16 at 45.
[64] See generally, S Atrill, "Who is the 'Fair Minded Observer'? Bias after *Magill*" [2003] CLJ 279.
[65] Above n 17.
[66] *Johnson v Johnson* (2000) 174 ALR 655 at 671.

to itself".[67] In keeping with the general theme of inconsistency, O'Brien notes that the Canadian courts have "imputed some technical knowledge upon the observer",[68] in particular in *R v Lippe*, where a majority of the Supreme Court attributed "full knowledge of the Quebec municipal court system, including all of its safeguards" to him or her.[69] Clearly, the comparative authorities reveal ambiguities which must be reasoned through in cases appearing in Irish courts, as well as the need to "out" certain flawed tendencies which may lead courts to produce a somewhat mystical, rather than reasonable, figure.

Defences

Necessity

The degree to which bias may be justified or at least moderated by a situation   [11–34]
of necessity produced by organizational capacity, limited pools of expertise and other practical considerations is contested. The defence of necessity will not usually be available to members of the judiciary, as was seen in the United Kingdom case of *Morrison and Another v AWG Group and Another*.[70] The trial judge, Evans-Lombe J, had upon reading the court materials the day before the matter commenced, realized that he knew one of the claimant's witnesses. They regularly interacted socially, and their children were friends. The next morning, the judge informed the parties, with the claimant voluntarily offering not to call the relevant witness. Despite this proposal, the defendant asked the judge to withdraw. Evans-Lombe J refused, based upon the withdrawal of witness, but also the cost and delay involved in reassigning the case. The Court of Appeal ultimately overturned this decision, and ruled out reliance on practical factors in such cases:

> "[such considerations are]....totally irrelevant to the crucial question of the real possibility of bias...In terms of time, costs and listing, it might well be more efficient and convenient to proceed with the trial, but... the paramount concern of the legal system is to administer justice, which must be, and must be seen by litigants and fair-minded members of the public to be fair and impartial."[71]

---

[67] *ibid* at 669.

[68] Above n 12 at 47.

[69] *R v Lippe* [1991] 2 SCR 114 at 152.

[70] *Morrison and Anor v AWG Group and Anor* [2006] EWCA Civ 6.

[71] *ibid* at para 29 per Mummery LJ. One might remark that the United Kingdom's preferred approach of automatic disqualification of judges for financial bias suggests more absolutist stance on bias than Ireland.

[11–35]   Notwithstanding this, courts have been sympathetic to the principle that a decision may not be void for bias where a decision-making body, including a court cannot constitute itself or proceed to a decision without the participation of the individual involved.[72] Necessity will not be entertained where there was an alternative panel of the decision-making body available, which could have been composed of persons against whom no claim of bias had been raised.[73]

[11–36]   Necessity can also make the courts reluctant to impugn an entire decision-making body, as was seen in *O'Neill v Beaumont Hospital*,[74] where Finlay CJ refused to accept that the ratification of a meeting's minutes by a disciplinary committee meant they carried the taint of bias:

> "[Necessity] is not a dominant doctrine, it could never defeat a real fear and a real reasonable fear of bias or injustice but it is a consideration in relation to the question of the entire board being prohibited, for if that were to be done there can be no other machinery by which something which is of great importance both to the board of the hospital and to the plaintiff and, I might add, to the public who will attend the hospital, namely the continuance or non continuance of the Plaintiff's services in the hospital, can be determined in accordance with the terms of the probationary agreement."[75]

[11–37]   This statement was cited with approval in an obiter portion of Smyth J's judgment in *O'Callaghan v Mahon & Ors*,[76] which involved an allegation of bias on the part of a Tribunal of Inquiry. While satisfied on the facts that no case of bias had been made out, Smyth J also commented that there was an "air of unreality" to the submission that the Oireachtas could simply appoint another Tribunal of Inquiry.[77] On the other side of the ledger, however, in cases where there was a "firm and concluded decision" that

---

[72] This was best embodied by the statement of Brennan J in the Australian case of Builders Registration Board of *Queensland v Rauber* [1983] 47 ALR 55, 71:
"The Common Law allows an exception as to the disqualifying effect of bias whether arising from an earlier prejudgment of a material question, from interest, or from some other cause where the exception is necessary to allow the functioning of the sole Tribunal with power to act."

[73] *O'Neill v Irish Hereford Breed Society Ltd.* [1992] 1 IR 431 at 628.

[74] Above n 48.

[75] ibid at 440.

[76] *O'Callaghan v Mahon & Ors* [2006] IEHC 311.

[77] ibid at para 62.

objective bias had been established, "then clearly the doctrine of necessity would not avail".[78]

Waiver

The case of *Balaz v His Honour Judge Kennedy & Anor*[79] represents a primary Irish authority addressing whether a person can waive their right to challenge a decision on grounds of bias when they fail to protest at the proceeding.[80] The Court endorsed the Australian case of *Vakauta v Kelly*,[81] a case which offers a colourful instance of ostensible bias. There the trial judge in a personal injury matter referred to the team of experts for the appellant as "the unholy trinity" and alleged their evidence was slanted towards the Government.[82] The High Court of Australia ruled that a litigant who was fully aware of the circumstances from which bias could be inferred should be taken as capable of waiving the right to object.[83] Dawson J[84] noted that the possibility of waiver reflects the overall assessment of bias: if "a party, being aware of his right to object, waives that right, there will be little danger of the appearance of injustice".[85] Hedigan J, approving of this approach, thus concluded:

[11–38]

> "I do not think that a party, who is fully apprised of all the facts necessary to mount an objection on the grounds of objective bias of the relevant judge, should be permitted to keep such a challenge in reserve, in case the result of trial is not in his favour. In the present case, the applicant contends that it was immediately apparent from the actions of the first named respondent that he had considered papers in an appeal which was not ultimately going to proceed. He made no objection or comment on this and proceeded to defend against the other charge in the usual

---

[78] *ibid.*

[79] *Balaz v His Honour Judge Kennedy & Anor* [2009] IEHC 110.

[80] An earlier authority was *DPP v O'Donnell* [1995] 2 IR 294, where Geoghegan J in *obiter* comments accepted that there might be circumstances in which a failure to challenge a tribunal's jurisdiction to consider a particular matter would constitute a waiver of the right of objection.

[81] *Vakauta v Kelly* (1989) 167 CLR 568.

[82] Other allegations included that that they belonged to "the usual panel of doctors who think you can do a full week's work without arms or legs" and that their "views are almost inevitably slanted by the [Government Insurance Office] by whom they have been retained consciously or unconsciously." *ibid* at para 6.

[83] *ibid* Toohey J at para 16.

[84] Who dissented on a separate issue.

[85] Above n 81, Dawson J at para 10.

manner. On this basis, I am satisfied that he has waived his right to challenge the ostensible impartiality of the first named respondent."[86]

Reflecting on the Institutional Elements of Bias Analysis

[11–39]   An ideal way to bring the chapter on the bias principle to a close is to consider the outer limits of the principle and how it should play a deeper role in institutional design. One issue which should be noted at the outset is that the courts have traditionally been very reluctant to grant any role to the concept of institutional loyalty in determining the existence or non-existence of bias. This is embodied by *Kelly v Visitors of Trinity College Dublin*, where Fennelly J strongly rejected the notion that the involvement of Pro Chancellor in a student disciplinary matter could give rise to an apprehension of bias:

> "…I fail to understand why her undoubted obligation and natural wish to vindicate the best interests of the College should render her more likely to favour a member of staff over a student. I specifically reject the suggestion advanced by the applicant in his affidavit that the Professor has an interest in the outcome of appeal to the Visitors. She has none whatever other than that of seeing that matters are justly and correctly decided."[87]

[11–40]   Nevertheless, a decision-maker's position or institutional location can often form the background in which a bias claim is raised. On certain rare occasions this can manifest itself as a claim of structural bias, which represents a claim that irrespective of the circumstances of a particular case, a body is, of its nature inherently biased. Some discussion of this possibility of "an in-built bias" has occurred in the context of debates regarding parliamentary inquiries, where some have felt that the possible application of a party whip and the elected representatives' responsibilities to their constituents can result in a reasonable apprehension of a lack of independence. This was raised as a side issue in the *Abbeylara* case[88] and was either not addressed or was rejected by the majority of the judges. Justice Geoghegan went furthest in stating that it was only in rare circumstances that such a body would be perceived by reasonable members of the public as capable of independent arbitration. This statement

---

[86] Above n 79 at para 26.
[87] Above n 59, un-annotated judgment.
[88] *Maguire v Ardagh*, above n 1.

represented however, only a starting point for considering the extensive curative actions that might need to be taken, for example, by ensuring that parliamentarians did not speak to the media and understood the seriousness of their legal obligations.[89] Chief Justice Keane was, perhaps, the strongest advocate of institutional inquisitorial competence, though this was rooted in the fact that the Constitution clearly contemplated adjudication by the Oireachtas in "two of the most solemn cases imaginable", namely the impeachment of the President[90] and the removal of the Superior Court judges.[91]

Structural Bias: Dual Regulatory and Policy Mandates

By far the most developed Irish case alleging structural or "in built" bias was brought in *Greenstar Ltd. v Dublin City Council, Dun Laoighaire Rathdown County Council, Fingal County Council and South Dublin County Council*.[92] The applicant was a waste management company who had been granted a waste collection permit by the respondents. The respondents were, however, also responsible for making and varying the Waste Management Plan (hereinafter "WMP") for the Dublin Region as per the Waste Management Acts 1996-2007. The respondents attempted to make a variation to the WMP, which the applicants sought to have reviewed on

[11–41]

---

[89] *ibid* at 721-722. The statement of Justice Geoghegan J appeared to endorse the possible conduct of an inquiry but underlined its difficulties:

"A sub-committee such as the respondent sub-committee would be reporting to the joint Oireachtas committee which in turn would be reporting to the Dáil and Seanad respectively. The joint committee, as was customary, was balanced in its membership according to the strength of the political parties. It would only be in rare circumstances that a body composed in that way would be perceived by reasonable members of the public as capable of independent arbitration. I appreciate that this court in approaching the problem of whether there is an inherent power or not has for the most part to consider the position as of 1937, when the present Constitution came into existence. In those days there was no "Questions and Answers ", little media probing of politicians but if anything the public was even more politically aware than they are now as civil war politics infused a large proportion of households. Then, as now, there may not have been a perception of great ideological differences between government and opposition. But political feelings at that time were such that the ordinary member of the public of reasonable disposition would have been even less likely to view an Oireachtas committee determination as truly independent. Even in cases where in the eyes of a reasonable observer bias might not exist merely from the composition of the body, the conduct of an inquiry by such committee or sub-committee is fraught with great practical difficulties if bias in the legal sense is to be avoided." [at 721]

[90] As provided for by Art 12 of Bunreacht na hÉireann.

[91] As provided for by Art 35 of Bunreacht na hÉireann.

[92] *Greenstar Ltd. v Dublin City Council & Ors* [2009] IEHC 589.

grounds that, *inter alia*, the respondents were structurally biased due to the fact they were both operators and regulators of a market.[93]

[11–42]   The variation of WMP in question was directed to stop what the respondents termed the "fracturing" of the waste disposal market in Dublin, whereby numerous private operators were entering the market. To that end the council proposed a variation which was to:

> "…include an objective in the Plan that the collection of household waste from single dwelling households (other than those in purpose built apartment blocks) will be carried out by the local authorities or that the local authorities will make arrangements by way of a public tendering process for the collection of such household waste (which may be on a geographical or area basis)."[94]

[11–43]   In support of the proposal, the authorities commissioned a market analysis which concluded that waste disposal should be approached as a "natural local monopoly", whereby a single supplier should be retained for each authority area.[95] The respondents then proceeded to vary the WMP by stating that collection should be by a single operator in each authority area, and that "single operator shall either be a Dublin Local Authority or the successful tendered under a competitive tendering process".[96] The applicants' submission regarding the state of affairs is worth quoting in full:

> "The applicant claims that by virtue of the fact that the respondents are both operators on the market and regulators thereof, there is structural bias built into the system. Decisions taken by the respondents in relation to this market could be said at least to give rise to a perception of objective bias; in those circumstances it is claimed that special care must be taken so as to avoid any suspicion that they have been influenced by external factors, and particularly in this case by their position as competitors in the market."[97]

---

[93] The case was decided in the aftermath of the related case of *Nurendale Ltd. t/a Panda Waste v Dublin City Council* [2009] IEHC 588, which held that the conduct of the respondent authorities breached competition law in abusing a dominant position in a market. The distinctive issues in *Greenstar Ltd* related to the failure to hold an oral hearing, the failure to provide a report and legal and economic advice from a law firm to the applicants and finally, the structural bias issue we analyse here.

[94] *ibid* at para 8.

[95] *ibid* at para 9.

[96] *ibid* at para 10.

[97] *ibid* at para 38.

The key authority influencing McKechnie J's eventual ruling was the British [11–44] case of *Steeples v Derbyshire Borough Council*.[98] There the English Court of Appeal had to assess the validity of a council effectively seeking permission from itself (or at least a sub-committee of itself). The council in the case had proposed to develop an area of parkland it owned with the help of a third party. An agreement was entered into between the council and the third party developer which provided that the council would take all reasonable steps to obtained the necessary planning permissions to enable the project to proceed, with damages to issue in the event they failed to make the necessary efforts. In finding that the later grant of permission was vitiated by a reasonable apprehension of bias, the Court then laid out the possible courses of action available to the council:

> "...the county council ask what else they could have done. One answer comes to mind immediately. They could have avoided committing themselves to KLF [the third party company] in any way until after the planning decision had been properly made or, if they were to make a contract with them, they could have ensured that the contract was subject to planning permission, that they had no obligation of any sort in connection with the obtaining of planning permission, and that they would be under no liability of any sort should planning permission not be obtained.
>
> Against the background of a contract already made, however, at least two further alternative courses come to mind as being far from inappropriate. They could have let KLF make the application, [to a neighbouring council, if possible] or they could have decided to hold a public meeting at which they, with members of the planning committee present, explained their proposals and the reasons for them and at which objectors were given an opportunity to air their views."[99]

In response, counsel for the local authorities in *Greenstar* argued that the [11–45] decision should be invalidated simply because at the outset of a process, the authorities considered a particular outcome desirable. The variation was based upon a legitimate concern regarding disruption to the market. Counsel then placed reliance upon the dicta of Lord Hoffman in *R (Alconbury Ltd) v Environment Secretary*:

> "It is the business of the Secretary of State, aided by his civil servants, to develop national planning policies and co-ordinate local policies. These

---

[98] *Steeples v Derbyshire Borough Council* [1984] 3 All ER 468.
[99] *ibid* at 494-5.

policies are not airy abstractions. They are intended to be applied in actual cases. It would be absurd for the Secretary of State, in arriving at a decision in a particular case, to ignore his policies and start with a completely open mind."[100]

[11–46]   The respondents argued that

"the relevant case law on bias applies in an attenuated form to administrative actions, particularly where the statutory framework makes it impossible for the administrators to have no view as to the desirability of what they propose".[101]

McKechnie J accepted that "decisions taken on policy issues are distinct and different from decisions of courts, tribunals or quasi tribunals".[102] On balance, His Honour refused to find that a structural bias arose, but underlined the value of *Steeples* as a precedent:

"...Ultimately I conclude that the dual role of the respondents, coupled with the statutory procedures for a Variation, are not such that they create objective bias. However, I would note that the situation of the respondents as both regulator and operator must inevitably increase the likelihood of objective bias, and in those circumstances, precautions, such as those suggested in Steeples, are to be encouraged where such a situation exists."[103]

[11–47]   Ultimately the fact that the relevant statute required the authorities to pay due regard to the submissions of those parties in reaching a decision on variation helped to avoid a ruling of bias. There is no doubt, however, that the existence of institutional interests which overlap with regulatory roles can make it less burdensome for applicants to raise the apprehension of bias. The "structural bias" frame is therefore useful for considering how the institutional design and overarching context can bolster arguments that a

---

[100] *R (Alconbury Ltd) v Environment Secretary* [2003] AC 295 at paragraph 123. Reference was also made to *Persimmon Homes Teeside Ltd. v R (Kevin Paul Lewis)* [2008] EWCA Civ 746, where the Court of Appeal emphasised the necessity "to be cognisant of the practicalities of local government" (at para 71).

[101] Above n 92 at para 43.

[102] *ibid* at para 45. McKechnie J cited Woolf, Jowell, Le Seuer, *'de Smith's Judicial Review* (6th ed) (Sweet & Maxwell, London, 2007) at p 530:

"The normal standards of impartiality applied in an adjudicative setting cannot meaningfully be applied to a body entitled to initiate a proposal and then to decide whether to proceed with it in the face of objections. It would be inappropriate for the courts to insist on maintaining the lofty detachment required by a judicial officer determining a lis inter partes"

[103] *ibid* at para 47.

reasonable apprehension of bias exists or require increased steps on the part of decision-makers.

Third Party Agreements: The *North Wall* Case

It is important to note that *Steeples*-type scenarios are not unprecedented in Ireland, indeed an Irish case with many shared elements is *North Wall Developments v Dublin Docklands Development Authority*.[104] This case illustrates the uncomfortable dynamics where a statutory body is at once performing public law functions, while being also tasked with an entrepreneurial focus which involves it in the "cut and thrust" of business negotiation. The case concerned the granting of a s 25 certificate as provided for by the Dublin Docklands Development Authority Act 1997. Such a certificate in effect accelerated the approval of certain development activities by exempting them from having to go through certain statutory procedures, such as the lodging of public objections. The respondent authority had granted a certificate to a third party, a rival of the applicant company. Before it had decided to do so, however, it had concluded a separate agreement with the third party, that, in the event a s 25 certificate was given, the third party would transfer some land to the respondent which would be used as public open space. Finlay Geoghegan J held that a reasonable apprehension of bias test applied to both judicial and administrative bodies, and such apprehension was raised as a result of the earlier agreement.[105] Nevertheless, Finlay Geoghegan J attempted to leave open room for a lighter application of the bias principle in certain administrative contexts:

[11–48]

> "...administrative bodies are subject to some limitation or exception in favour of a bias of necessity or structural bias, by reason of relevant statutory provisions."[106]

This statement seems in line with McKechnie J's above statement regarding the need to view policy decisions as distinct from judicial or quasi-judicial ones above. Both statements are framed very generally however, and it may be that abstract principle will not be especially helpful here. Rather, the nature of the statute which the relevant administrative body is operating under may be the key determinant of the outcome. Where the statute is

[11–49]

---

[104] *North Wall Developments v Dublin Docklands Development Authority* [2008] IEHC 305. Hereinafter "*North Wall*".
[105] *ibid* at para 98.
[106] *ibid* at para 99.

detailed and requires that the authority reason through public submissions, as in *Greenstar*, this may be sufficient evidence that the authority has located its prior agreement in the broader policy context and tested any initial perception of the public interest that underlay its earlier negotiation. Active steps to ameliorate the appearance of bias, such as the obtaining of an independent report on the benefits of the agreement and ensuring full transparency of the earlier agreement,[107] should be recommended to public bodies who are *necessarily* embroiled in such scenarios.

Conclusion: The Principle Against Bias and Institutional Design

[11–50]   As the *North Wall* case underlines, the individualistic focus of many bias cases should not obscure the need to ensure independence and impartiality is woven into statutory schemes. In the past fifteen years, the Refugee Appeals Tribunal has attracted enormous controversy due to a lack of transparency regarding its operation.[108] In *Nyembo v Refugee Appeals Tribunal*,[109] a refugee applicant sought leave to injunct a Tribunal member from hearing his appeal. Using statistics compiled by two leading legal practitioners in the area of refugee law, they alleged that the Tribunal member had not found in favour of an applicant in an oral hearing in the past three years, a period during which he would have heard hundreds of cases. The Tribunal settled the case and two other cases featuring similar allegations in December 2007.[110] The case underlined ongoing issues with

---

[107] The agreement at the heart of *North Wall* did not satisfy this, as it stated that:
> "The parties agree with one another that they will keep confidential the contents of this Agreement and will not, without the prior consent of the other party (such consent not to be unreasonably withheld or delayed), divulge to any third party whatsoever the details thereof (other than to necessary professional advisors and others who are necessary for NQIL in connection with its funding and other dealings with the development e.g. respective tenants and in any proceedings issued or intended to be issued or as required by law."

ibid at para 104.

This, along with other provisions, may explain why Justice Finlay Geoghegan described the terms of the agreement as "crucial" to the case. *ibid* at para 104.

[108] *The Irish Times*, "Members of refugee appeal body considered taking legal action", 8 March 2008. For a look at the birth of the current system see Byrne, "Expediency in Refugee Determination Procedures" (2000) 35 *Ir. Jur.* 149

[109] *Nyembo v Refugee Appeals Tribunal* [2006] IEHC 388.

[110] As Ward has written it later emerged that several Tribunal members intended to become notice parties to this case to dispute the Tribunal Chairman's assertion that the Tribunal member in question's record was not at variance with the record of other tribunal members. Tanya Ward, "Independence and Accountability of the Irish Judiciary" (2008) 8 (1) *JSIJ* 1

the operation and design of the tribunal, despite the fact that s 91 of the Refugee Act 1996 states that the Tribunal shall be independent in its functions. At the time of the *Nyembo* action there were wide divergences in the volume of case assignments given to tribunal members,[111] which added to the fact that members are paid on a case by case basis, led to widespread criticism and calls for reform. The need for proactive action in this area was underlined by retired Justice Catherine McGuiness who, writing in 2011, strongly condemned the operation of the system:

> "In reality, the tribunal affirms more than 95 per cent of negative decisions and has been widely criticised for its questionable independence, lack of transparency and scant or poor reasoning. Firstly, tribunal members are appointed by the Department of Justice so that, in essence, the department acts as judge, jury and executioner in the asylum system. Secondly, the manner in which the tribunal operates is opaque. There are no clear published guidelines for the allocation of cases to any particular member, some of whom have had 100 per cent refusal rates. Nor are there procedural guidelines for the conduct of proceedings."[112]

The indefensible political and administrative torpor which had existed   [11–51]
around the Tribunal's operation may now show some signs of dispersing. In August 2013, a new Tribunal Chairperson was appointed following a competitive selection process, and upon installation commenced a major review of Tribunal practices, procedures and guidelines. In September 2013, the Assigning Policy of the Tribunal was published, detailing how cases are assigned amongst the members of the Tribunal.[113] Furthermore, a Tribunal Users Group has been established, made up of the chairperson and representatives nominated by the Law Society and Bar Council. At time of writing the Group was considering the draft procedural guidelines which will set out the core practice and procedure of the tribunal.[114] These measures represent basic steps towards making the asserted independence

---

at p 9, citing in support *The Irish Times*, "Evidence of disharmony among members of refugee appeals process", 17 May 2008.

[111] Members must be solicitors or barristers of at least five years post-qualification experience.

[112] Justice Catherine McGuiness, "Effective Asylum Reforms would reduce reliance on the courts", *The Irish Times*, 2 September 2011.

[113] Available at: http://www.refappeal.ie/website/rat/ratweb.nsf/page/JWKY-9CDLLS16513311-en/$File/Guidance%20note%20no%202013-2.pdf (date accessed 30 June 2014).

[114] An improved training programme for members has also been launched in co-operation with the UNHCR.

of the Tribunal more concrete and removing the legitimate apprehensions of users. Enormous concern must be expressed at the manner in which a mere statutory statement of "independence" was treated as a passive statement of reality rather than as a duty to be delivered upon. As we discuss later in the context of the Social Welfare Appeals Tribunal,[115] independence is a complex objective conditioned heavily by legal, administrative and financial factors and should not be treated in a declarative manner by the legislature. Litigation regarding bias often struggles to stir this debate, but as we see later in this book, the requirements of independence and impartiality under the European Convention on Human Rights are stricter (though they remain hobbled somewhat by the remediating effects which the availability of enhanced judicial review may have). They also point to the imperative of tackling not just the vice of bias, but ensuring the virtue of independence.

---

[115] This discussion is featured in chapter 15 on the European Convention on Human Rights and Irish administrative law.

LEGITIMATE EXPECTATION

Introduction

On first encountering the term "legitimate expectation" many observers [12–01] may react by viewing it as a concept rooted in common sense: a device for imposing an obligation on Government to stand by its specific promises to act in a particular way. After all, at its simplest level, it provides that where a public body indicates it will conduct itself in a particular way that representation may be the basis of a legitimate expectation and the public body may be required to give effect to that expectation. Yet, the doctrine is, in fact, highly technical and has swiftly acquired a number of formal criteria which attach to its invocation. This reflects the journey travelled by a variety of initially loose equitable concepts, many of which exist as fairness-centred counterbalances to the more forceful tides of statutory provisions and discretionary decision-making powers. Legitimate expectation therefore exists to mediate in a certain amount of fairness to a number of specific and bounded situations.

While the doctrine is somewhat encrusted with restrictive requirements, it [12–02] is, intriguingly well positioned to engage with a number of emerging trends and patterns in postmodern governance. The first of these is the rapid process of amendment and obsolescence through which many regulatory schemes are now put. This legislative (and regulatory) hyperactivity sees statutory and non-statutory schemes appear, disappear or change, often in a non-transparent or bureaucratic manner that may blindside those subject to them. A related trend that the doctrine of legitimate expectation seems well positioned to interact with is the increasing dominance of "soft law" and policy guidance in the making of Government decisions. As we have already seen, key judicial review principles generally facilitate the creation of policy guidance and its application to the individual. The requirement that the decision-maker not close their mind to the individual circumstances of the case and that the policy not be *ultra vires* the parent Act provides some limited constraints on this process. Yet, there is an argument that soft law forms present some imbalances in the relationship between citizen and Government, the most basic of which is that there may not be any obligation to apply policy principles in all cases. Some comparator jurisdictions have reflected on the question of whether the citizen can have a legitimate expectation that such policies will be applied to their case.[1] This may represent a mechanism to ensure that Government discretion is structured by the principles laid down in key policy documents, and that policy is weighed and reasoned through in all cases. The lack of a systemized merits appeals system in Ireland, together with reliance upon decentralised or local bodies may often make consistency difficult to obtain.[2] Thus legitimate expectation may discipline the process of creating soft law guidance, ensuring that the documents are drafted to promote quality decision-making and not to drive institutional convenience.

[12–03]   Finally, in introducing the doctrine, we have already referred to its equitable heritage. This requires some further comment in order to understand both the doctrine's pedigree and its other, public law related, taproots. The interlinkage with the principle of estoppel was most strongly stated by Finlay CJ in *Webb v Ireland*, where he held the doctrine was "but an aspect of the well-recognised equitable concept of promissory estoppel".[3] This statement must, however, be supplemented by other judicial *dicta* which recognise the evolution and adaptation of legitimate expectation produced by its distinctive (public law) field of operation. In *Lett & Co. Ltd v Wexford Borough Council*,[4] Clarke J stressed that the doctrine is "often seen as the public law counterpart"[5] of estoppel. The basic result of the two doctrines is similar: both modify formal legal rights of a party by barring their enforcement in circumstances in which unfairness may arise. In *Abrahamson v Law Society of Ireland*,[6] however, McCracken J noted that the two concepts now rely upon the application of different legal grammar in achieving this common project:

> "While there is no doubt that the doctrine of legitimate expectation is similar to and probably founded upon the equitable concept of promissory estoppel, I would respectfully suggest that it has in fact been extended beyond the bounds of that doctrine. Promissory estoppel is largely defensive in its nature, and has been described as 'a shield and not a sword'. Its use is basically to ensure that a person who has made a

---

[1] M Groves, "Substantive Legitimate Expectation in Australian Administrative Law", (2008) 32 *Melbourne University Law Journal* 470.

[2] This has been seen recently in relation to the operation of medical cards, for example the Office of the Ombudsman report *Local Rules for National Schemes – Inequities in the administration of the Long Term Illness Card Scheme*, (Office of the Ombudsman, Dublin, 2014) highlighted that the HSE acknowledged that the relevant scheme operated differently around the country.

[3] *Webb v Ireland* [1988] IR 253 at 384.

[4] [2012] 2 IR 198.

[5] *ibid* at 216.

[6] [1996] 1 IR 403.

representation that they will not exercise some legitimate right is in fact bound by that expectation, and cannot exercise the right."[7]

In contrast, it will now be seen that legitimate expectation may at times be used to ground a benefit or compensate for the loss of a benefit.

Legitimate Expectation: Prerequisites for its Invocation

In the landmark case of *Glencar Exploration v Mayo County Council*,[8] the [12–04] Supreme Court laid down the three essential prerequisites for the successful making of a claim of legitimate expectation:

> "Firstly, the public authority must have made a statement or adopted a position amounting to a promise or representation, express or implied, as to how it will act in respect of an identifiable area of its activity. I will call this the representation.

> Secondly, the representation must be addressed or conveyed either directly or indirectly to an identifiable person or group of persons, affected annually or potentially in such a way that it forms part of a transaction definitively entered into or a relationship between that person or group and the public authority, or that the person or group has acted on the faith of the representation.

> Thirdly, it must be such as to create an expectation reasonably entertained by the person or group that the public body will abide by the representation to the extent that it would be unjust to permit the public authority to resile from it."[9]

Importantly, however, these requirements are open for future refinement, with Fennelly J expressly preserving space for this in his judgment in *Glencar*:

> "…refinements or extensions of these propositions are obviously possible. Equally they are qualified by considerations of the public interest, including the principle that freedom to exercise properly a statutory power is respected. However, the propositions I have endeavoured to formulate seem to me to be preconditions for the right to invoke the doctrine."[10]

---

[7] *ibid* at 418-19.
[8] [2002] 1 IR 84.
[9] *ibid* at 162-3.
[10] *ibid* at 163.

[12–05]   We will now move to explore the three established requirements in the context of specific cases, and then to reflect upon the underlying public interest factors which the judiciary have had recourse to in mapping and applying the doctrine.

[12–06]   The *Glencar* test was recently applied in *Curran v Minister for Education and Science*,[11] a case concerning the modification of an early retirement scheme for teachers. The scheme in question had operated from May 1997 as a pilot, and a circular issued by the Department in 2007 stated that the scheme would continue to include teachers retiring in 2007/8. The Court held that this express statement amounted to a representation as to how the Department planned to manage the scheme. The second requirement — that this promise relate to an identifiable person or group of persons — was also held to be satisfied despite the fact that the group involved could extend to up to sixty thousand teachers. Finally, the Court held that the scheme did confer an expectation of a substantive benefit. Despite satisfying all three criteria the Court held that the overriding public interest outweighed any established expectation. Dunne J ruled that "the declining economic circumstances" represented an overriding public interest. Her Honour noted that in some circumstances such an absolute override would not be acceptable and instead "it would be appropriate to have a reasonable period of notice or transitional arrangements in place" for those affected.[12]

[12–07]   Another case providing an accessible application of the *Glencar* criteria is *McCarthy v Minister for Education and Skills*.[13] The applicants in this case were students who had up until recent changes, qualified for a non-adjacent student support grant, the level of which was based on, *inter alia*, the distance between their ordinary residence and the third level institution. In December 2010, the Government indicated its intention to alter the specified distance required for qualification for obtaining a non-adjacent student support grant.[14] Under s 6 of the Student Support Act 2011, which amended existing legislation,[15] the Department took the decision to extend the distance criteria for qualification from twenty four to forty five kilometres.

---

[11] [2009] IR 300.

[12] *ibid* at 319.

[13] [2012] IEHC 200.

[14] A non adjacent grant provides the individual with a higher level of financial support than an adjacent grant, with the distinction intended to reflect the greater costs of someone who lives a greater distance from their third level institution.

[15] Local Authorities (Higher Education Grants) Acts 1968-1992.

The amendment also removed the automatic entitlement of mature students to the higher non-adjacent grant rate. The applicants contended, *inter alia*, that they had a legitimate expectation that the grant would continue to be provided to them and that they had relied upon that expectation in pursuing their studies. In particular one of the applicant stated by way of affidavit that

> "whilst I appreciated the amount of the grant would vary from year to year I never expected nor envisaged the distance criteria for the non-adjacent maintenance rate varying and whereby I would be excluded from the non-adjacent rate".[16]

Other applicants stated that the availability of the non-adjacent rate was "one of the fundamental reasons we both considered returning to full-time education".[17] However, despite these statements the Court held that applicants failed to identify any particular representation by the respondents, which amounted to a promise of non-revocation. Furthermore, the third element of the *Glencar* test, was not made out. This required the applicants to establish that they had formed a reasonable expectation that the respondent would stand by the alleged representation, and that it would be unjust to permit the Government to resile from it. In this regard Hedigan J held that even if the regular practice could somehow be held to constitute a representation: **[12–08]**

> "The applicants must have been aware of the worsening economic situation. The rates of grant in general, and in the higher education sector, have been reduced, including a reduction of 4% for all grants in the year 2011/2012. Rates of grant were also reduced by 5% in 2009/10. The alteration in the distance criteria and the position of mature students, the subject matter of this challenge had been signalled in the 2010 Budget. In these circumstances, it is my view that it was not reasonable for the applicants to expect the regular practice to continue."[18]

Finally, the Court stressed that even if the *Glencar* preconditions were established the case would have failed on public interest grounds. The affidavits sworn by members of the Department outlined the "the perilous state of the public finances at the time this decision was taken". Thus the   **[12–09]**

---

[16] *ibid* at para 6.4.
[17] *ibid*.
[18] *ibid* at para 6.5.

allegation of unfairness could not stand as "the obvious requirement" for reduced spending gave "a clear public policy basis" for the decision.[19]

[12–10] *McCarthy* underlines the reluctance of the courts to effectively imply a representation or promise where there has not been an express assurance.[20] As seen in *Curran* such a representation does not need to be made directly to the individual but can extend to classes of individuals such as applicants to a particular scheme. Another factor is that the relevant individual or individuals should have been at least aware of the statement or circumstances that gave rise to the legitimate expectation. In *Abrahamson v Incorporated Law Society of Ireland*,[21] McCracken J doubted whether detrimental reliance upon the representation was formally required,[22] but one can state that a claim for legitimate expectation will be stronger if the individual or individuals involved did, as a matter of fact, suffer a detriment as a result of their belief in the representation. Such reliance aids in proving that the expectation was "reasonable" and in raising the comfort level of the court with the argument that holding the Government to its promise would be in interests of justice.

[12–11] The Courts have also indicated their reluctance to find representations have been made when the communication occurred in a commercial context. In *Triatic Ltd v Cork County Council*,[23] the respondent, during a negotiation regarding a development project, represented that they would deal exclusively with the plaintiffs in exploring possible tourist or amenity uses for the site in question. After the company submitted a proposal, the Council contacted them expressing disappointment with the quality of their plans, and indicated they would seek other proposals through a fresh

---

[19] *ibid* at para 6.6.

[20] Biehler notes an exceptional case, *Phillips v Medical Council* [1991] 2 IR 115, where the Medical Council adopted new rules which practically precluded a doctor's already filed application from succeeding. Costello J held that the council had impliedly represented its intention to determine the plaintiff's application on the basis of the earlier rules. To allow the Council to rescind the rules with the application pending would be "grossly unfair". See H Biehler, *Judicial Review of Administrative Action: A Comparative Analysis* (3rd ed.) (Round Hall, Dublin, 2013) at p 184.

[21] Above n 6.

[22] *ibid* at 423. This is also supported by ruling of O'Hanlon J in *Fakih v Minister for Justice* 1993 2 IR 406. A judge who leans towards viewing legitimate expectation as inherently related to promissory estoppel is more likely to search for and possibly require detriment. For a more extensive analysis see Biehler, above n 20 at pp 189-191.

[23] *Triatic Ltd v Cork County Council* [2007] 3 IR 57. Such reluctance is also seen in *Lett & Company Ltd*, above n 4, Clarke J.

advertisement campaign. Laffoy J ruled that a claim of legitimate expectation would not be entertained in the particular context of the case. Her Honour expressed concern at any use of the doctrine to somehow moderate "the ordinary commercial risks which are inherent in negotiations".[24] *Triatic Ltd* highlights the reluctance of judges to extend the public law doctrine of legitimate expectations to cover the commercial activities of public bodies.

Substantive Legitimate Expectations and the Statutory/Non-Statutory Discretion Distinction

In *Glencar*, Fennelly J highlighted "the principle that freedom to exercise properly a statutory power is respected" as a highly significant part of considering whether a legitimate expectation can be enforced in a particular case.[25] This strongly valued need to protect the free exercise of statutory power is at the core of two interrelated restraints upon the use of the doctrine of legitimate expectation, namely:

[12–12]

- A traditional position whereby the doctrine of legitimate expectation could be applied to ensure that certain procedures are followed as per the decision-maker's representation, but that the doctrine could not function to secure a substantive benefit or right for an individual, particularly where a statutory discretion was being exercised by the decision-maker;
- Judicial discomfort with the idea that legitimate expectation could require a statutory discretion to be exercised in a particular way, a result which would seem to offend the separation of powers, given that the Oireachtas had intended the discretion to be vested in the addressee of the statute.

Recent High Court cases indicate that the first principle, barring what may be termed substantive legitimate expectation, is being relaxed. This, however, appears to apply in the context of non-statutory discretionary decisions, with the second principle, at least in the absence of further case law, still holding back the enforcement of a substantive legitimate expectation in the exercise of *statutory* discretions.

---

[24] *ibid* at 87.
[25] Above n 8 at 163.

[12–13]   The leading case upholding a legitimate expectation entailing the conferral of a substantive benefit in a non-statutory decision-making context is *Power v The Minister for Social and Family Affairs*.[26] The applicants in this case were full time students who were recipients of the Back to Education Allowance Scheme operated by the Department of Social and Family Affairs. The Scheme was administered in line with terms and conditions laid out in a 2002 booklet entitled "Back to Education Programme SW 70". This booklet stipulated that the allowance would be payable for the entire calendar term of the relevant educational course, including during the summer. In March 2003, however, the scheme was modified to henceforth exclude payments during the summer holidays. McMenamin J ruled that those individuals who had, before the change to the scheme, returned to education on the basis that the allowance would be payable during holiday periods, were entitled to a declaration that the decision to change the scheme was contrary to her legitimate expectation. His Honour stressed a number of core principles that had led the Court to enforce a substantive benefit. Firstly, the power in question was a non-statutory discretionary power. Secondly, in the context of such a scheme, the Court could carry out a balancing exercise between the interest to the claimant and the public interest in the unfettered exercise by the Minister of his discretionary decision-making power.

[12–14]   McMenamin J noted that the balancing process should aim at asking "whether there is a sufficient overriding interest to justify departure from what has been previously promised".[27] On the facts his Honour concluded that while the change was related to budgetary constraints, the detriment suffered by the applicant was such that the expectation should be enforced. The removal of the substantive benefit/procedural matter distinction in relation to non-statutory discretions was also supported by Clarke J in the 2011 case of *Atlantic Marine Supplies Ltd v Minister for Transport*.[28] Nevertheless, his Honour underlined that the public interest balancing which will occur must be conducted on the basis that

> "the public policy requirements which need to be given significant weight are much more likely to be present and are much more likely to weigh heavily in the case of a substantive rather than a procedural legitimate expectation".[29]

---

[26] [2007] 1 IR 543.
[27] *ibid* at 557.
[28] [2010] IEHC 104.
[29] *ibid* at para 7.9.

The orientation of the balancing process in a manner sympathetic to   **[12–15]**
Government interests was also signalled by McMenamin J's statement in
Power that "a legitimate expectation will arise only if the court thinks that
there is no good reason of public policy why it should not".[30] There remain
a number of clear statements ruling out the extension of substantive
legitimate expectation in statutory decision-making context.[31] The
separation of powers concerns underpinning this stance were most clearly
underlined by McCracken J in *Abrahamson v Law Society*:

> "Where a minister or public body is given by statute or statutory
> instrument a discretion or a power to make regulations for the good
> of the public or of a specific section of the public, the court will not
> interfere with the exercise of such discretion or power, as to do so
> would be tantamount to the court usurping the discretion or power to
> itself, and would be an undue interference by the court in the affairs of
> the persons or bodies to whom or to which such discretion or power
> was given by the legislature."[32]

We would underline, however, that this fundamental restriction is not   **[12–16]**
necessarily beyond future modification, particularly given some decisions
in comparative jurisdictions. As Biehler has argued:

> "There is clearly merit in the argument that giving effect to a legitimate
> expectation in a substantive manner may well have the effect of
> fettering the free exercise of discretionary powers but it is too simplistic
> to suggest that the latter principle must inevitably take priority over
> the former. A more nuanced approach would be to hold that where a
> specific representation has been made it should be honoured, even if
> there has been a change in policy in the interim and even if this involves
> some fettering of the free exercise of discretionary powers, unless the
> overriding public interest requires that the authority should be entitled
> to resile from the assurance given."[33]

---

[30] Above n 26 at 556.
[31] Costello J supplied an unambiguous statement of principle in *Tara Prospecting Ltd v Minister
for Energy* [1993] ILRM 770 at 788:
"In cases involving the exercise of a discretionary statutory power the only legitimate
expectation relating to the conferring of a benefit that can be inferred from words or
conduct is a conditional one, namely that a benefit will be conferred provided that at
the time the minister considers that it is a proper exercise of the statutory power in the
light of the current policy to grant it. Such a conditional expectation cannot give rise to
an enforceable right to the benefit should it later be refused by the minister in the public
interest."
[32] Above n 6 at 423.
[33] Biehler, above n 20 at pp 223-4.

[12–17]   Interestingly, one mooted solution is that the courts could require a decision-maker to take a legitimate expectation into account in the decision-making process.[34] The installation of proportionality review in Irish law could increase the practical usefulness of requiring this — a reviewing court could find that the unfairness raised by the legitimate expectation was not properly valued in making the decision or that its non-enforcement was disproportionate, rather than ruling that the legitimate expectation *de jure* limited the discretion of the statutory anointed decision-maker. This clearly represents a somewhat tortured semantic exercise, but might somehow raise the comfort level of the judiciary with enforcing substantive legitimate expectation in statutory contexts. Of course, it remains open to the courts to move beyond the categorical exclusion and elect to decide on a case-by-case basis, as Biehler notes above. Above all, we believe that this is an area where the Office of the Ombudsman should be particularly active as such a state of affairs represents a classic example of the inertia that can be produced by the separation of powers doctrine.

[12–18]   The existence of an alternative, individual rights centred way of looking at the doctrine was highlighted by the rather bracing intervention into the area by the European Court on Human Rights in the decision of *Stretch v United Kingdom*.[35] In Ireland (and other comparative jurisdictions), it has long been viewed as obvious that an individual or individuals cannot expect a legitimate expectation to confer a benefit where this would represent the bestowing "upon a statutory authority a power which that authority does not have under the terms of the relevant statute".[36] The ECtHR held that a legitimate expectation of a property right was to be understood as "a possession" to which Article 1 of the First Protocol applied. As a result, wherever a legitimate expectation was established, a balancing exercise between the effects on individual rights and the public interests at hand must be undertaken. This decision reveals the difficulties

---

[34] As was mooted in the English Court of Appeal decision in *R. (Bibi) v Newham London Borough Council* [2002] 1 WLR 237, 248.

[35] (2004) 38 EHRR 12.

[36] Hedigan J in *Cork Opera House Plc v The Revenue Commissioners* [2007] IEHC 388. In this case the applicant argued that the Revenue Commissioners could continue to grant it a licence to sell alcohol on its premises, despite the fact that the Commissioners in purporting to do so were misinterpreting the relevant statute which, as a matter of law, required separate District Court approval. See also the case of *Wiley v the Revenue Commissioners* [1994] 2 IR 160 whereby the applicant sought to enforce by way of legitimate expectation the continuation of a practice whereby the respondent would pay him refunds of an excise duty to which he was not, properly speaking, entitled.

which the ECtHR can face in harmonising its reasoning with common law doctrines. Regardless of the appropriateness of requiring a balancing test, the approach of the ECtHR seemed uncharacteristically insensitive to the differing conceptions of the separation of powers within its State Parties, and, in particular, the fundamental nature of the *ultra vires* principle to the UK. There is a strong argument that the possible enforcement of a legitimate expectation to permit an otherwise *ultra vires* act should fall within the margin of appreciation of the State Parties. This would permit a national court to take the lead role in considering whether, in an exceptional case, their constitutional doctrine should be relaxed to ensure compliance with the Convention. Regardless, even if a balancing process were to occur, it is unlikely that an Irish court would find that the weight of interests fell in favour of enforcing a representation of an unenforceable nature.

Having focused upon the limited prospects for enforcing substantive **[12–19]** legitimate expectation in statutory contexts, it is important to also recognize the way in which a legitimate expectation as to a procedural matter can deliver outcomes for an individual client, and practically deter State actors from cynical and rushed amendments to policies or schemes. This is illustrated by the High Court decision in *Glenkirren Homes v Dun Laoghaire Rathdown County Council*.[37] There, Clarke J stressed the procedural rights attaching to legitimate expectations:

> "I am satisfied that an implied representation can derive from the universal following of a particular practice for a prolonged period of time. It is, of course, important to note that the executive enjoys a constitutional entitlement to change policy. Furthermore bodies exercising a statutory role…also enjoy an entitlement to alter the policy within which they exercise their statutory functions subject only to the overall requirement that whatever policies are adopted must be consistent with their statutory role as defined. It is clear, therefore, that a legitimate expectation cannot arise to the effect that a policy will not be changed. Thus in *Hempenstall v Minister for Environment* [1994] 2 I.R. 20, Costello J determined that notwithstanding the fact that a new policy in respect of the issuing of taxi licences would have the effect of very significantly reducing the value of existing licences, nonetheless the overriding entitlement to change policy prevented a legitimate expectation arising. I should, therefore, emphasise that the existence of a longstanding practice does not give rise to any legitimate expectation that that practice will not change. However, where third parties

---

[37] [2007] IEHC 298.

reasonably arrange their affairs by reference to such a practice it seems to me that such third parties are entitled to rely upon an expectation that the practice will not be changed without reasonable notice being given. The notice that would be required is such as would reasonably allow those who have conducted their affairs in accordance with the practice to consider and implement an alternative means for dealing with the issues arising."[38]

[12–20]   The possible availability of damages is also a key factor in evaluating the practical utility of the doctrine's invocation. The Supreme Court has already endorsed this remedy on the facts in *McGrath v Minister for Defence*.[39] It is important to note that, due to the wording of Order 84, rule 25(1)(1) damages appear to be viewed as ancillary to *mandamus* or a declaration in the context of judicial review.[40] The judgment of Clarke J in *Atlantic Marine Supplies Ltd v Minister for Transport*,[41] likely carves out space for the awarding of damages as part of the general discretion of the courts to provide an equitable outcome.[42] Noting prior support for the provision of damages in the judgment of McCracken J in *Abrahamson*, his Honour held that:

> "I see no reason in principle to depart from [McCracken J's] view… to the effect that a claim in damages can, in an appropriate case, lie in respect of a breach of legitimate expectation. Indeed there may well be cases where an award of damages, rather than a substantive interference with the statutory or administrative system under review, may be more appropriate. It is possible that there may be circumstances (particularly where a claimant has significantly changed his position as a result of a legitimate expectation) where it would be unjust not to provide the claimant concerned with some remedy. There may well, in those circumstances, be cases where it would not be appropriate to afford a substantive remedy as such in the sense of a remedy which interfered with the statutory or administrative process under review. In at least some of those cases it may well be that damages would be the appropriate remedy."[43]

---

[38] *ibid* at para 5.6.

[39] [2010] 1 IR 560.

[40] See G Hogan and DG Morgan, *Administrative Law in Ireland*, (4th ed) (Round Hall, Dublin, 2010), pp 956-7.

[41] Above n 28.

[42] This recalls the statement of O'Donnell J in *Lett & Co. v Wexford Borough Corporation*, where he stated that "there is sufficient authority and principle to justify a court, once it has determined that there has been a breach of a legitimate expectation, to give such remedy as the equity of the case may demand". Above n 4 at 254.

[43] Above n 28 at para 7.10.

Conclusion

In this chapter, we have seen how the doctrine of legitimate expectation is   [12–21]
positioned to engage with key accountability themes such as consistency
and the remedying of errors. In concluding, it is important for the reader
not just to reflect upon the use of the doctrine in court cases, but how
Government authorities should take steps to ensure that their conduct is
litigation proofed. At a minimum, recent cases underline the need to treat
all communications with citizens with the utmost seriousness, to ensure
that soft law schemes are well considered and that there are clear
procedures for their amendment. As the doctrinal rigidities clinging to the
use of legitimate expectations begin to loosen somewhat, cases involving
its use now require increased engagement with overall fairness, and with
the public interest in holding Government to, or releasing it from, its prior
promises. The core normative question of when, as a matter of good public
policy and practical fairness, should a Government be required to live
with its mistakes? is of increasing centrality. Thus, a doctrine once
dominated by legalistic distinctions now offers greater potential for the
judiciary to reflect on how the courts should most effectively intervene to
regulate Government errors.

CHAPTER THIRTEEN

JUDICIAL REVIEW: PROCEDURES AND REMEDIES

Introduction

In delivering an analysis of judicial review principles, one must not neglect [13–01]
the reality that the practical utility of the review mechanism as a corrective
to Government misconduct is dependent upon procedural gateways,
together with the eventual provision of effective redress. In this chapter we
will provide a breakdown of the fundamentals of accessing judicial review,
the remedies that can be sought, while also reflecting on the degree to
which judicial review is effectively available to the citizen. The issue of
access to judicial review, often considered to be a matter of mere procedural
rules, is of critical importance given the central systematic role of judicial
review to securing administrative justice. The reader will recall that in the
opening chapter of this book we stressed that the rule of law is the "driving
force behind — and the normative basis of — administrative law."[1] Given
this, the receptivity of institutional actors to facilitating access to judicial
review is a crucial determinant of adherence to the rule of law.

Judicial review procedure and remedies has been heavily intertwined [13–02]
historically. Indeed the latter represented the most challenging procedural
hurdle for an applicant. Prior to the reform of judicial review procedure in
1986 an applicant wanting to challenge an administrative decision was
required to choose between two types of remedies. Firstly there were the
prerogative writs[2] — *certiorari, mandamus,* prohibition, *quo warranto* and
habeas corpus. These remedies were closely connected to the Crown and
provided entirely at the discretion of the court. The *prerogative writs* were
originally issued by the Court of the King's Bench, and were in part a
function of the King's exercise of justice and administrative control.[3]
Eventually the functions carried out in this area were transferred to the
High Court of Justice.[4] In the alternative there were the private law remedies
— declaration and the injunction — which were "so called because they

---

[1] M Elliott, *The Constitutional Foundations of Judicial Review* (Hart Publishing, Oxford, 2001) at
p 104.

[2] The use of the term *prerogative* derives from the fact that these remedies arose from the
Crown and were developed under the UK system of judicial review. As de Blacam notes,
the term was used from "at least the middle of the eighteenth century" onwards. M de
Blacam, *Judicial Review: A Guide to Irish Law* (Tottel Publishing, Dublin, 2013) at para 13-01.
Hereinafter "de Blacam".

[3] *ibid.*

[4] Initially under the Supreme Court of Judicature Act (Ireland) 1877, s 21 and upon independence
the Courts of Justice Act 1924. When in 1961, Courts (Supplemental Provisions) Act 1961, the
present-day High Court was established Order 84 of the Rules of the Superior Courts 1962
created the category of "state side" orders from these prerogative remedies.

were originally used only in private law and only later came to be used in public law."[5]

[13–03]　These six remedies overlapped to some extent but serious difficulties arose as to which remedy an applicant should apply for. If the incorrect type of remedy (prerogative/private) was requested then the application would be dismissed by the court regardless of the merits of the challenge.[6] So if an applicant was seeking to prevent a public body acting in a certain way they would have to choose between an order of prohibition (prerogative) and an injunction (private). In addition, the rules governing when a particular remedy was appropriate were technical. Indeed, the centuries of accreted doctrinal technicality which marred the prerogative writs, in particular, provoked Professor Kenneth Davis to assert that

> "either Parliament or the Law Lords should throw the entire set of prerogative writs into the Thames River, heavily weighted with sinkers to prevent them from rising again".[7]

[13–04]　These procedural problems arose largely as a product of judicial review's common law foundations. Over the years, many jurisdictions have chosen to enact statutory frameworks for their judicial review processes.[8] However, our jurisdiction has retained a system that grew organically and somewhat haphazardly both here and in Britain. This is not to say that the system has been without review and new procedures. Central to this was the Law Reform Commission (LRC) working paper — *Judicial Review of Administrative Action: the Problem of Remedies,*[9] which shone a critical spotlight on the operational problem of judicial review.

[13–05]　The LRC summed up the problems of the old system thus:

> "The present system cannot be defended on any rational grounds; its foibles and imperfections result from no conscious policy choices but

---

[5] P Cane, *Administrative Law* (4th ed) (OUP, Oxford, 2004) at p 86.

[6] Although remedies between categories could not be substituted, remedies within a category could be.

[7] K C Davis, "The Future of Judge-made Public Law in England: A Problem of Practical Jurisprudence" (1961) 61 *Columbia Law Review* 210 at, p 204.

[8] For example, the USA judicial review system operates under the Administrative Procedure Act 1946 and the Australian system under the Administrative Decisions (Judicial Review) Act 1977 although even under these frameworks the common law can still exert a powerful influence.

[9] LRC, *Judicial Review of Administrative Action: the Problem of Remedies* (LRC WP 8/1979) (LRC, Dublin, 1979). Hereinafter "LRC (1979)".

solely from the accidents of history. Reform is essential and relatively simple. *What is required is a single comprehensive procedure enabling the aggrieved citizen to bring his case – whatever its nature – before the courts. It will then be for the judge to decree that form of relief, including where appropriate an order for payment of damages, which seems best adapted to the particular case."*[10]

This working paper ultimately prompted the creation of the 1986 reforms and produced a new procedural framework which provided an important codification of judicial review procedure.[11] It has, to some extent been successful in that regard although it affords no overarching legislative framework. We therefore conclude that although the field of judicial review procedure was in the past studded with a series of "doctrinal tank traps",[12] present day actors are committed to move towards more concretely defined, modern frameworks.

Applying for Judicial Review

The following section provides the reader with an overview of some of the key issues arising in relation to the application for judicial review procedure. It is not designed to be absolutely exhaustive.[13] As will be discussed, Order 84 provides for a two stage application process. Firstly there is an *ex parte* application for leave and only where the court grants the applicant leave will the second substantive application be heard. It is important to note that the rules were intended to streamline the process providing citizens with an effective procedure which should operate efficiently. [13–06]

Sufficient Interest

Before examining the procedure set out in Order 84 RSC, we must first note the importance of *locus standi* to this process. Rule 20(4) provides that only where the court concludes that the applicant has "sufficient interest" in the issue(s) at stake in the case can leave be granted. The procedure was designed to ensure that *locus standi* requirements were the same for [13–07]

---

[10] Emphasis in original. LRC (1979), *ibid* at para 1.9.
[11] The Rules of the Superior Courts 1986 (SI No 15 of 1986) enacted following recommendations by the Law Reform Commission in their working paper, *Judicial Review of Administrative Action: The Problem of Remedies*, (Law Reform Commission, Dublin, 1979).
[12] This entertainingly accurate term was coined by Former Chief Justice of Australia, Sir Anthony Mason, in his foreword to P Keyzer, *Open Constitutional Courts* (The Federation Press, Sydney, 2010).
[13] For those in search of greater detail, see de Blacam, above n 2 at Part IX.

all remedies.[14] This is because traditionally, the rules varied depending on the type of remedy being sought. As Hogan and Morgan highlight, public law remedies such as *certioriari* tended to include an element of *"action popularis*, as the purpose of these remedies was not merely to avoid injustice *inter partes*, but also to maintain order in the legal system."[15] In practice, however, this did not mean that anyone could apply to the court. Rather the applicant needed to be an aggrieved person. Private law remedies operated under a narrower approach with the applicant needing to show "the existence of a legal right or other cognisable interest"[16] being threatened. With the development of a single application the rules around *locus standi* have in recent years been inclined to allow at least some opportunity for public interest challenges thus allowing judicial review to provide a wider administrative justice remit than just righting individual wrongs.

[13–08]   The rules operating in this area are judge made and the courts have stressed the need for flexibility "so as to be individually applicable to the particular facts of any given case".[17] In recent times, the rules have also taken a more liberal turn in relation to both public and private remedies with the courts looking for an applicant who has suffered some harm or prejudice going beyond that which members of the general public would suffer. However, as we will see, there is no longer a requirement that the applicant be a victim and the courts have also opened up the possibility of representative actions.

[13–09]   The relationship between *locus standi* in constitutional review cases and in judicial review of administrative actions has been considered in a number of cases with courts indicating that they are similar, if not completely alike.[18] The leading case on standing, from a constitutional review context, is *Cahill v Sutton*[19] in which the plaintiff sought to challenge s 11(2)(b) of the

---

[14] As the Law Reform Commission Consultation Paper on judicial review procedure highlights, prior to the 1986 rules the general approach was that the test for standing was "broadly speaking the same" for private and public law remedies. However, rule 20(4) sought to establish clearly that the approach would be the same. Law Reform Commission, *Judicial Review Procedure* (LRC CP 20/2003) (LRC, Dublin, 2003) at paragraph 1.53. Hereinafter "LRC (2003)".

[15] G Hogan and DG Morgan, *Administrative Law in Ireland* (4th ed) (Round Hall, Dublin, 2010) at para 16-196. Hereinafter "Hogan and Morgan".

[16] *ibid* at para 16-197.

[17] *State (Lynch) v Cooney* [1982] IR 337, per Walsh J at 369.

[18] See *State (Sheehan) v Government of Ireland* [1987] IR 550, *Duggan v An Taoiseach* [1989] ILRM 710.

[19] *Cahill v Sutton* [1980] IR 269. Hereinafter "*Cahill*".

Statute of Limitations 1957 which time barred applicants in medical negligence cases. However, the applicant was not personally able to claim the basis of her challenge - that the constitutional right to sue was infringed by a failure to provide an exception to those who become aware of the facts after the time limitation had expired.[20] Henchy J stated that:

"The plaintiff is seeking to be allowed to conjure up, invoke and champion the putative constitutional rights of a hypothetical third party, so that the provisions of s.11, subs. 2(b), may be declared unconstitutional on the basis that constitutional *jus tertii* – thus allowing the plaintiff to march through the resulting gap in the statute."[21]

The Court found that she did not have standing, Henchy J stating that an applicant   **[13–10]**

"must show that the impact of the impugned law on his personal situation discloses an injury or prejudice which he has either suffered or is in imminent danger of suffering".[22]

However, his Honour went on to find that that rule was subject to exceptions "when the justice of the case so requires."[23]

The approach adopted in *Cahill* has, however, been expanded upon in a number of cases. Thus in *State (Lynch) v Cooney*[24] Walsh J found that it was enough for an applicant to be "a person aggrieved" and that that term was to be widely interpreted: **[13–11]**

"The question of whether or not a person has sufficient interest must depend upon the circumstances of each particular case. In each case the question of sufficient interest is a mixed question of fact and law which must be decided upon legal principles but, it should be added, there is greater importance to be attached to the facts because it is only by an examination of the facts that the court can come to a decision

---

[20] The plaintiff had been aware of the injury during the relevant statutory time period.

[21] *Cahill*, above n 19 at 280.

[22] *ibid* at 284.

[23] *ibid*. In the constitutional context this was because:

"the paramount consideration in the exercise of the jurisdiction of the Courts to review legislation in the light of the Constitution is to ensure that persons entitled to the benefit of a constitutional right will not be prejudiced through being wrongfully deprived of it, there will be cases where the want of the normal locus standi on the part of the person questioning the constitutionality of the statute may be overlooked if, in the circumstances of the case, there is a transcendent need to assert against the statute the constitutional provision that has been invoked." (at 284).

[24] Above n 17.

as to whether there is a sufficient interest in the matter to which the application relates."[25]

Both *Cahill v Sutton* and *State (Lynch) v Cooney* were decided before the reform of judicial review procedure. However, their liberalising impact on *locus standi* continued after 1986.

[13–12]   The courts have had to consider the challenge to the *locus standi* rules where an applicant is taking an action more as a representative than a direct victim. These cases have tended to arise in the environmental/planning context.[26] In *Lancefort Ltd v An Bord Pleanála (No.2)*[27] Denham J found that there had been a line of cases that indicated a retreat from an approach requiring the applicant to be a victim of some kind to one which takes a more public interest focus.

[13–13]   The Supreme Court in *Mulcreevy v Minister for the Environment*[28] considered the standing of an applicant seeking to prevent the respondents from proceeding with construction work on a motorway which would damage a national monument. The applicant had no private interest:

> "It has been made clear in decisions of the High Court and this court in recent times that it is not in the public interest that decisions by statutory bodies which are of at least questionable validity should wholly escape scrutiny because the person who seeks to involve the jurisdiction of the court by way of judicial review cannot show that he is personally affected, in some sense peculiar to him, by the decision. It is in that sense, I think, that the requirement in Order 84, rule 20(4) of the Rules of the Superior Courts, 1986 should be read.... It is at the same time essential to bear in mind that, while it is undesirable that invalid legislation or unlawful practice should escape scrutiny because of the absence of an indisputable qualified objector, it is also important to ensure that unfounded and vexatious challenges are not entertained."[29]

[13–14]   An alternative approach can be found in the case of *Construction Industry Federation v Dublin City Council*[30] where the respondent successfully argued that the Construction Industry Federation ("the CIF") did not have standing

---

[25] *ibid* at 369.

[26] As such they operate under slightly different statutory rules which require applicants to show a *substantial interest* in the matter – s 50(4)(b)(iv) Planning and Development Act 2000.

[27] *Lancefort Ltd v An Bord Pleanála* [1999] 2 IR 270.

[28] *Mulcreevy v Minister for the Environment* [2004] 1 IR 72.

[29] *ibid* at 78.

[30] *Construction Industry Federation v Dublin City Council* [2005] 2 IR 496.

to challenge its decision to make a development contribution scheme on the basis that the CIF did not in itself engage in development despite being an unincorporated association of builders and developers. McCracken J found that although the applicant claimed its standing came from the fact that its members were affected by the proposed scheme and as such it had a common interest with its members:

> "...it appears to me that to allow the applicant to argue this point without relating it to any particular application and without showing any damage to the applicant itself, meant that the court is being asked to deal with a hypothetical situation, which is always undesirable. This is a challenge which could be brought by any of the members of the applicant who are affected and would then be related to the particular circumstances of that members. The members themselves are, in many cases, very large and financially substantial companies, which are unlikely to be deterred by the financial consequences of mounting a challenge such as this. Unlike many of the case in which parties with no personal or direct interest have been granted *locus standi*, there is no evidence before the court that, in the absence of the purposed challenge by the applicant, there would have been no other challenger. Indeed, the evidence appears to be the contrary."[31]

This case clearly indicates the impact of policy factors and the wider question [13–15] of public interest and appropriateness of representative applications. Where the members of the association are in a position to take a case themselves in relation to the specifics of their own situation the court has a preference for this rather than a more generic application. Equally, "opportunistic or unmeritorious" cases are far less likely to be treated liberally:

> "All citizens have a right of access to the Courts which, in other cases, the Courts have been sedulous in protecting. But this right of access is for the purpose of resolving justiciable issues and not for the purpose of constituting the Courts as a sort of debating society or deliberative assembly for the discussion of abstract issues."[32]

The significance of a liberal approach to standing should not be [13–16] underestimated. Judicial review plays a key role in upholding the rule of law in the context of "public wrongs" and in ensuring the responsibility and accountability of Government to the people.[33] In such cases the

---

[31] *ibid* at 526-7.

[32] *Riordan v Government of Ireland* [2009] 3 IR 745.

[33] See C Mac Eochaidh, "Procedural Obstacles to Public Interest Litigation", *FLAC Public Interest Seminar Series*, 12 May 2006.

applicant needs to show themselves to be a genuinely concerned citizen. However, the majority of judicial review cases are not about the public interest but ultimately about individual claims. In this category the applicant has to show that she or he has a sufficient interest based on the personal impact (injury or prejudice) of the matter complained of. Thus it is important to acknowledge that a representative interest may suffice in such cases, whilst in other cases a direct interest is more appropriate. The courts have long recognised the importance of flexibility in this area.

[13–17]   A particularly strong example of the need for this flexibility from England/ Wales is *R v Secretary of State for Foreign and Commonwealth Affairs, ex parte World Development Movement Ltd*[34] where a pressure group successfully challenged a decision of the UK Government to commit money to a defective overseas development scheme. Significantly this case is an example of a situation where if the pressure group did not challenge the decision it would be hard to find someone else in a position to do so. Rose LJ referred to the "importance of vindicating the rule of law" as a central element for finding standing. Leyland and Anthony highlight the point that such cases "arguably allow the courts to fill in part the accountability void".[35]

When Should the Court Consider the Applicant's Sufficient Interest?

[13–18]   The courts have had to consider the issue of whether sufficient interest can be addressed at the leave stage or whether it is best considered in the substantive proceedings, or both. The reader should recall that rule 20(4) requires the court to only grant leave when it has found that the applicant has sufficient interest in the case. However, we have already noted that in

---

[34] *R v Secretary of State for Foreign and Commonwealth Affairs, ex parte World Development Movement Ltd* [1995] 1 WLR 386.

[35] P Leyland and G Anthony, *Administrative Law*, (7th ed) (Oxford University Press, Oxford, 2009) at p 206. See in our jurisdiction *Murphy v Wicklow County Council* [1999] IEHC 225, High Court — the applicant sought to challenge the development of a dual carriageway road through the Glen of the Downs. The High Court found that the applicant had standing given he was "genuine and bona fide" with a "passionate commitment to the eco system and to the protection of the Glen of the Downs" and could also provide expert evidence on a range of matters that were relevant to the case. Although here the court did stress that the decision should not be seen as a "green light" for similar protests/challenges. Also *Digital Rights Ireland Ltd v Minister for Communications & Ors* [2010] IECH 221 where the court regarded the applicant as having *locus standi* because (a) the applicant was "a sincere and serious litigant" raising important constitutional issues and seeking to protect the public good, (b) the Court had a duty to uphold the Constitution and to scrutinise questionable actions and (c) the high costs associated with a legal challenge of this type meant it was unlikely that one mobile phone user would bring the case.

many cases the question of whether an applicant has leave is often "too complex and controversial to be resolved at the hearing of the application for leave".[36] In addition, as Biehler highlights,

> "it seems to be accepted that, at least where leave is granted on an *ex parte* basis, the issue of whether an applicant has a sufficient interests cannot be conclusively determined at this stage."[37]

The courts have tended to adopt such a position — Lord Diplock in *R v Inland Revenue Commissioners, ex parte National Federation of Self-Employed and Small Businesses Ltd*[38] stated

> "the discretion that the court is exercising at this stage is not the same as that which it is called upon to exercise when all the evidence is in and the matter has been fully argued at the hearing of the leave application".

This approach by the UK House of Lords was approved by Denham J in *G v Director of Public Prosecutions*.[39]

The reader will recall that in *State (Lynch) v Cooney*[40] Walsh J highlighted [13–19] that the question of *locus standi* was one of both fact and law but that more emphasis would be placed on the facts and that for a detailed examination to take place it should be done during the substantive application. This view was followed by Keane J in *Lancefort Ltd v An Bord Pleanála*,[41] where the court stated that the leave stage would operate to remove the obviously weak cases.[42]

Application for Leave

In this section we take the reader through the process of applying for leave [13–20] for judicial review. This is not quite as straightforward as the reader might

---

[36] A Collins and J O'Reilly, *Civil Proceedings and the State in Ireland: A Practitioners' Guide* (Thomson Round Hall, Dublin, 2004) at p 119.

[37] H Biehler, *Judicial Review of Administrative Action* (3rd ed) (Round Hall, Dublin, 2013) at p 441.

[38] *R v Inland Revenue Commissioners, ex parte National Federation of Self-Employed and Small Businesses Ltd* [1982] AC 617, 643-44.

[39] *G v Director of Public Prosecutions* [1994] 1 IR 374.

[40] Above n 17.

[41] *Lancefort Ltd v An Bord Pleanála* [1997] 2 ILRM 508.

[42] Note however, that Keane J highlighted a difference between standard judicial review and the statutory schemes where the court would be looking for "sufficient evidence" at the leave stage "to enable the judge to determine the question of standing". The case being considered by Keane J was a judicial review under planning legislation. *ibid* at 311.

expect, not least because there has been a recent amendment to Order 84 RSC. We will therefore review the operation of the process, including that amendment, and also note some possible reforms that might be made to improve the application procedures.

[13–21]   Order 84, rule 20(1) states that an application for judicial review may only be made if the court has given leave to the applicant.[43] The leave procedure requires that the applicant makes a motion *ex parte*[44] submitting the *Statement Required to Ground Application for Judicial Review* (Statement of Grounds).[45] This involves the submission of Form 13 which informs the court of the relief sought and the relevant grounds upon which the request for relief is based and Form 14 — an affidavit verifying the facts relied upon.[46] If the applicant is seeking interim relief they must also include a statement setting out what relief is sought and the relevant grounds for the request.[47] All forms must be filed with the Central Office of the High Court before the application for leave is made.[48] Where the court refuses to allow an *ex parte* application for judicial review, either in whole or in part, the applicant can appeal to the Supreme Court.[49] The application must be made within four days from the date of refusal although the court can extend that time limit. The process requires the applicant to provide details of the grounds of appeal in writing to the registrar of the court. However, it would appear that a respondent in a judicial review case does not have a right to appeal a leave decision.[50]

---

[43] Rules of the Superior Courts (Judicial Review) (SI No 691 of 2011), Ord 84 r 20(1).

[44] The respondent is not informed of the application and is not present at the leave hearing.

[45] The required forms for the Statement of Grounds are found in Appendix T of the Rules of the Superior Courts — SI No 691 of 2011: Rules of the Superior Courts (Judicial Review) 2011, Form 13. Available at: http://www.courts.ie/rules.nsf/SuperiorAmdLookup/NoT-S.I.+No.+691+Of+2011:+Rules+Of+The+Superior+Courts+(Judicial+Review)+2011+-+Forms+13+&+14 (date accessed 30 June 2014).

[46] Hearsay evidence should not be relied upon as part of the application, Ord 40, r 4.

[47] Rule 20(2)(1)(iii).

[48] Practice Direction HC02 — Judicial Review. Available at: http://www.courts.ie/courts.ie/library3.nsf/66d7c83325e8568b80256ffe00466ca0/52b148d2d9d6dd0480256ff60040906d?OpenDocument (date accessed 3 September 2014).

[49] Rules of the Superior Court, Ord 58, r 13. As Hogan and Morgan note the granting of leave can also be understood as being a "decision" of the High Court and therefore appealable under Art 34.4.3° of the Constitution. Hogan and Morgan, above n 15 at para 16-61.

[50] Hogan and Morgan, *ibid* highlight the decision in *State (Hughes) v O'Hanrahan* [1986] ILRM 218 where the Court indicated that it was unlikely that anyone other than the applicant could appeal against an *ex parte* order. However, no reasons were provided for this view. The course of action open to a respondent would be to bring a motion for the Court to set aside, see *Adams v DPP* [2001] 2 ILRM 401.

The leave stage is designed to prevent frivolous and meritless cases [13–22] clogging up the court system by removing them early; this is one of the reasons for having the application made on an *ex parte* basis. However, changes to the application process in 2011 have provided that the Court may:

> "having regard to the issues arising, the likely impact of the proceedings on the respondent or another party, or for the other good and sufficient reason, direct that the application for leave should be heard on notice and adjourn the application for leave on such terms as it may direct and give such directions as it thinks fit as to the service of notice of the application for leave (and copies of the statement of grounds, affidavit and any exhibits) on the intended respondent and on any other person, the mode of service and the time allowed for such service".[51]

In addition, the rules go on to allow for an application for leave to be treated as a full application stage of judicial review if the parties consent.[52] At the present time, we have little or no guidance as to what circumstances the Court will regard as being appropriate to proceed a leave hearing to take place on notice.

The principal changes introduced by the new rule 20 which came into force [13–23] at the start of 2012 relate to the drafting of the statement grounding the application, as well as the question of whether an interlocutory injunction or stay should be granted alongside leave. In terms of the pre-existing position, the classic case of *G v Director of Public Prosecutions*[53] provided an oft cited summary of the issues which should be *prima facie* established in the applicant affidavit in order that leave can be given. While stressing that his enumerated criteria were not intended to be exhaustive, Finlay CJ highlighted the following issues as requiring determination:

a) That the applicant has sufficient interest in the matter to which the application relates to comply with rule 20(4);

---

[51] Ord 18 r 24(1).

[52] Ord 18 r 24(2).

[53] Above n 39. The facts of G were as follows: the applicant sought an order of prohibition/injunction to prevent his trial on 27 charges of sex abuse from proceeding arguing that the delay in prosecution caused him incurable prejudice. Lavan J in the High Court had refused to grant leave to apply for judicial review on the basis that the offences charged did not include a time limit for prosecution. On appeal to the Supreme Court leave was granted, Finlay CJ holding that in applying the tests laid out the question of whether the lapse of time created a presumption of prejudice was a sufficient prima facie case to be determined at a full hearing.

b) That the facts averred in the affidavit would be sufficient, if proved, to support a stateable ground in the form of relief sought by way of judicial review;

c) That on those facts an arguable case in law can be made that the applicant is entitled to the relief which he seeks;

d) That the application has been made promptly and in any event within the three months;

e) That the only effective remedy, on the facts established by the applicant, which the applicant could obtain would be an order by way of judicial review or, if there be an alternative remedy, that the application by way of judicial review is, on all the facts of the case, a more appropriate method of procedure.[54]

[13–24] On point (d) above this is provided for in Order 84, rule 21(1), with an extension available where the court is satisfied that there is good reason for doing so.

While the appropriateness of available remedies may feature prominently at the leave stage, Finlay CJ reiterated that the remedies in judicial review remain at all times discretionary in nature. Ultimately it is key that the applicant establish that s/he has an arguable case in law, which is generally seen by the courts as being a "light" requirement.[55] In addition, the applicant must establish good faith; meaning that s/he should "make full and fair disclosure of all of the relevant facts of which he knows".[56]

[13–25] The 2012 amendments specified a number of required elements to be included within the statement grounding an application to judicial review. Under Order 84, rule 20(2)(a) a statement must contain, *inter alia*:

"(ii) a statement of each relief sought and of the particular grounds upon which each such relief is sought.

(iii) where any interim relief is sought, a statement of the orders sought by way of interim relief relief and a statement of the particular grounds upon which each order is sought".

[13–26] In addition to setting out mandatory details to be included in applications, both the courts and now the rules, have crafted a set of categories for which information is expected, though not obliged, to be provided by the applicant to the court. While these requirements are of course important in and of

---

[54] *ibid* at 377-8.

[55] *Per* Denham J, *ibid* at 381.

[56] *Adams v Director of Public Prosecutions* [2001] 2 ILRM 401 at 416 per Kelly J.

themselves to any practitioner, the reader will also see that they provide an interesting insight into the baseline level of professional conduct which the courts expect from counsel in public law matters. The years prior to the amendment of Order 84 saw a number of strongly worded statements by the courts regarding the paucity of detail and information, perhaps the most memorable of which was that of Cooke J in *Lofinmakin v Minister for Justice and Law Reform*:

> "The Court would take this opportunity to emphasise that judicial review under Order 84 of the Rules of the Superior Courts is not a form of forensic hoopla in which a player has at once tossed large numbers of grounds in the air like rings in the hope that one at least will land on the prize marked '*certiorari*'. In the judgment of the Court a Statement of Grounds under Order 84, is inadmissible to the extent that it fails to specify with precision the exact illegality or other flaw in an impugned act or measure which is claimed to require that it be quashed by such an order".[57]

Such statements may, in requiring greater specificity, correct the pattern **[13–27]** evident in many recent High Court judgments, where a matter, in addition to a core claim, features a sootfall of duplicative, under-developed grounds which are disposed in short order by the relevant judge.[58] Rule (20)(3) now further injuncts counsel against over general approaches:

> "It shall not be sufficient for an applicant to give as any of his grounds for the purposes of paragraphs (ii) or (iii) of sub-rule 2(a) an assertion in general terms of the ground concerned, but the applicant should state precisely each such ground, giving particulars where appropriate, and identify in respect of each ground the facts or matters relied upon as supporting that ground".

The standards of drafting required by rule 20(3) also receive a supporting **[13–28]** mechanism for enforcement in rule 20(4). Alongside the well-established

---

[57] [2011] IEHC 38 at para 8. Quoted by Daniel Donnelly BL, "Changes to Judicial Review Procedure", *Bar Review*, 2012 at p 3. Donnelly also cites the judgment of Murray CJ in *AP v Director of Public Prosecutions* [2011] 1 IR 729 where he stated, at 733:
> "In short it is incumbent on the parties to judicial review to assist the High Court, and consequentially this court on appeal, by ensuring that grounds for judicial review are stated clearly and precisely and that any additional grounds, subsequent to leave being granted, are raised only after an appropriate order has been applied for and obtained."

[58] We might note in addition, that stronger jurisprudence from the courts regarding the operation of different yet often overlapping grounds of judicial review would also assist this drafting process.

discretion to allow a statement of grounds accompanying an application to amended, this rule also allows the court to require amendment where it is of the view that further particulars regarding the reliefs sought are necessary.[59]

Granting of Leave and Interim Relief

[13–29] As evidenced by rule 20(2)(a)(iii) above, the preparation of a leave application also requires the question of interim relief to be addressed. The new rules have strengthened the functional separation between the granting of leave and provision of interim relief, with rule 20(8) stating:

> "Where leave to apply for judicial review is granted then the Court, should it consider it just and convenient to do so, may, on such terms as it thinks fit:
>
> (a) grant such interim relief as could be granted in an action begun by plenary summons,
> (b) where the relief sought is an order of prohibition or certiorari, make an order staying the proceedings, order or decision to which the application relates until the determination of the application for judicial review or until the Court otherwise orders."

[13–30] In *obiter* comments in the case of *PI & EI v Minister for Justice and Law Reform*,[60] Hogan J noted that under the new rule 20(8) the "just and convenient" requirement is now installed more firmly than in the previous wording. Thus, the long established *Campus Oil* test,[61] seemed to apply to requests for a stay or interlocutory injunction, requiring the applicant to make out that an arguable issue has been raised, that the provision of damages would not suffice and that the balance of convenience justifies the

---

[59] In *Babington v Minister for Justice* [2012] IESC 65 at para 7, McMenamin J, referring to the requirements in Form No 13 that the applicant should precisely set out the grounds, rather wearily bemoaned the poor state pleadings coming before the court:

"Regrettably, these explicit stipulations are frequently not complied with, and the same grounds are set out in as many different, varying, (and wearying) reformulations of the same point as can be conceived. Practitioners should realise that, in this entirely counterproductive and unnecessary process, there is a real risk of not being able to see the wood for the trees. A good point does not gain force by repetition. In fact, the contrary is true. What is required is simply a succinct statement of the grounds. ... Once the precise grounds are set out, succinctly, practitioners should then, simply set out and identify in respect of each ground, "the facts or matters relied upon as supporting that ground". Thus, no material issue will be omitted."

[60] *PI & EI v Minister for Justice and Law Reform* [2012] IEHC 7 at para 9.

[61] *Campus Oil v The Minister for Energy* [1983] 1 IR 88.

interim remedy. In the recent case of *Okunade v Minister for Justice, Equality and Law Reform*,[62] however, the Supreme Court appeared to indicate that some adaptation of the *Campus Oil* requirements are required. Emphasising the second (damages) and third (balance of convenience) elements of the *Campus Oil* test, the Court outlined how judges should tailor their analysis for the specific context of judicial review.[63] In relation to the adequacy of damages, Clarke J stressed that as a result of *Kennedy v Law Society*,[64] an individual can only obtain damages from a public authority in "very limited circumstances". In relation to the "balance of convenience" the court highlighted the distinct interest of a public authority to carry out its statutory remit:

> "There is a further feature of judicial review proceedings which is rarely present in ordinary injunctive proceedings. The entitlement of those who are given statutory or other power and authority so as to conduct specified types of legally binding decision-making or action taking is an important part of the structure of a legal order based on the rule of law. Recognising the entitlement of such persons or bodies to carry out their remit without undue interference is an important feature of any balancing exercise. It seems to me to follow that significant weight needs to be placed into the balance on the side of permitting measures which are prima facie valid to be carried out in a regular and orderly way. Regulators are entitled to regulate. Lower courts are entitled to decide. Ministers are entitled to exercise powers lawfully conferred by the Oireacthas. The list can go on. All due weight needs to be accorded to allowing the systems and processes by which lawful power is to be exercised to operate in an orderly fashion."[65]

The Role of the Leave Stage

The leave stage is a well established feature of judicial review in common law jurisdictions. In some ways, it can be understood as operating to protect public bodies from vexatious litigation, as identified by Denham J in *G v Director of Public Prosecutions*[66] when she stated that the leave stage was to "effect a screening process of litigation against public bodies and officers" **[13–31]**

---

[62] *Okunade v Minister for Justice, Equality and Law Reform* [2012] IESC 49.

[63] *ibid* at paras 9.25-9.30.

[64] *Kennedy v Law Society* [2005] IESC 23.

[65] Above n 62 at para 9.30. See G Simons, (2013) 1 "Aspects of New Judicial Review Procedure", *Irish Jurist* 227 in which he concludes his article with this extensive quote, which represents, in our view, an excellent encapsulating the overarching emphasis of many of the 2012 changes to Order 84. Hereinafter "Simons".

[66] Above n 39.

and "to prevent an abuse of the process, trivial or unstateable cases proceeding and thus impeding public authorities unnecessarily".[67]

[13–32] There are, however, arguments against it; including one that it allows viable claims to potentially be rejected.[68] This significant problem should not be under estimated, and can be exacerbated where there is inconsistency in the decision-making process at the leave stage.

[13–33] The extent to which the leave procedure might be better used to encourage resolution of cases prior to court should also be explored. As Bondy and Sunkin note in relation to the experience in England and Wales the leave process is:

> "not designed to encourage early resolution of disputes. The structure of the pre-trial procedure was principally intended to enable weak cases to be filtered from the system, in order to protect the court from unwarranted litigation and to save defendants from having to expend resources responding to unarguable cases. While these aims were laudable in themselves, they led to a system that did little to promote early engagement between the parties."[69]

[13–34] The UK Law Commission noted in its 1993 Consultation Paper that the leave requirement was meant to filter the "hopeless applications" which was "essential" in terms of the management of cases.[70] A year later it published a report which critiqued the procedures as operating

> "as a disincentive to public authorities to review their decisions at an early stage with a view to reaching settlements with prospective applicants for judicial review".[71]

[13–35] As a result the UK introduced reforms in 2000[72] to include more involvement of defendants at the leave stage. Thus, the "pre-action protocol" (PAP) allows for applicants to send a letter to the defendant setting out the

---

[67] *ibid* at 383.

[68] M Sunkin, L Bridges and G Meszaros, *Judicial Review in Perspective* (Public Law Project, London, 1993).

[69] V Bondy and M Sunkin, *The Dynamics of Judicial Review Litigation: The Resolution of Public Law Challenges Before Final Hearing* (Public Law Project, London, 2009) at p 34. Hereinafter "Bondy and Sunkin".

[70] United Kingdom Law Commission, *Law Commission Consultation Paper No. 126* (1993) HMSO at para 2.16.

[71] Law Commission, *Administrative Law: Judicial Review and Statutory Appeals* (Law Commission No 226, 1994) at para 1.11.

[72] Part 54 of the Civil Procedure Rules.

decision being challenged, a summary of the facts on which the claim is made, aspects of the information being sought and the disputed issues. The idea of such contact, which is not compulsory but is expected by the courts, is to see if the dispute can be resolved without resort to litigation.[73] These reforms were, in turn, criticised for making the leave stage more complex leading it to be used both for controlling access to judicial review and in relation to "managing the substantive dispute".[74]

The LRC considered the possibility of developing such a system although   [13–36]
its report on judicial review acknowledges that "there is ordinarily little scope for alternative dispute resolution in judicial review."[75] Nevertheless the report recommended a similar pre-action protocol approach to that adopted in the UK whereby:

> "the applicant should send to the respondent a letter informing the respondent that failure to concede the claim within 10 days will result in the applicant proceeding to seek leave to apply for judicial review."[76]

To date this has not been adopted.

The idea of pre-action contact is present in other areas of administrative   [13–37]
justice. For example in our chapters on the Ombudsman (chapter 4) and the Information Commissioner (chapter 3) we highlight that the procedures adopted by both of these bodies actively encourage a "fresh look" approach by which the public body revisits their decision in light of a viable complaint. However, judicial review, as it currently operates, does not readily facilitate this tending instead towards a crystallisation of positions by the parties.

The possibility that applicants for judicial review might opt for an   [13–38]
alternative dispute resolution system over judicial review, such as the Ombudsman, is attractive in a system where judicial review is costly and likely to be subject to delays. However, it should be remembered that ADR may in many cases be unsuitable:

---

[73] Pre action protocol is described at: www.justice.gov.uk/civil/procrules_fin/contents/protocols/prot_jrv.htm (date accessed 30 June 2014). The defendant should respond within 14 days.

[74] T Cornford and M Sunkin, "The Bowman Report, access and the recent reforms of the judicial review procedure" [2001] *Public Law* 11 at p 15. Waiting times in England/Wales have grown during the 2000s suggesting that the procedure has not successfully reduced delays overall.

[75] LRC (2003) above n 14 at para 4.03, referencing a similar review by the Lord Chancellor's Department in the UK: *Review of the Crown Office List* (Lord Chancellor's Dept, London, 2000).

[76] *ibid* at para 4.06.

> "ADR is not a panacea, and its use in administrative disputes should not undermine the overriding function and goal of administrative law to maintain government accountability. In some circumstances ADR is simply inappropriate, for example, where the dispute raises issues of public concern, such as ecologically sustainable development, and where the parties wish to test a statutory provision or establish a legal precedent."[77]

On this last point, the authors note with concern the fact that some judicial review cases never do proceed to a full hearing before the High Court, being settled on the steps of the court house, not as a pre-action resolution but as a last ditch action.[78] Practice such as this by public bodies undermines the point stressed by Preston J in the quote above regarding the goal of administrative law being to maintain Government accountability.

Time Limits

[13–39]   The imposition of strict time limits within the judicial review process is designed to ensure that the remedy operates as a quick and efficient process. Nevertheless it remains the case that delay can be a significant factor. This can impact upon applicants, respondents and third parties. A challenge to a decision of a public body will suspend the decision-making process, leaving licence holders unable to do business, public bodies unable to implement decisions and applicants deprived of claimed entitlements. In the recent Supreme Court case of *Shell E & P Ireland Ltd v McGrath*, Clarke J highlighted the broad public interest factors at play in any imposition of a time limit:

> "The underlying reason why the rules of court impose a relatively short timeframe in which challenges to public law measures should be brought is because of the desirability of bringing finality to qustions concerning the validity of such measures within a relatively short timeframe. At least at the level of broad generality there is a significant public interest advantage in early certainty as to the validity or otherwise of such public law measures. People are entitled to order

---

[77] Hon. Justice Preston, "The Use of Alternative Dispute Resolution in Administrative Disputes", Paper presented to Symposium on *Guarantee of the Right to Access to the Administrative Jurisdiction*, March 9 2011, Bangkok, Thailand.

[78] D O'Donovan, "Silent, Everyday Scandals: Appealing Departmental Decision Making in Ireland", *Human Rights in Ireland Blog*, February 28 2014. Available online at http:// humanrights.ie/children-and-the-law/silent-everyday-scandals-appealing-departmental-decision-making-in-ireland/ (date accessed 30 August 2014).

their affairs on the basis that a measure, apparently valid on its face, can be relied on. That entitlement applies just as much to public authorities. The underlying rationale for short timeframes within which judicial review proceedings can be brought is, therefore, clear and of sufficient weight. By permitting time to be extended the rules do, of course, recognise that there may be circumstances where, on the facts of an individual case, a departure from the strict application on whatever timescale might be provided is warranted. The rules do not purport to impose an absolute time period."[79]

Until recently Order 84, rule 21(1) provided that an application for judicial review should be made   **[13–40]**

"promptly, and in any event within three months from the date when grounds for the application first arose, or six months where the relief sought is *certiorari*, unless the court considers that there is good reason for extending the period within which the application shall be made".

Somewhat controversially, in amending Order 84 in 2012[80] the time limit for *certiorari* was reduced from six months to three. The amended rule 21 thus requires that an application for leave for judicial review should be made within three months of the date when the grounds for review initially occurred. In addition, the rule no longer states that the applicant should apply "promptly".   **[13–41]**

The court may now extend the three month period firstly if it is satisfied that there is "good and sufficient reason", with due regard to the effects of such an extension on the respondent and or any third party. Secondly, if it is satisfied that the circumstances giving rise to a delayed application were outside the control of the application, or could not be reasonably anticipated. Such variation has been seen previously in the planning context. In *Brady v Donegal County Council*,[81] the applicant was technically "timed out", having applied after the eight week deadline for planning law actions. It was successfully argued that the time limit should not be absolute, however, due to the fact that there had been a defect in the public notices which the developer was required to publish, which had contributed to the applicant having had delayed notice of the planning application at issue. In the circumstances, the Court exercised its discretion and found that the delay was not, in the circumstances, fatal to the action.   **[13–42]**

---

[79] *Shell E & P Ireland Ltd v McGrath* [2013] IESC 1, Clarke J at para 7.6. Hereinafter "Shell".

[80] Rules of the Superior Court (Judicial Review) 2011 above n 43.

[81] *Brady v Donegal County Council* [1989] ILRM 282.

[13–43]   Clearly, a crucial issue regarding any time limit is the question - when does the clock begin to tick? Rule 21 states that the time period runs from the "date when the grounds for the application first arose" rather than the time when the applicant first became aware of the grounds.[82] It is important that the approach taken to the time limit is reflective of values underpinning our schema of constitutional justice. Simons argues, in our view correctly, that

> "if a public authority wishes to avail itself of the benefit of the time limit, then it should ensure that it communicates any *decision* it makes in a formal document".[83]

[13–44]   Construing Order 84 therefore directs us back to the proper conduct of public authorities towards the individual. Simons instances[84] the recent judgment of *Pearce v Westmeath County Council*,[85] a case concerning a planning condition, as particularly instructive. There Hedigan J ruled that, while a public authority possesses a "broad discretion" in how such a decision should be recorded:

> "...a decision should at the every least be recorded in a document that:
>
> (a) clearly identifies itself as a formal record of a decision on compliance with a specific condition or conditions of a planning permission granted.
> (b) Unambiguously and precisely states that in the view of the local authority a specified condition has been complied with.
> (c) Is signed and dated by an officer indicating that he/she is authorised to make such a decision."[86]

[13–45]   In practice, in situations where a decision might not be entirely finalised or subject to a review, the applicant may not have to apply until the decision becomes active. For example, in the case of *CC v Ireland (No 1)*[87] the applicant was not out of time in relation to his application for judicial review because he could wait until the indictment was served. There is some potential difficulty with the new framing of the time limit, rooted as it is in the key phrase "the date when the grounds for the application first arose". This

---

[82] *Veolia Water UK Plc v Fingal County Council* [2007] 1 ILRM 216.
[83] Simons, above n 65 at p 227.
[84] *ibid* at p 228.
[85] *Pearce v Westmeath County Council* [2012] IEHC 300, See Simons, *ibid* at 229.
[86] *ibid* at para 5.7.
[87] *CC v Ireland (No 1)* [2006] 4 IR 1.

wording does not actually use the term "decision", raising the question as to whether the clock begins to run on interim decisions or steps when they are completed. Finally, it should be noted that should new facts emerge this can be taken into account by the court in relation to the question of the extension of time limits.

The key phrase "the date when the grounds for the application first arose"   [13–46] also raises a further potential difficulty. As we highlight in chapter 14 on European Union law and judicial review, where possible some traditional substantive doctrines have been influenced by a judicial desire to ensure compatibility with European Union law understandings. Such considerations may influence the interpretations of the courts here, with Simons highlighting the examination of the application of Order 84 to public procurement proceedings by the Court of Justice in *Commission v Ireland* (C-456/08) as particularly significant.[88] The High Court in this matter had held that the three month time limit applied to interim decisions taken by the public authority during the procurement procedure, with the applicant not entitled to wait until the final decision. The CJEU held that the EU law principle of legal certainty required an express statement of this limitation in *relevant national legislation.*

Further controversy attaches to the possibility that the High Court may   [13–47] dismiss an application for leave on grounds of delay even where it is made within the three month limit. Three months is the maximum time but the application needs to be timely and the Court can reject an application on the basis that delay in bringing the application for leave caused or is likely to cause the respondent or a third party to be prejudiced. Under the 1986 scheme the Court had found that an applicant who had applied within the time limit might still be ruled to have failed to act promptly. Although the 2011 rule change drops the reference to promptness it continues to state that an application can be rejected within the time limit if "the applicant's delay in applying ... has caused or likely to cause prejudice".[89] Under the pre-existing rules, the courts had found that speed would be of the essence in cases such as where the case relates to the awarding of a licence to a third party and delay will impact on trading.[90] The deletion of the express promptness requirement in 2011,

---

[88] *C-456/08 Commission v Ireland* [2010] ECR I-859 340. Simons, above n 65 at p 229.
[89] Rule 21(6).
[90] *Dekra Éireann Teo v Minister for the Environment* [2003] 2 IR 270.

arguably brings Ireland closer to compliance with the requirements in EU law matters. Some have alleged similar difficulties here as pertained to the discretion regarding interim matters, with the European Union law principle of legal certainty requiring some predictability be identifiable to key Order 84 phrases such as "at the earliest opportunity". Simons nevertheless concludes that based on England and Wales case law "the courts may retain a discretion to dismiss proceedings where delay has adversely affected third parties".[91]

[13–48]   Returning to broader issues, the recent Supreme Court judgment in *Shell E & P Ireland Ltd v McGrath*,[92] has clearly signalled a firming up of the application of time limits to cases. In the past it was possible to apply for judicial review by way of plenary proceedings commenced without leave. The courts had previously restrained the use of such plenary action by declaring that Order 84, rule 21 will be applied by analogy, and that the court in its discretion could choose to view the action as an inappropriate evasion of the leave procedure.[93] With the tightening of time limits in 2012, some practitioners had speculated about the benefits of instituting a plenary action to circumvent the three month rule. Such a course of action has been expressly rejected by the Supreme Court in *Shell*, where Clarke J supported the application of the *O'Donnell* case, the authority had originally laid down the principle that the application for a plenary hearing would be treated as analogous to a judicial review application:

> "[His Honour discussed the status of *O'Donnell* as a precedent, noting its approval by Fennelly J in *Murphy & Ors v Flood*]… It seems to me that *O'Donnell* was rightly decided in any event. It would make a nonsense of the system of judicial review if a party could by-pass any obligations which arise in that system (such as time limits and the need to seek leave) simply by issuing plenary proceedings which, in substance, whatever about form, sought the same relief or the same substantive ends. What would be the point of courts considering applications for leave or considering applications to extend them if a party could simply by-pass that whole process by issuing a plenary summons?"[94]

---

[91] Simons, above n 65.

[92] *Shell*, above n 79.

[93] The ruling that a plenary action could be treated as analogous to a judicial review application was made by Costello J in *O'Donnell v Dun Laoighaire Corporation* [1991] ILRM 301. This approach was, in his Honour's view justified by the need to ensure the application of time limits consciously created to protect public authorities. See 314-315.

[94] Above n 79 at para 7.11.

Thus, while there could be circumstances when an individual faced with **[13–49]** "proceedings brought placing reliance on a public law measure"[95] might be justified in challenging the validity of the measure outside the Order 84(21) time frames, the Court could not countenance sanctioning a broad based pathway which could grow into an alternative pipeline to the leave process. The Supreme Court has also exercised its right to supervise the commencement of proceedings in *Arklow Homes Ltd v An Bord Pleanála*,[96] where it underlined that courts can dismiss proceedings where a litigant could have argued a point of law in earlier proceedings but chose not to. Where the litigant then embarks on further litigation, this prohibition, commonly referred to as the rule in *Henderson v Henderson*,[97] operates to prevent the "reheating" of issues which should have been brought to the boil in the earlier matter.

Given the complexities of getting a matter up and running, there is, of **[13–50]** course, provision for applications for an extension of time. Under the 1986 draft of the rules, a non-exhaustive list of key policy factors that were to be considered in deciding whether there was a good reason for extending the time limit was set out by Denham J:

> "In analysing the facts of a case to determine if there is a good reason to extend time or to allow judicial review, the court may take into account factors such as; (i) the nature of the order or actions subject of the application; (ii) the conduct of the applicant; (iii) the conduct of the respondents; (iv) the effect of the order under review on the parties subsequent to the order being made and any steps taken by the parties subsequent to the order to be reviewed; (v) any effect which may have taken place on third parties by the order to be reviewed; (vi) public policy that proceedings relating to the public law domain take place promptly except when good reason is furnished."[98]

In this case the applicant sought to challenge his summary dismissal from the Defence Forces 29 years after it had taken place. The court noted that delay in itself could operate to refuse relief.[99]

---

[95] *ibid* at para 7.12.

[96] *Arklow Homes Ltd v An Bord Pleanála* [2011] IESC 29.

[97] *Henderson v Henderson* (1843) 3 Hare 100.

[98] *De Roiste v. Minister for Defence* [2001] 1 IR 190 at 207.

[99] This decision went against the decision of McCarthy J in *State (Furey) v Minister for Defence* [1988] ILRM 89 at 100 that delay would not "of itself disentitle ... any applicant ... who can demonstrate that a public wrong has been done to him".

[13–51]   Where an applicant can provide evidence to the court that they have attempted to resolve their case through other means, this will generally be regarded favourably. Thus, if the applicant has tried to use other political,[100] legal[101] or alternative dispute resolution methods[102] this can "justify" a delay. However, this does not mean that the courts will allow any length of delay to be ignored just because the applicant was communicating with the other party:

> "... it cannot be the case that simply by corresponding with the respondents the applicant indefinitely extends the period within which he is obliged to commence proceedings .... If the case were otherwise, then the applicant could extend the time indefinitely, merely by engaging in letter writing. It must be remembered that O. 84, r.21(1) is not there simply for the convenience of the parties. It has a public dimension and it has been adopted to ensure the expeditious administration of justice."[103]

[13–52]   The test for an extension of time has, however, been made more stringent under the 2011 rules. Rule 21(3) states that the courts will only extend the time period if satisfied that:

> "(a) there is good and sufficient reason for doing so, and
> (b) the circumstances that resulted in the failure to make the application for leave within the period ... either
> (i)   were outside the control of the appicant
> (ii) Could not reasonably have been anticipated by the applicant for such extension."

As noted earlier, the court must also look at the possible impact on the respondent and/or third parties. These requirements appear more restrictive than the previous rules — for example, the word "sufficient" is now added to the previous requirement of "good reason".

[13–53]   A number of precedents have laid out the factors which bear upon the assessment of whether there is a good and sufficient reason for an extension. In *FA v Refugee Appeals Tribunal*,[104] Peart J stressed the length of the relevant delay, the reason for it, the *prima facie* strength of the applicants case and

---

[100] *O'Donnell v Corporation of Dun Laoghaire* [1991] ILRM 305.
[101] *Murphy v District Justice Wallace* [1993] 2 IR 138.
[102] *Bane v Garda Representative Association* [1997] 2 IR 449.
[103] See *McCarthy v Irish Prison Service* [2009] IEHC 331.
[104] *FA v Refugee Appeals Tribunal*, Unreported, High Court, 27 July 2007.

any other personal circumstances. Significantly, in the context of legal aid and access to justice, Peart J also noted the significance of whether legal advice was available to the applicant during the limited time period allowed for initiating review.[105] In *Kelly v Leitrim County Council*,[106] Clarke J highlighted similar factors, as well as the time limit laid down by the relevant statute, whether any third party rights were affected, the centrality of the time limit to legislative policy, the blameworthiness of the applicant and the nature of the rights involved. In *JA v Refugee Applications Commissioner*,[107] Irvine J acknowledged these factors, while also highlighting the need for a holistic consideration of the extent to which an injustice might be perpetrated were the court to fail to grant the extension. Finally, in *S v Minister for Justice, Equality and Law Reform*,[108] Denham J noted that the fact that the delay may be attributable to the applicant's legal advisors will not automatically suffice as a good reason. An individual's non-culpability for the delay did not render an extension automatic:

> "The delay in issue is essentially delay by legal advisors. Legal advisors have a duty to act with expedition in these cases. In general, delay by legal advisors will not prima facie be a good and sufficient reason to extend time. Circumstances must exist to excuse such a delay and to enable the matter to be considered further."[109]

In the event, the Court allowed an extension due to the complexity of legal issues involved, and the fact that there the decision had been made at a time when the law relating to asylum decisions was in a transitional period.[110]

Availability of Alternative Remedies

The existence of an alternative remedy that can be availed of by the applicant does not automatically prevent them from bringing an action for judicial review. Although in some jurisdictions this has been developed as

[13–54]

---

[105] The relevant time period for judicial review of asylum decisions was fourteen days.

[106] *Kelly v Leitrim County Council* [2005] 2 IR 404 at 412-3.

[107] *J.A. v. Refugee Applications Commissioner* [2009] 2 IR 231.

[108] *S v Minister for Justice, Equality and Law Reform*, Unreported, Supreme Court, 5 March 2002.

[109] *ibid* at para 11.

[110] The *S* case is discussed by Simons, above n 65 at p 230. He also cites the case of *Marshall v Arklow Town Council* [2004] 4 IR 92 as a rare example of a substantial, written judgment concerning this issue. In this case the limitation period had run over the Easter vacation and the court held that the difficulty accessing legal counsel should not, as a matter of fairness, count against the applicant.

a strict requirement,[111] in our jurisdiction the courts have tended to adopt a position whereby they have regard to the availability of adequate alternatives. In practice, as de Blacam states, there may be good reasons for requiring an applicant to exhaust her or his alternatives but a failure to do this does not automatically disbar the application for judicial review.[112]

[13–55]   In practice the courts have adopted competing approaches to the question. In many ways these different approaches are embodied in the differing Supreme Court justices' decisions in the *Abenglen* case.[113] This case is often used as the embodiment of the hard line approach requiring applicants to exhaust their remedies before a judicial review could be brought. The applicant sought an order of *certiorari* to quash planning conditions which had been attached to a grant of planning permission given by the respondents. As we have already noted in chapter 7, the decision of the Supreme Court in this case was heavily motivated by their dislike of the applicant's attempts to circumvent the appeal system operated by An Bord Pleanála. Henchy J found that the Oireachtas had provided "a self-contained administrative scheme" which was sufficient to meet the needs of the applicant and so the Court should not intervene[114] and refused to grant a remedy on the basis that the applicant should have appealed under the planning legislation.

[13–56]   An alternative approach was put forward by O'Higgins CJ in the same case when he concluded that whether the existence of a right of appeal or an alternative remedy should lead to exclusion was a matter best left to the discretion of the Court taking into account all the circumstances of the case:

> "The question immediately arises of the existence of a right of appeal or an alternative remedy as to the effect on the exercise of the court's discretion. It is well established that the existence of such a right or remedy ought not to prevent the court from acting. It seems to me to be a question of justice. The court ought to take into account all the circumstances of the case, including the purpose for which certiorari has been sought, the adequacy of the alternative remedy and, of course,

---

[111] This is the case for instance in England and Wales. See T Endicott, *Administrative Law* (2nd ed) (Oxford University Press, Oxford, 2011) at p 61 where he quotes Lord Scarman in *R v Inland Revenue Commissioners, ex parte Preston* [1985] AC 835 at 852: "a remedy by way of judicial review is not to be made available where an alternative remedy exists. This is a proposition of great importance."

[112] De Blacam, above n 2 at p 398.

[113] *State (Abenglen Properties Ltd) v Dublin Corporation* [1984] IR 381 at 393.

[114] *ibid* at 405.

the conduct of the applicant. If the decision impugned is made without jurisdiction or in breach of natural justice then, normally, the existence of a right of appeal or of a failure to avail of such, should be immaterial. Again, if an appeal can only deal with the merits and not with the question of the jurisdiction involved, the existence of such ought not to be a ground for refusing relief. Other than these, there may be cases where the decision exhibits an error of law and a perfectly simple appeal can rectify the complaint, or where administrative legislation provides adequate appeal machinery which is particularly suitable for dealing with errors in the application of the code in question. In such cases, while retaining always the power to quash, the court should be slow to do so, unless satisfied that, for some particular reason, the appeal or alternative remedy is not adequate."[115]

This approach seemed to hold sway in *P&F Sharpe v Dublin City and County Manager*[116] where the Court underlined the differing goals of the appeals and review systems:

[13–57]

"The powers of An Bord Pleanála on the making of an appeal to it would be entirely confined to the consideration of the matters before it on the basis of the proper planning and development of the area and it would have no jurisdiction to consider the question of the validity, from a legal point of view, of the purported decision of the county manager."[117]

The Court therefore concluded that excluding a judicial review in such circumstances would be unjust. Although a restrictive approach was seen in *Abenglen,* other more flexible rulings have been evident since, as illustrated by the statement of Denham J in *Tomlinson v Criminal Injuries Compensation Tribunal*:

"The existence of the alternative remedy does not prevent the Court from exercising its discretion as to whether or not to grant judicial review. While a court would lean towards requiring that the remedies available under the scheme be exhausted, the ultimate decision depends on the circumstances of the case."[118]

---

[115] *ibid* at 393. On the facts of *Abenglen* the court found against the applicant. This approach was followed in a series of planning cases as set out by Hogan and Morgan above n 15 at paragraph 16-174, footnote 438 although more recent cases have adopted the discretion based approach found elsewhere — see *McGoldrick v An Bord Pleanála* [1997] 1 IR 497.

[116] *P&F Sharpe v Dublin City and County Manager* [1989] IR 701.

[117] *ibid* at 721.

[118] *Tomlinson v Criminal Injuries Compensation Tribunal* [2006] 4 IR 321 at 327. The applicant in this case applied to the respondent for compensation under the Scheme of Compensation for Personal Injuries Criminally Inflicted in respect of the death of her husband. The

[13–58] The Supreme Court rowed back from the High Court's decision that a court could not intervene before the process envisaged under the scheme has been exhausted. Thus, even though the applicant had not utilised the alternative remedy to judicial review, this fact alone was not enough to exclude the applicant from the court. Here the "more just remedy" was not that provided under the scheme but that potentially offered by judicial review.

[13–59] The later High Court decision in *O'Connor v Private Residential Tenancies Board and another,*[119] a case involving a refusal of an extension of time, did display a preference for a strict approach. In this case the applicant could have appealed the respondent board's decision, but he did not avail of this right even though he had received a letter informing him of his appeal rights. Hedigan J held that the fact "the applicant may have decided that judicial review was the more convenient remedy cannot avail him here".

[13–60] In practice the Court will have regard to the purpose of the relief sought and the nature of the error alleged. Where a complaint relates to procedural unfairness or a jurisdictional error the courts may take the view that an alternative remedy is not relevant. Thus in *Stefan v Minister for Justice,*[120] Denham J stated:

> "[T]he original decision was made in circumstances which were in breach of fair procedures and which resulted in a decision against the appellant on information which was incomplete. The appeals authority process would not be appropriate or adequate so as to withhold certiorari. The applicant is entitled to a primary decision in accordance with fair procedures and an appeal from that decision. A fair appeal does not cure an unfair hearing."[121]

---

respondent found in her favour, but made a significant deduction from her award. Notwithstanding that there was an appeal *de novo* under the scheme to a panel of three members of the respondent; she applied for judicial review, challenging the jurisdiction of the respondent to make that deduction.

[119] *O'Connor v Private Residential Tenancies Board and another* [2008] IEHC 205.

[120] *Stefan v Minister for Justice* [2001] 4 IR 203

[121] *ibid* at 218. The case involved an asylum application in which not all documents were set before the decision maker because of a translation error. However, in practice the courts have tended to adopt a position in relation to immigration cases that it is preferable that an applicant should exhaust his or her right of appeal to the tribunal unless there are compelling reasons for suggesting that this would otherwise be unjust or that the error could not be satisfactorily corrected on appeal.

Such rulings are still presented, however, as exceptions to the general rule. **[13–61]**
This was underlined by Clarke J in the recent case of *EMI Records (Ireland)
Ltd. v The Data Protection Commissioner*:

> "...the overall approach is clear. The default position is that a party
> should pursue a statutory appeal rather than initiate judicial review
> proceedings. The reason for this approach is ... that it must be presumed
> that the Oireachtas, in establishing a form of statutory appeal, intended
> that such an appeal was to be the means by which, ordinarily, those
> dissatisfied with an initial decision might be entitled to have the initial
> decision questioned."[122]

However, the Court went on to stress that there would be "exceptional **[13–62]**
cases" where "the justice of the case will not be met by confining a person
to the statutory appeal and excluding judicial review".[123] Although Clarke J
noted that the courts have not confined themselves to such circumstances,
they have acknowledged that recourse to judicial review may be available
where:

> "...because of constitutional difficulties or other circumstances where
> the body to whom the statutory appeal lies would not have jurisdiction
> to deal with all the issues. Likewise, there may be cases where, in all the
> circumstances, the allegation of the aggrieved party is that they were
> deprived of the reality of a proper consideration of the issues such that
> confining them to an appeal would be in truth depriving them of their
> entitlement to two hearings."[124]

Despite these various authorities, the courts have generally been seen to **[13–63]**
move towards a position that balances the competing interests and takes
into account the issues raised by the applicant. Thus, as Delany notes, the
Court will consider whether those issues

> "can be adequately dealt with in an appeal on the merits or whether
> questions of legality have been properly put forward which can only
> be addressed in judicial review proceedings".[125]

Finally it is worth noting that here, as in other areas of judicial review, there **[13–64]**
are different ways of understanding the approaches taken by the courts.

---

[122] *EMI Records (Ireland) Ltd v The Data Protection Commissioner* [2013] IESC 34 at para 4.8.
[123] *ibid.*
[124] *ibid* at para 4.9.
[125] H Delaney "The relevance of the availability of an alternative remedy in judicial review
proceedings" ILT 2009, 27(1), 10 at p 11.

Indeed, Hogan and Morgan highlight that the two main lines of authorities are grounded on difference policy approaches.[126] The restrictive approach, exemplified by the majority view in *Abenglen*, considers that if an applicant has a fair full appeal available to them then the law is adequately responding to any concern regarding the original decision. The more nuanced approach, as set out in *Sharpe* is that the applicant is entitled to have an initial decision made correctly — thus avoiding the cost and upset of an appeal.

[13–65]   Hogan and Morgan argue that the differing approaches are attributable to two separate justifications: the first focussed upon the rights of the individual applicant, the second and anchored in a broader desire to strengthen the administrative decision-making system. Under this second approach, the availability of an alternative remedy should not prevent the court exercising its discretion to hear the case. Ultimately they argue that both approaches can be housed in one over-arching principle:

> "[s]ome consistency can be built upon a reasonable principle by considering, in the context of a given case and the alleged blemish, exactly how comprehensive and appropriate is the right of appeal provided."[127]

[13–66]   In many ways the courts have in recent times moved to adopt this approach; Barron J in *McGoldrick v An Bord Pleanála* set out the following:

> "The real question to be determined when an appeal lies is the relative merits of an appeal as against the granting of relief by way of judicial review. It is not just a question whether an alternative remedy exists or whether the applicant has taken steps to pursue such remedy. The true question is which is the more appropriate remedy considered in the context of common sense, the ability to deal with the questions raised and principle of fairness; provided, of course, that the applicant has not gone too far down one road to be stopped from changing his or her mind."[128]

[13–67]   As we noted at the start of this discussion, the above should not be regarded by the reader as a full account of the procedure for judicial review. However, the reader should note some key themes, in particular the fact that although the procedure is now framed by Order 84 RSC, it remains

---

[126] Hogan and Morgan above n 15 at paras 16-184 – 16-185.
[127] *ibid* at para 16-185.
[128] *McGoldrick v An Bord Pleanála* [1997] 1 IR 497 at 509.

highly flexible and able to respond to the wider issues of the rights of applicants and the public interest in ensuring good public administration. We turn next to the issue of remedies, which are deeply intertwined with the wider procedure.

Remedies

The scope and impact of remedies in judicial review are of course critical to their overall impact. The courts are generally cautious in expanding remedies too far, despite the pressures that may be placed on them by applicants who may seek novel interventions. A core theme that runs through the area of remedies is their fundamentally discretionary nature. In this section we will set out a general overview of the core remedies available to an applicant, and some of the central issues which influence the court's discretion in granting them.[129]   [13–68]

There are primarily six remedies available: four traditional public law remedies of *certiorari, mandamus, quo warranto*, prohibition and two private law remedies of declaration and injunction. In addition, damages may also be available, as can restitution,[130] in appropriate cases. Following the adoption of Order 84 of the Rules of the Superior Court in 1986 the remedies are now interchangeable and an applicant cannot be refused on the basis that they have chosen the incorrect type of remedy.   [13–69]

Certiorari

Certiorari is the most commonly sought remedy in judicial review proceedings[131] and it operates to quash a decision taken in excess of legal authority by a body exercising an adjudicatory function within the public sphere. As the Law Reform Commission Report on Remedies stated this idea of "excess of ... legal authority" has been broadly understood to include: (a) where there is a complete absence of jurisdiction; (b) where the procedure used was in breach of constitutional justice; and (c) where there   [13–70]

---

[129] The following review is not intended to be an extensive review of remedies in this area, for more detail see de Blacam, above n 2 part VIII.

[130] For more detail on restitution see Hogan and Morgan, above n 15 at paras 18-184 – 18-206.

[131] This is largely based on the views of those within the profession and the authors' own bibliographies of judicial review jurisprudence. It must be noted, however, that the Courts Service do not provide a detailed breakdown of data on remedies in judicial review cases.

is an error on the face of the record.[132] O'Higgins CJ described the remedy in the *Abenglen* case as being "the great remedy available to citizens" with its purpose being "to supervise the exercise of jurisdiction by such bodies or tribunals and to control any usurpation or action in excess of jurisdiction".[133]

[13–71] The impact of an order of *certiorari* is that the parties should be restored to their original positions. Assuming the body remains vested with the power, the decision will need to be made again. Given the nature of judicial review as a mechanism there is nothing to prevent the same decision being made so long as the body has the power to do so and on the second attempt carries out that power in the correct way. Of course, the decision of the court may provide some indication to the deciding body as to how the decision making process should be carried out. In addition, if the court regards it necessary to ensure that the decision making body reconsider the matter it may also make an order of *mandamus* to compel the decision maker so to act.

[13–72] Under Order 84 rule 26(4) RSC the court may, after quashing a decision, remit it back to the decision-making body.[134] The High Court may direct that the reconsideration of the case be done by a differently constituted body thus ensuring that the issue is considered afresh. Clearly the reconsideration needs to be done in line with the High Court's decision; however case law does suggest that new material may be considered.[135]

Mandamus

[13–73] This order operates to compel a public body to carry out a duty imposed on it by law. The duty may arise through statute,[136] common law or contract. One problem arises in relation to this is the nature of the duty and whether it is sufficient to form the basis of the remedy. As de Blacam notes, some duties are absolute and will therefore straightforwardly give rise to a claim

---

[132] LRC (1979) above n 9 at para 2.4.

[133] *Abenglen*, above n 113 at 392.

[134] For more detail see de Blacam above n 2 at paras 39.05 – 39.15.

[135] de Blacam, *ibid* at para 39.15 notes the English cases of *R v Immigration Appeal Tribunal, ex parte Singh* [1987] 1 WLR 1394 and *R v Birmingham Juvenile Court, ex parte G* [1989] 3 WLR 1024.

[136] For example in *R (Jackson) v Sligo County Council* (1990) 34 ILTR an order of *mandamus* was made in relation to a duty to repair a court house.

of mandamus.[137] However, in other cases the courts will have to have regard to a duty that is framed in wide terms.[138]

Before this remedy can be provided the law required that there must have been a demand made on the body or person to carry out their duty which has been refused. A refusal can be inferred from the circumstances.[139]   **[13–74]**

Finally it should be noted that the courts are often reluctant to grant this order particularly where an alternative "equally effective and convenient remedy"[140] exists. This reluctance is particularly apparent where the failure to fulfill the duty arises due to a lack of available resources. In such a situation the court will be more at ease with ordering a declaration. Equally, if it is unlikely that an order of *mandamus* can be followed by the respondent the court will not grant relief. Thus, Maguire CJ in the Supreme Court stated   **[13–75]**

> "It is, of course, correct that an order will not be made if it is clear that it would be impossible of performance by reason of the circumstances that the doing of the act will involve a contravention of law or if the defendants have not the means of complying with the order."[141]

Prohibition

An order of probation operates to restrain a person or a body from starting or continuing a particular course of action which is in excess of jurisdiction. It is related to *certiorari* in that it operates to keep inferior courts within their jurisdiction. The only difference between the two remedies is whether the remedy is forward looking or backward looking. Thus *prohibition* seeks to prevent an order before it comes into effect rather than quashing the order afterwards as with *certiorari*. The use of this remedy is rare as it is not often that an applicant is aware of the unlawfulness before action is taken.   **[13–76]**

In practice the primary use of the remedy of prohibition is in relation to criminal prosecutions where the applicant seeks to prevent a trial going ahead on the grounds that there is a real or serious risk of unfairness should   **[13–77]**

---

[137] de Blacam, above n2 at para 29.03.
[138] *State (Modern Homes (Ireland) Ltd) v Dublin Corporation* [1953] IR 202.
[139] *R (Butler) v Navan U.D.C.* [1926] IR 466.
[140] *R (Tipperary North Riding and South Riding County Councils) v Considine* [1917] 2 IR 1 at 6.
[141] *State (Modern Homes (Ireland) Ltd) v Dublin Corporation* [1953] IR 202 at 229.

it proceed. Cases in this area have arisen because of excessive delay,[142] safeguarding evidence[143] and adverse publicity.[144]

Quo Warranto

[13–78]   Order 84 of the RSC allows for a procedure by way of *quo warranto*. The application relates to a method of deciding whether someone has the right to claim a particular office, franchise or liberty. Thus Kenny J noted the extent of the process historically thus:

> "when the holder of an office was removed and he claimed that this was not justified, he applied for the issue of an information in the nature of a *quo warranto* directed to the new holder of the office to show how he held the office from which the prior holder had been removed."[145]

In practice the remedy has rarely been used in recent history and an injunction has become the preferred remedy.[146] As the LRC acknowledged in 1979

> "no application for such an order [had] been made for many years, and it would appear to be obsolescent, if not indeed obsolete. Anyone wishing to raise the kind of issue determinable in such proceedings would probably now do so by seeking a declaration that the office had not been lawfully filled, and an injunction to restrain the holder from acting therein."[147]

In its later report of 2004 the LRC recommended that we follow other jurisdictions and formally abolition the order; to date this recommendation has not been followed.[148]

---

[142] *State (O'Connell) v Fawsitt* [1986] IR 362.

[143] *Bowes v Director of Public Prosecutions & McGrath v Director of Public Prosecutions* [2003] 2 IR 25. The cases were considered together by the Supreme Court; in the first case prohibition was denied, in the second case it was granted.

[144] *Clune v Director of Public Prosecutions* [1981] ILRM 17, prohibition available only where publicity causes a real and serious risk of injustice which cannot be avoided through a direction from the trial judge to the jury.

[145] *Garvey v Ireland* [1979] IR 266 at 113-4.

[146] It has been abolished in Australia and England.

[147] LRC (1979), above n 9 at para 5.2.

[148] Law Reform Commission, "Report on Judicial Review Procedure" (Dublin, LRC 71-2004) at p 101.

Private Law Remedies

Traditionally the private law remedies were regarded as secondary remedies operating to fill the gaps created by the often restrictive rules that operated around the State side remedies. While the reforms to the judicial review application procedure in 1986 went a long way to unifying the process there remains a difference between the two types of remedy.[149] As Hogan and Morgan note, this indicates that the hierarchy between the two types of remedy appears to linger, although without clear authority from the courts it is unclear as to the exact nature of this.[150]

[13–79]

Declaration

The declaration is a private law remedy which is extremely wide-ranging in nature and in recent years has come to occupy a central place in the remedial arsenal of the courts in judicial review proceedings. Hogan and Morgan describe it as "a safety net"[151] fitting into spaces where the older remedies could not. It is remarkably simple and extensive — allowing the court to state the law based on the facts brought before it. It applies to decisions already taken, those about to be taken, and where decisions have not been taken. It does not, however, quash a decision nor does it mandate action by the respondent. Thus it does not have a coercive element to it: rather the court expects the public body to follow the declaration made. As a result, a failure to abide by a declaration does not result in proceedings for contempt of court. This lack of a coercive component does not however render the declaration worthless. In practice, public bodies do follow the law as set out by the Court in a declaration.

[13–80]

---

[149] RSC Ord 84, r 18(1) states "An application for an order of certiorari (etc) shall be made by way of application of judicial review." While Ord 84, r 18(2) states:

An application for a declaration or an injunction may be made by way of an application for judicial review, and on such an application the Court may grant the declaration or injunction claimed if it considers that, having regard to -

(a) the nature of the matters in respect of which relief may be granted by way of an order of mandamus, prohibition, certiorari, or quo warranto,

(b) the nature of the persons and bodies against whom relief may be granted by way of such order, and

(c) all the circumstances of the case,

it would be just and convenient for the declaration or injunction to be granted on an application for judicial review.

[150] Hogan and Morgan, above n 15, at para 16-30.

[151] *ibid* at para 16-24.

[13–81]   Order 19, rule 29 RSC states that

> "No action or pleading shall be open to objection on the ground that a merely declaratory judgement or order is sought thereby, and the Court may, if it thinks fit, make binding declarations of right whether any consequential relief is or could be claimed or not."[152]

In practice the courts operate a flexible and wide approach to the granting of a declaration, having rejected an earlier cautious approach.[153]

[13–82]   The court has an absolute discretion as to whether to award a declaration and will consider a number of factors in exercise of that. Thus the court must be presented with a question of substance rather than a hypothetical.[154] The applicant must have a sufficient interest in seeking the declaration, although what a sufficient interest is remains highly flexible.[155] The court will take account of the availability of alternative remedies,[156] the behaviour of the applicant, the timing of the application[157] and whether the declaration will ultimately be useful[158] in terms of resolving "a real difficulty with which the... applicant is faced".[159] However, it is possible for the court to make "an advisory declaration".[160]

[13–83]   One emerging area in relation to declarations is whether an interim declaration can be awarded by the court. Traditionally these have not been available because of the finality of the legal finding made by the Court. In Ireland, de Blacam notes that the terms of rules under Order 84, rule 20(7)(b) do not appear to prevent such a development.[161] However, to date there has been no clear development in this area. In England and Wales the civil procedure rules do allow for these declarations[162] and it is clear that they

---

[152] The modern source of the declaration in Irish law is the Chancery (Ireland) Act 1867, s 155.

[153] See judgment of Walsh J in *Transport Salaried Staffs' Association v Córas Iompair* Éireann [1965] IR 180 at 202.

[154] *Maguire v South Eastern Health Board* [2001] 3 IR 26: the Court refused to consider declaratory relief in a case where the respondent had refused to offer home birth midwifery services because the birth had taken place by the time the case came to court.

[155] *Transport Salaried Staffs' Association v Córas Iompair* Éireann [1965] IR 180.

[156] *Creedon v Dublin Corporation* [1984] IR 428: the applicant was refused a declaration by the Supreme Court where she had failed to use an available statutory appeal system against a decision by the corporation for a change of use of her property.

[157] It needs to be neither too late nor too early.

[158] *Shannon v McGuiness* [1999] 3 IR 274.

[159] SA DeSmith, H Woolf and J Jowell, *Judicial Review of Administrative Action* (5th ed) (Sweet & Maxwell, London, 1995) at para 18:023.

[160] *Condon v Minister for Labour* [1981] IR 62.

[161] de Blacam, above n 2 at para 31.23.

[162] Civil Procedure Rule 25.1(1)(b).

provide an opportunity for the court to provide some certainty as to how the parties should proceed pending the outcome of a case.[163]

Injunction

As with the declaration, the injunction is a private law remedy: its source in Irish law was the Supreme Court of Judicature (Ireland) Act 1877, s 28(8) which stated that where it was "just and convenient to do so" an injunction could be granted.[164] Although an injunction is most often ordered to prohibit the performance of a particular act (prohibitory), it is possible for an injunction also to direct the performance of an act (mandatory).

[13–84]

Permanent injunctions are described as permanent or perpetual but in fact may be time limited. They are granted at the end of a case upon the final determination of the rights at issue. An injunction will be available if the applicant has shown that there has been an interference with their rights, that the respondent intends to continue with that infringement and damages would not amount to a suitable alternative remedy.[165] Thus, a central question for the court is whether damages would be an adequate remedy in the circumstances.

[13–85]

As regards temporary injunctions, we have already provided an analysis of the applicable tests earlier in this chapter at paragraph 13-30 above. This remedy provides temporary relief in order to preserve the status quo of the parties subsequent to the case being heard in full. Within this category there are two types of temporary injunction. The "interim injunction" is awarded by the Court on an *ex parte* application with the respondent not being provided advance notice of the hearing. Given the potential for injustice arising from this type of order the interim injunction will normally only operate for a short period — until a hearing involving both parties can be conveniently arranged. The "interlocutory injunction" is awarded following a hearing involving both parties and will last until the full hearing takes place.[166] In practice, where an applicant obtains an interim

[13–86]

---

[163] *R v Secretary of State for Trade and Industry, ex p. Trades Union Congress* [2001] CMLR 8: the Court of Appeal made an interim declaration pending the ruling of the Court of Justice of the European Union that certain elements of domestic law amounted to an improper implementation of a directive and therefore without legal effect.

[164] The present High Court is vested with the powers of the previous High Court under s 8(2) of the Courts (supplemental Provisions) Act 1961.

[165] See de Blacam, above n 2 at para 32.03.

[166] In awarding an interlocutory injunction the court must have regard to what are known as the *Cyanamid* principles which operate a three stage test: (i) whether there is a serious

injunction this will often result in the dispute being settled between the parties prior to the full court hearing. The advantage of the injunction lies in the fact that it can provide an applicant a remedy (even if it is a temporary one) within a short time frame. So although Hogan and Morgan note that

> "[a]s the specialist public law remedies of prohibition and mandamus often fulfil the role which might otherwise be discharged by the injunction, applications for injunctions in public law are not very common."[167]

De Blacam highlights the fact that they are likely to grow in importance.[168] The flexibility of the injunction over its equivalent state side orders is important here too.

Damages

[13–87]　It was traditionally a fundamental principle of judicial review that it did not of itself provide any basis for the award of damages; there was no provision for damages to be awarded alongside one of the state side orders. Instead, an applicant wanting to apply for damages would have to do so via a plenary action (either solely for damages or in conjunction with a private law remedy). The justification for this position was that judicial review was meant to operate as a check on the exercise of the powers of public bodies rather than as a compensatory remedy for individuals:

> "The justification for not giving damages for judicial review is that the proceedings are brought for the benefit of the public as a whole, good administration being for the benefit of the public as well as the individual applicant."[169]

[13–88]　However, following a recommendation by the Law Reform Commission[170] that has now changed and the Court can make an award of damages to the

---

issue to be tried; (ii) whether damages would be an appropriate remedy; (iii) whether the balance of convenience lies in granting or refusing an injunction. *American Cyanamid Company v Ethicon Ltd.* [1975] 1 All ER 504 adopted into Irish law by the Supreme Court in *Campus Oil v The Minister for Energy* [1983] IR 88.

[167] Hogan and Morgan above n 15 at para 16-26.
[168] de Blacam, above n 2 at paragraph 32.16.
[169] Lord Woolf, "Has the Human Rights Act made Judicial Review Redundant?" Alba Annual Lecture, 23 November 2005.
[170] LRC (1979) above n 10 para 6.6.

applicant if a number of conditions are met.[171] Thus, the court must be satisfied that if the claim had been made in a civil action the applicants would have been awarded damages. Further, the rules[172] require that the applicant set out the particulars of the claimed wrong doing and items of special damages. This is the same approach as is required in a civil action.

It is important to stress that the 1986 rules did not create an independent [13–89] remedy of damages in judicial review cases. However there are distinctions between situations where the applicant has suffered an economic loss because the public body has committed a tort and where the fault arises from an *ultra vires* decision. In the latter case the case law indicates that damages are not available where the action was only *ultra vires*. In *Pine Valley Developments Ltd. v Minister for the Environment*[173] the plaintiff was refused damages in a context where he had purchased land with outline planning permission that had been awarded *ultra vires*. Despite the loss in the value of the property caused by the invalid grant, the Supreme Court ruled that there was no negligence on the part of the Minister. This judgment indicates that to establish a claim for remedies in such situations an alternative approach is needed — this is found in the tort of misfeasance in public office. Thus, the Court had stated that damages might have been available if the plaintiff could show that the power had been exercised either maliciously or knowing that it was outside jurisdiction. This approach was clearly adopted, albeit narrowly, in *Glencar Exploration plc v Mayo County Council (No 2)*.[174]

Conclusion

Having provided an overview of some of the key issues around procedure [13–90] and remedies we would finally like to stress that legal commentary on this topic should not be allowed to constantly fragment into separate micro-issues without some consideration of the larger picture. In our view, few areas cry out for greater socio-legal or empirical study than judicial procedure and remedies. The Irish legal system is lacking research on the

---

[171] Ord 84, r 25, as amended by the Rules of the Superior Court (Judicial Review) 2011 (SI No 691 of 2011).

[172] Rules of the Superior Court Order 19, rules 5 & 7.

[173] *Pine Valley Developments Ltd v Minister for the Environment* [1988] IR 23.

[174] *Glencar Exploration plc v Mayo County Council (No 2)* [2002] 1 IR 84. The Court (at 149) required there to be a "deliberate and dishonest wrongful abuse of powers given to a public officer".

practical utility of judicial review within an overall system of regulation and Government accountability. To what extent do high levels of judicial review actions in particular areas correlate with poor internal or external appeal systems? Once a judicial review decision is handed down, to what extent are the consequences of that decision effectively communicated to ground level decision-makers in Government? The lack of answers to such questions means that if, in the future, attempts are made by government to limit access to judicial review, those defending judicial review's regulatory function will be forced to rely on anecdotal evidence of its ability to deliver individual justice, as well as its centrality to fundamental constitutional principles.

[13–91] System level monitoring and debate has featured more strongly in the UK over the past number of years. Our neighbouring jurisdiction has seen a dramatic increase in applications for judicial review and the number of cases proceeding past the leave stage. As Bondy and Sunkin report[175] there was an 11 fold increase in judicial review applications in England and Wales between 1981 and 2006, a 25 year period.[176] In addition, despite the huge rise in applications, only twice as many cases were permitted to proceed past the leave stage.[177]

[13–92] The extent of judicial review litigation in England and Wales has recently led the UK Government to make efforts to curb access.[178] Concerns about the increase in applications for leave which rose from 6692 in 2006 to 11,359 in 2011 with one in six applicants being granted leave to proceed were conflated with a view that applicants were being motivated by considerations of "PR" and using judicial review as a "delaying tactic".[179] Despite the proposals being widely criticised by academics, practitioners and the judiciary both on their specifics and on the wider basis that there was a "lack of evidence underpinning the reforms and the generally poor

---

[175] Bondy and Sunkin, above n 69 at p 2.

[176] Official statistics state that in 1981 533 applications for leave were made rising to 6,458 in 2006.

[177] 3390 cases in 2006 were considered at the leave stage with 752 granted permission to proceed – 22%.

[178] See https://www.gov.uk/government/news/action-on-time-wasting-judicial-reviews (date accessed 30 June 2014).

[179] Secretary of State for Justice/Lord Chancellor Grayling quoted in UK Department of Justice Press Release available online at http://www.bbc.co.uk/news/uk-politics-22260063 (date accessed 30 June 2014).

quality of the recommendations",[180] the Government has pressed ahead with significant reform, albeit not as extensive as first proposed.[181] The antagonism of political actors towards judicial review is of course in line with our discussion of the treatment of the Office of the Ombudsman in chapter 4. The point, as made by Mark Elliot in a blog post on the debate, is that:

> "Judicial review is—and *should be*—an unwelcome irritant from the perspective of Government; if it wasn't, then there would be something wrong. Indeed, judicial review is perhaps the pre-eminent manifestation of what Conor Gearty has recently termed the "important inconvenience of the rule of law". The Government, however, appears intent on smoothing out judicial review's rough edges in order to make it less of an inconvenience."[182]

In our jurisdiction, we have not seen a steady rise in the number of applications for judicial review of administrative action. Instead there have been fluctuations:

[13–93]

Year	Applications	% difference on previous year
2013	973	⇧ 3%
	385 (asylum)	⇧ 13%
2012	998	⇧ 16%
	440 (asylum)	⇧ 37%
2011	1193	⇧ 24%
	703 (asylum)	⇧ 25%
2010	1571	⇧ 20%
	936 (asylum)	⇧ 25%
2009	1317	⇧ 5%
	749 (asylum)	⇧ 5%

---

[180] A Wagner, "Government's 'war' on Judicial Review panned", UK Human Rights Blog 2 February 2013 available online at http://ukhumanrightsblog.com/2013/02/02/governments-war-on-judicial-review-panned/ (date accessed June 30 2014).

[181] See Part 4 of the Criminal Justice and Courts Bill 2014.

[182] M Elliot, "Government pressing ahead with (most of) its proposals to restrict access to judicial review", UK Human Rights Blog, 23 April 2013, http://ukhumanrightsblog.com/2013/04/23/government-pressing-ahead-with-most-of-its-proposals-to-restrict-access-to-judicial-review-mark-elliott/#more-18197 (date accessed 30 June 2014), referencing C Gearty, "The Important Inconvenience of the Rule of Law", UK Constitutional Law Group Blog, 30 March 2013, http://ukconstitutionallaw.org/2013/03/30/conor-gearty-the-important-inconvenience-of-the-rule-of-law/ (date accessed 30 June 2014).

2008	1379	⇧ 25%
	785 (asylum)	⇧ 30%
2007	1730	⇧ 12%
	1024 (asylum)	⇧ 12%
2006	1541	⇧ 9%
	909 (asylum)	⇧ 20%

[13–94] What is observable from the table above[183] is the prominent position occupied by cases related to the asylum process. These include judicial review applications brought under legislation related to asylum, immigration and refugee status. Haynes highlights the fact that the Refugee Appeals Tribunal (RAT) is the most judicially reviewed public authority in Ireland making up for 21.6% of all judicial reviews commenced between 2007 and 2011.[184] Although politicians blame the high levels of judicial review on overly litigious lawyers[185] those working in the system highlight the fundamental problems that exist around decision making and the accountability and openness of the system. What is clear is that the RAT has failed to provide information on the operation of judicial reviews in this area since 2002. Whatever the reasons, it seems clear a failing system has had to rely on judicial review as a form of appeal, as is borne out by the relatively high levels of pre-trial settlement by Government. Beyond this specific area however, the lack of empirical study and reflection extends across most thematic areas and while the Courts Service provides basic figures on applications there is little disaggregated information on why cases fail, for example, to progress past the leave stage. In order to fully

---

[183] Data taken from Courts Service Annual reports between 2006-2013.

[184] SM Haynes, "The prevalence of judicial review in the asylum arena", (2013) 18(1) *Bar Review* 29-32.

[185] Haynes, *ibid*, quotes former Minister of State for Integration Lenihan:

"The major delays in settling and dealing with asylum applications at the moment is principally focused on the legal challenges that are being taken by a very active and voracious group of barristers down in the Bar library who are representing clients virtually on a 'no foal, no fee' basis … Vulnerable asylum seekers were being given unrealistic hopes by some lawyers when in most cases their chances of a successful appeal were limited."

The Irish Times, "Lenihan blames barristers for delays in asylum appeals", 4 January 2008. Note the proposed changes to the rules for judicial review in asylum cases Part 4 of the Employment Permits (Amendment) Bill 2014 to amend s 5 of the Illegal Immigrants (Trafficking) Act 2000. The reforms are specifically aimed at reducing delays in judicial review cases and include an extension of the time limit for applying for judicial review (from 14 to 28 days) and an increase in the use of *ex parte* hearings.

map the practical operation of judicial review both in and of itself and as part of the wider accountability structures of the State it is essential that a stronger and deeper knowledge base is developed regarding the issues raised in this chapter. The reforms we have seen in the procedural and remedial context should be viewed as ongoing rather than an end point. Filling in the knowledge gaps in this area will only assist this process.

CHAPTER FOURTEEN

THE IMPACT OF EUROPEAN UNION LAW ON IRISH JUDICIAL REVIEW

Introduction

One of the more challenging aspects of any administrative law text is to [14–01] move between specific contexts and general principles of review. While respecting the specificity of particular subject areas, in writing this chapter we wish to consolidate and articulate the systemic challenges which EU law has raised for the Irish administrative State. This account can be read alongside the study of the substantive directives and regulations which apply in particular contexts. We therefore attempt to look at the overall "grammar" of judicial review in the EU law context, in that way encouraging readers to appreciate the increasing presence of legally pluralist review actions.

The ever expanding corpus of EU law means that judicial review in a [14–02] range of areas from the commercial sphere (financial regulations, telecommunications, public procurement), to employment and social security law, immigration and asylum and environmental law often involves the application of EU law. This is mandated by the twin founding principles of the EU, that of supremacy[1] and direct effect. Our approach in this chapter is to establish the systemic impact which EU law now has upon standards of review, availability of remedies and the protection of fundamental rights. It is worth recalling in this context the extra-judicial statement of Cooke J, a former member of the Court of First Instance:

> "Membership of the Union involves radical transfer of regulatory competence to the organs of the Community from the Member states… the far-reaching effects of this hand-over of power to the institutions is balanced by the guarantee that the legal order of the Treaty will protect the individual against the excessive and oppressive exercise of that power in a manner which is incompatible with superior rules of

---

[1] As mandated by Bunreacht na hÉireann, Art 29.4.10°:
"The State may become a member of the European Coal and Steel Community …, the European Economic Community…, and the European Atomic Energy Community…No provision of this Constitution invalidates law enacted, acts done or measures adopted by the State necessitated by the obligations of membership of the Communities, or prevents laws enacted or acts done or measures adopted by the Communities or the institutions thereof, from having the force of law in the State."

law and of fundamental human rights which the European Court will imply into the legal order of the Community for the purpose."[2]

[14–03]   The requirement of an effective remedy for breaches of European Union law represents a key fault-line between traditional Irish public administration and European Union structures. In important areas such as environmental law and anti-discrimination there remain question marks regarding the ability of Irish administration and its dispute resolution mechanisms to reach the enforcement expectations within the EU legal order. The degree to which traditional judicial review complies with the requirement of an effective review of initial decisions is prominent here. This is largely because EU law understandings of proportionality can be as expansive as those under the European Convention on Human Rights, which are outlined in chapter 15. Other European Union law protections, such as legitimate expectation, legal certainty and the protection of fundamental rights under the Charter of Fundamental Rights and Freedoms, also require the Irish courts to adapt traditional review approaches in order to ensure a closer level of scrutiny of a Government decision than would be adopted if a purely domestic cause of action was raised. Lastly, EU law offers, as we have mentioned, not merely a broadening of the grounds for challenging decisions, but may, in certain circumstances, offer potentially more far-reaching remedies.

Reviewing Actions in Contravention of the EU Treaties or Legislation

[14–04]   At the basic level judicial review may be sought in relation to Government actions which contravene EU law. The supremacy of EU law requires that a decision or act of a public body, and domestic legislation, be susceptible to challenge by way of judicial review on the ground that it infringes the Treaty on the Functioning of the European Union (TFEU), or a provision of European Union regulations or directives. Direct effect is provided for in Irish law, through s 2 of the European Communities Act 1972:

---

[2] Quoted by McKechnie J, *Digital Rights Ireland v Minister for Communication & Ors* [2010] IEHC 221 at para 43.

"From the 1st day of January 1973, the treaties governing the European Communities and the existing and future acts adopted by the institutions of those Communities shall be binding on the State and shall be part of the domestic law thereof under the conditions laid down in those treaties."

This was echoed internationally by the statement of the European Court of Justice in the landmark case of *Simmenthal*,[3] where it held that in case of conflict that supremacy resulted in:

"a national court...[being] under a duty to give due effect to those provisions, if necessary refusing of its own motion to apply any conflicting provision of national legislation, even if adopted subsequently, and it is not necessary for the court to request or await the prior setting aside of such provision by legislative or other constitutional means."

Thus, a national rule is not rendered invalid, but in the case of conflict must be dis-applied. These provisions have been internalized into Irish judicial practice, as Costello J stated in *Pigs and Bacon Commission v McCarren*: **[14–05]**

"The effect of [s 2 of the European Communities Act 1972] is that Community law takes legal effect in the Irish legal system in the manner in which Community law itself provides. Thus, if according to Community law a provision of the Treaty is directly enforceable so that rights are conferred on individuals which national courts must enforce, an Irish court must give effect to such a rule. And if, according to Community law, the provisions of Community law take precedence over a provision of national law in conflict with it an Irish court must give effect to this rule. That Community law enjoys precedence over a conflicting national law has been made clear in a number of decisions of the European Court and most recently in Case 106/77, *Amministrazione delle Finanze dello Stato v Simmenthal*."[4]

Justice Henchy, writing extrajudicially stated in 1977:

"Because Community law is part of domestic law, it is the duty of the courts set up under the Constitution to implement it; but it is the exclusive function of the European Court to interpret and determine conclusively the validity of the Treaties and of acts put forward as Community law; and where there a conflict is found between

---

[3] *Simmenthal SpA v Amminstrazione delle Finanze dello Stato* (Case 106/77) [1978] ECR 629 at para 24.
[4] *Pigs and Bacon Commission v McCarren* [1978] JISEL 109.

national law and Community law, it is an absolute imperative that the Community law shall prevail."[5]

[14–06] For a provision of EU law to be directly effective, it must be sufficiently clear and precise, be unconditional and leave no scope for discretion as to its implementation.[6] Clearly regulations raise fewer issues, as under Article 288 TFEU, they are "directly applicable in all Member States". In respect of directives, which are drafted with the intention that they be implemented by legislation at a national level, their terms must be examined to determine if direct effect arises.[7] One of the more prominent Irish considerations of these requirements occurred in *McBride v Galway Corporation*.[8] Quirke J refused to hold that EU directives applying to a decision on where to locate a sewage plant for Galway city were directly effective. He rather found that the provisions were not unconditional and not sufficiently precise. In contrast, the European Court of Justice has not been overly stringent in its treatment of some provisions of European law. For example, Article 45(3) TFEU, which allows for the free movement of workers, is made "subject to limitations justified on grounds of public policy, public security or public health". While determining the scope and scale of such limitations seem to be committed primarily to Member States, the Court of Justice refused to hold that free movement is a conditional right which is incapable of being directly effective. This was largely based on the fact that the provision was subject to judicial review in the courts of the Member States, which was suggestive of an objectively legal, rather than discretionary, character.[9] The final limb of the test for direct effect has also been read quite openly by the European Court, which has held that where further action by the states is specified, and a date for implementation is attached, the provision becomes directly effective once the period expires. Ultimately as Auburn *et al* note "the test for direct effect is, essentially, the practical one of whether the provision in question lends itself to judicial application".[10]

---

[5] S Henchy, "The Irish Constitution and the E.E.C." (1977) (1) *DULJ* 20-25, 23.

[6] As set out by Advocate-General Mayras in Case 2/74 *Reyners v Belgium* [1974] ECR 631.

[7] Art 288 TFEU, "a directive shall be binding, as to the result to be achieved, upon each Member State to which it is addressed, but shall leave to the national authorities the choice of form and methods".

[8] *McBride v Galway Corporation* [1998] 1 IR 458.

[9] Case 41/74 *Van Duyn v Home Office* [1974] ECR 1337 at para 7.

[10] J Auburn, J Moffett and A Sharland, *Judicial Review: Principles and Procedure* (Oxford University Press, Oxford, 2013) at p 83.

The directly effective nature of directives has been incrementally expanded [14–07] by the Court of Justice. In Case C-129/9 *Inter Environmenient Wallonie ASBL v Region Wallonie,*[11] the Court ruled that in the period granted to Member States to implement, they must refrain from taking any measures liable to seriously compromise the result sought to be achieved by the directive.[12] A partial or incomplete attempt to implement a directive also does not affect the entitlement of individuals to rely upon the full requirements of it in litigation. In a ruling which is particularly important in the Irish equality law context, in Case *C-62/00 Marks and Spencer plc v Commrs for Customs & Excise,*[13] the Court held that a sufficiently precise and unconditional directive can be invoked by an individual litigant even in circumstances where national measures have correctly implemented it. This iteration, thus, requires public administrators and judges to ensure full application of the directive *in practice.* Any future emergence of cases under this heading involving Ireland, will concretely illustrate the divergence between the judicially led red light, Diceyan vision of administrative law and more expansive notions of administrative *justice* which we discussed in chapter 1. Finally, it is important to note that an unimplemented directive does not merely collapse into a bald finding of violation of EU law by the Court of Justice, it may also require the courts to interpret existing law, so far as is possible, in the light of the wording and purpose of the directive.[14]

So far we have identified the impact of direct effect upon State actors. It is [14–08] important for public-private partnerships however, to discuss the concept of horizontal direct effect. This refers to the possibility that a private individual may invoke the provisions of EU law against another private individual. This has been rejected in *Marshall No 1*[15] and *El Corte Ingles SA v Rivero,*[16] with the Court noting the right of the individual to seek damages for any loss incurred from the Government which failed to implement the directives' provisions. The Court of Justice has nevertheless taken steps to ensure that the private entities which are engaged to provide public services are made subject to direct effect. The first modification made was the

---

[11] *Inter Environmenient Wallonie ASBL v Region Wallonie* [1997] ECR I-7411.
[12] Though there remains no obligation to disapply national laws in such a period.
[13] *Marks and Spencer plc v Commrs for Customs & Excise* [2002] ECR 1-6325.
[14] *Konstantinious Adeneler et al v Ellinikos Organismos Galaktos* (ELOG) [2006] ECR 1-6057.
[15] *Marshall v Southampton and South-West HampshireAHA* [1986] ECR 723 (Marshall (No 1).
[16] *El Corte Ingles SA v Rivero* Case C-192/94 [1996] ECR I-1281.

"emanation of the State" doctrine. In *Foster v British Gas*,[17] the Court of Justice held that the term "Member State" includes any emanations of it, that concept would therefore bring within it a body that is "controlled" or "owned" by the State or a body which was granted "special powers" by the State:

> "a body, whatever its legal form, which has been made responsible, pursuant to a measure adopted by the State, for providing a public service under the control of the State and has for that purpose special powers beyond those which result from the normal rules applicable in relations between individuals is included in any event among the bodies against which the provisions of a directive capable of having direct effect may be relied upon."[18]

[14–09]　Thus, local and regional authorities, State owned business entities and health authorities have all been held to be bound by directly effective EU directives. The restriction on horizontal direct effect was also moderated by the recognition of what has been termed "indirect effect", or what may be termed the "duty of consistent interpretation". This is a similar, but far less inhibited, version of the interpretative obligation contained in the European Convention on Human Rights Act 2003. In *Marleasing SA v La Comerical Internacional de Alimentacion SA*,[19] the ECJ held that this obligation applies not only in respect of legislation passed in order to implement a directive but also to legislation predating it.

[14–10]　Finally, it is important to stress that the successful transposition of EU law is also dependent on broader socio-legal processes such as an active parliamentary posture. As the Fine Gael/Labour *Programme for Government 2011-2016* states:

> "The situation can no longer be tolerated where Irish Ministers enact EU legislation by statutory instrument. The checks and balances of parliamentary democracy are by-passed. The parliamentary treatment accorded home-produced draft legislation must be extended to draft legislation initiated within the EU institutions."[20]

---

[17] *Foster & Ors v British Gas* [1990] ECR I-3313.
[18] *ibid* at para 20.
[19] *Marleasing SA v La Comerical Internacional de Alimentacion SA* [1990] ECR I-4135.
[20] Department of An Taoiseach, *Programme for Government 2011-2016* at p 25. Available at: http://www.taoiseach.gov.ie/eng/Work_Of_The_Department/Programme_for_Government/Programme_for_Government_2011-2016.pdf (date accessed 22 October 2014).

Practical measures to ensure this include the forwarding of Regulatory Impact Assessment to the relevant sectoral Oireachtas Committees, which should then advise on whether transposition should be undertaken through secondary or primary legislation. In this manner the visibility of directly applicable EU legislation in Irish public life can be improved.

General Principles of EU Law

In certain legal circumstances, Irish administrative decision-makers must respect the general principles of EU law in exercising their statutory discretion. These represent norms of constitutional status developed by the Court of Justice, according to which norms must be interpreted and with which measures must comply.[21] These include the protection of fundamental rights, the principle of proportionality, the principle of non-discrimination, the protection of legitimate expectations, the principle of legal certainty and the rights of the defence. While this book cannot deal with substantive pieces of EU legislation, we here attempt to provide some reflection upon these general principles, and how they might exceed or expand existing principles of review and statutory interpretation as applied in Irish administrative law. [14–11]

The obligation to respect the general principles is triggered where an administrative action measure falls within the scope of application of the TFEU. This phrase covers actions taken by public bodies when they are implementing EU law through administrative decisions, as well as national Government when it adopts implementing primary or secondary legislation.[22] The extremely broad area of application of even the TFEU should remind students and practitioners that there exists a very wide range of domestic measures which may be amenable to judicial review for breach of general principles of EU law. Perhaps the most infamous illustration of this was the challenge mounted to the ban on hunting with dogs in the UK under the Hunting Act 2004 in *R (Countryside Alliance)* [14–12]

---

[21] In *Nold v Commission* (Case 4/73 [1974] ECR 491) the Court cited the inspiration for the general principles of EU law as comprising: i) common national constitutional traditions and ii) international human rights agreements. The increasing status of fundamental rights was secured by the passage of the Charter of Fundamental Rights in the Lisbon Treaty. The judicial comfort level in evolving such general principles is also bolstered by the accretion of legislation in areas like non-discrimination.

[22] In effect they are operated as "agents of the EU" and are bound by the general principles. See *Case 5/88 Wachauf v Federal Republic of Germany* 1989 ECR 2609.

v Attorney General.[23] There the House of Lords held that the free movement provisions of the EU Treaty were engaged, and reviewed the Act to ensure it complied with the general principle of proportionality, eventually ruling in favour of the Government. Clearly therefore, in this chapter we will return to whether the *Meadows* version of proportionality outlined in chapter 9 is compatible with the version contemplated by EU law.

[14–13]   Returning to the Court of Justice case law on the "scope of application", perhaps the broadest approach was taken in *Herbert Karner Industrie Auktionen GmbH v Troostwijk GmnH*,[24] where the Court accepted the argument that a measure which was a potential impediment to intra-EU trade could be assessed for compliance with the general principles. In *R (Zagorski) v Secretary of State for Business, Innovation and Skills*,[25] Lloyd Jones J was called upon to evaluate a UK Government decision to export a drug used to administer the death penalty in the US in the light of the Charter of Fundamental Rights. He ultimately refused to do so, but on the narrow grounds that the claimants (US citizens on death row) were not protected individuals under the Charter. Earlier in the judgment he had held that the decision fell within the scope of application of EU law as relevant Treaty provisions restricted the ability of States to ban exports.

The EU Charter of Fundamental Rights

[14–14]   The category of "fundamental rights" was already in existence prior to the final creation of the Charter of Fundamental Rights on 12 December 2007. Article 6 TFEU states that the provisions "shall have the same legal value" as the Treaties and will not "extend in any way the competences of the Union as defined in the Treaties". Article 6(3) now expressly states that:

> "Fundamental rights, as guaranteed by the European Convention for the Protection of Human Rights and Fundamental Freedoms and as they result from the constitutional traditions common to the Member States, shall constitute general principles of the Union's law".

The Charter therefore encompasses all the rights in the ECHR, as well as many rights of a socio-economic character including fair and just working conditions. The principle of harmonious interpretation of the Convention

---

[23] *R (Countryside Alliance) v Attorney General* [2008] 1 AC 719.

[24] *Herbert Karner Industrie Auktionen GmbH v Troostwijk GmnH* [2004] ECR I-3025.

[25] *R (Zagorski) v Secretary of State for Business, Innovation and Skills* [2010] EWHC 3110 (Admin).

with the Charter is secured by Article 52(3) of the latter. However, while not allowing for reductive readings of the ECHR the provision "does not preclude the grant of wider protection by European Union law". We will discuss the Charter in depth in a later section of this chapter.

Equal Treatment

The general principle of equal treatment will now clearly be less freestanding [14–15] following the creation of the Charter. Its initial growth as a general principle had its taproots in Articles 18 and 19 TFEU.[26] According to the Court of Justice ruling in *Case C-127/07 Societe Arcelor Atlantique et Lorraine v Premier Ministre*,[27] a degree of deference should be applied to European institutions such as the Parliament or Commission in areas of involving political, economic or social choices.[28] The same deference may not be accorded to national authorities in judicial review of a decision falling within in the scope of EU law. A proportionality analysis will apply assessing if the measure is objectively justified, in the sense of being based on an "objective and reasonable criterion", namely

"if the difference relates to a legally permitted aim pursued by the legislation in question and it is proportionate to the aim pursued by the treatment".[29]

In Ireland some of the most visible applications of the general principle of [14–16] equal treatment have occurred in public procurement matters, where even though the Procurement Directive did not directly apply, the general

---

[26] Art 18 TFEU prohibits discrimination by the Union on the basis of nationality. Art 19 TFEU, introduced by the Treaty of Amsterdam, extends the non-discrimination prohibition to "any discrimination based on any ground, such as sex, race , colour, ethnic or social origin, genetic features, language, religion or belief, political or any other opinion, membership of a national minority, property, birth, disability, age or sexual orientation".

[27] *Societe Arcelor Atlantique et Lorraine v Premier Ministre* [2008] ECR I-9895.

[28] See *ibid* para 57:
"The Court acknowledges that in the exercise of the powers conferred on it the Community legislature has a broad discretion where its action involves political, economic and social choices and where it is called on to undertake complex assessments and evaluations (see Case C-344/04 *IATA and ELFAA* [2006] ECR I-403, paragraph 80). In addition, where it is called on to restructure or establish a complex system, it is entitled to have recourse to a step-by-step approach (see, to that effect, Case 37/83 *Rewe-Zentrale* [1984] ECR 1229, para 20; Case C-63/89 *Assurances du crédit v Council and Commission* [1991] ECR I-1799, para 11; and Case C-233/94 *Germany v Parliament and Council* [1997] ECR I-2405, para 43) and to proceed in the light of the experience gained."

[29] See Case C-127/07 *Arcelor Atlantique and Lorraine and Others* EU:C:2008:728 at para 47, and Case C-101/12 *Schaible* EU:C:2013:661 at para 77.

principle still subsisted. It is illegal under Irish law to discriminate in a public procurement decision on the basis of nationality when the competing businesses are from EU Member States.[30]

Legal Certainty and Legitimate Expectations

[14–17]   The first of these two principles received its clearest definition in *R (International Air Transport Association) v Department for Transport*:

> "[legal certainty] requires that rules should be clear and precise, so that individuals may ascertain unequivocally what their rights and obligations are and may take steps accordingly".[31]

Legal certainty must be uppermost in legislators' minds when implementing directives, given the Court of Justice's ruling in the *Commission v France*, that directives must be implemented with "unquestionable binding force", and with "specificity, precision and clarity".[32] While entitled to create limitation periods, the principle of legal certainty requires that these must be fixed in advance and not subject to ad hoc volatility.[33]

[14–18]   Legitimate expectation is clearly a related concept to legal certainty, the Court of Justice described it in *Duff v Minister of Agriculture, Ireland* as "the corollary of the principle of legal certainty"[34] and may be defined as ensuring that:

> "...situations and relationships lawfully created under Community law are not affected in a manner which could not have been foreseen by a diligent person".[35]

[14–19]   Perhaps the most prominent instance of a legitimate expectation action in the Irish courts is *Duff (No.2)*[36] which concerned the implementation of EU law regulating milk quotas. The plaintiffs claimed that having expended

---

[30] C-45/89 *Commission v Ireland* [1988] ECR 4929.

[31] Case C-344/04 *R(International Air Transport Association) v Department for Transport* [2006] ECR I-403, para 68.

[32] Case C-197/96, *Commission v France* [1997] ECR I-1489, at para 15.

[33] *ACF Chemiefarma v Commission of the European Communities* (Case 41/69) [1970] ECR 661 at para 19. The European Union principle of certainty received prominent recent consideration in the UK Supreme Court in the decision of *FII. Test Claimants in the Franked Investment Income Group Litigation v Inland Revenue* [2012] 2 WLR 1149, [2012] UKSC 19 (23 May 2012).

[34] Case C-63/93 *Duff v Minister for Agriculture and Food, Ireland* [1996] ECR I-569 at para 15.

[35] *ibid* 582 *per* Advocate-General Cosmas.

[36] *Duff v Minister for Agriculture (No 2)* [1997] 2 IR 22, hereinafter *Duff (No 2)*.

money in achieving goals set by the EU schemes, they had a legitimate expectation that they would not be frustrated in achieving these by the operation of another community scheme. The Minister had approved plans to develop the relevant farms, on the assumption that there would an expanded milk quota available to the owners. The resulting error is best summarized by Barrington J, for the majority, who noted:

> "The facts of this case are not in dispute. The plaintiffs are a group of small farmers. The State, on its own behalf and as agent for the European Commission induced them to borrow money and to develop their farms on the basis that there would be an expanded outlet for the sale of their milk. Now, after they have incurred heavy expenditure they find that they will not get the outlet for the sale of their milk which they expected and were induced to believe they would receive."[37]

Clearly, there could be no legitimate expectation that the law would not be changed. In this case however, the Minister had given them a reference quantity out of the national quota upon which they had relied. Thus the plaintiffs suffered damage and loss for the failure to implement the special reference quantities to which they felt entitled.[38]   **[14–20]**

O'Flaherty J strongly condemned the Minister's failure to apply his discretion to grant the reference quantity to the farmers: **[14–21]**

> "In effect, the Minister had said to the plaintiffs: "if you modernise and develop your holdings and so forth, I will see you right". Along comes the super-levy regime and he has a Regulation with a provision at his disposal with which he can keep to his commitment. As a matter of national law (as regards Community law, see the judgment of the Court of *Justice in Deutsche Milchkontor v. Germany* (Joined Cases 205-215182) [1983] ECR 2633), the plaintiffs had a legitimate expectation that the Minister would honour that commitment. The fulfilment of that promise would have required only that the Minister would exercise his discretion in a particular way. It is true, as held by the Court of Justice, that he was not bound as a matter of Community law in the abstract to exercise his decision in favour of the plaintiffs- but, as a matter of national law on the facts as proved in this case, he could hardly have done anything else. In order for him to honour his commitment to the development farmers to give them the fair deal that he had always held

---

[37] *ibid* at 73.
[38] *ibid* at 89.

out to them, he would not, of course, have been involved in breaking any statutory, or other, duty or obligation..."[39]

[14–22]   The recent case of *Cromane Seafoods Limited and O'Sullivan McCarthy Mussel Development Ltd. v The Minister for Agriculture, Fisheries and Food*,[40] saw a similar finding emerge. There the proceedings concerned a decision by the Minister to prohibit fishing for mussel seed in, *inter alia*, Castlemaine Harbour (Cromane) in County Kerry. This decision necessitated the closure of the harbour for the duration of mussel seed fishing season in 2008 and in 2010, leading to substantial losses for the plaintiffs. The Harbour had been designated as a "Natura 2000 site" by the EU Habitats Directive.[41] A ruling of the Court of Justice in 2007[42] had found that Ireland had not correctly transposed or applied Article 6(3) and (4) of the Habitats Directive, which established a mandatory requirement for appropriate impact assessment for any project or plan which could have a significant effect on the designated site. This decision triggered concern in the Department of Agriculture and Fisheries and in the Department of the Environment causing them to pass statutory instruments which prohibited the mussel seed fishing. A marine scientist gave testimony that a relatively simple screening test assessing possible negative impacts should have been carried out, and would have taken an estimated two months. In the years up to 2008 however, the Departments had not sought to undertake such a scientific investigation. In the years 2008 and 2010, during which the plaintiffs suffered financial losses, there was still no scientific study commissioned. During this period the defendants were making regular representations to the Minister, adducing evidence of the impact on their livelihoods, and questioning the failure to analyse the question of environmental impact. Assessing the experience, the plaintiffs argued:

> "...if the relevant Government department had started with an appropriate assessment, which normally involves a desk study, they would have been appraised of the information which had been accumulated from 1993 onwards, especially the Dúchas report of 2000, and the fact that nothing much had changed since then, it could have been satisfied that there was in reality no adverse impact from mussel seed fishing in Cromane Harbour over the 20 days of dredging activity

---

[39] *ibid* at 74.
[40] *Cromane Seafoods Limited and O'Sullivan McCarthy Mussel Development Ltd. v The Minister for Agriculture, Fisheries and Food* [2013] IEHC 338, hereinafter "*Cromane*".
[41] Council Directive 92/43/EEC.
[42] *Commission v Ireland Case* C-418/04, 13 December 2007.

associated with it. The plaintiffs claim that their vulnerability would not have been so acute if the Department had properly equipped itself, as it should previously have done, by having appropriate baseline data rather than relying simply on ad hoc subjective observations by coastal staff. There was no ordered decision making process or scheme allowing for the best use of existing information which could have afforded better protection to the plaintiffs."[43]

Thus, the ban was not "a matter of law" but was the product of "poorly informed decision making" of a department which had not constructed or appreciated the necessary evidence base.[44]

In ruling that a legitimate expectation had been established in this case, the Court stressed that "no new law came into being as a result of the judgment of the European Court delivered in December 2007" as the Court was interpreting the directive which had been in place since 2000.[45] In 2008, the Minister found himself barred from exercising his discretion to open the harbour to fishing "as a result of not having carried out an appropriate assessment", despite the fact that he did so in previous years even if it was under a mistake of law on his part: [14–23]

> "The mistake of law in the present case is more than just a pure mistake of law in the legal sense. It is a mistake of law in how the Minister thought it was appropriate to manage the aquaculture business in a balanced way with protecting the environment; the mistake of law that we are looking at here has a relevance in terms of how the regime was managed. There was operational negligence in failing to carry out the regular scientific tests or monitoring that would have provided the baseline data to equip the Minister either to have a proper screening test or to have a fully informed appropriate assessment. The delay could have been avoided if the Minister had not been guilty of operational negligence, which was part and parcel of his mistake of law."[46]

The Court noted that, on the basis of the "compelling" testimony of the marine scientist, Dr O'Connor,[47] a screening test could have been undertaken quickly and would have found no adverse consequences to the [14–24]

---

[43] *Cromane* above n 40 at para 23.

[44] *ibid* at para 24.

[45] *ibid* at para 48.

[46] The Court was fortified in this finding by the ruling of the Court of Justice in the *Commission v Ireland*, above n 42 at para 236, that Ireland "has systematically failed to carry out a proper assessment of [Special Protected Areas]"

[47] *Cromane* above n 40 at para 50.

environment would occur. While "everyone was hugely energised at a high level in 2008", on the ground "nothing happened" until 2010 when scientific information was generated.[48] The plaintiffs had operated lawfully and were entitled to expect the usual course of events to continue. The situation was ruptured by the operational negligence on the part of the State in failing to carry out proper scientific investigations between 2000 and 2008, so baseline data would be available to carry out the assessment necessitated by the Habitats Directive:

> "The State did not operate the regime in an orderly way which would have allowed harmony between environmental protection and the plaintiffs continuing with their business. The sequence of events points out what should have been a necessary state of knowledge on the part of the defendants, who nevertheless decided to sit on their hands and allow matters to carry on in what appears to be defiance of the clearly stated will of the European Court of Justice. Failure to comply with obligations with European law is relevant in flavouring the state of knowledge of what the parties understood as being *their modus vivendi* that came to a screeching halt in June 2008."[49]

This all grounded a requirement that decision-makers not:

> "...make sudden, unmeasured, haphazard and arbitrary decisions; the process should be managed in an orderly way by regularly gathering information, so that all parties can organise their affairs in an appropriate way with minimum disruption."[50]

[14–25]   It is important to reiterate that legitimate expectation cannot defeat the operation of a statutory duty, so if there had been a change in the law through legislation, the claim would have been defeated. This was stressed in Barrington J in *Duff (No. 2)*:

> "After the decision of the Court of Justice one must accept that the community legislator has power to change European law and that people such as the plaintiffs whose activities are subject to European law can have no legitimate expectation that the law will not be changed."[51]

---

[48] *ibid* at para 51.
[49] *ibid* at para 55.
[50] *ibid* at para 56.
[51] *Duff (No 2)* above n 36 at 81.

The examples we have given, therefore apply where the Minister retained a discretion to fulfil the expectation and was not legally precluded from doing so.

Rights of the Defence

This category largely involves a number of general procedural fairness [14–26] principles, which may equal, but largely do not exceed, those subsisting in the ECHR and other national legal systems. This is particularly the case in a country like Ireland, whose Constitution protects such rights. Nevertheless, this principle may operate to ensure the right to a fair hearing, the right not to self-incriminate, the right to reasons and the right to access documents. The main advantage of these provisions is possible enhanced remedies (when compared to domestic systems) which are available upon breach rather than more substantive entitlements.

Proportionality Under EU Law

Proportionality, as could have been predicted with the influence of the civil [14–27] law systems, (particularly Germany), has been a central principle of the European Court of Justice case-law.[52] Its role is now also expressly acknowledged in Article 5(4) TFEU which states:

> "Under the principle of proportionality, the content and form of Union action shall not exceed what is necessary to achieve the objectives of the Treaties".

In the formative case of *R v Ministry for Agriculture, Fisheries and Food, ex* [14–28] *parte Fedesa*, the Court of Justice provided the clearest statement as to how proportionality analysis is to proceed[53]:

(1) the measure in question must be appropriate and necessary in order to achieve the objectives legitimately pursued

(2) where there is a choice between several appropriate measures, recourse must be had to the least onerous

---

[52] A discussion of the role of proportionality in EU law features as early as 1970, see *Internationale Handelsgesellschaft Gmb v EInfuhr- und Vorratsstelle fur Getreide and Futtermittel* [1970] ECR 1125. It was recognized as a general principle in *R v Minister for Agriculture, Fisheries and Food, ex parte Fedesa* [1990] ECR I-4023, para 13.

[53] *R v Ministry for Agriculture, Fisheries and Food, ex parte Fedesa* [1990] ECR I-4023, para 13, hereinafter *ex parte Fedesa*.

(3) the disadvantages caused by the measure must not be disproportionate to the aims pursued.

[14–29] It must be commented that this statement suffers from the same circularity
as other proposed methods discussed elsewhere in this book, particularly
in chapter 9. The volatile disappearance and reappearance of the third limb
across the case-law, in particular, has been subjected to very strong
criticism.[54] Furthermore, while the statement does not include any role for
a sliding scale of review, it is at least arguable that the Court has subjected
different areas of EU legislative intervention to varying intensity of
review.[55] Measures taken within the Common Agricultural Policy or other
polycentric areas of discretion have often attracted a deferential approach,
with the Court appearing to ask whether the decision was "manifestly
inappropriate".[56] The extent of interference with the relevant EU law right
is also a primary consideration, with decisions involving the application of
penalties, however, tend to attract more searching judicial scrutiny. Clearly
the pattern of reasoning of the Court of Justice discloses a number of
categories where the Court attaches particular weight and deference, such
as issues involving public morality, public policy or the application of
political judgment. In contrast where a measure is discriminatory on the
ground of nationality it will receive more rigorous scrutiny.

[14–30] Given that at times inconsistent treatment of proportionality by the Court
of Justice it is unsurprising to see relatively fragmented discussion of the
principle appearing in Irish authorities. Nevertheless, it is clear that the
Irish courts are comfortable with the principle that it requires a more
searching standard of review, one often exceeding the *O'Keeffe/Keegan*
reasonableness test. Thus we have observed at times a calibration of the
standard of review for reasonableness allowing Irish judges to harmonise
their proceedings proportionality principle under EU law.

---

[54] See A Turk, *Judicial Review in EU Law*, (Edward Elgar, Cheltenham, 2009) at p 136. See
generally P Craig, *EU Administrative Law* (Oxford University Press, Oxford, 2012) at
chapters 19 and 20. Harbo argues that the variability of the treatment of the principle by the
Court of Justice means that "the dissection of the principle reveals that the principle has no
clear or fixed substantial meaning" T I Harbo, "The function of the proportionality principle
in EU law", (2010) *European Law Journal* 158 at p 160.

[55] See the discussion by of how the intensity of the proportionality varies according to the
nature of the interest involved, and the extent of the restriction in J Jans "Proportionality
Revisited", (2000) *Legal Issues of Economic integration* 239.

[56] *ex parte Fedesa* above n 53 at para 14.

A context in which the need for more invasive review has been **[14–31]** acknowledged by the Irish courts is in the oversight of public procurement contracts. Thus in *SIAC Construction v Mayo County Council*,[57] despite the prima facie narrowness of the key test of "manifest error" — which had been laid down within Court of Justice jurisprudence, the Supreme Court nevertheless ruled that an elevated standard of reasonableness review was required. Fennelly J noted that the word "manifest...should not be equated with any exaggerated description of obviousness".[58] The usual standard of review would have to be raised as the *Keegan/O'Keeffe* unreasonableness test might not be exacting enough and would:

> "run the risk of not offering what the [the Procurement Remedies Directive][59] clearly mandates, namely a judicial remedy which will be effective in the protection of the interests of disappointed tenderers".[60]

In *Sweetman v An Bord Pleanála*,[61] Article 10a of Directive 85/337/EEC **[14–32]** required a review of the "substantive and procedural legality" of relevant decisions be put in place by Member States. This provoked a discussion of the adequacy of *O'Keeffe* reasonableness in discharging this obligation. Clarke J pointed out that in considering whether sufficient review was available in accordance with Article 10a, it was necessary to take fully into account all grounds of judicial review, not merely unreasonableness. Furthermore, in a decision which fits within the broader debate regarding the flexibility of the reasonableness ground, Clarke J stressed:

> "[t]o the extent that it may be argued successfully that there are substantial grounds to the effect that a greater level of scrutiny is mandated by the Directive in relation to environmental judicial review applications, then such greater level of scrutiny can, by analogy with the position adopted in respect of fundamental human rights cases, be accommodated within the existing judicial review regime."[62]

In finding that standard judicial review was sufficiently flexible, Clarke J **[14–33]** also stressed that the Court of Justice had itself adopted a "manifest error"

---

[57] *SIAC Construction v Mayo County Council* [2002] 3 IR 148, hereinafter *"SIAC."*

[58] *ibid* at 176.

[59] Directive 89/665/EEC of 21 December 1989 on the co-ordination of the laws, regulations and administrative provisions relating to the application of review procedures to the award of public supply and public works contracts ([1989] OJ L395/33).

[60] *SIAC* above n 57 at 176.

[61] *Sweetman v An Bord Pleanála* [2008] 1 IR 277.

[62] *ibid* at 299.

test in reviewing decisions in the environmental context, a phrase which fell short of merits review. [63] Thus, Clarke J stressed that standard judicial review could be deployed to cover a large number of the reviews contemplated by the directive. Furthermore, where necessary, the courts could abandon the strict confines of *O'Keeffe* and shift to a more searching review.[64]

[14–34]   Ironically, the decision in *Meadows v Minister for Justice, Equality and Law Reform*,[65] while *generally* moderating the *O'Keeffe* standard, actually provided some mandate for that standard's application in the *specific* context of planning decisions. This was due to comments of Denham and Fennelly JJ which noted that *O'Keeffe* standard could still be employed for decisions involving "special skill and knowledge", with the technical expertise of An Bord Pleanála being expressly mentioned. This approach was endorsed by Hedigan J in *Scanlon v Sligo County Council*,[66] where Keegan was held to apply to areas of special skill and knowledge such as planning and development. In contrast to this, McMahon J accepted the need to shift from the *O'Keeffe* standard in *Klohn v An Bord Pleanála*, a case concerning review of environmental impact assessment procedures.[67] Recognising the deferential nature of *O'Keeffe* reasonableness, McMahon J noted that discretionary action taken under EU should be reviewed using "the standard of review adopted by the EU itself in reviewing the decisions of its own officials".[68]

---

[63] *ibid* at 300.

[64] *ibid*.

[65] *Meadows v Minister for Justice, Equality and Law Reform* [2010] 2 IR 701.

[66] *Scanlon v Sligo County Council* [2011] IEHC 143.

[67] *Klohn v An Bord Pleanála* [2009] 1 IR 59.

[68] *ibid* at 71. This was also viewed by McMahon J as furthering the uniformity of application and interpretation of EU legislation (at 70-71 of the report):

"In Irish law, in the planning area at least, the courts have shown huge deference to the decision of the appropriate authority, and will normally only interfere when the decision is irrational (the *O'Keeffe* standard). Though not without its critics, this is the general rule as set down in the case law. More recently, when the national legislation was inspired by an EU directive and the decision maker is exercising its discretion the question has arisen whether the non-demanding *O'Keeffe* threshold is appropriate when an EU measure is involved. It would seem more appropriate, in these circumstances, to adopt the standard of review adopted by the EU itself in reviewing the decisions of its own officials. Two reasons can be advanced for such a position: first, the *O'Keeffe* standard is too low; second, the adoption of the EU standard will go some way to ensuring uniformity throughout the community in these matters..."

The unsteadiness of the prevailing approaches was underlined by Hogan J [14–35] in *Keane v An Bord Pleanála*,[69] which was a challenge to, inter alia, a condition being attached to a grant of planning permission, which the applicant argued was in breach of the Environmental Impact Assessment Directive 1985:

> "it is not here necessary to express any concluded view as to whether the review of the exercise of the Board's discretion in a case such as this should be governed by the test enunciated in *O'Keeffe v An Bord Pleanala* [1993] 1 I.R. 39 or whether the somewhat more relaxed "manifest error test" should be applied in view of the approach taken by the Supreme Court in *SIAC Ltd v Mayo County Council* [2002] 3 I.R. 148, a public procurement case. As Clarke J seemed to hint in *Sweetman*, the case for applying the manifest error test would seem to be a powerful one in this context, not least given that the relevant discretionary powers vested in the Board with regard to the environmental impact assessment contained in the 2001 Regulations cannot be regarded as purely autonomous, autochthonous items of secondary legislation, but rather derive their root of title from the 1985 Directive".[70]

It may be that further refinement and conceptual clarification is necessary [14–36] in order to harmonise the EU and national approaches. It is also clear, however, that the inconsistent practice of the Court of Justice in relation to proportionality analysis makes the conflict more fragmented and obscure than the consolidated vision of balancing advocated by the European Courts on Human Rights. While environmental law has triggered most engagement on the question, the collision between the *Keegan* (post *Meadows*) standard and the expectations of European actors will arise across multiple litigation contexts, particularly with cases involving the Charter of Fundamental Rights now arising with greater regularity.

EU Law Remedies and Judicial Review

The TFEU does not address directly the question of what specific remedies [14–37] should be available when a public body acts in a manner contrary to EU law or violates an individual's rights under EU law. The general position, as stated by the Court of Justice, was of national procedural autonomy, such that

---

[69] *Keane v An Bord Pleanála* [2012] IEHC 324.
[70] *ibid* at para 18. Referring to the Planning and Development Regulations 2001.

> "it was not intended to create new remedies in the national courts to ensure the observance of Community law other than those already laid down by national law".[71]

This general approach however, is substantially modified by three significant principles which have concretely influenced and guided the forms of remedy available in actions involving EU norms: the principle of supremacy of EU law, the principle of equivalence and the principle of effectiveness.

[14–38]   *Supremacy* has already been discussed as a general principle, but in the context of remedies, it requires a national court to give immediate effect to EU law and not to make the execution of judgments contingent upon the repealing or quashing of conflicting national law.[72] There is an obligation to repeal legislation which conflicts with EU law so as to avoid confusion.[73] Furthermore, similar to the ECHR Act 2003 there is an obligation to interpret domestic legislation, where possible, in a manner that is compatible with EU law.

[14–39]   *Equivalence* mandates that remedies afforded by national law and by national courts for breaches of rights under EU law are no less favourable than those attaching to equivalent domestic law rights. The latter category of "equivalent domestic law rights" must be determined by reference to their "purpose, cause of action and essential characteristics".[74] The principle requires only that EU law claims are not singled out for less favourable treatment, and it does not bind national courts into extending the most favourable remedies to EU law claims.[75]

[14–40]   *Effectiveness* is a principle which requires a practical inquiry into the exercise of EU law rights: States must ensure their full and effective protection and not to, through procedural hurdles, render impossible their exercise or vindication. In the famous case of *Marshall v Southampton and South West Hampshire Area Health Authority*, the Court of Justice required that

---

[71] Case 158/80 *Rewe-Handelsgesellschaft Nord mbH v Hauptzollamt Kiel* [1981] ECR 1805, at para 44.

[72] *Simmenthal* above n 3.

[73] Case 167/173 *Commission of the European Commmunities v French Republic* [1974] ECR 359, paras 41-48.

[74] Case C-326/96 *BS Levez v TH Jennings (Harlow Pools) Ltd* [1998] ECR I-7835, para 43.

[75] Case C-231/96 *Edilizia Industriale Sidergurgica Srl (Edis) v Ministero delle Finanze* [1998] ECR I-4951, paras 36-37.

compensation for discrimination be awarded above the national statutory limits:

> "the objective [of EU Equal Treatment Directive] is to arrive at real equality of opportunity and cannot therefore be attained in the absence of measures appropriate to restore such equality when it has not been observed…those measures must be such as to guarantee real and effective judicial protection and have a real deterrent effect on the employer…When financial compensation is the measure adopted…it must enable the loss and damage to be made good in full in accordance with the applicable national rules."[76]

Effectiveness also requires that the national legal system does not render the exercise of EU rights excessively difficult. A significant judgment against Ireland for non-compliance with this principle occurred in *Impact v Minister for Agriculture and Food and Others*.[77] This case examined the question of when a specialized tribunal, such as the Labour Court, should integrate consideration of EU law matters into its rulings and when it may require a complainant to take a separate action to the High Court. The Court of Justice held that a legal system may not require the complainant to make two separate complaints concerning a matter if the costs, duration and representation entitlements of taking the two actions rendered the taking of the EU law based elements excessively difficult. Thus a specialized tribunal may have to extend its jurisdiction to matters affecting EU law rights in order to satisfy the principle of effectiveness. Having established this principle, the Court remitted the matter to the Labour Court, leaving it to determine whether the separation in the particular matter at hand was overly burdensome.

[14–41]

Another defined limb of the effectiveness principle is the entitlement to seek damages from the State in certain instances. In *Francovich v Italian Republic*,[78] the Court ruled that the principle would be impaired if injured parties could not obtain compensation for violations of EU law by the State. The three requirements for triggering such a circumstance are: firstly, that the provision of EU law which has been infringed must have been intended to confer rights on individuals; secondly, the breach must be "sufficiently serious"; and finally, there must be a direct causal link between the breach and the damage suffered.

[14–42]

---

[76] Case C-271/91 [1993] ECR I-04367 at para 24.
[77] Case C-268/06, *Impact v Minister for Agriculture and Food and Others* [2008] ECR I-2483.
[78] Cases C-6 and 9/90), *Francovich & Ors v Italy* [1991] ECR I-5357.

[14–43]   An example of where the first requirement was held not to be established was in *Paul v Bundesrepublik Deutschland*,[79] where the directive imposed obligations on national authorities to conduct financial supervision of banks, it was held that the directive was not intended to confer rights on individual depositors if their money was lost as a result of defective supervision, therefore, the state was not liable in damages. The "sufficiently serious" requirement was outlined by the Court of Justice in *Brasserie du Pecheur v Federal Republic of Germany*,[80] where that it required the following factors to be taken into account:

> "...the clarity and precision of the rule breached, the measure of discretion left by that rule to the national or Community authorities, whether the infringement and the damage caused was intentional or involuntary, whether any error of law was excusable or inexcusable, the fact that the position taken by a Community institution may have contributed towards the omission, and the adoption or retention of national measures or practices contrary to Community law".[81]

[14–44]   Clearly, there are categories of violation which are firmly established in terms of their seriousness: such as continuing to enforce legislation which the Court ruled to be incompatible with EU law[82] or failing to implement a directive within the relevant time limit. The Court of Justice also ruled in *Kobler v Austria* that judicial decisions may trigger damages.[83] Instances which will require a contextual analysis include when a Member State has incorrectly attempted to implement a directive[84] or where the state fails to take into account clear rulings of the Court.[85] The European Court must however, ensure that the rulings are clear enough for such breaches to be identified. For instance, in the recent Irish High Court case of *O'Connor v Environmental Protection Agency*,[86] Hogan J found that the Court of Justice had not sufficiently clarified the meaning of the phrase "not prohibitively

---

[79] Case C-222/02 *Paul and Others v Bundesrepublik Deutschland* [2004] ECR I-9425.

[80] *Brasserie du Pecheur SA v Germany and R v Secretary of State for Transport, ex parte Factortame* (Cases C-46 and 48/93) [1996] ECR I-1029.

[81] *ibid* at para 56.

[82] *ibid* at para 57.

[83.] *Kobler v Austria* [2003] ECR I-10239.

[84] Case C-392/93 *R v HM Treasury ex p British Telecommunications Plc* [1996] ECR I-1631, paras 42-45.

[85] Case C-466/04 *Test Claimants in the FII Group Litigation v Commissioners of Inland Revenue* [2006] ECR I-11753, para 215.

[86] *O'Connor v Environmental Protection Agency* [2012] IEHC 370.

expensive" in Article 11(4) of Directive 2011/92/EU so that a domestic court could choose between a range of possible meanings:

> "…enough has been said to demonstrate that the meaning of the phrase 'not prohibitively expensive is at present uncertain and requires further clarification from the Court of Justice".[87]

A recent UK judgment, *R(Negassi) v Secretary of State for the Home Department*, held that damages would only be available if an incorrect construction of a directive was based on arguments "which are entirely devoid of merit".[88] The best understanding of this ruling is perhaps that the Court was attempting to account for the "fog of law" which surrounds much statutory interpretation, rather than requiring an intention to breach the directive on the part of the State authorities.   **[14–45]**

Another related aspect to remedies is the question of who may have standing to enforce a provision of EU legislation. The European Court of Justice has been anxious to ensure the full effectiveness of EU law and has tended to allow actions to enforce a directly effective legal provision taken by particular individuals or classes of individuals. In *Antonio Munoz y Cia SA and Superior Fruiticola SA v Frumar Ltd*,[89] the claimant argued that a competitor had breached an EU food quality regulation by selling grapes in the UK. English and Welsh law tied enforcement actions taken under the regulation to public authorities, which in this case had refused to act. The Court, reasoning that the purpose of the regulation was to ensure the practical protection of food quality, endorsed the right of the claimant to initiate its own proceedings in the domestic courts.   **[14–46]**

One of the core mechanisms for ensuring the enforcement of EU law is the reference procedure, whereby the domestic court will refer a matter to the Court of Justice for a preliminary ruling. The Court of Justice will then provide the national court with a ruling, supplying all the interpretive guidance necessary to ensure the enforcement of EU law. A culture and practice of referring matters to the Court of Justice emerged very slowly in Ireland. As described by Elaine Fahey in the 25 years following the enactment of the European Communities Act 1972, only a small number of   **[14–47]**

---

[87] *ibid* at para 18.
[88] *R(Negassi) v Secretary of State for the Home Department* [2011] EWHC 386 (Admin) at para 18.
[89] *Antonio Munoz y Cia SA and Superior Fruiticola SA v Frumar Ltd* Case C-253/00, [2—2] ECR I-7289.

agriculture related matters were referred.[90] The pace has since quickened markedly, however, with 19 cases being referred from 1998 to 2010, and a significant rise to ten being recorded from 2011-2012.[91] A referring court must have power to grant interim measures including the suspension of statutory provisions. In *Zuckerfabrik Suderdithmarchen & Zuckerfabrik Soest* it was held that a national court may suspend the enforcement of the relevant EU measures pending a Court of Justice ruling on the preliminary issues referred.[92] One key reform introduced by the Lisbon Treaty was the additional requirement placed within Article 267 TFEU mandating that the Court of Justice decide with "the minimum of delay" whether a preliminary question raised in a case pending before a national court has impacts on a person in custody. This further enhances the ability to obtain an accelerated reference procedure in cases involving imminent harms, such as deportations or extraditions.

The Charter of Fundamental Rights

[14–48]   The Charter of Fundamental Rights of the European Union, originally agreed in December 2000, is the first single text statement of the fundamental rights of European citizens and persons resident in the EU. It was given full effect on 1 December 2009, as part of the Lisbon Treaty. It is now installed as a legally binding instrument of primary EU law, equivalent in stature to the EU Treaties. Its provisions consolidated the EU's existing "obligation to respect fundamental rights", incorporating existing principles of EU law, together with international treaties, such as the European Convention on Human Rights. While the Charter effectively echoes the protections afforded under the ECHR, it also includes some additional rights such as the right to asylum, the integrity of the person, the rights of the child and the protection of personal data.[93] Both instruments are now effectively

---

[90] E Fahey, *Practice and Procedure in Preliminary References to Europe: 30 Years of Article 234 EC Caselaw from the Irish Courts* (Firstlaw, Dublin, 2007).

[91] G de Búrca, "The Domestic Impact of the EU Charter on Fundamental Rights" (2013) 48(1) *Irish Jurist* 49 at p 59.

[92] *Joined Cases C-143/88 and C-92/89, Zuckerfabrik Suderdithmarchen & Zuckerfabrik Soest* [1991] ECR I-415.

[93] The Charter has seven chapters, with six of these containing substantive rights, and the seventh outlining interpretative and procedural provisions. The rights chapters are entitled: I Dignity, II Freedoms, III Equality, IV Solidarity V Citizens' Rights and VI Justice. The Dignity Chapter mirrors the early articles of the ECHR, protecting against torture and slavery. Chapter II refers to classical civil and political rights such as freedom of association, expression, private and family life. Chapter III, embraces the EU's extensive prohibition on

cross-pollinating through judicial dialogue, a process which could be further secured if the challenging negotiation of the EU's formal accession to the ECHR are successful.

The Scope of Application of the Charter

For Irish administrative law, the central impact of the CFR will be the obligation of national courts to ensure that national measures falling within the field of operation of EU law accord with respect for the relevant fundamental rights as interpreted by the Court of Justice. The key gateway term to the invocation of the CFR is contained in Article 51. It provides that the Charter is binding on Member States and European institutions when "they are *implementing EU law*": [14–49]

1. The provisions of this Charter are addressed to the Institutions, bodies and agencies of the Union with due regard for the principle of subsidiarity and to the Member States only when they are implementing Union law. They shall therefore respect the rights, observe the principles and promote the application thereof in accordance with their respective powers and respecting the limits of the powers of the Union as conferred on it in the other Parts of the Constitution.

2. This Charter does not extend the field of application of Union law beyond the powers of the Union or establish any new power or task for the Union, or modify powers and tasks defined in the other Parts of the Constitution.

The potential ambit of the "implementing EU law" phrase provoked much academic commentary, but the Court of Justice recently went some distance to removing uncertainty with its judgment in the case of *Aklagaren v Fransson*.[94] The case, in which Ireland was one of five Member States intervening to argue for a narrow interpretation of Article 51(1),[95] considered whether the imposition of charges for domestic tax offences constituted an [14–50]

---

discrimination across a wide variety of grounds, but fails to include any targeted minority rights protections. Chapters IV and V enumerate existing EU protection of labour rights and citizen's rights, including the right to good administration. Chapter VI focuses upon fair process rights in the criminal and administrative context, including the right to a fair trial, the presumption of innocence, the proportionality of penalties and the right to an effective remedy.

[94] *Aklagaren v Fransson*, Judgment of 26 February 2013 (Case C-617/10), [2013] 2 CMLR 46. Hereinafter "*Fransson*".

[95] Significantly, the European Commission also joined the matter, supporting the position of the five Member States.

"implementation of EU law". The Court preferred a broader approach to the scope of the Charter and placed the terms "governed by EU law" and "within the scope of application of EU law" at the centre of considering whether the Charter would apply. In particular, the relevant taxation provisions were within the Charter's scope due to EU legislation regulating the collection of VAT, encouraging anti-fraud and laundering activities and due to the fact that Member State contributions to the EU budget were drawn from VAT and other taxes. In essence, while the process of collection and enforcement of VAT was not specifically regulated by specific provisions of EU legislation, it was sufficiently linked with EU law for the Charter to apply.

[14–51] Furthermore, it is important to note that the Charter covers Member States implementing or enforcing an EU law provision, but also may apply to circumstances in which they seek to derogate from it.[96] The Charter of course, does not apply to Member State measures or actions undertaken in purely national situations. The most developed engagement with the Charter in the Irish Courts has occurred in the context of the European Arrest Warrant system. In *Minister for Justice, Equality and Law Reform v Josef Adam*,[97] the High Court ruled that Ireland is acting within the scope of EU law when it has to execute a European Arrest Warrant.[98]

[14–52] The *Fransson* judgment has however been further developed by a range of recent cases[99] which further explore the Charter's "scope of application". Of these, perhaps the most significant is *Siragusa*.[100] This case concerned a challenge to an Italian administrative law which requires the demolition of unauthorized developments conducted in areas covered by landscape conservation safeguards. This law represented an absolute prohibition,

---

[96] Case C-26089 *ERT* [1991] ECR I-2925. This was endorsed more recently by the Opinion of Advocate General Sharpston in *Gerardo Ruiz Zambrano v Office national de l'emploi*, 30 September 2010. The first Charter case to invoke these cases is the recent judgment in *Pfleger v Austria* C-390/12 *Pfleger* Case E-16/11, April 30 2014.

[97] *Minister for Justice, Equality and Law Reform v Josef Adam* [2011] IEHC 68.

[98] This case concerned an arrest warrant issued by the Czech Republic. The Court also held that The Charter was to be respected even if the procedure leading to the issuing of the warrant was initiated before the entry into force of this Charter (in these proceedings parties relied on Art 47 CFR).

[99] *Siragusa v Regione Sicilia - Soprintendenza Beni Culturali e Ambientali di Palermo* (C-206/13) [2014] 3 C.M.L.R. 13 (ECJ (10th Chamber)), *Julian Hernandez v Spain* (C-198/13) [2014] All E.R. (EC) 971 (ECJ (5th Chamber)) and Pfleger (C-390/12) (ECJ) (30th April 2014). These cases are analysed by T Fontanelli, 'Implementation of EU law through domestic measures after Fransson: the Court of Justice buys time and "non-preclusion" troubles loom large' (2014) 39(5) *ELR* 682.

[100] *Siragusa, ibid.*

and did not allow public authorities to grant retrospective planning permission even if the works were found, after litigation, to be compliant with the relevant landscape protections. The question before the Court of Justice was whether the inflexibility of this law contradicted the principle of proportionality in connection with the Charter protection of private property.[101] The reference from the Italian court to the Court of Justice requested a ruling on whether there was sufficient connection between the matters and EU law to apply the Charter, given that the Environmental Impact Assessment Directive, other environmental law provisions relating to the Aarhus Convention and broader European Union environmental policy seemed to have some legal bearing[102] upon the national safeguarding of landscape. Clearly, the complainants viewed their situation as similar to *Fransson*.

Despite this, the Court held that there was an insufficient link between the dispute and EU law, such that it did not attract the protections of the Charter under Article 51(1). In so ruling, it held that: **[14–53]**

> "the concept of 'implementing Union law', as referred to in Article 51 of the Charter, requires a certain degree of connection above and beyond the matters covered being closely related or one of those matters having an indirect impact on the other".[103]

The Court of Justice then attempted to lay down a multifactorial test for when national legislation is sufficiently connected to EU law, and thereby attracts the Charter protections. As Nic Shuibhne notes, in identifying such factors, the Court was drawing upon pre-existing caselaw which had reflected on when domestic legislation might be characterized as **[14–54]**

---

[101] Art 17 of the Charter provides:
"Everyone has the right to own, use, dispose of and bequeath his or her lawfully acquired possessions. No one may be deprived of his or her possessions, except in the public interest and in the cases and under the conditions provided for by law, subject to fair compensation being paid in good time for their loss. The use of property may be regulated by law insofar as is necessary for the general interest."

[102] As will no doubt the term "legal bearing" is carefully chosen to avoid contradicting the reasoning within the ruling in the *Siragusa* judgment.

[103] In explaining indirectness, the Court cited its previous decision in *Kremzow* C-299/95 [1997] ECR I-2405 at para 16, where it held that the fact that a person who had been accused under domestic law, and might thereby have his right to freedom of movement restricted, did not suffice to raise an issue under the TFEU. The Court also cited the cases of C-144/95 *Maurin* [1996] ECR I-2909 and *Daniele Annibaldi v Sindaco del Comune di Guidonia & Presidente Regione Lazio* (Case C-309/96) [1997] ECR I-7493. *Siragusa*, above n 99 at para 26 which involved similar findings.

implementing European Union law.[104] Firstly, in terms of assessing where the connection between national measures and EU law, the Court of Justice held that it should be determined whether:

> "that legislation is intended to implement a provision of EU law; the nature of that legislation and whether it pursues objectives other than those covered by EU law, even if it is capable of indirectly affecting EU law; and also whether there are specific rules of EU law on the matter or capable of affecting it".[105]

In finding that a sufficient connection was not established, the Court of Justice also stressed that EU law did not create any obligation applicable to the facts of the main proceedings:

> ".... the provisions of EU law in the subject area concerned did not impose any obligation on Member States *with regard to the situation at issue in the main proceedings*".[106]

Thus the Court stressed the fact that national legislation may not be sufficiently connected to fall within the scope of the Charter where the domestic law could have an indirect effect on a system established by EU law. Finally, the Court stressed that the overall purpose of EU fundamental rights framework was to preserve the "unity, primacy and effectiveness" of EU law, and the scope of the Charter should be construed in the light of this objective.[107] We further discuss this element of the analysis, which was more prominently considered by the Court of Justice in the earlier judgment of *Melloni*,[108] when we consider the interaction of the Charter and the Irish Constitution at paras [14-59]-[14.62].

[14–55]   These factors must now be applied by national judges to assess the sufficiency of the connection between EU law and the national dispute before it. The *Siragusa* judgment offers more concrete reasoning than *Fransson*, but one must also criticise the failure to address the relative weight between factors which are to be taken into account. The factual matrix of the case contributed to this, as the safeguarding of landscape failed virtually every aspect of the test. Thus, as Fontanelli comments "the multiple

---

[104] N Nic Shuibhne, "The Constitutional Weight of Adjectives", (2014) 39(2) *ELR* 153 at p 153. This existing case-law included *Maurin, Annibaldi* and *Kremzov, ibid*.

[105] *Siragusa*, above n 99 at para 25.

[106] *Siragusa*, above n 99 at para 26.

[107] *Siragusa*, above n 99 at para 32.

[108] *Melloni v Ministerio Fiscal* (C-399/11) [2013] QB 1067 (ECJ (Grand Chamber)).

rationales for non-application offered...provided no additional clarity, because they all applied at once".[109] It may be that the presence of these revolving factors may permit the Court of Justice to narrow the openness initially signaled by *Fransson*. This shift from the superficially permissive generality of *Fransson* to the dense multifactorial analysis of *Siragusa* is memorably encapsulated in the title of a recent piece by Steven Peers analysing the case: "They paved paradise, they put up a parking lot".[110]

The Interpretive Obligation: National Laws and the Charter

The impact of the Charter on domestic judicial review is likely to prove most visible in cases regarding the proper interpretation of legislation implementing EU directives. The interpretive duty placed on national courts as a result of the Charter has been outlined by the Grand Chamber of the Court of Justice in the following manner: **[14–56]**

> "Member States must, when transposing the directives...take care to rely on an interpretation of the directives which allows a fair balance to be struck between the various fundamental rights protected by the Community legal order. Further, when implementing the measures transposing these directives, the authorities and courts of the Member States must not only interpret their national law in a manner consistent with those directives but also make sure that they do not rely on an interpretation of them which would be in conflict with those fundamental rights or with the other general principles of Community law, such as the principle of proportionality."[111]

Thus, there is an obligation to integrate the norms of the Charter into administrative practice and not place formalistic reliance upon the abstract terms of the directive. In effect administrators', when applying such legislation, must choose the option which protects the Charter rights of those affected. In interpreting a statute or delegated legislation, the national court must prefer the interpretation which facilitates the Charter. While a national court can be assertive and take its own positions, there is no doubt that preliminary reference procedure may also be relied upon to generate the Charter compatible interpretation or decision. It is important to recognize   **[14–57]**

---

[109] *Fontanelli*, above n 99 at p 694.

[110] S Peers, *They Paved Paradise, They Put up a Parking Lot*, Available at: http://eulawanalysis. blogspot.com/2014/03/they-paved-paradise-they-put-up-parking.html (date accessed 13 October 2014). The title for this blog is a lyric from Joni Mitchell's song *Big Yellow Taxi*.

[111] Case C-275/06 *Produtores de Musica de Espana (Promusicae) v Telefonica de Espana SAU* 2008 ECR I-271 at para 68.

however, the more expansive nature of national court's interpretive obligations under the CFR as compared with s 2 of the ECHR Act 2003.[112] This interpretive obligation received its most direct discussion in *N.S. v Secretary of State for the Home Department* December 2011, at paragraph 1977:

> "The Member States must not only interpret their national law in a manner consistent with European Union law but also make sure they do not rely on an interpretation of an instrument of secondary legislation which would be in conflict with the fundamental rights protected by the European Union legal order or with the other general principles of European Union law...."[113]

[14–58]   Yet a survey of the Irish cases which involve the Charter would suggest that this interpretive obligation has yet to be fully grasped. The recent preliminary reference of the High Court in *Digital Rights Ireland v Minister for Communications, Marine & Natural Resources* contained a direct query regarding the obligation's nature and scope.[114] It provided Court of Justice with an opportunity to give an account of how the compatibility of national implementing measures and acts with the Charter should be carried out. In the event, however, this aspect of the case was rendered redundant by the Court's landmark ruling that the relevant Data Retention Directive was itself, a disproportionate interference with the fundamental rights to respect for private life and to the protection of personal data, a broad finding which meant the case did not discuss the interpretive obligation.[115]

The Interaction of the Charter and the Constitution

[14–59]   The final overarching issue which we must discuss prior to moving to the substantive administrative justice obligations under the Charter is the question of how its provisions interact with the Irish Constitution. It is observed in chapter 15 that the passage of the ECHR Act 2003 resulted in prominent judicial reiterations of the primacy of the Irish Constitution in

---

[112] See Case C-92/12 PPU *Health Service Executive v S.C. and another*, 26 April 2012. Where the Brussels II regulation on conflict of law issues in family law and the combatting of abductions was held to be interpreted according to the principle of the best interests of the child.

[113] Joined Cases C-411/10 *N.S. v Secretary of State for the Home Department* and C-493/10 *ME v Refugee Applications Commissioner* [2012] 2 CMLR 9, citing in support of this principle (see, to that effect, Case C-10101 *Lindqvist* [2003] ECR I-12971, para 87, and Case C-305/05 *Ordre des barreux francophones et germanophone and Others* [2007] ECR I-5305, para 28

[114] *Digital Rights Ireland v Minister for Communications, Marine & Natural Resources* [2010] IEHC 221.

[115] Joined cases C-293/12 and C-594/12 *Digital Rights Ireland and Seitlinger and Others*.

the fundamental rights protection.[116] It is clear that the status and substantive provisions of the Charter position it to have a far more fundamental and extensive impact upon the rights protection landscape in Ireland, where matters fall within its sphere of application. The primary provision on constitutional interaction is Article 53 of the Charter which states:

> "Nothing in this Charter shall be interpreted as restricting or adversely affecting human rights and fundamental freedoms as recognised, in their respective fields of application, by Union law and international law and by international agreements to which the Union or all the Member States are party, including the European Convention for the Protection of Human Rights and Fundamental Freedoms, and by the Member States' constitutions."

The interaction between the Charter and domestic constitutions was considered by the Court of Justice in the *Melloni* case which was a reference from the Spanish Constitutional Court concerning the European Arrest Warrant system.[117] The question addressed to the Court of Justice was whether Article 53 of the Charter could be interpreted as permitting the national court to refuse to execute a European Arrest Warrant in order to vindicate the higher standards offered by the domestic constitutional protection of the right to fair trial. If the answer to this question was yes, then the Charter would function as a minimum floor on the protection of rights in Europe, but national courts would be able to rely upon the more protective constitutional rights provisions to strike down national measures taken to implement EU law. In his opinion conducted prior to the Court of Justice ruling Advocate General Bot rejected this, centering his analysis upon the phrase "respective fields of application" in Article 53.[118] He therefore held that within its sphere of application, the Charter amounted to the sole relevant rights provision, and superceded national constitutions. **[14–60]**

In its eventual ruling, the Court of Justice pursued a different approach. While not permitting national courts to strike down national implementation measures based upon national constitutional rights protections, it differed **[14–61]**

---

[116] See paras [15-03]-[15.05].

[117] Spanish Constitutional Court, STC 26/2014, 13 Feb. 2014 and the ECJ decision in *Melloni*, above n 107.

[118] Opinion of Advocate General Bot – Case C-399/11 – *Criminal Proceedings against Stefano Melloni*. The role of the Advocates General attached to the Court of Justice is to present independent opinions on the cases before the Court. The opinions are not binding in any way. The office is taken from the French legal system.

from the Advocate General, in holding that the combined reliance upon constitutional and Charter protections was possible in certain circumstances:

> "(…) Article 53 of the Charter confirms that, where an EU legal act calls for national implementing measures, national authorities and courts remain free to apply national standards of protection of fundamental rights, provided that the level of protection provided for by the Charter, as interpreted by the Court, and the primacy, unity and effectiveness of EU law are not thereby compromised."[119]

Thus, while domestic constitutional rights may not be cited to undermine the level of protection offered by the Charter, the court did allow for their application where their enhanced protection did not endanger "the primacy, unity and effectiveness" of EU law.

[14–62]   While this book is focused upon administrative law rather than constitutional law, or EU law, some comment must be made upon this balance. Firstly, we note that the requirement that the "primacy, unity and effectiveness" of EU law is also central to the *Siragusa* sufficient connection requirement. It thus affects when the Charter can be pled and its interaction with the Constitution. Both are key issues for the invocation of the Charter in domestic judicial review. Secondly, it is clear from the Court's ruling in *Melloni* that "effectiveness" is a standard which needs further judicial exploration in the context of fundamental rights. In that case it was held that the Spanish constitutional prohibition on trials in absentia[120] could not be relied upon to stop the execution of the European Arrest Warrant requiring Mr Melloni to be returned to Italy. The Court stressed that as the relevant Framework Decision[121] which regulated his return, was a consensus document, concluded to define in a uniform manner the procedural rights of those who were to be extradited. As further case law builds however, we may get a greater sense for how the Charter and the Constitution blend together in particular contexts, with Thym arguing that *Melloni* indicates that the Court may be willing to provide Member States with "breathing space for country-specific solutions under the umbrella of

---

[119] *Melloni*, above n 108 at para 60.

[120] Art 24 of the Spanish Constitution

[121] Council Framework Decision 2009/299/JHA of 26 Feb. 2009 amending Framework Decisions 2002/584/JHA, 2005/214/JHA, 2006/783/JHA, 2008/909/JHA and 2008/947/JHA, thereby enhancing the procedural rights of persons and fostering the application of the principle of mutual recognition to decisions rendered in the absence of the person concerned at the trial.

the Charter".[122] The Court of Justice will likely be called upon again to reflect upon how national constitutional framework can be accommodated, especially given that Article 4(2) of the TFEU mandates the union to respect national constitutional identities.[123]

Administrative Law within the Charter of Fundamental Rights

It is important to note that the Charter was initially intended as a framing document — it subsumes the existing general principles of EU law and interlinks with the rights of the ECHR. It may also possess its own free-standing energy, with an enhanced mandate for the development of new general principles and enhanced interpretations.[124] While it is beyond the scope of this book to provide an in-depth analysis of discrete provisions of the Charter,[125] it is clear that Article 41, the right to good administration together with Article 47, the right to an effective remedy, require some direct consideration as "administrative law" protections. The latter provision provides that:

[14–63]

> "Everyone whose rights and freedoms guaranteed by the law of the Union are violated has the right to an effective remedy before a tribunal in compliance with the conditions laid down in this Article.
>
> Everyone is entitled to a fair and public hearing within a reasonable time by an independent and impartial tribunal previously established by law. Everyone shall have the possibility of being advised, defended and represented.
>
> Legal aid shall be made available to those who lack sufficient resources in so far as such aid is necessary to ensure effective access to justice."

---

[122] D Thym, *Blending National Autonomy into the EU Charter. A Reply to Leonard F.M. Besselink,* VerfBlog, 2014/8/19, http://www.verfassungsblog.de/blending-national-autonomy-eu-charter-reply-leonard-f-m-besselink/ (date accessed 13 October 2014). For a contrary perspective, which views the Court of Justice as having taken an aggressive stance on the primacy of the Charter over national constitutions see: L Besselink, "The Parameters of Constitutional Conflict after Melloni" (2014) 39 ELR 531.

[123] "The Union shall respect the equality of Member States before the Treaties as well as their national identities, inherent in their fundamental structures, political and constitutional, inclusive of regional and local self-government..."

[124] While the standards of the ECHR represent a floor below which the protection, Art 52(3) notes that rights protection under EU law may be more expansive.

[125] Though, clearly we have also enjoyed the opportunity to discuss many substantive areas of law, as we considered the consequences for public administration of the growing Europeanisation of our judicial review. Our chapter on the European Convention on Human Rights can also be employed given the express links between the two systems.

[14–64]   Article 47 subsumes the principle of equivalence and effectiveness which we have already discussed in this chapter.[126] It also can be read together with Article 6 ECHR, in that Strasbourg jurisprudence will play a powerful role in setting out and refining its core requirements. An early Irish illustration of the significance of Article 47 was the initial High Court ruling in the aforementioned *Digital Rights Ireland Ltd v Minister for Communications Marine & Natural Resources*.[127] The applicant company was attempting to make out that it possessed *locus standi* to take the action. The defendants objected, relying upon past judgments which had excluded corporate

---

[126] See Case C-432/05 *Unibet (London) Ltd and Unibet (International) Ltd v Justitiekanslern* [2007] ECR I-2271, paras 37-45:

"[A]ccording to settled case-law, the principle of effective judicial protection is a general principle of Community law stemming from the constitutional traditions common to the Member States, which has been enshrined in Articles 6 and 13 of the European Convention for the Protection of Human Rights and Fundamental Freedoms ... and which has also been reaffirmed by Article 47 of the Charter of fundamental rights of the European Union, proclaimed on 7 December 2000 in Nice (OJ 2000 C 364, p 1).

Under the principle of cooperation laid down in Art 10 EC, it is for the Member States to ensure judicial protection of an individual's rights under Community law. ... It is also to be noted that, in the absence of Community rules governing the matter, it is for the domestic legal system of each Member State to designate the courts and tribunals having jurisdiction and to lay down the detailed procedural rules governing actions for safeguarding rights which individuals derive from Community law. ... Although the EC Treaty has made it possible in a number of instances for private persons to bring a direct action, where appropriate, before the Community Court, it was not intended to create new remedies in the national courts to ensure the observance of Community law other than those already laid down by national law. ... It would be otherwise only if it were apparent from the overall scheme of the national legal system in question that no legal remedy existed which made it possible to ensure, even indirectly, respect for an individual's rights under Community law. ... Thus, while it is, in principle, for national law to determine an individual's standing and legal interest in bringing proceedings, Community law nevertheless requires that the national legislation does not undermine the right to effective judicial protection. ... In that regard, the detailed procedural rules governing actions for safeguarding an individual's rights under Community law must be no less favourable than those governing similar domestic actions (principle of equivalence) and must not render practically impossible or excessively difficult the exercise of rights conferred by Community law (principle of effectiveness)...

Moreover, it is for the national courts to interpret the procedural rules governing actions brought before them, such as the requirement for there to be a specific legal relationship between the applicant and the State, in such a way as to enable those rules, wherever possible, to be implemented in such a manner as to contribute to the attainment of the objective...of ensuring effective judicial protection of an individual's rights under Community law."

[127] *Digital Rights Ireland Ltd v Minister for Communications Marine & Natural Resources* [2010] 3 IR 251, paras 43-49.

persons.[128] Ruling for the applicants, McKechnie J highlighted the discrete impact of the principle of effectiveness on the matter before him:

> "It is therefore clear that where issues of EU law arise in litigation, the Courts may be required to take a more liberal approach to the issue of standing so that a person's rights thereunder are not unduly hampered or frustrated. The rules on standing should be interpreted in a way which avoid making it *"virtually impossible"*, or *"excessively difficult"*, or which impedes or makes *"unduly difficult"*, the capacity of a litigant to challenge EU measures of general application under Art. 267 TFEU (see also *Van Schijnel v. SPF* [1995] ECR I-4705, para. 17; *Amministrazione delle Finanze v. San Giogio* [1983] ECR 3595, para. 14). That is not to say that where questions of EU law are raised and a preliminary reference requested, the Court is automatically precluded from refusing a plaintiff standing. However, as was the case with regards to the power to grant interim relief in *The Queen v. Secretary of State for Transport, ex parte Factortame Ltd & Ors.* [1990] ECR I-2433, if the Court would be otherwise minded to allow standing in relation to the questions raised, but for a strict application of the national rules on *locus standi*, the Court should nonetheless grant standing where to do otherwise would render the plaintiff's Community rights effectively unenforceable."

One of the most significant features of Article 47 is its express guarantee of legal aid. While the right is clearly balanced by the requirement that "such aid is necessary to ensure effective access to justice", the Charter requires that a specific and coherent proportionality analysis be carried out on funding decisions. While decisions such as *Carmody*[129] successfully preserved existing Irish approaches in the ECHR Act context, the Charter (through its accompanying interpretive obligation) represents a binding source of potential provision for matters falling within the scope of EU law. In the early case of *DEB*,[130] the Court of Justice held that Article 47 was to be interpreted as applying to decisions to require or waive advance payment of costs. A national court is bound to consider whether the impact of such a decision is such that it undermines the right of access to the courts without proportionate justification. In particular, the amount of advance payment must not represent an insurmountable obstacle to securing an **[14–65]**

---

[128] In particular the Supreme Court decision in *Construction Industry Federation v Dublin City Council* [2005] 2 IR 496. The plaintiff in that case was an unincorporated association representing the interest of parties involved in the construction industry.

[129] *Carmody v Minister for Justice* [2010] 1 IR 635.

[130] *DEB, Deutsche Energiehandels v Bundesrepublik Deutschland*, Case C-279/09, *DEB* [2010] ECR I-13849.

effective remedy. Key elements of any legal aid proportionality analysis are whether the applicant has a reasonable prospect of success, the nature and seriousness of the personal interests involved, the complexity of the law and procedure and the ability of the applicant to represent herself or himself.[131]

[14–66]   Article 41, the right to good administration, embraces the right to a fair hearing and has already had a powerful impact on Ireland's asylum procedures, triggering reform of the manner in which decisions on subsidiary protection were taken. In the case of *MM*,[132] the Court of Justice expressly condemned Ireland's then bifurcated system, holding that where there were two separate procedures for determining asylum applications and applications for subsidiary protection, an applicant applying for subsidiary protection following a failed asylum claim had to be granted a fresh hearing during this second phase wherein his views would be taken into account. The following determinations were made regarding Article 41:

- "Article 41(2) of the Charter provides that the right to good administration includes the right of every person to be heard, before any individual measure which would affect him or her adversely is taken, the right of every person to have access to his or her file, while respecting the legitimate interests of confidentiality and of professional and business secrecy, and the obligation of the administration to give reasons for its decisions"[133];

- The right to be heard "must apply in all proceedings which are liable to culminate in a measure adversely affecting a person"[134];

- Observance of the right "is required even where the applicable legislation does not expressly provide for such a procedural requirement"[135];

---

[131] In the case of corporate bodies, the Court held that national courts should take into account whether the body in question is not-for-profit, the financial means of partners or shareholders and the practical likelihood of raising the advance fee.

[132] Case C-277/11 (22 November 2012), judgment not yet reported.

[133] *ibid* at para 83.

[134] *ibid* at para 86. Relying upon, inter alia, Case 17/74 *Transocean Marine Paint Association v Commission* [1974] ECR 1063, para 15; Case C-7/98 *Krombach v Bamberski*, [2000] ECR I-1935 para 42; and *Sopropé - Organizações de Calçado Lda v Fazenda Pública*, (Case C-349/07) [2008] ECR I-10369 at para 36.

[135] *ibid* at para 87, citing in support *Sopropé*, above n 111 at para 38.

- The right "requires the authorities to pay due attention to the observations thus submitted by the person concerned, examining carefully and impartially all the relevant aspects of the individual case and giving a detailed statement of reasons for their decision… the obligation to state reasons for a decision which are sufficiently specific and concrete to allow the person to understand why his application is being rejected is thus a corollary of the principle of respect for the rights of the defence".[136]

Using these principles, the Court of Justice rejected Ireland's submission that a fresh hearing was unnecessary as "the formality of a hearing in a sense replicates the hearing which he has already had in a largely similar context".[137] Having received the preliminary reference ruling of the Court of Justice, the national proceedings continued, and in *MM v Minister of Justice & Anor*, Hogan J quashed the Minister's refusal of subsidiary protection.[138] The Minister had relied on adverse credibility findings made during the separate asylum application and had failed to undertake a second hearing of the Mr MM's claims. Acknowledging the substantial practical impact of the decision, Hogan J noted that a fresh and effective hearing required that the applicant have the opportunity to respond to the adverse credibility findings and to express views on all matters relevant to his subsidiary protection claim.[139] [14–67]

Despite these examples of the Charter's successful invocation, it is clear that the prevailing sense is one of possibility rather than centrality. As De Búrca has argued, Irish Courts have so far been "much less ready to interpret and apply" its provisions despite its growing use by counsel. She submits that this is largely "based upon the relative novelty and unfamiliarity of the Charter…and their uncertainty about its scope of application".[140] At the everyday level, during the initial period after its introduction it appeared that "the courts have often sought to avoid the arguments based on the Charter", with only a brief treatment of any Charter arguments raised.[141] While we remain in an initial bedding-in phase, the co-existence and complementarity of the Charter and the ECHR lends an [14–68]

---

[136] *ibid* at para 88.
[137] *ibid* at para 90.
[138] *MM v Minister for Justice* [2013] IEHC 9.
[139] *ibid* at para 49.
[140] Above n 91.
[141] *ibid*.

established corpus of jurisprudence and a track record of proportionality analysis to the former. Given the interpretative obligation and the direct effect of EU law norms, the Charter is more hard-edged than the ECHR Act 2003. It will also be interesting to observe how the provisions which merely affirm existing general principles of EU law evolve. Their interpretation remains more dependent on existing Court of Justice precedents relating to the subject matter at hand, and it remains to be seen whether the Court will value rights in a more direct manner than prior to the Lisbon Treaty. The accumulation of jurisprudence will ultimately trigger many litigants to frame their applications for review to embrace Charter claims. In view of this, the use and influence of EU legal principles is only likely to grow in the domestic administrative law arena.

CHAPTER FIFTEEN

THE EUROPEAN CONVENTION ON HUMAN RIGHTS AND GOVERNMENT DECISION-MAKING

Introduction

The introduction of the European Convention on Human Rights Act 2003   **[15–01]**
added a new wrinkle to Government decision-making in Ireland. Clearly,
for the everyday Government employee, the rumour that defined statutory
schemes and tasks would be supplemented by the obligations contained
within a separate international instrument was no doubt imposing. Yet, as
perhaps indicated by the description of an "added wrinkle", it is clear that
the Act has not, as yet, had a far-reaching impact beyond certain defined
areas. This limited impact may be attributed both to certain qualifications
included within the 2003 Act and to a number of court decisions which
have affected its broader application. One must stress however, that
acknowledging the limited impact of the domestic Act is not to imply
that the Convention itself, as enforced by litigation before the European
Court on Human Rights, does not, as an international legal instrument,
exert considerable influence over Irish law and policy.

The recognition of the Convention exposes Irish administrative law to   **[15–02]**
different philosophies regarding discretion and the rule of law. As we
shall see in this chapter, the ECHR's "administrative law" centric
provision, Article 6, is not of the broadest scope and its development
is somewhat clouded by conceptual concerns. Despite this, however,
the Convention's provisions, with their emphasis upon balancing and the
broader process of reasoning with and through Convention rights, have
exposed a number of previously unquestioned statutory relationships and
processes to critique. Given the growing role of the Charter of Fundamental
Rights and the increasing competences of the EU, Irish public
administration may yet be grateful for the ECHR Act providing as it has a
cushioned test run for integrating international obligations and European
principles of public decision-making into Government Departments.
Furthermore, if the legal complexities surrounding the mooted accession
of the European Union to the European Convention on Human Rights are
resolved, a growing unity may be generated in the future.

As we begin our assessment of the law in this area it is useful to start with   **[15–03]**
the case of *X(R) v Minister for Justice and Law Reform*[1] in which Hogan J
provided a number of helpful baseline statements regarding the ECHR's
status and role in the Irish legal system, based on the Supreme Court cases

---

[1] *X(R) v Minister for Justice and Law Reform* [2010] IEHC 446, hereinafter "*X(R)*".

of *Carmody*[2] and *McD v L and ors*.[3] Firstly, he restated the accepted principle that pleadings based on constitutional rights will be heard prior to ECHR grounds of action, a process which reflects the fact that "the Convention comes into play only where the Constitution does not provide an adequate remedy in its own right".[4] He stressed that:

> "The Oireachtas has, of course, decided to give legal effect in the manner contemplated by the 2003 Act to the European Convention of Human Rights in accordance with Article 29.6 of the Constitution. The Convention is, of course, a central feature of the European legal patrimony and the jurisprudence of the European Court of Human Rights serves — among other things — as a salutary warning to the dangers of legal parochialism in matters of fundamental rights. But, as both Murray CJ and Fennelly J pointed out in *McD v L.*, the Convention does not have direct effect in our domestic law. Nor did the Oireachtas intend — and could not constitutionally have intended — to create a form of parallel Constitution via the 2003 Act. Rather, the whole thrust of the 2003 Act was to provide a form of failsafe mechanism to deal with those — hopefully rare — cases where it has been actually established that the Constitution does not meet the international obligations to which we have solemnly committed as a State".[5]

[15–04] The rejection of the idea that the ECHR could represent a "supplemental Constitution" is a rather strident expression of a fundamental principle: that a piece of legislation cannot overrule or qualify Constitution rights. It is perhaps also something of an *obiter* straw man which the judiciary can renounce in a manner which underlines its inter-institutional *bona fides* in interpreting the 2003 Act. A second point which may be made is the need to rule out any undertones which may accompany the expressions "failsafe mechanism" or "last resort".[6] These expressions should not be viewed by the reader as carrying with them the idea that the ECHR is not central or is unlikely to be determinative in many cases. It is important to underline that these comments concern the sequencing of grounds of action, rather than representing efforts to parse the future role of the 2003 Act or the overlap between the Convention and the Constitution, something which is best determined on a case by case basis.

---

[2] *Carmody v Minister for Justice* [2010] 1 IR 635, hereinafter "*Carmody*".
[3] *McD v L and ors* [2010] 2 IR 199.
[4] *X(R)* above n 1 at para 32. Citing *Carmody* above n 2 at 650.
[5] *X(R) ibid* at para 35.
[6] *ibid* at para 37.

Of course the primary focus in most cases taken under the ECHR Act will be on the discrete question of whether the conduct of the Government was compatible with the Convention. In such instances where the validity of an administrative decision is challenged, the Constitution first principle also applies as:

> "…it would be anomalous and at odds with the appropriate and established system of legal norms if, for instance, Article 8 ECHR came to be regarded *de facto* as the primary guarantee of family life with the result that Article 41 of the Constitution came to be effectively replaced or supplanted in such cases. This would, however, be the practical consequence of permitting litigants to invoke the ECHR as a first resort, instead of — as I believe the Oireachtas clearly intended with the 2003 Act – as a last resort".[7]

This chapter will commence somewhat unusually, in that, rather than extolling the virtues of pleading the ECHR in the Irish courts, we will focus on the difficulties of so doing. The language of the 2003 Act, combined with the prevailing judicial interpretation of its key terms, has significantly restricted its practical impact. For practitioners, it quickly becomes clear that using the 2003 Act is an ambiguous business, and those who do use it will often find their heads bumping on frustrating interpretative and remedial ceilings. Indeed in invoking the ECHR before the Irish courts, many a practitioner may feel like they have arrived on floor seven and a half in the movie *Being John Malkovich*. Escape from this world is, of course through the cupboard to the Strasbourg Court, the abiding weight of whose findings were embodied by recent high profile cases such as *A, B, C v Ireland*[8] and *Louise O'Keefe v Ireland*.[9] The public debate following both cases underlines that the Strasbourg avenue continues to deliver concrete outcomes for individual clients and have the ability to trigger broader legislative reform. They also underline that, regardless of the technicalities of the 2003 Act, Government policy makers must integrate consideration of the ECHR into their decision-making processes.

How Does the ECHR Enter the Irish Legal System?

The European Convention on Human Rights Act 2003 installed a number of mechanisms to promote compliance with the Convention obligations.

[15–05]

[15–06]

[15–07]

---

[7] *ibid.*

[8] *A, B, C v Ireland* (2011) 53 EHRR 13.

[9] *Louise O'Keefe v Ireland* Application No 35810/09 Grand Chamber judgment of 28 January 2014.

Firstly, there is the qualified obligation to interpret legislation in accordance with the provisions of the Constitution (the *interpretive obligation*):

> "In interpreting and applying any statutory provision or rule of law, a court shall, in so far as is possible, subject to the rules of law relating to such interpretation and application do so in a manner compatible with the State's obligations under the Convention provisions."[10]

Secondly, there is an obligation placed upon the organs of the State to act in a manner compatible with the State's obligations (the *performative obligation*):

> "(1) Subject to any statutory provision (other than this Act) or rule of law, every organ of the State shall perform its functions in a manner compatible with the State's obligations under the Convention provisions.
>
> (2) A person who has suffered injury, loss or damage as a result of a contravention of *subsection (1)*, may, if no other remedy in damages is available, institute proceedings to recover damages in respect of the contravention in the High Court (or subject to subsection 3, in the Circuit Court) and the Court may award to the person such damages (if any) as it considers appropriate."[11]

Thirdly, s 4, bearing the title "Interpretation of Convention Provisions" provides that:

> "Judicial notice shall be taken of the Convention provisions and of:
>
> (a) Any declaration, decision, advisory opinion or judgment of the European Court of Human Rights established under the Convention on any question in respect of which that Court has jurisdiction,
>
> (b) Any decision or opinion of the European Commission of Human Rights so established on any question in respect of which it had jurisdiction,
>
> (c) Any decision of the Committee of Ministers established under the Statute of the Council of Europe on any question in respect of which it has jurisdiction,
>
> and a court shall, when interpreting and applying the Convention provisions, take due account of the principles laid down by those declarations, decisions, advisory opinions, opinions and judgments."[12]

---

[10] s 2(1).

[11] s 3(1) and s 3(2). The damages recoverable under this section in the Circuit Court shall not exceed the amount standing prescribed, for the time being by law, as the limit of that Court's jurisdiction in tort.

[12] s 4.

Lastly, legislation can be declared incompatible with the Convention but this declaration of incompatibility does not interrupt the operation of the legislation.

The Interpretive Obligation

Upon its creation, s 2 could be immediately adversely compared to its equivalent provision in the UK Human Rights Act 1998. This latter provision stated:

[15–08]

> "So far as it is possible to do so, primary legislation and subordinate legislation must be read and given effect in a way which is compatible with Convention rights."[13]

The Irish s 2 is more qualified, noting that any duty to interpret the "subject to the rules of law relating to such interpretation and application". The consequences of this qualification were accurately predicted by then Chief Justice Keane, who noted that the qualification might

[15–09]

> "inhibit the courts in doing violence to the actual language used by the Oireachtas in an attempt to bring a statute into conformity with the Convention".[14]

The restricted horizons of s 2 were underlined by O'Neill J in *Dublin City Council v Gallagher*:

> "...the consequences of this difference are important because it means that in this jurisdiction a Court, when attempting to construe a law in a Convention compatible way, is still bound by the rules of law which heretofore have governed such interpretation, whereas in the U.K. no such restriction is imposed by Parliament. The range of manoeuvre available to a U.K. court...is not available to an Irish Court. The practical consequence of this is that, whereas in the U.K. it would appear that a Court can impose a Convention compatible meaning unless that meaning clearly conflicts with the express terms, or the necessary implication of such terms of the law in question, in this jurisdiction, a Court is required by the Oireachtas to adhere to existing rules of interpretation which means that the

---

[13] s 3(1) of the Human Rights Act 1998.

[14] Chief Justice Ronan Keane, *Issues for the Judiciary in the Application of the ECHR Act, 2003*, Paper presented at the Human Rights and Law Society of Ireland Conference on New Human Rights Legislation 2003. Available at: http://www.ihrc.ie/download/pdf/paper200310_actconf_ronan_keane.pdf (date accessed 30 June 2014).

dominant rule of statutory construction must still prevail i.e. that effect must be given to the will of Parliament, such intent being derived from the natural and ordinary meaning of the language used in the law concerned. Other rules of interpretation may have an equally or indeed more restrictive effect depending on the law under consideration. In effect, the kind of creative interpretation permitted under s.3 (1) of the U.K. Act may not be permissible under s.2 of the Act of 2003 unless [it] could be said to have been intended by Parliament".[15]

[15–10] The main case exploring the scope of s 2 to secure Convention compliant interpretations of domestic legislation is McKechnie J's High Court judgment in *Foy v An t-Ard Chlaraitheoir*.[16] *Foy* was an action taken by a post-operative transgendered person, who sought to amend her birth registration to reflect her identity. Amendment in such circumstances was not provided for under the Civil Registration Act 2004, despite the 2002 ruling of the European Court on Human Rights in *Goodwin v United Kingdom*,[17] that a refusal of recognition was a violation of the right to private and family life under Article 8. McKechnie J stated:

> "...section 2 of the Act is not free from doubt, in particular where it uses the expression 'in so far as possible...' Less wide ranging phrases such as in so far as is 'reasonable' or 'practicable' or some other such similar wording is not used. Therefore in my view, the Oireachtas intended the courts to go much further than simply applying traditional citeria, such as e.g., the purposeful rule of giving ambigious words a meaning which accords with convention rights; something like the double construction test."[18]

Nevertheless, McKechnie found that the wording of s 2 functioned to ensure:

> "...the section cannot extend to producing a meaning which is fundamentally at variance with a key or core feature of the statutory provision or rule of law in question. It cannot be applied *contra legum* nor can it permit the destruction of a scheme or its replacement with a remodelled one. In addition, a given legal position may be so well established that it becomes virtually immutable in the landscape. It seems to me that to apply the section in any of these, circmstances,

---

[15] *Dublin City Council v Gallagher* [2008] IEHC 354 at 10.
[16] *Foy v An t-Ard Chlaraitheoir* [2012] 2 IR 1, hereinafter "*Foy*".
[17] *Goodwin v United Kingdom* [2002] 35 EHRR 447.
[18] *Foy* above n 16 at 36-37.

which are but examples, would be to breach the threshold, even one set as expansively as this one is. When the court finds itself so restricted the only remedy is a declaration of incompatibility."[19]

It is sobering to conclude that *Foy* is the high point of interpretive duty in Irish law. Section 2 had not been the focus of the submissions of counsel for Ms Foy, and McKechnie J in the circumstances, felt that it was a sounder approach to issue a declaration of incompatibility.

[15–11]

A narrower approach to s 2 was supported in the Supreme Court judgments in *McD v L*, where Murray CJ stressed that s 2 is limited:

[15–12]

"In exercising its jurisdiction pursuant to s.2 a court must identify the statutory provisions or rule of law which it is interpreting or applying. Even then it is subject to any rule of law relating to interpretation and application".[20]

McD v L also contains valuable reflections on whether s 2 can be applied to areas of administrative discretion which are not regulated by the express terms of a statute. Fennelly J held that there must be a positive rule of law that can be the object of re-interpretation under s 2 of the Act.[21] Murray CJ however, stressed in *obiter* comments that:

[15–13]

"Although it may not be necessary to do so, I should add that the mere fact that the law could be said to be silent as regards a specific situation does not necessarily mean that it is unaffected by the law or the Constitution. Silence of the law may speak volumes for the legal status to be accorded or not to be accorded to a particular subject matter or situation...In short to say that the law is silent on a specific matter is not to say that such a matter necessarily exists in a legal vacuum so as to be unaffected by other rules of law."[22]

---

[19] *ibid* at 37.
[20] *McD v L* above n 3 at 251. Doyle and Ryan note also the judgment of MacMenamin J in *McB v LE* [2010] IESC 123 where a litigant sought to use the interpretive duty to expand the current legal provisions relating to unmarried fathers under family law:
  "the interpretive obligation could not go so far as to require the Court to pronounce new rights where statute law does not confer them and current jurisprudence expressly precludes them" [at paragraph 126].
  O Doyle and D Ryan, "Judicial Interpretation of the European Convention of Human Rights Act 2003: Reflections and Analysis", (2011) 18(1) DULJ 369.
[21] This was a criticism of Hedigan J's approach in the High Court, which his Honour regarded as failing to anchor itself in any specific rule of law.
[22] *McD v L* above n 3 at 255.

[15–14]   Doyle and Ryan correctly stress the significance of the comment, noting that "the apparent absence of a positive rule of law does not mean that a legal situation is unregulated by a rule of law".[23] In particular they note the common law principles that "whatever is not legally prohibited is legally permitted" and "that no person has a legal right as against another person, unless the law specifically accords her that right".[24] The authors would endorse this point, which reflects the powerful undertow which Ireland's nature as a republican state should carry as well as the rich and evolving common law principles which it inherited and continues to develop. Furthermore, as perhaps seen in our earlier discussion of the nature of executive power, discretion should be perceived as in some way structured or contemplated by statutory or constitutional authority. One would also note that the Constitution itself allows the entry of international law norms at the level of common law, and the ECHR Act 2003 heightens the legitimacy of relying upon such resources. In addition, such use of ECHR case-law cannot be assailed on grounds of separation of powers: if the Oireachtas disagreed with the interpretation of the courts regarding the subsisting common law norms, it would merely have to pass legislation modifying them. The attempt to adopt a restrictive interpretation of "rule of law" therefore outstrips the professed justifications for the narrow reading of s 2 more generally. Regardless, it is clear that the ruling of Fennelly J underlines the depth of the dominant judicial perception that s 2's language forbids expansive approaches. It is clear that the provision's qualified language cannot gain a firm enough foothold to disturb the continued application of the "ordinary meaning" approach to statutory interpretation.[25]

Performative Obligation (Section 3)

[15–15]   Section 3 of the ECHR Act requires "organs of the state" to carry out their functions in a Convention compliant manner "[s]ubject to any statutory provision...or rule of law". Section 1(1) of the Act defines the organs of the state including:

---

[23] Doyle and Ryan above n 20 at 373.

[24] *ibid.*

[25] This conclusion is one made a few years ago by F de Londras and C Kelly, *European Convention on Human Rights Act: Operation, Impact and Analysis'* (Round Hall, Dublin, 2010), chapter 4.

"...a tribunal or any other body (other than the President or the Oireachtas or either House of the Oireachtas or a Committee of either such House or a Joint Committee of both such Houses or a court) which is established by law or through which any of the legislative, executive or judicial powers of the State are exercised;"

This is a broad provision that eschews the approach in the UK, which looks to whether the body is engaging in a public function. As de Londras comments "it is not, however, at all clear that the bodies seemingly included under s 3 would be aware of their inclusion therein".[26] In the absence of further judicial clarification of s 1(1), speculation on its ambit will continue.

[15–16]

Turning to the substantive obligation under s 3, we meet an initially significant obligation which is again, in the manner of s 2, hand-braked by the qualifying phrase "[s]ubject to any statutory provision...or rule of law". The first way in which this can be interpreted is that a relevant Government decision-maker is entitled to rely on interpretations of the legislation under s 2. In other words, a breach of s 3 cannot be found where the decision-maker made the decision under existing lawful authority. Thus in litigating before the courts, s 3 would exist in the shadow of s 2: if a successful interpretation which expands the obligations of the decision-maker is obtained, a section three breach would follow. If the court finds it impossible to adopt a Convention compliant interpretation, s 3 would not be breached.

[15–17]

An alternative, more expansive approach was seen in the *Pullen (No 2)* case,[27] where it was held that s 3 requires organs of the State to perform their functions in the least violatory manner possible. Thus, in applying discretions, the administrative decision-maker would have to choose the course of action which least damaged Convention rights. The damages so far made available for breaches of s 3(1) have been substantial. In *O'Donnell v South Dublin County Council*,[28] Laffoy J indicated that damages could be

[15–18]

---

[26] F de Londras, "Using the ECHR in the Irish Courts: More Whisper than Bang", paper presented at the Public Interest Law Alliance, Seminar "Using the ECHR: where are we now?", 13 May 2011 at p 5. Available at: http://www.ucd.ie/t4cms/pilaechrseminar130511fdelondras.pdf (date accessed 30 June 2014), hereinafter "de Londras". She instances the Electricity Supply Board, established under the Electricity Supply Board Act 1927, asking "Is the ESB therefore under an obligation to ensure that when, for example, it cuts off someone's electricity supply it is cognizant of the Convention-based rights of that individual?".

[27] *Pullen v Dublin City Council (No 2)* [2009] IEHC 452, hereinafter *"Pullen (No 2)"*.

[28] *O'Donnell v South Dublin County Council* [2007] IEHC 204, hereinafter *"O'Donnell v South Dublin"*.

assessed to a level sufficient to purchase a mobile home, while in *Pullen v Dublin City Council*,[29] two local authority tenants were awarded €20,000 each for a breach of s 3.

[15–19] One positive aspect of s 3 has been the manner in which a range of remedies beyond damages can be made available to litigants. In *Bode v Minister for Justice & Law Reform*,[30] *certiorari* was initially granted by Finlay Geoghegan J.[31] In *MacFarlane v DPP*,[32] Kearns J was open to a grant of prohibition where "a serious breach" of the applicant's Article 6(1) Convention rights was established, although this position was *obiter*. In *Pullen (No.2)*,[33] Irvine J rejected the idea that courts could ever grant an injunction where a public authority's conduct represented a breach of s 3. It is important to note that these comments were also *obiter*, as there were justifiable reasons as to why an injunction should not be available on the facts of *Pullen*.[34] In making the broader finding, Irvine J relied upon the fact that the declaration of incompatibility remedy designed by the Act did not reach so far as to render the legislation as invalid. This appeared to indicate a legislative desire to avoid remedies which reached so far as to restrain the operation of otherwise valid legislation.[35] This was further supported by the focus upon a declaration accompanied by damages in s 3(2). This reading of the Act was further reinforced for Irvine J by broader separation of powers concerns, which in her Honour's view, required that statutes must be continued to operate unhindered unless and until they were struck down under the Constitution.[36]

[15–20] Doyle and Ryan are highly critical of this reasoning however, positing three reasons why it is flawed:

---

[29] *Pullen* above n 27.

[30] *Bode v Minister for Justice & Law Reform* [2008] 3 IR 663.

[31] Leave to seek *certiorari* was similarly granted in *Agbonlahor v Minister for Justice* [2006] IEHC 56 by Herbert J (though the relief was refused on the merits by Feeney J in the eventual action, [2007] 4 IR 309).

[32] *MacFarlane v DPP* [2008] 4 IR 117.

[33] *Pullen* above n 27.

[34] In the particular case, the relevant injunction requested was that s 62 of the Housing Act 1966 should never be utilized by a housing authority given the existence of s 14 of the Conveyancing Act 1881, which permitted owner re-entry following proceedings which would have allowed consideration of the relevant individuals Art 8 ECHR rights.

[35] *Pullen* above n 27 at 24. Irvine J held that the Oireachtas "did not intend to provide any remedy that would have the effect of displacing or curtailing the operation or enforcement of any constitutionally valid provision of national law".

[36] This principle was laid down by O'Flaherty J in *McDonnell v Ireland* [1998] 1 IR 134.

"First, the courts frequently prevent public authorities from acting in a particular way on foot of a statutory provision, notwithstanding that the provision must be presumed constitutional. There is — in terms of the separation of powers — no difference between holding that it is *ultra vires* for a public authority to act in breach of natural and constitutional justice and holding that it is *ultra vires* for a public authority to breach section 3(1) of the 2003 Act, by failure to observe fair procedures protected by Article 6 of the Convention. Neither conclusion questions the validity of the statutory power which was exercised, but merely imposes certain restraints on how that power can be exercised. Second, where a public authority's power is restrained, this restraint comes not from the court's decision to issue an injunction but from section 3(1) itself. We may assume that the Oireachtas was not intending a 'law and economics; approach to section 3 whereby section 3(2) is to be read as charging public authorities a small fee for the privilege of breaching the Convention rights of citizens and others. Presumably section 3(1) is actually intended to restrain behaviour and presumably public authorities — given their respect for the rule of law — will observe the strictures of section 3(1) even if the only remedy which could be granted is an award of damages. Third and most important, the granting of an injunction to remedy a breach of section 3(1) could only be said to breach the separation of powers if it is contrary to the meaning of section 3. If on a proper construction, section 3 does not preclude the granting of an injunction, then it would be equally a breach of the separation of powers to stymie legislative intent by precluding the grant of injunctions. Ultimately, the separation of powers concerns collapse into a question of what section 3 means."[37]

The decision in *Pullen (No.2)* perhaps underlines the Irish judiciary's tendency to view the ECHR Act as carrying with it overtones of judicial activism and a traditional dualist association of international law related legislation as carrying immediate implications for legitimacy. The rush to characterise restraining of administrative decision-makers from exercising their discretion in a manner incompatible with s 3 as representing something beyond a standard *ultra vires* action is indicative of a broader judicial discomfort refusal to treat the ECHR Act as just another statute. It underlines the itchy trigger finger of Irish judges, who seem to harbour a recurring wish to register the fact that they are not amenable to granting the Act a major role within the Irish legal system.   [15–21]

---

[37] Doyle and Ryan above n 20 at pp 376-377.

Judicial Notice of ECHR Case-Law (Section 4)

[15–22]   The obligation placed upon the courts by s 4 is to pay due regard to any relevant ECHR decisions which bear upon matters before it, regardless of whether a substantive claim under the ECHR Act 2003 is pleaded or not. As Doyle and Ryan note s 4 can "create an enhanced impetus for the already-developed practice of the infusion of Convention protection into domestic constitutional analysis".[38] Writing extrajudicially,[39] Judge Thomas O'Donnell highlighted the case of *McCann v The Judges of Monaghan District Court and Others*,[40] which involved a challenge to the constitutionality of the Enforcement of Courts Orders Act 1940. While the ECHR leg of this case was rendered moot by Laffoy J's finding of unconstitutionality, Justice O'Donnell praised the manner in which "the Convention points are woven into the case".[41] Clearly s 4 has a small part to play in ameliorating past oppositional tendencies in Irish judicial culture towards legal pluralism. This has often seen judicial reasoning regarding international legal norms to collapse into broad conclusory statements presenting two narrow alternatives: bindingness or subordination, rather than productive interaction between systems and actors.

[15–23]   A note of concern however, must be registered regarding the *manner* in which reliance is placed upon the Strasbourg case-law and its relationship to Ireland's Convention obligations. The cases of the ECtHR represent rulings of an international court, whose reasoning process is expressly structured to pay due deference to all national authorities — including national courts. Crucially, this includes the doctrine of the margin of appreciation, which is the area of judgment the ECtHR accords to national authorities due to their closer proximity to the relevant facts, administrative

---

[38] *ibid* at p 378. As an example of best practice in this regard they cite the judgment of Laffoy J in *O'Shea v Ireland*, [2007] 2 IR 313 where reliance was placed upon *B and L v The United Kingdom*, (2006) 42 EHRR 11, Laffoy J held at 329-330:

> "While…the interpretation or application of the Convention provisions is not in issue, so that the Court is not obliged to take account of the principles laid down in the judgment of the European Court of Human Rights, as would otherwise be the case by virtue of s.4 of the Act of 2003 if Convention rights were invoked, in my view the reasoning of the European Court of Human Rights in *B and L v United Kingdom* is persuasive in the context of the issue before the court."

[39] Justice Thomas O'Donnell, "The District Court, the European Convention on Human Rights Act, 2003 'Cause and Effect'", [2010] *Judicial Studies Institute Journal* 97, hereinafter "O'Donnell".

[40] *McCann v The Judges of Monaghan District Court and Others* [2009] IEHC 276.

[41] O'Donnell above n 39 at p 106.

structures and public interests involved. Thus reasoning with ECHR case-law begins with identifying the role which the margin of appreciation played in the relevant case, and considering how the judgment may be integrated into the reasoning of a *national* court. The UK courts have been more discerning in dealing with this distinction, and have ensured that the margin is not applied domestically. Instead, they have developed the entirely separation doctrine of a "discretionary area of judgment" which a national court must accord other domestic governmental institutions. It is most interesting to see that where successful cases have been taken under the ECHR Act, UK's domestic case-law has played an important role in raising Irish courts comfort level with expansive interpretations.[42] This also reflects some crossover between the terms of the Irish ECHR Act and the UK Human Rights Act. Yet reliance on UK case-law cannot be reflexive, due to the fact that those cases are structured around the UK-centric doctrine "discretionary area of judgment". The design of such a doctrine reflects the UK's approach to separation of powers, rather than our own. Thus, the process of taking notice of contains notable complexities, and identifying Ireland's obligations under the Convention does not entail merely the superficial consultation of the results of recent ECtHR case-law. The terms of s 4 of the ECHR Act itself reflect this noting that when interpreting and applying the provisions of the Convention, due account must be taken of the "principles laid down" in such decisions.

Declarations of Incompatibility (Section 5)

The ideal starting point to commence a discussion of the declaration of incompatibility mechanism is in de Londras' summation of it: [15–24]

> "the Irish Declaration of Incompatibility is like a cubic zirconia engagement ring: shiny, splendid looking and attractive but practically worthless apart from its sentimental value."[43]

Section 5 installs the declaration of incompatibility as available only where "no other legal remedy is adequate and available". Thus one must transit unsuccessfully through s 2 and s 3 for it to arise.

---

[42] For an example of this see *O'Donnell v South Dublin County Council*, above n 28.

[43] De Londras above n 26 at p 7.

[15–25]   The first declaration of incompatibility was *Foy v An t-Ard Chlaraitheoir*,[44] issued in the High Court by McKechnie J. The first response of the Government was to signal a desire to appeal to the Supreme Court, but following extensive delays (and a change of Government), draft legislation finally issued on 17 July 2013. The Gender Recognition Bill was still under discussion in the Oireachtas at the time this book went to press. Clearly the declaration of incompatibility is a remedy which is dependent upon the vagaries of political will. This is further underlined by reaction to the Supreme Court's declaration in *Donegan v Dublin City Council*,[45] that s 62 of Housing Act 1966, which allows for the accelerated removal of a tenant from a property without provision of a hearing, was incompatible with the ECHR. This also lay un-remedied for a sizeable period, until the introduction of new statutory provisions discussed at para [15–80].

[15–26]   Finally, the practical utility of a declaration of incompatibility was further reduced by the ruling of the Strasbourg Court in *A, B, C v Ireland*,[46] where the Grand Chamber held that the failure to seek a declaration under s 5 could not constitute a failure to exhaust domestic remedies. The Court held:

> "The Court does not consider that an application under the 2003 Act for a declaration of the relevant provisions of the 1861 Act, and for an associated *ex gratia* award of damages, could be considered an effective remedy which had to be exhausted. The rights guaranteed by the 2003 Act would not prevail over the provisions of the Constitution...In any event a declaration of incompatibility would place no legal obligation on the State to amend domestic law and, since it would not be binding on the parties to the relevant proceedings, it could not form the basis of an obligatory award of monetary compensation. In such circumstances and given the relatively small number of declarations to date...only one of which has recently become final, a request for such a declaration and for an *ex gratia* award of damages would not have provided an effective remedy to the first and second applicants."[47]

Administrative Law and the European Convention on Human Rights

[15–27]   With this chapter having commenced by noting the effectiveness of the ECtHR and then having established the general mechanics for using

---

[44] *Foy* above n 16.
[45] *Donegan v Dublin City Council* [2012] IESC 18.
[46] *A, B, C v Ireland* above n 8
[47] *ibid* at para 134.

the ECHR in the domestic courts, we are now in a position to consider the substantive norms relating to administrative law which are contained in the Convention. One should comment that this is an imposing task to undertake — which no existing administrative law textbook has engaged in. The first feature of the ECHR/ administrative law nexus is the single article which is clearly designed to ask many of the traditional questions posed by administrative law in this country — Article 6. As we shall illustrate Article 6's development is decidedly patchy, and is somewhat dwarfed by the domestic constitutional protection of procedural fairness. Yet, more broadly we wish to underline that the entire Convention is an instrument preoccupied with rule of law principles, and on the role of administrative decision-making in enforcing rights. In many ways, the hunt of administrative lawyers for an easily demarcated, fenced off administrative law section is bound to fail. What follows is our attempt to highlight the importance of exploring in any particular case, how the ECHR challenges existing arrangements in Irish public administration and judicial review.

Article 6 — The Civil Limb

Article 6(1) of the ECHR provides for a right to fair procedures: [15–28]

> "In the determination of his civil rights and obligations...everyone is entitled to a fair and public hearing within a reasonable time by an independent and impartial tribunal established by the law."

The immediate difficulty for a common law judge, is the manner in which the Article is anchored in rather alien term "civil rights". The term is difficult to define, as acknowledged by Millet LJ in the UK case of *Begum*:

> "the Strasbourg Court has not proceeded by reference to principle or on policy grounds; instead it has adopted an incremental and to English eyes a disappointingly formalistic approach, making it difficult to know where the line will finally come to be drawn."[48]

One can identify a number of approaches which have been taken by the   [15–29]
Strasbourg Court in construing the term. The dominant approach would seem to require that the interest affected by the decision in some way

---

[48] *Begum v Tower Hamlets LBC* [2003] 2 AC 430 at para 87, hereinafter "*Begum*".

resemble rights in private law. This, as Craig argues,[49] contrasts with the common law approach whereby a judge considers the seriousness of the matter balanced against other policy considerations such as the need to ensure adequate freedom for the decision-maker.

[15–30]   Lord Bingham spoke directly of the discomforts many common law judges feel when confronted by Article 6. For him, a narrow interpretation of "civil rights" would allow certain areas of Government decision to be subjected to rigorous requirements, but an overbroad interpretation carries with it another danger:

> "The narrower the interpretation given to "civil rights", the greater the need to insist on review by a tribunal exercising full powers. Conversely, the more elastic the interpretation given to "civil rights", the more flexible must be the approach to the requirement of independent and impartial review if the emasculation (by over-judicialisation) of administrative welfare schemes is to be avoided."[50]

[15–31]   In the absence of leadership by the Strasbourg Court many domestic judges have therefore proceeded with caution. Yet the case-law of the ECtHR continues to expand the ambit of "civil rights". For instance the case of *Feldbrugge v Austria*,[51] held that the right to social security benefits was to be regarded as a full civil right, despite some earlier cases refusing to recognise it as such. This expansion was accompanied by a strong dissenting opinion, which held that "civil rights and obligations" was to be confined to rights that were adjudicated by the civil courts.[52] The majority in *Feldbrugge* stressed their finding was related to the fact that "the right in question was a personal, economic and individual right, a factor that brought it close to the civil sphere".[53] This explanation received detailed treatment by the UK courts, with Lord Hoffman stressing in *Begum* that the "most important feature" of *Feldbrugge* was that it pertained to "[a social welfare payment that was] individual, economic and flowing from specific statutory rules."[54] Thus, while some social welfare adjudications may attract the full range of

---

[49] P Craig, "The Human Rights Act, Article 6 and Procedural Rights", (2003) *Public Law* 753, hereinafter "Craig".

[50] *Begum*, above n 48 at para 5.

[51] *Feldbrugge v The Netherlands* [1986] 8 EHRR 425.

[52] The joint dissenting opinion of Mr Ryssdal, Mrs Bindschedler-Robert, Mr Lagergren, Mr Matscher, Sir Vincent Evans, Mr Bernhardt and Mr Gersing. *ibid.*

[53] *ibid* at para 37.

[54] *ibid* at para 65.

Article 6 protections, more discretionary schemes "where utilitarian considerations could be taken into account when deciding on the regime of administration" could receive more flexible treatment.[55] In *Croydon,* Baroness Hale commented that attempts to rely on Article 6 by the applicant were adversely affected by the fact the decision involved "an evaluation of some very 'soft' criteria rather than specific rules", rendering it "difficult to say at what point the applicant may consider himself to be the holder of such a right".[56] In *Ali v Birmingham City Council,*[57] the UK Supreme Court invested heavily in this distinction stating that Article 6 could be focused upon benefits whose substance was defined precisely and benefits which required the exercise of more subjective discretion by the relevant authority.

Ironically, such an approach by the judiciary would encourage the creation of discretion and the removal of structured policy guidelines. In looking to ensure that the ambit of Article 6 does not over judicialise, judges must also act responsibly to ensure that Article 6 does not encourage creative non-compliance by governments. While there appears to be some mandate for restraint within Article 6's text, it must be balanced against its underlying purpose. Craig has argued strongly against the removal of discretionary decisions, as the distinction for him, "provides no basis for the conclusion that process rights should be inapplicable".[58] [15–32]

Can the Availability of Judicial Review Cure Flaws in the First Instance Process?

A key point in determining the reach and consequence of Article 6 is that any flaws in an initial hearing process can be remedied by the availability of an appeal process. The ECtHR has long established, since the 1983 case of *Albert and Le Compte v Belgium*[59] that compliance with Article 6 must be assessed by evaluating the decision-making process as a whole, rather than a single element of it. Crucially therefore, where an administrative body does not comply with Article 6(1), the existence of appeal rights or judicial review may, in certain circumstances, suffice to cure the flaws of the initial decision-making body. For this to occur, the judicial or appeal body must have "full jurisdiction", embracing the guarantees of Article 6(1). "Full [15–33]

---

[55] Craig, above n 49 at p 768.
[56] *R (A) v Croydon LBC* [2009] UKSC 8 at para 62.
[57] *Ali v Birmingham City Council* [2010] 2 AC 39.
[58] Craig above n 49 at p 758.
[59] *Albert and Le Compte v Belgium* (1991) 13 EHRR 415.

jurisdiction" continues to be explored, but its key elements are that the reviewing court must have the ability to consider the complaint for itself: it must be able to quash the decision being challenged and find that a new decision should be made by an impartial body. The power to make *de novo* or substitute findings is not required however. As a result a number of authorities have examined whether the availability of judicial review is curative of any flaws in the initial decision-making process.

[15–34]   In the UK, House of Lords judgment of *Alconbury* sought to establish a key distinction between policy and fact-finding in the role of the decision-maker. Lord Hoffman held that where the issues involved in the decision are matters of policy, judicial review will suffice.[60] Where, however, the decision represents "findings of fact, or the evaluation of facts", Article 6 requirements will not be discharged by the availability of review. Thus Juss notes that "Alconbury demonstrates that matters of national policy make it difficult to apply the strictures of Article 6 with full vigour".[61] This was further explored in *Friends Provident*,[62] where the Court held that judicial review of a planning permission decision would not suffice where there were contested issues of fact. However, the point at issue in the proceedings at hand was the impact assessment of the required building work, which the Court viewed as principally a matter of "local planning judgment, policy and expediency".[63]

[15–35]   The *Begum* case further underlined the anxieties of the UK judges regarding the implications of a finding that judicial review is inadequate to ensure compliance. The decision in this case related to an offer of housing by a local authority to the applicant, who had refused it. The relevant officer in the authority ruled that this refusal was unreasonable and disentitled the applicant to further offers. In a ruling which illustrates the ambiguities in the interplay of factual and policy issues, Lord Hoffman found that it was "inappropriate" to demand that findings of fact should be made by a body independent of the authority responsible for the administration of homelessness scheme. His Lordship argued that the overall procedure

---

[60] R *(Alconbury Developments) v Secretary of State for the Environment, Transport and the Regions* [2003] 2 AC 295.

[61] SS Juss, "Constitutionalising Rights Without a Constitution: the British Experience Under Article 6 of HRA 1998" (2006) 27(1) *Statute Law Review* 29, at p.34.

[62] R*(on the app of Friends Provident Life Office) v Secretary of State for the Environment, Transport and the Regions* [2001] EWHC Admin 820.

[63] *ibid* at para 94.

needed to be "lawful and fair".[64] Thus, even where findings of fact are raised, Article 6(1) may not be violated where the factual findings are only "only staging posts on the way to the much broader judgment".[65] Furthermore, Article 6(1) should not mandate "a more intensive approach to judicial review questions of fact". As Juss notes *Begum* illustrates that the "policy/fact-finding distinction is not necessarily a neat and happy one". The failure to make a finding of an Article 6(1) violation even where a factual dispute was raised, illustrated judicial discomfort with the potentially systemic impact of Article 6(1), especially where this could require judicial review to move into fact finding.

At this point the Strasbourg Court re-entered the fray, with its judgment in *Tsfayo v United Kingdom.*[66] Ms Tsfayo, a refugee from Ethiopia was initially granted housing benefit and council tax benefit but failed to apply in time for this to be renewed. When her situation was realised, she was again granted the benefit but her retrospective application to cover the period when the benefit lapsed was refused on the basis that she had not shown good cause for failing to apply in time. She was threatened with eviction for non-payment of rent and proceedings were issued by the local authority for non-payment of council tax. Her case was reviewed by the Council's Housing Benefit and Council Tax Benefit Review Board which rejected her appeal against refusal to pay the backdated benefits. Leave to appeal for judicial review was also rejected. **[15–36]**

The Strasbourg Court unanimously held that the Board was not an independent and impartial tribunal and that there had been a breach of Article 6. It held that the Board was not merely lacking in independence from the executive but was directly connected to one of the parties in the dispute (the Council) since it included five Councillors from the local authority that would be required to pay benefit if awarded. Further, it held that the safeguards built into the Appeal Board procedure were not adequate to overcome this fundamental lack of objective impartiality. While the concept of "full jurisdiction" permitted some flexibility, the ECtHR found that since the High Court as a second tier body had no jurisdiction to rehear the evidence or substitute its own views as to the applicant's credibility, there was never the possibility that the central issue **[15–37]**

---

[64] *Begum* above n 48 at para 47.

[65] *ibid* at para 9.

[66] *Tsfayo v UK* [2009] 48 EHRR 18, hereinafter *"Tsfayo"*.

would be determined by a tribunal that was independent of one of the parties to the dispute.[67]

[15–38] *Tsfayo* also has the consequence of introducing another analytic distinction, alongside the fact/policy one. The Court found that when determining compliance with Article 6(1), regard should be paid to whether the decision-maker is deciding non-specialist issues of fact or specialist issues. Whereas the issues in the earlier UK cases required "a measure of professional knowledge or experience and the exercise of administrative discretion pursuant to wider policy aims",[68] the question in *Tsfayo* was "a simple question of fact" determined by local councilors.

[15–39] The second Strasbourg case decided in the same period, *Crompton v United Kingdom*,[69] also complicated the picture. It acknowledged that findings under Article 6(1) were context-specific:

> "The Court has previously held that in order to determine whether the article 6-compliant second-tier tribunal had 'full jurisdiction', or provided 'sufficiency of review' to remedy a lack of independence at first instance, it was necessary to have regard to such factors as the subject-matter of the decision appealed against, the manner in which that decision was arrived at and the content of the dispute, including the desired and actual grounds of appeal."[70]

[15–40] In response to the above quote, Baker argues that "the approach to compliance is open-textured. It is a factor-based approach, but the choice of factors and their relative weight are at large".[71] In the specific case at hand the Strasbourg Court found that the availability of judicial review sufficed to defeat the argument that a violation of Article 6(1) had occurred. The applicant had sought compensation for redundancy from the Territorial

---

[67] *ibid* at para. 48 of its judgment the Court stated:
"The applicant had her claim refused because the 'Review Board' did not find her a credible witness. Whilst the High Court had power to quash the decision if it considered, inter alia, that there was no evidence to support the 'Board's' factual findings, or that its findings were plainly untenable, or that the Board had misunderstood or been ignorant of an established and relevant fact…it did not have jurisdiction to rehear the evidence or substitute its own views as to the applicant's credibility. Thus, in this case, there was never the possibility that the central issue would be determined by a tribunal that was independent of one of the parties to the dispute."

[68] *ibid* at para 46.

[69] *Crompton v United Kingdom* (2010) 50 EHRR 36.

[70] *ibid* at para 71.

[71] C Baker, "Tomlinson: a supreme case of clutching at straws in the wind: Part 2", (2010) 13(6) *Journal of Housing Law* 101 at p 102.

Army under a military scheme allowing complaints to be brought through the commanding officer to an Army Board. Following an unsuccessful judicial review which had sought to challenge the calculation of the compensation, he appealed to Strasbourg. The ECtHR found that while the Army Board lacked the necessary "structural independence" for Convention compliance, this had been remedied by the court review process.[72] It held that the Court had, in fact, examined the method and data used for the calculation "even though it could not substitute its own view as to an appropriate award in the circumstances of the case".[73] While the matter was not "specialist", the dispute itself "did not centre on a question of fact determined by the Army which the High Court had no jurisdiction to revisit", but whether the approach of the Board had been "appropriate" given its "large degree of discretion".[74] In addition, the particular factual dispute raised (which related to the salary level of the applicant at the time of the redundancy), had actually been examined by the Court, which had then accepted an undertaking on behalf of the Army Board to reconsider the figure it had used, with a subsequent increase actually having occurred.

These issues have not been overly prominent in Irish cases involving ECHR claims. This is due to the fact that most of these have been centred on the right to a home under Article 8. In the case of *Connors v UK*,[75] the Strasbourg Court held that as the provision of sufficient procedural safeguards is a core part of the protection of Article 8 rights, the requirements of Article 6, are effectively subsumed into the Article 8 analysis.[76] This has led to Article 6 case-law often being crowded out in the domestic courts. The *Donegan* judgment modelled the correct course of action, with McKechnie J, having noted the desirability of one consolidated Article 8 analysis, then proceeding to note how the ruling in *Tsfayo* fortified his conclusions under Article 8:

    [15–41]

> "...insofar as the requirements of Article 6 are incorporated in the determination with regards to the fair procedures required to vindicate infringements of Article 8 rights, the ECtHR case in *Tsfayo* is instructive... [McKechnie J proceeded to quote paragraphs 46 and 47 of the *Tsfayo* judgment]...Thus where a conflict of facts arises, which is required to be determined in relation to an alleged illegitimate infringement

---

[72] *Crompton* above n 69 at para 77.
[73] *ibid* at para 79.
[74] *ibid* at paras 78 and 79.
[75] *Connors v UK* (2004) 40 EHRR 189.
[76] *ibid at* paras 102-3.

of Article 8, it is necessary that there be some independence between the decision-maker and those, on either side, who make, support or seek to rely on the allegations in question. It is clear that any review undertaken in this regard, must be performed by a person who is rationally unconnected to those whom I have mentioned. This however should not be interpreted as requiring that a court must be the body to determine upon the matter. This could not be so; once there are in place procedures to ensure that where such questions of fact arise, there is access to an independent decision-maker acting within a process which is otherwise safeguarded, such will suffice. This requirement will only arise where the factual dispute is genuine, and where it is materially central and related to the Convention rights at issue."[77]

[15–42]   There are some examples where Irish litigants have perhaps failed to adequately integrate the core requirements of Article 6 into their Article 8 analysis. The recent case of *Reid v Industrial Development Authority*[78] perhaps illustrates some discomfort with the interrelationship between the articles on the part of counsel and the Court. There, the applicant sought to have the decision of the respondent authority to compulsorily acquire his property quashed. While the second named respondent, the Attorney General, placed extensive reliance upon *Alconbury* and other UK case-law on the adequacy of judicial review to cure a lack of independence at first instance, counsel for the applicant does not appear to have invoked any Article 6 case-law to support their Article 8 arguments. The Court in turn, did not reference *Tsfayo* in its judgment, relying instead on earlier case-law:

"A similar question to that raised by the applicant in this case was rejected in the UK House of Lords in R (*Alconbury Developments v Secretary of State for the Environment, Transport and the Regions* 2001 UKHL 23) namely whether a decision to acquire land compulsorily may only be made by an administrative body which is independent and impartial. The House of Lords found that the Secretary of State's jurisdiction to make compulsory purchase orders was consistent with article 6 of the ECHR. The House placed emphasis on the fact that the Secretary of State's decision is amenable to judicial review before the courts and this was sufficient to constitute "full jurisdiction" for the purposes of article 6." [79]

---

[77] *Tsfayo* above n 66 at para 135.
[78] *Reid v Industrial Development Authority* [2013] IEHC 433 (Hedigan J).
[79] *ibid* at para 6.2. A fact which may be attributable to the failure of the applicant to plead *Tsfayo*.

While compulsory acquisition decisions will involve issues of policy judg- **[15–43]** ment and especially, as the Court in *Reid* stressed, statutory criteria, the Court could have recognized the established inadequacy of judicial review where factual issues are raised. It must be noted however, Article 6 was not the focus of the *Reid* case, and we discuss the Article 8 elements later in this chapter.

In concluding this section, the reader may wonder whether Article 6(1) **[15–44]** retains much practical utility. Clearly more cases are required to disentangle key concepts and to reconnect with the overarching purpose of the provision. Patient identification of factually-centred administrative decision-making is required from practitioners. The possible accession of the European Union institutions to the ECHR may also prove fascinating, as EU regulators in spheres such as competition law encounter Article 6(1). Domestically, where Article 6 arguments appear in the Irish courts, there is a need to be more reflective regarding the use of UK case law, as *Alconbury*, in particular, reflects heavily upon the UK constitutional identity; especially the doctrine of parliamentary sovereignty.[80] It may be that Irish judges share the viewpoints of such cases, but they should provide their own free-standing justification. Finally, it is important to remember that the possible expansion of judicial review for errors of fact may strengthen arguments that judicial review can suffice for Article 6(1) compliance.

The Substantive Requirements of Article 6

We now move to provide an account of the substantive requirements of **[15–45]** Article 6(1), which are quite demanding, a fact which explains some of the tension regarding the adequacy of judicial review and "civil rights and obligations". The main guarantees offered by Article 6 may be grouped under the following headings:

- Tribunal independence;
- Equality of arms and equal access to information;
- The right to an oral hearing;
- Legal assistance and representation;
- Precedent and consistency;
- Protection against excessive delay.

---

[80] The authors of course, note that other considerations, such as the terms of the Human Rights Act itself or the normative development of common law rights may press the UK courts to be more expansive. The point is that this baggage should be unpacked by Irish judges.

Independence

[15–46]   In the case of *Belilos v Switzerland*, the ECtHR stressed the importance of:

> "…independence, in particular of the executive; impartiality; duration of its members' terms of office; guarantees afforded by its procedure."[81]

The leading case of *Dauti v Albania* laid down the fundamental touchstones for an analysis of independence.[82] It found that Article 6(1) had been violated in a case involving the refusal of incapacity benefit. Following an initial refusal, the applicant had applied to an Appeals Commission, consisting of medical practitioners appointed by the Albanian Ministry of Health. The Court stressed that the Commission contained no legally qualified or judicial members, finding that it did not constitute an independent or impartial tribunal:

> "The law and the domestic regulations contain no rules governing the members' term of office, their removal, resignation or any guarantee for their irremovability. The statutory rules do not provide for the possibility of an oath to be taken by its members. It appears that they can be removed from office at any time, at the whim of the ISS and the Ministry of Health, which exercise unfettered discretion. The position of the Appeals commission members is therefore open to external pressures. Such a situation undermines its appearance of independence."[83]

[15–47]   The requirements of impartiality and independence were also defined in the case of *Findlay v United Kingdom*, where the ECtHR stated:

> "In order to establish whether a tribunal can be considered as 'independent', regard must be had inter alia to the manner of appointment of its members and their term of office, the existence of guarantees against outside pressures and the question whether the body presents an appearance of independence…As to the question of 'impartiality', there are two aspects to this requirement. First, the tribunal must be subjectively free of personal prejudice or bias. Secondly, it must also be impartial from an objective viewpoint, that is, it must offer sufficient guarantees to exclude any legitimate doubt in this respect."[84]

---

[81] *Belilos v Switzerland* [1988] ECHR 4 at para 64.
[82] *Dauti v Albania*, Application No 19206/05, 3 February 2009.
[83] *ibid* at para 53.
[84] *Findlay v United Kingdom* (1997) 24 EHRR 221 at para 73.

In an Irish context, the Free Legal Advice Centre has argued that the current **[15–48]** arrangements for Social Welfare Appeals are not sufficiently independent.[85] The Appeals Office is administered by civil servants working in the Department of Social Welfare, who are not insulated from departmental policy and employment structures.[86] In 1986 the Commission on Social Welfare recommended that a separate independent appeals office be formed, with an independent chairperson. In 1991, the current Appeals Office was introduced and a Chief Appeals Officer appointed by the Minister.[87] This would appear to raise issues in terms of independence under Article 6(1). The case of *Sramek v Austria*[88] held that where a tribunal's members include people in a subordinate position in terms of their duties and organisational position, this raises legitimate doubts regarding that person's independence.

An Article 6 analysis is a strongly context-specific one, and it is clear from **[15–49]** the above that many factors will be taken into account in making a final assessment on independence. One of these will be public confidence in the mechanism:

> "In order to determine whether a tribunal can be considered to be independent as required by Article 6, appearances may also be of importance...Where in the present case, a tribunal's members include a person who is in a subordinate position, in terms of his duties and the organisation of his service, vis-à-vis one of the parties, litigants may entertain a legitimate doubt about that person's independence".[89]

It is important to remember the greater ability of a national court to scrutinise its own administrative culture; and thus the national courts may be more demanding than an international court like the ECtHR, which is more distanced from the national context.

Equality of Arms Between the Parties

This component of Article 6 has been invoked to ensure adequate legal **[15–50]** representation, equal access to information and other protections necessary

---

[85] *Not Fair Enough: Making a Case for Reform of the Social Welfare Appeals System* (FLAC, Dublin, 2010).

[86] Appeals Officers would normally transfer into the Office from another part of the Department. An Appeals Officer may also transfer back following a period of service in the Office.

[87] Prior to this, the practice had been that refusals would be appealed directly to the Minister.

[88] *Sramek v Austria* (1985) 7 EHRR 351.

[89] *ibid* at paras 41-42.

to ensure that both sides to participate in any proceedings on an equal footing. That such protections are directed towards the goal of ensuring equality between the parties was recognised in *Dombo Beheer v The Netherlands*:

> "It is clear that the requirement of "equality of arms", in the sense of a "fair balance": between the parties, applies in principle to such cases as well as to criminal cases".[90]

[15–51] In the *Dombo Beheer* case, the Court stressed that each party must be given "a reasonable opportunity to present his case...under conditions that do not place him at a substantial disadvantage vis-à-vis his opponent".[91] Furthermore in line with the Irish jurisprudence, the ECHR grounds the entitlement to an oral hearing, where the issues raised make this a practical requirement. In *Salomonsson v Sweden*, it noted that an oral hearing is often a default requirement, "if not an absolute one":

> "Thus, a hearing may be dispensed with if a party unequivocally waives his or her right thereto and there are no questions of public interest making a hearing necessary...Furthermore a hearing may not be necessary due to exceptional circumstances of the case, for example when it raises no questions of fact or law which cannot be adequately resolved on the basis of the case-file and the parties written observations".[92]

[15–52] The most prominent Irish example of Article 6 clashing with accelerated or fast track procedure has been in relation to the standard High Court orders inscribing the process for obtaining a final judgment against a debtor. The current provision for a "fast track" summary court procedure, whereby banks and other creditors apply for liberty to enter final judgments, clearly has the potential to raise Article 6(1) issues. This is due to the fact that under the summary procedure, judgements are decided on the basis of the judge's view of the "credibility" of any defence outlined in sworn written documents. Only in the event that an 'arguable' case is found is plenary hearing held, which includes the right to present oral evidence. In both

---

[90] *Dombo Beheer v The Netherlands* (1994) 18 EHRR 213.

[91] *ibid* at para 33.

[92] *Salomonsson v Sweden* (App 38978/97), Judgment of 12 November 2002 at para 34.

2011[93] and 2014,[94] the Master of the High Court made rulings stressing the possible violation of Article 6(1) where traditional approaches were applied without notice being taken of the Convention:

> "...in my view, for a lay litigant the minimum requirement for effective participation is to be allowed an opportunity to give his evidence in the witness stand. That is an absolute *sine qua non*: it would seem to follow that the test for leave to defend should not be the test dating from 1875 (*"is it very clear the defendant does not even have an arguable case?"*) but a new test derived from Human Rights principles: *"is it very clear the case can be fairly decided without an evidentiary hearing?"*[95]

While it was "probably not open" to the Master of the High Court to make a declaration of incompatibility, he nevertheless held that he was bound by the performative obligation under s 3, which in the 2011 case of *AIB v Collins* required that he remove the case from the fast track and list it for plenary hearing.[96]   **[15–53]**

The early disclosure of relevant information is also required, as was seen in *McMichael v United Kingdom*,[97] which related to child placement decision. There the failure of authorities to disclose reports by social services which included information relating to the factual background to the case, the child involved and the recommendations of care workers was found to represent a violation, despite the content of the reports had been shared with the parents at the oral hearing.   **[15–54]**

Another aspect of this is legal representation and legal aid, an issue which generated one of the most prominent judgments against Ireland from the Strasbourg Court — *Airey v Ireland*.[98] There the Court held that a breach of Article 6 had occurred where Mrs Airey had been denied legal aid for a judicial separation matter which was to be heard before the High Court. The Court stated that: **[15–55]**

---

[93] MR 4 - *AIB v Collins* 2010 1035 S (1). Available at: http://www.courts.ie/offices.nsf/(WebF iles)/8D658EB07A17B43A8025799E003E2328/$FILE/%5B2011%5D%20MR%204%20-%20 AIB%20-v-%20Collins%202010%201035%20S.doc (date accessed 30 June 2014).

[94] "High Court Warns on Fast Track Procedures", *The Irish Times*, 9 May 2014. Available at: http://www.irishtimes.com/news/crime-and-law/courts/high-court-warns-on-fast-track-procedures-1.1790270 (date accessed 30 June 2014).

[95] *AIB v Collins* above n 93 at para 22, original emphasis.

[96] *ibid.*

[97] *McMichael v United Kingdom* (1995) 20 EHRR 205.

[98] *Airey v Ireland* [1979] 2 EHRR 305.

> "Article 6 may sometimes compel the State to provide for the assistance of a lawyer when such assistance proves indispensable for an effective access to court either because legal representation is rendered compulsory…or by reason of the complexity of the procedure or of the case."[99]

[15–56]   In this case due to the involvement of complex points of law and the requirement to present evidence the court held that without legal assistance Mrs Airey would be unable to effectively present her case. A similarly celebrated case is *Steel and Morris v United Kingdom*,[100] where two anti-McDonald's activists were sued by the corporation for defamation, after they distributed leaflets outside its premises in Scotland. Defamation matters were excluded from the relevant legal aid scheme. The Strasbourg Court ruled that this represented a violation of Article 6. The requirement to fund legal assistance, it stated, is dependent upon:

> "what is at stake for the applicant in the proceedings, the complexity of the relevant law and procedure and the applicant's capacity to represent himself or herself effectively".[101]

Delay

[15–57]   As indicated by its express reference to "reasonable time", another core element of Article 6(1) is the protection against undue delay in the hearing of civil actions. A lack of efficiency in the provision of court services in Ireland has led to a number of cases where a violation against Ireland was found under this aspect of Article 6. In *Salesi v Italy*, the Strasbourg Court stressed that the goal of the provision is to protect the individual against "excessive procedural delays…to avoid a person remaining too long in a state of uncertainty about his fate".[102] In judging whether a delay is excessive the Court will assess the complexity of the case, the importance of the competing interests involved (which may increase the diligence required), the conduct of the authorities as well as the conduct of the applicants. In *Zimmerman and Steiner v Switzerland*,[103] the ECtHR ruled out taking into account a lack of resources as a factor, as in its view such a consideration would not reflect the fact that Article 6(1) required State

---

[99] *ibid* at para 26.
[100] *Steel and Morris v United Kingdom* [2005] 41 EHRR 403.
[101] *ibid* at para 61.
[102] *Salesi v Italy* (1993) Series A no.257-E para.24.
[103] *Zimmerman and Steiner v Switzerland* (1983) 6 EHRR 17 at para 29.

parties to "…organise their legal systems so as to allow the courts to comply with the requirements of art.6(1)".[104]

Examples of instances where Ireland was held to have violated Article 6(1) due to unreasonable delay include *Superwood Holdings plc v Ireland*.[105] The matter at the centre of that case was one of the longest civil cases in Irish legal history, with the ECtHR ruling that the case had continued for twenty two years, with an assessment of taxation of costs still ongoing at the time it heard the matter. The case involved a plaintiff company seeking damages from a number of different insurers after fire damage to a factory. The twenty two year total was arrived at following an initial judgment, a Supreme Court appeal, a High Court retrial, all accompanied by time extensions and adjournments.[106] The ECtHR appeared to associate the Supreme Court appeal track with the excessive delay, a finding which no doubt dovetailed with the case for a Court of Appeal, recently created by referendum. [15–58]

Procedural Justice Across the Convention as a Whole

Having outlined the ambiguities of Article 6(1), the administrative lawyer may lean towards regarding the ECHR as largely duplicating common law protections, alongside some narrow circumstances where future litigation may prove productive. Yet, as we have seen, the administrative law contained in the Convention is not merely housed in one discrete article, rather it is embedded in the structure of the entire instrument. In a profound sense, most of the cases to which Ireland has been a party have been administrative justice cases — focused upon rule of law criteria or the process of administrative reasoning. Thus the ECHR has, despite the well-guarded statutory choke-points warding off extensive use in the domestic courts, offered a continual rejoinder to traditional patterns of governance and legislative action in Ireland. In what remains of this chapter, we will discuss the most prominent case-law concerning Ireland under the Convention, and how the findings relate to administrative law themes and values. [15–59]

---

[104] *ibid.*

[105] Application No 7812/04, 8 September 2011.

[106] As Khan and Connolly note, however, it was hardly praiseworthy that the ECtHR itself took over seven years to reach its judgment. See S F Khan and B Connolly, "Justice Delayed, Justice Denied – The Case for a Court of Civil Appeal", (2013) 31(1) ILT 178.

Article 8

[15–60]   The natural starting point is Article 8, which as we have noted, overlaps heavily in terms of underlying themes with Article 6. The Strasbourg Court, has in variety of different factual contexts, stressed that Article 8 requires that a decision-maker not merely reaches the correct outcome but does so using the correct *process*. This was seen, for instance, in the landmark family law case of *W v United Kingdom*:

> "It is true that Article 8 contains no explicit procedural requirements, but this is not conclusive of the matter. The local authority's decision-making process clearly cannot be devoid of influence on the substance of the decision, notably by ensuring that it is based on the relevant considerations and is not one-sided and, hence, neither is nor appears to be arbitrary. Accordingly, the Court is entitled to have regard to that process to determine whether it has been conducted in a manner that, in all the circumstances, is fair and affords due respect to the interests protected by Article 8."[107]

[15–61]   The Court thus held that the decision-making process concerning children in care must ensure that parents':

> "views and interests are made known and duly taken into account by the local authority and that they are able to exercise in due time any remedies available to them".

[15–62]   The most visible instance of Ireland being held in violation of the procedural rights of Article 8 is of course, *A, B and C v Ireland*.[108] The Court found that the State's failure to legislate for what it determined to be constitutionally permitted abortions constituted a breach of C's Article 8 rights. It found that under Article 8, the State bore an obligation to provide

---

[107] *W v United Kingdom*, App. No. 9749/82 Eur Ct HR (1987) para 62. Note that our selection of Art 8 as a case study does not imply that other Articles have not seen a similar emphasis on procedure. For example in relation to right to property under Art 1 of the First Additional Protocol to the ECHR, the Court held in *AGOSI v United Kingdom*, App No 9118/80, [1986] ECHR 13:

> "[A]lthough the second paragraph of Article 1 contains no explicit procedural requirements, the Court must consider whether the applicable procedures in the present case were such as to enable, amongst other things, reasonable account to be taken of the degree of fault or care of the applicant company or, at least, of the relationship between the company's conduct and the breach of the law which undoubtedly occurred; and also whether the procedures in question afforded the applicant company a reasonable opportunity of putting its case the responsible authorities".

[108] *A, B and C* above n 8.

an *effective* and *accessible* means of protecting the right to respect for private life. Where the State decided to permit abortion,[109] it was necessary to ensure that a legal framework was put in place which was "shaped in a coherent manner which allows the different legitimate interests involved to be taken into account adequately".[110] The availability of High Court action to secure an abortion in circumstances where the life of the mother was under threat did not compensate for "the uncertainty generated by the lack of legislative implementation of Article 40.3.3".[111] The decision therefore, is to be understood as one anchored in administrative law and the rule of law.

It is therefore clear that Article 8 and indeed, other provisions of the Convention, pursue discrete administrative justice values such as accuracy, neutrality and participation, as well as the crucial criterion of correctability.[112] The main successful Irish case in this area is *Donegan v Dublin City Council*, where the Supreme Court held that s 62 of the Housing Act 1966 infringed Article 8 of the European Convention on Human Rights. Section 62 allowed a local authority to secure a court order for possession of a council house without an independent inquiry.[113] *Donegan* and its related case-law[114] represent the most advanced instance of the distinctive

[15–63]

---

[109] In relation to applicant's A and B, the Court had held that the state enjoyed a margin of appreciation as to whether to permit or restrict forms of abortion.

[110] *A, B and C* above n 8 at para 249, citing *SH and Others v Austria*, Application No 57813/00, 1 April 2010 at para 74.

[111] *ibid* at para 264.

[112] For a more general discussion see E Brems & L Lavyrsen, "Procedural Justice in Human Rights Adjudication: The European Court of Human Rights", (2013) 35 *Human Rights Quarterly* 176.

[113] *Donegan* above n 45. The District Court judge is mandatorily required "shall" to order possession on the production of required proofs.

[114] The actions began in *Dublin City Council v Fennell* [2005] IESC 33, where the Supreme Court held refused to consider the ECHR Act arguments, finding that the 2003 Act could not be applied retrospectively to cover a possession instituted prior to its introduction. There then followed four section 62 challenges in the High Court. *Leonard v Dublin City Council* [2008] IEHC 288, where Dunne J held that there was no violation of Article 8 by reference to the *specific facts* of the case. The case of *Pullen v Dublin City Council (No.2)*, saw Irvine J rule that Art 8 was violated by s 62:

> "the use of s. 62…to interfere with the plaintiffs' right to respect for their home following an in-house investigation, in circumstances where such procedure did not afford the plaintiffs any opportunity to dispute the lawfulness or the proportionality of the defendant's decision to evict them, was not justified as being necessary in a democratic society and was disproportionate to the defendant's stated aims having regard to the significance of the rights interfered with".

As mentioned above, the Court refused to grant the family an injunction restrain the Council from repossessing the home, and granted damages and a declaration.

contribution of the 2003 Act, a claim further underlined by the fact that the provision had been subjected to domestic judicial scrutiny over an extended period prior to the ECHR Act's introduction.[115] The eventual repeal of s 62, and its replacement with s 12(9)(a) of the Housing (Miscellaneous Provisions) Act 2014 is ultimately attributable to sustained litigation efforts under the 2003 Act.

[15–64]   The Supreme Court decision commonly referred to as *Donegan* actually involved the conjoined cases of *Donegan* and *Gallagher*, which were appealed by the State following rulings in the High Court by Laffoy J and O'Neill J. *Donegan* involved a council tenant who was subjected to an s 62 order, following a Garda finding that there were substantial evidence had been uncovered in his son's bedroom to suggest that heroin was being prepared for sale in the house.[116] The Council proposed that Mr Donegan get his own son legally excluded from staying at the house, but Mr Donegan rejected this alternative. Crucially, rather than make an application to have the son excluded from the house itself, the Council persisted in the s 62 application. *Gallagher* involved the repossession of a house from the son of long term tenant, where the son did not satisfy the relevant Council test to inherit the tenancy following his mother's death.[117] The District Court held that the council had factually erred in its contention that Mr Gallagher had not resided at the house for a period of two years prior to his mother's death. The District Court judge then asked the High Court whether, inter alia, the Court could enter into the merits of the decision to seek delivery of possession of the relevant dwelling.

[15–65]   Writing on behalf of all five judges who heard the case, McKechnie J ruled that the section was structured in a manner which prevents Convention compliant review by the District court where the application is made:

> "...an occupier has no right or entitlement to raise any defence to...
> an application [for possession], other than by way of challenging

---

[115] See *The State (O'Rourke) v Kelly* [1983] IR 58, where the Supreme Court held that "such legislative provisions are within the competence of the Oireachtas". The later case of *Dublin Corporation v Hamilton* [1999] 2 IR 486 confirmed that the District Court had no discretion once the necessary proofs had been tendered, holding that it was reasonable for the Oireachtas to legislate for an accelerated procedure to recover possession.

[116] No illegal drugs were actually found. Mr Donegan contended throughout the process that his son was not a drug dealer, but a drug addict, who was attempting to deal with his problem.

[117] These criteria were set out in the Council's Scheme of Letting Priorities for succession to tenancies created under s 60 of the Housing Act 1966.

the housing authority on…[certain] formal proofs. In addition, the absence of judicial discretion means that the personal circumstances of such occupier must be disregarded as being irrelevant; equally so with questions regarding the reasonableness or fairness of making the Order: these simply have no part in this statutory procedure."[118]

The Court strongly rejected the submissions made by the Council and the [15–66] Attorney General that judicial review of the s 62 decision provided an adequate safeguard. This was due to the core factual disputes identified above: the matters requiring resolution was whether Mr Donegan's son was a drug dealer or whether Mr Gallagher had been resident for the requisite period prior to his mother's death. Given the nature of these disputed issues, McKechnie J stressed that:

> "It is therefore difficult to see how a remedy like judicial review, modelled in the manner in which it is, could in any way make a decision or reach a conclusion on these issues. At most, it could set aside a decision unlawfully made but such would leave quite unresolved the basic dispute. It could never, of itself, substitute its own findings of fact for those made by a decision-maker. Therefore, judicial review is not, in any meaningful sense, a forum to which recourse can be had in the presenting circumstances."[119]

McKechnie J also supplied a clear statement of how a court will analyse the [15–67] adequacy of administrative procedures where a decision interferes with Article 8 rights:

> "In determining whether an interference is Article 8 compliant, the regulatory framework procedure sufficient to afford true respect to the interests safeguarded by the Article, (ii) is the decision making process fair in such a way as to respect that right, (iii) has the affected person an opportunity to have any relevant and weighty arguable issues tested before an independent tribunal and (iv), has that person an opportunity to have such an issue considered against the measure, to determine its proportionality.
>
> Where any one or more of these requirements, when considered collectively and having regard to the margin of appreciation, is absent, it may be considered that the safeguards necessarily attendant on Article 8 for the purposes of its vindication have not been satisfied. A violation in such circumstances may follow." [120]

---

[118] *Donegan* above n 45 at para 93.

[119] *ibid* at para 124.

[120] *ibid* at para 143.

[15–68]   Having found that judicial review was an inadequate safeguard, the Court ruled Mr Donegan's Article 8 rights had been violated as the contact he had had with the Council had been "ad hoc, unstructured and unregulated" and "solely in the nature of an investigation".[121] McKechnie J stressed that

> "the issue [of whether his son was involved in drug dealing] is of extreme simplicity but requires a mechanism to determine factual conflicts".[122]

[15–69]   Mr Gallagher, however, was not successful when the Court applied the same principles to him. It was stressed that the factual dispute (whether he had been in residence prior to his mother's death) was only one factor in determining whether he should be permitted to remain in occupation. A second element of the matter — whether he had been on the rent account for the premises for two years prior to her death — had not been satisfied. Mr Gallagher did not deny that he had not been on the rent account, but sought to have this requirement waived in his case. As he had no proprietary interest in the property and had never in fact been a tenant of the Council, McKechnie J distinguished his circumstances from Mr Donegan and found no violation had occurred because his Article 8 rights *were not engaged*.

[15–70]   *Donegan* thus established that the availability of judicial review to challenge a s 62 order was insufficient *in cases where the core dispute between the parties is factual in nature*. It was inevitable that a case would look to expand this finding to include an argument that judicial review is insufficient in cases *where the applicant believes the eviction to be disproportionate*. This was recently argued in the case of *Webster v Dun Laoighaire Rathdown County Council*.[123] *Webster* was no doubt provoked by a number of recent ECHR cases, which occurred after the Supreme Court judgment in *Donegan*, and which appeared to further consolidate the requirement to make available an independent tribunal with the ability to carry out a proportionality analysis.

[15–71]   In the case of *Bjedov v Croatia*, the ECtHR stressed that:

> "...any person at risk of an interference with her right to home should in principle be able to have the proportionality and reasonableness of the measure determined by an independent tribunal in the light of the

---

[121] *ibid* at para 148.

[122] *ibid* at para 149.

[123] *Webster v Dun Laoighaire Rathdown County Council* [2013] IEHC 118, hereinafter "*Webster*".

relevant principles under Article 8 of the Convention, notwithstanding that, under domestic law, he or she has no right to occupy a flat."[124]

In *Buckland v United Kingdom*, it held that:

"In conclusion the applicant's attempt to contest the making of a possession order failed because it was not possible at that time to challenge the decision to seek a possession order on the basis of the alleged disproportionlity of that decision in light of personal circumstances. Accordingly, the Court finds that the procedural safeguards required by Article 8 for the assessment of the proportionality of the interference were not observed. As a result, the applicant was dispossessed of her home without any possibility to have the proportionality of her eviction determined by an independent tribunal."[125]

The applicants in *Webster* were council tenants who were significantly [15–72] behind on their rent. They argued that s 62 was inconsistent with Article 8, as the procedure did not give them the opportunity to dispute the lawfulness or proportionality of the Council's decision to evict. Furthermore, the decision was clearly disproportionate due to the fact that the Council, instead of invoking the summary s 62 procedure, could have achieved the eviction under s 154 of the Conveyancing Act 1881, which would have supplied the requisite procedures for Article 8 compliance. The Court framed the issue in the following manner:

"the issue which the court must deal with is whether the respondents can pursue an eviction under s.62 where the facts of the matter are undisputed i.e. the tenants are in breach of a condition of the tenancy agreement in that they have failed to pay rent".[126]

Hedigan J refused to issue a declaration of incompatibility:

"I do not think that the facts of this case, had they been present in *Bjedov* or *Buckland*, would have led to a finding of a violation. On the facts herein, I consider it is possible to predict what decision would have been reached by the District Court had it been able to consider the proportionality of the order to evict. I do not think, therefore, that in this case an eviction order could give rise to a finding of incompatibility on the grounds of non-consideration of the proportionality of the eviction measure".[127]

---

[124] Application No 42150/09, 29 May 2012 at para 66.
[125] (2013) 56 EHRR 16.
[126] *Webster*, above n 123 at para 6.2.
[127] *ibid* at para 7.9.

[15–73]   In distinguishing the case at hand from *Bjedov* and *Buckland*, His Honour noted that there was no evidence that Ms Webster was in advanced years, suffered from poor health or likely to suffer irreparable harm to her health from her eviction.[128] Furthermore, the respondent had put forward arguments "demonstrating that the applicants' eviction was necessary in order to protect its own property rights and to manage its housing stock efficiently".[129]

[15–74]   Having found that, in the event of an analysis, proportionality would not have availed here, Hedigan J was provoked to comment:

> "It may well be that in the light of *Bjedov* and *Buckland*, the Irish courts may eventually find that the absence of an independent tribunal to determine the proportionality of an eviction from a home may give grounds for a declaration of incompatibility even where there is no factual dispute. The circumstances here, however, do not support such a finding".[130]

[15–75]   The reasoning in *Webster* did not seem to place much value upon the existence and availability of the 1881 Act. In a sense, the case underlines our argument in chapter 9 of this book that the approach to proportionality is largely one of substantive balancing and not overly focussed upon the availability of alternative means. Nevertheless, a proportionality analysis conducted at the District Court level, could have addressed the question of the availability of the 1881 Act as an alternative mechanism to obtain the result desired by the council. It may well be that the Irish courts would have determined that the need for speed here made the choice of s 62 proportionate,[131] but we find it difficult to state that "there is, to put it quite simply, no proportionality case to argue here".[132] We would respectfully suggest that future judges avoid engaging in a "what if" parsing of what would occur if proportionality analysis were undertaken, with the *Webster* approach ultimately being attributable to the facts of that case. In such a hypothetical scenario counsel for Ms Webster would have had the opportunity to more squarely and extensively address proportionality than

---

[128] Such evidence as to the harm likely to follow eviction had been advanced in *Buckland* and *Bjedov*.

[129] *Webster* above n 123 at para 7.8.

[130] *ibid* at para 7.9.

[131] Though one would comment that the use of accelerated procedures in cases of arrears – which by definition build up over time, is difficult to make out.

[132] *Webster* above n 123 at para 7.9.

in a High Court hearing directed at the more abstract question of the need for a declaration of incompatibility.[133] Perhaps the overarching signal from *Webster* is that judges prefer to proceed incrementally and cautiously in handling ECHR arguments.

Ultimately, however, as Hedigan J accurately predicted, the strengthening of the Strasbourg case-law would produce domestic judicial acknowledgement of the requirement for an independent proportionality analysis to be carried out. This finally occurred in *Lattimore v Dublin City Council*,[134] where Justice O'Neill held that the current arrangements could not amount to an independent inquiry into the proportionality of an eviction:

    [15–76]

> "In my view the clear thrust of all of the jurisprudence, establishes that a housing authority in these circumstances, cannot be the "independent Tribunal" for the purpose of making a determination on the proportionality issue in these circumstances. Thus, while, in my opinion, Ms Conlon carried out her task well, the simple reality is that she did not have or should not have had jurisdiction in the first place to embark upon this task. That should have been left to another body, independent of the respondent."[135]

The question of how to remedy this, now lay before the Court. Justice O'Neill held that in the aftermath of *Meadows*, the Court itself on a judicial review application could expand its standards of review to function as the independent tribunal contemplated by the Convention. The result being that there would be no breach of Article 8 on grounds of a lack of independent review of proportionality.[136]

The plaintiff in *Lattimore* was a seventy year old man who had lived at his three bedroom family home since 1991. His family had been occupying the house for the previous sixty years,[137] with his sister being the sole named tenant since 1990. From 1991 until the death of his sister in 2012, Mr Lattimore had resided there with the consent of Dublin City Council, managing the household and providing care to his sister during her

    [15–77]

---

[133] This argument is furthermore bolstered by the fact that the Council had moved away from an initial argument relating to anti-social behavior on the part of the Websters.

[134] *Lattimore v Dublin City Council* [2014] IEHC 233.

[135] *ibid* at para 53.

[136] *ibid* at para 54.

[137] They had moved in when Edward Lattimore was twelve years old, he had left to live in the UK in 1962, returning in 1991. *ibid* at para 42.

lifetime. Upon her death, he lodged an application to succeed to the tenancy. The Council rejected this, offering him a one bedroomed home nearby, and advising him that a notice to quit the three bedroom house would follow. It acknowledged that he had not breached any terms in the tenancy agreement, and was not in arrears. He was also suffering from a variety of significant ailments. The council held that the three bedroom house was "not appropriate to the needs of a single person", and reallocation was necessary due to demands for housing generally and the needs of other applicant families. It was an accepted fact that there were in excess of 1,400 eligible persons seeking accommodation from the council, with 134 of these seeking a three bedroomed house.[138]

[15–78]   Justice O'Neill undertook a consideration of the facts before him, acting as the independent tribunal. He ruled that

> "having regard to the weighty factors favouring either potential choice, and having regard to the necessity to balance these and then make the difficult choice to allow or refuse succession",

the administrator had observed the principle of proportionality. His Honour stressed that she had before her all relevant material "for the purposes of making a reasonable and proportionate decision".[139] In the context of what was in his Honour's view, a well-resourced decision, O'Neill J offered only a short holistic analysis of the overall situation, which can be quoted in full:

> "In that context, it would seem to me that what I have to do, having regard to what has been described in the words of Henchy J, as the *"implied constitutional limitation of jurisdiction"*, is to consider whether or not the decision made in this case by Ms. Conlon was proportionate to the objective to be achieved, and if disproportionate, to set it aside.
>
> All of the relevant material was before Ms. Conlon and, I am satisfied, considered by her, and in the balancing exercise she was required to do, she had to make a decision which was either favourable to the applicant or adverse to him. There was no middle ground, although in this context, the fact that a one-bedroom apartment was offered to the applicant, in close proximity to 21 Ennis Grove ensured that in the decisions that were made, the respondent was fulfilling its obligation to

---

[138] *ibid* at para 43.

[139] *ibid* at paras 50-51, emphasis in original.

the applicant to provide him with suitable housing, whilst at the same time, accommodating the needs of a family requiring a 3-bedroomed house. I am quite satisfied that the decision that was made by Ms. Conlon, as reflected in her letter of 23rd April 2013, was not in any sense disproportionate".[140]

These two paragraphs seem to encapsulate the notion of overall "fair balance", with O'Neill J supporting the decision made by the administrator. Reading the above portion of the judgment, there may be a temptation to regard *Lattimore* as supporting the idea that even though courts will now carry out an analysis, findings of disproportionality will be rare. This is a concern we raised in our detailed discussion of proportionality in chapter 9. Setting that to one side, we would stress however, the significance of the earlier finding by O'Neill J that all relevant material necessary to carry out a proportionality analysis had been before the administrator. Any evidence of a failure to weigh matters relevant to proportionality (for example if there had not been such extensive medical evidence before the decision-maker), could have led to a finding that the initial proportionality exercise was not carried out fully, and increased the willingness of the court to intervene with its own view. It may also be that, as we argued in chapter 8 at paras [8–43]-[8–47], a synergy will develop between pleas of proportionality and the ground of relevant considerations. [15–79]

The acceptance, in the *Lattimore* judgment, of the principle that proportionality must be independently assessed has had broader impacts outside the confines of direct litigation. This is reflected *Housing (Miscellaneous Provisions) Act 2014* which repealed the s 62 procedure, allowing a review of the proportionality of the eviction to be carried out by the District Court.[141] This embodies a wider acceptance of the implications [15–80]

---

[140] *ibid* at paras 56-57. Emphasis in original.

[141] s 12(9) states:

> "(a) ...the District Court shall make a possession order in respect of the dwelling the subject of a possession application under this section if it appears to the Court that the housing authority has grounds for the recovery of possession and that it is reasonable having regard to all the circumstances of the case to make the order.
>
> (b) In considering the reasonableness of making a possession order under this section, the District Court shall, where appropriate, have regard to the following:
>
> (i) the steps taken by the housing authority to secure the cessation or non-repetition of the breach of the term of the tenancy agreement or rent-related obligation, including the issue of any tenancy warning;
>
> (ii) the response of the tenant to the steps taken by the housing authority referred to in subparagraph (i)

of Convention proportionality and the administrative arrangements needed to implement it than has previously been evident in Irish law.

[15–81]   In bringing our analysis of Article 8 to an end, we must stress that s 62 was of course, an example of a narrow statutory scheme which curtailed the scope of judicial review. Once the statutory context shifts, the availability of judicial review may suffice, particularly where the statutory language regulating the relevant authority's decision is more open-textured and judgment centred. In such circumstances, the expanded reasonableness test outlined in *Meadows* may function to ensure the court can engage in sufficient proportionality analysis. It is thus productive to outline another domestic Article 8 case, that of *Reid v Industrial Development Authority*,[142] already mentioned earlier in this chapter. In determining whether a decision to compulsorily purchase Mr Reid's home, the IDA had established what the court referred to as "a form of inquiry" to look into the proposed acquisition presided over by a Senior Counsel.[143] This ran for five days, and allowed the Reid family to make objections, with legal representation also being supplied. Following this hearing the Senior Counsel made a report to the IDA which then took the decision under s 16 of the Industrial Development Act 1986.[144] In assessing the adequacy of such a procedure, Hedigan J made the following ruling:

    (iii) the effect, if any, that the breach of the tenancy agreement had or is having on the quality of life of those in the locality of the dwelling;

    (iv) whether in the circumstances it is just and equitable to make the order notwithstanding that—

        (I) the housing authority did not issue a tenancy warning in respect of the breach of the term of the tenancy agreement or the rent-related obligation,

        (II) a tenancy warning issued by the housing authority in respect of a breach of the term of the tenancy agreement or the rent-related obligation of a similar nature to the breach to which the possession application relates is under review, or

        (III) in accordance with subsection (3) (b), the housing authority did not issue a notice to the tenant under subsection (3) (a);

  and

    (v) the proportionality of making a possession order under this section, having regard to the grounds for the possession application.

[142] *Reid v Industrial Development Authority* above n 78.

[143] *ibid* at para 3.6.

[144] s 16 effectively provides that the IDA can make a compulsory purchase order where this is required for the development or maintenance of an industrial undertaking based upon foreign direct investment. Once satisfied of this, it formalizes a decision in a "record of decision" and notifies the affected parties. It does not have to seek a Compulsory Purchase Order from An Bord Pleanála in the manner of a local authority under the Planning and Development Act 2000.

"Is the IDA or was the independent inquiry such an independent tribunal? It seems to me that the independent inquiry was a part of the IDA decision-making process. As noted above, it was a fair and proper forum in which the applicant was given every opportunity to make his case on any ground that he wished. It must be noted that no plea *ad misericordiam* in relation to the loss of his home was actually raised at that hearing. I would have some doubt as to whether this whole process could be regarded as an independent tribunal which could consider the Article 8 issues that the European Court of Human Rights has decided is required. Although it has no particular interest in preferring one site over another, nonetheless the IDA does have its own particular interest in the sense of its perception of what or which land was most suitable in the light of its policy in relation to industrial development. I do not think, however, that the Court needs to resolve this issue. In my view, if there was any doubt as to the jurisdiction of this Court in judicial review to consider the reasonableness and proportionality of compulsory purchase, that doubt has been resolved. Firstly, the Supreme Court in O'Brien (cited above) required the IDA to act with due fairness of procedure and with proper consideration for the rights of the applicant. In the event it did not do so, clearly this Court can intervene. Secondly, in *Meadows v Minister for Justice* [2010] 2 I.R. 701, the Supreme Court harking back to the essence of Henchy J's seminal judgment in *The State (Keegan) v Stardust Compensation Tribunal* ([1986] I.R. 642, found that the proportionality of any act that interfered with constitutional rights was something the Court of judicial review could examine."[145]

Administrative Processes and Convention Reasoning

As noted in our discussion of the *A, B and C* decision, analysing the administrative law implications of the ECHR requires an appreciation of the overall "grammar" of reasoning under the Convention, not merely the "syntax" of particular articles or case-law. One aspect of this is how issues of fair procedure influence the construing of the extent of the margin of appreciation the court will grant to the national authorities in carrying out decisions affecting rights. A wide margin of appreciation lightens the burden of justification on the state. Thus, the margin of appreciation doctrine and proportionality analysis interact, with the former effectively functioning in a manner similar to deference in a domestic context. As we discussed in our chapter on reasonableness, ideas of deferring to expertise are part of Irish judicial review, but too often it remains implicit in the

[15–82]

---

[145] *Reid* above n 78 at para 7.6, emphasis added.

judges reasoning. Where expressed, it is often based on the identity, rather than the specific conduct of the body in question. The foremost example of this accepted "spatial deference" is the well-established reluctant of reviewing judges to interfere with complex planning decisions.

[15–83] Academics have highlighted the need for the Irish judiciary to reflect more extensively on the idea of deference, and how it interacts with the need proportionality test, particularly following the rejection of the "sliding scale" model of review in *Meadows*.[146] The reasoning of the ECtHR regarding the margin of appreciation may offer some useful resources in achieving this more extensive explanation. Nevertheless we must caution that the margin of appreciation, is motivated not, as might be the case in a national context, only by deference to expertise, but also by the need of a distant, international court to show appropriate deference to the national context. There is, however, no doubt that the invoking of deference in the UK courts has often been influenced by elements of Strasbourg judgments. The UK courts apply a distinctive doctrine of the "discretionary area of judgment", which is granted to the decision-maker based on a range of contextual factors.

[15–84] Turning back to the ECtHR's approach, we see instances of where the Court examined the conduct of decision-maker in assessing the margin of appreciation. In effect, there are a number of cases where the Court seemed to identify that the decision-maker had, in effect, earned deference through the application of conscientious procedures. Amongst the most prominent of these was the case of *Leyla Sahin v Turkey*,[147] noting that the process of introducing the prohibition of headscarves in Turkish universities was wide-ranging and extensive:

> "the process...took several years and was accompanied by a wide debate within Turkish society and the teaching profession...It is quite clear that throughout that decision-making process the university authorities sought to adapt to the evolving situation in a way that would not bar access to the university to students wearing the veil, through continued dialogue with those concerned".[148]

---

[146] See generally, H Biehler, "Curial Deference in the Context of Judicial Review of Administrative Action Post-Meadows", (2013) 49 *Irish Jurist* 29.

[147] *Leyla Sahin v Turkey* (2007) 44 EHRR 5.

[148] *ibid* at para 120.

Yet it is clear also that such a view of the process could be disputed, as **[15–85]**
Tulkens J stated in her dissent:

> "Freedom to manifest a religion entails everyone being allowed to
> exercise that right, whether individually or collectively, in public
> or in private, subject to the dual condition that they do not infringe
> the rights and freedoms of others and do not prejudice public order
> (Article 9 § 2).
>
> As regards the first condition, this could have not been satisfied
> if the headscarf the applicant wore as a religious symbol had been
> ostentatious or aggressive or was used to exert pressure, to provoke
> a reaction, to proselytise or to spread propaganda and undermined —
> or was liable to undermine — the convictions of others. However,
> the Government did not argue that this was the case and there was
> no evidence before the Court to suggest that Ms Şahin had any such
> intention. As to the second condition, it has been neither suggested nor
> demonstrated that there was any disruption in teaching or in everyday
> life at the university, or any disorderly conduct, as a result of the
> applicant's wearing the headscarf. Indeed, no disciplinary proceedings
> were taken against her."

The exchange illustrates the value of assessing claims to expertise in the **[15–86]**
context of particular decisions. Furthermore, in a complex area full of
sensitive questions relating to equality and religious freedom, it centred
the judges of the court in assessing matters of evidence and process with
which they are familiar. It also permits more incremental and subtle
rulings by courts, rather than abstractly endorsing the ability of
governments to enforce secularism or the individual's freedom to express
their religion in all contexts. This processural approach was also seen in
its handling of the *A, B and C v Ireland* case. Ultimately, in asking the
question "what did the authorities do to earn deference?" a court is
arming itself for a richer proportionality analysis — including questions
such as what alternatives were explored and whether the decision actually
furthers the professed aim.

The conceptual space opened up by this case-law is intriguing. In an Irish **[15–87]**
context, the grounded nature of the analysis, the notion that expertise must
be proved not merely asserted, would seem to counterbalance the tendency
towards more impressionistic approaches which rule the matter non-
justiciable or inappropriate for intervention due to its very nature. Of
course, as Allan has argued, there is a danger that the notion of deference
risks crowding out the need for an eventual evaluation of the substantive

issues.[149] Yet, the idea of earned deference opens up intriguing regulative potential, whereby factors such as the provision of appropriate training and or community participation are integrated into the courts' reasoning and weighed in balance. This may nudge Government bodies to consider the quality of their decision-making process in broader perspective. Though of course, a court must be wary of creating box-ticking requirements or as Lord Hoffman once commented placing an obligation that every decision-maker have a human rights textbook at their elbows.[150] While easily parodied, however, reflecting on such procedural steps may be a welcome counterbalance to an approach that merely leaves decision-makers to wonder whether their decision will be an exceptional one found disproportionate under an impressionistic application of the *Meadows* standard.

[15–88] The other administrative justice theme which runs through the Convention is the recurring requirement that where interferences with rights occur these are to be "in accordance with the law". There is a clear "rule of law" orientation to this requirement — the existence of a legal basis for the decision does not suffice, rather the court's analysis will extend to the quality of the law. Thus, legislation for example, while not entirely extinguishing discretion, must be accessible and foreseeable. The balancing between these two competing aims is best discussed by reference to surveillance cases, such as *Malone v UK*, where the Court held that the relevant law must be:

> "...sufficiently clear in its terms to give citizens an adequate indication as to the circumstances in which and the conditions on which public authorities are empowered to resort to this secret and potentially dangerous interference with the right to respect for private life and correspondence."[151]

---

[149] TRS Allan, "Human Rights and Judicial Review: A Critique of Due Deference", (2006) 65(3) *Cambridge Law Journal* 671.

[150] *R(Begum) v Denbigh High School* [2007] 1 AC 100 at para 68.

[151] *Malone v UK* (1984) 7 EHRR 14 at para 67:
"The Court would reiterate its opinion that the phrase 'in accordance with the law' does not merely refer back to domestic law but also relates to the quality of the law, requiring it to be compatible with the rule of law, which is expressly mentioned in the preamble to the Convention ... The phrase thus implies – and this follows from the object and purpose of Article 8 – that there must be a measure of legal protection in domestic law against arbitrary interferences by public authorities with the rights safeguarded by paragraph 1 ... Especially where a power of the executive is exercised in secret, the risks of arbitrariness are evident..."

While the Court has stressed that this "cannot mean that an individual   **[15–89]**
should be able to foresee when the authorities are likely to intercept his
communications so that he can adapt his conduct accordingly",
nevertheless, it has also created, in *Kruslin* extremely detailed requirements
on how the relevant legal rules are to be drafted:

> "the Court has developed the following minimum safeguards that
> should be set out in statute law in order to avoid abuses of power: the
> nature of the offences which may give rise to an interception order; a
> definition of the categories of people liable to have their telephones
> tapped; a limit on the duration of telephone tapping; the procedure
> to be followed for examining, using and storing the data obtained, the
> precautions to be taken when communicating the data to other parties;
> and the circumstances in which recordings may or must be erased or
> the tapes destroyed".[152]

The Court has also noted that in decisions affecting Article 8 rights it would   **[15–90]**
"be contrary to the rule of law for the legal discretion granted to the executive
to be expressed in terms of an unfettered power".[153] For students of
administrative law therefore, the ECHR offers an interesting perspective on
the balance between procedure and substance in the oversight of Government
decisions. As Tulkens and Van Droogenbroeck argue, the Strasbourg Court
has often, due to its distance from the facts, been drawn into the
"proceduralisation of substantial rights".[154] A focus on procedural requirements
seems to legitimise the claim that the court is engaged in a dialogue with State

---

> ... Since the implementation in practice of measures of secret surveillance of
> communications is not open to scrutiny by the individuals concerned or the public
> at large, it would be contrary to the rule of law for the legal discretion granted to the
> executive to be expressed in terms of an unfettered power. Consequently, the law must
> indicate the scope of any such discretion conferred on the competent authorities and
> the manner of its exercise with sufficient clarity, having regard to the legitimate aim of
> the measure in question, to give the individual adequate protection against arbitrary
> interference."

[152] *Kruslin v France* (1990) 12 EHRR 547 at para 33. General statement of the court in this regard
found in *Weber & Saravia v Germany*, Application no 54934/00, admissibility decision of
29 June 2006.

[153] *Amann v Switzerland* [2000] ECHR 88 at para 56.

[154] F Tulkens and S Van Droogenbroeck, "La Cour Européenne des Droits de l'homme Depuis
1980. Bilan et Orientations" in W Debeuckelaere and D Voorhoof, eds., En Toch Beweegt het
Recht, Tegenspraak-cahier 23, (Die Keure, Brugge, 2003) at p 224. Murphy, to whom we are
indebted for highlighting this overarching point in an Irish context, provides an excellent
analysis of this dynamic in the specific context of ECtHR decisions on surveillance in M
Murphy, "The Relationship between the European Court of Human Rights and National
Legislative Bodies: Considering the Merits and the Risks of the Approach of the Court in
Surveillance Cases", (2013) 3(2) *IJLS* 65.

Parties. However, de Hert and Gutwirth note that such deferring of substantive issues can lead to "the formalisation, bureaucratisation and depoliticisation of human rights questions", and that if the Convention is centred on substantive protections, it will need to recognise that for some governments "meeting formal constraints and conditions is never a hurdle too high to take".[155]

The Standard of Review in Domestic ECHR Actions

[15–91]   One final but central issue to the use of the Convention in judicial review is the overarching question of what should constitute the standard of review in ECHR-related matters. Clearly, as we indicated in our discussion in chapter 9, the relevant standard of review under Irish law is that approved by the Supreme Court in *Meadows*.[156] It is important, however, to assess a number of ECHR specific concerns which emerge from that judgment, something that takes us somewhat beyond the subject matter of our earlier discussion. Firstly there is the issue that in some respects, pre-*Meadows* case law on reviews under the 2003 Act could be viewed as more expansive in its treatment of proportionality. Thus in the case of *Pullen*, Irvine J stated that interferences with Convention rights would be found proportionate where:

> "(a) ... the objective of restricting the right is so pressing and substantial that it is sufficiently important to justify interfering with a fundamental right;
>
> (b) ... the restriction is suitable: it must be rationally connected to the objective in mind so that the limitation is not arbitrary, unfair or based on irrational considerations;
>
> (c) ... the restriction is necessary to accomplish the objective intended. In this respect the public authority must adopt the least drastic means of attaining the objective in mind, provided the means suggested are not fanciful; and
>
> (d) ... the restriction is not disproportionate. The restriction must not impose burdens or cause harm which is excessive when compared to the importance of the objective to be achieved."[157]

Given our argument in chapter 9 that *Meadows* proportionality is of an impressionistic character, it can be argued that the conception of

---

[155] P De Hert and S Gutwirth, "Privacy, Data Protection and Law Enforcement. Opacity of the Individual and Transparency of Power" in E Claes, A Duff and S Gutwirth (eds.), *Privacy and the Criminal Law* (Intersentia, Brussels, 2005) at p 88.

[156] *Meadows v Minister for Justice* [2010] 2 IR 701. See paras [9.19]-[9.39].

[157] *Pullen v Dublin City council (No 1)* [2008] IEHC 379 at para 39.

proportionality outlined by Irvine J has been marginalised by the impacts of the *Meadows* ruling.[158] It must also be stressed however that *Meadows* is a framework which allows for proportionality to be applied in a manner reflecting particular statutory contexts.

The broader implications of this have been extensively canvassed by Biehler and Donnelly, who argue that the *Meadows* standard of review, as currently practiced by the courts, is not sufficiently protective of Convention rights.[159] In support of this, they rely upon the ECtHR decision in *Smith and Grady*, where the Court held that the then prevailing UK approach to judicial review did not provide an adequate remedy for breach of Convention rights (as was required by Article 13 of the Convention):

[15–92]

> "...the threshold at which the High Court and the Court of Appeal could find the Ministry of Defence policy irrational was placed so high that *it effectively excluded any consideration* by the domestic courts of the question of whether the interference with the applicants' rights answered a pressing social need or was proportionate to national security and public order aims pursued, principles which lie at the heart of the Court's analysis of complaints under Article 8 of the Convention".[160]

---

[158] See chapter 9 at paras [9.41] to [9.66].

[159] H Biehler and C Donnelly, "*Proportionality in the Irish Courts: The Need for Guidance*" (2014) 3 EHRLR 272, hereinafter "Biehler and Donnelly".

[160] Emphasis added. *Smith and Grady v United Kingdom Smith v United Kingdom* (2000) 29 EHRR 493 at para 138. It should be noted that this statement was preceded in paras 135-137 by an analysis of the domestic court cases, which stressed the fact that the judges had been unable to value what they admitted were "powerful" arguments raised by the applicants. This broader sense that the UK judges' hands were tied in the consideration of proportionality seems to have been central in the overall finding:

"The test of "irrationality" applied in the present case was that explained in the judgment of Sir Thomas Bingham MR: a court was not entitled to interfere with the exercise of an administrative discretion on substantive grounds save where the court was satisfied that the decision was unreasonable in the sense that it was beyond the range of responses open to a reasonable decision-maker. In judging whether the decision-maker had exceeded this margin of appreciation, the human rights context was important, so that the more substantial the interference with human rights, the more the court would require by way of justification before it was satisfied that the decision was reasonable.

It was, however, further emphasised that, notwithstanding any human rights context, the threshold of irrationality which an applicant was required to surmount was a high one. This is, in the view of the Court, confirmed by the judgments of the High Court and the Court of Appeal themselves. The Court notes that the main judgments in both courts commented favourably on the applicants' submissions challenging the reasons advanced by the Government in justification of the policy. Simon Brown LJ considered that the balance of argument lay with the applicants and that their arguments in favour of a conduct-based code were powerful...Sir Thomas Bingham MR found that those submissions of the applicants were of "very considerable cogency"...Furthermore, while offering no conclusive views on the Convention issues raised by the case, Simon

[15–93]   Thus the doctrine of *Wednesbury* unreasonableness, with its focus upon irrationality, could not suffice when reviewing Convention rights, even when teamed with the doctrine of anxious scrutiny[161] which permitted the Court to raise the intensity of its reasonableness review. Yet the phrase "effectively excluded *any* consideration" suggests that *Wednesbury* was condemned for its inflexibility; not least the fact that it rules out on its terms the undertaking of proportionality balancing. It is possible therefore to argue that while the ECtHR was requiring proportionality to be assessed, it was not directly installing a defined methodology for its assessment. As Loveland puts it; "the case law of the European Court does no more than tell us that a *Wednesbury* intensive review of substantive merits is not sufficient".[162] The key question for Irish courts is whether, as Biehler and Donnelly argue,

> "the formulation of proportionality which is now widely adopted by the Irish courts does not reflect the standard of review identified by the European Court".[163]

[15–94]   The question of what standard of review satisfies the Convention received further treatment in a chain of cases, before the courts of England and Wales and the ECtHR, which challenged, under Article 8 of the Convention, the system for obtaining possession of public tenancies. In the early case of *Qazi*, the House of Lords decided, albeit by a bare majority, that the public authority's owner's contractual and proprietary rights could not be defeated by Article 8 ECHR protection of the right to family life.[164] The relevant domestic legal framework therefore did not seem to allow for the consideration of proportionality. This led to the ECtHR making a finding of

---

Brown LJ expressed the opinion that "the days of the policy were numbered" in light of the United Kingdom's Convention obligations and Sir Thomas Bingham MR observed that the investigations and the discharge of the applicants did not appear to show respect for their private lives. He considered that there might be room for argument as to whether there had been a disproportionate interference with their rights under Article 8 of the Convention.

Nevertheless, both courts concluded that the policy could not be said to be beyond the range of responses open to a reasonable decision-maker and, accordingly, could not be considered to be "irrational"."

[161] The principle of anxious scrutiny held more substantial the interference with human rights, the more the court would require by way of justification before it was satisfied that the decision was reasonable. As we discuss in chapter 9, the concept was not accepted by the Supreme Court in *Meadows*, and was, in fact, subjected to quite stinging criticism.

[162] I Loveland, "The Shifting Sands of Article 8 Jurisprudence in English Housing Law" (2011) 2 EHRLR 151 at p 160, hereinafter "Loveland".

[163] Biehler and Donnelly, above n 159 at p 283.

[164] *Harrow v Qazi* [2004] 1 AC 983

violation against the UK in the case of *McCann v United Kingdom*, with the ECtHR stressing:

> "The loss of one's home is a most extreme form of interference with the right to respect for the home. Any person at risk of an interference of this magnitude should in principle be able to have the proportionality of the measure determined by an independent tribunal *in light of the relevant principles under art.8 of the Convention*, notwithstanding that, in domestic law, his right of occupation has come to an end."[165]

We would argue that the statement that proportionality must be assessed "in the light of the relevant principles under art. 8 of the Convention" is the closest the ECtHR has come to requiring the structured model of proportionality be used in reviewing Article 8 rights.

In response, the UK House of Lords further refined its approach in the **[15–95]** cases of *Kay*[166] and *Doherty*,[167] which led the court to rule that exceptionally, it would be possible for an individual subject to a possession order to challenge that order "as an improper exercise" of power by the housing authority, on the basis that "it was a decision that no reasonable person would consider justifiable". This defence would only be available to a defendant in the county court where their personal circumstances were of such a nature that it was "seriously arguable". The decision represented a narrow gateway through which proportionality could be raised as was underlined by Hope LJ in *Doherty*, who admitted that it:

> "...would be unduly formalistic to confine the review strictly to traditional Wednesbury grounds. The considerations that can be brought into account in this case are wider. An examination of the question whether the respondent's decision was reasonable, having regard to the aim which it was pursuing and to the length of time that the appellant and his family have resided on the site, would be appropriate. But the requisite scrutiny would not involve the judge substituting his own judgment for that of the local authority. In my opinion the test of reasonableness should be...whether the decision to recover possession was one which no reasonable person would consider justifiable."[168]

---

[165] *McCann v United Kingdom* (App no 19009/04), 13 May 2008 (2008) 47 EHRR 40 at para 50.
[166] *Kay v Lambeth* [2006] 2 AC 465. The judgments of the minority in *Kay* were later to shape much of the approach eventually approved by the Supreme Court.
[167] *Doherty v Birmingham* [2009] 1 AC 367.
[168] *ibid* at para 52.

[15–96]   In its later case of *Kay v UK*, the ECtHR praised the efforts to expand the ground of review to allow the personal circumstances of the individual to be taken into account:

> "The Court welcomes the increasing tendency of the domestic courts to develop and expand conventional judicial review grounds in the light of Article 8. A number of their Lordships in *Doherty* alluded to the possibility for challenges on conventional judicial review grounds in cases such as the applicants' to encompass more than just traditional *Wednesbury* grounds…"[169]

[15–97]   Perhaps as a result of this encouragement by the ECtHR, the UK Supreme Court, in its judgments of *Pinnock*[170] and *Powell*,[171] gave further insight into the heavily constricted nature of proportionality analysis in the context of a possession order. It is clear that pleading the defence of disproportionality will only be *permitted* in exceptional circumstances, with instances where it will succeed obviously being even rarer.[172] Where it is allowed, the Court effectively held that a repossession always constitutes a measure pursuing the legitimate aim of increasing the availability of housing stock and enforcing the legal rights of the authority. In addition, the Supreme Court stressed that county courts evaluating orders should focus upon the question: "is making a possession order a proportionate means of achieving a legitimate aim?" In *Powell*, the Supreme Court expressly refused to require that the County Court undertake a structured proportionality analysis, as had been required by the Court in the immigration context in *Huang*.[173]

---

[169] *Kay v The United Kingdom*, App. No. 37341/06, September 21, 2010. European Court of Human Rights (Fourth Section), [2012] 54 EHRR 30 at para 73. Citing the following portions of the *Doherty*, ibid Lord Hope at para 55; Lord Scott at paras 70 and 84 to 85; and Lord Mance at paras 133 to 135. In the event, as the particular case before had been determined prior to the innovations in the *Doherty* case, the Court held that there had been a violation of Article 8 on the facts before it.

[170] *Manchester City Council v Pinnock* [2010] UKSC 45.

[171] *Hounslow v Powell; Leeds v Hall; Birmingham v Frisby* [2011] UKSC 8.

[172] The ECtHR has expressly approved this notion of exceptionality in *McCann* above n 165 at para 55, stating that "it would be only in very exceptional cases that an applicant would succeed in raising an arguable case which would require a court to examine the issue". As Loveland argues, this hardly represents a defence of the centrality of structured proportionality analysis: "Whether one characterises this as putting the cart before the horse or allowing the tail to wag the dog is not of much import; one cannot conceal the profoundly unsatisfactory nature of this proposition. In doctrinal terms it is feeble." Loveland, above n 162 at p 160.

[173] *Huang v Secretary of State for the Home Department; Kashmiri v Secretary of State for the Home Department* [2007] UKHL 11, [2007] All ER (D) 338 (Mar). Huang proportionality may be

The chain of cases ultimately culminated in the ECtHR judgment in *Pinnock*   **[15–98]**
and Walker v UK,[174] where the Court ruled inadmissible an argument that a
possession order was in violation of Article 8. Most importantly for our
present purposes however, the applicant's submissions included the
argument that in hearing the case:

> "...the Supreme Court had failed to apply the established principle
> of proportionality; indeed, according to the applicants, the principles
> actually applied were impossible to ascertain from its judgment."[175]

The ECtHR held that the UK Supreme Court had in fact carried out the   **[15–99]**
proportionality analysis accurately. This was established by the presence of
three factors in its reasoning:

> "When assessing the proportionality of making the order, the Supreme
> Court identified the relevant facts which supported the seeking of a
> possession order, pointing to the "many and serious" events which had
> occurred..."[176]

> "The Supreme Court also examined the first applicant's arguments
> against the making of a possession order."[177]

---

understood as including four steps: legitimate objective, rational connection, minimal
impairment and overall fair balance. It is thus equivalent to *Pullen* in the Irish context,
above n 157.

[174] *Pinnock and Walker v the United Kingdom* [2013] (Application no 31673/11) (Fourth Section)
Decision of 24 September 2013.

[175] *ibid* at para 25. They specifically based part of their claim around the idea that the Court
had failed to properly carry out the rational connection step of the proportionality analysis:
"They claimed that the court had failed to apply the principle that there must be a rational
connection between the proposed interference with the right to respect for the home
and the legitimate aim relied upon. As the legitimate aim in their case was to prevent
recurrences of criminal and anti-social behaviour connected with the applicants' home,
it was clear that when the possession order was finally made in February 2011 there was
no rational connection between eviction and the achievement of that aim. The aim had
been achieved when the first applicant's sons ceased to reside at the property, and there
had been no allegations of nuisance, criminal activity or other anti-social behaviour for
three years."
This was regarded as a flawed argument by the ECtHR as it failed to appreciate a second
legitimate aim of the authority in this instance "namely the local authority's right to manage
its housing stock and to apply properly the statutory scheme for housing provision for the
protection of other intended beneficiaries of the complex arrangements put in place under
domestic legislation." (para 30 of the judgment).

[176] These involved inter alia the criminal activities and anti social behavior of the first
applicant's sons in the property and its immediate vicinity. *ibid* at para 31.

[177] These mainly centred around the fact that none of the applicant's sons were resident
at the property, but the possession order was based mainly upon their behaviour. The
ECtHR noted that "although there were alternative remedies available to deal with the

"It is clear from the foregoing that the Supreme Court had regard to all relevant factors when making the possession order and weighed the first applicant's interests in remaining in the property against the interests of the local authority in seeking his eviction. It provided detailed reasons which, far from capable of being taxed as arbitrary or unreasonable, were relevant and sufficient for its conclusion that the applicants' eviction would not be disproportionate. In so far as the applicants complain about the failure of the Supreme Court to resolve disputed matters of fact, it is evident from the court's judgment that, even if the matters had been resolved in the first applicant's favour, this would not have affected the outcome of the case."[178]

[15–100]   Thus it would seem that even without adhering to the structured approach, the Supreme Court had assessed proportionality appropriately. The three above elements of the Supreme Court is reasoning appeared to amount to a sufficient consideration of proportionality, *at least in this factual and statutory context*. The message of *Pinnock and Walker* would appear to be that the ECtHR will intervene where the eventual finding of the Court is incorrect, but will not always require a more structured, doctrinally clear method of analysing proportionality. Thus, we would argue that while the UK generally applies a structured four step analysis, the Supreme Court has successfully seized upon the ability of this model to be diluted or amended according to the statutory context.[179] This is further underlined

---

first applicant's sons, the [Supreme Court] did not consider it disproportionate to decide instead to remove the parents whom they undoubtedly visited." *ibid* at para 32.

[178] *ibid* at para 33.

[179] This "chameleon" or shifting nature of proportionality has recently been underlined by the Supreme Court in *Kennedy v The Charity Commission*, [2014] UKSC 20, Judgment of 24 March 2014, where the Court argued, at para 54, that such flexibility reveals the deep connections between proportionality and reasonableness:

"Whatever the context, the court deploying them [proportionality and reasonableness] must be aware that they overlap potentially and that the intensity with which they are applied is heavily dependent on the context. In the context of fundamental rights, it is a truism that the scrutiny is likely to be more intense than where other interests are involved. But that proportionality itself is not always equated with intense scrutiny was clearly identified by Lord Bingham of Cornhill CJ in *R v Secretary of State for Health, Ex p Eastside Cheese Co* [1999] 3 CMLR 123, paras 41-49, which Laws and Arden LJJ and Lord Neuberger MR cited and discussed at paras 21, 133 and 196-200 in *R (Sinclair Collis Ltd) v Secretary of State for Health* [2011] EWCA Civ 437, [2012] QB 394, a case in which the general considerations governing proportionality were treated as relevantly identical under EU and Convention law (paras 54, 147 and 192-194). As Lord Bingham explained, at para 47, proportionality review may itself be limited in context to examining whether the exercise of a power involved some manifest error or a clear excess of the bounds of discretion – a point taken up and amplified in the *Sinclair Collis* case, at paras 126-134 and 203 by Arden LJ and by Lord Neuberger."

by the explanation of the *Pinnock* proportionality analysis provided Arden LJ in the recent case of *Akerman-Livingstone v Aster Communities Ltd*:

> "The proportionality exercise is generally divided into three (or even four) steps but it does not require every step in the exercise to be carried out: the steps are cumulative and if the court finds that any one step is not met there is no need to go to the other steps. That is what in my judgment happened in Pinnock and Powell: the court went straight to the balancing exercise because the weight to be attached to the twin [legitimate] aims was almost overwhelming: it would outweigh any consideration based on Article 8 save in exceptional circumstances."[180]

Having assessed this long chain of case law, we must now return to reflect on the adequacy of the *Meadows* approach under the Convention. At the time of writing, Hogan J appears to be the only Irish judge who has sought to link Irish approaches with the UK possession case-law, with his comment in *Efe v Minister for Justice, Equality and Law Reform*: **[15–101]**

> "[The decision of the ECtHR in *Kay*] clearly signals that judicial review providing for a proportionality analysis of administrative decisions affecting fundamental rights will fully satisfy the Convention's requirements. Whatever might have been the case prior to *Meadows*, it is obvious in the wake of that decision that in this respect the scope of review articulated in cases such as *Meadows* and *I.S.O.F. v Minister for Justice, Equality and Law Reform (No. 2)* [2010] clearly meets this standard."[181]

Biehler and Donnelly refer to this as an instance of where the "Irish courts derive unwarranted comfort from Meadows".[182] While agreeing with general thrust of this, we would also argue that *Meadows* itself illuminates ambiguities within the ECtHR jurisprudence. It could be said that the *Pinnock and Walker* decision is limited to the specific context of possession proceedings, and that a structured proportionality approach is broadly required. Yet it is also possible to argue that permitting an impressionistic consideration of proportionality, rather than the uniform adoption of the structured methodology, currently appears sufficient to satisfy the ECtHR **[15–102]**

---

[180] *Akerman-Livingstone v Aster Communities Ltd (formerly Flourish Homes Ltd)* [2014] EWCA Civ 1081 (30 July 2014), at para 27. This statement occurred in the broader context of a judgment which sought to require that attempts to rely upon the Equality Act 2010 to prevent possession orders being issued should be assessed under the same requirements as Article 8. It is currently under appeal to the Supreme Court.

[181] *Efe v Minister for Justice Equality and Law Reform* [2011] IEHC 214 at para 48, referring to the case of *ISOF v Minister for Justice, Equality and Law Reform (No. 2)* [2010] IEHC 457.

[182] Biehler and Donnelly, above n 159 at pp 281–282.

in certain circumstances.[183] While the UK has often been depicted as a legal order which has sought to resist the Strasbourg court's approaches to reviewing rights, the judicially cultivated ambiguity which marks *Meadows* proportionality also fits within such a trend. It may be described as oppositional and minimalist, but, the use of the formula, of itself, does not always constitute, at least without further intervention by the ECtHR, a direct violation of the Convention. Biehler and Donnelly have correctly identified an empirical trend whereby *Meadows* proportionality is not being extended to include four step balancing. A possible defence of the Supreme Court would be to view this as not attributable to the *Meadows* formula, as it is the responsibility of the individual reviewing judge to determine what form of proportionality is required in a particular context. Assertions of flexibility are not enough to secure Convention consistent practice, however, particularly when accompanied by general statements which seem to view disproportionality as an exceptional finding. Such conclusory parsing of proportionality's proper, subsidiary place in judicial review, encourages the individual judge to focus upon a general assessment of the overall character of the decision before them. Proportionality is thereby reverse engineered into the traditional reasonableness analysis, rather than representing a separate reasoning process.

[15–103]   In concluding this section, we return to the point we have already argued in chapter 9 that many proportionality assessments post *Meadows* are unduly impressionistic.[184] Carrying out a compressed version of proportionality anchored in substantive balancing when the relevant Strasbourg case law relies upon the more structured approach seems unacceptable as a matter of common sense. The unstructured nature of Irish proportionality analysis may ultimately result in more actions concerning Ireland being taken to the Strasbourg court. This argument is further underlined by the fact that while the rulings of the UK courts were based upon the particular statutory framework relating to possession, the test in *Meadows* is general in nature.[185] Finally, while the reader will note our pessimism regarding its current status and future prospects, we

---

[183] This phrase is meant to convey the idea that the ECtHR will not find the standard of review immediately insufficient, but may find applications of it incorrect.

[184] See paras [9-41] to [9-66].

[185] This difference can be strikingly expressed: the UK courts stated that findings of disproportionality will be rare *in the context of possession proceedings*. The Supreme Court in Meadows is arguably, on one interpretation, stressing that findings of disproportionality will be rare *in the context of the entire 2003 Act*.

underline our overarching support for the structured approach to proportionality, the reasons for which are set out in chapter 9, in particular the desirability of uniting the default standard for assessing the constitutionality of legislation and of administrative decisions.[186]

Conclusion

In this book we committed to a two-fold separation of the administrative law subject: dealing with issues which involve a system wide perspective on administrative justice and then with specific grounds under judicial review. It is interesting to reflect that our account of the ECHR involves an overlap between these two elements. The impact of the ECHR has been seen in both areas, even if it has not always been as profound as was first anticipated by lawyers or feared by administrators. [15–104]

While we have identified a number of successful instances of reliance upon the Convention within the Irish courts, there is no doubt that the volume of litigation is destined to be far more limited than under the UK Human Rights Act 1998. This reflects the fact that Ireland's 2003 Act corralled domestic invocations of the ECHR into a judicial review framework of limited pathways and remedies. Nevertheless from a systemic perspective, the ECHR has triggered important reflections upon traditional closures, normative and institutional, within our administrative system. Ultimately, the core reason for this lies with the abiding political impact of a successful application to the ECtHR in Irish public life. Such rulings have resulted in system wide or legislative change, underlining the fruitful relationship which can exist between litigation and administrative reform. This, together with our reflections upon European Union law in the previous chapter, underline that the influence of the European integration and co-operation upon Ireland's administrative law framework has been profound and will continue apace. [15–105]

---

[186] See paras [9-38]-[9-40].

CHAPTER SIXTEEN

Into the Future: Reforming Irish Administrative Law

"What I propose, therefore, is very simple: it is nothing more than to think what we are doing."

Hannah Arendt.[1]

Introduction

This book has been written with multiple communities in mind, whose   [16–01]
members may approach administrative law with many different
motivations and perspectives. This diverse group includes the practitioner
looking to resolve particular cases, administrators looking to avoid legal
tripwires, and those engaged in more broadly framed political or legal
study. Often these multiple perspectives fragment and are not placed
alongside each other or considered on a holistic basis. Thus the critical is
often arbitrarily separated from the instrumental: the "political" set apart
from the "legal". We hope that in our discussion of the boundary concepts
of judicial review, and of integrity mechanisms such as Commissions of
Inquiry and of parliamentary review, this book has, in a small way, affirmed
the position of Boyle that:

> "Administrative law is about the exercise of power in society, it cannot
> be divorced from broader political choices about the structure of
> government and the constitutional order."[2]

In such a context, the above quote by Arendt can be understood to represent   [16–02]
a core mission statement for the study of administrative law. In it, Arendt
warns us against the dangers of all-encompassing, reactive pragmatism or
adherence to traditional standards, which can lead to "drift and
inadvertence" dominating our actions.[3] In the context of Irish administrative
law, legal actors can fall into this trap by adopting an overly formalist
approach to reviewing administrators' actions. Political actors, meanwhile,

---

[1] H Arendt, *The Human Condition,* (University of Chicago Press, Chicago/London, 1958), at
p 5. It might be said that, at times, Irish administrative law reflects the viewpoint of Alfred
North Whitehead in *an Introduction to Mathematics,* who rejected such link between thought
and action as an "erroneous truism", arguing that "operations of thought are like cavalry
charges in a battle — they are strictly limited in number, they require fresh horses and must
only be made at decisive moments". Alfred North Whitehead, *An Introduction to Mathematics,*
(Williams and Norgate, London, 1911) at pp 45-46.

[2] AE Boyle, "Sovereignty, Accountability and the Reform of Administrative Law" in G
Richardson and H Genn (eds.) *Administrative Law and Government Action* (Clarendon Press,
Oxford, 1994) at p 103.

[3] Above n 1 at p 5.

can be prone to allow their constitutional role to be crowded out by party political considerations. While we would not describe Irish administrative law as "thoughtless", we are, as the reader will have noted, concerned at some of the key silences that mark certain critical junctures. For Arendt, while the past experiences embodied by traditional concepts must be reasoned through, it is also crucial to take up the vantage point of "our newest experience and our most recent fears" and to avoid "the complacent repetition" of traditional truths.[4] If administrative justice "is today the work of many hands",[5] then the unified engagement of all actors combined in an interdisciplinary dialogue seems essential.[6] It should be the function of administrative law to legally institutionalise the conditions necessary for contestation, justification and mutual questioning between the public, courts, politicians and administrators.

[16–03]   The final element lying within Arendt's deceptively simple statement is the importance of connecting between *values or ideas* and practical *action*. In considering both the operation of administrative law as it currently stands, and in looking forward to its reform we would stress the vital importance of each actor in the system reflecting upon "how legal rules, doctrines, legal decisions, institutionalised cultural and legal practice work together to create the reality of law in action".[7] Those working within this area should not merely passively contemplate the state of administrative law by clinging onto the lifebelt of "practical rules"; instead we must confront the engagement of theory and practice, bringing it together in revealing and mutually critical ways. This should happen not only at the micro level of grounds of review, or methods to accountability, but also at the macro level of what we understand administrative law to be. We highlighted in our first chapter the rather under-defined relationship between administrative law and administrative *justice*. This lack of definition is unwelcome. Judicial review, for example, should not merely be perceived as an internally sovereign logic belonging only to lawyers, but must be connected to, and

---

[4] *ibid.*

[5] The Rt Hon Dame Sian Elias, GNZM, Chief Justice of New Zealand, *National Lecture on Administrative Law*, Australian Institute of Administrative Law Conference, 2013, at p 7.

[6] In teaching administrative law ourselves, we have often been troubled by the deep split between judicial review and the broader law of public administration. The increase in semesterisation in Irish universities may now enhance this separation, with judicial review being offered as a separate unit.

[7] R Banakar, "Studying Cases Empirically: A Sociological Method for Studying Discrimination Cases in Sweden 'Data and Method of Investigation'", in R Banakar and M Travers (eds), *Theory and Method in Socio-Legal Research*, (Hart Publishing, Oxford, 2005) at p 140.

must itself constantly be seeking connection with, actual administrative contexts and broader constitutional dilemmas. In trying to draw an extensive and diverse book to close, we wish to underline a few of the recurring reform issues we have discussed.

Alleviating the Rigidity of the Separation of Powers Through Institutional Innovations and the Recalibration of Judicial Review Principles

As we highlighted in chapter 1, the doctrine of the separation of powers in Ireland is a label which papers over many contradictory principles and functions. In particular, as Carolan argues persuasively, that it is "unclear as to whether it instinctively demands a system of separation or one of checks and balances".[8] It is our belief that judges must recognize the need for a diverse conception of the separation of powers, one which acknowledges that the tripartite model does not, and cannot exist in pure form, and that its borders must be attended to. A constitution is fundamentally about the positive exercise of public power, not its placement within non-interacting silos. Yet, as Carolan has also stated a "focus on separation and restraint, rather than supervision and checks and balances", has at times encouraged the judiciary to withdraw to an "inactive formalist position" in reviewing administrative action.[9] While we may wish for institutional innovation to break the inter-institutional deadlock, carefully executed judicial review is also required to "help counter failures of inclusiveness and responsiveness in the political process"— termed by Dixon as "blind spots" and "burdens of inertia".[10] In making this point we are clearly acknowledging and defending the of role of courts in vindicating rights. However, it also points us towards the vital need to consider how legal judgments can encourage greater legislative engagement with administration, implementation and oversight.

[16–04]

Even for those who prefer the red light understanding of judicial review, which we explored in chapter 1, this book has suggested alternative reform options, underlining the point that inaction cannot be acceptable, regardless of one's understanding of the appropriate division of labour under the

[16–05]

---

[8] E Carolan, *The New Separation of Powers* (Oxford University Press, Oxford, 2009) at p 32.

[9] *ibid* at p 51.

[10] R Dixon, "Creating Dialogue about Socioeconomic Rights: Strong-form Versus Weak-form Judicial Review Revisited", (2007) 5 *International Journal of Constitutional Law* 391 at p 406.

Constitution. Throughout this book we have returned again and again to the idea of an integrity branch of Government. If firmly established, such bodies can secure "horizontal accountability" of un-elected officials, which in turn leads to more concentrated democratic engagement with the intricacies of ever more bureaucratic and technocratic forms of modern administration. We believe that the recent experiences of the Office of the Ombudsman, in particular, illustrate both the imperative for their strengthening, and the practical barriers which they face. A key part of constitutional renewal lies in such institutions which, in driving administrative justice, muster the powers of our Constitution to accountable action, and stop the shading of the comparatively uniquely value-laden Bunreacht na hÉireann into an inert map of designated institutional spheres and formalist, bureaucratic divisions.

Reinvigorating Parliament as an Accountability Mechanism

[16–06] It is clear that the traditional structures of the Oireachtas are struggling to manage the increasingly complex administrative system. Rising to Arendt's challenge, we must measure the theoretical constitutional model of parliamentary scrutiny against the actual functioning of our Government. We see this in particular in the idea of ministerial responsibility and the impact of the political party upon the separation of powers. While there are efforts underway to strengthen committee structures and inquiry powers, the Oireachtas has a long way to go in self-critically rebuilding a parliamentary culture which engages seriously and effectively with accountability and oversight. However, even where structural change is developed, it is important to recognize the limits of the law against the wider cultural context. We need to acknowledge that we cannot simply constitutionalise or legislate our way to effective parliamentary scrutiny, such change may ultimately raise false hopes where there is no overarching change in the political and administrative cultures.

The Need for a Renewed Focus Upon First Instance Justice in Ireland

[16–07] Given that half of this book is devoted to the operation of judicial review, we clearly acknowledge and reflect on its importance for administrative oversight. However, it is also important to avoid court centrism — not least as judicial review is an expensive remedy of limited availability. It is, of course, vital to understand how law is disseminated within Government Departments and how rulings are integrated into administrative practice. Any effort to write a book, particularly one looking to serve the diverse audience we acknowledged at the start of this chapter, will result in exclusions of certain areas or the adoption of an emphasis upon particular issues. While we used our discussion of the Ombudsman, and of the fact scenarios of particular judicial review actions, to give the reader a sense of errors which might occur at first instance, this book reflects the legal curriculum in centering itself upon review mechanisms. For all that, however, "getting it right" is just as much an imperative as "setting it right", as Marc Galanter has argued:

> "Just as health is not found primarily in hospitals or knowledge in schools, so justice is not only to be found in official justice-giving institutions. Ultimately, access to justice is not just a matter of bringing cases to a judge, but of improving the relations and actions between people".[11]

We also need to acknowledge at this stage the fact that an examination of [16–08] first instance justice in Ireland — both departmental and public body decision-making and internal appeal mechanisms — is both extremely difficult and often impracticable. This is in large part due to the extraordinary complexity of these decision-making and appeal arrangements. Indeed to engage in drawing up a typology of appeal mechanisms one would be rapidly exasperated by the sheer variety and inconsistency of appeal avenues, levels of independence, security of tenure, the extent of discretion or the departmental policy versus law balance that the reviewer is bound to apply. As was mentioned in the first chapter, this space could be filled by the creation of an Irish Administrative Appeals Tribunal,[12] along the lines of that which exists in Australia. Such a body would, if designed correctly,

---

[11] M Galanter, "Justice in Many Rooms: Courts, Private Ordering, and Indigenous Law", (1981) 19 *Journal of Pluralism* 1 at p 17. The need for accessible legal information, self-help strategies, the role of non-legal advisers as gateways to legal services and integrated responses to legal and non-legal needs are all elements of this larger challenge of prioritising the early resolution of legal questions and of empowering citizens to engage with the administrative state.

[12] Another innovation could be the creation of subject specific bodies such as an Irish Environmental Court, a possibility that has been acknowledged by Denham CJ (speaking extrajudicially) See Chief Justice Denham, 'Some thoughts on the Constitution of Ireland at 75' was published in E Carolan (ed) *The Constitution of Ireland: Perspectives and Prospects* (Bloomsbury Professional, Dublin, 2012).

offer a centralized, co-ordinated vision of independent merits review, modelling the proper exercise of discretion by primary administrators. Regardless, it is important to seek proactive compliance by civil servants with the principles of good administration — a process which may be termed the socialisation of administrative law.

Into the Future

[16–09]   Throughout this book, we have seen evidence of reform efforts in various sectors, but the tide of such change so far has been ambiguous and selective. While there have been extensive constitutional convention debates proposing referenda to reform the state's constitutional framework, these have largely failed to address questions of administrative justice. This emphasis on the constitutional to the detriment of the administrative is extremely disappointing, as while it may be said that we have a constitutional vocabulary of rights and values, we have not yet formed an effective administrative and inter-institutional grammar for their delivery. We must not forget that, as Mashaw points out, "a robust internal law of administration is always necessary to systemic legality".[13] Much has been written regarding Ireland's economic crash and the entrance of the Troika, often carrying within it a sense of despair regarding Ireland's governance structures. Yet as Aldous Huxley pointed out "experience is not what happens to you. It is what you do with what happens to you".[14] In this sense, the key to making sense of the events of the past years does not solely lie in the "Anglo Tapes" or in hindsight oriented inquiries, but in the unwritten project of reforming the Irish State. Future generations will judge us not by our rhetorical condemnations, but by our practical reforms.

---

[13] J L Mashaw, "Administration and 'The Democracy': Administrative Law from Jackson to Lincoln, 1829-1861", (2008) 117 *Yale Law Journal* 1568 at p 1693.
[14] A Huxley, *Texts and Pretexts* (Chatto & Windus, London, 1932) at p 5.

INDEX

A

abortions
European Convention Article 8,
breach of, 15–62—15–63
absolute discretion, 10–31—10–42
academic institutions
discretionary powers, abuse of,
9–42
fair procedure, application of,
10–15—10–16, 10–66
breach of examination rules,
10–71—10–75
disciplinary matters, 10–107,
11–39
religious freedom in,
manifestation of, 15–84—
15–86
accountability
administrative-policy interface,
1–08—1–10
executive-elected council,
6–20—6–29
of civil servants, 1–08—1–10,
2–21, 2–42—2–51
of civil servants, inquiries,
2–52—2–59
of government, 2–01—2–02
instruments of, 1–06, 2–01—
2–02, 2–04. *see also* **Dáil
Éireann: formal control of
government; freedom of
information; parliamentary
oversight; public inquiries**

of Ministers. *see* **ministerial
responsibility**
parliamentary sovereignty and,
1–16
of state-sponsored bodies, 2–41
Ackerman, B, 1–37
actio popularis, 13–07
actual bias, 11–02
administrative decisions. *see also*
discretionary powers
European Convention
Article 6 rights and, 15–28—
15–32
Article 8 rights and, 15–60—
15–81
individual decisions, 9–39—
9–40
legislation and, contradictions
between judicial review of,
9–38—9–40
notice of, requirement to give,
10–64—10–70
notion of, 1–04
Ombudsman's review of,
"defects" in, 4–13—4–14
policy and fact-finding,
distinction between, 15–34—
15–38
policy decisions and, distinction
between, 2–45—2–47
reasons for decisions, duty to
give. *see* **reasons, right to**
administrative discretion.
see **discretionary powers;**